Violence, Inequality, and Human Freedom

Praise for *Violence, Inequality, and Human Freedom*, third edition

"I've used previous versions of this book successfully for a decade in a university class on violence. Iadicola and Shupe have created a very good analytical tool to study violence from a sociological perspective—better than any book in this area. This updated version will be a much-needed contribution in analyzing various forms of structural violence in light of the worldwide social changes following the global economic crisis of 2008."
—**Gunnar Valgeirsson**, California State University, Los Angeles

"Peter Iadicola and Anson Shupe provide a holistic discussion of violence incorporating a theoretically well-grounded interdisciplinary approach. The authors recognize and illuminate the interplay between interactional, institutional, and structural levels, moving beyond the traditional scope of violence to include the often overlooked aspects such as empire harm and corporate harm that have been constructed as legitimate but that nonetheless are forms of violence."
—**Dawn L. Rothe**, Old Dominion University

Violence, Inequality, and Human Freedom

Third Edition

Peter Iadicola and Anson Shupe

ROWMAN & LITTLEFIELD PUBLISHERS, INC.
Lanham • Boulder • New York • Toronto • Plymouth, UK

Published by Rowman & Littlefield Publishers, Inc.
A wholly owned subsidary of The Rowman & Littlefield Publishing Group, Inc.
4501 Forbes Boulevard, Suite 200, Lanham, Maryland 20706
www.rowman.com

10 Thornbury Road, Plymouth PL6 7PP, United Kingdom

British Library Cataloguing in Publication Information Available

Library of Congress Cataloging-in-Publication Data

Iadicola, Peter.
Violence, inequality, and human freedom / Peter Iadicola and Anson Shupe.—3rd ed.
  p. cm.
Includes bibliographical references and index.
ISBN 978-1-4422-0948-0 (cloth : alk. paper)—ISBN 978-1-4422-0949-7 (pbk. : alk. paper)—ISBN
978-1-4422-0950-3 (electronic)
1. Violence. 2. Civil rights. I. Shupe, Anson. II. Title.
HM886.I18 2012
303.6—dc23
2012029547

♾™ The paper used in this publication meets the minimum requirements of American
National Standard for Information Sciences Permanence of Paper for Printed Library
Materials, ANSI/NISO Z39.48-1992.

Printed in the United States of America

Contents

Preface

Violence has been and continues to be a central issue that concerns people throughout the world. Whether it is the violence that exists within one's own home, community, or nation or the violence that exists throughout the world, it is a problem that has plagued humanity throughout recorded history and as overwhelmingly reported in today's mass media. Some scholars have claimed that it is has increased throughout history. They describe the litany of mass murders, wars, and genocides that have occurred during the past century and that continue today. Others claim that earlier times were far more barbaric and destructive of human life. However, all these works that attempt to measure the fluctuation in rates of violence over history are fundamentally flawed because only in recent history have governments and scholars been able to systematically collect information on the occurrence on just a few of the forms of violence. Furthermore, few of these works attempt to comprehensively define violence and to include all its various forms in their measurements of the occurrence of violence. Thus, the estimates that are developed are incomplete in that the focus is principally on either levels of interpersonal violence (murder) or the state violence of warfare, and even for these areas of violence only recently has there been little systematic collection of data on these forms throughout the world, especially those countries that are the least developed. Thus attempts to measure violence over time using incomplete information from only the most developed areas of the world lead to mere speculation more informed by ideology than any comprehensive scientific measurement.

The recent work by Pinker that attempts to measure violence and determine its trend throughout history is the latest example in this incomplete, flawed analysis (Pinker, 2011). Drawing upon a broad range of information from archaeological records of war deaths among early humans to rates of homicide and war deaths in modern societies, he concludes that violence is down as a result of the power of democratic states, the transition to agrarian societies, and the rise in feminism. However, this work has been criticized, like others, of being selective in which information is presented and relying upon the idea that we should look at relative impact of violence (deaths per population size) as opposed to absolute numbers. Given that the world's population did not reach one billion persons until the early 1800s but has increased rapidly during the past century, the current estimate is seven billion, and the rate of growth is estimated to be one billion persons every fifteen years, it would be difficult despite the increased power of weapons of mass destruction not to find that the relative rates of violence have declined. Nevertheless, this estimate of violence, like previous estimates, is flawed because of the lack of a comprehensive conceptualization and measurement of violence historically and in the present period worldwide. This work attempts to first develop a comprehensive definition of violence and to describe its many forms. Once the reader realizes the many forms that violence takes in the world, they will recognize that attempts to measure the overall frequency of violence in the world historically and in the present using the data that is available is an impossible task. The best that scholars can do is speculate on the patterns based on what we have learned about the causes of violence that we currently understand to be true.

This book tells the story of the violence that harms people throughout the world. It tells the story of the violence that most people think of when they hear the words *murder* and *rape*. But it also tells the story of the forms of violence that most people do not think of when they hear the word *violence*. In these categories of violence we discuss the violence that is the product of institutional actions (family, economy, state, and religious organizations) and violence that is the product of the very organization of societies (structural violence). Most writings about violence focus on interpersonal violence. This book is unique because the focus is principally on those other, more devastating forms of violence. As we are writing this preface, the news of the day is that the highest officials of Penn State University, including the idolized Coach Joe Paterno, were aware and covered up a ten-year history of sexual abuse by Jerry Sandusky, one of the coaches of their famed college football program. In Philadelphia, Monsignor William J. Lynn, a former archbishop's aide, was found guilty Friday of endangering children, becoming the first senior official of the Roman Catholic Church in the United States to be convicted of covering up child sexual abuses by priests under his supervision. In the West Virginia coal mining area, there is a dramatic increase in the number of black lung cases. We learn that in southwestern Niger, there is a massive famine that is unfolding, killing thousands of people. These are the forms of violence that we don't think of and don't include in our understanding or measurement of violence. This book examines the broad range of violence from the interpersonal to institutional to structural forms.

This book also moves beyond considering only humans as victims of violence and looks at the systematic killing of other species as violence as well. We confront the speciesist bias in the conceptualization of violence that is based on only humans as victims and ignores the vast amount of killing that humans do of other species for their entertainment or sport or to be used as food or articles of dress. Violence directed at other species is such a part of human modern existence that the level of violence as measured by species extinction rates threatens not only the survival of other species but the survival of our own species as well.

Another story that this book tells is how the forms of violence are linked together. We have learned in the course of our study that there is an important linkage between the many different forms of violence that occur throughout a society and the world. Although we can think of a form of violence in isolation, in reality the forms of violence that exist in the society and the world are linked together. We discuss the idea of a chain of violence that links the interpersonal forms of violence with the institutional and structural violence. The more we understand the nature of this linkage, the greater our ability to address the problem of violence.

The book also tells the story of how violence is related to inequality. At the most fundamental level, what allows us to violate another is our ability to define those others as separate and less than ourselves. The hierarchical structures that we have created and act to maintain and extend create this ability and teach it to the next generation. The story of violence is a story of inequality. We have learned that inequality is both a cause and an outcome of violence. How we respond to the structures of inequality in the society and world will determine the nature of violence within these systems.

Lastly, this book tells the story of how violence is related to freedom, a value that we in the United States celebrate and in our public messages to the world promote. Our wars of liberation are not exceptions to this relationship. The U.S. government has often committed itself to wars to "liberate" or "free" people. However, as we attempt to liberate people by providing them with the right to own property and to profit from it in a capitalist system unfettered by government and by the creation of a system of selection of rulers through a process that those with the most wealth in and outside of the system have the greatest power to influence, we create other structures of inequality and use increasing violence, which restrict the freedom to maintain the newly imposed system. This can be seen in our most recent wars in the Middle East.

Violence is fundamentally about control and the control over freedom of action. Violence is ultimately a form of power that at the same time extends and denies freedom to the actors involved. As we commit ourselves to war to "liberate" people by transforming their society to one that creates structures of other inequality based on the system that we are imposing, there is a loss of freedom for some and the occurrence of violence. And overall, the more violence that occurs in the world, the less freedom exists for us all.

We view this book as an introduction to the subject of violence. It is not intended to be a theoretical treatise on the topic. Instead, our goals are more modest. It is to provide the reader with a new way of looking at the phenomenon and to gain an appreciation for the scope and complexity of the topic. The book is written to begin a conversation about why violence in its many forms occurs, a conversation beyond the psychology or presumed evil of those who commit such acts. This book is rooted in the sociological disciplinary perspective. For those who are not as familiar with this perspective, the introductory chapter will provide the reader with the necessary disciplinary lens to gain a better understanding of the phenomenon of violence.

Chapter One

The Domain of Violence

In 1999 two male seniors at Columbine High School near Denver, Colorado, went on a planned shooting spree inside the school that killed twelve students and one teacher and directly injured twenty-one other students. Similar attacks against students and instructors at elementary, junior, and senior high schools as well as at universities begin occurring across the United States and soon after in various European countries.

In Jasper, Texas, three white men chain a black man to the back of a pickup truck and drag him until his body is torn apart.

It is learned that industrial factories that produce radioactive elements for nuclear weapons have been systematically and knowingly polluting their surrounding communities for years, with no one punished.

Unarmed Chinese university students are ruthlessly gunned down by government troops in Tiananmen Square because they dare to demonstrate for democracy.

A coordinated attack by terrorists from a Middle Eastern terrorist group sends four planeloads of passengers to their fiery deaths. Two of the planes crash into the World Trade Center in New York City, killing almost three thousand people; another crashes into a section of the Pentagon, killing another 288 people.

In the People's Republic of China starting in March 2010, a series of unrelated violent attacks against elementary school children and high school youths, usually committed by knife-wielding middle-aged men, leave over a brief period of several months a total of at least twenty-one dead and more than ninety injured. Chinese analysts blame everything from mental illness to motives of revenge.

Violence against individuals, against minorities, against nations, against even our home planet is the overarching problem of our age. It is no exaggeration to say that every conceivable social problem interfaces with this destructive phenomenon. Violence's myriad forms consume the attention of news media reports and cost us dearly as citizens as we try to cope with or prevent their destructive effects. Many other social problems—drug addiction, the breakup of the American family, deteriorating city schools, corporate corruption, terrorism, religious intolerance, and exploitation—are interwoven with violence. Violence is not simply linked to such obvious controversies as building larger prisons, tightening criminal sentences, or passing gun control laws. It is also linked to problems of famine, pollution, overpopulation, and the advanced technology of nuclear destruction in the hands of increasing numbers of countries.

The various behavioral sciences, from anthropology and psychology to economics and political science, have developed theories about the causes of destructive actions. Considerable research has accumulated, especially during the past thirty years. Most important, a rich scholarly legacy of testing and refining concepts has made it abundantly clear that the sum of violence in any society must be understood as multiply determined. No single viewpoint, no solitary theoretical "slant," will suffice.

For example, psychology is better able to address questions about imitation and the learning of actions, innate drives, and personality as these relate to interpersonal violence than about the economic, social, political, and historical circumstances most conducive to political revolution. Anthropology tempers our Western understandings of violence with analyses of the roles and function violence and conflict play in cross-cultural settings. Political science casts violence in the rational, decision-making mold of being a conscious policy alternative used by statespersons, instead of simply serving as a physiological release of frustration, anger, or sadism.

Ball-Rokeach (1980) notes that because "the phenomenon of violence cuts across many disciplines and fields of inquiry, it tends toward a fragmented inquiry into this or that form of violence." There is a need for a more unitary approach, discussing violence as a phenomenon in and of itself. The sociological perspective, which we believe permits the most comprehensive understanding of violence, is the likely place for such a unitary approach to develop.

Sociology examines the phenomenon as a pattern of behavior that emanates fundamentally from the very organization of society. For sociologists, the pattern of violence in a given society is unique to that social system. Thus violence originates in structural and institutional sources that are supra-personal but, to most persons, are experienced at the interpersonal level.

There are several reasons why the sociological perspective lends itself to the development of this unitary approach. First, sociology facilitates the viewing of action from the position of an outsider or an objective position by providing us with a lens to see what is strange in what is familiar to us. All of our behavior can be viewed as unusual or strange when taken out of the cultural context in which we are immersed. The foods we eat, the dwellings we reside in, and the style of fashion—all can be viewed as unusual. What we define and consider violent or nonviolent also can be seen as strange. In fact, what is violent may often not be defined as violence by those socialized to accept it as natural, justifiable, or sacred. For example, the spanking, slapping, or even belt lashing of children by their parents when they are deemed to be unruly is not viewed as violent unless it exceeds some established norm. Yet in Sweden the spanking of children is considered an act of violence and is criminal. In many societies, and in our own in a not-so-distant past, husbands striking their wives was not considered violence. In colonial America, wife beating brought severe corporal punishment by the community on the abusing male. Today, courts and the police are compelled by social pressure to treat spousal abuse as a serious case of assault that requires criminal justice intervention. Yet in other parts of the world wife beating is seen quite differently. Harris notes that among the Yanomamo, no "woman escapes the brutal tutelage of the typical hot-tempered, drug-taking Yanomamo warrior-husband. All Yanomamo men physically abuse their wives. Kind husbands merely bruise and mutilate them; the fierce ones wound and kill" (Harris, 1974, 74).

Similarly, the denial of medical care to those in need because of their economic status is not considered violent. Infant mortality rates for African American infants that are twice that of white infants are not considered violent. Neither is paddling children in school for their misbehavior, nor the dumping of industrial waste into the nation's waterways. Often we do not even think of capital punishment as violent. Yet from another perspective, all these acts can be considered forms of violence. Sociology helps one to view the "social reality" from the position of a stranger, inviting the viewer to step back and "out" of the social situation so that what was first viewed as nonviolent and even commonplace comes to be viewed in a different light.

Alternately, not only does sociology allow us to view the world from the vantage point of a stranger but it also helps the viewer to be cognizant of the different positions that the actors occupy in the violence. It furthermore allows one to assume the subjective positions of the actors themselves in order to understand the social reality from the position of the victims and perpetrators of violence in the performance of roles in the violent interaction. For example, how is an act of violence defined differently because of the different statuses and roles of the actors participating in the interaction? How is the form of violence understood by the actors involved? What social processes and contexts allow actors to see some forms of violence and not others, or to judge violence differently as a result of the different roles they are performing in the violent interaction? How are the roles of victim and offender socially defined in each form of violence?

If one individual were struck by another as a result of an altercation, we would define this as an assault. If the perpetrator were a mugger using violence as a way to get money from an elderly woman, this would be clearly understood. The victim and perpetrator would experience the violence as violence. In contrast, if the perpetrator was an adult woman, a mother, and the victim was a small child, her son, we would think of the violence another way, and the victim and perpetrator would experience the violence differently. Or say that the perpetrator was a police officer and was using violence to apprehend a suspect who was resisting arrest. What about the case of a soldier using harsh interrogation techniques on a prisoner during the time of war: do we consider this violence? Again, the objective violent act of striking another is the same; however, in viewing the subjective phenomenon from the vantage point of the different actors, we understand the violence differently.

A second characteristic of this unique disciplinary perspective is that sociology searches through various instances of action for patterns. In short, sociology looks for the general in the particular. What are the patterns of violence in our society? Who is more likely to participate in violence? What kinds of people are more likely to be offenders or victims of a particular form of violence? Under what social circumstances or contexts are people more likely to be violent or to be victimized by violence?

Although we often hear about the "random" act of violence, random violence is a rarity. Violence is patterned. Some people are more likely to be victims of violence than others because of social, temporal, and geographic positioning. For example, today the leading cause of death among African Americans aged ten to twenty-four is homicide; it is the second leading cause of death for young people in general in this age group (Center for Disease Control, 2010). Almost half of homicide victims are African American (Bureau of Justice Statistics [BJS], 2010a). Approximately three-quarters are male (BJS, 2010b). In reviewing homicide victimization for 1976 to 2005, 63 percent of persons victimized were under the age of thirty-five. The rate of victimization for aggravated assault for persons in households with annual incomes of less than $7,500 was eight times greater than persons in households with incomes of $75,000 or more (BJS, 2010b).

Thus, violence is hardly random. It is patterned. The more we know about the patterns of violence, the greater insight we have as to the causes. Sociology also looks for the interrelationship among the patterns. How may one pattern of violence be related to another? Are the patterns of violence noted above related? Is the violence within the minority population related to income? Are there relationships between types of violence? For example, are the patterns of violence between parents and children at all related to the patterns of violence between husbands and wives? Does the violence that children experience today with their parents prepare them to be violent with their own children in the future? Does it prepare them to be violent with their spouse? At a more macro level, are the patterns of violence we see between nations related to the patterns of violence experienced within nations? In short, how are patterns of violence related within a society and between societies? Sociology as a discipline directs us to look for the relationship between such patterns of violence.

Last, sociology facilitates our understanding of individual behavior as it is the product of the way society is organized and functions. In the language of sociology, the discipline depersonalizes the personal. Sociology helps us see how our individual behavior is the product of the nature of the society. This does not mean that social forces are deterministic. As individuals, we choose our behavior, yet social forces limit the range of choices available to us and influence us to choose one option over another. Every day we make individual decisions as to which actions to choose. We decide what time to wake, what and when to eat, whether and how to clothe ourselves, and what to do once we have awakened, eaten, and dressed. Nevertheless, there are forces that make us choose to get up at a certain time, to eat one food as opposed to another, to wear a particular article of clothing, and so forth. Some of these forces are a product of cultural expectations as they define diet and style of dress or are a result of the statuses we occupy and the role expectations that stem from these positions. Other reasons may be because of our relationship to others and their expectations for behavior. Still others may be a result of the resources that we have available to define the diet and style of dress. These are some of the social forces that limit the range of choices of our action and direct us to choose from a more limited range of alternatives that we may have available to us. All our actions, including violence, are seen as personal decisions, but what choices we have available to us and what choices we are likely to choose are products of the social forces that compose the society.

Sociologists ask: how are the patterns of violence that exist in our society the product of the social forces rooted in how our society is organized? How is it that the family, the school, the economy, and the religious and political systems are organized and actually work to limit the range of choices of people and influence some to choose acts of violence as opposed to other routes to accomplish their goals? Moreover, not only is the pattern of violence in a society a product of how that society is organized, but also the people's understandings of violence is the product of the nature of that society's system of shared meanings and knowledge, their culture. Culture provides a lens through which we define or do not define acts as violent. In short, sociology facilitates our understanding of violence as a societal phenomenon with particular attention to how violence is linked at all levels within the society and how it is fundamentally a product of how society is organized and functions.

In addition to the general sociological perspective, the basic assumptions that underlie the disciplinary viewpoint facilitate the conceptualization of violence as a unitary phenomenon. First, sociologists assume that individuals are by their nature social beings. Children enter the world totally dependent on others for their survival. They have a longer period of dependency than any other animal. Our need for an association with a "group" is an essential element of human nature. Human beings can survive only in social groups of one kind or another. The importance of group affiliation is most clearly evident in primitive societies, where the most severe punishment was banishment from the group.

A second disciplinary assumption is that individuals are, for the most part, socially determined. During infancy, the child is at the mercy of adults, especially parents. These persons shape the infant in an infinite variety of ways, depending on their proclivities and those of their society. Parents will have a profound impact on the child's way of thinking about him- or herself and about others. Parents will transmit religious views, political attitudes, and attitudes toward other groups. Most significantly, parents act as cultural agents, transferring the ways of the society to their children. These processes

continue beyond the primary group level to all the groups of which we are a
member. Thus, how we define ourselves and the world of which we are part
are products of our society.

According to sociologists, we are the products of the groups of which we
are members. The groups we are members of provide the most fundamental
social forces that direct our behavior. Whether we are talking about the
family, the nation-state or country, the ethnic group, or a school class, they
all provide the social forces in constraining our actions. It makes little sense
to conceive of us apart from such group affiliations. For example, today
many babies born in poorer countries to parents of little means are taken
from birth and adopted by parents of higher status in wealthier countries.
Babies born to poor parents in Guatemala, Romania, Bolivia, or the Philippines and then adopted by people in upper-class positions in advanced capitalist countries experience a dramatic change in who they are and who they
are likely to become. This affects not only what language they will speak but
also how long they are likely to live, how healthy they will be in their lives,
how they are likely to live in terms of quality of life, how they will be
educated, what occupation they will choose, whom they will marry, how
large their family will be, and so on. Who they are and what they think of
themselves change because of the change in the social groups of which they
are a part. In this way, we are socially determined.

A third disciplinary assumption is that individuals create, sustain, and
change the social structures within which they conduct their lives. Social
groups of all sizes and types are human creations. The social world in which
we are immersed is a human creation. All the structures, beliefs, norms, and
institutions we are a part of are a social creation, a creation of the groups we
are participating in or that were participated in by previous generations of
members of the society. We are born into a society that is a product of the
social creation efforts of previous generations. The social world we are born
into becomes the context in which we interact with others. Thus, we act to
change, sustain, and create new structures, beliefs, norms, institutions, and
the like that then set the social context for interaction for ourselves and other
new members of the society. This is a continuous ongoing phenomenon of
creating, maintaining, and changing the social structures in which we live our
lives.

It is important to qualify this last statement by noting that we do not all
have the same amount of power or ability to create, maintain, and change the
social structures within the society. Our position via systems of stratification
provides us with differences in the amount of power we have to create,
maintain, and change social structures. Nevertheless, it is important for the
reader to recognize that the social reality that they experience is human-
made.

The significance of these assumptions as they relate to the issue of violence is that, first, violence is a problem because it fundamentally weakens
the social web that is the basis of human life. Furthermore, violence that
reaches a critical level threatens the interconnectedness of people necessary
for human survival. Second, violence in a society is ultimately a product of
social organization. All social or antisocial behaviors can ultimately be
understood only as products of the nature of the society and the nature of the

social relationships within. Thus, we may discuss acts of interpersonal violence that appear on the surface to be a clear expression of individual behavior, but this level views a phenomenon out of its societal context. Sociology provides the viewer with this context. Violence ultimately is a result of the nature of the social relationships or social connection the victim and/or offender have with the group in which the violence occurs. This is the case whether we are discussing the violence of gangs or the violence of a lone killer. As humans act to create, sustain, and change the social world, they also create, maintain, and change the patterns of violence within it. Furthermore, if the social forces that create the patterns of violence are ultimately human creations, the question then is what social forces would need to be changed to change the patterns of violence within the society. Or, more to the point, what is the nature of a society that would have the least amount of violence?

ORDER, CONFLICT, AND SYMBOLIC INTERACTIONIST APPROACHES WITHIN SOCIOLOGY

We will discuss three paradigms or theoretical perspectives that provide a framework to understanding the nature of violence. Two of these paradigms, order and conflict, focus our view of violence at the macro level. That is, they are viewing the phenomenon of violence as it manifests itself as a product of large-scale social forces. The third paradigm, symbolic interactionist, focuses at the micro level, viewing violence as it manifests itself as a product of small groups and social interaction. Each approach establishes a framework for us to view violence, and in many ways their implications for addressing violence are radically different. However, seen together they provide a holistic view of the nature of violence. Within all societies there is both order and conflict, and to achieve a comprehensive understanding of human behavior, it must be viewed though both a macro and micro lens in order to see all the forces that impact it.

Table 1.1 presents a comparison of the two macro approaches to the study of society. The order approach views the society as normally stable. All members of the society have, relatively speaking, the same culture and interests in maintaining the order. The primary social process in the society is cooperation. All individuals are performing roles within the formal institutions contributing to the ongoing maintenance of the social order. The organismic analogy best describes how the order approach defines how a society functions. It refers to the idea of viewing the social system in the same way one views a biological system. For example, the human body is made up of organs. Each organ carries out a specific physiological function. The heart functions as a pump to move or circulate the blood throughout the system. The lungs function to transfer gases, removing carbon dioxide from the blood and replacing it with oxygen. Processes link the organs to one another: respiratory processes, digestive processes, circulatory processes, and so forth.

When all organs are appropriately carrying out their function, working in coordination with one another, linked via processes, we say that the organism is in a state of health.

The society is composed of institutions, organizations that perform valued functions to the society that are analogous to organs. Each institution carries out a specific social function. Organizations within the education institution function to enculturate and provide the skills necessary for neophytes to assume statuses or positions within social institutions. Organizations within the economic institution function to produce and distribute the human creations (services and products) necessary for humans to participate in the society. Organized family units function to reproduce and provide primary socialization for new members of the society. Organizations with the governing institutions or state function to create and execute the rules that govern human relations and behavior. Lastly, organizations within the religious institution function to provide humans a connection to the spiritual and provide their members with an understanding of life's purpose and goals.

As in the case of organs, institutions are linked via processes (e.g., socialization processes, exchange processes, governing processes, etc.). Like organisms, when all the institutions are working appropriately and in coordination with each other via these processes, the society is normatively in a state of balance. All parts of the system are carrying out their designed function, linked via processes, all working for the maintenance, growth, or reproduction of the whole system.

To continue our description of the order approach, the foundation of the society is the cultural system, the system of language, knowledge, beliefs, and values that unify the population. The divisions that exist in the society along class, ethnicity, and gender lines are viewed as either basically natural to people in the society and/or necessary or functional to the nature of the society (Jensen, 1969; Hernstein, 1973; Davis and Moore, 1945).

For the order approach, the functioning and organization of institutions are manifestations of the cultural system. For example, the structure and the processes within education systems in this country emphasize individual achievement, as it is a product of competition in the classroom and self-interested/rational action by the student, as well as an assumption of inequality in the quality of students and their academic achievement. These are all central cultural values of our society and key elements of the dominant ideology that legitimates the society. Thus, the educational system is organized to produce these results. Furthermore, the order approach focuses on how the institutions are linked via processes. It asks: is the nature of the linkages efficient given the functioning of the institutions in fulfilling the needs of the larger social order? For example, do the methods we use to socialize our children in the home and their outcomes complement the methods used in the schools and the outcomes expected? Or do they conflict? If they conflict, how do these methods need to change to produce the desired results? Last, the order approach emphasizes how institutions serve to create and maintain boundaries that separate members of this society from other societies and give members of the society a sense of unity or cohesiveness

Table 1.1.   Order and Conflict Approaches to the Study of Society.

Conception of the social order	Homogeneity, stability, and in balance. Organismic Analogy is applied. Primary social process is cooperation.	Heterogeneity, instability, and in imbalance. Primary social process is conflict/competition.
Foundation of social systems	Cultural system/knowledge system (idealism). Cultural values/ideals/traditions are the foundation of the order.	Structural divisions rooted in system of material and human reproduction; class and gender systems (materialism) are the foundation of the order.
Position of divisions	Natural, necessary, and functional to the social system.	Product of historical development. Dynamic foundation of the social order. Ultimately maintained by means of oppression and social control.
Position of institutions	Structural reflections of cultural/knowledge systems. Stress of linkages and functional efficiency. Also stress on their integrative/boundary-maintaining function.	Mechanisms to maintain and reproduce the order, including the structural divisions that are its foundation. Institutions seen as mechanisms of coercion or social control.
Origins/method of change	Evolutionary/natural progression. Originates from the top down to the masses. It is a product of innovation of the elites (intellectual, political, economic, etc.).	Product of conflict between the divisions within the order that develops because of the clash of forces of (re)production with relations of (re)production. Change comes from the bottom up, product of social movements.
Political orientation	Conservative/liberal (solutions to problems come from within the ideological parameters of the system).	Radical (solutions to problems come from outside of the ideological parameters of the system).

Central questions	What is the nature of the social bond? What holds society together? How is stability and development maintained?	What conditions provoke the conflicts between the structural divisions? What conditions promote structural position consciousness?

(Parsons, 1991). One's participation in the social institutions in the society provides him or her with a common experience that unites the society as a distinct group and with common socialization to function within the society.

The order approach emphasizes and views social change as part of a natural, evolutionary progression of the society. Change principally comes from the top down, a product of the innovation of elites who govern the basic institutions of the society. In any particular case, elites may be responding to social pressure from below. However, they, through their power and actions, are the engine of change. The political orientation of the order approach is within the ideological parameters of the system it is describing; therefore, it is either conservative or liberal. The order is seen as good; problems within the society are a result of dramatic changes often initiated outside the system that disrupt the functioning of institutions. Both the content and speed of change are defined as the primary sources of social problems.

The central questions for the order approach are: What is the nature of the social bond? What holds society together? How do we maintain the social order? More precisely, for developmental or modernization theorists (order theorists that focus on the nature of societal development), how is stability and development maintained by a society?

In sociology there are two general conflict orientations: pluralist conflict and structuralist conflict. The difference between these two orientations is principally in the identification of the dimensions of conflict. For the pluralist conflict approach, the conflict of values and interests stems from the diversity of the population. Because the population is diverse along a series of dimensions—age, gender, occupation, lifestyle, religion, locality, ethnicity—members of the society are likely to come into conflict over issues and interests. The specific dimensions of the diversity of the population are not as important as the amount of dimensions of diversity of the population. Thus, one dimension is not necessarily more important than another as it relates to the organization of society and the nature of the conflict within it. What is important in accounting for the occurrence of conflict is the amount of diversity of the population. In contrast, structural conflict analysis argues that although diversity of the population is important, the major dimensions of conflict are along the structural divisions or systems of stratification that form the foundation of the society: class, gender, and race or ethnicity.

In the following description we discuss a structural conflict approach. The conflict approach conceptualizes the social order in a very different manner. As opposed to homogeneity of interests and values, the conflict theorist sees heterogeneity of interests, values, and cultural orientation. Or, more precisely put, the conflict theorist sees conflicting values, interests, and cultural orientations, especially along the divisions within systems of stratification or inequality within a society. The primary social process here is conflict or competition.

We can extend the order approach's organismic analogy to the conflict approach to illustrate the differences in the approaches. The institutions function like organs of an organism, linked via processes, functioning to maintain the whole system. For the conflict approach, however, the question is: whose values or interests dominate the functioning of the institutions of the society? Which position or positions within the society have the greatest power in the functioning of organizations within the various institutions of the society? The structural conflict approach focuses on the divisions as they define the positions as based in the systems of material and human reproduction that are the foundation of the society. The conflict approaches rooted in a Marxist theoretical orientation are fundamentally materialist.

For a materialist, understanding any system begins with describing what that system needs to exist and how it goes about meeting its needs. All societies need to organize themselves to reproduce their populations. Human reproduction has two fundamental components or modes to accomplish— physical reproduction and cultural reproduction. A society also needs material resources to sustain human life and the tools to access or transform these resources. That is, society first must be organized for procreation and socialization (mode of reproduction) and for the production of the necessities of survival for the population (mode of production). Without an organized way for this to occur the society will not exist for more than a generation (see figure 1.1).

Each of the modes has two components: the relations and forces of production and reproduction. The forces refer to the technology, the skill level of the actors, and the energy and material resources necessary for the production of things and the reproduction of people (physically and culturally). The relations refer to how the population is organized to produce things and reproduce people. For the relations of production, the fundamental organizing principle is social class. The social-class system in any society specifies

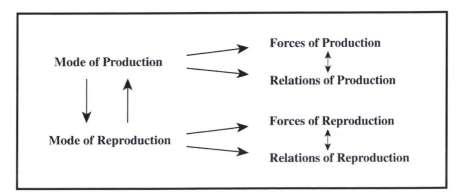

Figure 1.1. Substructure or Societal Base.

the relations that people have to production. Social class simply refers to a category of people who have a common relationship to production. A social-class system is a hierarchy of positions defined in terms of one's relationship to production.

For example, in describing the class structure of the United States as a capitalist society, we can identify two essential class positions. The first class position, the one that is in the dominant power position, is the capitalist or owning class. The capitalist or owning class refers to a category of people who own and control production and receive their income or wealth through a right of expropriation of the surplus produced by others. The right to hold private (productive) property is fundamental to the ability of members of the capitalist class to expropriate the surplus produced by those who work the property. This is the basis of the profit that is the driving force for capitalists to accumulate private property. Marxist conflict theories refer to this process of expropriation of surplus by owners from those who produce it as exploitation. Although the surplus is produced at the site of production, the realization of this surplus takes place in the marketplace. This is why a free market, one without interference of this right of expropriation by government or any other collectivity, is crucial to the functioning of capitalism.

Those who produce the surplus are in the second essential class position: the working class. The working class refers to a category of people who do not own or control production, but sell their capacity to labor or work to those who do or their representatives. Although workers are free to work for anyone that they choose in a capitalist society, as opposed to slaves and serfs under two previous modes of production, workers are fundamentally coerced to work. Choice to work or not for members of the working class is limited to select groups that are either dependent upon another who works (children and a spouse in one-worker home) or the state (state workers, welfare recipients, prisoners) for their survival and participation in the society. Since capitalists control the means of production, the only means by which workers are able to survive is by selling their capacity to work to a capitalist or state or by assuming a dependent status. Capitalist class interest is to limit the size of the state sector through privatization of state operations and welfare sectors in order to increase the size of the working class seeking work. Generally speaking in a capitalist society, the more competition for work, the lower the price of labor. The two class positions are fundamentally in conflict. The goal of the capitalist is to generate increasing amounts of surplus (the basis of profits) by means of increasing control over work in order to increase levels of efficiency and increase levels of surplus produced by the worker. The goal of workers is to have more control over their labor and to get an increasing share of the surplus they produce.

Two other class positions are managers and independent producers (petite bourgeoisie or, more commonly, the self-employed). Although not essential class positions, they add stability to capitalist systems as they develop. For managers, their specific relationship to production is that they do not own but they do control production for those who do own. The goal of management is to generate efficiency over their unit to reduce the costs of production relative to the surplus produced. Some define the managerial class position as an in-between or contradictory position. This means that their interests can be divided between the two opposing classes. Because managers do not own production, like workers they sell their labor to those who do or their representatives via a labor market. They can also be fired for their management work. However, they are paid to represent the interest of owners and are rewarded for increasing the levels of exploitation of workers. Managers at the highest levels also will receive portions of ownership as an incentive for their success in management. Thus at the highest levels the differences in position with the capitalist class disappear. In these positions most of the income that these managers receive comes more directly from stock options and bonuses. Independent producers (sometimes referred to as small business or petit bourgeoisie) are like capitalists in that they own and control production. Unlike capitalists, however, they do not receive their income principally from the expropriation of surplus produced by the labor of others; instead, the surplus is for the most part produced by their own labor. In the United States, this is the group that we define as "self-employed." They essentially employ themselves to work to produce a surplus that they directly own. There are few or no other workers who are part of the production of surplus. As more workers are added and more surplus is produced by these additional workers, the position changes into that of capitalist position, sometimes transitioning through an "owner-manager position."

In terms of the relations of reproduction, the fundamental organizing principle is gender. Gender refers to the social transformation of the biological category of sex. It refers to the role and behavioral expectations associated with one who is a member of one gender or the other. Generally speaking, in all societies of the world there is the institutionalization of dominance of male over the female gender. This institutionalized pattern is called patriarchy. Patriarchy refers to the institutional pattern whereby men have more power than women in the functioning of the family and schools, two spheres of physical and cultural reproduction of the population, as well as all other institutional spheres (economy, polity, and religious institutions). Conflict theorists define our own society as patriarchal capitalist. This refers to a specific level of development and organization of the forces of production and reproduction and relations of production and reproduction. For the conflict approach, the relations of production and reproduction, the divisions along class and gender lines, are at the foundation of the social order. The character of these divisions (numbers of positions within the divisions and distances between them) is a product of the historical development of the forces of production and reproduction and the struggles and conflict between and within the divisions in the society.

Ethnic or "racial" designation is also an important organizing principle of the population and cuts across class and gender divisions. In the United States and many other capitalist nations, labor markets have been organized in terms of ethnic/racial categories. The origins of these systems are traced to the legacy of empires with populations that occupied the positions of conqueror, settler, and conquered. During periods of occupation systems of overt discrimination were institutionalized, in some cases creating separate places (reservations in the case of the United States) to contain the conquered populations. In these most overt cases, laws were passed to establish discriminatory treatment of categories of people who occupy a particular ethnic/racial group. The legal discriminatory treatment of Native Americans, African Americans, Hispanics, and Asians through the system of apartheid or legal segregation within the educational institution in the United States was outlawed with the *Brown v. Board of Education* Supreme Court decision in 1954. In the United States this system of institutionalized discrimination continued to be eroded throughout the economic and political institutions with the Civil Rights Acts of 1964 and 1968 and the Voting Rights Act of 1965. The system of apartheid in South Africa was more recently dismantled at the end of the last century and, like the system of apartheid in the United States, will leave a legacy affecting citizens for a very long time. Today, legal forms of discrimination around the world have given way to patterns of subordination that are a product of these historical experiences, cultural traditions, and institutional practices that are ethnically discriminatory in outcome but not necessarily by intent. When we look at patterns regarding the distribution of power across the various institutions within a society, they fall along these divisions of class, gender, and ethnic stratification. The intersection of these divisions defines specific positions along a power hierarchy. Those at the top are capitalist, in most cases male and of white European ancestry; those at the bottom are working class, usually female and of minority ethnic status (Native American, African American, Latin American in the United States).

From the conflict perspective, the institutions of the society are mechanisms to maintain and reproduce the social order. In particular, the institutions function to reproduce the divisions that are at the foundation of the society (i.e., relations of production and reproduction). In this way, institutions are seen as mechanisms of coercion and social control. For example, whether we are discussing education or the criminal justice system, both function to maintain and reproduce the order either through the promotion of ideas or ideologies that legitimate the order, as in the case of schools, or through threats of violence directed at those whose actions threaten the order, as in the case of the police, courts, and the prison system. In this way, both institutional spheres are principally fulfilling a social-control function.

Furthermore, the institutions of the society function systematically to benefit those with the most power in the society based on their position and function to the disadvantage of those with the least power in the society based on their position. Thus the economy is structured as in the functioning of a market, to be more responsive to those with more power (money) to participate and least responsive to those with the least power (money) to participate. The political system in the United States, although based on a system of universal suffrage for adult citizens, is intimately connected to the distribution of economic power. We know that the amount of money individuals have to contribute to candidates influences election outcomes. Furthermore, those who are in the highest offices in local, state, and federal governments are disproportionately drawn from the economic elite positions of those respective jurisdictions. Last, Miliband (1983) notes that aside from the economic power of the capitalist class and the importance of the shared culture among the elite, there is the power that capitalists have in influencing the state as a result of their control of production. Economic activity is the tax base of government funding. Furthermore, if the state acts in ways that are counter to the interest of capital, capital has the ultimate power of reducing its investment in production or shifting it to sites outside of the jurisdiction of specific governmental bodies. This will have serious impact on the economic well-being of the populace and the political careers of those in control of the state (Miliband, 1983).

In terms of the educational institution, we know that all citizens have a right to an education in the United States, but we also know that the quality of schooling in the United States is very much tied to school resources and the income and wealth of the school population it serves. Kozol's *Savage Inequalities* documented the tremendous disparities in resource distribution across public schools throughout the nation. The inequities between public schools that are best funded and the elite private schools are even greater (Kozol, 1991).

Change is caused by the conflict between the divisions within the society. This conflict is stimulated because of what is referred to as contradictions that develop within and between modes of production and reproduction. In regard to the contradictions that develop within the mode of production, as the forces of production develop they come into conflict with the relations of production. There is constant pressure for capitalists to develop the forces of production in order to produce the higher levels of surplus that is the basis of their profits. Capitalists are also in competition with other capitalists for the sale of their products in the marketplace. Only through the sale of products in the marketplace can capitalists realize the surplus produced in the production process through the exploitation of labor.

To garner a larger and larger share of the market to maximize the realization of surplus, the capitalist attempts to produce in a more efficient manner. This efficiency may refer to the introduction of increasing mechanization of production to streamline and speed up the production process. With increasing mechanization, workers working at the same time intervals can produce a larger amount of products than workers who are producing without the machinery. This refers to increasing the relative surplus of production. Efficiency also can be achieved by paying workers less for the same labor. This can result directly by redefining the nature of work from skilled to semiskilled or machine operator status. It can also be caused indirectly as a result of the increasing levels of unemployment as workers are increasingly displaced by machines in the production process, thus lowering wages. These latter methods are referred to as increasing the level of absolute surplus. For the capitalist, the fundamental rule of the market is that you grow or you die. What this means is that if you, as a capitalist, do not continue to garner a larger and larger share of the market at greater and greater levels of surplus produced and realized, you risk being beaten in the market by capitalists who have more capital to expand and improve the generation of surplus. These forces push the further development of the forces of production. Thus, capitalists are pushed to produce increasing amounts of surplus at increasing levels of efficiency in order to continue to expand their capital. If they do not, they risk losing it. This is the nature of the capital accumulation processes that are at the heart of capitalist systems. This further development of the forces of production has consequences on the relations of production, or as Marxist conflict theorists describe it, the forces of production come into contradiction with the relations of production.

An example of a contradiction that can develop as a result of this fundamental dynamic of capitalist society results from the fact that as production develops, it requires less and less human labor. Machines are increasingly taking over work that humans used to perform. On the one hand this is progress; less human labor is required for the material reproduction of the society, and humans will have more leisure time to develop their talents and interests. On the other hand, this poses a serious problem for our society and is the basis for the stimulation of conflict that has the potential of leading to fundamental changes in the society. If less labor is required in the society, how will the increasingly large segment of the society without work be able to acquire the necessities of survival? This is a fundamental contradiction that develops because of the nature of the mode of production in our society. Other examples of these contradictions inherent to our mode of production take us beyond the scope of our discussion at this time. These contradictions all serve to stimulate conflicts between the divisions in the society that, for the conflict approach, are the basis of change in the society.

Regarding contradictions that develop within the mode of reproduction, the same dynamic is present. As the forces of reproduction develop, they come into contradiction with the relations of reproduction or gender relations. For example, the impact of changes in the technology of birth control affects the power relations between men and women. Many sociologists have pointed to the development of the birth control pill as a factor that led to the women's movement during the late 1960s that created changes in the nature of the relations between men and women in our society (Mauss, 1975; Tallman, 1976). As women gain more control over their reproduction, their power increases relative to men in the society. They have the ability to choose not to have children, to seek employment, and thus be less dependent on men in their role as breadwinner. This reduces the power disparity between women and men and thus has the potential of changing the nature of gender relations in the society. Thus, as the forces of reproduction develop, they come into conflict with how we have organized the population in terms of gender to physically and culturally reproduce the population.

Contradictions may develop between the modes of production and reproduction. Both systems are linked as part of a whole system. As one system changes in response to the conflicts stimulated by contradictions within, it reverberates back to the other system. For example, as women have increasingly entered the workforce in part because of changes in birth control technology, this has had an effect on gender relations. Women, who were once entirely dependent economically on men, are no longer as dependent, if at all. This independence has affected the distribution of power between men and women in the home. Divorce rates have climbed dramatically in this country from the 1950s, and the rate of marriage has also been in decline, reaching its lowest level in the United States in 2009 (UPI, 2010). Furthermore, as capitalists have mechanized and automated production and have increased in size and holdings (tendency toward monopolization), they have been able to shift production continually to cheaper labor areas, increasingly outside of the

United States to poorer developing countries. This has resulted in an increasing displacement of workers, especially male workers, as a result of deindustrialization. The fall in the standard of living of the working population resulting from deindustrialization and the increasing internationalization of the labor market has pushed women into the labor market in order for families to maintain their economic position or slow down their decline. This increased entry of women workers as a result of both forces affects not only gender relations but the relations of production: as more women enter the workforce, increasing the pool of available workers, it affects the price of labor and the nature of work conditions; it is also changes the gendered nature of the workplace. Conflicts over sexual harassment and hostile work environments are a result of the increasing participation and power of women in the workplace. Thus, as one mode changes in response to contradictions that develop between forces and relations and the resultant conflict that develops, so does the potential for change in the other mode.

The political orientation of the conflict approach is radical, that is, outside the ideological parameters of the system. Problems within the society are endemic, a product of the organization of the society, not incidental to the society. They fundamentally occur because of the class, gender, and ethnic divisions within the population. The central questions for the conflict approach are: What are the conditions that provoke conflicts between the structural divisions? What are the conditions that provoke a class, ethnic group, or gender's awareness or consciousness of their interest and action that attempts to realize their interests in opposition to the dominant interests? The focus is on the forces for change in the society.

How does each of these two approaches view violence? Table 1.2 contrasts the two approaches on the concept of violence. First, regarding the conceptualization of violence, the order approach sees violence as principally the result of actions of people acting alone or within small groups. Violence as a product of institutional action or the structural organization of society is not usually considered a focus of the problem, unless it threatens the order.

Also, according to the order approach, the intent of the action is crucial to understanding the behavior. The actors must intend violence for it to be violent behavior. Action that is willful but not intended as violence is not considered a violent act. Thus, actions by corporations that are not intended to be violent but have violent consequences, such as knowingly selling unsafe products to unsuspecting consumers or operating unsafe mines or factories, would not be considered violence. Moreover, definitions of violence are system specific. What is defined as violence in one society does not necessarily apply to another. Violence is defined in terms of the cultural system, often in terms of a violation of law. Thus, from the order approach, the study of criminal violence and violence are one and the same. Generally, violence not defined as criminal is not considered an object of study.

The conflict approach, in contrast, sees violence as principally the result of the organization of society. Here, the principal causes of violence in a society are systems of stratification that are the basis of the organization of that society. Also, the violence of individuals is only one source of violence. More important to the conflict theorist are institutional and structural forms or levels of violence. Thus, violence by the state or economic institutional

Table 1.2. Order and Conflict Approaches to the Study of Violence.

	Order	Conflict
Conceptualization of violence	Individual and collective action. Intent of action is of primary importance. Stress is on cultural relative definitions of violence. A certain level of violence is innate to humans.	Individual, institutional, and structural action. Outcome is of primary importance. Stress is on universal definitions of violence tied to human rights. Violence is not innate but learned.
Cause of violence	Incidental to the social order. Violence is principally seen as a deficit of the individual. Deviant forms of violence are seen as a product of physical, psychological, and/or socially adaptive deficits together with natural tendencies.	Social forms in which we live our lives are the causes. Hierarchies and exploitative relationships are the fundamental causes of violence.
Role of violence in the society	Focus is principally on its disruptive role. Violence that is used to maintain the order is seen as legitimate and necessary and not defined as an area of study.	Constructive, adaptive, and disruptive to the social order. Violence is seen as playing a role in reproducing hierarchical/exploitative relations within the order and as a form of adaption and rebellion to those relations.

actors in the pursuit of power and profit is recognized to be more destructive than acts of interpersonal violence. Also, the violence of poverty, sexism, and racism is seen as the greatest form of violence. Furthermore, these higher levels of violence are ultimately the causes of interpersonal violence.

For conflict theorists, the intent of action is secondary to the outcome. Although violence may not be intended by the actors, their actions are willful, and the violent outcomes are the same. In many cases, we can say that the violence is institutionalized in the society. For example, businesses that knowingly engage in selling unsafe products to unsuspecting consumers would still be violent, regardless of whether or not the intent of the sale was to cause violence to consumers. The violence to "maintain order" is nevertheless violence. Similarly the violence in other organizations performing other institutional actions, whether it is in the school, home, or church, is still violence.

For the conflict approach, the stress is on seeing the forms of violence as interdependent or interrelated. Violence of an interpersonal nature is linked to institutional and structural levels of violence. Additionally, violence is defined in terms of universal criteria. For example, conflict theorists conceptualize violence as actions or conditions that are threatening to the well-being of individuals or groups and as actions that are a violation of fundamental human rights. The distinction between normative and deviant forms of violence is not central to the definition of violence for the conflict approach as it is for the order approach. Therefore, an act of female infanticide among the Yanomamo would be defined as an act of violence by those using a conflict approach, as well as the denial of needed medical services to the poor and uninsured that leads to premature death. Or the violence that results from the dumping of toxic wastes unsafely near residential areas is defined as violence by the conflict theorist, whereas in societies where these acts occur, they may not be defined as violence and are thus not violent by the conceptualization of order theorists.

Pepinsky notes that "if indeed crime and punishment are arbitrary distinctions for forms of violence, and if indeed the distinctions are politically partisan, then it is morally and epistemologically unacceptable for criminologists to accept any of these distinctions; instead, nonpartisan criminologists ought to develop a theory of violence which presupposes that the only way to reduce the level of crime or punishment in any person or any group is to reduce violence generally" (1991, 17). This is ultimately the goal of a conflict analysis of violence.

Regarding criminal violence, the order approach views violence as fundamentally a problem of an actor's adaptation or maladaptation to the social order. Usually this is a result of individual deficiencies or the individual's immediate environment. The root of this maladjustment may be biological. For example, acts of violence have been attributed to genetic defects as in the case of Klinefelter's syndrome (XYY chromosome), hormonal or dietary imbalances, or as a result of a physiological illness (e.g., linking epilepsy and violent behavior) (Fishbein, 1990). Or the root cause may be psychological. A plethora of research focuses on the psychopathic personality and acts of violence, and other research focuses on deficiencies in one's personality and violence. Last, order theorists may see the root cause as sociological. Violence may be seen as caused by a disorganized social environment, anomie (a sense of normlessness or a condition where means are insufficient to achieve societally defined goals), the learning of violence from intimates, or from the absence of social control as a result of inadequate bonds to the social order. In all these cases, however, the basic organization of the society is not seen as the central problem, but the focus is on a deviation from normality either in the individual or the immediate social environment of the violent individual or both. All of these deviations are correctable within the parameters of the social system.

Ball-Rokeach (1980) lists the most common deficit theoretical approaches as biogenetic deficits, ecosystem malfunction (e.g., crowding, hampered territoriality), deficits of person (psyche, insufficient internal controls), source of socialization or learning, and social system malfunction (breakdown of control or the authority system). In most cases, violence is understood as incidental to the way society is organized. It is not because society is organized in a certain way that we have violence; it is because of individuals' adaptation to the way in which society is organized.

For the conflict approach, the pattern of violence in a society is endemic to the way society is organized or ordered. Violence is a mechanism to protect and extend the social relations that are at its foundation. It is also a product of an individual's adaptation or rebellion to the way society is organized. In the first case, both institutional and structural acts of violence are mechanisms that reproduce the society. For example, the violence over protecting property here and abroad serves to maintain property relations that are at the foundation of class systems. Oftentimes tyranny or the lack of freedom refers directly or indirectly to threats to the rights of ownership and the exploitation of labor and an open market to realize the surplus produced. Violence committed by the police and military is in the vast majority of cases ultimately a defense of property rights and market access. The police use violence to apprehend a thief or stop illegal markets in drugs. The violence is used to defend property rights and the distribution of income that results from these rights. The use of violence by the military to redress the threat to national interests is usually translated to mean property rights of U.S. citizens or corporations or the functioning of the market, whereby the surplus controlled by capitalists is realized.

In the second case, violence is understood as a product of individual adaptation to or rebellion against the way society is organized. Violence is a form of striking back at society and how society reduces the range of choices of action for individuals to reach their goals, as well as defining what the appropriate goals to be achieved are. In many cases, violence can also provide a sense of power that has been stripped away by the functioning of institutions in the society as they reproduce the structural divisions within the social order. In either case, the violence can be instrumental or expressive, or an adaptive or rebellious response to the social context or position in which one lives.

Remember, as noted earlier, conflict theorists view institutions as fundamentally acting to reproduce the divisions that are at the foundation of the social order. For example, conflict theorists, in viewing the nature of the education system in our society, focus on how it functions to reward and enrich those who enter schools with the most educational resources and punish and impoverish those who enter with the least, through mechanisms of individual competition, "ability" grouping, and norm reference testing. Another example of the reproductive function of institutional processes is how the political system responds to different interests in the society as a result of the influence of money in elections. Political rulers follow their self-interest by responding favorably to the interests of those who have the greatest wealth and thus will preserve and reproduce the order that produces this wealth distribution. These reproductive processes reduce the range of choices for those who are seeking economic opportunity through education and those who are seeking political empowerment through democracy in a capitalist society.

Although order theorists in some cases have viewed deviance as functional to the social order (Durkheim, 1938; Dentler and Erickson, 1959), order theorists principally view violence as disruptive to the social order. Solutions to the problems of violence are defined in terms of improving the efficiency of agencies of social control, improving the integration or connection between institutions (connections between schools and family, schools and the economy, etc.), and reducing the problems of maladjustment to the social order.

Although conflict theorists see violence in society as personally disruptive, they view violence as constructive to reproducing the social order, as a vehicle for social change, or as a destructive adaptation to the system. In the first instance, violence is an important tool for social control and the maintenance and defense of the social order. Violence and the threat of violence are also tools by which those with little power are able to disrupt the system and potentially change it. Social welfare reform has often come about in the aftermath of riots. A report by the National Advisory Commission on Civil Disorders (1968), a commission appointed by Lyndon Johnson, identified more than 150 riots or major disorders between 1965 and 1968. In 1967 alone, eighty-three people were killed (most of them black), 1,800 were injured, and property valued at more than $100 million was destroyed. These riots preceded a significant expansion of the welfare sector during the late 1960s and early 1970s, defined as a war on poverty.

Last, violence can be destructive to the life chances of those who commit it, furthering the oppression and exploitation within the system. The use of violence by relatively powerless males to exert the rights of patriarchy (spouse abuse and rape) is an example where violence is a learned response to exploit those who have less power than oneself. The legitimation of the use or exploitation of another is learned from a system based on contractual relationships of exploitation; the violence is used to enforce a right that stems from capitalist and patriarchal relations. Ultimately, conflict theorists see the solution to violence in terms of changing the nature of the social order as defined in terms of the social divisions that form the foundation of the order and the functioning of institutions in reproducing these divisions.

This book takes a conflict approach to the study of violence. Beginning with the development of a definition of violence, the conflict approach guides us in our investigation of the phenomenon. Although we could have developed both approaches throughout the book, we found this to be too cumbersome and awkward. Furthermore, the order approach limits the study of violence by defining violence only within the definitional parameters of the society it is studying. In this way, the most severe forms of violence are excluded from study.

The third approach to the study of violence focuses at the micro level of social organization and interaction, one highly relevant to our discussions in later chapters. The symbolic interactionist (SI) approach views society as being composed of symbols that people use to establish *meanings* for themselves, events, and everything else making up their social world. The SI approach emphasizes how these meanings arise through communication (human beings accepted as the most sophisticated of animals in creating, manipulating, and exchanging symbols) and how persons in groups as small as only two literally create a *social reality* with real implications for their lives alongside the physical reality surrounding them.

Indeed, for sociologists the symbolic or social reality in which every human being is immersed from birth to death is the more important reality in most cases for understanding interpersonal relationships and social interaction. Symbols, from obvious manifestations like vocal sounds and writings-etchings to insignia, physical gestures, and body posture, are employed to provide cues for what behavior is anticipated and/or ideally expected from ourselves and others in "situations." Human beings use symbols literally to define what new and familiar situations mean to themselves as social actors.

Language is an element critical to establishing and maintaining any culture's social reality. For human beings the spoken language is a rich trove of phonetic symbols that can be further symbolically transcribed by physical marks agreed upon to represent actual sounds (and their meanings). These marks in turn can be saved indefinitely, thereby communicating the stored heritage of meanings (particularly when they stand for abstract ideas) to other persons of current and future generations. Because language as a symbolic system conveys meanings about the world around us, it is also the most important source of socialization and hence forms a salient factor in how we describe, interpret, and respond to social reality, including ourselves, or how we think about who we are.

Therefore, not only do we use language to define the situations in which we act, but we also symbolically define ourselves as to who and what sort of persons we are and what is to be expected in terms of our behavior. This self-concept develops through interaction with others, particularly in communicating our needs, desires, and perceived intentions of *us* and *them*, of self and others. Language is critical, for through it we not only individually come to learn how we (our appearances, our performances, and the consequences of our actions) appear in others' eyes; but through it we also are provided with the means to internalize others' definitions of us (not necessarily always passively but certainly interactively). Without the ability to symbolically communicate with others, regardless of the medium of communications, an individual will not develop a conception of his or her self nor be able to manipulate the presumed image in the eyes of others (optimally to his or her benefit). Without language there would be no way to express the thoughts, emotions, and attitudes that make up the realm of the individual mind. Thus, the key to human uniqueness in the SI perspective is the ability to use language and the symbols that comprise it. To employ an aquatic analogy, human beings are like fish, and a symbolic environment is the sea in which we all swim as naturally as fish do in water.

What is also important for symbolic interactionism is learning the definition of situations that we act in the context of and the symbolic cues that define the situation. In considering violent actions, the symbolic interactionist would consider the importance of learning the symbolic cues and definitions of situations that would provoke or rationalize violent behavior. Later in the next chapter we describe the importance of learning roles as they relates to violence and the definition of situations that communicate to the actors the meaning of violence in that social interaction context.

Finally, symbolic interaction offers a valuable dimension to any understanding of violence. It leads us to ask such questions (or to be sensitive to such considerations) as: Does the definition of violence differ from group to group, society to society, and era to era? Or does the acceptability of some levels of violence also follow such cultural and temporal or any other situationally defined relativity? Clearly the definition and accepted view of violence by any group are central to understanding the phenomenon. In others words, the interactionist approach leads us to consider that violence is not simply some objective thing, with standard properties of physical reality such as one finds in the elements within the periodic table. For the symbolic interactionist the context of the behavior is more important than understanding the nature of the physical act of violence. It is the context that defines the behavioral expectations for the violence to occur. Lastly, symbolic interactionists focus our attention on the fact that violence is learned, just as any other behavior is learned, and it is defined as appropriate or inappropriate in different socially defined situations. Violence is learned in the context of groups that define its meaning to the actors involved in the social interaction as participants or audience to the act.

IMPORTANCE OF CROSS-CULTURAL ANALYSIS IN SOCIOLOGY

Cross-cultural analysis is an important tool of the sociological perspective. It facilitates our ability to see the strange in the familiar. In looking at patterns of violence in different societies, cross-cultural comparisons allow us to make the transition in viewing the violence in our own society as an outsider to our own society.

Furthermore, cross-cultural analysis facilitates our ability to see the general in the particular. In viewing the violence in another society, it is much easier to see patterns of behavior. We are less likely to get lost in the trees and not see the forest. In viewing patterns of violence in other societies, we are more able to make this transition to gain a better understanding of the patterned violence in our own society, whether the subject is suicide, rape, or state violence.

Last, cross-cultural analysis makes it easier to depersonalize the personal. It is much easier to view the patterns of violence in another society as the product of that society than it is to see the patterns of violence in our own society as the product of our own society. In discussing how violence, say, in South Africa, is part of the legacy of their system of apartheid, we may see some parallels in our own society and how violence may relate to the racial divisions within our society. Without the benefit of cross-cultural analysis, we are more likely to engage in reductionism, seeing the violence of African Americans as a product of choices of individuals. Comparative approaches are crucial to the conflict approach. Again, the conflict approach sees the pattern of violence in a society as an artifact of that society. In particular, we start this analysis by looking at the organizational structure and, more specifically, the hierarchical arrangements that are at the foundation of the society under study. Only by means of cross-cultural analysis do we see how these structures vary and have different consequences for patterns of violence. Unfortunately, since most of the research on violence is conducted from an order approach, there is little comparative research. Nevertheless, we integrate some of the research that has been conducted into our discussions of violence to highlight the importance of social system variables in understanding violence.

WHAT IS VIOLENCE?

Violence is a phenomenon that is often taken for granted—"I know it when I see it." Such commonsense understandings can be both time and culture bound. For example, in 1934, when Adolf Hitler and the Nazi Party assumed control of Germany, the *Encyclopedia of the Social Sciences* defined violence as "the illegal employment of methods of physical coercion for personal or group ends" (Hook, 1934, 264). The explicit understanding was that a sovereign state, by definition, could not commit violence, whether in its own defense or in an effort to "control" its citizenry to maintain the order. "State violence" was assumed to be a matter of expediency, not a subject for social ethics. Violence committed by the state, in other words, was in the minds of sociologists at that time an oxymoron, a contradictory pairing of two terms. Incredibly, by that 1934 definition, the Nazi genocides of Jews and other ethnic and sexual minorities would not have met with the then current "social scientific" criteria to have been labeled violence.

Even today, most social science definitions of violence as they are rooted in the order paradigm are conservative and biased in favor of the status quo. Only deviant forms of violence are considered violent. Violence is largely conceived in social psychological or interpersonal terms, with individuals the primary perpetrators. Psychologists prefer the term "aggression" to violence and, unlike (at least conflict) sociologists, rarely look beyond the individual level (which is understandably their usual level of analysis) at macro-contextual dimensions facilitating or promoting violence at individual and supra-individual plateaus. As a result, neither state (i.e., governmental) nor corporate-based actions are subject to much discussion in studies of violence. Violence is seen basically as a breakdown in individual self-control or in the social control mechanism external to the individual. In this view, violence is problematic only when it is directed against the social order and "law-abiding" citizens. As Archer and Gartner note:

> The term violence conjures up the image of dangerous individuals. We tend to think of violent acts and violent actors in concrete, personalized form. This individualistic bias obscures the very real violence committed by authorities in the pursuit of domestic social control, or by governments in the pursuit of foreign war. Serious violence, including homicide, is produced routinely in the course of law enforcement, criminal punishment and executions, crowd and riot control, political subversion and assassination and, of course, war. (Archer and Gartner, 1984, 63)

With the development of the conflict approach to the study of crime, in part, stemming out of the development of labeling theory in the 1960s and the expansion and further development of the critical school of criminology during the 1970s and 1980s, the political nature of the definition of crime has been a central focus of discussion. A central tenet of conflict theory is that those with the most power in a hierarchically ordered society have the most power to define crime, and those acts that threaten their interests ultimately become defined as criminal. They have, in symbolic interactionist terms, the power to define and enforce the definition of the situation. Furthermore, acts that are in the interests of those who have power, even though they may cause harm to others (especially those with least power), are less likely to be defined as criminal. As conflict or critical theorists have moved beyond the critique of what is crime, they have struggled with developing a definition of crime that is inclusive of all the harms to people in a society or in the world as a whole. Thus there has been an increasing focus on defining crime in terms of acts that are a violation of universal standards or rights (Schwendinger and Schwendinger, 1975; Michalowski, 1985). Nevertheless, the definition of crime implies a legal foundation and thus a legislative body that defines law. Critical theorists have increasingly focused on international bodies that create laws or conventions as the basis of this definition. As in the case of a law within a society, however, if it is not enforced, acts violating it are not considered crime in terms of the consequential reaction to offenders.

There has been less attention by critical theorists to the phenomenon of violence as an area of study. Yet by focusing on violence instead of crime, critical criminologists may avoid some of the problems of definition that plague them in defining crime. Ball-Rokeach presented a conflict analysis of violence. She focused on how violence was a product of the hierarchical arrangements of society. She defined violence as "a struggle to maintain, change, or protest asymmetric social relations governing the distribution of scarce resources, by the threat or exertion of physical force" (1980, 46). Although her work was very significant in initiating a study of violence from the conflict analysis, her definition focused on the fundamental cause of violence as opposed to defining the concept itself.

Another definition of violence offers a broader, more inclusive view. Criminologists Weiner, Zahn, and Sagi (1990), in an anthology entitled *Violence: Patterns, Causes, Public Policy*, define violence as "the threat, attempt, or use of physical force by one or more persons that results in physical or nonphysical harm to one or more other persons" (xiii). This definition, because it considers action completed or attempted and psychological as well as physical effects, broadens the domain of violence. The authors omit the issue of a person's intent, claiming that being concerned about motives (i.e., whether the harm done is or is not violence if he or she did not mean to do it) renders violence a subjective concept depending on the actor's viewpoint, instead of permitting it to be a behavior that can be identified by independent observers. The definition, nevertheless, is limited in that the focus is principally on interpersonal forms of violence. Institutional and structural violence are not excluded by the definition; however, they are not explicitly included.

Weiner, Zahn, and Sagi view their definition as a useful heuristic device for expanding the classification, analysis, and discussion of violence. We agree. They deal, in one way or another, with those elements that need to be considered in any definition of violence: the degree and type of injury, the issue of the intentionality of violent participants, the object of the attack, and whether the harm occurring is the result of acts committed or omitted (i.e., failed to be performed). Although we agree with the basic thrust of this definition, we see a need for modification in expanding the definition of actors beyond that of individuals and groups to include institutions and the structural foundations of societies. Regarding the latter category, violence that is an outcome of social structure (systems of stratification) is not necessarily a result of actions by individuals or groups but more a result of lack of access to requirements for health and safety because of an individual's position in the society that results in death or injury. For example, infant mortality rates in the United States that are higher for African American infants than for white infants are a product not as much of individual action as of the structural arrangements based on class and ethnic minority status that limit or deny access to prenatal and postnatal medical care. Differences in the rate of AIDS between countries in the Northern and Southern Hemispheres of the world would be another example of structural violence.

Given this problem with Weiner, Zahn, and Sagi's definition, we propose the following general definition with the necessary specifications: Violence is any action, inaction, or structural arrangement that results in physical or nonphysical harm to one or more animals. Incorporated in its simplicity are seven important points of elaboration.

First, action, inaction, or social relationships based on structural arrangements that result in harmful outcomes must be willfully or deliberately committed or condoned by an actor or agent of the actor. Harmful effects need not be the primary goal of an actor, but the action, inaction, or social relationship must be within the sphere of control of the actor. Otherwise, it would have to be thought of as an accident. To be sure, accidental patterns can be regarded as social problems; that status alone does not qualify them to be included within the domain of violence.

Thus a traffic accident that occurs because the brakes in a driver's car suddenly fail on a curve, causing the car to veer off the road into a group of children waiting at a bus stop, does not meet the willful criteria of our definition, however harmful the effects might be. The same automobile accident caused by a driver who was intoxicated would be considered violence. In this case, although the killing of children was not willed, the drinking of alcohol to impairment was willed. Or another instance would be a traffic accident that occurs because a manufacturer-known defect in the design of the car that makes it difficult to control when navigating a curve at high speed, causing the driver to veer off the road into a group of children waiting at a bus stop. Again, there is willful action in the manufactured defect that ultimately causes the violence to occur. Furthermore, the denying of food by a shopkeeper to poor children because they do not have the money to pay for it is violent because of the structural position of these children in relation to the shopkeeper (a product of the class structure of the society). The action is willful and has violent outcomes: the premature illness or death of the children as a result of malnutrition. Another example would be a hospital's staff's denial of medical services to indigent patients. Again, the status of indigence is based on a structural relationship (a product of the class structure of the society); the inaction or action of denial of medical services is willful and has violent outcomes rooted in the class structure of the society.

To see how this action is violence, consider the same action outside the institutional context or in another society where the structural divisions are not present. For example, let's say you are walking down the street when you come across an individual lying on the sidewalk seriously injured and in need of help. If you choose to ignore the individual and keep on walking, your action has a violent outcome, an outcome of harm to the individual in need of help. But would it be defined as violence? Now place yourself in the context of a community of the San of the Kalahari. The San are a people of southern Africa who traditionally have lived as hunters and gathers. They are grouped in small bands of thirty to one hundred. The effective organizational unit in traditional San society is the band, the members of which are linked by elaborate kin networks. You are a member of this community and are injured and asking for help. It would be considered very wrong and an act of violence if other members of the band ignored your request for help. Questions about whether you had enough resources to pay for the help would not enter the mind of members of the band (Lee, 1979).

Second, as a corollary to the first point, violence can be intended or not intended by the actor. Here we are addressing intent, not consciousness and deliberation, as in the previous point. For example, in instances of rape or homicide, where violence is intended, we would have little problem in regarding these acts as violent. But what of the act that was never intended to produce violence? Take the example of the automobile company who manufactures a product it knows to be unsafe. It produces the product to increase profits, and the product causes damage to those who consume the product. Two examples would be the Ford Pinto, with its faulty design of a gasoline tank that could turn the vehicle into an incendiary bomb in a collision, and the Dalkon Shield birth control device that produced deadly infections in the women who used them. Both are instances where the fatal consequences were never intended by corporate decision makers, yet were nevertheless the results of the willed action of producing a product that they knew had violent consequences. Similarly, in the examples of structural violence, the actors who deny food or medical services do not intend violence; they are merely following the rules of the structural relationships that have violent consequences. The action is willed, nonaccidental action; however, the violence is not the intent of the action.

Third, the violence may be justified or unjustified. Sociology has long maintained the importance of any viewer's possible positions in age, gender, educational, economic, and power hierarchies, as well as the influence of the vested interests caused by such positions on his or her interpretations of social action. Often, there is widespread agreement that a violent action is justified, such as when a person defends himself or herself against assaults by muggers, rapists, or burglars. Likewise, government's use of violence as a mechanism to maintain social order can be perceived as justified, for example in response to looters who rampage through the streets after a hurricane or earthquake. Capital punishment would also be an example of what has been defined as justifiable violence by a state. Thus, the execution of more than four thousand persons in the United States since 1930 would be considered four thousand acts of state violence, regardless of the issue of justification.

Usually, judgments that actions are unjustifiably or justifiably violent depend on whose interests are at stake or who stands to lose or gain by the violence. The state or government in distinguishing criminal violence from noncriminal violence defines itself as the arbiter in determining which violence is justified and which is not. Those who only study criminal violence study those forms that are defined as unjustified as defined by the state. Of course, "justifiability" is undoubtedly the most negotiable of meanings for violent actions. For example, the eighteenth-century revolution by the North American colonies began as an illegal insurrection from the British point of view. Likewise, the 1989 Tiananmen Square student demonstrations in the People's Republic of China were sternly but, from the Chinese government's standpoint, necessarily suppressed in the interest of civil order. The deaths of thousands of Afghani citizens who were killed as a result of the U.S. attack and overthrow of the government of Afghanistan in the wake of the September 11, 2001, terrorist attack on the United States would be another example in which the violence was defined as justified by the government of the United States.

As a result of the subjective nature of social life that underlies our everyday, "taken for granted" social reality, any definition of violence must not allow for a shifting, never-final yardstick of the "justifiability" dimension—because that yardstick will vary depending on the power and interests of the interpreters of violence. Thus violence is violence whether it is justified or unjustified as defined by either the actors or the audience to the action.

Fourth, violence and its harmful effects impact one's physical, psychological, and social well-being. What unites these forms of well-being in regard to violence is that the safety and security of the person is damaged or threatened to the point of impairment. Obviously a physical attack of a man pummeling his wife or, after a series of such beatings, threatening to do so again can injure her body, not to mention her sense of personal security. Likewise, persistently demeaning her with insults that question her self-worth and threatening the relationship between them has serious consequences in regard to her well-being and whether she acts to further the development of herself or sublimates her interests and will to that of another. As often noted by sociologists and psychologists researching family violence, the long-term traumas and injuries from forcible rapes and domestic violence are often social and psychological and not just physical. Thus, physically, psychologically, and socially oriented actions (though, practically speaking, it is not always easy to separate them) can unquestionably damage a person's well-being. Well-being also refers to thriving and progressing. Thus, when we refer to violence, it is not only damage to one's current state of existence, but also damage to one's ability to progress and develop one's human potential. Here violence may be action that denies a minority group's access to education, health care, housing, an adequate diet, and other necessities of survival and human development.

Fifth, there is the issue of perception or awareness. Violence may or may not be recognized by either the recipient of the action or the actor. Certain forms of violence may be so integral to the structure of society and the functioning of its institutions that they may not be recognized as violence per se, just as the more important racial/ethnic forms of discrimination in the post-1960s United States have been almost invisibly institutional compared to more obvious forms of bigotry and prejudice on an interpersonal level that was more open prior to this period. Thus, practices by banks and insurance companies that serve to discriminate on rates or availability in certain areas of a community may have just as much if not more of a serious detrimental effect on the ability of residents of an area to maintain the quality of their housing and prevent neighborhood deterioration as forms of individual discrimination by actors who were following racist social conventions. Often, the long-range effect of such discriminatory action is an increase in the risk of violence to residents as a result of the social disorganization that accompanies the physical deterioration of neighborhoods. It is here that we may recognize the violence that occurs from "criminal acts" of individual offenders victimizing residents of the deteriorated neighborhood. However, the acts of institutional discrimination is hardly ever seen as an act of violence by these companies; it may be seen as just good business in reducing their risk and increasing their profits. Another case is the dramatic increase in homeless populations throughout the country, which is in part related to government decisions to reduce funding for low-income housing and the impact of deinstitutionalization of the mentally ill. In both cases, the policy changes result in violent outcomes to segments of the community, who are denied access to adequate shelter, and thus are recognized to be acts of violence. It is a sociological truism that ideologies or interest-based perspectives of social groups often create blinders that prevent individual members from seeing violence that is a result of the system(s) of hierarchy or inequity and associated rationalizations that affect them. These ideologies often are supportive of institutional actions and the structural arrangements that have violent consequences for people.

For example, however surprising it might seem to students of the late twentieth century, wife beating has had a mixed history of being defined as violence, both by the men who committed it and by the women who endured it. Prior to the women's movement of the 1960s and '70s, kicking and punching/slapping a woman was not legally defined as assault. It was most likely regarded as "necessary, if regrettable, discipline." Yet, during colonial times and even during the nineteenth century, women battering was viewed as a serious social problem (viewed, that is, by men, no less, who ran the legal establishments), and punishments (in terms of fines, prison terms, and even public whippings) were also much harsher than today. Marital rape, the phenomenon of "honor killings of women," and slavery as defined in terms of bonded labor in countries in the Middle East, Asia, and South America are other forms of violence that are changing in relation to their perception by the public and governing elites within those areas.

Anthropologist Paul Heelas (1982) argues that we cannot define violence outside its cultural context. Heelas contends that there are two perspectives on violence: that of the perpetrator and that of the victim. Problems occur when these two perspectives are not in agreement as to whether the violence existed or not. However, a larger problem occurs when neither victim nor perpetrator defines the act as violent, yet by universalistic standards it is violence. For example, in the Amazonian Yanomamo tribe, the husband, the wife, or the community as a whole would not define wife beating as violence. Nevertheless, these actions would be considered acts of violence under our proposed definition. Another example would be the outcomes of a system of institutionalized racism, such as that which until recently existed in South Africa. This system of institutionalized racism resulted in an infant mortality rate for black South Africans that was and still is many times higher than it is for white South Africans. Under our proposed definition this would be considered violence. In all these cases, the term *violence* may not be used by the victimized, the perpetrators, or benefactors of the relationship; however, the action is violent. In the same way, raping one's wife in a large portion of the world is not considered violence; by the definition proposed, it is a form of violence. Also, the widespread occurrence of young girls forced into prostitution to help pay off the debt of poor peasant families in Thailand would be considered violence.

This is not to say that the perceptions of perpetrators or victims of violence are not relevant to the study of violence. How violence becomes defined in a society is indicative of how a society is organized. Nevertheless, a definition of violence must be fundamentally separable from the perceptions of the actors involved. Thus, in principle, some acts may be perceived as violent by the perpetrators and the recipient, some acts by the recipient but not the perpetrators, and some acts by neither.

In our conceptualization of violence we do not intend to limit the domain of violence to instances where the actors, recipients, or perpetrators agree that violence has occurred. Indeed, we suspect that because of how ideology may alter perceptions, actors or recipients do not recognize most of the violence in a society. The effort to flesh out the existence and social consequences of violence is part of what the late C. Wright Mills termed the "sociological imagination," sometimes as much an art as a science but nevertheless using the humanistically informed scientific method (Mills, 1959, 4). As such a method, the goals in the case of violence are to define violence in such a way as to encompass all actions, inactions, and structures that damage current and future well-being.

Sixth, the proposed definition of violence is a universal as opposed to a relative definition of violence. Following from the above point regarding the recognition of violence, violence must be defined as a culturally universal phenomenon as opposed to one that is defined specifically in terms of the particular culture of the society in which it occurs. Although this clearly violates the cultural relativistic value premise of anthropology, it is consistent with the movement of international bodies (United Nations Universal Declaration of Human Rights, International Labor Organization, International Criminal Court, and Human Development Program of the United Nations) attempting to develop international standards of rights, trade, and law to judge and influence the development of social systems throughout the world to promote the greatest human development and well-being. In short, our position is that we can and must define violence by focusing on voluntary actions, inaction, or social arrangements that injure well-being regardless of (1) the intent of the actor, (2) whether it is recognized as violence by any of the actors involved, (3) whether it is defined as legitimate or illegitimate, or (4) whether it is justified or unjustified.

Seventh, violence is not restricted to human animals. Other animals are both violent and the victims of violence. Predation refers to the killing and consuming of other animals. Obviously, predation and the violence that results are not unique to the human species. However, there is a pattern whereby those species that are most powerful as defined in terms of their predatory skills are the most violent. Other species of animals are more likely to be targets of human violence than the opposite. The systematic violence to other nonhuman animals perpetrated or perpetuated by Homo sapiens is a form of *speciesism*. Speciesism, as Peter Singer first defined the term in his classic work *Animal Liberation* (1975), is the exploitation of one species by another more powerful species for the latter's benefit and interests. The more powerful species, in other words, assumes a preference for its own material enrichment, comfort, or even amusement that overrides the pain and suffering, fear, lack of freedom, or even death itself of other less powerful species. The result of speciesism, however justified by human values, governments, industries, or even religions, is that nonhuman animals become *objectified* (i.e., treated as objects to be used) and *commodified* (i.e., to be amassed as units and processed in batches) as depersonalized marketable goods rather than as otherwise legitimate sentient occupants of planet Earth.

Speciesism in that sense takes its place alongside other "isms" of exploitation that many modern social scientists often view as pernicious. For example, *racism* in American history and elsewhere has justified the wholesale capture, sale, and enslavement of persons and communities as consumer goods and ultimately power-holders' private property. *Sexism* has traditionally legitimated a commodified view of women as literally men's property (for example, to control and/or trade with other men for their possessed women) or, in more recent times, treated them as integral human beings but with limited physical and psychological attributes compared to more socially powerful men. Both racism and sexism have at times developed elaborate ideologies and justifications for denying blacks, yellows, browns, and other nonwhites as well as women full civil rights and political liberties as well as equal access to important social institutions of the military, education, politics, and fields of employment. Another of the isms, *ethnocentrism*, one could argue, has been a driving factor behind most wars of conquest that make up most of the history of the civilized world, as power groups (backed by military force) conquer and take the resources of those that they deem less human, religiously enlightened, or civilized.

Violence against nonhuman animals, including other primates like gorillas and chimpanzees, occurs at the interpersonal, institutional, and structural levels. Animals have long been and still are violently exploited and killed in a variety of ways, directly or indirectly, such as: for *amusement and sport* (open vs. caged hunting; falconry; dog/horse racing; fighting in Roman gladiatorial games and otherwise, as in dog/cock/bear/fish fighting; puppy mills and for-profit breeding; circuses); *for transportation* (dogs, horses, mules, oxen, elephants, llamas, and camels); *for educational purposes* (zoos, carnivals, television programs); *for medical and other research* (genetics, toxicology, vaccines, medicines, behavioral psychology, and cosmetics); *for bodily products* (skins and hides, bones and teeth, organs, secretions); *for food* (milk or meat from cows, pigs, fowl, sheep, goals, ostriches, amphibians and reptiles); *for religion* (old and modern sacrifices of various cultures); *for work* (horses, mules, oxen, dogs, camels, llamas, not just as beasts of burden but also for manure for fertilizer and/or burning); *for law enforcement* (as in dogs employed in criminal tracking, apprehension, and drug detection); and *for various ameliorative/therapeutic purposes* (such as "leader" dogs for the blind and therapy dogs in hospitals).

Speciesism, in the way the term is typically used, is always one way; it is uniquely human and perpetrated on other animals. True, nonhuman animal-on-animal violence is frequent, even ubiquitous, but it is beyond our sociological purview to explore other nonhuman animal patterns, motives, and psychology concerning their violence in this book. Our interest in this introductory chapter is to delimit our coverage of the violent effects of speciesism at different analytic levels and prepare the reader to consider violence directed at nonhuman animals in ways contrary to our otherwise rarely questioned (or even noticed) daily dependence on their bodies and lives.

At the same time, we do not wish to trivialize dominant human interaction with nonhumans by considering horse racing or pet/companion ownership alongside the brutal extermination of exotic animals (with no chance of escape) trapped in "caged hunts" or the often painful preparation of cattle for slaughter (having their horns ripped off, branding their faces, and so forth, without anesthesia). Likewise, there may be compelling reasons on both sides of the debate over employing animals and animal products for research to save human lives (see, e.g., Croce, 1999; Carbone, 2004; Scully, 2002), and resolution of the morality of sacrificing animals for such ends is not easily resolved sociologically, ethically, or even theologically (Linzey, 1976; 1995). Certainly it cannot be accomplished here nor by us. We are keenly mindful of Stephen Budiansky's (1992, 166) caution against simplistic moralizing in the matter of living alongside and using animals, domestic or wild. Budiansky warned about "the pretentiousness of our believing that we can even make clear moral choices about a system as complex as the natural world." Nevertheless, it is important to recognize that, whether justified or for a higher purpose or greater good, the acts of harm directed at nonhuman animals is violence, and to exclude them from a field of study ignores an important area of violence that is linked in interesting ways to the violence that occurs between humans.

CONTEXTS OR SPHERES OF VIOLENCE

Now that we have defined violence, let's discuss the social contexts in which violence occurs. These contexts can be understood as representing different interactional spheres. We can think about these contexts as the symbolic interactionist would define them as different social interactional situations. The definition of the situation is defined by the positions and role behavior that is expected of the actors in that particular social interaction. Let's think of the various situations that we find ourselves in during daily social interaction. There are home and family situations; there are workplace and school situations. There are situations in which we are engaged in interaction with those who are strangers to us in public places. There are also situations that are defined as different contexts as a result of the positions of others in the larger society. Situations are often defined differently if one or both genders are represented in the interaction. Does our behavior change if we are interacting with someone of the same gender rather than interacting with someone of the other gender? Situations are also defined differently if we are interacting with someone of a different class or ethnic position as these are important systems of stratification in a society. What this means is that just as with gender, class relations and ethnic relations create different contexts or situations of our action.

By discussing the context or sphere of violence, we are not specifically addressing the cause of the violence. However, in the sense that the context describes the rules and expectations of behavior of actors, it is accordingly part of an explanation of the cause of violence. Let's take the case of violence in the home, for example child or spouse abuse. Would violence have occurred if it was not a family situation? Would the parent who beat the child attack any other child that was not his own, or the husband who attacked his wife attack someone else's wife? What about a soldier in the situation of war? Is the definition of the situation or the context related to their violent behavior? What about those who are soldiers but not at war? Are they as violent as they would be on the battlefield? Of course not—the situation is different, and thus the expectations of behavior and positions to which they are attached are also different.

Similarly, in the institutional context of a corporate officer who decides to authorize a product that he or she knows to be unsafe, the context describes the rules of behavior of actors that are part of an explanation of the cause of violence. All violence takes place in social contexts. The social contexts of our interaction, including violent interaction, are a part of the organization of the whole social system. In this work we will focus on three general areas or contexts of social interaction: the interpersonal context or sphere, the institutional context or sphere, and the structural context or sphere. Furthermore, although we discuss violence in separate contexts, many forms of violence overlap two or even three contexts. Thus, at separate points in this book we examine family violence within the institutional context of the family and later consider family violence as a manifestation of gender violence at the structural context or level. Let's first discuss each sphere of violence. Figure 1.2 depicts the three contexts or interactional spheres of violence.

Interpersonal violence is violence that occurs between people acting outside the role of agent or representative of an organization within a social institution. The aggravated assault between strangers at a bar, a gang fight between rival gangs, the rape by a stranger in the parking lot of a shopping mall, the road rage that turns into an assault—all are examples of interpersonal violence. Interpersonal violence is violence that is occurring outside of an institutional context. The violence may be organized, as in the case of gang violence or the violence of a Mafia, but neither group would be considered an institutional agent. However, in many cases it is not organized, but rather in response to emotions as in the case of road rage.

Institutional violence is violence that occurs by the action of an organization and their agents within the context of societal institutions. Institutional violence is violence by individuals whose actions are governed by the roles that they are playing in an organizational institutional context. Institutions represent a collective response to common problems in the society. They represent organizational mechanisms to solve problems that all members of the society confront. Turner defines social institutions as "a complex of positions, roles, norms and values lodged in particular types of social struc-

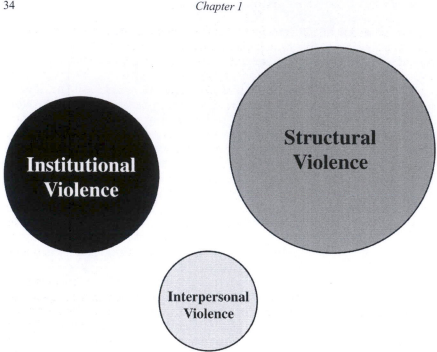

Figure 1.2.   Spheres of Violence.

tures and organizing relatively stable patterns of human activity with respect to fundamental problems in producing life-sustaining resources, in reproducing individuals, and in sustaining viable societal structures within a given environment" (1997, 6).

Sociologists recognize five important institutions in society: economy, polity or government, family, education, and religion. Within the broad categories of institutions, there are organizations that are carrying out an institutional role. For example, within the category of the educational institution, there are schools of various levels. It is the school that sets the specific context for individual action. In this way institutional violence is always violence by an organization. However, not all organizations are institutional actors. Each one of these listed institutions, the organizations within them, and their agents may be actors in enacting violence.

Violence in the economic institution would include violent acts by agents of corporations, such as producing a product that the manufacturer knows to be defective and not informing the consumer of the defect or forcing workers to work under conditions that may result in their harm and not informing them of the dangers of their employment. Violence in the political institution or by the state includes violent acts by government, such as conducting assassinations, executions, torture, wars against foreign nations, genocide, drug or chemical warfare experiments conducted by the government without the knowledge of the victims, and harm resulting from police riots that occur during civil unrest. Violence in the religious institution includes acts by religious organizations, such as intersect violence, witch hunts, heresy persecutions, religious ritualistic suicides, cult violence, forced religious conversions, rape and molestations, and patriarchal religious systems that encourage violence in the home under the guise of discipline. Violence in the family institution includes acts by family members acting within the contexts of their familial institutional role, such as child abuse by parents, spousal abuse, elder abuse, and marital rape. The least obvious forms of institutional violence are in the educational institution. Violence in the education institution would include violence enacted by members of a school acting within the context of their school roles. One example is the use of corporal punishment by schoolteachers and administrators. There is further the growing concern over the prevalent practice of bullying of some students by other students. Another area of violence within schools that is of growing concern is the violence by students directed at students or school personnel. The recent rash of school shootings during the 1990s in the United States in places like Littleton, Colorado; Pearl, Mississippi; West Paducah, Kentucky; Jonesboro, Arkansas; Edinboro, Pennsylvania; and Springfield, Oregon, raised public concern about this type of violence.

Structural violence is violence that occurs in the context of establishing, maintaining, extending, or reducing the hierarchical ordering of categories of people in a society. For example, violence directed at a racial or ethnic minority that establishes, maintains, or extends the system of hierarchy is structural violence. The 1989 episode in Bensonhurst, New York, where Yusuf Hawkins was gunned down because he was an African American male in a "white neighborhood" is an example of structural violence (Trippett and Painton, 1989). There were 4,742 recorded lynchings in America between 1882 and 1968. All but 10 percent of the victims were black (Allen, 2000). Although this is clearly interpersonal violence, the roots of the violence are in a system of racism that legitimates and maintains the racial divisions in this country.

The active subjugation and enslavement of native populations on contact by Christopher Columbus and his soldiers is an example of structural violence. Zinn notes that in 1495 Columbus went on a great slave raid, rounding up 1,500 Arawak men, women, and children. He placed them in pens and then selected the 500 best and sent them back to Spain to sell to pay off his creditors. Two years after this initial raid, half the estimated 250,000 Indians on Haiti were dead. Less than one hundred years later, no Indians remained on the island (Koning, 1976; Zinn, 1980). Here violence was used to establish a hierarchy between European and native or indigenous populations in the Western Hemisphere. Many other instances of this active subjugation and creation of structural divisions as defined in terms of ethnicity occurred on every continent of the world.

Structural violence is also violence when the harmful action is an outcome of the hierarchical ordering of categories of people. Here structural violence takes less obvious forms. For example, the different infant mortality rates and differences in life expectancy between African Americans, Native Americans, Hispanics, and those of European ancestry in this country are examples of violence that manifests itself because of the class and ethnic stratification systems that exist in this country. The same pattern of poverty is found throughout the Southern Hemisphere of the world where the poor whose life expectancy is many years shorter and who experience the highest rates of infectious diseases are the indigenous population who are at the bottom of the social structure as a result of conquest and institutionalized discrimination.

Structural violence also can be directed at women, youth, and workers. The systematic abortion of female fetuses in India because of male child preference is another case of structural violence. The act of rape, although clearly a case of interpersonal violence, systematically furthers the hierarchy between men and women in this society. Rape threatens principally women, not men (with the exception of male prison inmates); as an act of violence and an act of domination by males, it serves to inhibit the social freedom of women in the public sphere of life and thus maintains and extends the hierarchy between men and women. The violence directed at children to "discipline" them for behavior that offends adults who are defined as having control and responsibility for them is another example. The violence directed at strikers by company agents and the violence directed at scab laborers by strikers are all products of the class system in capitalist societies and thus structural violence.

INTERSECTION OF THE SPHERES OF VIOLENCE

Although we can think of spheres of violence as conceptually distinct, in reality there is a great deal of overlap between them. Figure 1.3 illustrates the overlap between spheres or contexts. In speaking of institutional structural violence, we are talking about violence by institutional organizations and their agents as they function to maintain, extend, or reduce the hierarchical ordering of categories of people within the society. One example of this is hospitals refusing to treat individuals who cannot afford their services. The action of the institutional organization damages the well-being and extends or maintains the differences in life expectancy of individuals that stem from their position in systems of stratification. Another example would entail worker safety violations that result in hazards in the workplace that lead to the death or injury of workers. Again this is a case of violence where institutional agents, typically owners or managers of an economic enterprise or organization, act to extend or maintain the differences in life expectancy of individuals that stem from their position in systems of stratification. A third and more obvious case is where the military, as in many Central and South American and African countries today and the United States in the not-too-distant past, acted in the interest of landowners to remove Indian populations, peasants, and hunters and gatherers from land they had utilized for generations. Death squads in many Central American countries, in many cases sponsored and supported by the police and military, performed the same function to intimidate and evict indigenous peasant populations throughout countries in Central and South America.

Another area of overlap is interpersonal structural violence. Here, individuals or groups acting outside the roles of institutional agents commit violent acts to maintain, extend, or reduce hierarchical structures in the society. A

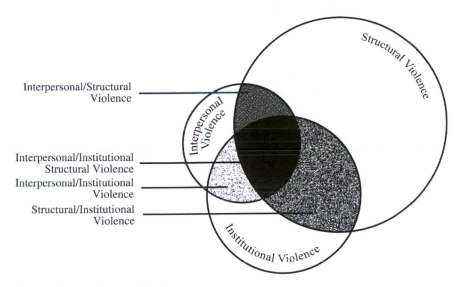

Figure 1.3.   Spheres of Violence.

typical example of this type of violence is a race riot. Race riots have occurred often in U.S. history and have functioned in most cases to further the
hierarchy, as did the riots in St. Louis in the first part of the twentieth century
where white workers attacked blacks because they were used as strike break-
ers by local capitalists. The New York City draft riots of 1863, when Irish
immigrant laborers refused to be drafted into the Union Army to fight for the
freeing of black slaves whom they saw as potential competitors for their jobs,
are another similar example. More than one thousand persons died during
these riots. The peak of race rioting in the United States occurred in the
summer of 1919 when riots erupted in twenty-five cities. In all these riots,
African Americans were the principal target of white working-class wrath.

Riots have also been instigated by minorities against the majority as in the
post–civil rights era in the United States and the anti-apartheid riots in South
Africa during the same period. The riots in Harlem (1964), Watts (1965),
Chicago (1966), Detroit (1967), Liberty City (1980) and Overtown (1986) in
Florida, Los Angeles (1992), and Cincinnati (2001) are examples where
minorities attempted to strike out against the establishment (usually precipitated by police force actions) and the system of stratification as it manifested
itself to the disadvantage of categories of people. Violence by members of
the Ku Klux Klan and other hate groups is another example. Silberman
(1978) notes that between 1882 and 1903, southern lynch mobs killed no
fewer than 1,985 blacks. Today, hate crimes are directed at ethnic and religious minorities, women, and gays and are an example of interpersonal structural violence.

A third area of overlap is interpersonal institutional violence, where the
interpersonal dimension overlaps with institutional violence. Here we are
talking about violence by individuals or groups acting outside institutional

roles directed at institutions and their agents. The deranged assassin, for example John Hinckley, who shot President Reagan and Press Secretary James Brady, would be an example of this. The intent was not to strike out at the institution or its agent to extend, maintain, or change a system of stratification. For John Hinckley, the goal was to achieve notoriety to win the affection of movie actress Jodie Foster. Another example is the murder of Salvo Lima, the sixty-four-year-old mayor of Palermo, Italy. Two Mafia gunmen gunned the mayor down March 12, 1992, as he drove through a beachside suburb in Palermo. There were allegations that Mayor Lima had worked with the Mafia. Similar murders of public officials have occurred in Colombia regarding the government's drug war with the Medellín cartel and most recently in cities in Mexico as part of the drug war there. In all cases, the organized group is not an institutional agent and therefore would be defined as an example of interpersonal, institutional violence.

Interpersonal institutional structural violence refers to violence by individuals or groups outside institutional roles, whose actions are directed at institutions or their agents for the purpose of maintaining, extending, or reducing hierarchical arrangements of people in society. The assassinations of Abraham Lincoln, Czar Nicholas II, Indira Gandhi, and Anwar Sadat illustrate cases of interpersonal institutional structural violence. Here an institutional agent, in these cases a government agent, is attacked to change or stop the changes in the social structure. Terrorist activities of the African National Congress and South African neo-Nazi groups that resulted in death or injury of institutional agents are another example. The coordinated terrorist attack by Al Qaeda that destroyed the World Trade Center and damaged the Pentagon and killed more than three thousand people is a more recent example. Here the organization, as indicated by their spoken and written justification for the attack, saw itself as waging a war against an imperial force, the U.S. government along with its allies, who increasingly were militarily occupying the Middle East. The more recent attacks by Al Qaeda terrorists on military and police headquarters in Afghanistan and Iraq, who are defined as working with the occupying powers, are another example. The terrorists define themselves as fighting a war to end their subjugation and control from an empire. This of course is not the definition that we use to define these acts of violence. From the perspective of the U.S. government, they represent madness or fanaticism or the efforts of a radical fringe group who is resisting progress in the nation's development, claims that are often made against groups that threaten the order.

In general, interpersonal violence is more likely to be defined as violent in the society and is viewed as more threatening by elites in the system. Institutional violence and structural violence are less likely to be defined as violent in the society and are viewed as least threatening by elites in the system. Yet as we will discuss in subsequent chapters, acts of institutional and structural violence are more destructive as measured by the amount and extent of the violence. Interpersonal violence directed at institutions and/or the social structure—as in the cases of interpersonal institutional violence, interpersonal structural violence, and interpersonal institutional structural violence—is generally viewed as more threatening than interpersonal violence alone, and punishments for these acts are more severe than for acts of interpersonal violence alone. For example, the attempted killing of a government official by assassins is deemed to be more serious than the killing of ordinary civilians by means of unsafe production or products, during times of warfare or through the actions of death squads, or by means of starvation or lack of access to medical care.

PRINCIPLES OF VIOLENCE

Ten axiomatic principles of violence form the basis of our conflict analysis. These principles outline a framework by which we can analyze violence. They are not propositions in the strict sense but are axioms or presuppositions that describe an understanding of violence rooted in the conflict paradigm within sociology.

The first principle of violence is that violence and the threat of violence are ultimately forms of power used to control the behavior of others. They are used by parents in controlling their children, by an abusive husband to control his wife, by a rapist to control a woman he wishes to take advantage of, by a robber who wishes to acquire money, and by the state to control behavior that threatens the social order. Violence is a form of coercive power based on the threat or enactment of physical harm. The central question for conflict sociologists is: under what social conditions will this form of power be used?

The second principle is that violence takes place within the context of the social structures in which we live our lives. Violence is a form of power that is an instrument for the maintenance of social structures in the society. In this sense, violence occurs in the enforcement of the social structures. Those who most benefit from these structures and have sufficient power will act to maintain the structures, ultimately by violence. In this way, violence occurs when there is violation or threatened violation of those structures. Thus, parents may use violence to force compliance to the family order they define as normative. The state may use violence to enforce the rules regarding the distribution of power that defines the social order. In capitalist societies, this distribution is fundamentally rooted in property relations. Most crimes in capitalist societies generally threaten property relations or rules regarding the distribution of property. Thus the state often uses violence to enforce these rules. In these cases, those with the greatest amounts of power—parents, governing elites, and owners of property—have a vested interest in the use of violence to maintain these structures.

Violence also occurs as an act of conscious rebellion or as an instrumental or expressive response to the structures. The responses may be an act of violence to challenge or change the structures. Examples of this include terrorist actions by the Palestinian Liberation Army, Al Qaeda, Irish Republican Army, and Italian Red Brigades, as well as the violence enacted by the Sons of Liberty, American revolutionaries against the British colonial governors.

The responses may also be an act of violence to achieve an end that the structural arrangement may create blockages to achieving. Organized crime is an example of this. Organized crime syndicates use violence to maintain, expand, or create black markets as a means to gain economic and political power in the society. Many organized crime syndicates are ethnically based, so they represent a path for social mobility for ethnic minority populations (Bell, 1953; Ianni, 1973). But it does not have to be an organized crime syndicate. The lone bank robber also uses violence as an instrumental response to the structures of the larger society as it relates to the distribution of income and wealth. In these ways, violence is an instrumental adaptive response to the structures.

The responses may be an act of violence as an emotional expression of frustration in response to social conditions stemming from the structures. The violence of gangs of economically and socially displaced youth in our society is one example of this. Violence often result from insults stemming from a lack of respect or recognition by another that connects to a sense of powerlessness as a result of the positions they occupy in systems of stratification. Even acts of violence by those who have power within an institutional context (the family) may stem from frustration in response to social conditions that the individuals have little control over. For example, child and spousal abuse are often connected to acts of frustration and a sense of powerlessness derived from economic displacement, poverty, and unemployment.

The third principle is that violence is more likely to occur in the context of hierarchical social structures. This is a further specification of the second principle. Not only do acts of violence occur in the enforcement of, rebellion toward, or adaptation to social structures, but they are more likely to occur when the structures are hierarchically arranged.

A hierarchical social structure refers to a ranking of people in terms of specific identifiable attributes that allows one category of people to possess more power in social interaction than another category of people. Systems of stratification of all kinds are by definition a hierarchical arrangement of social positions. In hierarchical structures, violence occurs because hierarchical structures are fundamentally based on relationships of exploitation between the positions that make up the hierarchy. An exploitative relationship by definition creates differential benefits and commitments for the actors involved. As a result of this inequality of benefits, there is ultimately a need for coercion to maintain them. This coercion may be latent—oftentimes exercised through the use of symbols, as in the role of ideologies that help those who are disadvantaged in the relationship to accept the structures as natural, necessary, or just. Or the coercion may be manifest or overt, as in the use of physical force by the military and the police to maintain order and the hierarchical relationships that form its foundation.

Hierarchical structures also can be more generally understood as rules that allow for the unequal distribution of a scarcity or power either based on chance, family position, a specific skill, or a specific attribute. Because differential benefits accrue from the rule, violence is more likely to occur. In foraging societies, which generally have much less developed systems of stratification, violence often occurs because of conflict over the rules of distribution of the scarcities. This is the same case as in more complex industrial societies. Although the rules may be more formally institutionalized in economic relations, there is a level of violence in maintaining and resisting them.

This third principle is consistent with the first five assumptions of the conflict analysis applied to violence as noted by Ball-Rokeach (1980, 50):

1. An unequal distribution of societal resources produces asymmetric social relations.
2. Asymmetric social relations produce conflict between constituent parts.
3. The asymmetric social relations that constitute a society's social structure generate and shape the unequal distribution of resources that produce asymmetric social relations between interacting subunits.
4. Therefore, conflict between strata in the social structure generates and shapes conflict between interacting subunits.
5. The transition from latent to manifest conflict is conditional upon: (a) legitimacy of asymmetric social relations; (b) perceived threat to established asymmetric social relations; (c) dissatisfaction with established asymmetric social relations; and (d) capacity to manifest conflict.

A corollary to this third principle is that the more hierarchical structures that exist within a society (ethnic, class, gender, age, etc.) and the greater the distance between positions within the hierarchical structures, the more violence will exist in that society as a means of preserving, adapting, or rebelling against these structures. Thus, in a society such as India, with complex systems of stratification, more violence will exist than in societies such as Iceland or Finland, which are more homogeneous and generally less stratified overall.

The fourth principle is that violence as a form of power is learned. It is learned first by the imitation of those who use violence to maintain power and control. In these instances we principally learn that power can be instrumental. As those with power use violence to maintain and extend their control and domination, we learn the appropriateness of violence for maintaining hierarchies or, more likely put, maintaining order and the control of the social relations that stem from these hierarchies. Thus, violence that is structural and institutional spreads to the interpersonal level as we learn to use violence to maintain the order in our own life that stems from these structures of domination. The violence directed at children is violence fundamentally committed by men or women, often directed by men, to maintain control. This violence is then learned by children as a means to control others with whom they engage in social interaction.

Violence also can be learned as an imitation of those who are dominated or controlled. In this instance, we learn that violence can be expressive in that it is defined as an "appropriate" response to anger or frustration. Our ability to enact violence allows us to experience the illusion that we have power, when usually it is because of the absence of power that we enact violence.

Learning provides the linkages between levels of violence noted earlier. Violence that we are accustomed to at the structural level becomes a matter of policy or practice at the institutional level and becomes a mode of personal behavior at the interpersonal level. As we learn the cultural and ideological justifications for the structural violence, and learn the legitimacy of the violent policy actions at the institutional level, the violence we enact in our personal life becomes "natural" or "normal." The violence that occurs in poorer families between parents (oftentimes mothers) and children as a way to gain control over their own lives and that is the product of their class and gender position is often passed on to the next generation as these children learn these same violent methods of control with their own children. Straus's research on child discipline patterns and their relationship to delinquency illustrates this pattern where violence by parents is used as a means of controlling order in the home and violence as a form of power is learned by their children as an appropriate method of exerting control in social interaction (Straus and Gelles, 1991a).

The fourth principle does not necessarily preclude the assumption that humans are innately aggressive, although this is an untestable assumption and is best relegated to the realm of ideology. Nevertheless, whether we are innately aggressive or not, we must learn when and how to be violent. Learning is the channel through which our biological inclinations or potentials manifest themselves into social action. We learn to be violent; we learn to exercise this form of power in social interaction. Ultimately, the culture of a society contains the curriculum of violence that we learn through the socialization processes and the structures that are legitimated by the systems of ideas that are part of this larger system of shared understandings. In the next chapter we discuss the role of culture in creating the lessons of violence.

We contend that an act of violence is not in the vast majority of cases a product of a physiological or psychological defect. Given the pervasiveness of violence at all societal levels, it would be difficult to argue that it is a product of individual pathology, unless one assumes that the vast majority of the population, including those in the highest positions within institutions (presidents and other government officials and corporate and religious leaders), are infected with physiological or psychological diseases that cause violence. Generally, all biological and psychological approaches suffer from the problem of not being able to draw connections between the defective gene or syndrome and the actual behavior. Furthermore, for biological and psychological approaches not to examine the pathological roots of legitimate or normative violence reveals their principal ideological bias and function of displacing attention from the nature of the social system and placing attention (and blame) for violence on those who are least powerful in the system. For example, if we are to use a biological or psychological argument to account for the actions of a violent gang member, why do we not apply the same model to account for the heroism of a soldier who is very effective in killing the enemy? Both individuals may see themselves as acting for the benefit of the group and acting to defend geographic or market position or territory, social status or position, or honor.

The fifth principle is that violence is defined as legitimate or illegitimate as it relates to whether it furthers or threatens the social structures and power relations that stem from them in the society. Robbery is defined as an illegitimate act of criminal violence because it threatens property relations. Assault is violent because it exerts control or power over another (not necessarily defined as assault if it is directed at women and children) outside of legitimate, institutional channels. Illegitimate rape threatens patriarchy. "Legitimate" rape—marital and date rape—that reinforces patriarchy is less likely to be defined as an act of violence. For example in Pakistan, rape is used as a means of punishment carried out by tribal leaders. On June 22, 2002, in the Pakistani province of Punjab, a tribal council convened to determine the fate of an eleven-year-old boy seen walking in the fields with a girl of the higher-caste Matsoi tribe.

> In a village like Meerwala, such an act is considered a great dishonor to the entire tribe. The boy's father tried to convince the council that his son had done no wrong. He even volunteered for his son to marry the girl in question and wed his own daughter to one of the Matsoi men. The council, however, could not allow a Matsoi girl to marry a lower caste male. After two hours of deliberation, the council ordered a ruthless punishment. Four Matsoi tribesmen, also members of the judicial council, were told to inflict dishonor on the family by raping Mukhtaran [the boy's sister]. Recounting that day, Mukhtaran says she fell to her knees, crying and weeping. She said she appealed to the council members' morality, reminding them that she taught their daughters to read the Koran. "But they tore my clothes and raped me, one by one." (Masood, 2002)

According to a recent human rights report in Punjab alone, a woman is raped every six hours and a woman is gang-raped every four days, yet only 321 rape cases were reported to the police last year (Masood, 2002).

Another example is that of state violence, which is often defined as legitimate and is often not defined as violent but rather as defensive or police (enemies are often referred to as "bad guys") or peacekeeping or humanitarian actions. Military interventions by the United States are all defined this way, including the military actions taken during the end of the twentieth century in Panama, Grenada, Iraq, former Yugoslavia, and Libya and recent actions in Afghanistan and Iraq, as well as the secret or covert wars in Guatemala, Nicaragua, El Salvador, or Colombia. The military now brands wars to sell them to the American public (Desert Storm, Enduring Freedom, Just Cause, Iraqi Freedom) and claims the use of smart weapons that have minimal impact on innocent citizens as a means to cover the violent nature of the warfare. Furthermore, civilian casualty counts are not reported because of concerns about public support for the violence and are referred to under such euphemisms as collateral damage.

A corollary to this last principle is that those who are more powerful in the society and in the world system have a greater ability to commit violence and the violence they commit is more likely to be defined as legitimate and thus not problematic. State violence is a large category of legitimate violence used by those who are most powerful. Conversely, those who are least powerful in the society have less ability to commit violence, and the violence they commit is more likely to be defined as illegitimate and thus problematic. This is consistent with the seventh assumption of Ball-Rokeach. She notes that the

> conflict behaviors of subordinates against superordinates are more likely to be defined as violent than conflict behaviors of superordinates against subordinates. . . . Control of the semantic politics of violence is a resource that usually resides with occupants of superordinate positions. While violence typically plays a role in the construction, maintenance, and change of asymmetric social relations, maintenance violence is likely to be labeled as something else. If superordinates relative to subordinates, have a greater capacity to define the violence out of their violent acts, then they would experience less psychological, social, and behavioral cost or be freer from social control forces when they engage in violence. Superordinates, especially those actively maintaining high positions in the social structure, should thus exhibit more violence than subordinates. (Ball-Rokeach, 1980, 51)

A sixth principle of violence is that violence takes place in the context of levels: interpersonal, institutional, and structural. All levels are a part of the general system of violence in a particular society. As we move from the interpersonal to institutional and to structural violence, the scale and scope of violence increase. At the same time, the higher levels of violence are less likely to be recognized as violence or are seen as less violent or as legitimate forms of violence and thus are not seen as problematic. One qualification to the above principle is where interpersonal violence intersects with institutional and/or structural violence. In this case, as mentioned previously, the violence is seen as more problematic and threatening than just interpersonal violence. Thus the individual who attacks representatives of authority of institutions is seen as more violent than the individual attacking his neighbor or a stranger. A race or class riot is more violent than a "just" war.

The seventh principle refers to the chain of violence. Most violence that occurs in a society is linked to other levels of violence. Violence begins at the structural level. What allows us to victimize others is our ability to think less of those we victimize, our ability to separate ourselves from those we victimize. Pepinsky notes in his description of violence as unresponsiveness: "Violence entails a willful disregard for one's effect on others. . . . Violence or disregard for others may be direct and personal or indirect and structural, as when the plight of impoverished classes remains unaddressed by privileged classes in a shared economic order" (1991, 17). Fundamentally, in the act of violence we think of our victim as less because we are conditioned to view others in our society differently, based on our perception of human differences of value or quality. This difference in perception in the evaluation of others is rooted in the structural divisions that form the basis of the social order. Inequalities of all kinds are social constructions. Differences exist between people on a whole range of attributes. The transformation of these differences into inequalities is a social transformation based on systems of stratification within the society. Thus men and women are different, those of African ancestry and those of white European ancestry are different, the poor and rich are different, and there are those who have different talents and abilities rooted in intellectual, physical, and psychological differences. What transforms these differences into a system of access to greater or lesser privileges and rights is a social construction.

The violence that begins at the structural level (e.g., differential illness rates, differences in infant mortality rates, differences in life expectancy rates, differences in life chances to develop one's human potentials) as illustrated in figure 1.4 is the first link in the chain of violence in the society. This violence is then linked to institutional violence. Those victimized at the structural level, at birth, are more likely to be victimized at the institutional level in families, schools, religious institutions, in the economy, and in the political system. Last, the violence manifests itself at the interpersonal level, sometimes directed at those perceived as victimizers at the higher levels, in most cases at those who experience similar or greater levels of victimization.

The dominant pattern of interpersonal violence, whether we are talking about murder, assault, or rape, is that those who are participants in violence at this level were likely previously victimized at higher levels. Thus, the causal chain of violence in any society begins with structural violence and ends with interpersonal violence. At this point in the chain the violence is more likely to be officially recognized and defined as violence. The earlier links are made invisible as defined in terms of violence. Thus, in searching for the causes of violence in a society, it is crucial to begin by assessing the society in terms of patterns of structural violence and institutional violence and then to look at the patterns of interpersonal violence and how they are linked to the other two. Unfortunately, because we have traditionally been blinded from understanding violence as anything but interpersonal, we often look only at the causes of violence at the interpersonal level. Thus our focus ends in a classic blaming-the-victim posture in explaining the violence in our midst.

A corollary to this principle is that societies with high levels of structural violence also have high levels of institutional and interpersonal violence. Conversely, societies that have low levels of structural violence have low levels of institutional and interpersonal violence. Thus to assess the level of violence in a society, it is crucial that we begin by measuring the levels of violence at the highest levels.

Figure 1.4. Chain of Violence.

The eighth principle of violence refers to the internationalization of violence. Although we can talk of violence as a societal phenomenon, it is crucial that we understand the phenomenon as a force that links societies throughout the world. Though these international linkages of violence occur at all three levels, the major links are at the structural level, followed by the institutional levels, and finally, the least important linkages, at the interpersonal levels. Structural violence at the international level refers to how the hierarchical divisions along major systems of stratification manifest themselves internationally in the positioning of nation-states and people within them and how these structures manifest themselves in differences in life chances. Life expectancies and morbidity and mortality differentials are much greater internationally, say, comparing Namibia or Afghanistan to the United States, than what you would find in any one society. Institutional violence internationally can be understood not only in terms of military violence between states but more pervasively in the economic arena: toxic dumping and the dumping of unsafe products and production overseas are examples of this. Another area not often discussed as international violence is the violent consequences of religious missionary work that has occurred throughout history and continues today. This is the often genocidal violence that results from the forced assimilation and destruction of indigenous cultures that is widespread throughout the Southern Hemisphere of the world.

Like interpersonal violence in general, interpersonal violence internationally is most likely of the three types to be recognized as violence and has received the most attention. As in all cases regarding levels of violence, enforcement networks have been well established for interpersonal violence. This is also true for international interpersonal violence and international interpersonal institutional structural violence (international terrorist activities). Similarly, as with institutional violence in general, enforcement is weak or nonexistent. This is also true for international institutional violence. Enforcement for international institutional violence is usually relegated to UN agencies such as the International Labor Organization (ILO), the World Health Organization (WHO), or the recently formed International Criminal Court, all of which have extremely limited power to enforce the international regulations and laws to prevent international institutional violence. For structural violence at both national and international levels, controls are even weaker or altogether nonexistent.

The ninth principle is that violence at the international level is defined as legitimate or illegitimate as it relates to whether it furthers or threatens the divisions between and within societies. Thus the invasion of Kuwait by Iraq was defined as illegitimate violence, but the more violent attack by the United States and its allies on Iraq that has continued for more than twenty years thereafter is defined as legitimate and necessary. As with violence at the societal level, international violence defined as legitimate is often not defined as violent but rather as a defensive or peacekeeping action. For example, after the Gulf War, there were a good many charges of rape, torture, and killings of Kuwaiti nationals and attacks on the Kurdish minority by Iraqi forces; however, there was little information regarding the level of destruction in Iraq and on its civilian population.

A corollary to this last principle is that nations and alliances among nations that are more powerful internationally have a greater ability to commit violence and the violence they commit is more likely to be defined as legitimate and thus nonproblematic. Conversely, those who are least powerful in the international community have less ability to commit violence and the violence they commit is more likely to be defined as illegitimate and thus problematic. Thus, the potential for and occurrence of violence by the weakest states are systematically exaggerated relative to the potential for and occurrence of violence by the more powerful states.

Herman (1987; 2010) makes this point in his discussion of the use of the terms *terrorism* and *genocide*. He illustrates in the many examples that he provides in the post–World War II era that the most powerful states define terrorism and genocide to exclude their acts and those of their friends and clients. He notes several ways that this is done in the case of terrorism. Two ways, in particular, are to confine the use of the term to nonstate actors and to distinguish between terrorism and retaliation. Thus, terrorists are understood to be principally small groups from the developing world who cross nation-state boundaries to inflict violence. The violence sponsored by the economically and militarily dominated states or by countries in alliances with these states, the violence of death squads composed of military and police, overt and covert military actions, legal and extra-legal executions, torture of prisoners, and so on are not defined as terrorism. Who is more likely to be defined as a terrorist group: the Palestinian Liberation Organization or the Contras during the war in Nicaragua, the Libyan government or the government of Great Britain? In all cases, it is the groups or governments that are defined as our enemies and not those who may be responsible for the greater numbers of civilian deaths as a technique of terror.

The U.S. State Department in the early years of the George W. Bush administration designated seven countries—Iran, Iraq, Syria, Libya, Cuba, North Korea, and Sudan—as state sponsors of international terrorism (U.S. State Department, 2001). Countries such as Colombia and Israel whose militaries during the same time had been linked to death squads, torture, and assassinations were missing from the list (Human Rights Watch, 2001; CNN, 2001; Lewis, 2001). Furthermore, by the criteria used by the U.S. government to determine which states would be terrorist states (for example harboring groups that have committed terrorist acts), the United States itself would be considered a terrorist state. Blum lists a number of individuals who have been accused of bombings of hotels and airlines, murder, and torture that would be considered terrorist acts in their home countries yet were living in the United States under the protection of the U.S. government. This in addition to the U.S. government's own assassination plots and attempts; funding, training, and directing mercenary armies to overthrow governments; possessing and distributing weapons of mass destruction; training and participation in torture of political prisoners; and so on would certainly raise serious questions about the U.S. government's righteousness in defining which states are terrorist states (Blum, 2000).

In the case of genocide, Herman and Peterson note when genocide is recognized and the role of political power: "The western establishment rushed to proclaim 'genocide' in Bosnia-Herzegovina, Rwanda, Kosovo, and

Darfur, and also agitated for tribunals to hold the alleged perpetrators accountable. In contrast, its silence over the crimes committed by its own regimes against the peoples of Southeast Asia, Central America, the Middle East, and Sub-Saharan Africa is deafening. This is the 'politics of genocide'" (Herman and Peterson, 2010, 112).

The tenth and last principle refers to the international chain of violence. Although violence principally has a societally specific causal chain, it is important to understand the international causal chain. In order to comprehend the pattern of interpersonal violence in our own society, we must first recognize how it is a part of an international chain. This chain of violence begins at the highest levels of international systems of stratification within a world political economic system (international structural violence). It leads to international institutional violence that reproduces, maintains, and extends the hierarchy in social relations between nation-states and sectors of the world system. This then leads to the pattern of structural violence within a given social system stemming from the patterns of stratification that are in part a product of world structural position as well as part of that system's history. This structural violence leads to the institutional violence that reproduces, maintains, and extends the hierarchy within nation-states. Finally, we arrive at the interpersonal violence between those who are acting in response to the social conditions and social relations that are a product of positions within social systems.

The impoverishment of nations and their people because of their structural position in the world economy and the enforcement of the maintenance of this position by imperialist relations between advanced industrialized societies and countries on the periphery is the beginning of this chain. The international structural violence of disease, famine, and lower life expectancies resulting from the impoverishment of people in Africa, South and Central America, and Asia begins the chain. This international structural violence may also manifest itself in the displacement of working-class populations in dominant countries of the world as a result of the super-exploitative relationships that multinational corporations are able to create with workers in poorer, less developed countries because of their victimization. This leads to international institutional violence as military forces from dominant nations, mercenary armies hired by these nation-states, or the military of the client states enact violence to maintain the hierarchical ordering between people and nation-states. Last, the interpersonal violence throughout the world by

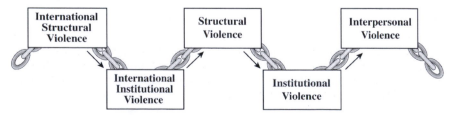

Figure 1.5.   International Chain of Violence.

those who are most displaced is a product of the structural and institutional violence that they have experienced. This occurs both within the poorest nations, where most of the world's population reside, and among those who are most displaced in the ghettos of the wealthiest nations.

If we focus only on the lowest levels, we see the trees but miss the forest of which they are a part. In so doing, we fail to understand the forces beyond the individual actors who are in their personal drama of violence. This is how we generally view the violence in our own society as we look for the defects in the individual actors or their immediate social situation. We fail to understand and see how the violence that is committed at the highest levels by those with the greatest power manifests itself in the violence of those with the least power in the society and the world. These ten principles form the basis of our analysis of violence. They provide the lens we use to understand the disparate forms of violence that exist in the society and the world.

CONCLUSION

Violence, as we have seen in this introductory chapter, can be perceived from different vantage points. It can be approached at increasingly abstract levels of conceptualization (interpersonal, institutional, or structural) that lend important insights into the contextual dynamics of how violence occurs and even point to forms not previously recognized. It also can be interpreted through separate disciplinary perspectives. A limitation of much previous treatment of the violence phenomenon, however, is that often it is considered only at one level (most frequently the interpersonal) within an order paradigm focusing only on criminal violence. Moreover, assumptions of the "abnormality" of violence are often implicit (usually from a pro–status quo orientation that views the sources of violence as located in aberrant individuals), and the official working data of violence are likely to be narrowly grounded in one culture or society.

Sociology offers a disciplinary perspective that follows the scientific method in describing the patterns of violence in societies and investigating the social forces that create these specific patterns. The goal of a sociology of violence is to sensitize us to ultimately recognize that violence is fundamentally a product of the organization of the society. This perspective challenges us to assess critically the nature of the social order for its contribution to creating the violence that threatens human existence.

Some of the instances of violence discussed in the following chapters are apparent, even familiar, to readers. Others, however, may be less obvious and perhaps never considered. To the extent that we can contribute a sense of connectedness to both the familiar and unfamiliar types of violence, movement toward a better theoretical realization of violence's pervasive and extensive sociological grounding will have been achieved, and consequently a better understanding of the nature of violence in this society and throughout the world will have been accomplished.

QUESTIONS FOR DISCUSSION

1. Think of a recent violent act in your community as reported by the media. Most likely it was presented as an interpersonal action. But what are the larger domains, structures, or contexts that surrounded that action? How was it a specific form of something more general?

2. A man enters a nightclub with his girlfriend and notices someone from a rival gang who has threatened to kill him because of a past altercation. He leaves the club but when he is waiting for a cab the rival gang member comes out and shoots him, killing him. How would this single act of violence be viewed differently from order, conflict, and symbolic interactionist approaches? How do they provide a more comprehensive understanding of the violent act than any one of them alone?

3. A farmer becomes angry at the dog that he acquired last year to protect his chickens from predators. The dog had killed one of his prize roosters, and he takes a gun and kills the dog. Is this an act of violence? What if the animal he killed was a fox? What about if it was pig and he sold the slaughtered meat to a butcher for a profit? At which point does the act no longer become violent? At which species of animal, and why?

4. Are people less responsible for their violent actions if they think that the violence is expected of them and they believe they are acting for the greater good? Forms of institutional violence oftentimes will take this quality. The offender sees that their actions are in the interest of the organization within which they have a position. So is a soldier who is operating a drone that kills a suspected terrorist and members of their family who are in the home seen as less violent than someone who kills someone in a bar fight over an insult? What about a mine safety inspector who ignores the safety violations of a large mining corporation because the political administration in power is discouraging the enforcement of these regulations, especially for a company and its owners who donated large sums of money to the political party in power? How are the levels of responsibility we assign to the perpetrators defined differently in these cases?

5. The authors contend that an act is violent in its consequence to the victim and that whether the offended intended his or her actions to be violent is not important in determining whether the act is violence. As long as the perpetrator was in control of his or her actions, intention is not important. Take the example of someone who is driving their friends to a baseball game. He gets a text and he responds back by texting while he is driving the car. He doesn't see that a child on a bicycle begins to cross the street as the light at the intersection turns red. He turns to avoid the child and his vehicle is struck broadside by oncoming traffic, killing his girlfriend in the front seat. Is there violence here? What if his girlfriend was not wearing a seat belt and she dies because she is thrown out of the car? Does that change the definition of violence as it pertains to her?

6. Is suicide an act of violence? If not, why not? If so, what type of violence is it? Is it interpersonal, institutional, or structural? Can you think of types of suicide that fit each type?

Chapter Two

The Cultural Roots of Violence

In 1971 a band of twenty-four people calling themselves the Tasaday was discovered living in a remote rain forest on the Philippine island of Mindanao. Believed never to have been exposed to the "outside world," the Tasaday allegedly possessed no weapons (nor even words to describe them) and had no history of war or conflict. They seemed to be living a primitive existence as simple hunter-gatherers, sleeping in caves, digging wild yams, foraging for nuts, and storing water in bamboo stalks. After two National Geographic *articles and a book entitled* The Gentle Tasaday *made the tribe a worldwide sensation, journalists and other observers flocked to Mindanao to investigate these nonviolent people. The Tasaday, it seemed, cut off from and uncontaminated by modern civilization, had found a way to survive successfully from some earlier, more harmonious age.*

But in 1986 a Swiss journalist named Oswald Iten revealed that the Tasaday were impostors, part of a hoax concocted by the politically ambitious head of the Philippine government agency in charge of that country's "indigenous peoples." When Iten encountered the Tasaday, they were wearing jeans and T-shirts, growing crops, and living in huts elevated above the ground just like other Philippine natives. He learned that the government official had paid the villagers of two Westernized tribes to smear themselves with dirt, clad themselves in the briefest of loincloths, and conduct themselves like classic Stone Agers.

The short-lived notoriety of the Tasaday illustrates the nostalgic value that such a pristine, if hypothetical, people possesses. These "savage innocents" seemed to confirm the myth of a basically nonaggressive human nature. They also lent support to countercultural critics who rejected modern materialism and its assumed relationship to crime and violence This was not the first time that Western observers (professional or otherwise) had idealized a tribal people as virtually free of violence when it later turned out that there was really considerable turmoil there all along (see, e.g., Barnouw, 1963, 39–58, 83–91).

It is no wonder that many persons want to believe that somewhere, somehow, such an idyllic nonviolent culture has survived or evolved. But sociologically, such a utopia is strictly wishful thinking. Even in the simplest societies studied by anthropologists there exist scarce resources, hierarchies along gender lines and family status, and (consequently) struggles that involve power and coercion.

And the documented conflicts even among so-called nonviolent people include interpersonal aggression, gender disagreements, corporal punishment of children, emotional and violent ostracization of deviants, and occasionally homicides (Montagu, 1978). These are patterns of social disturbance familiar to us all.

Yet at the same time cross-cultural analyses show that societies do manifest a wide variation in the prevalence, acceptance, and even valuation of violence. Anthropologist Ashley Montagu (1978, 6), in surveying more than two dozen relatively nonviolent, non-Western societies, asked; "How can one account for the marked differences in the expression of violence?" He concluded that the answer lay in "the environmental stimulation" (or culture) of a social group rather than in its members' genes. No one starts out life developing his or her own language without reference to other people, and likewise, no one adopts aggression and violence as social tactics without the influence of others in the context of performing roles or outside institutional role performance.

Culture, in its symbols, values, and traditions, sets the definitions and contexts of appropriate roles within social institutions. It also demarcates the appropriateness of violence in those roles and the inappropriateness of violence outside those roles. Thus, culture and its learning are important areas to investigate for an analysis of violence, particularly for conceptualizing the forms that violence takes.

CULTURAL ROOTS

The Symbols of Violence

Human beings are symbol-creating, symbol-manipulating creatures. It is a truism in symbolic interaction theory that we do not live merely in a world of physical reality but, more important, in a world of social reality. In every society members attach a myriad of negotiated or constructed meanings to all facets of their interpersonal relationships, and they use symbols to represent those meanings, whether the latter are the presumed intentions of others as they act or the shifting power and statuses of various social actors. Given the cognitive and speech capabilities of human beings, symbols can stand for nearly anything, such as concrete objects (e.g., a swastika or a cross representing a political and religious creed), and, conversely, nearly anything can become a symbol. Voice tone, facial gestures, body posture, skin color, numerous insignias, flags, uniforms, car models, clothing brand names, colors, lights, occupational titles, hairstyles—all can serve as symbolic guideposts affecting persons' treatment of each other and the flow of their interactions.

Consideration of symbols is important in the study of violence because so much aggression occurs between persons involving stimuli in the physical environment that have broader symbolic meanings within their shared social reality. Take, as a simple example, insulting gestures. The meanings of derogatory body gestures to insult people are not universal but particular to specific cultures (as symbol systems). The various individual physical movements involved would be inconsequential minus their symbolic power to arouse emotions.

Thus, the familiar North American hand gesture of touching the tips of the index finger and thumb to form a circle while extending the other three fingers together, an innocuous way to signal "OK" or approval/understanding, represents something altogether different and possibly offensive in some South American countries. There it may stand for *la sena* (mark or sign) *del burro*, meaning the anus of the animal. Likewise, raising a rigid middle finger while simultaneously curving the others, unquestionably North Americans' favorite obscene gesture meaning "Fuck you!" elicits virtually no reaction from non-Westernized Japanese. Nevertheless, in that Far Eastern culture, muttering *yotsu* (the number four, referring to the number of legs on a nonhuman animal) implies that the person spoken about is a despised member of the former medieval outcast burakumin stratum of society. Worse yet, curling the thumb and two middle fingers inward while extending the index and little fingers symbolizes horns (also a sign for the allegedly subhuman outcast minority) and can provoke a literal riot in a crowded Tokyo subway car (Devos and Wagatsuma, 1972). In France, a driver responding to another angry motorist's horn or vocalizations will stick his arm out the window and straight up. By patting the roof of the car directly over him, he signals: "Put your testicles up here for me to smash!" As is well known, Italians, Spaniards, and East Europeans, among many others, have their own special gestures to express rejection, disagreement, and contempt that often establish provocation for aggression. Possibly spitting is the only candidate for a universal motion of contempt. Admitting that one exception, obviously none of the other physical movements described is inherently threatening or insulting. Instead, over time they have come to serve as symbolic "shorthand" ways for expressing aggressive emotions.

Another case in point is art. Not long ago two European scholars examined ancient (mid-ninth to seventh century B.C.E.) Assyrian art and concluded that the Assyrians' artistic renditions of themselves in war and victory parades as well as on the hunt were symbolic statements of power and violence deliberately communicating those themes (Bersani and Dutoit, 1985). Likewise, Nazi propaganda extolled so-called Aryan virtues in posters that displayed robust men and women in heroic poses suggesting determination, strength, and even belligerence. Interestingly, the above authors compared the 2,800-year-old Assyrian bas-reliefs to the German filmmaker Leni Riefenstahl's classic *Triumph of the Will*, a propaganda movie that Hitler commissioned to record and glorify the 1934 Nazi Party Congress meeting in

Nuremberg. Both ancient Assyrian sculptors and Nazi propagandists under-stood the manipulation of violence and aggression in symbolic ways to pro-mote fear and awe of the regime.

The important point here is that a symbol can become a proxy for in-tended or implied violence. The closer such a proxy resembles the act or potential effects of violent acts, the greater is its salience and its power to elicit an equally violent reaction. A fist shaken in another's face, thumbing one's nose during a bar disagreement, or the North American middle-finger gesture (which could be used literally to penetrate someone either vaginally or anally) are all common examples. The range of possible violence proxies, and their deep integration into our daily physical and vocal expressions as well as our literature and popular entertainment, is considerable indeed.

The Value of Violence in Culture

The Yanomamo are a primitive polygynous tribe of approximately fifteen thousand Indians who inhabit the rain forests straddling the borders of Vene-zuela and Brazil. They have the unparalleled distinction in anthropological research of being the meanest, fiercest, and most relentlessly violent people ever studied (Chagnon, 1968; Shapiro, 1971; Harris, 1974, 74–75). The men are habitual users of a hallucinogenic powder that they blow through tubes into each others' noses, a drug that serves as an analgesic (dulling pain) and induces a stupor that leaves the users draining long trails of green mucus from their nostrils. When not raiding the villages of their fellow tribesmen, Yanomamo males constantly pick fights with each other. They challenge each other to physically punishing duels over the slightest matters: first trad-ing hard punches into each other's pectoral muscles, sometimes escalating to taking turns delivering blows with heavy poles to an unresisting adversary's bowed head, and then occasionally culminating in fights with six-foot-long spears. Constantly eager to demonstrate their aggressiveness, Yanomamo males are proud of their scars, even shaving the crowns of their heads and rubbing red pigments into the skin to make the lesions stand out.

The Yanomamo illustrate one extreme on a continuum of culturally ap-proved interpersonal violence, the opposite, say, of Quakers or Australia's famously cooperative hunter-gathering aborigines. It is unlikely that any so-cial group of any size is totally violence free. The members of societies have always had to accommodate themselves to some certain level of violence perceived as "necessary." As anthropologist Catherine H. Bernadt (1978, 158) notes, "The problem . . . is not whether there is some modicum of aggression in any given society, or whether there are expressions of what could be called aggression. It is whether there are checks and balances that restrain or contain these, how successful or otherwise they seem to be, and how they are transmitted."

Clearly social institutions prescribe rather broad roles of sanctioned vio-lence and even may promote violence as entertainment. In Elizabethan Eng-land, for example, "bear baiting" (placing a defenseless bear in a deep pit and gradually stabbing it to death with long poles) was a popular form of amuse-ment alongside Shakespeare's plays. The gladiatorial extravaganzas of Impe-rial Rome, sometimes pointed to as simply a more brutal and fatal extension of the aggressive drama in modern professional football, hockey, or mixed martial arts matches on television, served up a considerable amount of aggression and occasionally blood for mass amusement.

Human sacrifice is another extreme of institutional violence that has been shown by scholars to have been a truly global phenomenon, although it is probably true that no one surpassed the Aztecs of pre-Columbian Mexico in the scale on which it was practiced. The most common Aztec ritual sacrifice was carving out the living victim's heart while he or she was stretched across an altar. Flaying (skinning alive) was another favorite form. Sacrifices of men, women, and children were offered to various gods to ensure fertility for crops, dedicate new public buildings, celebrate military victories, coronate emperors, and perform funerals for elites. When Ahuitzotle, a powerful fif-

Figure 2.1.   Aztec ritual human sacrifice portrayed in the page 141 (folio 70r) of the Codex Magliabechiano.

teenth-century leader and warrior, died, two hundred slaves accompanied him into the afterlife. Ahuitzotle, once dedicating a temple to the War God, participated in innumerable removals of hearts until, wading in blood, he finally became exhausted and passed his dagger to a replacement. Countless more unfortunate individuals were sacrificed during the four-day celebration when the last Mexican emperor, Moctezuma II, was crowned (Davies, 1981, 216). Moreover, the Aztecs and their Meso-American neighbors understandably conducted war for conquest and tribute, but they also institutionalized human sacrifice to the point that the capture of prisoners to receive cardioectomies became in itself the main purpose of many military actions. The ritual combat called the "War of the Flowers" was really more like a medieval European jousting tournament, a mock battle staged by armies using weapons more likely to wound than kill. A warrior's status and rank resulted from the number of prisoners for sacrifice that he captured, not slew (Davies, 1981, 216–17).

Human sacrifice, in fact, has been a culturally respectable and "normal" phenomenon within prescribed institutional roles in societies from India to Africa to Polynesia to East Asia to Europe to the New World. The famous Hindu ritual of suttee, in which a man's living widow was burned on a funeral pyre along with her husband's corpse, was in no way unique. The bodies of Indian rajahs were frequently accompanied into the fires by a host of wives and concubines. Human sacrifices have also been regarded in many societies as desperate but mandatory ways to cope with military emergencies, droughts and natural disasters, and epidemics. Anthropologist Nigel Davies reports that the ancient Phoenicians and Carthaginians believed that the gods would improve their chances in war through sacrificial appeasement. Thus, at one point during the Punic Wars with Rome, noble Carthaginian families offered up two hundred of their sons for sacrifice to the god Baal out of altruistic patriotism. Pre-Christian Scandinavians buried children alive to stop plagues, while small children in Peru's pre-Columbian empire were sacrificed both to "cure" the emperor if he became ill and otherwise to preserve him in good health. Likewise, the rite of interring both children and adults within the foundations of new buildings, under city gates, and in the supports of bridges was common in pre-Christian Europe and the Far East and is even reported to have been practiced by the Israelites in the Old Testament (Davies, 1981, 61ff).

Not to be outdone by the past, there have been horrendous instances of mass slaughter in modern times. Some cases, like the two atomic bomb attacks on the civilian populations of Hiroshima and Nagasaki or the firebombings of Dresden and Tokyo, have been defined as within the normative bounds of institutionalized warfare. Other instances, such as Adolf Hitler's Nazi depredations on "non-Aryan" Europeans (including his genocidal holocaust that exterminated six million Jews) or Stalin's murder of millions of Soviet minorities and political prisoners, have been internationally condemned as violence falling outside the pale of any institutional legitimacy, hence branded "crimes against humanity" or "war crimes." Meanwhile, technological sophistication of the instruments of violence has grown exponentially since even these recent examples.

Yet, at the same time, as we've entered the third Christian millennium, the case could be made that the citizens of most industrialized nations are increasingly becoming sensitized to, and concerned about, violence. Indeed, there may be movement in narrowing the boundaries of its acceptability even into the areas of institutional violence. As sociologists Jack D. Douglas and Frances C. Waksler observe,

> The most striking change (in American violence) has been the rapid increase in social disapproval of violence, particularly in its illegal forms, and in repressive social reactions toward it. Social definitions of deviant behavior have been expanding to include more and more forms of action, while definitions of nondeviant violence have been contracting; this development has led many people to believe that there has been a great upsurge in violence. (Douglas and Waksler, 1982, 230–31)

The twin problems of spousal and child abuse, which we will take up in greater detail in chapter 4, are evidence of this new awareness. Woman battering, for example, has at various times in American history been considered a serious social offense requiring harsh corporal punishment and imprisonment or, alternately, a man's prerogative, that is, for "necessary disciplining" of a woman. The women's movement, among other factors, has been effective in changing the definition of domestic interpersonal violence as illegitimate (Stacey and Shupe, 1983).

At the same time, the rash of school shootings during the past fifteen years, including Colorado's Columbine High School rampage of random, wanton murders of students by an indisputably disturbed pair of students, has alarmed educators and parents. Whether similar events were independently inspired or following a copycat pattern, they are equally alarming. To a time traveler forwarded from the 1960s, the extent of "security" consciousness now part of public life, whether in our schools or courthouses or even in our airports following the 2001 attacks on New York's World Trade Center towers, would be astonishing and, given the taken-for-granted assumptions of safety of several decades earlier, would appear paranoid. Yet to twenty-first-century Americans, routine metal detection screenings before entering a school or boarding an aircraft have become acceptable, even desirable.

A further example is the growing concern over media violence, particularly as CGI (computer-generated imagery) has greatly increased filmmakers' ability to "perfect" and magnify special effects that glorify explicit, even exaggerated, portrayals of aggression and its grisly, splattering aftermath in shootings, slashings, explosions, and crashes. Since the 1960s several federal commissions and numerous independent studies (see, e.g., Goldstein, 1986; Rowland, 1983; Cater and Strickland, 1975), including one conducted by the American Academy of Pediatrics (Jubera, 1991), have confirmed that a constant diet of violent entertainment can have deleterious effects on audiences, particularly children. At least, this stylized violence desensitizes many members of any audience and prevents them from fully empathizing with characters in dramas. But this change, in turn, is generalizable to real life when these persons are then blocked from being emotionally affected by real occurrences. At worst, such violence has been found to offer role models for antisocial behavior and can lead to increased aggressive behavior during teenage and adult years (for a readable review of such findings, see Goldstein, 1986, 35–51, 170–75). Given studies that claim the typical American child watches more than twenty-seven hours of television each week and by age sixteen will have been exposed to fifty thousand attempted murders as well as approximately two hundred thousand acts of violence (simulated and real), there has been great concern voiced by behavioral scientists, family advocates, and governmental representatives. Virtually all research by the end of the twentieth century confirmed these findings.

Various women's advocates have voiced additional justifiable concern, arising out of this "new sensitivity" to violent themes in modern Western culture, over violent pornography. Research on adults demonstrates, among other things, that such aggressive erotica provides subtle (and sometimes not so subtle) images to males depicting females masochistically enjoying and inviting rough treatment during sexual intimacy. Moreover, experimental research has reliably found disturbing evidence that repeated exposure desensitizes both men and women, leading them to consider such violence as forcible rape a less serious criminal offense than they would otherwise have felt (see, e.g., Gubar and Hoff, 1989; Malamuth and Donnerstein, 1984). Some years ago, when one major publishing house, Alfred A. Knopf, was arranging to publish *American Psycho*, a novel in which women are kidnapped and dismembered, cannibalized, and sexually tortured (one victim has a starving rat inserted into her vagina, which then eats its way out of her body; another is literally nailed into captivity on the floor), one magazine columnist wrote in disgust:

> The real issue is our increasingly degraded and brutal popular culture. The fact that our rape and murder rates are triple those of other Western nations has a lot to do with the violent images and fantasies flooding our culture. . . . Why is Knopf dealing in violent junk? Because pots of money can be made by brutalizing the culture. (Leo 1990a, 62)

Popular music has likewise repeatedly come under fire, particularly rap lyrics. Although critics assailing rock lyrics is nothing new, in 1990 controversy flamed over 2 Live Crew, a black (male) rap group that sang about (among other things) damaging a girl's vagina during intercourse, anally raping her, and forcing her to lick human excrement. The group was banned in various communities and arrested in Florida for obscenity. "Why should our daughters have to grow up in a culture in which musical advice on the domination and abuse of women is accepted as entertainment?" one commentator lamented (Leo 1990b, 32).

Even violence in children's video games became controversial in the 1990s. Two games of that era in particular, *Night Trap* and *Mortal Kombat*, raised concern. In *Night Trap*, three men in black masks charge into the bedroom of a woman dressed in a flimsy negligee. The player's challenge is to prevent the men from dragging her off and holding her down while a companion drives an electric drill into her neck. In *Mortal Kombat*, a gruesome extension of martial arts street fighting videos, opponents splatter blood with their blows and winners can triumphantly rip out the spinal columns of the defeated. One newspaper columnist wrote, "Profit, of course, is the only motivation that matters. That's why companies are in business, right? They have no obligation to be socially responsible" (Kolson, 1993).

Video game violence (or violent video games) continues to be argued over as a major contributor (or not) to youth violence. Many psychologists and even the FBI consider video game violence (particularly in games that call for the players to identify with the game's violent character or hero) a definite factor contributing to youth violence, from bullying to school shootings. At Video Games ProCon.org, the website of a nonpartisan nonprofit group that monitors the debate, arguments for and against such violent games as *Grand Theft Auto* and *Doom* are even-handedly presented. There is reason for concern, given the huge market for video games. In 2008, almost 300 million video games were sold in the United States, earning a total of almost $12 billion, and six of the top ten best sellers included violence. But the evidence, as ProCon illustrates, is far from consistent.

For instance, during the years 1995–2008 sales of violent games more than quadrupled while arrest rates for juvenile murders fell 77 percent and arrest rates for all juvenile crimes declined 49 percent. Yet one 2008 study found that 60 percent of middle school boys who played at least one mature-rated game hit and beat up someone, compared to 39 percent of boys who had not watched such games. Another study in 1998 found obvious violence against women in 21 percent of video games sampled. Yet studies comparing video game playing in the United States and Japan found that, controlling for prior aggression, youths who played more violent video games during the beginning of a school year were more likely to engage in aggressive behavior sometime later in that same year than nonplaying peers. Yet while the per capita amount of money spent for video games was $5.20 per American teenager compared to $47 per Japanese youth in 1998, there were 2,279 murders committed by U.S. teenagers compared to only 73 in all of Japan. And almost two-thirds of the American video game consumers are over eighteen years of age, certainly not impressionable adolescents (Video Game Procon.org, 2010). And just to muddy the waters with more contradictory facts: the two teen shooters at Columbine High School who on April 29, 1999, killed thirteen persons and wounded more were avid video players of two violent games, *Wolfenstein 3D* and *Doom*, while the perpetrator of the Virginia Tech shootings in April 2007 did not play video games. Moreover, lists of the ten most frequently played games feature such titles as *Guitar Hero*, *Solitaire*, and *Dance Dance Revolution*, ones that hardly promote violence.

Dr. Henry Jenkins (2006), director of the Comparative Media Studies Program at the Massachusetts Institute of Technology, in a classic web article entitled "Reality Bytes: Eight Myths about Video Games Debunked," points out that 90 percent of boys and 40 percent of girls play video games, the vast majority of whom are not violent. Further, video games now have been around at least a generation, with most youth growing into adulthood and parenthood and becoming nonviolent adult players. Jenkins argues that various studies show viewing video violence can be cathartic escapism or harmless release, that it is often done with family members (including spouses) and/or friends (dismissing the disturbed loner stereotype) in multiplayer games, and that the video game market not only is largely adult but caters to adult tastes. All but a tiny proportion of adults, he maintains, can readily distinguish between escapism and reality. Even considering a violent realistic war-oriented game, such as *Doom II*, used as battlefield training for soldiers in the U.S. Marine Corps and for recruitment by the U.S. Army, we have to acknowledge a host of other factors (many more important, Jenkins believes, than merely a "diet" of violent games for amusement), such as the existence of a stable nuclear family in the viewer's life, the context of viewing, and so forth. Professor Jenkins feels that some politicians and what sociologists term "moral entrepreneurs" are creating a "moral panic" out of video *entertainment*.

The truth seems to be that most professionally conducted studies are limited, suggestive but inconclusive. True, such video games may desensitize viewers to violent images, but is that the same thing as causing, partially or entirely, real-life violence? And heavy viewing of violent video games could represent more of an effect of already existing violent tendencies and personalities rather than a cause.

Meanwhile, in 2005 the American Psychological Association passed a resolution calling for a reduction in video game violence. That same year, then-U.S. Senator (from New York) Hillary Clinton introduced a bill to criminalize selling "mature" (often violent) or "Adults Only" (sometimes combining sex and violence) video games to minors, calling video violence "a silent epidemic of desensitization." The bill was named the Family Entertainment Protection Act, but it eventually died in committee. Nevertheless, whether it is a cause or effect, the popularity of video game violence for vicarious amusement can be understood as a symptom, or a characteristic, of a society and world plagued daily by violence.

Violence in sports—although estimated to be less than the days of early sport as in the gladiatorial contests of ancient Rome or the violence of lacrosse of native American tribes, and less than the violence of early American baseball, football, and hockey—is certainly a part of our cultural heritage. Smith (1983) describes a typology of sport violence: (1) brutal body contact like in the case of hard checking in hockey, spiking in baseball, hard tackles in football, etc.; (2) borderline violence, which involves acts that are prohibited by the rules of the game but are part of the sport like fighting in hockey, helmet to helmet tackles in football, intentional fouls in basketball, or bean balls in baseball; (3) quasi-criminal violence of sport; and (4) criminal violence where the case is clearly outside the margins of acceptability and is handled as criminal in the courts. Young (2000) claims that incidents considered "quasi-criminal violence," "borderline violence," or merely "brutal body contact" when Smith did his classification are being more closely scrutinized today by the authorities and when litigated are dealt with under criminal rather than civil law.

Sports violence among athletes, once controversial but contained to the playing fields or in arenas, has spilled over into the audiences. So-called little league or peewee baseball/football/soccer parents' emotions have, of course, long been a staple of children's amateur sports. Adults who exhort their children and even become heated and profane are considered part of the sports ritual. Such adults are as much or more so driven for victory than their children. Americans were shocked, however, in early 2002 when Thomas Junta, a forty-four-year-old father, came out of the bleachers and attacked the hockey coach. Junta, weighing 270 pounds, literally pummeled 156-pound Michael Costin to death in front of numerous witnesses, including children. The issue was over roughness in both their sons' hockey practice that day. Junta reportedly punched Costin a number of times and slammed his head against the floor between locker rooms, rupturing an artery in Costin's neck. Americans could even witness the criminal trial live for either a sense of vicarious justice or titillation on the CNN cable network (Associated Press, 2002).

Junta's violent behavior was extreme but by no means abnormal. Syndicated newspaper columnist Bonnie Erbe wrote:

> They say adult violence surrounding kids' sports is on the rise. . . . Parents who attend children's practice or games have become inured to other pushy parents yelling at the coach or chastising children in public for poor performance. Kids, in turn, seem to have become more violent as well. [Sympathizing with Junta's conviction for involuntary manslaughter, she added:] Those parents who cannot control themselves at kids' sports events should stay away or face official retribution. (Erbe, 2002)

And just as many persons are concerned over the rise in violence surrounding children's sports, likewise there are animal advocates outraged over recent exposure of various incidences of humans encouraging animal violence toward fellow animals for humans' wagering and amusement: bull-fighting, cock-fighting, and dog-fighting, to name just a few examples (none of which are "new"). All such forms artificially exploit wild and semi-domesticated animals' natural (but in the wilds biologically and instinctually regulated) aggressive tendencies. Ancient Roman gladiatorial games famously served as an opportunity to pit trained human fighters (*bestiarii*), often with swords, spears, or whips, against a wide assortment of captured animals, such as lions, tigers, leopards, boars, and elephants. There were also animal-against-animal matches—the more exotic the animals, the better (Kyle, 1998; Potter and Mattlingly, 1999; Futreli, 2006).

Cock-fighting—the setting of two roosters (or gamecocks) in a pit and taking advantage of their natural inter-male aggression—has a long history. The natural ferocity of the gamecocks (and their potential for damage) is enhanced by removing one of the spurs (or nails) from each of the cock's feet and strapping in its place a metal spur (or small razor-sharp knife) ranging from one to two and one-half inches. Typically the cocks fight until one kills or seriously wounds the other. There are records of cock-fighting as early as 2000 B.C.E. in the Indus Valley of ancient India. Cock-fighting was accepted as a venue for gambling and entertainment for all social classes in the British Isles as recently as the late 1800s. In modern times cock-fighting is illegal in most of the United States (though it has been traditionally popular in southern and southwestern regions) and in Europe. However, it is still frequently found (sometimes with government approval) in much of Southeast Asia as well as Mexico and Latin America and most of South America (with the exception of Brazil; see Sherman, 2002; Collins, 2005).

As another example, human breeding and training of dogs to fight one another in enclosed pits, both a rural and urban phenomenon, has a hoary legacy and still exists today (although outlawed) in the United States. This fact was dramatically shown in April 2007 when Michael Vick, star quarterback for the Atlanta Falcons football team, was implicated (along with a cousin who managed the "Bad Newz Kennels") in a dog-fighting ring that had operated for more than five years. In court Vick admitted financing and overseeing the fighting and sometimes the execution by hanging, drugging, and electrocution of six to eight dogs who did not (in Vick's words) "perform well," though he inconsistently denied wagering on the outcomes of fights. Vick pleaded guilty to federal felony charges and served twenty-one months in prison. After serving jail time, Vick lost his multi-million-dollar endorsements, the Falcons' owners no longer wanted to play Vick in games, and Vick filed for Chapter 11 bankruptcy. Unable to trade the stigmatized Vick, the Falcons released his contract. Ultimately in 2009 Vick was signed by the Philadelphia Eagles football team. His first few games at least were loudly and visibly attended by sign-carrying, hooting pickets made up of animal rights protesters.

As a final example of humans' speciesistic exploitation of animals, a quasi-wildlife-hunting preserve has sprung up in various countries, including the United States, exemplified in Safari Club International (SCI). What SCI (with a claimed 45,000 members) offers those more interested in a trophy head or horns as opposed to physical challenges and possible danger are "caged hunts." A variety of exotic animals are captured or, when old and possibly ailing, purchased from zoos and circuses and stocked in an enclosed area with no meaningful chance of escape (these trapped victims would include elephants, rhinoceroses, lions, leopards, and so forth). SCI, now established in the United States and elsewhere, while declaring itself a promoter/benefactor of wildlife conservation, advertises a no-kill-no-pay guarantee policy to its customers. Needless to say, "real" hunters of free-range wildlife (who have a generally agreed-upon code of ethics on what constitutes a "fair" kill) as well as the Fund for Animals and the Humane Society of the United States vehemently oppose this sort of "artificial" hunting (likening it to gratuitous slaughter) and are promoting legislation to bar it in various states. Meanwhile, former U.S. President George W. Bush has been an SCI member, has spoken at its conferences, and during his administration even appointed an SCI official as deputy director of the U.S. Fish and Wildlife Service (Scully, 2002; Humane Society of the United States, 2010).

These examples demonstrate an increasing willingness on the part of many Americans to hold a more inclusive definition of violence, a definition that on the popular level closely resembles our sociological one and that devalues violence in interpersonal and institutional role relationships. We are not suggesting that Americans should expect the cultural pendulum to swing away anytime soon from an entertainment industry often steeped in sensationalist violent imagery. As sociologist Michael Parenti observed about American mass media some years ago when this trend was fully under way, in general, private profitability instead of social need or responsibility is the driving fact in capital investment. And thus far, there is considerable profit in providing the novelty, titillation, and vicarious thrills associated with media violence. This is an ongoing economic fact of modern North American culture (Parenti, 1986).

But it is also true that new conflicts are arising as interest groups, sometimes aligned, are protesting violence merchants in modern American culture. Indeed, this reaction against profit-driven violent entertainment may prove to be one of the most powerful emerging social movements of the late twentieth and early twenty-first centuries.

The Heritage of Violence

In a sense all of us living in modern industrialized societies, regardless of our language or specific nationality, are inheritors of a violent tradition. This tradition began when humankind made the transition from hunting-gathering bands to a more settled agrarian existence, creating a more complex division of labor and specialized "agencies" of coercion (warriors) and learning/legitimation (priests) apart from resource producers (farmers). This major agricultural revolution occurred during the Neolithic Age (9000–6000 B.C.E. in the Middle East and around 6000 B.C.E. and 2000 B.C.E. in South America and North America, respectively). It irrevocably set in motion many issues new to human groups that have never left us since, such as how to deal with crop surpluses, storage, wealth, and class hierarchy. As historian Ernest Gellner (1988, 154–55) writes in *Plough, Sword and Book: The Structure of Human History*: "Agrarian society is doomed to violence. It stores valuable concentrations of wealth, which must be defended, and the distribution of which has to be enforced . . . during the agrarian age, most of mankind was not free and on the edge of starvation. It was oppressed and half-starving. It starved in accordance with rank."

Yet even with the similar archaic economic origins of inequality and coercion, historical traditions of violence do not necessarily lead to common contemporary outcomes. A case in point is the United States, where serious problems of urban gang- and drug-related violence, interpersonal assault, occasional "spree" shootings, race riots, and widespread gun possession are commonly accounted for by referring to the nation's "frontier tradition." The latter includes Indian (and other) wars, slavery, untamed mining and cattle towns and outlaw raids, frequent absence of law enforcement officials, and lynch mob and vigilante actions. During the 1960s, in particular, when the U.S. government enlisted historians and social scientists to help make sense of violent student and minority demonstrations, antiwar protests, and assassinations, the interpretation in vogue at that time was that America had a very violent heritage that still pervades the many forms of interpersonal aggression in modern times (see, e.g., Pierce, 1970; Brown, 1969; Frantz, 1969; Elliot, 1944). For example, the historian David Brion Davis (1970, 56), after analyzing violence in American literature, wrote that it has always been difficult to conceal the fact that the nation was conceived in violence, that its birth was accompanied by mobs and confiscations, and that a burden remained on the people collectively to validate their rebellion against lawful authority. The same author perceived the telltale effects of this nation's violent birth running rampant in its literary history: "Critics who interpret violence in contemporary literature as a symptom of a sick society may be reassured to know that American writers have always been preoccupied with murder, rape, and deadly combat" (Davis, 1970, 66). Some regions of the United States have even been singled out as particularly steeped in violent traditions. One such region, in addition to the frontier West, has been the Old South, with its cavalier codes of defending one's honor, dueling, vendettas, vigilante night-riders, and racial conflict both pre– and post–Civil War (Newman, 1979, 42–43; Hofstadter and Wallace, 1971; Hackney, 1969; Franklin, 1956).

But other scholars have rejected some deterministic link between current (admittedly severe) patterns of American violence and the nation's alleged past. McGrath (1984), in *Gunfighters, Highwaymen and Vigilantes: Violence on the Frontier*, has observed that while there were many assaults and homicides between armed, inebriated men in mining town saloons, nevertheless rape, robbery, burglary, and what we moderns would call "muggings" were rare, chiefly because (respectively) women were often few in number and men were frequently armed. Even stagecoach robberies were usually aimed at the stage's commercial freight, not at the possessions of the passengers themselves. Calculating crime rates for two Trans-Sierra mining towns (using categories of the FBI Uniform Crime Reports) and comparing them to similar statistics for such modern urban metroplexes as Miami, Atlanta, Chicago, and San Francisco, McGrath found the frontier towns unstereotypically low in many offenses we usually think of as violent. In addition, vigilante actions, as others have noted (Burrows, 1976, 19ff; Hofstadter and Wallace, 1971, 22; Brown, 1969), were disciplined, involved many of a community's elite members (Dimsdale, 1953), and hardly resembled the rough "mob justice" caricatures of popular imagery. Contrary to conventional wisdom, frontier communities actually saw more violence overall as they became more "civilized" and urbanized (McGrath, 1984). McGrath blames our popular fixation about frontier violence on fictional television and film portrayals of such flamboyant deviants as Billy the Kid, Wyatt Earp, and Wild Bill Hickok.

Other scholars agree that claiming a causal connection between modern American violence and an alleged frontier tradition is overblown. Hofstadter and Wallace warn:

> The conventional attribution of American violence to our long history should not be given too much credence. It is true, of course, that frontier conditions somewhat enhanced the American disposition to violence, as they did, for example, in the history of Indian warfare and the attitudes it engendered. Yet it is worth emphasizing that over the whole course of our history only a small portion of the total American population—and always a decreasing portion—has ever seen or been on a frontier. (Hofstadter and Wallace, 1971, 11–12)

These authors attribute American culture's heavy emphasis on violence in its entertainment and literature to a popular legacy of "acceptance" of violence's purported widespread existence. Likewise, Lynn (1969) has acknowledged the "pleasures of hyperbolic exaggeration" that American audiences have persistently craved in their fiction and fantasy, be these the famous "dime novels" of the late nineteenth century that romanticized such characters as stagecoach and train robbers or the twentieth century's glamorization of martial arts movie stars such as Bruce Lee, Chuck Norris, Steven Seagal, and Jean-Claude Van Damme. Criminologist Graeme Newman (1979, 39) has even bluntly accused historians of the 1960s of fabricating a culture of violence somehow integral to North American society in order to explain the waves of riots and civil disorder they were witnessing rather than consider class warfare or institutional discrimination.

It is instructive to contrast America's indisputably high rates of interpersonal violence and its contested history of violent actions with those of Japan, an equally industrialized urban society that has a much longer history of civil disturbances, peasant uprisings, dynastic wars, and the famous samurai warrior ethic but also much lower rates of nearly all forms of interpersonal violence. Despite its legacy of bloodshed, Japanese society's interpersonal "style" of relating involves individual self-effacement and personal control in the face of authority, emotion, and egocentric desire. This does not mean that the Japanese do not joke or become angry, jealous, or ambitious. Nor do they lack individual desires, competitiveness, or even aggressiveness. They are simply more thoroughly conditioned, and constantly reinforced, to live within a culture that values restraint, self-sacrifice for the greater good of the larger group, and a public "face" of courtesy, as they have for centuries (Nakane, 1970; Benedict, 1946). Thus, there exists the irony that grueling martial arts, such as judo, karate, and kendo (broadsword fencing) are taught almost everywhere in the country in junior and senior high schools (often to females as well as males), yet Japan's levels of officially documented interpersonal violence are modest. In a classic comparative analysis of crime and police work in the United States and Japan, Bayley (1976, 5) noted that in 1973 there were four-and-a-half times as many murders per 100,000 persons in the United States as in Japan (population-wise, half the size of the latter country). In fact, the New York metropolitan area alone during the early 1970s had three-fourths as many murders as all of Japan.

One important factor in explaining such differences is the heritage from medieval Japan of only elites (the aristocracy and samurai warrior castes) being entitled to carry weapons, whereas not only America's frontier tradition but also our Second Amendment in the Bill of Rights guarantees every adult not convicted of a felony the right to own almost every imaginable weapon. In Japan only police officers, soldiers in the self-defense forces, and a few hunters and Olympic shooters possess firearms. Swords and even knives beyond a certain length must be registered with the government.

Perhaps just as important a factor in Japan's low levels of interpersonal violence is its cultural emphasis on loyalty to a larger group, such as the family and by extension one's employer or company, which exercises much greater and more thorough social control on emotional outbursts and actions than most Americans understand or would tolerate. Outbursts of emotion and anger are discouraged by long-established social norms. For example, Bayley observes about males' connection to their occupational world:

> Responsible behavior is secured in Japan by developing the allegiance of the individual to the work group in such a way as to legitimate its disciplinary claims on him and to intensify his feeling of obligation not to offend against it. The work group in Japan dominates personal life. It has the emotional overtones of a family—a word policemen use frequently to describe the kind of emotional fulfillment they want to achieve in the group. (Bayley, 1976, 71)

This illustrative comparison between the United States and Japan has not been made to suggest that generalizations about the social sources and circumstances of interpersonal violence among societies, or even within a single society's culture over time, are impossible to make. The point is that they require our explanations to be more complex. Culture and history clearly prepare, but do not completely determine, how each generation of a society interprets its collective experience of violence. The range of popular acceptance of violence being quite varied over time and place, any social science analysis must recognize the role of culture in prompting a society's members to receive instances of violence as either normative (i.e., acceptable) or deviant (i.e., nonacceptable). Before moving to specific examples of violence, therefore, we briefly turn to the general phenomenon of learning such normative boundaries.

SOCIALIZATION TO VIOLENCE

Most social scientists have abandoned the nature versus nurture, or instincts versus learning, debate over the source of human violence. Attempts by such ethologists as Konrad Lorenz and some socio-biologists as Edward O. Wilson to demonstrate a strong continuity of biologically determined aggression from lower animals through primates to Homo sapiens have proved largely fruitless because, in the words of psychologist Jeffrey H. Goldstein (1986, 6), "to argue that because we can behave like lower organisms, we must behave like them is preposterous. While human beings possess diffuse innate biological urges, they also have extremely malleable psychological potentials. The same human mind can devise a fishing pole or a throwing spear, a telephone or a ballistic missile, a hypodermic needle or a flame-thrower." There is no question that even if individuals were born with some genetic predisposition to be aggressive, and we are not suggesting they are, it would be well within their rational, cognitive capabilities to learn to restrain, suppress, or creatively divert such urges. Thus the key to understanding how individuals deal with aggressive feelings as well as "make sense" out of the violence they see and in which they may even become involved is socialization, or learning.

In particular, much of this socialization occurs through what social psychologists term social learning. That is, persons do not have to be directly involved in violence to learn that it can be effective, rewarding, and even satisfying. Alternately, they can come to regard it as destructive, painful, and horrifying. Unlike Pavlov's classical conditioning, where learners are passive, or direct operant conditioning, where learners are given positive or negative reinforcement immediately after performing a response, social learning is vicarious or indirect. Essentially one watches another who is a perpetrator or victim, sees the consequences of the violent action, and then internalizes a reaction to the outcome as well as, in many cases, the techniques of committing the violence. This modeling process is akin to imitation in everyday parlance, and a good deal of social psychological research has been amassed to explain its dynamics.

Learning the Role of Perpetrator

Laboratory experiments have conclusively demonstrated that children, after being exposed to an adult acting out aggression and not being punished, will imitate that aggression. The most famous type of such experiments was developed by psychologist Albert Bandura (1963, 1965, 1973, 1977) and several colleagues in the early 1960s. For example, in one typical experiment (Bandura, 1965), sixty-six children of nursery school age were shown one of three five-minute films. All children witnessed an adult attacking a plastic Bobo doll (a tall rubber inflated clown figure with sand in its base as weight to keep it upright) and yelling specific words like "Pow!" and "Socko!" In one condition of the experiment the adult model received rewards of candy and soft drinks following the repeated striking of the doll. In a second condition the adult was verbally punished and even spanked after the doll attacks. In a third condition children saw no rewarding or punishing of the model after aggression against the doll. All children then were permitted ten minutes of "free play" in a room in which had been placed a variety of toys, including a Bobo doll. After experimenters observed each child, they said that he or she would receive a drink and colorful picture booklets after imitating the behavior acted out in the film. The findings showed that: (1) the "spontaneous" behavior during the ten minute free-play period was significantly aggressive both among children in the first model-rewarded condition and among children in the model-neither-rewarded-nor-punished condition; (2) the least aggression was seen by experimenters in the model-punished condition; (3) yet when promised rewards for imitating the film's aggression, all children, regardless of their experimental condition, were equally able to replicate the model's aggression, even down to the details of incorporating specific expressions uttered by the model while striking the doll.

The findings of Bandura and his colleagues, as well as those of many other social psychologists, demonstrate that children's learning to imitate aggressive acts can take place regardless of whether there is some immediate reward or punishment to the violent actor or the viewer. If there is either a rewarding outcome to the violence or at least no punishment, however, the probability of the aggression being repeated is significantly enhanced.

While this type of laboratory experiment using nursery schoolchildren may seem artificially simplistic, its basic logic has been repeated successfully on adults as well (see, e.g., Eron et al., 1972; Cater and Strickland, 1975). Clinical studies of violent men, for example, found that adult men who responded violently to their wives or girlfriends during domestic quarrels often experienced "generational transfer," or social learning, of physical and verbal abuse in their families as a way of settling arguments. In a study of more than two hundred men who had beaten their female significant others, the authors wrote:

> Most of these men had witnessed violence between their parents during arguments. They saw violence used as a strategy by the father to win those arguments with the mother, or at least to get his way. They saw it portrayed as manly, as the man's right, and associated it with a male parent figure whom they naturally wanted to imitate. Thus as boys many of these men learned (indirectly or vicariously) the appropriateness of men's using violence against women as well as its effectiveness. Little in what they were to learn from American culture, either in how power and resources are distributed by gender or through the mass media with its macho heroes and docile female stereotypes, contradicted those impressions. (Shupe, Stacey, and Hazlewood, 1987, 38)

The famous Milgram obedience experiments may also provide some insights into acts of institutional violence. Psychologist Stanley Milgram (1974) was examining the extent of obedience to authority among people who were led to believe their own obedience would harm another person. Milgram told volunteer subjects that they were to be involved in an experiment in learning and memory. The subjects (the teacher role) were told to give electric shocks to another subject, the learner, who was part of the experimental team, when he failed to provide the correct answer to a word-association test. The learner in reality received no shocks and merely faked the response when a shock was supposedly emitted. On a desk in front of the subject teacher was a series of switches labeled from 15 to 450 volts (thirty switches altogether) with the last six marked with a warning of the danger of severe shock. The subject teacher was called on by an experimenter dressed in a white lab coat to pull a progressively higher voltage switch each time the learner provided an incorrect answer. There was also a prearranged response that the learner gave out in the next room, where he could not be seen. The responses began with a simple "Ouch." At 150 volts the learner would plead, "Experimenter! That's all. Get me out of here. I told you I had heart trouble. My heart's starting to bother me now." This type of prearranged response continued until the subject reached the 330-volt switch. After this point, all succeeding shocks at higher levels received no response on the part of the learner. After the initial cries of protest from the learner at 150 volts, virtually none of the teacher participants wanted to continue applying the shocks. But the experimenter (the person in authority) told them to continue. On average, over 60 percent of the teacher subjects continued applying the shocks through to the 450-volt level.

The Milgram experiments provide insight into how individuals acting in the context of institutional roles such as soldier, executioner, or police officer can commit acts of violence because they were told to do so by someone in authority. One can still hear the testimony of war criminals at Nuremberg testifying about their role in the atrocities in the Holocaust, stating that they were just following orders. More recently, in the My Lai massacre, one of the grimmest episodes of the U.S. involvement in the Vietnam War, more than three hundred unarmed Vietnamese civilians were massacred by an

American infantry company. The Americans, under the command of Capt. Ernest L. Medina and Lt. William L. Calley Jr., entered the village of Son My, and in the hamlet they called My Lai 4, they lashed out at whomever they found, mostly women, children, and old men. Some villagers were herded into ditches where they were shot. After Calley was court-martialed, a significant segment of the American public felt that he was unjustly prosecuted because he was just following orders (Bilton, 1992). More recently, after Colonel Oliver North was convicted in May 1989 of three of the twelve criminal counts involving his role in the Iran Contra scandal, a large segment of the American public contended that he should not be prosecuted because he was just following orders (Lacayo, Duffy, and Holmes, 1989).

An extreme example of learning the role of perpetrator of institutional violence is discussed by Browning in his work on the Order Police of Nazi Germany, who were assigned the task of rounding up Jewish populations in Poland and Russia and killing them or transporting them to death camps. Browning details the killings of Jews by a number of battalions of the Order Police. He cites the case of Police Battalion 309, which undertook the slaughter of between two thousand and three thousand Jews in the city of Bialystok. Jews collected at the marketplace were taken to a park, lined up against a wall, and shot. The killing sometimes lasted until dark. At the synagogue, where at least seven hundred Jews had been collected, gasoline was poured at the entryways. A grenade was tossed into the building, igniting a fire. Police shot anyone trying to escape. The fire spread to nearby houses in which Jews were hiding, and they too were burned alive. The next day, thirty wagonloads of corpses were taken to a mass grave (Browning 1992, 12). In another case, two battalions of Order Police murdered more than thirty-three thousand Jews in the ravine of Babi Yar in Kiev.

Browning focuses his research on one particular unit, Battalion 101. His research discussed the difficulties encountered by these working-class and middle-class older men, many of whom had joined the Order Police to avoid military service, in carrying out their orders of conducting a mass murder of Jews. He discusses the first major massacre the battalion participated in, the killing of 1,800 Jews in Jozefow, Poland. The commander of the battalion would not witness the killings, but stayed in his headquarters and wept openly. Older men were initially given the option of not participating. About a dozen asked for reassignment to other duties. As the slaughter began, many others sought permission to be reassigned. The soldiers were specifically instructed as to how to execute the Jews. Each was to place his bayonet on his rifle, place it at the base of the head of the victim, and fire. However, many of the police missed their target, intentionally in many cases. This resulted in the back of the heads of the prisoners exploding, spraying the soldiers around them with skull fragments and pieces of brain tissue. The soldiers were also instructed to kill infants, young children, and the elderly in their homes as opposed to bringing them to the market square. Browning reports that this order was rarely followed as in the case of infants and the children who were later brought to the market square where they were murdered along with their mothers. The men were sent into the woods where they were told to lie down on the ground and then shot in the back of the head. Browning notes that as darkness came, the task was not finished and it became increasingly difficult for the squads of police to find a spot where Jews were not lying about dead. Officers supplied the executioners with alcohol to ease the process. Browning notes that after the killings in Jozefow, the men were despondent. The commanding officer and his superiors in Lublin had to deal with the broad demoralization of the battalion as a result of the reaction to the horror of the killing process. The battalion was reassigned for a time to ghetto clearing and deportation, instead of carrying out the executions. After a time the battalion was again participating in executions. Browning observes that in the end, the five hundred men of Battalion 101 had directly participated in the deaths of thirty-eight thousand Jews and the deportation of forty-five thousand Jews to death camps.

What can account for the behavior of these five hundred men? According to Browning, like the rest of German society, the men of Battalion 101 were immersed in a deluge of racist and anti-Semitic propaganda. Browning notes that Order Police were provided with additional indoctrination as part of their training and as an ongoing practice within the units. Browning contends that such incessant propagandizing must have had a considerable effect in reinforcing general notions of Germanic racial superiority and a certain aversion toward the Jews. This is consistent with what was discussed in the previous chapter regarding the importance of defining the victim as less, as deserving of violence. Browning also notes that conformity to authority (as discussed in the Milgram experiments) was a factor. The battalion had orders to kill Jews, but each individual did not. Yet 80 to 90 percent of the men proceeded to kill, though almost all of them, at least initially, were horrified and disgusted by what they were doing. To break ranks and step out, to adopt overtly nonconformist behavior, was simply beyond most of the men. It was easier for them to shoot (Browning, 1992, 184).

In later chapters, when we discuss institutional violence, it will be important to recall the importance of the systems of thought that allow us to define victims as less "human" and think about the power of the group within the institutional agency to promote conformity to the role expectations. Whether we are discussing the violence of police or military or priests or ministers or corporate executives, the dynamic is similar. The lesson of Battalion 101 is that perpetrators of violence must be able to separate themselves from their victims. Ideologies that teach us to accept and perpetuate through our actions inequalities and separateness between people are crucial in this regard. Furthermore, when engaged in repetitive forms of violence, as in the case of many forms of institutional violence, social supports of the group or agency may be crucial to reinforce the mandates of the roles they are performing.

Social learning research tells us that aggressive attitudes and violent techniques are learned, just like other behaviors. Relatives, friends, media personalities, actors, political leaders, and others in authority all can be role models. Given our culture's heavy saturation with values, symbols, and instances of violence (real or fictionally glorified), together with the pervasiveness of systems of thought that divide people along hierarchical dimensions, perhaps we should ask why more do not commit acts of violence given the overwhelming opportunities for learning violence. Violence, after all, can serve as a satisfying, even cathartic, shortcut that bypasses many frustrating problems and social responsibilities. Perhaps nonviolence more urgently requires an explanation.

Learning the Role of the Victim

It might seem commonsensical to say that no one consciously prepares to become the victim of violence. A family that has had its possessions stolen during a burglary, a man mugged on a subway platform, or a woman raped— none of these persons deliberately invited their own victimization. To suggest otherwise might seem like engaging in a not-so-subtle game of "blaming the victim," placing at least some causal blame for the event on the victim rather than on the perpetrator. The women's movement has been particularly insistent on this point in countering the (predominantly male) conventional wisdom that female rape victims often somehow "ask for it" by their dress or presence in a given location. As the movement's spokespersons have stressed, susceptibility and vulnerability do not equal culpability.

Likewise, despite early speculation in the 1970s about little girls learning that being the victim of domestic violence is part of an adult woman's role (just as little boys learn that violence toward women is a man's prerogative), in fact research shows just the opposite. Many adult women who are victims of batterings by husbands or boyfriends were raised in nonviolent homes, and many who fled to women's shelters or sought help elsewhere manifest no signs that they somehow thought the abuse they received was "normal," appropriate, or part of a woman's role (Pagelow, 1981; Stacey and Shupe, 1983, 41–46). Why they remain in violent relationships, as we discuss in the next chapter, is more a matter of economics than psychology.

On the other hand, we have cross-cultural and historical instances of persons being deliberately indoctrinated to accept their own victimization. The practice of human sacrifice was an important part of the religious rituals of the Aztecs and Incas prior to the sixteenth century (Davies, 1981). It is estimated that for the Aztecs alone, more than twenty thousand humans were sacrificed annually, the vast majority of them children. For the Incas such violence occurred twice a year at the solstice celebrations in June and December. Then the empire's best crops, most prized livestock, most precious artwork, and finest clothes, along with the most beautiful children of the empire, were gathered together at Cuzco, the Incas' 11,000-foot-high capital. Everything, including children, was herded into a corral to be inspected. The children were examined for deformities and signs of disease. Those who were not in excellent shape were weeded out. The remaining children listened to speeches from the Inca high priest about the benefits of their upcoming sacrifice to the empire. During this time they learned the role of victim. There were then ten days of festivities in the capital during which the children were celebrated as semidivine. The children were then sacrificed at the highest altars as payment for the Inca rulers' sins. Is something similar in victim socialization happening during the recruitment, training, and indoctrination of Islamic suicide bombers who are the same time both perpetrators and victims of their own violence? In a later chapter we will be examining just such a socialization effect in the production of suicide terrorists.

There are also some situations when the repeated experience of interpersonal violence, or the expectation of such violence, can become a real factor in the social roles one acts out on a regular basis. Fear of muggings, for example, leads many residents of such metropolises as New York City to adopt abrupt, defensive interpersonal styles, like refusing to talk to strangers or avoiding certain public places. Likewise, clinicians who have studied violent marriages have noted a sort of symbiotic relationship that develops between abuser and victim. It is not that the woman enjoys being slapped or hit by the stronger male during an argument but that the violence comes to be part of an overall role (e.g., wife) that she is unwilling to give up.

Perhaps more significant is how all of us learn the cultural distinctions between persons who are "legitimate" or innocent victims of violence (they did nothing to deserve violence, thus we can hold empathy for their plight as "true victims") as opposed to those who are technically victims but who fall outside the limits of "legitimacy" (thus they do not deserve our sympathy). In the latter case, victimization is actually regarded as a well-deserved punishment. For example, in 1990 and 1991, the citizens of Kuwait who were shot, tortured, and raped by invading Iraqi troops were portrayed as victims by the American media and became recognized as victims in most Americans' eyes. Hardly so the starving Iraqi soldiers in the trenches abandoned and in some cases buried alive by the allied forces equipped with bulldozers and tanks, or the civilian casualties that occurred during and after the war as a result of the intense allied bombing runs over Baghdad. The semantics of victimization is the propagandist's art: invaders and aggressors (i.e., those outside our own politically drawn "circle") rarely produce martyrs or heroes in our eyes. Defenders do that.

The role of the victim is a culturally defined one, and vested interests may seek to restrict the definition for their own purposes. Americans trapped in exploding Ford Pintos struck from behind, for example, were not initially regarded as legitimate "victims" of any corporate violence due to a faulty gas tank design in the early 1970s. They simply had the bad luck to be in traffic accidents. Their identity as victims emerged when it was revealed that the Ford Motor Company knew ahead of time that the design was dangerous and finally discontinued production of Pintos (Dowie, 1977). Similarly, the major manufacturing scandal of the late 1990s involving Bridgestone/Firestone tires that spontaneously lost their tread and caused accidents at first appeared as "driver error" for dozens of deceased drivers until National Highway Traffic Administration investigators found that the tires were defective. Recall of the tires cost the firm hundreds of millions of dollars, not to mention the loss of sales to the Ford Motor Company, whose Explorer line came equipped with those tires (Wood, 2001).

In a sense, more and more North Americans are coming to appreciate learning the role of victim. Indeed, it portends to be a trend in our increasingly litigious society. Futurist Alvin Toffler (1990) notes than in the United States more than one thousand new lawsuits are processed every working day. And the United States now possesses 5 percent of the world's population yet 70 percent of the planet's lawyers. Complained one American observer of his litigation-happy fellow citizens: "No other industrialized nation permits such arrant nonsense. The United States has thirty times more lawsuits per person than Japan. . . . In Japan there are more than twenty engineers for each lawyer. We have a ratio of 2.5 to 1, and it is falling fast" (Gergen, 1989, 43). What angered him, among other things, was the case of a burglar, who, in the process of looting a California high school, fell through a skylight and sued the local school board for personal damages. Shockingly, he won $260,000 in damages plus a $1,200 per month stipend!

There is another twist on learning the role of the victim and that occurs when the individual has not been a victim. In several cases prosecuting attorneys have led children into believing that they were the victims of child molestation. In the McMartin case of California, the longest and one of the most expensive trials in U.S. history, after two of the defendants working in a daycare facility spent two and five years in jail respectively, they were acquitted of child endangerment and molestation. There has been a similar problem of therapists convincing clients in the process of therapy that they were victims of child abuse (Baker, 1992). Shupe (1991) reports of one particular episode among the Mormons in Utah, the Lehi case, where a therapist's coaching of her child clients into making false charges of sexual abuse against their parents resulted in the state of Utah passing legislation making it a crime for persons to raise false accusations of child abuse or to induce children to make false accusations thereof. Thus, learning the role of the victim may no longer be the straightforward social psychological phenomenon it was once thought to be.

Learning the Role of the Audience

The audience to violence is not merely a passive group of witnesses but has become an integral part of the definition, discovery, and interpretation of violence. And an audience possibly desensitized or sensitized regarding specific forms of violence by a steady stream of disclosures about street crime and glorified entertainment violence is not the only audience issue. There is also fear arousal.

During the past two decades sociologists have substantially documented the role of journalistic and entertainment mass media, both newspapers and television, in inadvertently socializing audiences to accept a particular image of violence in American society that leaves them anxious and concerned. Dominick (1978) found in one study that murder, assault and armed robbery were the most frequent crimes portrayed by the media. And studying newspaper coverage of crime, he discovered that major metropolitan newspapers devoted 5 to 10 percent of all available space to individual violent crime. Alternately, less than 5 percent of the crime news was devoted to the causes and remedies of crime that social science has investigated. Ironically, individual violent crimes, always the more sensational and easiest for readers to identify with, were emphasized at the expense of more widespread and costly property, white-collar, and corporate crimes.

Sanford Sherizen (1978), in a similar analysis of media reports of crime, has written of the "unreality" of their portrayal. Crime reporters, he concludes, are often mere conduits for official views of crime (relying as they do on police sources for crime news). Researchers have also generally agreed that the unreality that is constructed has two aspects: first, blacks, young people, and lower socioeconomic "types" are stereotypically overrepresented (compared to FBI statistics); and second, particularly in the television "world" of criminal justice, the legal process is unrealistically pictured as ending, for all intents and purposes, with police capture of suspects that the audience already "knows" are guilty. Sherizen has commented on the "scare" effect much non–supermarket tabloid newspaper coverage of crime has: "Crimes are that which occurs outside of the potential for the police to prevent, especially homicides found in the newspapers were presented as being 'caused' by passions and insanities. For an individual reader who absorbs this imagery, crime appears to be violent, probably rampant, out of control, and likely to strike physically at any moment" (Sherizen, 1978, 215).

Barak (1994, 34) notes that the news discourse surrounds itself with very subtle "explanations" that appear in enclosed forms that do not enhance causal understanding. Barak describes the common portrayal of crime in the news: "Serious crime has been 'diagnosed' as having little or no relationship to political economy. Not only is the presentation of crime and crime control severed from its underlying socioeconomic conditions; it is also disconnected from its own historical development" (Barak, 1994, 249). Erickson notes that when an explanation can be read into the news, it "is more likely to be tacitly evoked by cues in the text or by the powerful master labels such as 'violent' and 'criminal' which carry unambiguous connotations and meld together disparate phenomena and their meanings. . . . They are deployed stereotypically. The stereotypes are blended with imputations of motives, whether noble or blameworthy. The imputations of motives, in turn, carry excuses and justifications for behavior" (Erickson et al., 1991, 269). In general, the violence that is represented to us focuses on interpersonal violence that is defined to be the most illegitimate by those who write and voice "official" opinions. The violence at the institutional and structural levels and the violence that is deemed to be legitimate are not usually represented to us as violence and, if so, are defined as unavoidable.

Images and stories about crime and especially violence dominate the news and entertainment industry. Studies that have been done over the years in the United Sates have documented the frequency of violent images in the media. According to an American Psychological Association task force report on television and American society (Huston et al., 1992), by the time the average child (i.e., one who watches two to four hours of television daily) leaves elementary school, he or she will have witnessed at least eight thousand murders and more than one hundred thousand other assorted acts of violence on television.

For the entertainment industry, television reality shows on crime do not appear to diverge much from the news programming in terms of frames or explanations. Fishman and Cavender (1998) note that television crime programs are informed by conservative ideologies that support current crime policies. The messages in these shows reinforce the idea that criminal violence is a serious problem, and longer prison sentences are offered as the solution. Criminals are presented as different from their victims. They are presented as stereotypical caricatures such as Satanists, drug dealers, and crazed, cold-blooded murderers. Victims are seen in equally stereotypical images—respectable and physically attractive. The final message of these shows is that what stands between order and chaos is the thin blue line of the police.

What is the social psychological effect on individual audience members and the ultimate social roles they fill as witnesses, internalizers, and evaluators of the violence in media? In the opinion of psychologist Jeffrey Goldstein, the end result is a mechanistic view of violent behavior:

> There is a consistent theme that (1) the causes of human violence exist within the individual, (2) that if only psychiatrists, psychologists, and biologists were clever enough, they could identify the genetic or personality factors that give rise to violent behavior, and (3) given the "fact" that the causes of violence reside within the individual's skin, it is assumed to be at least theoretically possible to identify potential offenders before they ever commit an offence by using some sort of early childhood screening procedure. (Goldstein, 1986, 215)

Viewers/readers, in other words, come away with the impression that "those who commit crimes or acts of violence are different in tangible and predictable ways from those who do not" (Goldstein, 1986, 15).

The upshot is that ordinary citizens are being slowly conditioned by the mass media to (1) expect more interpersonal violence potentially in their lives than will likely occur, (2) overestimate rates of interpersonal violence in their communities, (3) think only in terms of lurid interpersonal violence when the overall subject is brought up, and (4) isolate violence as a phenomenon within the realm of the bizarre and pathological rather than a product of the nature of our society. That, essentially, is what has happened in creating the "new sensitivity" of America to much interpersonal violence.

Michalowski (1985) adds to this discussion regarding what our cultural understandings of crime and violence are and what forces create them. Although he is discussing the imagery of crime, the same forces are responsible for creating our image of violence. He notes that the systematic generation and dissemination of crime statistics is culture work. For Michalowski, culture work refers to activity that serves to create or maintain widely accepted perceptions of the nature of reality. Insofar as our cultural understanding of crime is shaped by the institutional mechanisms for gathering and disseminating crime data, those institutional mechanisms play an important role in shaping what we perceive to be the "reality" of crime. The same logic applies to our understanding of violence. As various levels of government disseminate reports about the problem of violence in our society and the world, and as this information is presented in the media through news items and television documentaries, it becomes part of our cultural understanding of what violence is. We are the audience for the orchestration of a particular image or cultural reality of violence.

Michalowski goes on to note that the production and distribution of crime data reflect distinctions between common crimes and crimes of capital or corporate crime. Only those institutions charged with controlling common crimes actively produce and publicly disseminate data about the offenses under their jurisdiction. This selective generation and dissemination of data on social harms in American society serves to shape our awareness of crime in such a way that the category of "crime" in American culture generally includes only those harms most often committed by the poorer segments of American society. Excluded from such a definition of the reality of "crime" are harms more often committed by the elite in America in pursuit of profit and power.

In regard to violence the same pattern would apply; only forms of violence (interpersonal violence) that are disproportionately committed by the poorer segments of the society are part of the social reality of violence created by the agencies who create and disseminate the statistics. Institutional violence and structural violence are not part of this social construction and therefore are outside our understanding of the reality of violence. For example, there are no statistics regularly collected and disseminated on economic violence (death resulting from production, death resulting from defect in design of products, death resulting from ill disposal or chemical wastes from production, etc.). Therefore, when we think of the problem of violence, this type of violence is excluded from our conceptualization.

Another example is the lack of information on killings by the police in this country. The U.S. government has just recently begun to collect information on the number of people killed each year by law enforcement officers. However, reporting of this information is not required of police departments. What about violence resulting from government military or military sponsored by the government? Again, if these types of violence were systematically reported, indicating trends, who are most vulnerable, and so forth, how would this change our understanding of violence? Why do we have this selective generation of images, and how does this relate to the structure of power relations of the society? How are cultural understandings that allow us to be a perpetrator, victim, and audience influenced by the power relations of the larger society? Do those who have more power in the society have more power to create and promote understandings of reality that better serve their interests and possibly not our own?

Another dimension of learning the role of audience to violence is learning not to see it as violence or to see it as necessary violence. In the former case, we are an audience to the structural violence that is part of everyday life. The violence of poverty, which manifests itself in the increasing mortality rates of the poor who cannot afford health care or live in conditions of squalor, is invisible as a form of violence. Scheper-Hughes and Bourgois (2004, 4) note that "structural violence is generally invisible because it is part of the routine grounds of everyday life and transformed into expressions of moral worth." In the summer of 1995, the city of Chicago experienced a deadly heat wave. By the end of the second week in July, medical examiners confirmed that more than five hundred residents of the city had succumbed to the extreme temperatures; public health workers reported seven hundred deaths in excess of the weekly average. Klinenberg (2004, 309) notes that though the devastating event was journistically constructed and conventionally remembered as the city's most deadly natural disaster, the destructive 1995 heat wave was, in fact, a sign and symptom of the new and dangerous forms of marginality and neglect endemic to contemporary American big cities and notably severe in Chicago, a structurally determined catastrophe for which sociological analysis illuminates not simply the obvious relationship between poverty and suffering, but some of the institutional and social mechanisms upon which extreme forms of American insecurity are built."

The audience also learns to see the violence as necessary and thus acceptable. Litwack describes lynchings in the American South during the turn of the twentieth century. During this period, two or three black southerners were hanged, burned at the stake, or quietly murdered every week. He notes that the executions of black men who were not tried for their alleged crimes became "public theater, a participatory ritual of torture and death, a voyeuristic spectacle prolonged as long as possible (once for seven hours) for the benefit of the crowd" (Litwak, 2004, 125). He notes that in some cases newspapers announced in advance the time and place of lynchings. There were excursion trains to transport the spectators, employees released their workers to attend, and parents sent notes to their children's schoolteachers asking to excuse their children so that they could attend the event. Families attended and photographers sold postcards depicting the hangings or the charred remains of the bodies. The lynching of black men was seen as a necessary violence to maintain the order of white supremacy at the time. Black men were seen as a threat to the order, oftentimes alleged to be rapists of white women (although rarely proved), and thus needed to be eliminated in the most public display to serve as a warning to others who might also have threatened the civilized order of the South.

Lastly, we learn the role of audience to violence as the violence becomes normalized. Kramer (2010) describes how the bombing of civilians during war has become normalized beginning with the bombing of civilians at Guernica in the Spanish Civil War by Franco and his fascist allies of Germany and Italy to the areal bombings during World War II, the most extreme case being the bombings in Japan (both the firebombings of Tokyo and the first use of the atomic bomb on Hiroshima and Nagasaki), to the massive bombings of Vietnam by the United States during the 1970s to the shock and awe bombing of Bagdad during the 2003 conquest of Iraq by the United States and Great Britain. During the most recent wars against Iraq at the end of the twentieth century and beginning of the twenty-first, the term *collateral damage* was introduced to the American public to define the massive civilian deaths and casualties as unavoidable outcomes of a necessary war.

IDEOLOGY: THE BRIDGE BETWEEN CULTURE AND SOCIAL STRUCTURE

A major focus of this book is the connection between how a society is organized in terms of social structure (i.e., its systems of stratification) and how this is related to patterns of violence. Our understanding of the structure of the society, our acceptance and support of it, and our understanding of violence (that is, what it is and what we believe causes it) are products of the ideologies we are taught as part of the socialization we experience in the society and are reinforced by the dominant media in the country. A society's dominant ideology is the cultural mechanism that defends, preserves, and legitimates the structural arrangements or, more specifically, the systems of stratification that form the foundation of the society and the normative systems that support and preserve them. We accept the differences we see in our society as they relate to living conditions, levels of power, and social status because we feel that the mechanisms that create these differences are legitimate. Hunt (1981, 3) refers to an ideology as "the ideas and beliefs that tend to justify morally a society's social and economic relationships." He notes that most members of a society internalize the ideology that is dominant in the society and thus believe that their functional role, as well as the role of others, is morally correct and that the method by which society divides its produce is fair.

Another way of defining an ideology is as a viewpoint based on one's vantage point in the social order. The vantage point of an individual in the society is based on the positions that one occupies relative to the systems of stratification in the society. In this sense, there are as many ideologies as there are unique structural positions in social space. Thus, throughout most countries of the world we can identify three major systems of stratification: class, gender, and ethnicity. The intersection of these systems of stratification creates unique vantage points or positions in that the life experiences of people who occupy these positions will be different because of these systems of stratification. For example, the life experience of a male capitalist of European ancestry, such as Henry Ford II or one of the male heirs to the Campbell Soup Company, will be different from the life experience of a black woman or male worker, a male or female worker of European ancestry, or a male or female worker of Mexican ancestry. They will experience social institutions and processes differently because of the different positions they occupy.

For example, an increase in unemployment in a society will affect the people who occupy these positions differently. The male capitalist of European ancestry benefits, in the short term at least, from an increase in the rate of unemployment. When unemployment is high, there is less demand for higher wages and better working conditions. The male and female workers and managers will experience unemployment differently because gender, ethnicity, and occupational position influence their different locations in the labor market.

The cost of health care is another phenomenon that people experience differently because of the differences in the positions they occupy. The same applies to all other areas of social life: education, housing, crime, the welfare system, and war. In short, society as a whole is experienced differently because of the positions we occupy, positions determined by the intersection of the systems of stratification in the society. Thus the fact that we experience our society differently because of the differences in the positions we occupy provides the basis for an understanding of our society or, more specifically, provides the basis of an ideology.

Each stratified society during periods of stability will have a dominant ideology. This dominant ideology will reflect, first, the mode of production and reproduction that is dominant in the society and, correspondingly, the interests of the dominant structural position as defined in terms of class, gender, and ethnicity (i.e., in this case white European ethnicity, male, capitalist class). The dominant ideology will also reflect the historical experience of the society as experienced by the dominant class, ethnic, and gender position; the history of conflict and compromise between the structural divisions within the society; and the history of conquest and colonization within the world system. The dominant ideology will also be colored by the cultural and religious heritage of the country. Thus, in looking at different patriarchal capitalist societies throughout the world, one sees a great deal of commonality in the dominant ideologies, which promote the importance of a human nature that is competitive, individualistic, and materialistic and acts on the basis of self-interest and a rational calculus of costs and benefits of the action. It is also an ideology that promotes private property and a free market as necessary for order and happiness. Despite the presence of differences in history, religious traditions, and culture, key elements of the ideologies of these various patriarchal capitalist society persist. They will have in common an ideology that serves to legitimate the nature of the order as organized in terms of class, gender, and ethnicity.

Just as there are dominant ideologies, so there are competing ideologies. The dominant ideology fundamentally reflects the interests of the dominant structural positions as defined in terms of class, gender, and ethnicity. Competing ideologies reflect the interests (or viewpoint of the society from the vantage points) of the dominated structural positions. The majority of the population during periods of stability will view their world through this dominant ideology or from the vantage point of this dominant stratum. Assuming a perspective that is based on the position that you occupy is referred to as having "true consciousness." Assuming a perspective that does not reflect one's structural position in the social system is "false consciousness." In most stable societies it is crucial that the dominant groups have the majority of the population perceiving their society from a position of "false consciousness" or more specifically viewing the society from the position of the dominant position. Thus in a patriarchal capitalist society it is essential for workers to see the world through the eyes of the capitalist class, for women to see the world through the eyes of men, and for the ethnic minority to view the world through the eyes of the ethnic majority.

As mentioned, the institutions play a role in integrating and socializing neophytes into the social order (educational, familial, religious, political, and economic via the mass media) and serve to reinforce and perpetuate the dominant ideology and thus promote false consciousness to the dominated groups. One's experience in the social system based on the social relations one enters, which in turn are rooted in structural divisions that form the basis of the social system, will also serve to reinforce the dominant ideology. For example, in a capitalist society we experience and define people's basic nature as fundamentally selfish, individualistic, rational, and competitive. This nature is reflective of the social relations that are rooted in a capitalist mode of production. People are taught, and it is demonstrated to them by those who have the most power, that in order to be successful in our society one must act this way. Furthermore, we are taught that this way of behavior is part of our basic nature. Media through both fictionalized and nonfictionalized portrayal of life will reinforce these ideas. Our role models from celebrities to sports heroes to the story of the ruling elite will also illustrate the importance of the ideals and ideas conveyed to us as part of the dominant ideology.

In contrast, Inuit (Eskimos) or American Indians prior to contact with white European people and still today many indigenous groups of Africa, South America, and Southeast Asia would describe people's basic nature in a very different light. The experiences in their own groups promote behavior and an understanding of their society and their lives as human beings that would be very different from our own. In band societies in general the members are more likely to be taught that to be successful in their society, one needs to be concerned with the welfare of others, to be cooperative, and to be spiritually conscious. Furthermore, they learn the importance of not transforming and exploiting nature but rather learn how to use and sustain nature (Turnbull, 1987; Brody, 2000). They would have a dominant consciousness or ideology that reflects what anthropologists would term a more acephalous, or consciously interdependent, society on which their social relations are based.

As people who are products of other societies that are ordered very differently from our own become members of our society, they are socialized to this different dominant ideology, and their own experience reinforces this new understanding. There is also likely to be a fear or concern about these newcomers since they do not share these same understandings of the world and themselves. Their religious beliefs, values, and norms of behavior all connected to their ideology may be perceived as threatening to the host or conquering society members' way of life. Historically, an early fear of immigrants spreading foreign ideologies during the turn of the twentieth century was important in the establishment of universal public education in the United States. Employers in particular were very concerned about the ideologies of working people in Europe, where socialist ideologies were more popular among the working class than in the United States. The concern was that these ideas might create problems of worker unrest in our capitalist society (Billington, 1974; Olson, 1979; Handlin, 1957). The forced "civilizing" by missionaries of indigenous populations who reside on lands that are being conquered is another example of the threat of different systems of understandings and assumptions about the nature of humans and the appropriate ordering of society. Prior to the universal education of the public schools were the development of the Indian schools throughout the United States and Canada specifically organized to rapidly assimilate these different groups into the dominant way of life and ideology. This drama of conquest, displacement, and assimilation is still playing out in many areas south of the equator where hunting and gathering and pastoral indigenous societies are being incorporated via the forces of "globalization," a new chapter in the expansion of empires (Iadicola, 2008).

FOUR CURRENT IDEOLOGIES IN U.S. PUBLIC POLICY DEBATES

Four different ideologies that are current in public policy debates in the United States and are rooted in different positions within the society allow us to discuss how one would understand the nature of violence from viewing this social reality from these different sets of lenses (Greenberg, 1985; Hunt, 1981; Williamson et al., 1985). Table 2.1 provides a summary description of the first two of these ideologies: organic conservative and individualist conservative. Table 2.2 summarizes the last two ideologies: liberal/feminist and egalitarian. It is important for the reader to understand that these are only four of the many different ideologies that exist in the United States and many other countries around the world. There are various nationalist, anarchist, communist, environmentalist, various religionist (Islamist, Orthodox Christian, and Jewish perspectives), and radical feminist ideologies that can be found in countries throughout the world. However, we will focus on these four because of how well represented they are in public policy debate in the United States in particular, but variations of them can be found in most countries of the world.

These particular ideologies principally represent perspectives derived from the class and gender positions within U.S. society. Also, recognize that these are general descriptions and that within each ideology there is a diversity of more specific viewpoints that represent the interests of a specific group or faction. In describing these four ideologies, we mention some of the variants within each; however, our major focus is on providing a general description of the ideology that glosses over the differences within. These ideologies are briefly discussed with regard to their views of human nature, their central values, the nature of the social order, the role of the state, orientation toward change, ideal system, cause and solution to social problems in the society, and finally their view of the problem of violence.

The Organic Conservative Perspective

The historical root of the *organic conservative ideology* is the Christian paternalism of feudal society as exhibited in the writings of Thomas Aquinas and Edmund Burke (Hunt, 1981). Traces of the ideology are also found in the writings and speeches of American royalists in the colonies and Southern aristocrats prior to the Civil War. The organic conservative ideology fundamentally legitimates a socioeconomic system that is primarily agriculturally based on landed wealth and pre-capitalist relations of production (slave, serf, and/or indentured labor systems). Gender relations are based on the traditional patriarchal gender division of labor that would be found among the elite in agrarian societies. Historically speaking, this perspective represents the worldview of the landed gentry.

Although the United States never experienced a period of feudalism, the period in the history of the United States that most closely coincides with the dominance of this ideology includes the colonial period up to the early part of the nineteenth century, the Civil War representing a transition in class dominance and dominant ideology. During the colonial period and until the

Table 2.1. Organic and Individualist Conservative Ideologies in the United States.

	Organic Conservative	Individualist Conservative
Human nature	Humans are inherently aggressive, selfish, hierarchical, and motivated principally by biological needs. Men and women have different natures. Women are more temperate in their qualities and also have nurturing, caretaker qualities. Men are more aggressive, rational, and dominant.	Humans are inherently selfish, competitive, rational, individualistic, and basically lazy or inert. Humans are motivated by a rational calculation of self-interest. Inequality is inherent to differences in humans. Inequality between men and women is seen in terms of different choices that men make relative to women. Differences are not inherent to gender.
Central values	Authority and tradition as rooted in terms of class and gender relations. Freedom *within* prescribed bounds.	Individual liberty and private property (laissez faire). Liberty is not possible without the right of private property and a free market. Freedom *from* restraint.
Nature of the social order	Humans need society to protect themselves from other humans, especially men. Gender and class structure/hierarchy is necessary for society and humans to exist. Society is founded on basic human principles that are reflected in customs and traditions.	Free market and private property are the foundation of the economic and political order. Government is the coercive force. The invisible hand of competition is the just allocator. Gender and class hierarchies are the outcomes of individual differences and choices. Society is no more than the sum of the individuals who make it up; it is a social contract.

Role of the state	Elites should guide the state according to basic human principles, in Judeo-Christian societies, as they are stated in either the Bible or natural law. *Anti-democratic traditions.*	State should abstain from free market and restrict activities to national defense and safeguarding private property rights, criminal justice/system of courts, and maintaining monetary system. *Limited democratic traditions.*
Orientation toward change	Change is disruptive. It should be gradual, from the top down, guided by institutional elites and consistent with principles that form the foundation of the society	Change occurs in a "naturally" slow and incremental way as a result of individuals acting in competition with each other, trying to realize their self-interest in the marketplace. Social change is cyclical, like the market.
Ideal system	Patriarchal capitalist— stability through class and gender elite-directed development.	Free-market capitalism. Increase production through individual decisions stimulated by competition in the marketplace that benefits everyone in the society.
Cause of social problems	Sudden changes that are in violation of the basic principles and resultant breakdown in social control mechanisms of the society.	Government coercion and disruption of the free market (the natural regulator of the social order). As government interferes with the system, misallocation of goods and services disrupts human incentives to produce leading to social problems.
Solution to social problems	Found in past traditions that reflect basic human principles.	Found in the basic principles of capitalist society (neoclassical economics), found in private property and unfettered free market.

early part of the nineteenth century, bonded labor systems (slavery and indentured) dominated social relations, especially in the southern part of the country. The economy was principally based on agriculture, while the manufacturing sector was at an early stage of development. Production was small-scale, with individualized workshops and simple technology. The class structure consisted of a large independent producer class of small farmers, a small landowning-gentry class that was dominant, a class of indentured or slave laborers, a growing merchant class, and small but growing classes of factory owners and free workers. In general, class development in the southern part of the country lagged behind the northern in terms of the dominance of more classical capitalist relations of production. Organic conservatism was dominant in the southern region because of this difference in class structure. In the North during the first part of the nineteenth century, classical liberalism or what we refer to as individualist conservatism provided the legitimation for the emerging merchant and manufacturing classes. In general, the organic conservative ideology is more developed in Europe and in many Latin American and Middle Eastern societies where a landed oligarchy once clearly dominated these societies.

The religious fundamentalism of today is tied to an organic conservative ideology that looks to past wisdom and social formation for direction. Swift (1990) notes that Christian (largely Protestant) fundamentalism grew up in the United States at the turn of the century. The Judaic version has only surfaced in the past fifty years while Islamic fundamentalism dates from just before World War II and has only grown in the past twenty years. Swift contends that fundamentalism is principally a reactionary movement. He notes that "cultural and economic confusion provide fertile ground for the growth of fundamentalism. Who would not want a return to certainty in an uncertain world?" (Swift, 1990, 2).

Today in the United States there are three divergent variants of the organic conservative ideology: (1) religious moral conservative (groups like Concerned Women for America, Focus on the Family, American Coalition for Traditional Values, Christian Voice, and Eagle Forum); (2) populist conservative (Ku Klux Klan, Christian Identity groups, National Alliance, and John Birch Society); and (3) traditionalist (a variant of classical conservatism—neo-conservatism—would be a more recent example of this variant; William F. Buckley and popular talk show host Rush Limbaugh would be well-known representatives, as well as think tanks such as the Heritage Foundation). The first two variants have been most popular among segments of the working-class population and independent producers who reside in more economically depressed and politically conservative regions of the nation (southern states and the Bible Belt especially). Although these variants are quite different, and the adherents of each would not recognize their common philosophical grounding, the points of commonality center on the central values and conception of human nature. Publications in the United States that generally represent these variants are represented by the following: moral conservatives: *Plain Truth, Saturday Evening Post*, and *Reader's Digest*; populist conservative: *Washington Times* and *The New American*; and traditionalist or classical conservative: *National Review, American Spectator*, and *Conservative Digest*.

The organic conservatives contend that humans are naturally prone to anarchy, evil, and mutual destruction. Humans are seen as inherently aggressive, selfish, and hierarchical by nature. Humans, in this view, are motivated primarily by their base biological urges. The moral/religious organic conservative will focus on humans as being motivated by the propensity to sin, which in turn may be motivated by biological urges.

Following from this cynical and negative view of human nature, organic conservatives see the social order as the only thing that stands between civilization and anarchy. The social order is an organic entity that is greater than the sum of its individual members. For the organic conservative, the social order takes primacy over the rights of its individual members. It represents the embodiment of the customs and traditions that reflect basic principles of human life.

For the *moral/religious organic conservative*, these basic principles are reflected in the Bible as the foundation of the Judeo-Christian heritage. In countries that are dominated by Islamic parties or elites, as in the case of Iran, Saudi Arabia, and Afghanistan, the Koran and Sharia Law is where these principles are to be found. In Israel and among the Orthodox community, it is the Torah and the interpretations in the Talmud or Midrash. For the *traditionalist/classical conservative*, they are found in the U.S. Constitution as it defines the founding principles of the nation and in Greek and Roman natural law as it provides the philosophical basis of Western civilization. The customs, traditions, and basic institutions of the society are rooted in these basic principles that are the founding principles of the social order and have guided its development. Social policy and the behavior of individual members of the society are evaluated in the light of these standards. Interpretations of these principles and documents are prescribed narrowly. Organic conservatives are generally strict constructionists of the principles that are embodied in these documents. The organic conservative values past wisdom in dealing with the social problems of the day and that this past wisdom is reflected in the customs, laws, and religion of the society (Williamson, Evans, and Munley, 1985).

Inequality and hierarchy in the society are natural and necessary for the proper functioning of the social order. Class, gender, and ethnic hierarchies are legitimated as a product of natural differences between people who occupy these positions. These hierarchies are also understood to be functional to the society. Following from this, organic conservatives argue that the elite have a greater responsibility to others in the society as leaders and benefactors of those who are unable to take care of themselves. They are to serve as a patriarch taking care of the poor and disabled, as a husband and father takes care of his wife and children.

Hunt also suggests that the Christian paternalist ethic that is an element of the organic conservative perspective can be understood by comparing society to a family: "Those with positions of power and wealth can be likened to the father or keeper of the family. They have strong paternalistic obligations toward the common people, the poor, or, in our analogy, the children. The common person, however, is expected to accept his or her place in society and to be willingly subordinate to the leadership of the wealthy and the powerful in much the same way that a child accepts the authority of his or her father" (Hunt, 1981, 5). The paternalistic analogy of the husband taking care of his wife and children was often used to describe the role of the lord in caring for the serfs during feudalism or a master caring for his slaves during ancient times or periods of slavery during the pre–Civil War United States. The same analogy would apply in describing how the organic conservative would see the role of the capitalist elite in taking care of the poor through the establishment of charitable foundations.

The elite are defined in terms of class, but also in terms of gender and ethnicity. Owners of production, men, and the ethnic or cultural elite have an obligation to lead and care for those who serve them in factories, in homes, and in service to the state. Hunt notes that this hierarchy was rationalized as the will of God, as the order of nature, in terms of the genetic and inherent differences between people, or in some combination of these explanations from the roots of this ideology in medieval societies to the capitalist societies of today.

The organic conservative ideology is also referred to as the law and order approach. What is central to this ideology is the maintenance of the social order, to conserve the past, and to protect people from their aggressive, evil ways. Individual freedom is possible only when there is social order as defined by the system of rules, values, and traditions that underlies the order. There is no freedom without order; it becomes anarchy. People are free only when they choose to act in lawful and valued ways, that is, consistent with the basic principles that underlie the society. Those ways can be defined in terms of religious doctrine or in terms of the principles of Western civilization as defined in terms of modern-day capitalist society. Freedom is discussed in terms of freedom within prescribed bounds. Boundaries are defined in terms of the system of norms or laws, values, customs, and traditions, as they are reflective of the basic principles that underlie the social order.

The central values of the organic conservative perspective are authority, order, and tradition. Authority is essential to the social order and is defined as legitimate coercion derived from the hierarchical positions within the society. Nisbet (1962) notes that, like power, authority is a form of constraint, but, unlike power, it is based on the consent of those under it. This consent is ultimately given as a result of the moral obligations of citizens to preserve the order and to be respectful and obedient to those who are in positions of power. Order refers to the institutionalized hierarchy of statuses and roles within the society. This hierarchy is understood as natural and necessary for human survival and is legitimated by the traditions reflecting those basic human principles firmly rooted in the cultural heritage.

The state is to be ruled by elites who guide it in the interests of all in terms of the time-honored traditions and customs of the society. Democratic processes are not consistent with the logic of this perspective. For the organic conservative, democracy often translates into mob rule, whereby those with the least abilities to govern have the ability to do so. *Organic conservatives* promote nondemocratic mechanisms (electoral colleges, appointed commissions, and so forth) to limit the potential harm to the social order from popular rule.

Social change is viewed with suspicion from this ideology, for it is seen as essentially disruptive to the social order. Change that is unavoidable or deemed necessary should be slow, within the institutional framework of the social order, and guided by elites who are acting in terms of the basic principles that underlie the society. Historically, the ideal system for the *organic conservative* is reflected in the social relations of feudal society with its notions of reciprocal responsibility, fixed duty, and noblesse oblige. Organic conservatives today in the United States accept the historical ascension of capitalism as the dominant mode of production while desiring to retain some characteristics of past feudal social relations. The ideal for the organic conservative is paternalistic capitalism: a basic stability in the social order brought about by adherence to traditional values that reflect the basic principles embedded in the Judeo-Christian heritage or the philosophical precepts of Western civilization and through elite-managed growth. In countries where military rule is aligned with a landed oligarchy, the organic conservative ideology will be dominant in public policy. Many countries in Latin America, Africa, and the Middle East follow this pattern.

Organic conservatives understand violent behavior to be endemic to humans. Violence stems from our aggressive nature that is part of our connection to the animal world or our proneness to sin resulting from our falling from grace, according to the Judeo-Christian heritage. In either case, the potential for violence is normal and inherent to our nature. The occurrence of violence is checked by the social order, which restrains and structures our behavior. The problem of violence occurs when the social order and the institutional controls have weakened or broken down. This can occur because of social changes that have been inconsistent or counter to the basic principles of the society as noted in the sacred texts or traditions or Constitution. Grassroots movements are particularly viewed with suspicion as they represent change without the wisdom of the elites within the system. Furthermore, change itself is seen as disruptive in that it creates disruptions of institutional mechanisms to control the natural, potentially violent impulses of humans.

The focus is on interpersonal violence. Most violence conducted by elites is deemed to be incidental and/or necessary for the maintenance of the order, although some elite violence is recognized to be a result of moral failings. This is the case for interpersonal violence conducted by the elite and forms of institutional violence, such as state, religious, and economic violence, deemed to be excessive or immoral, that is, not justifiable in terms of preserving the social order.

The solutions to the problem of violence are to reinforce the order, to strengthen the bonds to the order, and to improve the efficiency of the mechanisms of social control that keep sin or aggressive, animal impulses in check. The organic conservative looks to the basic principles that underlie the order as providing insight as to how to control violence. Stress is placed on promoting steps to educate or inculcate morals and traditional values among the masses. Often this is done by increasing the role of religion in public life. Another strategy is to increase the level of external restraints by promoting more criminalization and the use of the criminal justice system in controlling disruptive behavior. Last, by promoting the obligations of individuals to the needs of the community (usually defined in terms of the state), organic conservatives hope to reduce violence and preserve the order. In short, solutions are ultimately defined in terms of strengthening institutional controls, applying further restrictions on behavior, and increasing the levels of punishment to control behavior that is threatening to the status quo. In criminology, the theory of crime control that is most rooted in the organic conservative ideology is control theory. The assumptions regarding the propensity to crime and the strategies to reduce crime by strengthening one's bond to the social order (Hirschi, 1969) and the strengthening of containment mechanisms (Reckless, 1962) follow from this ideology.

The Individualist Conservative Perspective

Individualist conservatism, classical liberalism, or what is referred to currently as neo-liberalism was the dominant perspective of capitalism during the eighteenth and nineteenth centuries. Although much of this perspective took root and gained wide acceptance during the transitional mercantilist periods, it was in the nineteenth century that classical liberalism dominated social, political, and economic thought in England at the start of the Industrial Revolution. The perspective reflects a temper of mind that found the essence of society to lie in the individual autonomous, self-sufficing, and rational action and the essence of history to lie in the progressive emancipation of the individual from the tyranny of the past feudal order. Competition, individualism, dislocation of status and custom, impersonality, and moral anonymity were hailed by the rationalist because through them the natural stable and rational individual would be given an environment in which he would develop without constraining his inherent potentialities.

The individualist conservative legitimates the dominance of capitalist social relations in the stage of competitive industrial capitalism and the interests of the dominant class of entrepreneurs. In the United States, this stage occurred between the early nineteenth and early twentieth centuries, though the ideology of classical liberalism had been a powerful influence on the founding fathers during the eighteenth century. The craft sector declined during the nineteenth century, and the scale, mechanization, and integration of coordinated manufacturing production increased rapidly. There arose simultaneously a small but powerful factory-owning class and a large industrial working class made up of immigrants, displaced farmers, and artisans. The ranks of the independent producers were shrinking in the wake of increasing periods of economic concentration. These changes left in their wake the destruction of the gemeinschaft of the previous colonial order where the remnants of feudal structures were legitimated by organic conservatism.

Today, the individualist conservative ideology or neo-liberalism is most representative of the viewpoint of owners of businesses, especially in competitive sectors of the economy, and the petite bourgeoisie (i.e., independent producers, small farmers, and shopkeepers). This viewpoint is represented in the positions of the National Association of Manufacturers, Rotary clubs (which are dominated by small business owners), and the U.S. Chamber of Commerce. Libertarians present a purer version of the individualist conservative ideology. Although they represent a relatively small number of American followers, their numbers have been growing since the 1980s. Publications that present an individualist conservative ideology are *Human Events, Commentary, The Economist, The Public Interest, U.S. News and World Report, BusinessWeek, Forbes,* and the editorial pages of the *Wall Street Journal*.

The individualist conservative ideology possesses a view of human nature that, in some respects, overlaps with the organic conservative ideology: humans are basically aggressive (individualist conservatives would define this as competitive) and selfish. There is, however, this crucial difference: individualist conservatives see humans as highly rational, individualistic, and basically inert or lazy. The utilitarianism of Thomas Hobbes and Jeremy Bentham is an important element of individualist conservatism. Individuals in this view are assumed to be motivated by their own self-interest and to engage in a completely rational calculation of the cost and benefits of alternatives before they engage in any action.

The free market and private property are the foundations of the social order and the basis of political freedom, according to this perspective. The free market, the competitive arena where individual producers are competing to sell their products at the best possible price and where workers are competing to sell their labor power at the best possible price, provides for the channeling of the individual's egoistic drives for the ultimate good of the social order. As Adam Smith observed:

> Each producer intends only his own security; and by directing that industry in such a manner as its produce may be of the greatest value, he intends only his own gain, and he is in this, and in many other cases, led by an invisible hand to promote an end which was no part of his intention. Nor is it always the worse for the society that it was not a part of it. By pursuing his own interest he frequently promotes that of society more effectually than when he really intends to promote it. I have never known much good done by those who affected to trade for the public good. It is an affectation, indeed, not very common among merchants, and very few words need be employed in dissuading them from it. (Smith, 1937, 423)

In this view, the free market untampered allows for a just allocation of goods and services, an allocation that serves the needs of the individual actors within the market and thus the social order as a whole. The primary coercive force within the society, according to individualist conservatives, is the state. The state, under both the previous policies of mercantilism and contemporary liberal policies, disrupts the market. For example, by establishing a minimum wage and regulating the marketing of goods and services, the state essentially coerces individuals to act in opposition to their interests, which, in the individualist conservative view, results in inflationary prices and depressed market conditions. This leads to further problems in the society as the rational behavior of individuals within the society become increasingly disruptive as they respond to the irrational outcomes of a disrupted market. The state is to serve three essential functions: (1) protect the country from external threats; (2) protect citizens against injustices committed by other citizens, such as violation of contracts and property rights; and (3) erect and maintain public institutions and public works that are in the public interest, such as currency, standards of weights and measures, and physical means necessary to conduct business.

Society for the individualist conservative is defined as no more than the sum of its parts (i.e., the individuals composing it). The social contract as described by Jean-Jacques Rousseau is the foundation of the social order.

The ideal is "to find a form of association that may defend and protect with the whole force of the community, the person and property of every associate, and by means of which each, coalescing with all, may nevertheless obey only himself, and remain as free as before" (Rousseau, 1967, 17).

According to the individualist conservative, inequality and hierarchy in the society are natural insofar as the market determines them. Each individual competes with others to nurture and develop the talents he or she was born with and each is assessed by the market as to his or her worth. Those with the greatest talent and greatest initiative compete for the highest income, their talents and acquired skills being in short supply and high demand. Those with the least talent and the least initiative receive the lowest income, their talents being ordinary, in great supply, and with little demand. Just as supply and demand determine the price of a product, so also do they determine the price of labor and thus one's income. Gender, class, and ethnic stratification are understood only as they are the products of individual choices in the marketplace. They are not understood as systems outside the context of the individual choices and actions that created them. The only exception to this is in describing forms and levels of inequality resulting from irrational discrimination that has occurred as a result of government actions that have blocked the market force and the individual's rational decision making.

Individual liberty and private property are the two central values of the individualist conservative ideology. In order for the social order to exist and progress, each individual must be free to realize his or her own interests, and by each individual having the ability to possess property, the means of production, he or she is less likely to be coerced by others. Individual liberty through ownership of private property can be realized only by the presence of a free market. It is in the marketplace where the benefits of one's free entrepreneurial action can be realized. Freedom is understood in terms of freedom from restraint. The primary agency of restraint is government.

For the individualist conservative change occurs in a naturally slow and incremental way as a result of individual actions. Social change is cyclical, like the cycles of the market. Change results from individuals acting as individuals in the pursuit of their own interests. The inventor and entrepreneur are viewed as the principal agents of change. The ideal system for the individualist conservative is free market or laissez-faire capitalism, a social order that allows individuals to manifest their egoistic drive for material accumulation (profit) through the market, which results in benefits to all members of the society.

How do individualist conservatives understand the problem of violence? Again, like the organic conservatives, the focus is interpersonal violence. Institutional violence and certainly structural violence are generally not recognized to be violence by individual conservatives. Especially in the case of structural violence, the positions and their consequences are an outcome that results from the irrational decisions made by individuals, either as a result of their own wrong choices or as a result of government actions that have insulated them from the consequences of their wrong decisions in the past. They see what we refer to as structural violence as less a result of an unchecked natural inclination than a conscious decision on the part of the victim. Violence is an action perceived to be rational by the actor, rational in the context of the relative value of the costs and benefits of action. The armed robber who kills a victim, the rapist, the contract killer, even the spouse abuser, evaluates the costs and benefits of the action and rationally chooses violence. For the individualist conservative, the key to the problem of violence is found in understanding how the costs and benefits of violence have been created. In most cases, individualist conservatives will charge actions by the state interfering with natural forces (market forces) as the cause of the distortion in the rational calculus. They also note that the breakdown of social control decreases the cost of violence to the offender relative to possible rewards, thus making violence rational in this context.

The solution to the problem of violence is then understood in the context of changing the costs and benefits of violent behavior for the individual offender. The principal focus in public policy from the individualist conservative approach has been changing the costs of the violent behavior, rather than in providing alternative ways to achieve the benefits that are the goal of the action. Thus the criminal justice system is the principal agency to address the problem of violence. Increasing the penalties and increasing the certainty that punishment will result from the action are ways promoted by individualist conservatives to control violence.

In regard to the issue of alternative means to achieve the benefits, individualist conservatives understand the problem of limited means to achieve the benefits as a problem of government interference with the marketplace. For individualist conservatives, government has limited the legitimate, appropriate means to achieve the good (through initiative and hard work) in the society. Government has limited employment opportunities by welfare and market regulation; it has discouraged individual initiative and drive by providing for people in a way that rewards their idleness and has destroyed families by making individuals increasingly dependent on the state for their well-being and not their own initiative and enterprise. All of these increase the likelihood that violence will be chosen by the individual in the exercise of illegitimate, disruptive alternatives to achieving wealth, status, and power.

Solutions to addressing the benefits side of the equation would focus on reducing the role of government in the marketplace in order to encourage further enterprise and initiative that would have the result of providing more alternatives to achieve the benefits that result from violent action. Even forms of violence that are a result of frustration and interpersonal conflict are understood as a result of the disruptive influence of government in the society, and again, with the reduced role of government in the marketplace, the level of conflict and frustration will be reduced as more opportunities for self-fulfillment are created through unrestrained individual initiative in the marketplace.

In criminological theory, the classical school of thought, or what is more commonly referred to as deterrence theory and the latest version, rational choice theory, is based on the ideological assumptions of individualist conservatism. The focus is on individual choice based on the calculation of costs and benefits of action. The policy implications of deterrence theory focus on changing the severity and certainty of punishment in response to the occurrence of criminal behavior.

The Liberal Ideology

Modern-day *liberalism* developed primarily in response to increasing problems of economic instability and, secondarily, to public outcry over increasing concentration of wealth and monopolization in the marketplace as industrial capitalism developed in the post–Civil War period of U.S. history. The historical context for the development of the reform corporate liberal ideology is the monopoly stage of capitalist development. The ideology reflects the interests of large-scale monopoly capital that looks to the state to stabilize the system and provide increasing amounts of subsidies to maintain its monopoly positions. The disruptiveness of the economic cycle that goes boom to bust takes on more gravity as the economy grows in size. With each recession the costs to employers and employees grows, and it becomes more difficult to resolve the crisis in order to begin the next boom period. Rapid acceleration of fixed capital costs as there is increasing mechanization of production, together with the normal operation of the business cycle, result in increasing concentration and centralization. Work becomes increasingly routinized with the introduction of mechanization and the transition from technical to bureaucratic control of the workplace.

New conflicts develop as a result of the division of the economy into monopoly and competitive sectors and as a result of the internationalization of capital, that is, center-dominant capitalist societies versus periphery-dominated, dependent-capitalist societies. There are not only increasing divisions within the owning class (nationally and internationally) but also increasing divisions within the working class. There is also at this stage the increasingly rapid growth of a relative surplus population and the need for the state to respond to this economic and political problem. Early development of liberalism in the United States is seen in the development of the Progressive Movement at the turn of the twentieth century. Later John Maynard Keynes's *The General Theory of Employment, Interest, and Money*, which was written during a time of worldwide crisis for the capitalist, legitimated the role of the state to resolve this crisis by means of increasing intervention in the marketplace.

This liberal perspective was the dominant perspective in the United States from the Great Depression up through the 1960s with President Lyndon Johnson's War on Poverty and the civil rights initiatives of that period. In recent times, beginning in the mid-1970s, the liberal perspective has suffered a serious setback in terms of its dominance in public policy. Greenberg (1985) notes that this fall of the liberal policy regime resulted from the combination of a sputtering economy, international retreat (Vietnam and Iran, reversal of the Bretton Woods agreement), and stagnant living standards (inflation and stagnation). Attempts have been made to dress up the perspective in new clothes or to make some fundamental changes in the economic tenets of the perspective. Traditional liberal U.S. periodicals are *Newsweek*, *Time Magazine*, *The Atlantic Monthly*, *Harper's*, and the editorial pages of the *New York Times, Boston Globe*, and *Washington Post*.

The liberal/feminist component is rooted in the first women's movement in the United States with the co-optation of the radical wing of the movement (represented by the thinking of Stanton and Anthony) into the National

Table 2.2.   Liberal and Egalitarian Ideologies in the United States.

	Liberal	Egalitarian
Human nature	Same as individualist conservatives with the exception that humans can be motivated by altruism under certain circumstances. Inequality is inherent to differences in humans. Inequality between men and women is the result of socialization differences, patterns of institutional discrimination, and differences in choices made. Differences are not rooted in biological differences.	Human nature defined in terms of needs and how they are realized through interaction with nature. Humans have projective consciousness (species need)—need to think, to imagine, to create. The essence of human nature is the capacity and realization of these needs. Humans have the same needs; differences that exist are a product of the gender and class divisions rooted in patriarchal, capitalist society.
Central values	Individual liberty (civil rights), private property, and equal opportunity. Freedom *of* opportunity.	Equality and community. Freedom *to* develop capacities and potentials.
Nature of the social order	Free market and private property are the foundation of the economic and political order. However, capitalism has tendencies toward instability and concentrations of wealth and power. The result is social injustices in the meritocratic structure of the society that require government fine-tuning to keep the system expanding and beneficial to all.	Modes of production and reproduction and their articulation are the basis of the social order. Patriarchal, capitalist society is based on inequality, coercion, exploitation, and alienation whereby those in dominant position determined by their relationship to production (class) and reproduction (gender) benefit at the expense of those in dominated positions.

Role of the state	By means of pluralistic democracy, the state serves everyone's interests. The state must act as a regulator of the system to make sure there is equal opportunity and stable growth. *Open contest democratic system.*	Politics and the state are dominated by the interests of the ruling elite as defined in terms of class and gender. *Nonpatriarchal democratic socialism—*class and gender position are irrelevant to democratic decision making. Society organized to meet needs of all, not the elite defined in terms of class and gender.
Orientation toward change	Collective action on the part of citizens in many cases mediated by government action is necessary to keep the system progressing. Social change is evolutionary, a result of government-directed capitalist growth and development.	Fundamental social change occurs as a result of conflict between the divisions within the society. This conflict of divisions is stimulated by contradictions within and between modes of production and reproduction. *Change is dialectical.*
Ideal system	Welfare state capitalism—capitalist society with an open meritocracy (open educational, economic, and political contests) and welfare safety net necessary to ensure stability and development.	Democratic-nonpatriarchal socialism—elimination of class, gender, and all other forms of oppression. Society organized and functions to promote the collective fulfillment of natural and species needs of all humanity.
Cause of social problems	Uncontrolled economy and lack of equal opportunity in the meritocracy.	Structured inequality and inherent contradictions create problems and have potential to stimulate conflict within the society that may force for change.
Solution to social problems	Government monitoring of the economy and the meritocracy and regulation to maintain fairness.	Elimination of hierarchical structures and exploitive social relations.

American Women's Suffrage Association (NAWSA) and the definition of the problem of women's rights as principally the right of suffrage. Today, in the wake of the second women's movement, the National Organization for Women (NOW) has succeeded the NAWSA as the paramount liberal/feminist political organization. Although today's liberal feminism embraces elements of the previous radical agenda of the first women's movement (Equal

Rights Amendment), this no longer appears to be central to its agenda. The focus of NOW, like its predecessor, is to work through the established institutional mechanisms within the state and corporate structure to achieve incremental gains for women as defined in terms of extending opportunities for women to be equal participants in the institutions of the larger society. Changing institutional structures is only promoted when they serve to block women's opportunities for participation. A critique of patriarchy as it manifests itself in the functioning of all institutions in our society including religion, state, and economy is not part of liberal feminism. Inclusion, not revolution, is the goal.

Reflecting their common roots in classical liberalism, the liberal/feminists' view of human nature is similar to that of individualist conservatives; it is not, however, as cynical. While liberal/feminism accepts the individualist conservative position that humans are fundamentally rational and self-interested, they believe that individuals can, under certain limited circumstances, be motivated by altruism, through an appeal to their "better nature." In regard to gender, differences between men and women are the result of socialization differences, patterns of institutional discrimination, and differences in choices made. Differences are not rooted in biological differences. Equality and sameness are stressed in viewing men and women. The same applies to ethnic stratification as it is principally a product of discrimination and lack of equal opportunity. However, liberals recognize that inequality of talent and ability is natural to humans and will manifest itself in class differences.

In terms of their conception of the social order, liberals believe, like individualist conservatives, that the capitalist system provides a foundation for its central value, individual freedom. However, unlike the individualist conservative ideology, which promotes laissez-faire, free-market capitalism, the liberal/feminist ideology supports a role for government to fine-tune the economic system in order to maintain freedom and opportunity for individual development. Liberals contend that because the economic system has tendencies toward economic instability and concentration of ownership and wealth, they see the role of the state as one of monitoring or fine-tuning the system to maintain steady or stable economic growth and safeguarding the competitive nature of the free market through slowing down the problem of concentration. Both liberal and conservative policymakers encourage promotion of trade and the strategic lifting of trade barriers in areas to create national economic advantage. The establishment of welfare (government subsidies for workers who are displaced) and wealth-fare (government subsidies for owners to support capital accumulation) and adjustments to the money supply to control the pace of economic activity are all liberal methods used to control the economic cycle. Antitrust actions and redistributive tax systems have been used (although less vigorously of late) by liberal policymakers to slow down the pace of concentration in the marketplace in terms of distribution of wealth and income.

This monitoring of the system is not restricted to the economic sphere. Liberals will also express concern as to the fairness of the meritocracy, the system of contests (education, work, and politics) that ensures the proper placement of individuals in the social order on the basis of their abilities and efforts. Liberals are concerned to ensure that the outcomes of these contests are fair in that all participants (including the poor, women, and ethnic minorities) have an "equal opportunity" to succeed. If the contests of the meritocracy are not fair, not only do individuals suffer in terms of their lack of opportunity but also the social order as a whole suffers, for human talent is not being used efficiently by the system.

Liberals assume that inequality is natural to the human condition; however, they hope that the outcomes of the meritocracy follow a model of distributive justice. Legal strategies disallowing forms of illegitimate discriminating practices (against racial and gender minorities) and social expenditures to assure equal opportunity in each of the contests are central elements of their strategy. Liberals are confident that their program can be implemented, despite the inconvenience to some individuals, by an appeal to the altruism inherent in human nature. However, liberals underestimate the competition between groups formed along class, ethnic, and gender dimensions that often undermines these efforts.

Pluralism best describes the nature of the political process from the liberal point of view. An open arena of competition in the policy sector with different interest groups, each representing the interests of their membership to the best of their ability, ensures that the state will serve everyone's interests. The state is the neutral arbiter of conflicting interests in a pluralistic society. Liberals conceptualize social change in terms of an evolutionary model. Society is modernizing as a result of the increasing political openness and following of a path of capitalist development guided by a political engaged civil society. For liberals the social system is inherently rational (or can be made so) and will progress as humans increase their knowledge and intervene (collectively by means of the state pressured by interest groups) to make appropriate modifications in the system. The two central values of the liberal ideology are individual civil liberties and equal opportunity. Freedom is discussed in terms of freedom of opportunity.

The ideal system for liberals is the corporate welfare state. Government works with business in a partnership with other interests in the society to maintain a pattern of stable growth and an increasing standard of living for working people and increasing profits for owners and investors. The countries of Norway, Sweden, Finland, Denmark, Belgium, France, and the Netherlands are examples of countries that have experienced a long period of liberal dominance in government policies.

Violence from the liberal/feminist ideology is understood as principally a result of a lack of equal opportunity in the meritocracy. Like the previous two ideologies, interpersonal violence is the principal focus. However, liberals will also recognize institutional violence by economic actors (corporate violence), by the state, and by men dominating women in the family. Violence is not seen as endemic to human nature, but a result of an uncontrolled economic system that leads to distortions in the meritocracy. Violence, principally committed by men, is understood as a response (not necessarily rational) to the blocked opportunities resulting from the undirected, unfettered market force. Specific focus of these blocked opportunities is in the area of employment and educational opportunities. Violence among minority populations and the young is understood in terms of lack of opportunities in these areas, which leads to frustration and violence as a means to seek alternatives or, more likely, as a means to strike out at the system that denies these opportunities. The violence in the institutional areas, especially economic, is viewed as a result of a lack of government regulation to ensure safe and least environmentally destructive production and wholesome and safe products in the marketplace.

The solution to the problem of violence in the society is the maintenance of fairness in the meritocracy through the regulating of market relations and enforcing laws that prohibit individual and institutional discrimination that denies opportunities for participation by women and ethnic minorities. Furthermore, general economic progression resulting from government regulation and actions to direct and subsidize investment in promising growth areas (high tech) is also seen as important. As the economic pie expands, there is more for everyone, reducing the societal pressures rooted in unequal distribution of income and wealth.

In criminological theory liberalism has been represented in the positivist school of thought. The stress is in identifying the defect in the individual or the immediate environment that leads to the individual not having access to equal opportunity for participation in the meritocracy. Biological and psychological positivist theories have been the more conservative approaches within this paradigm in that they see the problem of violence as more fixed within the individual as a result of his or her deficiencies. There is little need to change the social environment to accommodate the individual's pathology. The implications of these theories are that there are biological and psychological interventions that will reduce levels of violence in individuals. The violence of the individual will be controlled directly by the therapeutic intervention or indirectly by providing access to opportunities once the physical or personality defect is corrected.

Sociological positivist theories have located the cause of violence in problems of the opportunity structure resulting from problems of the immediate environment or the individual's adaptation to it. Strain or opportunity theory is a good example of this latter approach. In strain or opportunity theory the problems of crime are rooted in lack of access to opportunities to achieve the goals of the society. This frustration can lead to adaptations, violence being one. Versions of strain theories of the violent delinquent focus on how aggression stems from the frustration resulting from blocked opportunities (Cohen, 1955; Cloward and Ohlin, 1960). Solutions are defined in terms of expanding opportunities in the meritocracy to reduce levels of crime and violence and correcting the deficits in the individual's adaptation to the environment.

In all three of the preceding ideologies, the problem of violence and the solutions are addressed within the context of the society. In none of the ideologies discussed thus far is the problem of violence understood as endemic to how the society is organized. Violence is ultimately seen as incidental to the fundamental organizational-political-economic structure as defined in terms of systems of stratification. Even the liberal analysis views the solution to the problems of the society, violence as well, in fine-tuning the system, making sure that women and ethnic minorities and the poor have access to participation in the system, not fundamentally changing the nature of class, gender, or ethnic relations or the rights of property or market relations that allow for the power of private property.

The last ideology defines the problems of the society, violence specifically, as endemic to how we have organized the society. This ideology is outside the ideological parameters of the system, and thus these ideas pose the greatest threat to elites within the system. The preceding ideologies are well represented on the editorial pages of local and national media and in public commentary heard on television and radio programs. This is not the case with this last ideology.

The Egalitarian Ideology

It is important to recognize that the *egalitarian* ideology discussed represents a merging of elements of radical feminism with a socialist ideology. The socialist ideology has a long tradition rooted in the utopian socialists going back as early as the fifth century. More well-known utopian socialists of the eighteenth and nineteenth centuries include Babeuf, Proudhon, Saint-Simon, and Fourier. The socialist ideology today is still dominated by a variant of scientific socialism based on the writings of Karl Marx.

Early Marxist feminists include Clara Zetkin and Rosa Luxemburg. The weakness of this perspective was in the theoretical primacy of the class dimension of stratification over the gender dimension. The institutionalization of private property was understood as the basis of all other forms of oppression and stratification, including the subjugation of women. A similar perceived weakness was seen in the radical feminist analysis, which contends that gender oppression and stratification is the basis of all other forms of oppression and stratification, including social class. However, socialist/feminist ideology circumvented the weaknesses of both analyses by integrating the centrality of the radical feminist agenda with the socialist agenda. This perspective represents a materialist analysis grounded principally in Marxist political economy and an incorporation of the radical feminist emphasis of patriarchy as a separate structure within a social system (Hartman, 1981; Vogel, 1981). In this ideology, both patriarchy and class oppression are seen as separate but interlocked systems of stratification that form the basis of patriarchal capitalist societies today.

Socialists, in general, proceed from the premise that human nature is rooted in human needs. Although the topic of human needs is one that has been a focus of great philosophical and psychological debates, from the socialist ideology we can simply identify two general areas of needs: physical or natural needs, which are similar to the needs of all animals, and species needs, that is, needs that are unique to humans (McMurtry, 1978). Humans' physical needs are reflected in their needs to fulfill their physical being. Humans' physical needs include sustenance and protection from the elements. Humans' species needs are reflected in the unique qualities of the human species. Species needs are defined in terms of the drive for members of the species to realize their species potentials. Species needs are based on the human abilities to think, create, and imagine. McMurtry refers to this species need as projective consciousness, the ability to imagine something that does not exist in nature and to project it into reality through the creative powers of humans.

Both human physical or natural and species needs are fulfilled through human interaction with nature. Humans objectify and re-create themselves through interaction with nature, developing themselves and developing nature simultaneously. Other human beings are a crucial component of nature. Humans need other human beings in order to exist, to fulfill their physical and species needs. This is sometimes referred to as the social nature of human beings (Azizah, 1981). For the egalitarian ideology, that is all that there is of human nature. It is a tabula rasa that is based on needs that reflect the essence of humanity and the need to be social, to interact with nature and especially other humans, to realize these needs. The idea that humans are selfish, individualistic, rational, competitive, and hierarchical in society today is not a result of human nature but the reflection of the nature of humans as they are a product of capitalist society.

The concept of alienation is at the core of a socialist conception of human nature (Ollman, 1972). Alienation essentially refers to the separation of humans from nature and thus from their ability to reproduce and fully actualize their needs and potentials through interaction with nature. All systems of stratification in societies, especially those based on class and gender, create problems of alienation in that they inhibit a segment of the population (workers and women) from reaching their potential as human beings through their interaction with nature. In all cases of alienation, the dominated interactions with nature are controlled for the benefit of those who dominate.

The inequality between men and women is not a reflection of differences in their natures per se but is a product of the gender stratification system rooted in patriarchy. Thus, as social systems change in terms of the nature of gender oppression (i.e., patriarchy), so does the nature of the inequality between men and women and the presumed differences in nature that are used to legitimate this inequality. The same is true for class inequality.

Both the modes of production and reproduction form the foundation of the social system. The specific nature of these modes of production and reproduction, as defined in terms of forces and relations of production/reproduction, defines the social system, thus American society is a capitalist patriarchy. Furthermore, although these systems can be described as independent of each other, they are articulated as part of a whole system. Today the vast majority of the world's societies are patriarchal capitalist systems, although the specific nature of these systems and their articulation are not the same from society to society. Nevertheless, one's position in the social order in patriarchal capitalist societies is characterized in terms of one's structural position in relation to each of the modes of production/reproduction: male worker, female worker, male capitalist, and so forth. Ethnic/racial and age stratification systems are significant as they intersect with these fundamental structural divisions. Racism and nationalism have been used by the capitalist class historically to maintain control over the workforce by maintaining a divided opposition and by furthering imperialist goals of domination of other social systems to meet the needs for expanding markets and access to resources. The origins of the ethnic/racial stratification system are fundamentally rooted in the legacy of conquest and inter-ethnic/racial group competition over scarcities.

Patriarchy for socialist/feminists and egalitarians is defined both ideologically and, more importantly, materially. Patriarchy is a set of social relations that has a material base and in which there are hierarchical relations between men. These hierarchical relations are institutionalized in the customs, norms, and structure of social relations in all arenas of human interaction. This hierarchy is also maintained through solidarity among men. The material base of patriarchy is men's control over women's labor power. Control over women is maintained by restricting women's access to necessary economically productive resources and restricting and controlling women's sexuality.

For any social system to survive and persist, there must be an articulation, a fitting together, of the modes of production and reproduction. This does not mean that the two systems do not come into conflict or contradiction with each other. Change in one ordinarily creates movement, tension, or contradiction in the other (Hartman, 1981). The gender and class systems change as a result of struggle between the dominant and dominated groups within each sphere that is stimulated by the contradictions that develop out of each respective mode, and as a result of the conflict that may develop as the aims of those who dominate in each sphere conflict (Dworkin, 1976). (For a further discussion on the concept of contradiction, the reader is referred back to the discussion in chapter 1.)

The major factor perpetuating gender inequality is that the modes of production and reproduction and the nature of the articulation of these two modes form the foundation of the social order. Institutional processes maintain the stability of the social order because those who dominate each system as defined in terms of the relations of production and reproduction benefit from the continuation of the domination and from the specific nature of the articulation of the two systems. For example, capitalists benefit from patriarchy because of a defined pool of workers who are excluded or discriminated against in gaining access to production (a reserve army of unemployed). The divisions between men and women serve to divide the workforce, making it easier to control. For example, the super-exploitation in women's wages and the unpaid labor by women in home maintenance serve to hold wages down and maximize profits for capitalists. Men benefit from the free labor at home, a psychology of domination, control over sexuality, and the production of their progeny. The articulation of the two systems benefits all men in that the super-exploitation of women in the workforce serves to maintain their dependence and powerlessness for the continued maintenance of patriarchy.

As each of the two modes change, so does the nature of the articulation between the two modes. Contradictions between the two modes develop and increase conflict between the opposing classes/genders within and between the modes of production and reproduction. Depending on the nature of the power differences between these opposing classes/genders, these contradictions have the potential to bring about fundamental changes in the overall social system.

The ideal system for the egalitarian ideology is nonpatriarchal democratic socialism. This implies a society that has eliminated class, gender, and all other systems of stratification. Society is organized and functions to promote the collective fulfillment of natural and species needs of all humanity.

What is the cause and solution to the problem of violence in our society? For the egalitarian, that violence that is larger in scope and severity is structural and institutional. Violence is not inherent to humans but is a product of the social organization of humans. In particular, it is a product of the hierarchical organization of the society whereby humans are valued and devalued relative to each other as they occupy positions within this hierarchy. Violence is fundamentally the means by which the hierarchies are established, maintained, extended, and ultimately challenged and changed. Thus at the highest level, violence (structural) is a direct outcome of this hierarchical organization in that the development of some (those in dominated positions) is sacrificed for the development of those who are dominant. The violent consequences of this arrangement, as it manifests itself in mortality and morbidity differences and differences in human development of those who occupy differing positions in the hierarchy, are recognized to be central to defining the problem of violence. At another level, violence takes the form of institutional practices that maintain and extend the systems of stratification. In this sense, violence is the use of force to acquire and maintain wealth, status, and power legitimately as they are defined in terms of the rules of the systems of stratification that underlie the social order. These rules of ownership, control, and power establish the parameters for the functioning of institutions of the larger society. This institutional violence is crucial for the maintenance and reproduction of systems of stratification. Last, violence is the illegitimate use of force to acquire wealth, status, power, and control over women through the violation of the rules of systems of stratification that underlie the social order. This is the problem of interpersonal criminal violence. Although not seen to be as large in scope and severity as institutional or structural, it is nevertheless violence that threatens human life and is a product of hierarchical relations of the larger society.

Solutions to the problems of violence focus on empowering those who are dominated to make change in the systems of stratification that are the basis of their oppression. Class and gender oppression is ultimately the basis of violence. As those who are dominated are empowered to change these structures and allow all members of the society to realize their species and physical needs, levels of violence will be reduced.

The critical school of criminology (Michalowski, 1985; Chambliss, 1988) and the emerging socialist/feminist criminological theories (Messerschmidt, 1986; Mullins, 2006) are rooted in the egalitarian ideology. The problem of crime is rooted in systems of stratification. Nonreformist reforms, those that appear to be reforms but fundamentally change systems of stratification, are seen as appropriate strategies to reducing crime. For example, reforms such as full employment would change the distribution of power between owners and workers so that it would have an impact on the pattern of crime in the society. The comparable worth reform, whereby wage differentials are determined on the basis of the amount of work required to attain the skill and not by means of the market alone, would have an impact on the economic position of men relative to women and thus be a nonreformist reform and would have an impact on patterns of violence in the society.

CONCLUSION

In conclusion, how we perceive and understand violence and the roles we play in relation to the violence we experience in our lives as actors, victims, and observers takes place through a cultural prism. This cultural prism is a social creation, like the violence we are observing. This cultural prism is constructed in part by the ideologies that are dominant in our society. These ideologies allow us to see some forms of violence and not others. To understand what violence is and how we experience it, it is first necessary for us to understand the nature of the prism and how it may restrict our recognition and understanding of violence.

In this book we are attempting to extend the reader's understanding of violence by first developing a definition of violence based on universalistic criteria. We are also attempting to allow the reader to go beyond the limitations of understanding created by the cultural and ideological lenses that one has acquired as a product and actor within a particularly society. As we discuss and describe different kinds of violence based on the definition of violence developed within the first chapter, the reader will sense the pull of the culture and more specifically the ideologies that are dominant in the society. We hope we have begun to provide the tools for stepping back and looking at this phenomenon from different ideological frameworks or vantage points to allow for a more complete understanding of what violence is.

DISCUSSION QUESTIONS

1. Considering the four types of perspectives laid out in chapter 2 (organic conservative, etc.), how would each one of them view the cause of and solutions to gang violence in our society? What about family violence?

2. Culturally in North America we have caged hunts, sometimes bloody Ultimate Fighter matches on pay-per-view cable outlets, and much hoopla over professional sports, such as football, where violence is explicitly encouraged and broadcast. How different are we North Americans regarding such entertainment from the Roman masses of the second century A.D. with their gladiatorial games?

3. In the chapter discussion on learning to be the audience to violence, what are examples of learning to be the audience to violence and does our learning to be the audience facilitate the occurrence of the violent behavior? How else could we learn to be the audience that would discourage the violence?

4. Do you think the real extent of violence in a society is related to that society's ideas of violence as entertainment?

5. In what positions do we learn the role of being violent and is there an alternative to this behavior in achieving the same end? If so, what would those alternative role behaviors be for each of the positions identified?

Chapter Three

Interpersonal Violence: Murder and Rape

Contractor Carey Kovacs was just a guy having a good time at a Saturday-night bachelor party in a strip joint on Detroit's Eight Mile Road. The twenty-five-year-old Kovacs was to have been the best man at his friend's wedding the next week. Then a fight broke out between Kovacs's friends and another group of men. Kovacs was knocked to the ground and repeatedly kicked in the head by Benny Jovanovic. Kovacs died of head injuries on Sunday morning (Adler, 1994, 41).

A fifteen-year-old Houston boy raped and murdered a sixty-six-year-old woman, then burglarized her home. A fifteen-year-old Detroit boy was charged with killing another teenager with a sawed-off shotgun, apparently in a dispute over a stolen bicycle. A sixteen-year-old boy drove 150 miles from his home in Princeton, Kentucky, and shot to death a woman he did not know. The boy, who came to be known as "Little Rambo" to his schoolmates, told police that he "just wanted to get away and kill somebody" (Toufexis, 1989, 52).

In Watsonville, California, Ignacio Vasquez Segura on Tuesday walked into a packing shed on a mushroom farm where a former girlfriend worked. She was not there, so he asked for one of her friends, Raquel Gutierrez, age twenty-four, shot her dead, and blasted away with a semiautomatic rifle, wounding two coworkers. Segura fled in a sports car and shot himself in the head as police were closing in (Church, 1989, 20).

George Hennard crashed his blue pickup truck into a Luby's cafeteria and in less than a ten-minute period randomly shot and killed twenty-two patrons before taking his own life (Woodbury, 1991).

These are some true instances of interpersonal violence, stories of human tragedy that occur regularly in the world today. How often do they occur? When are they likely to occur? Who is likely to be the offender(s) and the victim(s)? Why does it happen? In short, what are the patterns of interpersonal violence in this country and in the world today? In this chapter we explore the patterns of interpersonal violence, focusing on murder and rape. Although distinct acts in themselves, we argue that both phenomena represent similar expressions of power. In general, those who are victims of rape and/or murder tend to be the least powerful as defined in terms of structural relations, and where rates of murder and assault are high, usually rates of rape are high as well (Kutchinkski, 1988). Thus, in our discussion of interpersonal violence it is first important to focus on these two severe forms of interpersonal violence: who, when, and where murder and rape occur. We look at these patterns historically and cross-societally in order to uncover the social forces that influence the formation of these patterns.

MURDER

We begin by defining what we mean by murder. Legally, murder and non-negligent manslaughter are both defined as the intentional and unlawful killing of a person or persons. This excludes what is considered to be justifiable homicide, whether it is committed in the act of duty, as in the case of a police officer or soldier, or as an act of self-defense by a private citizen. Nevertheless, whether justified or unjustified, this is an act of interpersonal violence. By the classification system suggested in chapter 1, murder as an area of interpersonal violence would focus on the killing that occurs outside the institutional roles the actors are performing. Thus the acts of violence committed by a police officer or a soldier would be considered appropriate institutional violence and would not be included in homicide statistics. On the other hand, other areas of institutional violence would be defined as illegal homicides yet are also institutional violence. One example is that of a husband or wife killing each other or killing one of their children during a domestic quarrel; family violence or violence among intimates composes a significant proportion of homicides. In most of these cases we are talking about institutional violence that maintains, extends, or challenges asymmetric gender/age/power relations. In these latter cases of violence, they are included in the statistics on homicide yet they are cases of individuals acting in the context of roles within a social institution. Why one type of institutional violence (killings by police and military), as opposed to another type of institutional violence (murders by husbands or wives), would not be counted as homicide may say more about which dimension of stratification is more threatened by these crimes and whether those who are dominant are threatened by the violence than about the actions themselves. Despite these problems of the data available, let us look at the patterns of homicide as indicated by government statistics.

There is also the issue of intent. In the definition used in the text what is important is not intent but willful action. Whether the offender intended to kill or injure the victim is irrelevant to the definition. However, whether the action was within one's sphere of control is central. So the individual who

Figure 3.1.   Lee Harvey Oswald being shot and killed by Jack Ruby as Oswald is being moved by police, November 24, 1963. Photograph by Jack Beers Jr., *Dallas Morning News* **photographer.**

fires a gun into the house next door to stop the noise coming from it and kills a small child would still be committing an act of violence whether they intended to kill or injure someone or not. The government statistics that are published contain only those acts that have been determined by the police, the prosecuting attorney, and the court to be acts of homicide. In the process of decision-making at all three levels, some acts which we would consider acts of homicide are defined as something else as a result of the issue of justifiability and intent. Nevertheless, it is the data that is used to inform the public and policy makers as to the nature of murder in a given community and society as a whole.

Murder rates as determined by the Department of Justice have been in decline for the past thirty years. The rate of murder and nonnegligent manslaughter in 1980 was 10.2 per 100,000 and in 2009 the rate was 5.0 per 100,000, a drop of more than 50 percent. This was pretty consistent across both genders and between majority and minority (U.S. Census Bureau, 2011; U.S. Department of Justice, 2010).

OFFENDER AND VICTIM CHARACTERISTICS

Gender

Who are identified as murderers? We find that those who are arrested for murder and nonnegligent manslaughter are overwhelmingly men. According to Department of Justice statistics of 2009 murder offenders where gender is reported, males were approximately nine times more likely to commit murder than females (U.S. Department of Justice, 2010). This is a pattern that will be repeated over and over again in all forms of violence. Overall, men overwhelmingly commit the majority of violence in a society (Maguire, Pastore, and Flanagan, 1993).

For victims of murder, we find a similar pattern. Most (77 percent) of the victims of homicide are males (U.S. Department of Justice, 2010). Both male and female offenders are more likely to target male victims than female victims. However, 89 percent of female victims of homicide were murdered by males (U.S. Department of Justice, 2010). Males are more likely to be victims of homicides when the relationship between victim and offender is more distant (Zahn and Sagi, 1987), such as outside the home. Females are more likely to be the victim when the relationship between victim and offender is characterized as intimate (Fox and Zawitz, 2001). Women are more likely to be murdered by men whom they know than by men who are strangers. About one-third of female murder victims were killed by an intimate; about 3 percent of male murder victims were killed by an intimate (Bureau of Justice Statistics, 2010). In every age group female murder victims were more likely than male victims to have been killed by an intimate. The greatest difference between male and female victims was at 18 to 24 years of age in which 2 percent of males were killed by an intimate while for female victims 29 percent were killed by an intimate. For male homicide victims, the percentage killed by intimates was at 9.2 in 1976 but decreased to 2.5 in

2005. The pattern was different for female victims. The percentage killed by an intimate in 1975 was 34.6; it decreased to its low in 1995 to 26.1 percent and then rose to a high of 33.3 percent in 2005.

There is also an interesting difference in this pattern between white and black victims. According to the Justice Department's statistics the number of homicide victims by intimate partners declined the most for black male victims (by 83 percent), white males by 61 percent, black females by 52 percent, and white females by 6 percent. Black husbands experienced the greatest decline in victimization from 18.07 in 1976 to 0.89 in 2005. For white husbands there was also a decline but not as great, from 0.95 in 1976 to 0.17 in 2005. The declines for the victimization of wives were not as great. For black wives the rate of victimization was 12.53 in 1976 and 3.02 in 2005. For white wives the rate of victimization had the lowest level decline from 1.73 in 1976 to 1.02 in 2005.

In regard to same-sex killings, males are almost nine times more likely to kill males than females killing females. Males are victims of men in single victim/offender murders in 88 percent of cases in 2009 when sex, race, and age of both victim and offender are known (Bureau of Justice Statistics, 2010). In general, Daly and Wilson point out that there is no known society in which the level of violence among women begins to approach that among men (Daly and Wilson, 1988, 146).

Age

American criminologists unanimously agree that younger persons are most likely to be the perpetrators of murder and lethal assault. The majority of offenders in this country are under thirty-five years of age. According to the 2009 Uniform Crime Reports (UCR), of those where the age of the offender is known, 64 percent of arrests for murder and nonnegligent manslaughter were of suspects thirty-four years of age or under, approximately 27 percent were for those thirty-five years and older, and approximately 9 percent were under eighteen years of age (Bureau of Justice Statistics, 2010). Now it is important to see these proportions in demographic context. While, those under eighteen accounted for 9 percent of arrests, they constituted almost 25 percent of the population in 2009. For those eighteen to thirty-four, who account for 64 percent of known murder offenders, they constituted approximately 25.5 percent of the population. Lastly, those who were thirty-five years and older, who accounted for 27 percent of known offenders, represented a little over 52 percent of the population. The age bracket with the greatest overrepresentation in rate of offending would be those between the ages of twenty to twenty-four, who compose approximately 7 percent of the population, yet compose approximately 25 percent of offenders where the age of the offender is known (U.S. Census, 2009; Bureau of Justice Statistics, 2010). This is more than three times their representation within the population. The next two highest age groups with high rates of offending would be those aged seventeen to nineteen and those aged twenty-five to twenty-nine, respectively. The greatest age underrepresentation in murder offending would be those who are seventy-five years and older. They compose approximately 6 percent of the population, yet are identified as less than 1 percent of those who are murderers.

The pattern of victimization parallels the pattern of offending. According to the 2005 data, eighteen- to twenty-four-year-olds experienced the highest homicide victimization and offending rates. This age group is followed by those who are twenty-five to thirty-four as having the next highest rates of victimization and offending. The offending and victimization rates for fourteen- to seventeen-year-olds has had an up-and-down pattern during the period 1985 to 2005. Offending rates for this age group increased rapidly after 1985 surpassing the twenty-five to thirty-four age group until 2000 when the rates were slightly lower for this age group compared to the twenty-five to thirty-four age group. The pattern of victimization for the fourteen- to seventeen-year-olds was not as dramatic; victimization rates increased significantly after the mid-1980s and declined to their previous position and leveled off after 2000. Those between thirty-five and forty-nine years of age have declined in both rates of offending and victimization since 1980, leveling off since 2000 (Bureau of Justice Statistics, 2010). Nevertheless, homicide is the second leading cause of death for those ten to twenty-four years of age (National Center for Disease Control and Prevention, 2010).

In general, the offender is usually younger than the victim. Wolfgang (1958) uncovered this pattern in his classic work on homicide in Philadelphia. This pattern has been replicated in more recent research. Fox and Zawitz (2001) note that a four-year difference between victim and offender persists during the twenty-four-year period that they analyzed; however, the ages decline for both victim and offender, dropping from thirty-five to thirty-one years of age for the victim and dropping from thirty-one to twenty-seven years old for the offender. Most recent government statistics for 2005 find that the difference is still approximately four years between offender and victim (Bureau of Justice Statistics, 2010).

In addition to this general age pattern, Zahn and Sagi (1987) found differences in this age pattern for the different types of murder. The greatest disparity in age between victim and offender was in the case of felony murder between strangers (robbery, murder) where the average age of the victim was forty and the average age of the offender was twenty-six, and the smallest distance was between acquaintances aged thirty-one and thirty, respectively. There is also a difference in the average age of homicide offenders. In stranger homicides, the ages of perpetrators are generally younger than in family homicides and the victims are older. Furthermore, Fox and Zawitz note that where there are multiple offenders as in the case of gang-related violence, over 25 percent of the victims were less than eighteen years of age. Young people are also disproportionately represented as victims in homicides that occur in the home, and the younger the age the more likely their victimization is to be at the hands of a parent.

This declining age of victimization has been found to be a pattern of developing capitalist societies. In earlier stages of capitalist development and in pre-capitalist societies, peak ages of victimization for murder were higher (Greenberg, 1985). In all acts of interpersonal violence, those who are in the most marginal positions in the society have the highest rates of involvement.

As youth have become more displaced and marginalized economically in a society as it develops along a capitalist path of industrialization, they are more likely to be involved in crime and delinquency, including acts of interpersonal violence.

Race or Ethnic Minority Status

There are clear ethnic patterns in homicide statistics. In Wolfgang's 1958 study of homicide in Philadelphia, he notes that the arrest rate for African Americans was approximately eight times the rate for whites. Bensing and Schroeder (1960) and Pokorny (1965) discovered similar patterns in Cleveland and Houston. In 2005, the arrest data by race indicates that African Americans have a rate that is a little more than seven times the rate for whites, 26.5 per 100,000 versus 3.5 per 100,000 (Bureau of Justice Statistics, 2010).

Although African Americans have a much higher rate of offending, they also have a disproportionate rate of victimization. For 2005, their rate of victimization was more than six times the rate for whites, 20.6 per 100,000 versus 3.3 per 100,000. In general murder, like rape and assault, is principally an intra-racial crime. In 2005, of the offenders known to police, approximately 93 percent of African American homicide victims were murdered by an African American assailant and 83 percent of white homicide victims were murdered by a white assailant (Bureau of Justice Statistics, 2010). Zahn and Sagi (1987) point to differences in racial characteristics of victims and offenders for different types of homicides. The authors point out that where the victim and offender know each other the homicide is most likely to be intra-racial (95 percent of homicides in the family and 92 percent of homicides among acquaintances); in the case of stranger homicides for white victims, 74 percent were inter-racial (black and Hispanic offenders), while for African Americans 89 percent were intra-racial. Felony homicides generally had the highest rates of inter-racial homicides for both African Americans and whites. But, when you combine all forms of homicide, about 80 percent of interpersonal violence occurs between persons of the same race or ethnic status. According to recent data, the leading cause of death for African American males between fifteen and thirty-four years of age is homicide (National Center for Injury Prevention and Control, 2010). Messner and Rosenfeld (1994) reported that 40 percent of all deaths of fifteen- to twenty-four-year-old African Americans were attributable to homicide.

The U.S. Department of Justice noted that from 1987 to 1992 the average annual rate of handgun victimization per one thousand young African American males was three to four times higher than the rate of victimization for young white males. Younger African American males (twelve to twenty-four years old) were fourteen times as likely to be a homicide victim than members of the general population in 1992. For older African American males, they were eight times more likely than the general population (Bastian and Taylor, 1994). According to 2006 data the rates of victimization were highest for black males at 40.6/100,000, then black females at 6.6/100,000, then white males at 5.4/100,000, and lastly white females at 1.9/100,000 (U.S. Census, 2011).

It is important to note that the rates of homicide have declined dramatically since 1993. Looking at more recent victimization figures the rates for African Americans declined 47 percent, from 38.7 per 100,000 in 1993 to 20.9 per 100,000 in 2007. For whites the rates declined 38 percent, from 5.3 per 100,000 in 1993 to 3.3 per 100,000 in 2007 (U.S. Census Bureau, 2011).

Social Class

When we discuss the research on the relationship between social class and homicide, the data available are based on either income or occupational status. Little research analyzes crime patterns and social class as classically defined categories discussed previously: capitalist, worker, independent producer, and manager. Generally, income and status differences are rather rough proxies for social-class differences. There is overlap in that capitalists generally make more than workers do, capitalists receive more income than managers and independent producers, and managers and independent producers generally receive more income than workers. Nevertheless, we can all list examples of workers who make more than managers and independent producers and in some exceptional cases receive more than capitalists do. Recognizing this weakness in the data, we discuss the patterns of homicide and rape in terms of income and socioeconomic status differences.

Research shows that most people involved in homicide in this country, as either victim or offender, are poor. Wolfgang (1958) estimated that 90 to 95 percent of the offenders came from the lower end of the occupational scale. More recent studies showed that 92 percent of those convicted of murder were semiskilled workers, unskilled laborers, or welfare recipients (Parker, 1989; Swigert and Farrell, 1976). According to the National Crime Victimization Survey for the year 2009, the rate of victimization for aggravated assault (which has similar patterns as homicide) for those who earned less than $7,500 was sixteen per one thousand, while the rate declines for each higher income grouping to a rate of two per one thousand for those whose household income is $75,000 or more (Bureau of Justice Statistics, 2010). Hawkins (1983) concluded after reviewing the literature that homicide victims and offenders are both more likely to be African American, poor, uneducated, and residing in the South. From all recent statistics, this overall pattern has not changed significantly in the interim years.

Victim/Offender Relationship

Thus far, we have seen that homicides are not simply random acts. Some of us, because of the position we occupy in society, as defined by age, class, gender, and ethnic position, are more likely to use interpersonal violence to exert power and are more likely to be victims of this form of violence. Another important factor in accounting for differences in the risk of victimization is the nature of the relationships we have with others. The majority of homicides in which we know the nature of victim/offender relationship involve people who know each other, and most often they were intimates. Homicide as a form of power is likely to be exerted over people with whom we are at least acquainted. Stranger relationships of victim and offender are consistently found to occur less frequently than relationships where the victim and offender are known to each other. This pattern is found in research on larger cities (Wolfgang, 1958; Pokorny, 1965; Block, 1981; Zimring, Mukhergee, and Van Winkle, 1983) and research on smaller cities as well (Hewitt, 1988). Fox and Zawitz (2001) found that for homicides that occurred in the years 1976 to 1999, 7.1 percent were between husbands and wives, 7.8 percent were between other family members, 4.3 percent between boyfriend and girlfriend, 33.2 percent between other acquaintances, 14 percent between strangers, and 33.5 percent where the relationship is unknown. The research of Daly and Wilson (1988) following up homicides that occurred in Detroit in 1972 gives further support to this finding. They found that by 1980, of cases that were solved, 370, or 72.8 percent, were between acquaintances or relatives, whereas 138, or 27.2 percent, were between strangers.

Research by Riedel (1987) contends that government statistics systematically underestimate the rate of stranger homicides. He has noted that there is a problem of lag in the reporting of stranger homicides and that there are problems in the accuracy of the robbery/murder classification. Riedel reviewed case studies of several large cities and found that the rate of stranger homicide was significantly higher (as high as 29.6 percent in Chicago) and that the trend in recent years is that the rate of stranger homicides is increasing.

The unknown category in Justice Department Uniform Crime Report statistics is largely an artifact of how the data is collected and recorded by the government. Barkan (2012) notes that most of the unknown relationship cases occur because of the timing of when information is sent to the FBI for recording in the UCR report. When the data is sent to the FBI, there are a number of cases that have not been solved. Unfortunately when they are solved and the relationship is known, the information is usually not forwarded to the FBI, thus the information is listed as unknown even though the relationship is actually known. Messner, Deane, and Beaulieu (2002) in utilizing a sophisticated statistical technique estimate that within the unknown category no more than 25 percent of the unknowns represent a stranger relationship. Overall, you are almost four times more likely to be murdered by someone who knows you than by a stranger.

As we noted earlier in our discussion of race patterns in victimization as it relates to relationship between victim and offender, overall rates of violence between intimates is on the decline. Fox and Zawitz (2001) find that the rates of violence by intimates have declined significantly over the period of 1976 and 1998. They note that on average for this period, the number of murders by intimates decreased by 4 percent per year for male victims and 1 percent per year for female victims. They note that the sharpest decrease in number of intimate murders has been for black male victims. There was a 74 percent decrease in the number of black men murdered between 1976 and 1998. The authors note, however, that intimate violence is primarily a crime against women—in 1998, females were the victims in 72 percent of intimate murders and the victims of about 85 percent of nonlethal intimate violence. In general about one-third of female murder victims were killed by an intimate, whereas only 4 percent of male murder victims were killed by an intimate. Women

aged sixteen to twenty-four experienced the highest per capita rates of intimate violence (19.6 victimizations per 1,000 women). This disparity between
men and women as victims of intimate murders has continued to decline as
noted earlier, especially with black males who had the greatest drop in victimization in this relationship category (U.S. Census, 2011).

THE ROLE OF ALCOHOL AND FIREARMS IN HOMICIDE

The Handgun and Homicide

Alcohol and firearms are indisputably and precipitously associated with
homicide. According to the most recent Uniform Crime Report (2009) more
than two-thirds of homicides are committed with a firearm, the vast majority
with a handgun. The next most likely weapon is a knife or a cutting instrument of some kind being used in another 13 percent. The risk of death from a
firearm is not uniformly distributed throughout the population. The Panel on
the Understanding and Control of Violent Behavior found that the risk of
homicide by a gun is highly elevated for adolescents in general, and black
male adolescents in particular (Reiss and Roth, 1993). They report that in
1988, the gun homicide rate was 8 per 100,000 for fifteen- to nineteen-year-
olds and less than 6 for the population as a whole. Among fifteen- to nineteen-year-olds, the rate was 83.4 per 100,000 for black males, an eleven
times greater risk of homicide by firearms than for white males (7.5 per
100,000). The council notes that the fraction of homicides committed with
firearms peaks for fifteen- to nineteen-year-olds, at 81 percent of homicides,
and consistently declines relative to other weapons used as the victim's age
increases. More recent UCRs (2010) confirm this pattern; 84 percent of
homicide victims who were seventeen to nineteen years of age were killed by
a firearm. Fox and Zawitz (2001) found that murders with the use of a
handgun peaked in the early 1990s for all age groups and have declined,
although levels for fourteen to seventeen and eighteen to twenty-four are still
slightly higher than they were in 1976; for those under fourteen and over
twenty-four the rates returned to these previous levels.

Handguns are also most common in homicides between strangers (Riedel,
1987). Regardless of the political controversy in the United States regarding
gun ownership, what is clear is that the presence of handguns increases the
likelihood that an assault will turn into a homicide. The Panel on the Understanding and Control of Violent Behavior concluded that in most circumstances, those who use a firearm did not choose the weapon with the intent to
kill but rather chose a weapon that was available and it is because of the
power of the weapon that the violent event ended up being a killing (Reiss
and Roth, 1993). Whether in domestic disturbances or felony murders, there
are indications that the availability of the type of weapon used was most
important in determining whether a homicide took place. Wright and Rossi's
(1985) survey of incarcerated convicted felons found that only 36 percent
reported firing a weapon with the intent to kill the victim.

The type of gun is also important in discussing the incidence of homicide. Two-thirds of guns owned in the United States are long guns, yet handguns are three times more likely to be used in a homicide than long guns. Generally, more than 80 percent of the time when the weapon is known, the handgun is the weapon used (Zawitz and Strom, 2000).

How does the availability of handguns relate to the incidence of homicide? One particular study comparing homicide and assault rates in Seattle and Vancouver, two cities of comparable size and demographic characteristics yet with very different regulations regarding handgun ownership, gives some insight into this question. The risk of being murdered in Seattle, where there is a significantly higher rate of handgun ownership, is approximately five times higher than in Vancouver (Sloan, Kellerman, and Reay, 1988). Another piece of evidence supporting the impact of availability of handguns as it relates to the occurrence of violence is an evaluation of the 1977 District of Columbia Firearms Control Act. This act prohibited handgun ownership among civilians, with the exception of previously licensed gun owners. During periods of vigorous enforcement of this act, gun homicides, robbery, and assault were significantly reduced (Jones, 1981; Loftin, McDowall, Wierseman, and Cottey, 1991). In the Loftin et al. research, homicides declined during the period of this law until an increase in homicides resulting from the cocaine black market. A more recent study looked at the impact of a ban on the carrying of firearms on certain days in Cali and Bogotá, Columbia, two cities with very high rates of homicide (Villaveces et al., 2000). Carrying of firearms was banned on weekends after paydays, on holidays, and on election days. Police set up checkpoints and searched individuals during traffic stops and other routine law enforcement activities. The days during which the ban took place had significantly lower rates of homicide in both cities, reduced the standardized homicide rates by 23 percent in Bogotá (from 102 to 79 per 100,000 person-years) and 18 percent in Cali (from 170 to 139 per 100,000). Another study on the effects of a gun seizure program in high crime areas of Kansas City also reported a significant drop in gun-related crime including homicide (Sherman and Rogan, 1995). Sherman (2000) also claims that the increase in arrests for illegal weapons possession may be one factor in the declining homicide rates in the United States since the early 1990s.

Other studies have substantiated that gun ownership facilitates occurrences of murder. The region of the country with the highest level of firearm ownership—the South—has the highest murder rate, and the region of the country with the lowest level of firearm ownership—the Northeast—has the lowest rate of murder (FBI, 1988). Furthermore, research has indicated that, over time, increases in murder rates are positively correlated with increases in firearm ownership (Farley, 1980).

In a cross-national analysis of thirty-six nations controlling for other factors that are related to rates of homicide, Hoskin (2001) found that homicide rates are consistently higher in countries that have a greater supply of firearms in private hands. His research provides additional support for the hypothesis that greater gun availability increases the likelihood that a gun will be used in an attack, which in turn increases the risk that the victim will die of his or her injuries.

Gun ownership has increased dramatically in the United States during the past forty years. According to government statistics, the number of guns increased from 54 million in 1950 to 201 million in 1990 (Bureau of Alcohol, Tobacco, and Firearms, 1991). The percentage of households who have a gun in their home has fluctuated between 35 to 50 percent of households. Gallup has been asking about gun ownership in households since 1959 and finds that overall gun ownership is highest since the previous peak period of 1993, where 51 percent of households reported having a gun in their home versus 47 percent in 2011 (Saad, 2011). According to Gallup one out of every three people owns a gun in the United States. As to who is more likely to own a gun? According to Gallup research the most likely person is male (46 percent of men vs. 23 percent of women), lives in the southern part of the country, lives in a rural area, is white as opposed to black, and is a registered member of the Republican political party.

It is important to state that we are not suggesting a causal relationship between the presence of handguns or guns in general and violence. We are suggesting that their presence increases the likelihood that existing violence will be escalated with the lethal force, thus serving as a catalyst or facilitator. The situation that led to the violence is not necessarily related to the presence of a gun. The presence of a gun is likely to make the violence more lethal.

Alcohol Abuse and Homicide

Of all drugs that are either outlawed or regulated, alcohol has the greatest link to violence. In this case, like guns, it can serve as a catalytic factor in violence. In Wolfgang's classic study of homicide, he found that more than 63 percent of the cases involved alcohol consumption. This pattern has been replicated in study after study of homicide (Greenberg, 1981). Dawson and Langan (1994) found that alcohol was present in 47 percent of the victims and 64 percent of the defendants. Barlow (1990) describes the significance of alcohol in the following way: "To the extent that alcohol lowers social inhibitions and reduces anxiety and guilt, people who have been drinking may act more aggressively than otherwise would have been the case. The underlying dispute may have erupted anyway, and the individuals concerned may well have been tempted to seek a violent solution. With the situational influence of alcohol missing, fear, anxiety, guilt, and social inhibitions are there to serve as constraints" (166). On the other hand, Kantor and Straus (1987) note that being drunk may indirectly help prepare an individual to commit an act of violence by providing a later rationalization for the act.

In sum, the overall pattern regarding the occurrence of homicide is that those who are in more marginal positions in the society in terms of income, age, and ethnicity are more likely to be both victims and offenders of homicide. This pattern is exemplified by the fact that the leading cause of death among young African American males is homicide. Furthermore, homicide is most often used to address interpersonal problems that stem from problems that may be institutional or structural in nature. Thus, what society officially defines as homicide is a phenomenon of power pursued by those who have less access to other forms of power (institutional). Homicide also is more likely to be exercised to exert one's influence over those with whom he or she has personal relationships. Finally, the presence of alcohol and handguns often serve as accelerators or catalytic factors to transform acts of violence into homicide.

HISTORICAL TRENDS IN MURDERS

What have been the historical trends in homicide? Are societies today more or less violent in terms of rates of homicide? As a generalization, most scholars contend that the earliest civilized societies were more violent than modern societies. Political scientist Ted R. Gurr states that

> homicide rates were three times higher in the thirteenth century than the seventeenth, three times higher in the seventeenth century than the nineteenth, and in London they were twice as high in the early nineteenth century as they are now. The decline in homicide has been particularly great in the towns and rural areas. And though Londoners today are more murderous than in the recent past, the metropolis remains a far safer place than it was in earlier centuries. (Gurr, 1979, 414)

Gurr (1990) further indicates that there were waves within this general trend, noting that high levels were reached during the fourteenth century after the Hundred Years War and partly as a result of the turmoil connected to the Black Death, later during Elizabethan times, and again in early-nineteenth-century London.

With regard to the United States, Gurr (1979) contends that violent crime in nineteenth-century America indicated a stable or declining trend for the first half of the century and a shift upward shortly before the Civil War that persisted into the 1870s. However, violent crime was not unheard of during the colonial era. In 1776, Benjamin Franklin petitioned the British Parliament to stop solving its crime problem by shipping convicted felons to the American colonies. He complained that transported felons were corrupting the morals of the poor and terrorizing the rest of the population (Silberman, 1978). Later, in the early 1800s, the problems of violent crime were still being noted in public speeches of politicians. In a speech that made Abraham Lincoln known in political circles, delivered in Springfield, Illinois, in January 1838, he argued that internal violence was the nation's major domestic problem (Silberman, 1978). Indeed, just before the Civil War, a U.S. Senate committee investigating crime in Washington, D.C., reported that "riot and bloodshed are of daily occurrence, innocent and unoffending persons are shot, stabbed, and otherwise shamefully maltreated and not infrequently the offender is not even arrested" (Silberman, 1978, 29).

While it is important to note that most of the data available for these earlier periods of U.S. history are from urban areas and principally eastern cities, there is nevertheless some indication that murder rates may have been higher in smaller cities and non-eastern areas. Silberman notes that in a fifteen-month period in the 1850s, forty-four murders were recorded in Los Angeles, then a town of only eight thousand inhabitants. This is about forty or fifty times as high as rates in the city today.

After the Civil War, there was a dramatic increase in violent crime. Silberman (1978) reports that in the twenty years after the Civil War, the murder rate quadrupled, far outstripping the growth in population. Family blood feuds kindled by hatreds generated during the war and refueled by political and economic conflicts became increasingly frequent. This rate continued to climb during a period of a high level of violence connected to labor unrest in the late nineteenth century through to the early twentieth century. The rate declined during the Great Depression in the 1930s until the 1960s and then the rate began to climb again. The rate doubled from 1962 (4.6 per 100,000) to 1980 (10.2 per 100,000). The rate fell slightly during the early 1980s, declining to 7.9 per 100,000 in 1984, but then rising again and peaking in 1991 at 9.8 per 100,000. The rates declined sharply again to 4.8 homicides per 100,000 in 2010, almost returning to the 1962 period. Two explanations for this pattern have been postulated by criminologists (Cooper and Smith, 2011).

One explanation is based on a contagion hypothesis where the increase in violence is a result of a spread of violence as a result of a period of warfare. War is an important factor in stimulating high levels of violence in all societies (Archer and Gartner, 1984; Gurr, 1990). Archer and Gartner (1984) found that most combatant nations, compared to a control group of noncombatant nations, experienced substantial postwar increases in rates of homicide. Furthermore, they found that the increases were pervasive and occurred regardless of the size of the conflict. Homicide rates increased in both victorious and defeated nations, in nations with either improved or worsened

Figure 3.2. U.S. Homicide Rate Trends per 100,000 population, 1900–2006. Source: National Center for Health Statistics, Vital Statistics.

postwar economies, among both men and women offenders, and across several age groups. Finally, postwar increases were most frequent among nations with large numbers of combat deaths. Archer and Gartner (1984) conclude that their findings regarding the effect of war on homicide rates is consistent with the legitimization of violence model. Wars provide concrete evidence that homicide under some conditions is acceptable in the eyes of a nation's leaders. This wartime reversal of the customary peacetime prohibition against killing may somehow influence the threshold for using homicide as a means of settling conflict in everyday life (79). In looking at the increasing involvement of the United States in wars both covert and overt since World War II, one may suspect that promotion of this war mentality may have contributed to the increasing levels of violence in the society throughout this same period.

Another explanation is that the increase in homicide is related to the increase in drug wars, which lead to black market conditions in which violence is an important means to control one's market share and to enforce the rules of the market for nonpayment or for bad product. Illegal black markets also lead to an increase in robbery targeting drug dealers or bootleggers, which can often lead to homicide. A review of figure 3.1 shows that during the periods of increased enforcement of laws prohibiting alcohol (prohibition years were 1920 to 1933) and the creation and enforcement of laws on a variety of drugs that were classified as drugs of abuse (from 1971 when Nixon declared the War on Drugs to mid-1990s period of reduction in enforcement of drug laws and marijuana medicalization movement beginning with California's first state law on medical marijuana in 1996), homicide rates were at their peak periods during their respective halves of the twentieth century. The link between drug wars and violent crime in the United States has been established by several researchers (Inciardi, 1981; Goldstein, 1985; 1997; Fox and Levine, 2001). This pattern of parallel fluctuations in homicide rates and alcohol/drug prohibition strategy is not present in European countries, possible a result of the differences in levels of enforcement and their resulting impact on black market conditions and other contingent factors such as poverty and inequality (Zimring and Hawkins, 1997). Ousey and Lee (2002) attempted to test the relationship between within-city change in mean levels of drug market activity and homicide rates over the 1984–1997 period in a sample of 122 U.S. cities. They also looked at the effect of between-city variation in preexisting social conditions including resource deprivation as well as the population structure, percentage aged fifteen to twenty-nine, percentage divorced, and Southern location on the magnitude of this within-city association. In general they found support for the relationship between drug activity and homicide rates and that the presence of high levels of numerous forms of disadvantage serves to create informal economies or illegal markets that are particularly competitive and violent.

In general, in the United States since the Civil War, rates of homicide have been increasing with the exception of the period of the Great Depression and the 1950s and the most recent decline beginning in the latter half of the 1990s. What explains these increases in homicide? The conflict perspective we employ suggests that as the structures of inequality increase so also will increasing levels of interpersonal violence in rebellion, adaptation, or enforcement of these structures. Furthermore, as violence is increasingly used by the state to repress and control populations that threaten these structures, nationally and internationally, violence is learned as an appropriate means to address interpersonal problems. Given the recent trends in increases in levels of inequality as a result of the changes in the economic structure (Wolff, 2010; U.S. Congressional Budget Office, 2011) and during the same period the increases in the use of the military to address international political problems (the United States has been involved in more than a dozen wars since 1980, five of which required overt U.S. military action—Grenada, Panama, Libya, Iraq, and Afghanistan), these facts, together with an increase in the use of domestic military-style policing to crack down on the drug trade, would all contribute to an escalation in interpersonal violence in the United States. Let's further investigate the connection between the occurrence of homicide and structures of inequality.

HOMICIDE AND INEQUALITY

It is important to reiterate that the relationship between homicide and inequality can be viewed in two ways: how inequality causes homicide and how homicide causes inequality. If members of a particular group are more likely to be victims of homicide than members of another group, this creates a disadvantage in terms of power and over access and control of scarcities. An example would be young African American male teens. It is, in part, because they experience a higher rate of homicide victimization that this group is disadvantaged relative to other racial and gender groups in terms of access to life chances and power. As African American males are increasingly victimized by violence and as violence increases in the communities that they reside in, they are less capable of achieving a quality education as well as economic and political opportunities for advancement. The violence serves to inhibit their development relative to groups that do not experience the same levels of violence, leading to further levels of inequality.

Similarly, in terms of gender stratification, as females are victimized or are more likely to fear victimization relative to males, this disadvantages them in the pursuit of human development. As we discuss later in this chapter, this is most evident in the case of rape. However, it is also present when we look at who murders women and under what circumstances. A woman's murderer is more likely to be a man she is at least acquainted with, and in most of these cases when they were at least acquainted, they were involved intimately. Fear of victimization inhibits women's ability to pursue careers and in general work outside the home and is a factor in the control of women by men in the home. In these ways, the differential homicide victimization by a category of people serves to create further inequity for that category and for those who are dependent on them in primary social relationships.

Inequality can also lead to higher levels of homicide victimization. Both poverty and inequality have been found to be related to rates of homicide across different cities in the United States (Blau and Blau, 1982; Lee, 2000; Ousey, 2000). Avison and Loring (1986) found that both ethnic heterogeneity and income inequality were important in accounting for variations in rates of homicide across nations. They note that "structural conditions such as inequality appear to be cleavages that increase the probability of social conflict. When cultural differentiation is also present, that probability is further increased substantially. In one sense, then, structure and cultural factors have more than just additive effects on cross-national homicide rates. It appears that cultural differences within societies tend to magnify the effects of inequality on homicide" (748). More recently Hoskin (2001) confirms this relationship between ethnic heterogeneity and homicide rates in the thirty-six countries in his sample. Krahn, Hartnagel, and Gartrell (1986), in their study on income inequality and homicide, find that income inequality has a moderate effect on levels of homicide. Furthermore, the authors find that the effect of income inequality on homicide rates is strongest in wealthier countries and countries with larger law enforcement systems. This relationship between homicide and inequality in cross-national research is well established (LaFree and Kick, 1986; Messner, 1989; Messner and Rosenfeld, 1997; Neapolitan, 1994).

Krug, Powell, and Dahlberg's (1998) analysis of countries using the World Health Organizations data on death statistics from the early 1990s concluded that the United States had the highest rate of homicide of the twenty-six high-income countries that reported rates. Countries that have significantly higher homicide rates are ones that have experienced large-scale popular unrest as a result of guerrilla warfare, death squads, or military activities connected to increasing levels of inequality and economic displacement, or those undergoing dramatic social transformations as a result of a change to capitalism as in the case of the former Soviet Union. For example, Chile, Guatemala, and the Philippines during the 1970s had significantly higher rates of murder, ranging from 45.7 per 100,000 for Chile to 20.8 per 100,000 for Guatemala. International data summarized by Foster, Siegel, Plesser, and Jacobs (1987) indicate that for 1987, other than Northern Ireland, no country had a rate that came close to that of the United States.

Baron and Straus (1988) concluded in their research that legitimate violence, poverty, and economic inequality are significantly associated with state-by-state differences in rates of homicide. They found that the more urbanized states, and states with higher levels of poverty and inequality, had higher rates of homicide. These relationships were reproduced in an analysis of murder rates across the fifty states and Washington, D.C. Winslow and Zhang (2008) found that murder rates were correlated with various measures of poverty and inequality including infant mortality (.78), Gini Index (.59), percentage of people living in poverty (.48), unemployment rate (.48), income inequality (.59), and black/white income gap (.84).

Blau and Blau (1982) note that socioeconomic inequalities between races and within them were positively related to higher rates of violent crime in standard metropolitan statistical areas (SMSAs), and when these factors are controlled, the rate of poverty is not related to levels of violent crime. "Thus, aggressive acts of violence seem to result not so much from lack of advantages as from being taken advantage of, not from absolute but from relative deprivation. Southern cities have higher rates of criminal violence not as the result of the historical experience of the South that produced a tradition of violence but owing to the greater economic inequality there" (126).

Loftin and Hill (1974) and Messner and Tardiff (1986) find that poverty, not inequality, is the major determinant of homicide. Loftin and Parker (1985) and Parker (1989) find that the relationship between poverty and homicide depends on the type of homicide. Parker finds that in looking at homicides between family intimates and acquaintances and nonrobbery felony homicide, rates of poverty are very significantly related. Only in the case of homicides committed in the occurrence of a robbery is poverty not significantly related. In general, what the research seems to confirm is that as segments of the population become increasingly powerless (relatively or absolutely), homicide is increasingly likely to occur.

Brenner's research (1978, 1979) gives further support to this pattern of homicide. His research points to the impact of economic recessions on homicide rates over the years 1900 to 1980. In a more recent work, Petras and Davenport (1991) examine the impact of economic transformation on crime in general. The authors find that as deindustrialization occurred in the five large cities they studied over a twenty-six-year period, homicide increased threefold.

Another interesting relationship is the relationship between welfare policies and homicide rates. Generally the more restrictive and conservative the welfare policies, the higher the rate of homicide (Fiala and LaFree, 1988; Messner and Rosenfeld, 1997). This pattern of the higher the welfare expenditures, the lower the rate of homicide was also found in Hoskin's (2001) cross-national study.

An interesting example of how economic inequality and gender inequality manifest themselves in homicide is the case of dowry deaths in India. McCoid has found that higher and higher dowry demands constitute one attempt by middle-class men to become upwardly mobile in India. Conflicts over the amount of the dowry can result in the murder of the wife. Women who are most economically dependent on their husband are most likely to be victims of homicide by their husbands or other members of the husband's family (McCoid, 1989).

Research on the relationship between gender inequality and female homicide victimization finds that as women's inequality increases, homicide of females declines (Baily and Peterson, 1995) This finding is also consistent with research on tribal societies that shows that the status of women is lower in more violent societies (Divale and Harris, 1976; Reiss, 1986). However, it is important to note that some research also shows a backlash phenomenon where women increasing status can also cause a violent reaction from men who are threatened by the increase in status relative to their own (Vieraitis and Williams, 2002).

What about band or tribal societies where levels of inequality in general would be much lower? How are their rates of homicide? What has the anthropological literature found as it relates to patterns of homicide? There have been investigations that attempt to calculate rates of homicide in non-Western, nonindustrialized societies (Bohannan, 1960; Knauft, 1987; Lee, 1979). Overall, the problems of calculating rates of crime in general and homicide in particular in these societies are complex. One major obstacle is the problem of definition. Often, what the community defines as an execution of a sorcerer is defined as a murder by anthropologists. This is well illustrated by the work on the Gebusi by Knauft (1987). A second problem is the reliability of the data. Most data in these societies are based on recollection of the past by informants or re-creation of rates based on the occurrence of murder during the time the society was being studied. For example, Gibson notes of the Buid, "I am aware of only one homicide occurring within a Buid population of one thousand in a ten year period, and that was carried out by a man with a fearsome reputation as a sorcerer" (Gibson, 1990, 131). Despite the limits of such research, the circumstances of murders can give us further insight into their cause.

For example, The !Kung, once described as the harmless people (Thomas, 1959), are in fact noted as having a rate of homicide of 29.3 per 100,000, almost three times the U.S. rate (Lee, 1979, 1984). This rate is based on twenty-two murders occurring between 1920 and 1955. All the killers were male and seventeen out of the twenty-two acted alone. Most of the killers were between the ages of twenty and fifty. A poison arrow was the primary weapon. Fifteen of the killings were part of feuds; seven were isolated killings. Likewise, Lee notes that most of the victims of homicide were not part of the conflict but were innocent bystanders struck by spears. Of the eighteen cases reviewed by Lee, eight were principals in an argument and ten were struck more or less at random in the process of observing the conflict, acting as peacemakers, or coming to the aid of someone. He says that of the eight homicides involving a principal in a prior dispute, the circumstances include the following: a man attacked and killed a non-San who had been sleeping with his wife, a man killed another man and ran away with the victim's wife, a man who had slept with another's wife was attacked by the husband but killed the husband, and a man killed his wife in an argument over her adultery (Lee, 1979, 392).

Another example is the Gebusi, a society of approximately 450 persons living in the lowland rain forest of south central New Guinea (Knauft, 1987). Subsistence is based on hunting and foraging, nonintensive agriculture, and small-scale husbandry of pigs. The population resides in a longhouse arrangement, with each longhouse holding approximately twenty-six persons. There are two to six longhouses to a settlement. Settlements are made up principally of kin as defined in terms of affinal or matrilineal. The political and economic life of the Gebusi is highly decentralized. Knauft (1987) observes that the Gebusi recognize no indigenous positions of secular male leadership. Men are highly self-effacing in social interaction and avoid taking a public stance that could be perceived as either ordering or pressuring other men in the community to conform to their point of view (460). The men of the settlement usually attempt to build consensus among themselves to solve problems.

Knauft also notes that the Gebusi are unusual for practicing no competitive exchanges and having no custom of material compensation to resolve disputes or to transact marriages (460). Furthermore, males among the Gebusi generally do not engage in status competition or rivalry. Males of a settlement generally have strong bonds of friendship. Furthermore, according to

Knauft, hostility and aggressive behavior is seen to be individualistic and antisocial, which conflicts with the central cultural values of communal sociality. Along with this, fear and withdrawal in the face of violence are strongly approved and encouraged.

Despite social patterns that are conducive to a relatively low level of violence, Knauft calculates the rate of homicide among the Gebusi prior to Western contact to be 683 per 100,000 per year; after contact, the rate drops to 419 per 100,000. Overall, Knauft estimates the rate of homicide among this New Guinea tribe to be forty times the rate of U.S. lethal violence including wars and executions for the same period. Why?

First, it is important to note that Knauft used a very broad definition of homicide. Of the total 129 homicides discovered by Knauft, 84, or 65 percent, were called sorcerer killings. Sorcerers are individuals accused of causing the death by sickness of another Gebusi. They are believed to be bad people motivated to kill their victim through illness because of general maliciousness or spite. Most of the killings recorded by Knauft were executions of sorcerers by members of the community. Can we define the killings of sorcerers as interpersonal violence, or are they more accurately classified as a form of institutional violence within this lesser developed society? Let us look more closely at these killings.

The identity of sorcerers is determined by an inquest that begins with a séance that lasts an entire evening. Mediums conduct séances. The body of the medium is inhabited during the séance by spirits who know of details of the sickness unknown by humans and know the identity of the sorcerer. The medium is believed to be unbiased and in particular not allowed to be a relative of the primary kin of the sickness victim. To assure this, given the kinship basis of this society, mediums often come from other settlements or communities. Mediums are not paid; seership is considered to be a civic duty. The position of medium is not given a special status within the community.

Indictment by the medium begins the process of divination. Knauft reports that this spiritual evidence must be validated by public divinations undertaken by the suspect, often done by the cooking of a large divination packet with meat or fish inside. The failure of a suspect to perform this part of the ritual properly may be regarded as a sign of his or her guilt. Public torture for the guilty is not unknown. Some have been killed on the spot.

> When a suspect is indicted for having caused the sickness death of a member of his or her own patriline, close kinsmen perpetrate the killing. In many instances, however, the closest kin of the alleged sorcerer are ambivalent about the suspect's guilt. Especially if the outcome of the public divination is not definitive, the potential of armed support for the suspect by these people precludes an immediate killing. In these cases, the accusers typically wait until the initial tensions of the situation wanes—perhaps for several weeks or months—and then organize a consensual plan in the community to ambush the suspect when he or she is in the forest, unsuspecting, with few supporters. . . . The kin of the alleged sorcerer, while often not completely convinced that the suspect is guilty, rarely risk their lives to resist or avenge a killing that has the consensual approval of the many different clans in the community at large. In

the great majority of cases, then, the killing of the suspect is accepted and goes unavenged. Indeed, there is a general feeling of relief in the community that a lethal sickness sender in the group has been expunged. (Knauft, 1987, 465)

Knauft reports that only 4 homicides out of the 129 resulted from revenge deaths. The remaining homicides were either battle deaths (9 percent) or deaths resulting from individual conflict (26 percent). This latter group would be considered homicide for comparative purposes. The other two categories, which compose 74 percent of homicides, would be considered acts of institutional violence. They are either executions by members of the community or killings resulting from warfare.

Whether we are talking about homicides, executions, or warfare, what unites them is the cause of the violence. Knauft (1987) observes that lack of marital reciprocity in sister exchange is a condition that is likely to lead to homicide via sorcerer inquest. Knauft finds that sorcery homicide is ultimately about male control of marriageable women. Similar patterns of homicide as they stem from male control over women are found in other societies that are essentially classless societies. Research on the Eskimo finds similar patterns whereby most of the violence is a result of conflict over issues of adultery, and then most of the murders occur as a result of retaliation for the killing (Hoebel, 1964; Rasmussen, 1932). Similar patterns are found among the Mbuti (Turnbull, 1961), the Semai (Dentan, 1978), and the Hadza (Woodburn, 1979).

As property relations become more developed, homicide stems from not only controlling women but also disputes over property. The assertion of witchcraft or sorcery is again a common mechanism to rid the individual or community of the threat to the distribution of power established by the class or gender relations. Among the Swazi, the Batsakatsi are the witches and sorcerers (Kuper, 1963). Kuper notes that the propensity for witchcraft is passed on through the female to her children. Ritual murders occur as sacrifices to enhance agricultural fertility or for personal aggrandizement. Kuper claims that where the murder occurs for medicine to doctor the crops, capital punishment is prescribed for the principals while others involved receive long prison terms. Where the crime is committed for personal aggrandizement, capital punishment is invariably imposed. Witchcraft and sorcery can be directed at anyone, but there are patterns. Conflict over the hierarchy established by class or gender relations often results in violence.

First, because they emanate from hatred, fear, jealousy and thwarted ambition they are usually aimed at persons who are already connected by social bonds. . . . In the polygynous homestead, the unsatkatsi (victim) is usually a jealous co-wife or an unscrupulous half-brother who is ambitious of the inheritance; outside the homestead, suspected evil doers are blatantly successful and aggressive peers. Important men do not need to use sorcery against insignificant inferiors, nor are they suspected of doing so. Sorcery is an indication of status and of the ambitions for improvement of status that operate within the limits of the stratified traditional society. (Kuper, 1963, 66)

Daly and Wilson (1988) describe research on the Bison-Horn Maria of India, citing Verrier Elwin's 1950s research account of 107 cases of murder that occurred between 1920 and 1941. Verrier Elwin estimated that the rate of homicide among the Bison-Horn Maria was sixty-nine homicides per million per year. This would be a rate that is slightly higher than the rate for New Zealand and Northern Ireland. Among these were very high proportions of family homicides. Out of 107 murder victims, only one was killed by a stranger. The rest were done in by spouses, stepparents, in-laws, cousins, and other blood kin. Most of the violence was precipitated by conflicts over land. The killing of Marvi Buti by his paternal half-brother, Marvi Chule, is a typical case:

> Upon their father's death, the elder Buti had inherited the family farm. Like many a disenfranchised younger brother through human history, Chule left home to seek his fortune. He did not find it, and so, after several years, the prodigal Chule returned to his father's land, there to rent a plot from his brother and farm it. So he did, but only for one year. When the lease came up for renewal, Buti at first doubled the rent, and then reneged on the agreement altogether, in order to bestow the land on a third brother. Defeated, Chule again moved away, but on a return visit to collect his possessions, he was confronted by Buti brandishing a knife. To be thus run off his natal farm was too much for the propertyless Chule, whose resentment at last exploded. Close at hand was an ax. (Daly and Wilson, 1988, 28)

Taylor (1979, 85) described some similar patterns of homicide in colonial Mexico. First, among the Indians of central and southern Mexico in the 1700s, males were generally the offenders in homicide. In both regions, no more than 4 percent of offenders were female, while approximately 18 percent of the victims were female. Furthermore, the age of offenders was significantly above what would be expected given today's patterns. For Indian offenders in the central Mexico region, the average age was thirty-three, while in the southern region it was twenty-nine. Seldom were victims and perpetrators strangers. A significant proportion were wives, sex partners, and sex rivals. Taylor notes that adultery and the jealousies of villagers caught up in sexual affairs—situations intimately related to the position of women in these village societies—appear to be the fundamental sources of violent conflict in both rural areas.

Furthermore, Taylor notes that the violence was more likely to be within the community and more specifically within the nuclear family. In general, for the two Indian regions of Mexico studied by Taylor, the conjugal unit was the principal site of conflict. Conflict over property also existed within these communities. Taylor reports that there was a difference between the two Indian communities as to whether such conflict spilled over into acts of violence. For the central region, property disputes rarely resulted in violence, whereas in the southern region violence occurred more frequently. Comparing the two regions of colonial Mexico overall, he found that violence was precipitated by sex-related and conjugal disputes, property disputes, insults to honor, and excessive consumption of alcohol (Taylor, 1979). This is a pattern that is not dissimilar from what would be found in Mexico and other societies around the world today.

Greenberg (1989) analyzes factors related to a very high rate of homicide in the Juquila District of rural Mexico. Between 1973 and 1977 he discovered a homicide rate in the village of Yaitepec of 511 per 100,000. Although this was the most severe rate for a village within the district, unexpectedly high rates were also found in Ixtapan (408 per 100,000) and Panixtlahuaca (450 per 100,000). In general, the average rate in seven villages in the district was 300 per 100,000. Greenberg's analysis lends further credence to the importance of hierarchies and their effect on increasing levels of violence. In particular, Greenberg sees the transition to capitalist relations as the major impetus for these increasing rates of homicide in these villages. Increasing conflicts between classes over land and increasing conflicts within classes due to economic displacement often resulted in acts of violence. He notes that in the late 1940s and early 1950s, when peasants in the region began to specialize in coffee as a cash crop, the inequalities created by changing land tenure violated village norms of sharing, cooperation, and reciprocity. Instead of casting these conflicts in class terms, people personalized them. They blamed their misfortunes on the greed, envy, and jealousy of evil people. They explained these changes as caused by witchcraft and saw them as personal attacks. Villagers began to suspect one another of witchcraft and, as Fortino notes, started killing witches in great numbers (Greenberg, 1989, 202).

Greenberg (1989) found that capitalist relations of production and exchange caused conflicts that corroded the social bonds within classes in more traditional agrarian communities. As capitalist forms have expanded and have rationalized systems of production and concentrated wealth in fewer and fewer hands, households and families in Juquila have come under growing pressure (214). He also found that the economic pressures were often at the root of domestic difficulties. These pressures can result in conflicts over the division of labor within the home and perceived unfulfillment of role expectations and disputes over the distribution of power along gender lines.

Other conflicts within the family resulted because of disputes over inheritance and issues of courtship. As the position of peasants becomes increasingly marginalized, the scarce resources they possess can become objects of intense competition. Regarding courtship, arranged marriages are still common, and families in general have a considerable stake in marriage alliances. Parents attempt to control female children's relations with males in order to maintain or increase family economic position. Greenberg notes that courtship involves delicate negotiations between families, and this can often result in conflict. Because of the pressure parents place on couples, elopement is not uncommon, although it is considered equivalent to rape. The crime involves not just stealing a women but also depriving her family of the compensation for the loss of a daughter that is ordinarily part of marriage arrangements. Because the family sees elopement as a form of theft, even where the woman is a willing partner, this act of "rape" can be a dangerous, even violent, enterprise (Greenberg, 1989, 216).

In addition to conflicts within family relations, Greenberg claims that increasing conflicts with friends and compadres are also a product of the transformations present with capitalist development. These relationships are based on a delicate balanced set of reciprocity that becomes altered. According to Greenberg (1989), the rationality of market relations intrudes on friendship relations, forcing individuals to choose between the former or economic self-interest. "Despite egalitarian attempts to mask inequalities and disjunctions of interest, money is often put ahead of friendship. Misunderstandings and conflicts among friends are common. This is especially true among men, because they are more prone to use friendship as an instrument to achieve economic and political ends" (217).

Two other major areas of conflict are politics and community disputes over common lands that were central to traditional agrarian societies. Beyond family and friends, an array of institutions are found in the district that preserve the community. Increasing concentrations of income and wealth become a corrupting influence of the functioning of these institutions. Greenberg found that a principal complaint about the traditional institutions is that authorities abuse their power and position. Few problems can be solved unless one has connections or cash or can repay favors in some way. Without these, unless one has a patron who can intercede, little help can be expected from institutions. Not only do individuals become entangled in conflicts with them, but conflicts frequently pit organizations against one another (Greenberg, 1989, 218). Mafia-style organizations develop based principally on client-patron relationships that function to control resources of institutions. Conflicts that lead to violence develop between Mafias for control over these resources.

Last, Greenberg notes that conflicts develop between communities over control of communal land. These conflicts can often lead to a scale that is best defined as warfare. But such conflicts do not occur exclusively between communities. As the process of capitalist development accelerated, conflicts developed over ambiguities about land tenure. Communal land that was available to villages for subsistence purposes began to be used by villages to plant coffee for the market. This led to conflicts within the community regarding the use of the land.

Greenberg (1989) mentions in the afterword of his book that since completing his fieldwork significant changes in the incidence of violence have occurred. Rates of murder have dropped dramatically. He attributes these changes to three forces: (1) land reform that gave peasants access to the communal lands that were a source of conflict; (2) an emerging women's movement with political clout that resulted in a ban on alcohol in the region and increased the power of women in the home; and (3) the increasing empowerment of the villagers through their struggles for land reform. All these factors are again related to changes in the pattern of inequality in the communities.

The importance of anthropological research on homicide is in the analysis of the precipitating cause of the act and how the experience and transformation of these societies to more hierarchical patterns are connected to increasing levels of violence. Generally speaking, when we review patterns of homicide in lesser developed and developed societies, we find that the precipitating conflict focuses on (1) disputes over sexual access or privilege—in most cases conflicts are over control of women by males; (2) disputes over access to property—control of material; and (3) disputes over access to power and status—control of position. Inequities as they relate to gender, class, and power/status provide the fertile soil for violence to grow. The conflicts that stem from the exploitation and assault on one's dignity can lead to death. Homicide is an ultimate outcome of conflict, conflict over control of material or power, where the resources to resolve the conflict in nonviolent ways are not present. In general, murder as a type of interpersonal violence is a technique used by those who do not have access to legitimized or institutional forms of power and violence to exert their will. Thus it is most frequent among poorer and more marginal segments of the society.

WHY PEOPLE KILL: A QUESTION OF MOTIVES

Another way of looking at the relationship between structures of inequality and violence is to examine the problem at a micro level by investigating the motives noted by the offender. Under what circumstances will lethal violence be used to assert one's will? By looking at the goals for the action, we may be better able to understand these circumstances. Wolfgang (1958) in his analysis of homicide in Philadelphia analyzed the motives of both the victim and the offender. Table 3.1 focuses on the motivations of the offender in the act of homicide.

The first striking fact is that the largest single category of motives is to resolve a relatively trivial dispute. There is often a verbal insult that leads to violence. The issue here is a threat to status or position. Daly and Wilson (1988) also conclude in their analysis that the most common type of homicide involves two acquainted, unrelated males in a dispute over status or face. Rutherford and Chapman note that such altercations are directly or indirectly tests of masculinity in a society where the accepted masculine man must adopt the values of male superiority (Rutherford and Chapman, 1988, 24).

This follows directly to the next homicidal motives. Both Wolfgang's categories of domestic quarrel and jealousy, 13.4 percent and 11.1 percent respectively, can be understood in terms of conflicts over controlling sexuality. This is what is found to be dominant in several of the acephalous societies we discussed earlier. Last, conflicts over property (combining altercations over money, 10.3 percent, and robbery, 7.9) would follow in frequency. Thus if we combine all homicides that are directly connected to conflict over status, property, and control of women, at least 80 percent are attributed to either creating, maintaining, or extending structures of inequality.

Polk and Ranson's (1991) analysis of homicides in Victoria, Australia, find a somewhat similar pattern, although their analysis is more refined in the specification of the typology. The authors find that most homicides in Victoria are between intimates. Slightly over one-half of the homicides occur where the victim and the offender are in a close personal relationship. Polk and Ranson further break down this category into three subtypes: homicide originated in an intimate relationship between (1) those whose relationship was sexual in nature (62 percent of intimate homicides or 32 percent of all homicides), (2) those who were linked together by family ties, mostly children (20

Table 3.1.   Offender's Motives in Homicide, Philadelphia, 1948–1952.

Altercation of relatively trivial nature	36.6
Domestic quarrel	13.4
Jealousy	11.1
Altercation over money	10.3
Robbery	7.9
Revenge	4.8
Accidental	4.5
Self-defense	1.3
Halting a felon	1.1
Escaping arrest	1.0
Concealing birth	0.8
Other	4.2
Unknown	3.1

percent of intimate homicides or 10 percent of all homicides), and (3) persons who had been at some earlier point bound together by friendship (17 percent of intimate homicides or 9 percent of all homicides).

Regarding the first subtype, the majority of victims were women, most of whom experienced intimate murder. In all cases, the conflict was over possessiveness, usually the male attempting to control the female in the relationship or in general defining the female as an object of possession. One unusual example cited by the authors is where an older man, experiencing extreme depression, decided to take his wife's life at the same time he took his own. Here the wife was viewed as a possession to be taken as a partner in death. Most homicides in this category are where the husband kills his wife because of sexual infidelity. Within this category of violence developing from sexual intimacy, the authors identify a minority of cases where a female is the victim of another female (two cases), where a male is the victim of the female (six cases), and where a male is the victim of another male (two cases).

In the second subtype of intimate homicide, family killings (excluding the husband and wife relationship) were entirely homicides between adults and children. The third subtype refers to murder among friends where the homicide can best be understood as stemming from a conflict within the relationship. The dominant example was where violence resulted from debts that were not resolved. The authors note that all these cases occurred between those who were on the margins of the society as a result of criminality, prison, drug use, or unemployment.

The second major pattern of homicide is referred to as confrontational homicide. In this type, the conflict itself defines the relationship that brings the victim and offender together. In other words, no personal relationship existed between the victim and offender. This is homicide that occurs as a result of an affront to position or honor. In all cases males are either the victim or the offender. Polk and Ranson (1991, 92) describe the homicide as occurring in the following general manner: in its simplest form, the parties come together, a challenge is laid down, and a fight ensues.

The authors apply Luckenbill's analysis of the situated transaction of a confrontation. Luckenbill (1977) identifies the following six stages that apply to confrontational homicide. The first stage is referred to as the opening move. This consists of one of the parties performing some act that the other party interprets as an affront or threat to his position, such as insults. The second stage occurs when the offended party recognizes that the affront was directed at him or her. Stage three is when a decision is made as to how to respond to the affront. If the offended party is not able to rationalize or excuse the other person's behavior, he or she will have to retaliate or retreat. If retreat is not the option taken, then retaliation takes place in stage four. In this stage the original offender may continue or escalate the insulting behavior, perhaps using violence. It is at the point of the fifth stage that it is difficult for both parties to break out of the confrontation without losing status or face. Weapons are likely to be produced during stage five, if they have not appeared earlier. In the sixth stage police enter the situation, influencing the behavior of the remaining actors. Using this six-step model, Luckenbill nicely describes the nature of the interaction over a conflict of position or status. He observes that murder is the outcome of a dynamic interchange between an offender, victim, and in many cases bystanders (185).

Overall, Polk and Ranson (1991) point out that the Luckenbill description accurately describes the pattern of confrontational homicide over a concern for masculine honor, face, or status. The authors furthermore note that those involved in confrontational homicide are more likely to be males in marginal positions in the society. Again, this is consistent with the observation that murder as a type of interpersonal violence is a technique used by those who do not have access to legitimized or institutional forms of power and violence to exert their will.

The third major pattern of homicide according to Polk and Ransom (1991) stems from another crime. Eighteen percent were connected to another crime. Most of these homicides were cases of felony homicide. A typical example would be one in which the victim of a robbery is murdered. Other murders within this type were (1) those in which the initial offender was killed by the police, security guard, or victim; (2) professional killings; and (3) police officers slain off-duty.

In concluding our discussion of homicide, there is repeatedly seen a pattern whereby violence occurs over conflict that stems from gender, status (position), and class relations. Homicide is seen as a solution to the conflict over maintaining, extending, or resisting interpersonal relations rooted in the power relations of the larger society as defined in terms of systems of stratification. These solutions may be seen as legitimate or illegitimate depending in part on the relative power of the victim and offender and whether the action serves to maintain or change the institutionalized power relations of the larger society. Brazil provides a good example of the legitimacy of homicide as it pertains to gender relations (Neier, 1992). A suitable defense for homicide in Brazil has traditionally been an affront to honor. Men dishonored by the adulterous behavior of their wives were legally justified in seeking revenge through violence. This situation is changing in Brazil as a result of women becoming increasingly powerful. In a recent case, after a husband stabbed to death his wife and her lover, the highest court in Brazil overturned the acquittal based on the defense of honor. Nevertheless, when the case was retried in the lower court, the killer again was acquitted.

RAPE: THE VICTIMS AND THE OFFENDERS

Let us now turn to the question of rape, another area of interpersonal violence. What are the patterns of rape? Who are the victims? Who are the offenders? And how do systems of inequality relate to these patterns? During the 1990s, the problems of rape and the sexual harassment of women in general increasingly appeared in the news. Trials involving two well-known males accused of rape, William Kennedy Smith and Michael Tyson, received daily newspaper and television coverage. The confirmation hearings of Supreme Court Justice Nominee Clarence Thomas became subject to much controversy when Anita Hill testified to being a victim of sexual harassment by the candidate.

The sexual control of women through acts of physical and/or verbal abuse is increasingly recognized as a very common form of violence in our society. Nevertheless, arrest rates for rape decreased dramatically from the 1980s. The forcible rape arrest rate reached its peak in the period from 1984 to 1991. Between 1991 and 2009, the rape arrest rate declined over this period by 56 percent. In 2009 the forcible rape arrest rate was at its lowest level in at least thirty years (Snyder, 2011). It is important to recognize that rape, like homicide, is not only a manifestation of interpersonal violence but also a form of institutional and structural violence. In traditional societies such as the Yanomamo, rape and abduction of women are frequent practices accompanying warfare (Chagnon, 1968). This is also the case in modern societies. For example, throughout history, rape has accompanied war, and in many cases has been part of the war policy of a nation. Brownmiller (1975) notes that rape has been an inevitable accompaniment of religious crusades, revolutions, liberations, and wars of imperial conquest. The systematic rape by soldiers of innocent women in towns and villages in the United States during the American Revolution; during the conquest and attempted genocide of native people on the North American continent; during the American Civil War; during World Wars I and II in Belgium, France, China, and Germany; and during the most recent wars of our time in Korea, Vietnam, Bangladesh, Nicaragua, El Salvador, Russia, former Yugoslavia, and the Congo are just a few examples. Rape has been used to punish the enemy and as a reward for the victors.

In some extreme cases, rape can also be a business strategy of the husbands or fathers of the women victims. The economic plight of a population can often lead to women being coerced into prostitution, as was the case during destitute conditions among Italians in Palermo, Italy, after World War II. The American troops set up their camps in public parks. Husbands

Figure 3.3.   Eighteen-year-old housemaid raped and murdered by an unskilled laborer in Dresden, Germany, on the night of October 14, 1904.

ought their wives to victorious troops and took the money. Soldiers queued in front of hastily erected tents. As soon as one man came out, another went in. Park keepers even provided the mattresses so that the Yanks would be comfortable (Brownmiller, 1975, 75).

Recently, there has been growing concern about the spread of AIDS among young women abducted in the countryside and placed in brothels in Thailand and Cambodia. Robinson (1993) reports that one study estimates that 50 percent of the child prostitutes in Thailand are HIV positive. She notes that sex workers are typically recruited from rural families, the sum given to the parents representing several months' advance salary, with the rest to be remitted after a ten-month or one-year term. The lump-sum payments provide subsistence for a family with few other resources and may even finance a new house, cultivation of the family land, or schooling for young siblings. This form of contract binds the sex worker to her job, the sense of family obligation overwhelming negative feelings about the work itself (493). A similar pattern of selling female children is present in Cambodia. A survey of 399 prostitutes in Cambodia by a local women's rights group reported that nearly half had been taken to brothels and were unable to leave. The epidemic is spreading rapidly in Southeast Asia as a result of expansion of the prostitution trade. We address these forms of rape when we discuss institutional and structural violence. For now, we concentrate on the discussion of rape as interpersonal violence.

What is rape? Who are those who rape? Who are those who are victims of rape? Why does rape occur? These are all crucial questions to take up in describing this form of interpersonal violence. Rape is defined in criminal law as the carnal knowledge of a female forcibly and against her will (FBI, 1988, 13). Beirne and Messerschmidt (1991) suggest that because the criminal law concentrates on the "against her will" threat component, the use of violence must be present for the charge of rape to be made. Thus the criminal law labels rape principally in terms of forcible rape. This is distinct from statutory rape, which refers to acts of sexual intercourse with a minor, that is, someone who is not legally able to give consent. At the time of this writing the FBI is undergoing a revision in the definition of rape to include males as victims as well as allowing for penetration with objects other than a penis (Johnson, 2012). This will broaden the definition to include many crimes that are currently classified as sexual assault.

The history of the development of rape laws reflects the power context of this form of violence and how that has changed over time as women have gained power to question the male privileges derived from patriarchy. From Old Testament Jewish codes to medieval Europe, rape was treated as a property offense committed against men who "owned" the woman who was raped (Porter, 1986). Usually the "owners" were fathers or husbands. In the case of a maiden, rape destroyed her property value on the marriage market and brought shame to her family. Financial compensation was usually awarded to address the compensation warranted by the damage done to the father or husband. Furthermore, most legal traditions, from Hammurabi's code to ancient Jewish law to British common law, exempted husbands from raping their wives, since a husband could not be held liable for stealing or damaging his own property.

Today, the definition of rape is still a highly charged political and moral issue. Battles are fought over whether married women can be raped by their husbands, the degree and type of force (physical and/or economic) that is necessary in establishing rape (Box, 1983; Hite, 1976; Bourgue, 1989; Finkelhor and Yllo, 1985), the relevance of the victims' sexual histories in court proceedings (Bourgue, 1989), the sexual versus nonsexual definition of the act (Bourgue, 1989), the inclusion of males as victims (Bourgue, 1989), and whether sexual acts that are pressured and forced in the context of a date are considered rape (Koss, Gidycz, and Wisniewski, 1987). Consider the following incident:

> It was late in the evening. Melanie was doing the laundry when it happened. Her husband had come home and flopped down on the bed—passed out. He had been out drinking most of the evening. She went to the next building where the laundry room was to put in another load. As she walked back into the apartment, a man jumped out of the closet, grabbed her from behind, and began to rip off her clothes. At first, she did not even realize that it was her husband. Though she screamed and struggled to get away, he used his superior strength and size to overpower her, tear her clothes off, and rape her anally. (Finkelhor and Yllo, 1985, 51)

Marital rape is a crime in all states; however, in thirty-three states, there are exemptions given to husbands from rape prosecutions. When his wife is most vulnerable (e.g., she is mentally or physically impaired, unconscious, or asleep) and is legally unable to consent, a husband may be exempt from prosecution in many of these thirty-three states (Bergen, 2008; Russell, 1990). Bergen (1999) notes that the existence of some spousal exemptions in the majority of states indicates that rape in marriage is still treated as a lesser crime than other forms of rape. Still, the women's movement worldwide has made a significant impact in redefining the legal concept of rape. But the enforcement of the definition is limited within our own society and even more so internationally. Additional legal views in the United States are changing in the following areas: (1) sex of offender and victim: new laws are gender neutral; (2) nature of penetration: new laws include any intrusion however slight and by any object at all, of genital or anal openings (including oral sex); (3) force: new laws focus on the behavior of the offender, including threats of violence and use of superior strength to restrain or confine a victim; and (4) resistance: victims no longer have to prove that they resisted and in some states the notion of "reasonable" resistance, which takes into account the age, strength, and other factors, is considered and includes nonforcible intercourse that may occur when someone is unable to consent because of their incapacitation (Beirne and Messerschmidt, 2011).

Nevertheless, popular definitions lag, possibly reflecting more the true nature of gender stratification in the society. Koss (1989), in a survey of six thousand students on thirty-two American college and university campuses, found that nearly 90 percent of males who admitted to using force to obtain sexual intercourse were adamant that their behavior was definitely not rape. Men were not alone in possessing more traditional definitions of rape. Koss

found that only 27 percent of the women whose experience met legal definitions of rape labeled themselves as rape victims, and only 5 percent reported
their victimization to the police.

In a more recent study of undergraduates at thirty colleges in the United
States, Koss and Cook (1998) found that in a twelve-month period 8 percent
of college women experienced one or more attempted or completed rape.
Eighty percent of the rapes were committed by a nonstranger and more than
half of the rapes or attempted rapes occurred on a date. The research also
indicated that one out of every four college men reported that they had used
some form of sexual coercion since the age of fourteen. Fisher, Cullen, and
Turner (2000) estimated that in the course of a college career (five years) the
percentage of completed or attempted rape victimization among women in
colleges and universities may be as high as 25 percent.

The problems of definition are magnified when we look at rape in less
complex societies. Levine notes that among the Gusii, legitimate sexual encounters may be considered rape within our own society. The following
passage describing the institutionalized sexual practices during the wedding
night illustrates the definitional problem.

> The bride usually refuses to get onto the bed. If she did not resist the groom's
> advances, she would be thought sexually promiscuous. At this point, some of
> the young men may forcibly disrobe her and put her on the bed. The groom
> examines the bride's mouth for pods or other magical devices designed to
> render him impotent. As he proceeds toward sexual intercourse she continues
> to resist and he must force her into position. Ordinarily she performs the
> practice known as ogotega, allowing him between her thighs but keeping her
> vaginal muscles so tense that penetration is impossible. If the groom is young,
> the young men intervene, reprimand the bride and hold her in position so that
> penetration can be achieved on the first night. . . . Once penetration has been
> achieved, the young men sing jubilation and retire from the house to allow the
> groom to complete the nuptial sexual relations. They are keenly interested in
> how many times he will be able to perform coitus on the first night, as this is a
> matter of prestige and invidious comparison. . . . Six is considered a minimally
> respectable number and twelve is the maximum of which informants had
> heard. . . . The explicit object of such prodigious feats is to hurt the bride. If the
> bride is unable to walk on the day following the wedding night, the young men
> consider the groom a real man and he is able to boast of his exploits, particu-
> larly the fact that he made her cry. (Levine, 1977, 194–95)

Levine notes that the use of force in the context of a resistant woman and the
causing of pain during coitus is not limited to the wedding night. It continues
to be an important part of marital sexual relations. Furthermore, Levine notes
that young husbands claim to desire coitus twice a night. When a wife stub-
bornly resists, husbands are eventually moved to beat them and possibly send
them back to their parents and demand return of the bridewealth. Levine
points out that, in addition to this marital rape, the rate of recognized rape in
Gusii society is almost four times the rate of rape in urban areas in the United
States.

Thus, this problem of definition plagues the interpretation of the data on
rape. If we confine ourselves to official statistics on rape, we of course
underestimate the violence because of reluctance to report rape, especially

marital and date rape. Unlike with murder, where the vast majority of murders are reported and the clearance rate is the highest of all crimes (usually 65 to 70 percent), only 30 percent of rapes are reported to the police, and the rate of clearance is significantly lower than in most other violent crimes (41 percent in 2009) (U.S. Department of Justice, 2010). As a result, victimization surveys are particularly important in providing additional information to validate and supplement the data collected via arrest reports, though we still overlook large areas of rape that are not always recognized as rape by the law enforcers or by victim or offender, such as marital rape, or by the victims in cases of rape recognized by the law, such as date rape. Nevertheless, it is worth examining the patterns indicated in official statistics as to who are officially defined as the offenders and who are officially defined as victims of rape.

Gender

Obviously, the dominant pattern is that males are offenders and females are victims. Of those arrested for rape, 98.8 percent are male. Rape is clearly an act whereby men victimize women in an act of violence. But it is important to note that rape does not fit this pattern exclusively and with the change in definition to include male victims of male sexual assault as victims of rape, we will have a better idea as to the scope of the problem in the United States. We do know that male and female homosexual rape is a problem in prison and jail settings. Here again, males are more likely to be the victimized and the victimizers. Kuper (2001) estimates that one in four male inmates has been raped. With increasing problems of prison overcrowding, longer sentences, and budget cutbacks leading to staff cuts, the rates are likely to continue to be high. Younger males in jails and prisons are particularly vulnerable to sexual assault (Scacco, 1982; Groth and Birnbaum, 1979).

It is in the prison setting where rape as an issue of power and control is unquestionable. Rape is a very important mechanism in establishing and maintaining the inmate hierarchy within prisons as well as in the larger society, where women are the victims. Donaldson (2004) describes the practice of "hooking up" in prisons, which he claims has existed since the early nineteenth century, whereby a vulnerable male will become a "punk" or "boy" to a senior male or "male." In this relationship, the "punk" or "boy" provides sexual services in exchange for protection from other male rapists in the prison.

Instances where women rape men or other women are quite rare (Groth and Birnbaum, 1979). When women are charged with rape, the vast majority of cases are of statutory rape. In 2009 arrests statistics, 148 women were arrested for forcible rape, approximately 1 percent of arrests. Of all offenders of statutory rape where the male is the victim, 95 percent of the offenders are female. However, it is important to note that male victims of statutory rape only compose 5 percent of the victims of statutory rape; in the vast majority of cases females are the victims (U.S. Department of Justice, 2005). Tjaden and Thoennes (2000) found that approximately 23 percent of the men who had lived with a man as a couple reported being raped, physically assaulted, and/or stalked by a male cohabitant, while 7.4 percent of the men who had married or lived with a woman as a couple reported such violence by a wife or female cohabitant.

Age

According to official statistics, rape offenders and victims tend to be young, usually under age twenty-five. Juveniles (under eighteen years) constitute approximately 16 percent of arrests for rape. This proportion has stayed pretty constant over the past thirty years, and as general rates of arrest for rape have declined, they have declined at the same rate for juveniles (Snyder, 2011). On the other hand, teenagers, those sixteen to nineteen years, were more than twice as likely as any other age group to be victims of rape or sexual assault. People age twelve to fifteen and twenty to twenty-four are also in high-risk groups; after age twenty-four, the rate of attacks steadily declines (Rennison, 2001). In terms of arrests, 43 percent of those arrested are under twenty-five years of age and 56 percent are under thirty years of age. The peak ages of arrest is for those eighteen to twenty-four years of age, composing 28 percent of arrests in 2009 (U.S. Department of Justice, 2010).

A similar pattern is found when we look at marital rape. Finkelhor and Yllo (1985), in their review of cases of marital rape in the first two years after the California statute went into effect in 1980, found that two-thirds of the offenders were under thirty years of age. Likewise, Russell (1982) found that approximately two-thirds of the sample of the husbands in the marital rape cases studied were under age thirty.

Race or Ethnic Minority Status

African Americans are overrepresented in rape arrest statistics. In 2009 almost 32.5 percent of those arrested were African American (almost three times their representation in the population), while 65 percent were white or of European ancestry (U.S. Department of Justice, 2010). As the Bureau of Justice Statistics reports, from 1980 to 2009, the black forcible rape arrest rate declined 70 percent, while the white arrest rate fell 31 percent (Snyder, 2011). Rape, like homicide, is predominantly an intra-racial act. African American women have a slightly higher rate of reported rape than white women. The rape and sexual assault victimization rate for whites in 2009 was 0.4 per 1,000; for blacks, the rate is 1.2 per 1,000 (Truman and Rand, 2010). Some research that is restricted to adolescent and more educated women finds that there are no differences in rates of victimization for white and African American women (Ageton, 1983; Hall and Flannery, 1984). This suggests that the racial victimization pattern may be a result of income and class differences between the two populations. In one case the opposite pattern is found. Russell's research on college women found that white women had the highest victimization rates (Koss et al., 1987; Russell, 1984; Sorenson et al., 1987). There is also a difference in the racial/ethnic pattern for Native American women. Amnesty International (2007) estimates one-third of Native American women will be raped in their lifetime compared to half that level for non–Native American women. According to a Bureau of Justice report analyzing victimization trends between 1992 and 2002, Native Americans experienced a victimization rate that was two and a half times greater than for whites and African Americans (Perry, 2004). Also, unlike the dominant pattern of rape being intra-racial for all other groups, for Native American women the rapist is a non–Native American. According to Justice Department statistics 80 percent of those who committed rape or sexual assault of Native American women were white (Perry, 2004).

There is also a difference in rates of reporting of rape by ethnicity. In a victimization study surveying twenty-six of the largest cities, the Department of Justice found that minority victims were more likely to report rape to the police than white victims (76 percent versus 62 percent) (McDermott, 1979). In the case of marital rape, Finkelhor and Yllo (1985) found in a state-by-state analysis that the racial breakdown of husbands arrested mirrored respective states' racial distributions. Russell (1982), on the other hand, found that white husbands were overrepresented in her study of husbands who had raped their wives. There are a number of issues, including differences in definition, law enforcement, and willingness of victims to report rape, that cloud the statistical picture.

Social Class

As with homicide, the most likely victims who report rape and offenders caught in rape incidents, regardless of race or ethnicity, come from relatively low socioeconomic neighborhoods in the nation's larger cities. Justice Department statistics indicate that the relationship is linear and direct (Rennison, 2001). As family income increases, the rate of rape victimization declines. The sexual assault/rape rate for those with a family income less than $7,500 is 5.2 per 1,000, while for the next highest income, $7,500 to $14,999, it is 1.7 per 1,000. The lowest rate of victimization is among women whose family income is $75,000 or more, 0.2 per 1,000.

As to the social-class background of the offender, a classic study on rape in Philadelphia for the years 1958 and 1960 found that more than 90 percent of offenders of both races belonged to the lower end of the occupational scale (Amir, 1971). In particular, 92 percent of African American offenders were unemployed. The obvious problems with generalizing from this data to the current era is the high level of unreported rape during this period and how this nonreporting may be, in part, class and racially biased. Rates of reported rape increased dramatically beginning in the middle 1960s through the early 1980s, principally as a result of changes in perception of rape and rape victims and increased sensitivity to the problem of rape. Yet there is little research that replicates the earlier research on rape as it relates to social class. We would suspect, however, that given the potential discretionary power of the police and prosecuting attorney, middle- and upper-class offenders would be systematically underrepresented. Some research suggests that there is bias in the judicial process whereby men of middle-class backgrounds are less likely to be successfully tried and convicted than men from traditional working-class backgrounds (Davis, 1979; Clark and Lewis, 1977).

Research on marital and date rape does not consistently reflect this same class pattern. Here social class is either irrelevant or relates only to the nature of the coercion in rape. For example, Russell (1982) found that 45 percent of wife rape victims were upper middle class, 35 percent were middle class, and 21 percent were lower class. On the other hand, Finkelhor and Yllo's research on marital rape in Boston (1985) found that 24 percent of the sample with incomes of less than $10,000 reported forced sex, whereas only 2 percent of families with more than $35,000 in income did. In reviewing cases where sexual assault occurred, only 5 percent of those who reported that forced sex and battering took place had business or professional jobs, whereas 46 percent of those who reported force only without battering had business/professional jobs.

Victim/Offender Relationships *Section 3*

According to Department of Justice statistics on victimizations, 79 percent of rapes (both attempted and completed) were committed by nonstrangers (Truman and Rand, 2010). Because of the problem of the nonreportage of rape as a result of official and unofficial perceptions as to whether or not the rape occurred in cases of marital and date rapes, the proportion of rapes that are nonstranger may be even higher. Recalling the Koss et al. (1987) survey of college students, most of the victims of rape who know their offender do not define what happened to them as rape. Generally, only one in four rape victims defines what they experienced as rape, despite the fact that such violence fulfills the legal requirements of rape. Koss also found that over half the women sampled had been victims of attempted or completed rape since the age of fourteen, and 84 percent of these rape victims knew their assailants.

Most victimization studies have indicated that the majority of rapes are among persons who are romantically involved (Tjaden and Thoennes, 2000). These types of rapes have the lowest probability of being reported to police (Ellis, 1989). On anonymous questionnaires, 20 to 25 percent of sampled college males admit to having used some degree of physical force at least once to make sexual advances beyond their dates' wishes; 10 to 15 percent have reported having actually forced a date to have sex against her will. Fisher, Cullen, and Turner conducted a large telephone survey of a randomly selected, national sample of 4,446 women who were attending a two- or four-year college or university during fall 1996. The questions were asked between February and May 1997. Based on their analysis they estimate that approximately 5 percent of college women will be raped or sexually assaulted during the course of a year at school (Fisher, Cullen, and Turner, 2000). *Ms. Magazine*'s nationwide survey of more than seven hundred college students on thirty-five campuses found that 13 percent of women had been raped and that 52 percent had experienced some form of sexual assault (Sweet, 1985). The research of Malamuth and Check (1985) follows this same pattern: between 40 and 50 percent of all high school boys in Los Angeles expressed the view that it would be acceptable to force a girl to have sex if she repeatedly sexually teased her date or if she agreed to have sex but changed her mind at the last minute.

The results of the National Survey of Violence against Women found that nearly 25 percent of surveyed women and 7.5 percent of men said they were raped and/or physically assaulted by a current or former spouse, cohabiting partner, or date at some time in their lifetime (Tjaden and Thoennes, 2000). Approximately, 1.5 million women and 834,732 men are raped and/or physically assaulted by an intimate partner annually in the United States. Overall the rate of rape or sexual assault remained generally stable from 2000 to 2007 before declining between 2007 and 2009 (Truman and Rand, 2010). Whether the victim is a female or male, the survey found that intimate partner violence is perpetrated primarily by men. The incidence of marital rape is more underestimated because most states still provide for a marital exemption in their rape statutes (Bergen, 1999), and law enforcement agencies haven't been as vigilant in publicizing the problem of marital rape.

As noted earlier, most countries throughout the world do not recognize marital rape legally or in practice. The following countries were noted in a UNICEF report (2000) on domestic violence as having legislated against marital rape: Australia, Austria, Barbados, Canada, Cyprus, Denmark, the Dominican Republic, Ecuador, Finland, France, Germany, Ireland, Mexico, Namibia, New Zealand, Norway, the Philippines, Poland, Russia, South Africa, Spain, Sweden, Trinidad and Tobago, the United Kingdom, and the United States of America. However, Russell (1982) notes that in both Norway and Denmark husbands who rape their wives are subject to milder penalties. This is similar to the pattern in the United States given the presence of the exemptions provided for married men under certain conditions of the rape. The Violence against Women Act signed in 2006 has led to some changes in states' laws that treated marital rape as less serious than rape. However, in countries like Kenya rape is widespread. In a 2002 report issued by Amnesty International, rapes reported to police have increased more than 300 percent since 1990. These statistics do not include marital rape in Kenya, which is not illegal (Amnesty International, 2002).

Even though the law has changed in many states, in this country enforcement is lagging behind. This does not mean that few cases occur since earlier research on marital rape indicates that it is a quite frequent occurrence. Russell (1982) reports that one in seven women who were or had been married were victims of at least one completed or attempted rape by a husband or ex-husband. Eighty-four percent of these rape incidents involved some physical force. Finkelhor and Yllo (1985) in their survey of 323 Boston-area women conducted in 1980 and 1981 found that 10 percent of married or previously married women said that their husband had used physical force or threat to try to have sex with them (6–7). In addition to this figure on marital rape, the authors report that 10 percent of the women in the sample reported that they had experienced date rape. The authors conclude that sexual assault by intimates is the most common form of rape. More recently Basile (2002) found that 34 percent of women indicated that they had unwanted sex with their partner. In most cases this was a result of a perceived marital obligation. Angela Browne's (1987) study on battered women who kill their husbands found that many had also been raped often and violently, indicating how rape and murder are intimately connected. Further indication of the link between rape and assault and murder is found in Frieze's research, which found that women who are battered are at greater likelihood of being raped by their partners (Frieze, 1983).

In sum, because the occurrence of date and marital rape is significantly underestimated and often undefined by both victim and offender, we would expect the true incidence of nonstranger rape to be much higher. Furthermore, as opposed to seeing rape as an isolated, unusual occurrence, rape and coercive sexual relations may be more accurately understood as normative in the context of patriarchal relations.

HISTORICAL TRENDS

Because of the differences in rates of reporting and the changes in perception and definition of crime, it is extremely difficult to measure the incidence of rape over time. For the year 2009, there were 88,097 rapes reported to police according to the Uniform Crime Reports (U.S. Department of Justice, 2010). This is translated into a rate of 28.7 per 100,000. The rate of rapes reported to police has declined 56 percent since 1991, 30 percent since 2000 alone (Snyder, 2011). It is important to remember that the estimate based on victim surveys is that 43 percent of rapes go unreported, indicating that the rate of rape is actually much higher. In 2009, 88,097 were reported to police, while in the victim survey the number of victims is 125,910. Nevertheless we find that the rate of victimization for forcible rapes has declined even greater than the rate of reportage, down 56.9 percent between 2000 and 2009 (Truman and Rand, 2010).

CROSS-NATIONAL CULTURAL PATTERNS

What is the pattern of rape cross-nationally? Is the United States unique or typical in its patterns of rape? First, the problem of comparing statistics from different societies with different definitions of rape is almost insurmountable. This is especially true for marital rape because, as noted earlier, relatively few countries recognize the social and legal existence of rape between marriage partners. Yet, despite these difficulties, we can form some conclusions. In looking at industrial societies with similar legal statutes pertaining to rape, we find considerable variability. The comparative research that has been done consistently shows that as in the case of homicide, the United States has a much higher rate of rape than any other industrialized country (Ellis, 1989).

Anthropological research on rape is quite scarce. Some anthropological research has focused on whether rape is a biological propensity (innate to the human species) (Shields and Shields, 1983; Thornhill and Thornhill, 1987) or learned and a product of nurture (Baron, 1985; Sanday, 1981; Sunday and Tobach, 1985). Anthropological research on rape in general suffers from two problems: little data on rape and problems of accuracy of the data that are available (Palmer, 1989). As Palmer notes, despite the problems with the research, it appears that rape is present in all societies to some degree. There are no societies that can claim to be rape-free.

WHY PEOPLE RAPE: A QUESTION OF MOTIVES

Research that attempts to classify rapes and rapists in terms of a typology focuses on the issue of motives. Groth identifies three major types of rape: (1) power rape, where sexual aggression is an assertion of control and domination; (2) anger rape, where coercive sex vents anger and frustration; and (3) sadistic rape, where violent sex satisfies a pathological need to inflict suffering (Groth and Birnbaum, 1979). Groth contends that power rape is the most common type. He furthermore notes that rape is always a symptom of some psychological dysfunction. But this view of rape as psychopathology has come under increasing attack. Barlow (1990) contends that there is little impressive evidence that rapists are in general psychologically abnormal and that the most promising approach is one that links structural and cultural factors with situational inducements, as was the case with explanations of violence in general (204). Barlow cites Russell's description of the "patriarch" as a common mental attitude of rapists.

> [Patriarchs] see themselves as superior to their wives because they are men; they believe their wives are their property and that it is the duty of their wives to accommodate them sexually whenever they want; they believe they should be the boss in the marriage, and that wives who behave in an insubordinate fashion deserve punishment. . . . They subscribe to a sexual double standard in which it is acceptable for husbands to have other sexual attractions or affairs, but it is totally unacceptable for their wives to do the same. (Russell, 1982, 123)

Scully and Marolla (1985) also critique the presumption of psychopathology of rape research. Citing Abel, they note that fewer than 5 percent of men were psychotic when they raped (Abel, Becker, and Skinner, 1980). Scully and Marolla (1985, 255) identify a number of motives for rape. The first motive they describe is revenge and punishment. In most cases, the rape victim was a substitute for the women on whom they wanted to enact revenge. The authors note an upsetting event, involving a woman, preceded a significant number of rapes. When they raped, these men were angry because of a perceived indiscretion typically related to a rigid, moralistic standard of sexual conduct, which they required from their woman but, in most cases, did not abide by themselves. The authors add that sometimes the target of the revenge is the rape victim's husband.

A second motive was sexual access. Here males felt that they were entitled to the sex withheld from them or that rape was the only means of getting sex from a particular woman. In many cases of date and marital rape, because they are lost in their own ideologies of dominance, men cannot see that rape could even exist in the context of marital or dating relationships. It is a product of an obligation that extends from the marriage contract or the exchange that occurs in a dating relationship.

Impersonal sex and power was another motive noted by Scully and Marolla. For the rape offender, rape required no concern for the victim in the act of sex. Said one rapist: "Rape gave me the power to do what I wanted to do without feeling I had to please a partner or respond to a partner. I felt in control, dominant. Rape was the ability to have sex without caring about the women's response. I was totally dominant" (Scully and Marolla, 1985, 259). A third motive noted was recreation and adventure. This occurs most frequently in gang rape. Here rape offenders noted that it was exciting or a challenge.

Overall, when we review the motives of men who rape and consider the frequent occurrence of marital and date rape, it is increasingly evident that we are not dealing with abnormal behavior but what has been defined as normal behavior based on acceptable ideas and beliefs that guide gender relations in this society. As Barlow (1990) notes,

> In virtually all areas of American life—family, work, politics, sports, education, and so on—males have traditionally found themselves in positions of power, domination, independence, and self-determination. Women, on the other hand, are expected to take subordinate positions and to acquiesce to the decisions and demands made by men. The world of sexuality is no different. The prevailing cultural image of maleness supports the idea of men as being dominating, powerful, and active and as the instigators of sexual interaction; the female as weak, passive, and submissive. (200)

Thus rape is a form of violence that stems from the nature of gender relations; that is, it is not a deviation from normal gender relations, as would be explained by the focus on the psychologically pathological causes of rape. Women in the context of patriarchy are defined as commodities to be acquired by men and to be owned in the context of marriage. Historically speaking, rape has been defined as deviant principally when it occurs in violation of these rights of ownership and control. This results in defining rape principally from a man's perspective. Rape is problematic not because it reduces the rights of males who control women, but because it is a technique of control by men in general in patriarchal society. Women are ultimately controlled by the occurrence of rape.

Women's movements around the world have attempted to redefine rape in the context of egalitarian gender relations, defining rape from the victim's perspective. Broadening the definition of rape to include women's understanding will provide women with greater freedom in the society. The issue of control over a resource, here women and sexuality, links rape to murder and, as we discuss in later chapters, other forms of violence as well. Both rape and murder represent forms of power to have access and control over a resource. In patriarchal class societies, men attempt to dominate each other through the control of the production of what is valued in the society and through the control of women, who produce their progeny and serve as an outlet for their sexual drive. This leads us to the discussion of rape and inequality.

RAPE AND INEQUALITY

The relationship between rape and inequality is complex. First, rape is a tactic that maintains inequality because one gender is predominantly victimized by another. In effect, the crime itself places one group at a disadvantage relative to the other. Women experience a loss of freedom and opportunity to develop because of the occurrence of rape or the threat of it. Riger and Gordon (1981) have found that women's fear of violence sometimes results in their not taking certain jobs, not visiting friends, and not venturing out at night for walks or entertainment. They found that 22 percent of men and 68 percent of women avoid doing necessary errands (such as shopping) because of the fear of criminal violence. In terms of recreational activities, 25 percent of men and 70 percent of women avoid them because of fear for their safety. Thus rape specifically limits the freedom of women to engage in social interaction and limits opportunities for women's advancement in our society. In general, it is women's time and space freedom that is limited by rape. Furthermore, the occurrence of rape serves to reinforce women's dependency on men to protect them from other males, thus reinforcing patriarchy. Thus, rape maintains or increases the level of inequality between men and women in a society.

On the other hand, rape may be regarded as a consequence of gender inequality. In this context, if women were not seen as the property of men, then rape in all social relations, including marriage and dating, would be unacceptable. Kokopeli and Lakey (1994) argue that masculine sexuality as it is defined by patriarchy involves the oppression of women, competition between men, and homophobia. The authors note that patriarchy shapes men's sexuality in terms of the importance of domination in sexual relations. Patriarchy tells men that their need for love and respect can only be met by being masculine, powerful, and ultimately violent. As men come to accept this, their sexuality begins to reflect it. Violence and sexuality combine to support masculinity as a character ideal. To love a women is to have power over her and to treat her violently if need be (Kokopeli and Lakey, 1994, 451). According to Kokopeli and Lakey, rape is the logical end of masculine sexuality.

Most of the research appears to give support to the link between patriarchy and rape. Baron and Straus's (1989) research is one of the more comprehensive studies testing the relationship. The authors compared rates of rape across the fifty states for 1980 to 1982. The authors found that social disorganization (measured by, among others things, level of geographic mobility, divorce, lack of religious affiliation, households headed by males with no females present, female-headed households with children, and the ratio of tourists to residents in each state) is positively related to rape. Other independent variables influencing the rate of rape were sex-magazine circulation (positively related), gender equality (inversely related), level of income inequality as percentage of population in SMSA (positively related), and percentage of the population unemployed (positively related).

Furthermore, the authors noted that the less economic inequality, the greater the gender equality and thus the lower the rate of rape. The authors concluded that the greater the disparity between men's and women's statuses, the higher the rape rate (a finding consistent with feminist theory). They suggested that gender inequality contributes to a social climate that is conducive to violence against women (Baron and Straus, 1989, 185). They called for equal rights with men in all spheres of life, including the passage of an equal rights amendment and the elimination of the income gender gap as a way to reduce the incidence of rape. This would be consistent with research on the nature of marital relations and violence within the home. As will be discussed more in the next chapter on family violence, egalitarian marriages, as opposed to male-dominant marriages, have the lowest incidence of violence (Coleman and Straus, 1986; Straus, Gelles, and Steinmetz, 1980).

Peterson and Bailey (1992) examined the relationship between rape rates and various measures of general, racial, and gender socioeconomic inequality for U.S. metropolitan areas for the year 1980. These authors concluded that the greater the income gap between males and females in metropolitan areas, the higher the rate of rape. They observed that if income equality between men and women were achieved, the rape rate would be reduced by 16.24 persons per 100,000 female population. In addition, both the general levels of economic inequality and racial inequality were strongly and positively related to levels of rape in metropolitan areas. Baron and Straus (1989), comparing differences in levels of violence across societies, noted that those societies with the highest levels of violence also have the highest levels of gender inequality.

Another indication of how rape is related to gender inequality is to look at how the definition of rape is related to women's relationship to men. For example, when women are in a relationship with men (either in a marriage or dating relationship), the definition of rape becomes problematic. In marriage it generally is not defined as rape, and in dating it legally can be defined as rape but in most cases is not recognized as rape in the context of law enforcement. When there is no relationship between men and women, then rape is clear. As discussed previously there is also ambiguity on the part of the victim and offender when there is a relationship between them. Thus, the nature of the relationship, a power relationship, either in marriage or dating, limits the definition of rape. It is as if the victims, in most cases women, have fewer rights when they are in a relationship with the person who rapes or sexually assaults them, in most cases men. The male defines her rights and, as noted earlier, has the greater power in defining rape. This is classically patriarchal. In the same way that the salutation for a woman (Miss and Mrs.) is important in defining women's relationship to men, so is the nature of the relationship important in the application of the definition of rape to the act of violence.

In regard to both date and marital rape, these are also more often considered areas of victim-precipitated rape. Here it is the women's fault for not acting in a way that is appropriate as defined in terms of gender relations that leads to rape. How is the appropriateness of one's behavior defined in terms of patriarchy? What are appropriate women's role responsibilities in terms of a dating relationship? Who is responsible when sexual petting goes too far?

What are women's obligations in marriage as it relates to sexual relations? Even in stranger rape, the victim precipitation argument is present. How she was dressed, where she was and at what time, or how she led the male on are considered in defining responsibility and whether the offender is truly guilty. Nevertheless, in general, the more distant the relationship, the less likely these role obligations are present and thus the victim is defined as truly a victim within patriarchal society.

Another way gender inequality is related to rape is how the law and law enforcement changed as a result of women's empowerment. Much of the increased concern regarding rape and the treatment of victims of rape is in part related to the increase in the political power of women in this society and their increasing entry into such professions as law and criminal justice. Another way of looking at how law changes in response to women's empowerment is to look at how the history of rape laws reflect the central importance of gender inequality, as discussed earlier.

Rape may also be related to how patriarchy is connected to other forms of stratification. How are class and ethnic inequality related to rape? Men who may be dominated by the nature of their class and ethnic position can still dominate women, and this may be important as a way to assert power and control over their lives as they experience class and racial/ethnic oppression. This pattern was supported by the research of Peterson and Bailey (1992) noted earlier. Another study on rape in South Africa highlights the dynamics of race and class inequality and rape. Vogelman's (1989) analysis of rape in South Africa found that in 1988 there were officially 19,368 rape cases. Official annual figures for rape in the 1980s record between 15,000 and 16,000 cases, 9,000 prosecutions, and 5,000 convictions. He notes that unofficially 399,000 rapes are committed annually in South Africa, meaning on the average more than 1,000 women are raped daily in South Africa—almost one every one and a half minutes. He furthermore notes that the figures for rape from 1986 to 1987 showed an increase of 14.7 percent. Vogelman concludes that the high incidence of rape in South Africa is attributed to the powerlessness of women that stems from patriarchy. This, together with the oppressive class and racial systems of stratification, makes women vulnerable to being victimized by black South African working-class men who are seeking to exert power over women to compensate psychologically for the powerlessness they experience as a result of class and racial oppression.

This interconnection of class, race or ethnicity, and gender stratification as it relates to violence directed at women is highlighted in critical criminology. In all social classes men learn to see themselves as privileged, yet society denies marginalized men a privileged economic position. Marginalized male youth experience disproportionately severe economic problems arising from the inherent mechanisms of capitalism. Given these conditions, for some males, the importance of manipulating and controlling women, by violence, if necessary, is elevated (Messerschmidt, 1986, 139). Also, the fact that women are more likely to be lower in class position (as defined in terms of income and occupational status) than men (two-thirds of the adult poor in the United States are women) does have an impact on their level of victimization (McDermott, 1979). Ethnic minority working-class women are more likely to be victimized than white upper-class women. Messerschmidt (1986) states that in a racist and sexist society, African American women, because they are viewed as less worthy of respect than other women, become rape victims in very high numbers (139).

Smith and Bennett (1985) conclude in their study on the relationship between rape and poverty that greater degrees of poverty are part of a community environment that is conducive to high rates of violence. They agree with the Schwendingers (1983) that conditions of poverty in general serve to promote contempt for others and that this contempt is likely to be directed at those who are less powerful, women in particular. Smith and Bennett further note that the percentage divorced is a powerful correlate of rates of rape in a community. They contend that divorce is a measure of interpersonal conflict between men and women, and that this conflict may manifest itself in rape. DeKeseredy, Rogness, and Schwartz (2004) review the literature on the relationship between divorce, separation, and sexual assault and conclude that "exiting a marital/cohabiting relationship or trying to exit increases women's chances of being sexually assaulted, especially if they are connected to patriarchal men."

CONCLUSION

In conclusion, rape, like homicide, is a learned strategy to exert power over another in interpersonal relations. Inequality contributes to the use of violence because it makes the victim vulnerable and because dominance of another is a normative characteristic of the society and the social relations that are endemic to it. Furthermore, as structured systems of inequality are legitimated through belief systems that define those who are dominated as less than those who are dominant—less in quality, less in talent, less in intelligence, and so forth—they contribute to the occurrence of violence by creating a disassociation between victim and offender and a legitimization for the use of force in controlling those who are less and may be in need of control because of their lower abilities.

Furthermore, we have discussed how this pattern of victimization increases levels of inequality, as those at the lower ends of the economic spectrum are in general more seriously affected. This is true for both homicide and rape. Last, we see how the structures of inequality may contribute to increasing use of violence, as those with the least power rely upon increasingly desperate and violent means to gain some measure of control for themselves and power over others, which is defined as a value in hierarchically structured societies. We learn the value of dominance as we are dominated by others. We learn that through the dominance of others, we gain control over our lives. We learn that power over others is a good and necessary feature of social relations in our society. Whether this is defined in terms of control over women, children, racial and ethnic minorities, or those with little status or property, violence may be more often chosen as a mechanism to exert power in situations of limited access to wealth, status, or control over one's life.

How do these patterns of victimization as they are a product of inequality carry over to the next level of violence, institutional violence? Who are the victims and who are the offenders of this type of violence? What are the patterns and how do they vary across different social systems? These are the questions we address in succeeding chapters.

DISCUSSION QUESTIONS

1. In the late nineteenth century the classic French sociologist Émile Durkheim wrote of *social facts*: patterns of group behavior that predictably involve categories of people in ways they may or may not even be aware of. What sorts of patterns in interpersonal violence are most obvious? Are these patterns (age, gender, minority status, and so forth) explainable?

2. Given what you know about the principal motives for murder, what would you suggest would be ways to prevent the occurrence?

3. Is there a culture of rape in our society? Is there a curriculum that we learn from the media (music and videos) in how men and women are portrayed that encourages rape and sexual assault on women?

4. Given the problem of date and marital rape, what would you suggest needs to be done to prevent these acts from occurring?

5. Given the relationship between the occurrence of murder and a country's involvement in war, what should be done to reduce this problem after a nation engages in war?

Chapter Four

Family Violence

Lee was always armed because he worked as a correctional officer at the Kankakee Jail, and he always carried handcuffs. He frequently tied Caroline up or handcuffed her before he beat her. The handcuffs, in fact, became such an integral part of his torture routine that he had only to give a signal—tapping his left wrist with his right hand and pointing to where they were kept—to tell her to get the cuffs and bring them to him so he could shackle her and begin the beating (Gillespie, 1981, 2).

Although she had been beaten so severely that she had been hospitalized on at least two occasions and had lost an eye and part of an ear, her assailant was released each time on his promise to the judge that he would not repeat the offense. The victim, I am told, finally solved the situation herself. She committed suicide (U.S. Commission on Civil Rights, 1982, 47).

William and Carrie present a clear case of mutual abuse, jealousy, and insecurity. He is a product of two alcoholic, verbally abusive parents. She was raised in a home in which her father had fistfights with her older brothers. William now has strong needs to control her behavior, afraid she will leave him for another man. She has a history of sexual promiscuity, knows his fears, and by acting flirtatiously in public plays to them. Within a year of their last violent incident she told him she had a lesbian lover to test his reaction. . . . Once, to punish her for her "waywardness" (his term), William dumped "goop" on her head, smearing a combination of "piss, tuna, and anything else I could get my hands on" into her hair (Stacey, Hazlewood, and Shupe, 1994, 108, 111).

Here is a vignette even older: Abigail Abbot Bailey wrote the first autobiographical account of family violence published in the United States. Born in 1746 and a deeply religious woman, Abigail married Asa Bailey at the age of twenty-two. Within one month of their marriage, Asa began physically abusing her. Over time he was to have an affair with a hired woman and attempt to rape another female servant. After Abigail had been married to Asa for twenty-one years and had borne fourteen children (all of whom the father regularly bullied), he began to abuse physically and sexually one sixteen-year-old daughter. Abigail described one such violent incident that she witnessed:

> In great rage, and with a voice of terror, he asked why she did not come to him, when he first called her? She respectfully told him that he called her to get up, which she immediately did, and went to her work. But she said she did not hear him call her to come to him. He seized his horsewhip, and said in a rage, he would make her know that when he called her, she should come to him. He then fell to whipping her without mercy. She cried, and begged, and repeated her assertion that she did not know he called her to come to him. . . . But he was not in the least appeased. He continued to whip her, as though he were dealing with an ungovernable brute; striking over her head, hands, and back; nor did he spare her face and eyes; while the poor girl appeared as though she must die. (Taves, 1989, 75–76)

Finally, in August 1793 Abigail obtained a divorce from Asa. While divorce was permissible in late eighteenth-century New England, it was not casually obtained. One of the marriage partners had to have broken the understood "covenant" established between them. This marital covenant clearly assumed that one partner (the woman) was subordinate to the other (the male), though within this two-tiered hierarchy both partners were recognized as having rights and responsibilities. Adultery, cruelty (wife beating), and desertion were all considered examples of breaches of these "rights and responsibilities." Interestingly, the primary grounds on which Abigail eventually secured a divorce from her abusive husband were not his violence toward her nor because of what we moderns would regard as his incest or his child abuse, but rather his adultery regarding his wife and daughter: that is, by engaging in incestuous relations with his own daughter, Abigail's husband had posed a threat to her, the marriage, and the larger social order. In this view, however curious it may seem to modern family advocates, the wife, not the child, was assumed to be the primary victim of the father-daughter incest (Taves, 1989, 26).

The experiences of Abigail Abbot Bailey two hundred years ago demonstrate a fundamental fact about the perception of family violence as a social problem:

> Historically, the greater the level of intimacy associated with partnerships in which violence was observed, the less likely the institutional response was to characterize the behavior as criminal. . . . The labeling of intimate violence as "domestic" not only creates the perception that it falls within the private realm of the family, but, further, that it is better treated outside the jurisdiction of the criminal justice system. (Cardarelli, 1997, 2)

Its definition as a social problem has differed tremendously throughout history and, as we show, continues to change.

FAMILY VIOLENCE IN BRIEF HISTORICAL PERSPECTIVE

Only within the past century or so has violence within the family been regarded as a serious, widespread problem and then largely in Western societies. Yet the phenomenon has existed probably as long as the domestic institution itself. Consider child abuse.

As David Bakan (1971) chronicles in grisly detail in his classic *Slaughter of the Innocents*, systematic exploitation and abuse of children is interwoven with the very history of civilization. The movement to establish children's rights to be safe from physical and sexual abuse is relatively young. In the United States it began just after the Civil War. Interestingly, the case that helped the movement gain visibility and momentum involved the Society for the Prevention of Cruelty to Animals. A little girl named Mary Ellen had to be taken from her family because in addition to being frequently beaten, she had been seriously neglected and had become malnourished. There were no social service agencies for children that could argue in court on her behalf, so the Society for the Prevention of Cruelty to Animals maintained that as a member of the animal kingdom she should be removed from her abusive parents, as was an animal's right by law. The Society won its case. The obvious need for an entirely separate advocate to safeguard children led to the formation of the Society for the Prevention of Cruelty to Children in 1871 in New York City (Radbill, 1974).

But it was not until 1962 that the term "battered child syndrome" came into our lexicon when it was introduced at a symposium for the American Academy of Pediatricians by Dr. C. Henry Kempe. Likewise, only in the past few centuries has woman battering been viewed as a problem at all, much less a serious problem. In fact, for much of history violence in the home was viewed as obligatory on the part of the husband to maintain control and chastise his wife with physical force.

The "right" of husbands to beat their wives has its roots in Roman law, which originally permitted a husband to kill his wife if she committed a variety of offenses, particularly adultery. This common law tradition was modified in medieval Europe, limiting male-directed punishment to beating women rather than taking their lives. For many centuries, during the Dark and Middle Ages as well as the Renaissance, women were routinely subjugated by physical violence. The physical punishment that accompanied their taken-for-granted inferior status, justified by the so-called laws of chastisement, went unquestioned. Such violence was simply regarded as part of the divinely ordained and natural order of things.

In his history of divorce in Western society, Roderick Phillips (1988, 525) describes a seventeenth-century English commentary on the law relating to women. The commentator states that just as a man might beat an outlaw, a pagan, or a traitor with impunity, so a husband might legitimately beat his wife, but only as long as he did not do "any bodily damage, otherwise than appertains to the office of a Husband for lawful and reasonable correction." And Phillips (1988, 328) quotes from a book published in London in 1612, entitled *A Godlie Forme of Householde Government*, that admonished (male) readers: "If she be of a gentle spirit, he may use gentle means which will then

Figure 4.1.   October 1815 London caricature by "Williams," whose title is an allusion to Shakespeare's play "The Taming of the Shrew." Mrs. Petruchio is shown confined to a canopied four-poster bed, whose head and foot are stocks, while Petruchio menaces her with cane and gag. On the table is Petruchio's patent, and the thumbscrews, while the books "Rule a Wife and Have a Wife" and a torn copy of "The Whole Duty of Woman" are on the floor. A placard reading "LOVE, HONOR, and OBEY" (with "Obey" written in larger letters) hangs along the wall inside the bed's canopy. This is a quote from the traditional wedding ceremony (in which only the woman promises to obey), and the way that the woman's shoes, corset, and red garment are strewn carelessly on the floor or over a chair may suggest that this is their wedding night. Source: Library of Congress

doe the most good, but if she be of a more hard nature, rougher means must be used and she must be dealt withal after a more round manner." He goes on to cite an old French proverb that said: "Don't expect any good from an ass, a nut, or a woman unless you have a stick in your hand."

In the New England colonies, only Massachusetts considered wife abuse a criminal offense. In general, North American legislators followed their British counterparts in shaping laws concerning woman battering. An example was the now-infamous "rule of thumb," an expression that has become a part of everyday speech. British common law during the nineteenth century, in a reform effort to put limits on how harshly a husband could legally chastise his wife, stipulated that the "reasonable instrument" to be used by a husband in a beating could be "a rod not thicker than his thumb."

Gradually during the nineteenth century, legislatures on both sides of the Atlantic began to remove males' "automatic entitlement" to use violence against their spouses. A series of marital laws appeared in England, such as the 1853 Act for the Prevention and Punishment of Aggravated Assaults on Women and the 1882 Wife Beaters Act, and mandated fines and imprisonment for woman-abusers. Likewise, various states in this country enacted quite severe statutes regarding husbands' assaults on wives. For example, a Maryland law passed in 1882 prescribed forty lashes or one year in prison for wife beaters. In Delaware an abusive man could be punished with five to thirty lashes at the whipping post, while in New Mexico he could be given a fine of $255 to $1,000 or one to five years in prison. By 1910 only eleven states still did not permit divorce by reasons of cruelty by one spouse toward the other.

FAMILY VIOLENCE AND INEQUALITY

For most of the history of Western civilization the family unit has resembled an asymmetric power hierarchy. It has been what Australian sociologist Robert W. Connell (1987) has termed a "domestic patriarchy" or a "gender regime" in which stratification is determined by both age and gender: adult males at the top of the pyramid, all children at the bottom (though they can be stratified also by age), and women somewhere in between. There may have been exceptions in individual households where strong-willed women "ruled the roost" and basically made the key decisions instead of men, and it is true that modern families are witnessing more egalitarian relations between the sexes. Nevertheless, as a system patriarchy (i.e., men holding maximum power and autonomy) has held sway as opposed to matriarchy (where women enjoy such resources and men are subjugated). But while matriarchy is a concept, patriarchy is far and away most often the reality.

It is also important to remember that domestic patriarchy is dependent for support from the larger society of which the family is merely one unit (Connell, 1987, 123–24). Inequality of power in marriage is a reflection of gender inequality in the larger society. This means that the culture's gender roles, its procedures for (and contents of) the socialization of children, its traditional

Figure 4.2. "JUDGE THUMB. or— Patent Sticks for Family Correction: War-ranted Lawful!," a 1782 caricature by James Gillray. Word balloons in graphic; Judge Thumb says: "Who wants a cure for a nasty Wife? Here's your nice Family Amusement for Winter Evenings! Who buys here?" Woman says: "Help! Murder, for God sake, Murder!" Man says: "Murder, hey? it's Law, you Bitch: it's not bigger than my Thumb!" Source: Library of Congress

patterns of educating and employing persons, and even its literary/folklore/ mass media portrayals reinforce for both men and women what they "should" expect of one another when they form families.

A related debate has been how universally dispersed across all socioeconomic levels family violence is. All surveys find, for example, that spousal violence appears to occur more frequently at the lower socioeconomic levels. Writes one author: "The theories that relate family violence to inequalities assume that life as an underdog is more stressful and frustrating" (Little, 1995, 257). Some have argued that the poorer elements of society versus the more affluent elements are more reluctant to report violent incidences to law enforcement officials out of traditional suspicion or pessimism, or vice versa those more affluent families fear the stigma of police involvement and thus underreport. The best that can be said at this time is that if there is a relationship between patriarchy and socioeconomic class and the use of violence in the family, then patriarchy is related to levels of violence, and those levels of spousal violence mirror inequality in the larger society.

As a consequence, no specific interpersonal act of family violence is unrelated to the larger institutional and cultural context. One has only to interview a cross-section of battered women who have become clients of a safe haven or shelter to appreciate how fundamentally the various sociocultural dimensions of family violence are interwoven into the pain and tragedy of an individual family. In any hypothetical case of woman battering in North America, for example, these would include:

- His enculturated macho ideal of male supremacy and control (accompanied by secondary predilections for violence, sexual aggression, and alcohol/drug consumption) versus her enculturated ideal of passivity, deference, tolerance, and reservation
- His inability to communicate openly and constructively about his male needs and feelings versus her mirror inability to communicate openly and constructively about her female needs and feelings
- His likelihood of earning all or most of the income (hence possessing greater resources, from checking accounts and income to employability to the mobility of an automobile) versus her likelihood of not having her own independent access to financial (and resultant) resources or having lesser resources
- His likelihood of being less involved in the daily responsibilities of feeding, cleansing, and caring for children versus her likelihood of being the primary caregiver for their children

This list is certainly not exhaustive. Also to be considered are the factors that intimate relationships allow a freer flow of emotions (including anger), there are minimal "inhibitors" of emotions, and man-woman living relationships inevitably bring to the front such issues as the division of labor in household chores and sexual access. But the point is that each of the previous comparisons can be linked sociologically to the institutional context of the modern family. At the interpersonal level they constitute the issues of stress, strain, anger, and hostility that fuel violence in an intimate situation. They are the stuff of police blotters, divorce courts, and files in women's shelters. But they are, in the larger picture, specific manifestations of macro-themes that exist in a hierarchical system of power.

How this asymmetric arrangement originated has generated a running debate among sociologists and anthropologists since the two disciplines began. The debate grew appreciably during the late 1960s into the 1970s with the advent of the modern women's liberation movement. The biological reductionists point to basic qualitative differences between the two sexes. Men are physically stronger and bigger than women (Collins, 1971); have an evolutionary tendency to band together, whether in hunting parties or at taverns (Tiger, 1970); and cannot become pregnant; and thus women raise boys who must ultimately reject femininity and seek masculine identity. Men's advantage that results in their predominant asymmetric power, in other words, is fundamentally physiological (and therefore somehow "natural"). The historicists, on the other hand, take a more materialist, or Neo-Marxist, point of view. What is produced in a society, how it is produced, who produces it, and who controls it after production are all factors that determine a lot about women's and men's statuses in any society.

Resolving this issue is beyond the scope of this chapter. At this time it appears that a recognition of both cultural-economic and biological factors provides the best working explanation for the persistence of patriarchy, particularly in modern industrial societies where women are not "inexorably" destined to be full-time "child producers" for most of their adult years. Anthropologist Alice Schlegel (1977, 27), in developing a theory of sexual stratification using both Western and non-Western case studies, came to just such a conclusion during the formative years of the women's liberation movement. She wrote of the "modern" situation: "In the industrial society the status of the woman is increasingly dependent on her roles in the public sector and depends very little on her procreative activities in the domestic." The result, as feminists have pointed out, is a conflict between the demands of the full-time workplace and the full-time home. Schlegel concludes that the hierarchy that subjugates women, or at best subtly limits their horizons beyond homemaking, is not based on their childbearing monopoly but rather on a male-oriented legacy of leaving an overwhelming proportion of the child care/primary socialization to women. As long as women are given such tasks, by default the "glass ceiling" of limited advancement and opportunity will confront them. With this view of the modern Western family as a hierarchy of asymmetrical power, many of the patterns found by family violence researchers become more easily understood.

SPOUSAL VIOLENCE

Assault between married partners or cohabiting adults has not readily been accepted by authorities as the same type of serious crime as assault between two strangers. Indeed, during the early 1980s, while Stacey and Shupe (1983) were researching a book on domestic violence, an incident occurred in Fort Worth, Texas, that illustrates this point. A man repeatedly struck and knocked down a woman in an alley off a city street. When citizens, both male and female, were attracted by her cries and stopped to see if they could help, the man reassured them with the statement, "It's okay. She's my wife." And they moved on without interfering.

And this has been as true of public officials as of the average citizen. In one study of 1,323 felony arrest bail decisions collected during 1983–1984, for example, the courts clearly discriminated in assault cases in ways that showed family violence to be considered less "serious" than other types of violence. The authors concluded:

> Violent crimes against a family member are handled differently at the bail-setting stage than the same crimes against unrelated victims. Although related and unrelated offenders are equally likely to obtain release from pretrial detention, suspects who are related to their victims and are charged with a violent offense are treated more leniently. Related suspects tend to be released on recognizance more often than unrelated ones and, if required to post a bond, are required to post a lesser amount. (Herzberger and Channels, 1991, 70–71)

But awareness has been changing during the past half century. The Attorney General's Task Force on Family Violence (1984, 4) stated: "The legal response to family violence must be guided primarily by the nature of the abusive act, not the relationship between the victim and the abuser." There is now considerably more concern generated and attention paid to violence against women (generally) and violence between spouses/cohabiting partners (in particular). Domestic violence as a social problem no longer runs up against the believability problem it faced in the 1970s. Advocates of victims in the anti–family violence movement no longer have to adopt a defensive stance in pressing their case for abused constituents. Still, the passage to a greater sensitivity about spousal violence has not been without controversy and argumentation.

Patterns

One often encounters in books and magazine articles dealing with family violence "official" statistics that state a women in the United States is beaten every so many seconds or somber pronouncements that one out of every two (sometimes three, sometimes four) females in this country will at some time in their adult lives become the victim of a man's violence in a relationship. Are such figures accurate, and where do they originate?

The fact is that such statistics are "guesstimates" put out by well-intentioned, concerned "experts" who want to impress on readers that spousal violence (and here we include cohabiting partners and same-sex partners [see, e.g., Renzetti, 1992, 1997; Island and Letellier, 1991] as well as married couples) is no trivial problem. No one really knows for sure how many battered women there are at any given moment or within any time frame. No official agency in the federal government acts as a clearinghouse for such information or comprehensively monitors the numbers on family violence. There is no Uniform Crime Report category for these kinds of assaults similar to the ones that the Federal Bureau of Investigation compiles annually on robbery, murder, and so forth. There is little doubt that domestic violence victims, *most* of them women and children, number annually in the millions.

Our ability to generalize about the patterns and dynamics of spousal violence comes primarily from two sources: victimization surveys and studies of women's shelter residents. Relying solely on either source can be misleading. Yllo and Straus (1991) has warned of both the representative sample fallacy and the clinical fallacy. In the first case the survey methods employing representative sampling will probably miss some of the more violent cases because respondents can be embarrassed and reluctant to talk about their experiences with total strangers, either face-to-face or by telephone. On the other hand, persons receiving treatment or assistance for a problem like violence to the point they have to flee their homes and take up residence elsewhere are often not representative of the entire population (as is true with most persons who turn to public agencies for assistance). Based on what we know from in-depth studies of battered women in shelters and from what women and men in national surveys have recounted about violence they experienced, it is apparent that many shelter residents display the more severe cases of violence, certainly many times worse than what a random sample survey would pick up. For example, in a 1985 survey Yllo and Straus (1991) found that only 13 percent of the 644 assaulted women among the thousands of respondents he sampled had ever gone to a shelter.

Thus, it is best to use both types of data on family violence, but with caution. Surveys give us a good picture of how widespread this violence is within the general population, while clinical studies help us understand the dynamics involved between family members. Unquestionably the most comprehensive and reliable survey research has been conducted by sociologists at the Family Research Laboratory at the University of New Hampshire. Over the past four decades Murray A. Straus, Richard J. Gelles, Suzanne K. Steinmetz, David Finkelhor, and many of their colleagues have given us a detailed analysis of incidents (acts committed within a specific period of time, such as a year) and prevalence (acts committed over the entire span of a relationship) of spousal violence in American families. What they have revealed are patterns that confirm the existence of what Stacey and Shupe (1983, 195–203) earlier termed a "cult of violence" in American society: an environment of patriarchy and cultural glorification of violence that serves as fertile soil for violence's cultivation. In both 1975 and 1985 Straus and his colleagues conducted extensive national surveys of American households, drawing on representative samples. Altogether they analyzed responses from 8,145 families. The results show a considerable amount of violence in the home. For example, one in six (or 16 percent) of American couples experienced at least one physically violent episode during 1985. Since there are approximately 64 million couples in the United States, that means (by extrapolation) an estimated 8.7 million couples had at least one violent act committed in their home in one year. Most of the violence was "minor": pushing, shoving, slapping, and throwing or smashing household objects. But 3.4 million households had "high risk" violence, such as kicking, punching, biting, and choking (Straus and Gelles, 1991b, 96–97). Almost one out of every eight North American husbands carried out one or more violent acts in 1985, and three out of every 100 women in their study that year (which translates into 1.8 million women nationally) were severely assaulted by their male partners. In fact, the 12 percent of the women interviewed who reported being beaten by husbands or partners during the year of the survey had been assaulted an average of six times.

Regarding serious violence, which involves life-threatening harm and often death, it is clear, *just from reported and investigated cases*, that on an average day in the United States three or more women and at least one man are murdered by their intimate partners. In 2000 that amounted to 1,247 women and 440 men (Bureau of Justice Statistics, 2006).

Another pattern in the 1985 Straus and Gelles survey was consistent with results from the 1975 survey (Straus, Gelles, and Steinmetz, 1980). Women committed roughly an equal amount of violence against men as men did against women. Straus and Gelles point out that many of the assaults by women against their husbands or partners were acts of retaliation or self-defense: "One of the fundamental reasons why women are violent within the family (but rarely outside the family) is that for a typical American women [sic], her home is the location where there is the most serious risk of assault. . . . Since women are so often the victims of murderous assault within the family, it is not surprising that women, who commit only about a tenth of the non-spouse murders in the United States, commit nearly half (48 percent) of the murders of spouses" (Straus and Gelles, 1991b, 98).

This pattern of female-initiated violence is controversial but not unique to Straus et al.'s surveys. Indeed, decades ago Steinmetz (1977) wrote of a "battered husband syndrome" in which men, not women, were the primary victims of physical abuse. Shupe, Stacey, and Hazlewood (1987) devoted an entire chapter in their book on family violence to the dynamics producing violent women who ended up in counseling. Indeed, they later devoted an entire book, entitled *The Violent Couple*, to the study of a sample of one hundred male/female partnerships in which both men and women were violent toward one another, often aggressively so (Stacey, Hazlewood, and Shupe, 1994). Several other researchers have documented female violence that is not always purely in self-defense (e.g., Dutton, 1988; McLeod, 1984). Such mounting findings suggest, as two social workers concluded in the journal *Social Work*, that the domestic violence problem is "a falsely framed issue" if we cling to the simplistic assumption that men "exclusively or nearly exclusively perpetrate domestic assaults" (McNeely and Robinson-Simpson, 1987). These authors also demonstrate how clinical studies of battered women (as Straus warned) can miss part of the overall picture: victimized women entering a shelter are rarely or never asked about their possible violence toward men.

This view has been criticized (falsely) as claiming that acknowledging women's violence against men also claims that there is a "symmetry" or equality of harm and danger to men and women from each other's violence (e.g., Dobash et al., 1992). Actually no one has made such an improbable assertion. According to government statistics, men are at a greater risk of violence from acquaintances and strangers than from girlfriends or family members, with the majority of their assailants being other males. Generally speaking the risk for men of being killed by their wives is very low and has decreased over the last thirty years (Fox and Zawitz, 2007). Two other social scientists have noted: "In a society characterized by high rates of violent crime, women experience the majority of the violence directed at them by those with whom they have ongoing relationships. In effect, intimate violence—violence committed by those individuals one is more likely to trust and have continuing social relations with—represents the type of violence most likely to be increasing for women" (Miller and Wellford, 1997, 17).

But the idea that women are (not just could be) contributing aggressively to violence in the home is anathema to feminists. It has been described as a "backlash against the challenge to male privilege mounted by the battered women's movement" (Gondolf, 1988, 5). For years most researchers in the area of family violence (who were also usually feminists) maintained that a marriage license is in reality a "hitting license" for husbands and that it is almost always women who are the victims of violence. They have resisted using terms like "mutual combat" in describing spousal violence, characterizing women's violence as a myth (Berk, Berk, Loseke, and Rauma, 1983). When Straus first presented his findings on female violence in the late 1970s, booing, shouting, and picketing protesters interrupted his presentations. Suzanne K. Steinmetz, who first coined the term "battered husband syndrome," received threatening phone calls, had a bomb threat called in to a conference where she was to speak, and had to face a negative letter-writing campaign to her university when she was being considered for promotion (Straus and Gelles, 1991c, 11).

But the indisputable fact is that Straus et al. as well as others show that women are violent, and not always in self-defense. In the 1985 survey the researchers asked who hit first in any violent episodes that year. According to husbands interviewed, they were the ones who struck first in 44 percent of the episodes, the wives struck first in 45 percent of the episodes, and the men were unsure in the remaining 11 percent of the episodes. According to wives interviewed, husbands struck first in 53 percent of the cases, the wives struck first 42 percent of the time, and the women were unsure in the remaining 5 percent of the episodes (Straus and Gelles, 1991b, 104–5). Regardless of men and women's different perspectives, it is clear that women's violence against men is not a negligible factor in spousal violence. All of this is not to say that men are at greater or equal risk compared to women. In fact, men are less likely to be seriously injured than women are when the former are assaulted in the home (Stacey, Hazlewood, and Shupe, 1994; Stets and Straus, 1991).

Yet there is one further interesting pattern that changed from the 1975 to 1985 studies. While Straus and his colleagues found a 22 percent decrease in wife beating over a decade's time, overall wife-to-husband violence increased slightly (Straus and Gelles, 1991a, 118–19). Straus and Gelles (1991b, 105) conclude: "Violence by women is a critically important issue for the safety and well-being of women. . . . [The] danger to a woman of such behavior is that it sets the stage for the husband to assault her. . . . Unless women also forsake violence in their relationships with male partners and children, they cannot expect to be free of assault. Women must insist as much on non-violence by their sisters as they rightfully insist on it by men."

The ugly truth is that an individual in the United States of America is far more likely to be murdered by a member of his or her own family than by anyone else (Straus, 1991, 20). For men, the likelihood of being assaulted by a family member is twenty times greater than being assaulted by a stranger; for women, that risk of being assaulted in the home rather than by a stranger jumps to more than two hundred times greater. Worse, based on his studies, Straus (1991, 21) considers the statistics from both 1975 and 1985 surveys to be underestimates. Incidences vary between one in six and one in eight families each year experiencing violence at least once but often more. The prevalence of such violence occurring at least once in a relationship is likely for approximately 60 percent of American families. Domestic violence in American homes is a reliably documented fact. With a phenomenon so prevalent, therefore, we must ask, what is generating it?

Dynamics

Three levels of social life contribute to spousal violence. (Notice we do not say "cause" because some levels provide more of a context than specific determinants of violence.) The social structural level is the system of patriarchy endemic in this country as well as in virtually every modern society. It is about inequitable distributions of power and access to opportunity within and outside the family unit. The cultural level is made up of stereotypical and normative ideas about gender-appropriate behavior. The social psychological level is concerned with the interaction between individuals' differences and their sociocultural influences in socialization, personality, and anger-management/communication skills. What is important to emphasize is that specific experiences of violence are embedded in a structural-hierarchical context reinforced by cultural definitions of what is "normal." In other words, family violence incidences are not isolated, unrelated phenomena.

For example, Shupe, Stacey and Hazlewood (1987) studied in-depth and over a period of several years 241 known violent men (supplemented with information about 542 other violent men taken from interviews with their wives and girlfriends) who had entered counseling either because of a court-mandated rehabilitation or because of family pressure (such as a partner threatening to leave). They found that the economic backgrounds of violent men covered the gamut: from homeless to the financially comfortable. The same range was true for education and occupation. While the unemployment rate among violent men, whether being counseled or not, was almost double that of the national level and more than double the state's rate, white-collar professionals as well as regularly employed blue-collar workers were also solidly represented in the nonrandom sample.

Most important for the social psychological level, Shupe, Stacey, and Hazlewood (1987, 33–44) identified four critical foundations for men's spousal violence:

1. Physiological factors
2. Trauma from abuse as a child
3. Childhood learning
4. Lack of communication skills and impulse control

Physiological factors included a high rate of alcohol/substance use (true for both men and women in violent households as well as in nonviolent families) with the drugs proving to be depressants and/or disinhibitors. Nevertheless, the authors concluded that in terms of actual causation "such factors played a minor role in influencing any of the family violence we encountered" (Shupe, Stacey, and Hazlewood, 1987, 35).

Trauma from abuse as a child was a more significant issue. It gave rise to an emotional dependence of adult men on women who, however inadequately, try to express their needs and codependency with maltreatment and violence. Write the authors:

> The love/hurt/rage reactions that helpless young boys felt toward their abusive, powerful parents (for whom the boys nevertheless felt attraction) were replayed by these men in their own marriages. . . . Because many of these men found their fathers to be cold, unresponsive, or indifferent, they turned to their mothers for warmth and the protective side of parental strength. Only the mothers would give the boys positive feelings of self-worth and genuine comfort. . . . These men typically had very little to do with their own children, particularly infants and young children, as if they were aloof from or uninterested in their offspring. Actually they lacked the ability to relate fully and effectively, just as their own fathers had. (Shupe, Stacey, and Hazlewood, 1987, 35)

Early childhood learning as well as lack of communication skills and poor impulse control constituted an even more important cluster of social psychological factors. For example, the intergenerational transfer hypothesis was a proposition initially taken for granted by many professionals in the family violence field during the mid-to-late 1970s and only empirically tested by the early 1980s. This hypothesis assumed that little boys learn to be adult batterers from watching their fathers successfully use violence in the home to settle husband-wife disputes (what social psychologists term "modeling") while little girls learn that beatings are part of the adult woman's lot in life from watching their mother-victims, a normal (however unpleasant) part of the female role as wife and homemaker. But social service providers who worked with spousal violence victims who did not have personal histories of domestic violence came to question this "conventional wisdom." Indeed, interviews with large numbers of women's shelter residents have shown just the opposite trend: they report relatively low rates of having experienced or witnessed inter-parental or childhood violence in their homes when growing up.

Thus, generational transfer of violence must become a modified concept: it only works for learning violence as an acceptable strategy of conflict resolution, not for learning victimization. The earlier, simplistic version of the intergenerational transfer hypothesis has been criticized by others (e.g., Cappell and Heiner, 1990; Herzberger, 1983) and, interestingly, in its most recent form appears to work in the same social learning way for women as well as men. In examining past research literature as well as their own clinical research findings on one hundred couples, Shupe, Stacey, and Hazlewood (1987, 45–62) found that, other than instances of women's violence committed in self-defense against men's violence, the dynamics of women's violence in general were similar to those of men. Violent women, in other words, struck out in jealousy, because of limitations in anger management, because of a lack of communication skills, or with histories of past childhood trauma and abuse. In these violent couples, both partners had witnessed and internalized the pragmatic lessons of male/female violence in the home. Correspondingly, they both had been raised without a surfeit of genuine, useful, constructive strategies for effectively communicating with the opposite sex. They had, in essence, learned hitting as a mechanism for gaining attention and (however dysfunctionally) resolving disputes.

But the spousal violence issue is more than a problem of poor communications. There are, more importantly, structural issues of patriarchy and inequality in the modern family. The two most common characteristics of violent spouses, reported in numerous published testimonies, studies, and interviews, are "the need to control" and "the need to dominate." Whether out of sexist macho ideals of male superiority in the home or from dysfunctional male feelings of overdependence on women, there is little question that male power to direct women is the central issue in most research on spousal violence. This fact emerges in both explicitly feminist and sympathetic as well as not necessarily feminist writings, and as in most cases of spousal violence, it crosses class and race/ethnic boundaries (Cazenave and Straus, 1991; Straus, 1991).

Sociological research provides insight into how these hierarchical issues have an impact on spousal abuse of women. Coleman and Straus (1991) found that when conflict (such as arguments) occurred in couples with "asymmetrical power structures" (i.e., either male-dominant or female-dominant), there was a much greater risk of violence than when conflict occurred in couples with "egalitarian" or symmetrical power structures. The latter power arrangement, they concluded, can tolerate a much greater amount of tension, conflict, and aggravation without the disagreements turning into physical violence. On the other hand, Coleman and Straus observed that the amount of agreement between both partners in an asymmetrical couple as to the "legitimacy" or "appropriateness" of the power inequity was a key factor in predicting the level of conflict over family responsibilities and, ultimately, subsequent violence. For example, if the man and woman both agreed that a given arrangement such as patriarchy was desirable or acceptable, then there was less violence than when the partners in a patriarchal relationship did not agree. (However, the patriarchal relationships overall still tended to be more violent than the egalitarian ones.) The authors concluded that "the results provide one more indication of the importance of including the power structure of intimate relationships as part of an analysis of marital violence" (Coleman and Straus, 1991, 301). Felson and Outlaw (2007) term the general issue one of "the control motive," in their opinion the primary sociological factor in power issues in intimate violence. Certainly it is as significant in female aggression against male marital partners as it is in male aggression against female partners. (See also Mooney, 2001; Sorenson and Taylor, 2005.)

In another study on a wife's marital dependency and possible abuse, Kalmuss and Straus (1991) examined the relationship between the resources a woman might or might not have (e.g., separate income, a job, presence of dependent children, and so forth) and physical abuse. Their findings confirmed the key role resources play in why women stay and endure physical violence in the home when they know it is not right or "normal." The likelihood of leaving the abusive situation is directly tied to the availability of resources "to go it alone." Earlier Stacey and Shupe (1983, 53ff) rejected the psychologically oriented theory of Lenore Walker (1979) that battered women stay in abusive relationships because they have become conditioned into states of "learned helplessness." Instead, they argued, look in her purse for cash, car keys, credit cards, and other signs of independent means. Likewise, Kalmuss and Straus (1991) determined that women with a high dependency on their marriages experience more physical abuse from their husbands than less dependent women.

Finally, support for the role of patriarchy in increasing physical violence against women in homes came from a study by Yllo and Straus (1991). They found in a state-by-state analysis, examining factors such as educational levels, employment/unemployment, and women's legal rights, that where women's economic-educational-political-legal statuses were lower, female victimization rates in spousal violence were higher. In fact, "the rate declines steadily as the status of women increases" (Yllo and Strauss, 1991, 394). States with the most male-dominant, traditional norms, as measured by a sophisticated set of scales, had double the rates of wife beating as did states with the more egalitarian cultures.

Thus, the relationship between spousal violence and the hierarchical structure of many American families has been empirically established. Next we consider the other aspect of violence in this hierarchy: the victimization of children.

CHILD ABUSE AND MALTREATMENT

Two sociologists who set out to study battered women in shelters in 1979 found themselves also having to examine child abuse (since most of the women in their sample brought at least two young children with them to safe havens). They recalled the visceral reactions to child maltreatment from a wide range of persons whom they encountered in their research:

> Excluding professionals working daily with child abuse cases, no one we talked to during our research reacted dispassionately to the problem. Indeed, it aroused extraordinary vindictive anger in otherwise respectable citizens whose backgrounds ranged across a broad spectrum, such as school teachers, police officers, college presidents, ministers, university students, auto mechanics, and landlords. This anger was vehement and unrelenting. Many acquaintances and colleagues suggested without so much as batting an eye that child abusers deserved castration, execution, or worse. These abusers were even condemned as subhumans. In short, no one seemed able to separate personal emotional outrage from objective attempts to understand the phenomenon. (Stacey and Shupe, 1983, 61)

Such reactions manifest a sensitized viewpoint of children's special vulnerability by modern Western standards. But it was not always so. A variety of scholars have traced the sad historical and cross-cultural patterns of child maltreatment (Boswell, 1989; Radbill, 1974). Two experts in human development relate: "When we examine the history of mankind, whether from paleontological evidence, documentary accounts such as the Bible, or culture-specific myths and fairy tales, we see evidence of children being mistreated, abandoned, sacrificed, or eaten to go along with evidence of their being cuddled, nurtured, and encouraged" (Burgess and Garbarino, 1983, 88). Many historians even argue that the very concept of childhood as we moderns understand it did not exist before the seventeenth century.

The source of much of this abuse can be located in the taken-for-granted perspective that has existed for millennia that children (particularly females) are the property of their families—patriarchal, hierarchical families (Tower, 1989). In Roman society, for example, the father's rights under the law included killing or maiming a son or daughter, sacrificing him or her to the gods, or even selling children as slaves. This ownership principle has receded slowly in Western civilization. The later European feudal system continued much of the Roman hierarchical principle giving adult men power over women and putting children, particularly poor children, at the bottom. It was not until the Renaissance that some recognition of children's special needs emerged. For example, only in 1548 and 1576, respectively, did England pass laws to provide some shielding of children (as we now define children) from sexual abuse. In the first instance a law was created protecting boys from forced sodomy; in the second instance a law was enacted prohibiting forcible rape of girls under the age of ten. And in 1601 the Elizabethan poor laws recognized orphaned or abandoned children as a class or group entitled to special relief (Tower, 1989, 2–5).

Yet maltreatment legally unacceptable today in the United States continued. In the nineteenth century it was still common for parents to indenture (or apprentice) their children from an early age into their teenage years under working conditions that were often appalling. One only has to read Charles Dickens's *Oliver Twist* to catch a flavor of such exploitation. Sociologist Dean Knudsen (1992, 6–10), summarizing the literature on this subject, observes that it was only during the period of high industrialization in North America during the 1880s and 1890s that the vulnerability and exploitation of children became issues. The rise of unions, Victorian perspectives that women belonged in the home rather than in the workplace, and the rising tide of immigrants from Europe all played roles in forging this new concern for children (recall the case of Mary Ellen mentioned earlier in this chapter). It is also not coincidental that both psychology and sociology—both disciplines that began to examine the dynamics of socialization and childhood development—arose during this era. Indeed, many of the early behavioral scientists were activists in "progressive" movements such as child labor reform.

But the problem of child labor, as just one form of child abuse or maltreatment, is still endemic on a global level. For years the United Nations International Labor Organization has reported that children continue to be at risk, not just from disease and malnutrition (see our chapter on structural violence) but also from systematic murder (see our later chapter on state violence).

Unfortunately, on the global level the problem will persist for the indefinite future. Poverty is too great a reality in many countries to spare families the necessity of their children working. And the United States, once a leader in pressing for laws ending the exploitation of child labor, is not helping. President George H. W. Bush refused to sign the 1989 UN Convention on the Rights of the Child that argued against such exploitation (curiously on the grounds that the UN law might not agree with U.S. laws). Likewise, U.S. Representative Dan J. Pease of Ohio introduced a bill forbidding importation of goods made by foreign exploited child labor, but the U.S. Congress stalled action on it. In 1995, UN Ambassador to the United Nations Madeleine Albright signed the Convention; however, it is yet to be ratified by the U.S. Senate and signed by President Obama.

So exploitation of child labor and physical and sexual abuse are still rampant worldwide. A recent report published by the International Labor Organization (ILO) estimated that there were some 306 million children ages five to seventeen in employment in the world in 2008 (Diallo, Hagemann, Etienne, Gurbuzer, and Mehran, 2010). The report points out that most of these children are poor recent migrants from rural areas and that they are most likely employed in unsafe conditions for long hours at a time. The ILO research indicates that 115 million children are working in the worst form of child labor (hazardous work). The authors note that in terms of absolute numbers of child laborers between five and seventeen years of age, the Asian-Pacific region has the most, 113 million, followed by sub-Saharan African with 65.1 million, and Latin America and the Caribbean with 14.1 million. However, the incidence (number relative to the child population) of child labor is highest in sub-Saharan Africa with one in four children involved. The largest proportion (68 percent of child laborers) are engaged in unpaid family work. There is more discussion of child labor and slavery in the structural violence chapter. Since most of this labor takes place in the context of the family, it is important to mention here as a form of abuse. Overall, most children are still helplessly at the bottom of an often-unkind hierarchy, with the youngest the farthest down.

Patterns

Given the extensive financial costs and personal care and attention that raising a healthy child usually entails, and considering the known amounts of abuse and neglect that many of our fellow citizens heap on the young children they have created, child maltreatment mirrors the emotional ambivalence many abusive spouses show toward each other. The child's dependence on the more powerful parent is both a source of affection and of frustration for many adults. Scholars and child advocates typically define child abuse as the deliberate and willful injury of a child by a caretaker adult, most often by hitting, binding, burning, cutting, or pushing (including sexual abuse). Neglect can be more passive and even subtle: treatment of the child that does not adequately (by pediatric and legal standards) care for emotional and physical needs or provide a healthy chance to pass into adulthood. It is a lack of basic nurturance, in other words, and as one might expect, legal definitions and opinions about what constitutes neglect are more variable from state to state and community to community than are ones for physical abuse.

As with the case of woman battering, the figures on the extent of child maltreatment are often rough estimates, for most child abuse and neglect is never reported or is covered up by the abusers. Many times the victims are too young to tell anyone outside the home or to leave home. The child may have been socialized by parents to believe that he or she deserved "appropriate" punishment for some mistake. There are also, to be sure, as with the case of men's traditional "right" to discipline women in the patriarchal home, cultural norms of the "spare the rod and spoil the child" variety that instruct fathers and mothers to incorporate corporal punishment into child rearing. And in reporting violence against the child there is also the problem that both parents can conspire to hide any maltreatment for what they perceive as the good of their overall family relationship, even if only one of them is directly abusing the young person.

Knudsen (1992, 40–47) points out that we basically have four sources of information on child maltreatment: self-reports of victims and perpetrators (sometimes retrospectively obtained), studies done of professionals/agents/clients that deal with the problem, official reports, and "evaluated reports" (that is, cases in which a thorough substantiation of each incident is made). What do all these sources tell us?

Sociologist David Gil has been one of the premier researchers on the subject of child abuse. He estimated as long ago as 1965 that there were anywhere from 2.5 million to 4 million abused children in the United States (1975, 1970). (There are approximately 63 million children aged zero to seventeen years in this country.) At that time critics quickly charged that Gil had greatly exaggerated the problem, but an official study published by the U.S. Department of Health and Human Services pushed the figures of known abuse incidents back toward Gil's original levels. The National Center on Child Abuse and Neglect reported that their estimate of 652,000 instances every year in this country was a bare minimum number. And in a footnote the report followed this figure with another estimate: "Very likely, the actual number of children abused and neglected annually in the U.S. is at least 1,000,000" (U.S. Department of Health and Human Services, 1988, 3). A report by UNICEF (Grant, 1994) noted that reported child abuse cases had tripled during the 1980s. James Grant, executive director of UNICEF, claims that today three children die each day from maltreatment in the United States.

Sociologists Murray A. Straus and Richard J. Gelles looked for evidence of violence against children in both their 1975 and 1985 surveys. They found that young children (zero to three years) were almost all struck (even if only spanked) during both 1975 and 1985. In 1985 (extrapolating to the general population) 6.9 million children aged zero to seventeen years experienced what the researchers rated as severe violence, and 1.5 million experienced what was termed very severe violence. And this the researchers learned in spite of the fact that all the acts of violence were self-reported by the parents!

Curiously, Straus and Gelles report a drop of 47 percent in reports of severely violent incidents against children from 1975 to 1985, but they consider such a drop to represent differences in the ways questions were worded in the two studies and many adult Americans' greater sensitivity to the child abuse issue, hence their reluctance to admit it (Straus and Gelles, 1991a). Nevertheless, despite the fact that there are now compulsory child abuse reporting laws in all fifty states, comparisons of the Straus-Gelles 1985 National Resurvey rates for child abuse with the rates of cases known to the Child Protective Services (CPS) agencies of each state reveal that the incident rates found by the former are about three and one-half times greater than the number of abuse cases known to the CPS agencies. Straus and Gelles (1991b, 111) report: "If child abuse is defined to include hitting a child with an object, then the survey rate is about sixteen times greater than the number of cases reported to protective service agencies in 1985."

Official rates of violence against children have risen dramatically in recent years. For instance, a 1988 national study sponsored by the U.S. Department of Health and Human Services, the National Center on Child Abuse and Neglect, and other federal agencies discovered that since the last major federally sponsored national survey in 1986, there had been significant increases in reporting various kinds of child abuse. To take one illustration: the number of reports of sexual abuse tripled in just two years (xiii–7.5). But many experts, such as Knudsen (1992, 26–37), do not see the United States suddenly undergoing any "epidemic" of adult violence against children. It is simply being recognized and reported more frequently. Douglas J. Besharov, former director of the National Center on Child Abuse and Neglect, has observed that "years of public awareness campaigns and professional education have had their intended effect. Americans are much more sensitive to the plight of maltreated children, and are more willing than ever to report suspected cases" (Besharov, 1988). In fact, some critics have charged that some overzealous "child-savers" are going overboard, creating a child abuse "industry" (Best, 1990; Pride, 1986), reading satanic ritual abuse into situations where violence against children may not even have occurred (Shupe, 1991), and creating a hysteria that, for innocent persons falsely accused by "child-savers," has become akin to the seventeenth-century Salem witch hunt (Gardner, 1991).

In 1989, the federal government established a centralized collection of information on child neglect and abuse, National Child Abuse and Neglect Data System (NCANDS). NCANDS collects case-level data on all children who received a CPS agency response in the form of an investigation response or an alternative response. The Children's Bureau in the Administration for Children and Families, U.S. Department of Health and Human Services, collects and analyzes the data voluntarily submitted by the states, the District of Columbia, and the Commonwealth of Puerto Rico. The first report from NCANDS was based on data for 1990; the most recent report at the time of this writing is for federal fiscal year (FFY) 2010 data, the twenty-first issuance of this annual publication (Children's Bureau, 2011).

According to this report 3.6 million reports of child abuse are made in the United States involving 6 million children (reports can include more than one child and can be reports of one child more than once) (Children's Bureau,

2011). In approximately 20 percent of these reported cases there is agency action taken. The victim rate was 10.0 victims per 1,000 children in the population (this is counting cases where there are repeated reports of abuse or duplicate cases [754,000]); the unique victim rate was 9.2 victims per 1,000 children in the population or 695,000 children (Children's Bureau, 2011). According to the report, the highest rate of victimization (20.6 per 1,000) was for children aged one and under. Of all cases reported boys accounted for 48.5 percent and girls were 51.2 percent of cases; in a little over 1 percent sex was unknown. The most common form of maltreatment was neglect with 78.3 percent, followed by 17.6 percent who suffered physical abuse and 9.2 percent who suffered sexual abuse. For the year 2010, based on the data submitted, there were 1,560 children who died as a result of abuse or neglect, 2.07 deaths per 100,000 children. The vast majority of these children were less than four years old, 79.4 percent. Boy children had a significantly higher rate of deaths than girls, 2.51 vs. 1.73 per 100,000. The ethnic breakdown of unique victims was the following: African American (21.9 percent), Hispanic (21.4 percent), and white (44.8 percent). However, when one calculates rates of victimization the highest rates of victimization are found for African American (14.6 per 1,000), American Indian or Alaska Native (11 per 1,000), and multiple racial descent (12.7 per 1,000). About a third of the deaths were attributed to neglect (32.6 percent). The vast majority of the perpetrators were parents (81.2 percent); of substantiated cases, another 6.1 percent were other relatives. The vast majority of the parents were biological parents, 84.2 percent. Most of the perpetrators were women (53.6 percent), and 84.2 percent of the perpetrators were between twenty and forty-nine years of age, most in the twenty to twenty-nine age group (36 percent).

Dynamics

All family members are capable of emotional maltreatment of one another, and most will have engaged in such psychological abuse at one time or another. Emotional abuse and neglect of children occur most often in families possessing the fewest resources, be these financial, interactive skill-related, or psychological (Knudsen, 1992, 95). The same is true of physical abuse of children. But precisely what causes adult violence toward children in some homes rather than others is a matter of debate. Actually the debate is not so much over what factors are involved as much as over which ones are the most important determiners. Confounding matters is the fact that the dynamics of violence are often not the same in different families. Here is a classic case of the interface of sociological (contextual) parameters within which psychological (individual) differences can operate. Furthermore, the twin notions of patriarchy/hierarchy play an important role in producing the violence.

In recent years there has been a move away from individualistic psychodynamic (i.e., personality) explanations toward more social psychological models that incorporate dimensions of the social environment (Tower, 1989). A recent review (Knudsen, 1992, 63–65) surveying dozens of clinical studies of psychological factors of batterers turned up the following characteristics:

(1) low self-esteem of the violent adult and poor self-concept that fosters feelings that one needs constantly to reinforce or "prove" one's control over the members of the family unit; (2) poorly developed perceptual/attentive/decision-making skills; (3) unrealistic expectations of children's abilities and self-control as well as of the rewards of child rearing in general; and (4) relatively low levels of adult emotional status and competence.

As Shupe, Stacey, and Hazlewood (1987, 33) observe, violence in the home is often "over-determined." This means that one spouse's violence against another, or against a child, "is likely to be a product of more than one cause or influence working simultaneously." Thus, in any single instance of child abuse it is statistically impossible to portion out precisely how much of any of the four factors above contributed to the violence.

Likewise, there have been investigations of victimization, that is, what characteristics of the young victims render them to become more likely targets of violence. These include (1) being born out of wedlock, hence resented by both father and mother; (2) being born prematurely, hence presenting special needs that require greater cost and attention; (3) being born with a congenital infirmity (i.e., deformed and retarded), hence less immediately attractive; and (4) becoming a stepchild (Tower, 1989, 62–63).

Finally, sociological factors in the adult violence-against-children problem include environmental stress, socioeconomic status, gender, and cultural reinforcers. Environmental stress works social psychologically through the phenomenon of excitation (arousal) transfer, which leads an adult already hassled or angered from some other source to take out (or displace) his or her frustration on a child who may simply be boisterous or in some other way behaving perfectly normally for his or her age. Socioeconomic status can be a stressor, particularly where one parent is unemployed, hospitalized, or imprisoned. For example, Stacey and Shupe (1983, 86) found in a study of battered women and their children (many of whom were also abused) that unemployment among abusive men was more than double the highest unemployment rate in their metropolitan area over a two-year period. Likewise, Straus and Smith (1991a, 249–51) found that while official reports show that child advocacy agencies process greater numbers of low-income persons, representative surveys also reveal that lower-income families experience greater rates of such violence. Some of the higher rate for violence against children in these families may be due to an authoritarian style of child rearing, greater acceptance of physical punishment, and less understanding of child psychology that sociologists have long documented (Kohn, 1969), but as Straus and Smith point out, low-income areas also have high rates of violence outside the home as well.

Gender is also an issue (however controversial): patriarchal family structure has traditionally placed women in a role primarily responsible for child rearing. In modern North America, where the family is often a mixture of patriarchal authority and egalitarian economics (i.e., both spouses work), stressors are even greater for women who find themselves in the role-conflictive position of being nurturer/bread-winner/social controller of children's behavior. Moreover, the factors of contraception and mechanization of much work have freed many women from the traditional caregiver domestic role, and the attainment of greater levels of higher education and technical training has accentuated such trends. Straus and Smith (1991a) found in the 1985 Straus-Gelles National Resurvey that women are essentially as abusive of their own children as are men. Such a finding emphasizes the significance of social (as opposed to psychodynamic) factors in making sense of child abuse. Women, it has long been established, are much less likely to be violent outside the home than men. Thus, Straus and Smith conclude, the reasons why women are violent in the home are better explained by their social roles than by any personality characteristics that would otherwise be expected to show up across various social situations within and outside the home.

As feminists have argued over the past five decades, cultural reinforcers (i.e., norms and values) play a critical contextual role in approving or excusing forms of family violence. The same logic that "permits" a man to beat his wife in the quest for domestic harmony and order also "forgives" him for exercising physical, even painful control over recalcitrant children. By extension of patriarchal logic, the woman (as an agent of the man's authority) then is also justified in exercising such control.

VIOLENCE AGAINST THE ELDERLY

Violent abuse and neglect of elderly citizens, or deliberate acts to injure their well-being and exploit their vulnerability, have become of heightened concern in recent years. A major problem in gathering even approximate estimates of much such abuse occurs is that many elderly persons are relatively immobile, essentially living within the somewhat "invisible" context of the home, or likewise "cloistered" in nursing homes where access to them (for reporting purposes) is often limited. During the mid-1970s and early 1980s, when violence within the family generally was becoming recognized as a serious problem, elderly victimization was also acknowledged to exist (Baker, 1975). But few researchers focused on that issue exclusively. Originally the separate problem of elderly abuse and neglect was conceived of strictly in physical terms. (In Great Britain the term used was "granny battering"; in the United States it was colloquially called "granny bashing.") Soon the accompanying psychological harms of battering and assault, or fear of such actions, including intimidation, social isolation, loss of self-esteem/self-confidence/psychological independence, and suicidal tendencies, were drawn into the understanding of this form of violence (Beckman and Adelman, 1992).

Kruger and Pascuahy (1997, 115) define elder abuse and neglect as actions (or deliberate acts of omission) "resulting in actual or threatened harm to the health or welfare of an elderly person." Kruger and Pascuahy claim that the life conditions of well over two million Americans each year fit this definition. Two other researchers, Chen and Koval (2002, 205), writing in an effort to alert orthopedic surgeons (who are often the best equipped specialists to recognize physical abuse symptoms when examining musculoskeletal injuries), said that mistreatment of individuals over the age of sixty-six is a widespread public health problem and that of seniors examined in health facilities "the prevalence of elder abuse is 32 cases per 1,000 persons and is increasing with the growing elderly population."

By the late 1980s every state in this country as well as Great Britain, other European countries (e.g., Bennett, 1992), and the World Health Organization recognized violence against the elderly as a significant concern (Pillemer and Wolf, 1986; Boyank and Berg, 2003; Cooper, Selwood, and Livingstone, 2008). In the United States alone, reported cases of elder abuse roles rose more than 300 percent, from 117,000 reported cases to over 470,000 reported cases between 1986 and 2000 (Lehman, 2002, 5). Such figures, of course, reflect the growing awareness and discovery of the problem. During the 1990s the criminalization of physical abuse against the elderly increased considerably. This criminalization has involved harsher penalties for deliberate and repeated abuse and neglect, more specific investigative procedures used by law enforcement officials, and mandatory reporting legislation affecting a variety of health care professionals. Advocates for the elderly also have directed concentrated efforts at detection of such abuse, not just in private homes by, say, adult children and other relatives, but also in facilities such as nursing homes.

One U.S. Senate Bill (S2933) was introduced in 2000 (sponsored by both Republicans and Democrats) to create special federal offices focusing on "elder justice," specifically to fund prevention, detection, and treatment of victims and increased prosecution of perpetrators. Sponsor Senator John Breaux (Democrat-Louisiana) said that compared to better recognized issues such as woman battering and child abuse, "elder abuse has not received sustained federal attention and resources." The bill provided for FBI criminal background checks for employees of long-term nursing facilities, funding projects addressing the shortage of staff in such facilities, incentives for attracting more health care professionals into gerontology, grants to educate law enforcement officials and prosecutors on this abuse problem, and forensic training for physicians and geriatricians (Lehman, 2002, 5).

Awareness of elderly citizens' vulnerability is growing. Anecdotally our own 2011 browsing on the Internet revealed a large number of law firms specializing in and advertising their services for nursing home neglect and elderly violence litigation. More significantly, in 2011 the North American Securities and Administrators Association and the National Adult Protective Services Association (the latter group made up largely of social workers) have started providing primary care physicians and other medical professionals a four-page informational packet providing names and websites for such groups as the National Center on Elder Abuse and the National Academy of Elder Law Attorneys.

One particular set of problems confronting elderly citizens is financial, not just in cases of adult children withholding welfare or Social Security checks from weaker parents, but more in cases of a host of persons trying to exploit the elderly who may be lacking in sound judgment about monetary issues. According to a 2008 Duke University study, one-third of people over the age of seventy-one are in some way cognitively impaired, making them more likely to make financial errors or to be persuaded to invest unwisely with their limited incomes. Con artists attempt to tap into the resources of this sometimes economically vulnerable segment of the population. The director of the Texas Consortium Geriatric Education Center of the Baylor College of Medicine (in Houston) observes: "[Elderly] people become less risk-averse and become victims of unscrupulous families, friends, people they know from church or real estate agents. . . . When we look more closely, we find they have lost their executive function, or their ability to plan, or organize and remember details" (Olson, 2011). The result is the possibility of predators seeking to take advantage of elderly persons with con games such as sure-fire-can't-lose business propositions, investment schemes, and other scams meant to separate gullible, even impaired seniors from their money. An Investors Protection Trust survey in 2010 found that one in five North Americans over sixty-five years of age had been defrauded at sometime, with almost 40 percent of these elderly persons reporting that they had received solicitations or letters asking for money from bogus charities and fly-by-night investments to manipulative television evangelists (Olson, 2011). Consistent with our earlier definition of violence in chapter 1, such abusive financial activities directed particularly at the elderly and diminishing their well-being qualify as violence.

SIBLING VIOLENCE

Rivalry and violence between siblings has a rich cultural legacy, from the Roman legends of Romulus and Remus to the biblical account of brutal fratricide in Cain's slaying of his brother Abel in the opening chapters of Genesis. Experts usually do *not* include in the category of sibling violence the prosaic "roughhouse" play behaviors of wrestling, pushing, and shoving that occur so frequently in homes but rather focus on severe aggression, such as one sibling getting another in a stranglehold or putting the other in a headlock and punching the face repeatedly. This type of violence can result in serious immediate harm and endangerment, not to mention immediate and later-life emotional damage.

Ironically sibling violence is a far more common form of family violence than other better publicized types, such as inter-adult violence and adult-child abuse, according to Caffaro and Conn-Caffaro (1998). In 1993, these authors report, there were 1,250,000 confirmed cases of serious sibling violence within the United States, but actually such estimates, even if doubled or tripled, are likely gross underestimates and represent merely the severest cases of *known* violence. There are several reasons for thinking that we are aware of only the tip of an enormous iceberg.

For instance, sibling violence occurs often (but not exclusively) within the home where the typical witnesses, if any, remain other family members. And if the perpetrator is an older brother or sister, which is typically the case, the younger-weaker siblings may easily be intimidated into silence. Sibling violence goes unreported so frequently because some amounts of competition, emotionally charged outbursts, and aggressive physical contact are so much a part of many American homes. Few parents wish to report even serious incidences to civil or school authorities because at the very least it implies a loss of parental control or skill on their part. And few victimization surveys "target" this specific form of family violence. Moreover, there is the fact that most forms of non-life-endangering sibling violence tend to taper off as siblings move through adolescence into their teenage years (Finkelhor, 1995; Whipple and Finton, 1995; Wiehe, 1997, 2002; Butler, 2006).

But researchers, as Butler (2006) states in her review of previous studies, acknowledge that in serious cases "sibling violence becomes a form of repeated, inescapable and emotionally damaging abuse." The debate as to gender differences in perpetration-victimization is ongoing. One study of 2,030 children conducted by the University of New Hampshire's noted family sociologist David Finkelhor found that overall 35 percent of the youthful respondents reported they had been attacked by a sibling; 13 percent had been injured; and 6 percent had been attacked by a sibling with a weapon. Victims are typically between six and twelve years old and male (Butler, 2006). Alternately, earlier researchers Goodwin and Roscoe (1990) found relatively few gender differences as to the extent of violence or perpetration. Statistics in sibling incest and sexual abuse are even murkier. The figure of 15 percent of all adults reporting having experienced some kind of youthful sibling sexual contact and/or incest (Katy, 2009) is questionably reliable due to vague definitions of the acts themselves, understandable reasons for psychological repression/denial and/or later-life reinterpretations of such events, and the passage of time diminishing memory.

Current victims' advocacy groups like SASIAN (Sibling Abuse Survivors Information and Advisory Network) monitor official and academic statistics, mindful that whatever the true statistical extent of the sibling violence problem, it is a harsh reality for many children, their families, and clinical counselors who must deal regularly with its consequences, even if sibling violence (as one review of past studies found; see Jaffe, Sudermann, and Reitzel, 1992, 314–16) is "merely" the result of children watching their parents violently abuse each other and then mimicking and redirecting that violence onto each other.

DATING VIOLENCE

Dating violence (or violence committed between intimate or casual partners who are not cohabitating) has been considered in recent years an important "barometer" or predictor of future family violence. During dating formally uncommitted young adults (it is mostly teenagers with whom we are concerned here) are conventionally thought to be on better behavior in such tentative relationships than they might otherwise be in more permanent arrangements. On the latter assumption, recent results from a variety of sources suggest otherwise.

In a widely cited study, Silverman, Raj, Mucci, and Hathaway (2001) found that one in three U.S. teens had experienced violence from a partner on at least one date. The dynamics seem to be that in teen relationships (sixteen to twenty years of age), when the partners are relatively inexperienced in life and often hold idealistic expectations of love and intimacy, considerable frustration arises. The primary issues revolve around decision making, or control, within the couple. (As we noted in an earlier section of this chapter about family violence *the control motive* is an important source of tension, argument, and ultimately violence: who has the final say, whose will is dominant, who charts the priorities of the relationship.) They found that young men tended to assume or insist that this control was a male prerogative; not all young women agreed to go along with such an asymmetrical power arrangement. Young women also tended to take more personal responsibility for relationships' problems and felt "reinforced" in assuming the normality of control issue conflict since so many of their female friends reported experiencing the same problems. These issues carried over, predictably, in decisions about sexual intimacy; indeed, reports of physical violence usually are couched by researchers as within the "physical and/or sexual" category in surveys.

A Bureau of Justice special report on intimate partner violence from 2006 found similar patterns. One in five couples reported purely physical aggression (punishment in the form of slaps, shoves, and so forth) and/or sexual violence, including rape. Between 30 and 50 percent of female high school students in the United States reported having experienced such behavior, with the ages sixteen to twenty-four experiencing the highest rates of intimate violence (20 per 1,000 respondents; Bureau of Justice, 2006). Moreover, data from 1993–2004 showed that teens who had been under the age of twelve while living in households where inter-adult violence occurred were more likely to experience later dating violence (about a 2-to-1 victimization likelihood for females as opposed to males).

The pattern seems explainable: whether dating violence reveals the likelihood of "copy-cat" violence by young persons (or what is formally termed *the generational transfer effect*) from family influences and/or is abetted by the influence of a cultural preoccupation with violence in news and entertainment (movies, television programs, fiction, video games and the Internet, and music), dating violence reveals a continuum of violence from pre-family heterosexual relationships to more established conventional marriages (Archer, 2000).

VIOLENCE AGAINST PETS

One of us co-authoring a book on family violence during the early years of recognizing the problem (Stacey and Shupe, 1983) began the first chapter with a dramatic "grabber": in *The Burning Bed*, author Faith McNulty told the harrowing story of battered wife Francine Hughes and her abusive, sometimes sadistic husband, Mickey. Before Francine eventually poured gasoline on Mickey after he had passed out in a post-beating drunken stupor, threw a lighted match on him, and burned him to death (along with destroying the entire house), Mickey had forced the pregnant family dog out into the backyard on a bitter winter's night just as the mother went into labor. Both mother dog and newborn pups froze to death.

Initially we thought this grotesque story was simply an extreme anecdote of callousness accompanying the sociopathic batterer's personality. Now, in hindsight, the incident takes on clearer meaning as part of an established pattern. Animal control and police officers, animal care advocates, women's shelter staffs, and violence experts in general acknowledge that violence against domestic animals is a frequent accompaniment of violence against other family members. Such groups as the Society for the Prevention of Cruelty to Animals are now firm allies with the movements to end violence against women, children, and others within the home. The link between cruelty to pets and general violence in the American home has been indisputably established by sociological, psychological, and psychiatric sources (Ascione, Weber, and Ward, 1997; Wilson and Norris, 2003).

The reasons and dynamics are interwoven. Household pets are *dumb* animals (which does not mean they are less intellectually developed or feeling for their evolutionary level but that they are simply unable to communicate symbolically in the same ways as more articulate humans). Thus they cannot report what they see, hear, or experience. They are vulnerable "at-risk" potential victims, often at the mercy of, or dependent upon, humans for the basic necessities of life, freedom of movement, and safety. In many ways pets become trapped in violent households with little recourse of summoning help or escaping. Often there are no witnesses to violence committed against them or the neglect they suffer as sentient beings.

Feminists, who have recognized that many physically smaller, relatively resource-poor women share the same vulnerability as household animals, have made common cause with animal advocates (see, e.g., Adams and Donovan, 1996). The issues of control, domination, explosive anger directed at weaker targets, and low impulse control are essentially the same. In addition, affection and bonding with pets has been found to be a "level" of control for abusive men to pressure women into committing illegal actions (for example, theft) by men threatening pets (Loring and Bolden-Himes, 2004). Possible endangerment of pets "abandoned" to more violence if the women leave home to flee to women's shelters can also be a decisive factor in battered women choosing to remain in the home since most shelters will not accept pets (Faver and Strand, 2003).

Moreover, children in abusive homes, either themselves directly hurt or modeling parental violent behavior, can transfer (or redirect) the violence against pets (Ascione, 1998). Some experts warn that childhood cruelty toward animals can serve as *desensitizing* or "anticipatory socialization" experiences for later adult violence in relationships. Certainly the lack of empathy mixed with unrestrained anger is unhealthy to experience or witness during younger formative years. Alternately, love of a pet is an additional source of terror for children when the animal is callously victimized in front of them. According to a survey by Ascione (1998), about one-half of incidences in the home involving violence against pets had a father, stepfather, or mother as perpetrator, and half the children in the survey said they had tried to protect pets from adult violence. Pet violence adds to a volatile crucible within which many children grow up.

At the very least, a battered partner who is concerned for herself or her children's safety, often physically and psychologically injured, is a less than effective steward of household animals' welfare and may dysfunctionally begin to scapegoat blame for her predicament onto a pet. The animals becomes in effect a convenient outlet, or "proxy," for human problems with violence and anger. Like abuse between adult partners or against the elderly or against children, the "invisibility" of much of the violent deviance against pets in the home renders any "official" statistics (based on reported cases city-by-city or state-by-state since there is no national or referral repository for such data) merely guesstimates of the real prevalence of such abuse

FAMILY VIOLENCE IN A GLOBAL HIERARCHICAL PERSPECTIVE

The family violence problem in the United States is widespread and, from a researcher's perspective, somewhat intimidating in its enormity. There are so many aspects that we cannot even touch on here. But out of all the rich data collected by the Family Research Laboratory at the University of New Hampshire, Straus (1983) stresses that one fact emerges: violence begets violence, so children in violent homes are more likely to be violent toward their siblings and later in their adult relationships with partners as well as with their own children and pets.

We indicated earlier that child maltreatment occurs worldwide. In some ways the United States sees fewer of the worst cases than many other countries. We have, for example, no teenage or preteen girls sold to legalized brothels by their parents. But there is evidence that men's violence against women in the United States may be closely equivalent to that of other Western countries as varied as England, New Zealand, Canada, Scotland (Burgess and Garbarino, 1983), France, and even Papua New Guinea (Neal, 1992). Likewise, studies have been done of Afro-Caribbean women (Morrow, 1992) and in South Asian families in the United States (Abraham, 1992). Denmark established its first "halfway house" for battered men in the late '80s. Today, there are men's shelters as well as gender-neutral shelters in at least five additional countries and nine states.

Violence against women is worse in non-Western societies where traditions of patriarchy are even more ingrained and concepts of equal rights for both sexes are less developed. Mary Daly (1978) catalogs in gruesome detail how men have subordinated women through the centuries by binding their feet (Manchu-dynasty China), mutilating (i.e., circumcising) their genitals, immolating them as "dutiful wives" in ritual funeral fires with the bodies of their deceased husbands (the Hindu ritual of suttee), and torturing them (along with males) in Nazi pseudo-scientific experiments. In modern India, dowry deaths, in which a woman who has contributed a dowry to her husband's family upon marriage is killed by her husband or in-laws, are becoming more common as women are becoming emancipated, increasingly involved in the labor force and exposed to nontraditional lifestyle options, and resistant to patriarchy (Rao, 1992; Kumari, 1989).

Thus, violence in the home, within a place usually thought of as a safe haven from an often unfeeling and even brutal world, can ironically feed on the properties of intimacy that most of us consider normal for a family. A major reason that such violence is so widespread and so systematic is that most families are hierarchies, with unequal distribution of power and decision-making authority. Perceived threats to that authority can be dealt with in a variety of ways, but obviously one strategy is the violence option. To that extent the relationships among power, conflict, and violence in the home resemble those in the large asymmetric hierarchy of society.

DISCUSSION QUESTIONS

1. What actions could you take in your own family arrangement that might reduce the possibility of violence in your own family and the future families your grown children might create?
2. What does the "up-and-down" historical awareness and concern about family violence say more generally about how our society perceives social problems?
3. What is the common thread running through a husband beating his wife, an older brother systematically frightening and hurting a younger sibling, or anyone in the family abusing a grandparent or pet?
4. If you were to create a violence-free household, what methods would you use to discipline your children if they misbehaved?
5. If you were to create a violence-free household, what methods would you use to prevent your children from using physical violence between each other?

Chapter Five

Educational Violence

On October 17, 2006, three weeks before her fourteenth birthday, a Dardenne Prairie, Missouri, teenager named Megan Meier hanged herself. Since the third grade Megan had been under the care (with supervised medications) of a psychiatrist for depression, attention deficit disorder, and continual struggles with her weight. By eighth grade she was attending Immaculate Conception Catholic School. In retaliation for supposedly spreading gossip about her own daughter (a classmate of Megan), Lori Drew (along with several accomplices) created a MySpace account and cultivated the image of a fictitious sixteen-year-old male named Josh Evans. This "Josh" character became Megan's online friend.

In the beginning "Josh"-Drew and Megan exchanged friendly messages. Gradually, however, "Josh" methodically began accusing Megan of gossiping about her friends, Megan found her more personal messages to the fabricated "Josh" posted elsewhere on the Internet, and "Josh" became hypercritical of Megan, calling her "fat" and a "whore." "Josh's" last message to her read "Everybody . . . knows who you are. You are a bad person and everybody hates you. Have a bad rest of your life. The world would be a better place without you." Greatly upset, Megan responded with a final message; then twenty minutes later she was found dead in her bedroom closest.

Eventually Megan's parents learned of Lori Drew's complicity in harassing their daughter. Drew was indicted, tried, and convicted in 2008 for contributing to the suicide, but later she was acquitted on appeal in 2009. This was the country's first major publicized case of cyberbullying (Megan Meier Foundation, 2008; Zetter, 2007).

Schools, public or private, were once thought relatively safe havens compared to life "on the street" or in "the real world." This notion now has been pretty much dismissed as fanciful at best. Once upon a time there were only drills for fires, possible Cold War air raids, and perhaps tornados. That was before armed guards, metal detectors, sniper drills, drug-sniffing dogs, and lockdowns became something unfortunately commonplace in schools, not just in the United States but around the world. Worse, the educational institution now has some forms of violence that can be considered unique to its hallowed halls.

In this chapter we consider several important forms of violence in schools. We will be describing forms of violence that occur between students and between student and teacher. Many forms of violence that occur within the institutional context of the school have been a recent focus of attention in the mass media. The violence of school shootings has been a focus since the shooting at Columbine High School. More recently the violence of bullying has come to the media's attention. But there also are types of violence within the school that are not seen as violence but fit the definition that is used in this text. The violence of corporal punishment is one example of a form of violence that is administered within the school as a means of direct social control. Most schools within the United States allow for some form of physical violence directed at students to control their behavior. There are also other forms of violence that occur within the schools that have a long history and are directed at those who are in minority positions within society. This is the symbolic violence that is part of the cultural and physical genocide of dominated populations or subgroups. These are all forms of institutional violence where the violence only occurs within the context of the school as it is defined by the role behavior of actors. In this chapter we examine several forms of educational violence: school bullying, rape (teacher-student and student-student), school massacres, corporal punishment, and symbolic violence.

SCHOOL BULLYING

Since the early 1990s, bullying behavior in schools has become recognized as a major dimension of educational violence and the one most young persons will encounter. It also presents a controversial subject: some say it is an exaggerated problem, or just a boyhood ritual of establishing a "pecking order" on the playground, or part of a leftist campaign to privilege gays and "sneak" the homosexual lifestyle into our schools, or a serious threat not just to the order in a school necessary for quality instruction but also a provable danger that has resulted in a number of publicized teenage suicides by bullied youths. Some call for congressional hearings, write legions of books on the subject (how to recognize it, how to prevent it, and so forth), and decry bullying as a significant menace undermining American education. The opinion that school bullying has reached alarming rates has at least convinced Nickelodeon, the popular children's television cable network, starting in 2011 to run public service announcements offering advice to young people who feel they are being bullied (Bauder, 2011).

Let us sort out some facts and positions. In the United Kingdom (where bullying behavior, or *bullycide* as it is known, is also a high publicized problem), bullying in schools is defined as "a pattern of behavior whereby one person with a lot of internal anger, resentment, and aggression and lacking interpersonal skills chooses to displace their aggression onto another person, chosen for their vulnerability with respect to the bully." (BullyingOnline.org).

There are several social science issues in this definition, both psychological and sociological: bullies have repressed anger and ongoing simmering resentment/frustration and lack the social skills and internal controls to deal with such feelings or express them appropriately (i.e., nonviolently); and as a result bullies select weaker (often younger) targets as scapegoats and safe victims because of an imbalance of physical or social power between the bully and victim.

Considerable research in the United States and across Europe has shown that school bullies often operate within a constellation of socio-personal problems: violent parental and sibling role models; frustrating/repressive/neglectful child-rearing experience; poor anger management and impulse control; violent peers; a mass media glorifying violence; and learning disadvantages that have previously lowered their self-esteem. Further, bullying behavior can be physical (assault, intimidation); verbal (constant taunting, teasing, and belittling criticism as well as attempts to isolate the victims and drive away other contacts); and/or emotional (actually establishing a codependent relationship with victims;—see Smith, 1999; Javonen, 2001; Smith, Pepler, and Rigby 2004; Jimerson, 2010). School bullies are also, at times, adept at manipulating adults, themselves capable of playing the role of misunderstood victims. Bullies can be masters of denial and rationalizing or minimalizing (neutralizing) their aggressive actions (Smith, 1999; Rigby, 2001).

In fact, researchers have found through the lens of role network theory and using such established measurement instruments as the Olweus Bully/Victim Questionnaire on large student populations that the image of the "lone" bully is a misnomer (even if the bully is not part of "pack bullying," which better resembles proto-gang behavior). Within the "domain" of the active bully is actually a web of interpenetrating relationships as "parts" or roles in the aggressive drama: Bully, Bully Reinforcer, Assistant to the Bully, Victim, Defender of the Victim, and Outsider Observer. Boys more frequently fill the first three roles, while girls more often take the last two roles. Interestingly most participants in whatever activity surrounds bullying incidents choose charitably to see themselves as either Defender of the Victim or Outsiders (Solberg and Olweus, 2003; Salmivalli, Lagerspetz, Bjorkvist, Osterman, and Kaukiainen, 1996).

The National Conference of State Legislators has estimated that in 2007 nearly one-third of students twelve to eighteen years of age reported having been bullied or have been bullies (NCSL, 2011). The characteristics of victims have been found to be varied: ethnicity, race, gender, physical size or disability, religion, and sexual orientation. Bullying seems to be more common among middle school rather than high school students and peaks in late adolescence (suggesting that it stabilizes and even begins to wane with greater psychological and physical maturity). Males are typically more physical in their bullying tactics than females (yet males are also more likely to cyberbully, i.e, aggressing by means of the Internet, cell phones, texting, and so forth) while young females use more subtle, indirect, nonphysical manipulative tactics. Females seem most likely to bully other females, while males are more likely to abuse *both* males and females (Pezanoski-Browne, 2010).

Bullying is also connected to the hierarchical structure of the peer social structure in middle and high schools. Based on a review of ethnographic studies of adolescent peer cultures, structured and unstructured interviews, and responses to survey questionnaires completed by nearly 100,000 middle school and high school students, Bishop and colleagues found that the violation of teen hierarchies by students will bring about bullying and harassment (Bishop et al., 2004). Furthermore, they found that students would achieve status within their groups by harassing and bullying students who were defined to be of low status because of their size, their appearance, the clothes that they wore, or just being classified as a "nerd." "Maybe they like to prove to their friends that they're cool, that they can put someone else down without [being put down themselves]" (Bishop et al., 2004, 237). The survey completed in 1998–1999 found that 13.1 percent of boys and 6.7 percent of girls were "teased, insulted, or made fun of to my face" almost every day. Another 19.5 percent of boys and 13.3 percent of girls reported that they were insulted to their face "about once a week." Another 16 percent of boys and 12.7 percent of girls indicated that "almost every day" they were "insulted or made fun of behind your back." Almost 4 percent of students (an estimated 890,000 students) reported being "pushed, tripped, or hurt by other students" almost every day. Another 4.3 percent reported it happened about once a week (Bishop et al., 2004, 237). Staff and Kreager find that the victims of bullying and different forms of shaming become alienated from social relations at school (Staff and Kreager, 2008). Milner (2004) claims that the cruelty that pervades social relationships at school is the product of the elitist peer-status systems and the competition resulting from a largely inexpansible resource such as prestige. This competitive environment perpetuates a sense of insecurity among students who don't possess the material accoutrements of high status and are classified as outsiders or marginal to the social structure.

Bullying is clearly a problem for teachers as well as students: as violence it disturbs and distracts students' attention/concentration on scholastics and occupies teacher time in intervening instead of spending time on instruction. As any kindergarten, middle school, or high school teacher, or even college professors, can attest, even one continually disruptive student (overtly violent or not) can interrupt the learning "flow" of an entire class meeting.

So what can be finally and succinctly said about bullying from a perspective that meaningfully sorts out myths, trends, and prospects for dealing with the problem in schools? Dr. Susan M. Swearer, educational psychologist, is the coauthor of *Bullying Prevention and Intervention: Realistic Strategies for Schools* (Swearer, Espelage, and Napolitan, 2009). She suggests that we recognize several "facts" about the prevalent problem of bullying:

1. Bullying, like any abuse, is somewhat subjectively experienced. Most teens are connected to the Internet, just as most are not cyberbullied (nor consider themselves to ever have been). In fact, most bullied youths are not cyberbullied. Bullying is usually face-to-face, whether verbal or physical.
2. The clear distinction between victims and bullies is often false. Many bullies are themselves victims of current or past bully behavior (at home, school, or elsewhere) so they are passing on the abuse they themselves experience(d). Eventually some bullying victims will also go on later in life to become bullies themselves, such as in the workplace, where such nonphysical aggressive behavior will be less easily identified as such.
3. Bullying as a pattern may recede later in the bully's life, but the emotional effects on victims can be long-lasting.
4. Contrary to what some spectacular youth suicides (such as our opening example) might suggest, we cannot directly blame most teen suicides solely on bullying. Bullied persons often possess a matrix of other problems. Bullying, however, may become a suicide trigger.
5. Bullying in schools can be reliably identified, steps can be taken to educate students and teachers, positive steps can be made to deal directly with the bullies themselves, *but ultimately bullying behavior itself can never be eradicated* because our definitions of what constitutes bullying are constantly evolving alongside our awareness of it. (See also Swearer, 2010.)

While most states have some form of anti-bullying laws, and in 2009 the House Education Committee of the U.S. Congress began holding a series of hearings to consider what, if anything, can be done legislatively through selective funding of anti-bullying measures at the federal level (Bruce, 2009), legislators at every level do not find the anti-bullying controversy a straightforward one to negotiate. In Indiana, for example, this conservative state already has anti-bullying laws in place. The suicide of bullied fifteen-year-old Billy Lucas of the Greensburg School District in 2010 inspired an initiative for more stringent punitive measures to be taken against bullies themselves (Brooks, 2010). Indiana law already prescribed that all schools present formal anti-bullying programs for students and teachers. A new bill (No. 538) was proposed by two conservative Republican state senators to include gender orientation as a recognized "target" of bullying. The bill died in committee in March 2011, but not before it provoked more controversy. It was opposed by conservative "family values" groups such as the Indiana Family Institute (an affiliate of the American Family Institute), which described the bill as part of a larger "homosexual left" agenda and labeled the two avowedly conservative senators as "far-left" sponsors. The Indiana Family Institute (IFI) said in a statement that "many bullying bills and programs have become a Trojan Horse for homosexual demands groups. . . . There is a danger in uniformly casting students with traditional values as bullies, silencing legitimate views, or creating specially protected classes of children as opposed to focusing on actual acts of bullying" (cited in Kennedy, 2011). One central Indiana newspaper dryly commented: "Senate Bill 538's undeserved demise illustrates how some legislation in the current session is being driven not by reason and testimony but by wild-eyed assertions." (*Fort Wayne Journal Gazette*, 2011)

As one former director of the Indiana American Civil Liberties Union, Sheila Kennedy, put it, this proposed gender orientation addition by the Indiana senators was intended (in the IFI's minds) to "stigmatize those who express their disapproval of homosexuality with enthusiasm." In other words, bullying against members of groups is not really bullying if it is done out of motives stemming from traditional conservative values. Kennedy recalls one bullying instance in a southern Indiana middle school where a twelve-year-old boy was routinely beaten up on the playground by those who identified him as gay. Though the young man's parents repeatedly complained to the school administration, the school principal bluntly told the ACLU lawyer handling the case that the victim brought it on himself "by acting different" (Kennedy, 2011).

Gender is a major element in defining the status structure of schools. According to Malaby, masculinity at school is constructed around dominant cultural discourses and ideologies that link with power relations within the school peer social structure. This masculinity is defined in terms of physical strength and bravado; suppression of certain feminized feelings such as re-morse, empathy, and uncertainty; strict heterosexuality; economic power; authority over women and other men; and capacity for violence and aggres-sion (Malaby, 2007, 158). Malaby notes that the males who are placed in nonmasculine categories are subject to a variety of disciplinary procedures whose purpose is to maintain them on the margins.

Gender orientation is not an issue isolated to conservative "red states" like Indiana. The American Principles Project executive director Andy Bloom spoke at the February 2011 Tea Party Policy Summit in Arizona and railed against anti-bullying laws *in general* at both state and national levels, basing his opposition on the Trojan-Horse-sneaking-gay-values-into-law ar-gument (Fang, 2011). Meanwhile, pop entertainer Britney Spears and other celebrities announced that the next month they were joining President and Mrs. Barak Obama in an anti-bullying campaign, meeting for its inaugural conference in Washington, D.C. (VH1, 2011). Recently, the Southern Pover-ty Law Center, a civil rights advocacy group, along with the Justice Depart-ment, won a landmark suit against Minnesota's largest school district to protect students, especially LGBT students, from bullying in the schools (Southern Poverty Law Center, 2012). The Anoka-Hennepin School District had at least four LGBT students die by suicide over a two-year period after they experienced bullying and physical assaults because of their sexual orien-tation. The case won by the Southern Poverty Law Center and the Justice Department requires that the school district take specific steps to address and prevent anti-LGBT harassment.

By the new millennium's second decade, the debate was ongoing, some persons conflating the sexual orientation issue with the entire school bullying problem. However, the seriousness of the bullying problem, in the minds of most schoolteachers, administrators, parents, and a good number of scholars and politicians, barely merits debate: bullying endangers the physical, emo-tional, and psychological well-being of students; fuels unnecessary tensions both in the classroom and on the playground; and wastes valuable instructional time. Concern with bullying is not the singular result of any uniquely homosexual initiative (though homosexuals have real concern that their sexual orientation has at times realistically been singled out for particular hate violence). That the entire bullying issue has become part of a conservative backlash flavored by part of the national political culture is unfortunate and, in the opinions of many concerned about this form of educational violence, regressive.

SCHOOL RAPE

School rape (of students by students, of students by teachers, and of teachers by students) is another clear indicator that schools are not the safe havens they were once thought to be. Most of these acts of violence also occur when actors are misusing their institutional roles for personal reasons. School rape occurs at all levels. There are cases of sexual violence directed at young children, like the case of English language instructors in Thailand who have been accused of raping young girls and boys in their charge (Goldman, 2007). In one study done on the incidence of sexual assault in rural schools in Zimbabwe, the author found that over the year period of police reports, 98 percent of the 108 victims were female; the modal age for sexual abuse was twelve years, which represents 46 percent of reported cases; and 69 percent of the cases were between eleven and thirteen years of age (Nhundu and Shumba, 2001). In the United States, most of the violence of rape occurs between students at the high school and college levels (see National Center for Educational Statistics, 2004, 18–19). By now fairly reliable statistics reveal a general pattern: between one in four and one in five college women report surviving rape or attempted rape (Warsaw, 1994; Douglas et al., 1997; Tjaden and Thoennes, 1998), and the statistics are similar for high school females (Davis, Peck, and Starment, 1993). Most of the victims are women; the numbers for young men claiming to be rape victims are in the very low single digits (Tjaden and Thoennes, 1998; Douglas et al., 1997; Greenfield, 1997).

Most victims of school rapes previously knew their attackers (Dunn et al., 1999), often not only from their same schools but also from their same neighborhoods (Greenfield, 1997). The various injuries of such rapes can be physical, mental, and social: ranging from actual bodily injury, eventual pregnancy, and/or contraction of venereal disease, to depression, guilt, and blaming oneself (some 55 percent of young women involved in acquaintance rape reportedly were drinking or taking drugs at the time [Warsaw, 1994]), to shame and even social ostracism as the attackers may boast to peers of their "conquests" and others blame the victims for somehow having "invited" the attacks.

This social ostracism is significant, particularly for teenage victims. Two recent cases in point illustrate this last tragic fact. First, in a 2009 incident in Richmond, California (a small city outside San Francisco), a fifteen-year-old girl attending a high school homecoming dance was gang-raped repeatedly outside the school while as many as twenty young men stood watching over a two and one-half hour period. Police immediately arrested and jailed two male suspects and soon after posted a $20,000 reward for informants to come forward. According to one police officer, "She was raped, beaten, robbed, and dehumanized by several suspects who were obviously OK enough with it to behave in that way in each other's presence" (Kates, 2009). Word about the attack spread quickly throughout the school as well as the stigma that became attached to her as the victim, as if she played some willing part in the atrocity.

A second case also illustrates victim shame and school insensitivity, yet also the victim's refusal to accept the stigma. A high school rape victim, a young woman on a cheerleading squad, was sexually assaulted by a star male athlete on the school's football team (and the assault became common knowledge to her classmates). Thereafter she refused as a matter of conscience to cheer for that athlete at home games and as a result was removed from the cheerleading squad. Her family sued school administrators for acting insensitively both to her victimization and subsequent squad removal as well as to the continual taunting by fellow students. The court "no-billed" the rape accusation because of lack of witnesses (common enough in such cases), and there was no conviction nor even any arrest of the alleged rapist. One of the victim's complaints was that school administrators criticized her for not "living up to her responsibilities as a cheer-leader" (Netter, 2010).

Most of the perpetrator-victim pairs represent student-on-student assaults. Some, however, involved teacher-on-student rapes. Male instructors engaged in statutory (i.e., nonviolent, noncoercive) rapes with young females, however consensual they may seem to participants, are the most frequent. Adults in such cases are, of course, legal fiduciaries, that is, persons in positions of superior authority and experience/knowledge with a responsibility for the well-being of their more vulnerable young charges. By sexually exploiting their positions of authority, no matter how consensual such liaisons superficially seem in the eyes of both partners, these fiduciaries betray their role responsibilities both interpersonally and institutionally as well as commit, technically in a criminological sense, sexual assault. As one anonymous commentator, angrily writing in a newspaper about a 2008 Clarksville, Tennessee, male high school teacher who in 2008 was convicted of statutory rape of a female student (but only received a 120-day jail sentence and two years' probation), expressed this fiduciary-betrayal sentiment: "I am especially appalled by this case. Teenagers may act grown up and may look grown up, but in many cases they are not adults. Teenage girls are under a lot of pressure to look thin, attractive and sexy. An older man could take advantage of their infatuation and inexperience. Teenagers have had crushes on their teachers for years—that is no excuse for a teacher to rape a student" (Commentary Guest, 2008).

One particular area of teacher-on-student sexual assault that has received an enormous amount of publicity in recent years has involved considerably older women fixating obsessively on adolescent and teenage boys, with many of these women perpetrators already married and sometimes with previous children of their own. Our own area of northeastern Indiana has been particularly replete with such cases, and we witnessed in communities surrounding Fort Wayne an avalanche not only of male coaches, principals, teachers, and guidance counselors molesting youths through love letters on the Internet, having sex with them on the wrestling mats, holding trysts in school classrooms after hours, sending them feminine underwear, meeting them in parked cars, and so forth, but also of females acting in kind.

One female molester, Kimberley Kleber, a forty-year-old guidance counselor at the Indian Village Woods Middle School, in 2000 was arrested and charged with two felony counts of sexual misconduct. Her victim was a fifteen-year-old boy in her charge. She had fondled the young man and had sex repeatedly with him between December 1999 and August 2000 on a school playground and in various school offices. The young man had a troubled past, having been shifted among various schools, and was eventually released from the Indiana Boys School. In 2000 Kleber faced a six- to twenty-year sentence if convicted; she pleaded guilty, but was never incarcerated and was instead put on probation. By 2001 she resumed the physical relationship with the boy. In one month she met with him three times, violating terms of her probation. By 2002 the male was seventeen years old and she was having sex with him repeatedly in her car, at her home, behind a shopping mall, and so forth. At her final tryst with him she was apprehended by authorities in an intimate act at a gas station and arrested yet again (*Fort Wayne Journal Gazette*, 2001, 2002). In 2011 another Fort Wayne female teacher, Kristi N. Metzger, twenty-eight, resigned after having been charged with having sex with a fifteen-year-old boy. She had sex with him at her home five times, plying him with beer on each occasion (Haynie, 2011).

But the record for notoriety and obsession for a teenage boy by a predatory female schoolteacher undoubtedly is held by Mary Kay Letourneau, at the time a thirty-five-year-old Seattle, Washington, woman who became enamored with a thirteen-year-old male middle school student. Letourneau at the time was married and had several small children. During the initial mid-1990s affair, Letourneau became pregnant with the boy's child and gave birth. (Her husband, meanwhile, disgustedly took their children and left her, successively obtaining divorce.) Having encountered the courts before (Mary Kay was first handed a six-month jail sentence after she pleaded guilty to child rape), she was released from jail on probation on the condition she have no contact with the young man (by now fourteen years of age). However, soon she was discovered by police in 1998 having sex with him (now fifteen years of age) in a car with the windows steamed in a parking lot along with $6,200 in cash and her passport. This time Letourneau was sent to prison for seven and a half years. She claimed she and the youth "were in love." The couple announced their intention to marry when she was released (*Fort Wayne Journal Gazette*, 1998), and they did so in 2005.

Not all adults see this pattern as sexual assault or rape. One judge opined: "I really don't see the harm that was done and certainly don't need to be worried. It's just something between two people that clicked beyond the teacher-student relationship" (*Philadelphia Inquirer*, 2002). This casual attitude is not totally isolated. One mother, as reported in 1996 in the Associated Press, even tried in 1994 to extort $15,000 in payments from a female school principal who she had learned had raped her twelve-year-old son when he was in the sixth grade. The principal was supposedly "counseling" the boy for misbehaving in class. The mother told reporters, "Part of his psyche was missing, and I wanted to make him whole. He said no one had ever loved him before" (Associated Press, 1996). Whether this was simple rationalization or not, she overlooked the assault, realized its possible benefit, and wanted hush money from the administrator.

Something similar to the Letourneau case occurred when CBS News reported that a twenty-seven-year-old married female physical education coach had sex with a thirteen-year-old boy (Dakss, 2005). However, the prosecutor in the case, who steadfastly refused to adopt a double standard on gender and maintained that adult female sexual assault on young males is no less heinous than adult male assault on young females, reasoned: "Some people don't look at it as serious, but if you reverse the roles and make it a male on a female, then everyone gets really upset, and it's considered really serious" (Dakss, 2005).

Meanwhile, despite the myth that sexually abusive female teachers' crimes are somehow considered more lightly by judges than if the sex roles are reversed, Saletan (2006) in a thorough review of such cases found that women in fact *do not* receive more reduced jail sentences. True, female adult educators (for psychological reasons we do not pretend to understand or explain) tend to become fixated on individual males for their repeated offenses, while male offenders tend to have more varied victims. But women's abuse is not generally considered less serious than men's, at least by the courts.

SCHOOL SHOOTINGS

Most adult North Americans have heard of the more spectacular school shootings in their countries within the past two decades, though most would be hard pressed to name more than a few, since there have been so many. For example, as a very brief sampler, North Americans have witnessed on nightly news broadcasts: Columbine High School in Littleton, Colorado (1998—fifteen students killed or injured); Dawson College in Montreal, Canada (2006—two students killed, including the shooter, and more than a dozen students and faculty members wounded); Westside Middle School in Jonesboro, Arkansas (1998—five killed, including a teacher, and ten students wounded); Thurston High School in Springfield, Oregon (1998—twenty-seven shot, four killed, including the shooter's parents); or Virginia Tech University in Blacksburg, Virginia (2007—thirty-three students and faculty members killed, as well as the shooter who killed himself, and fifteen others wounded, making it the most deadly school shooting rampage in U.S. history (Freydis, 2011; *New York Times*, 2009; High Beam, 2011).

If one includes all documented shootings and attacks at primary (elementary), secondary (middle and high school), and colleges/universities, just in the United States since World War II, the numbers are well past the dozens moving toward over one hundred. Moore, Petrie, Braga, and McLaughlin (2003) estimated that between 1992 and 2001, thirty-five incidents of lethal violence occurred in which students showed up at their school or at a school-sponsored event and started firing at their schoolmates and teachers. According to the National School Safety and Security Services (2010), 445 school shootings of this type occurred in the United States between 2000 and 2010. For colleges and universities alone, between 1990 and 2008, fourteen incidents of multiple fatality shootings occurred on college campuses in the United States (Fox and Savage, 2009).

Several facts need to be kept in mind about the prevalence of such violence.

First, not all parallel acts of violence in schools involve students shooting students. School principals, janitors, teachers, guidance counselors, and even parents have also been victims.

Second, school shootings (despite arguments against the relative ease of obtaining firearms in the United States) are not uniquely North American. Many shootings occur in a worldwide context in places as disparate as Finland, Austria, Yemen, Australia, Ireland, Canada, Israel, Scotland, and various Asian nations. Indeed, as this book was in its final stages of preparation, twenty-three-year-old Wellington Olivera, a former student (with no previous criminal history) at the public Tasso Da Silvera Middle School in Rio de Janeiro, walked into the school with two unspecified guns and fired off at least thirty rounds of ammunition, killing at least eleven students (mostly girls) and gravely wounding at least half a dozen others. Two police officers chased Olivera, and one wounded him before Olivera, as most school shooters do, took his own life (Barbassa, 2011).

Third, school shootings are not some uniquely modern phenomena. There are documented instances just in the United States going back to the early years of the twentieth century (High Beam, 2011).

Fourth, most shootings are committed by males, though occasionally females are attackers, such as a Baton Rouge nursing student who shot and killed two women and then herself at Louisiana Tech College in 2008 (High Beam, 2011).

Fifth, in keeping with our emphasis on inclusive definitions for considering the global domain of violence in general and educational violence in this chapter, we prefer the term "school massacres" to "school shootings" since worldwide an enormous amount of educational violence involves weapons other than firearms. Asian countries, like Japan and China, where individual possession of guns is less frequent than in America and European cultures, see a tremendous number of school attacks involving students or outside adults or perpetrators using various forms of knives, swords, machetes, and other edged weaponry.

The People's Republic of China, for example, in recent years has experienced a series of savage attacks on schoolchildren and their teachers, not infrequently the youngest children such as kindergarteners, by men wielding dangerous, sharp objects. In May 2010 a man wielding a meat cleaver killed seven children and two teachers at a kindergarten in northwest China (Ford, 2010). In northeastern China later that year a similar attack occurred on kindergarten children and teachers by a man with a two-foot-long knife, killing three children and a teacher and injuring twenty staff members and other children. Another attacker stabbed eight primary school students to death and was executed by the state *on the same day* that sixteen children and their teacher were attacked at a primary school in southern China (CDT, 2011). There were six such attacks just between the months of March and May 2010 in China (Ford, 2010). Most attacks involved knives or meat cleavers, though in April 2010 a male farmer went into a nursery school in eastern China with a hammer and injured five pupils of a preschool. Like Americans after their tragedies, the Chinese were asking, "Why?"

If we consider such documented *recent* cases from a variety of educational, Internet, and other sources, they number well over a thousand on a worldwide scale. There are cases from North America (United States and Canada); Central and South America (Haiti, Jamaica, Costa Rica, Argentina, Brazil); Asia (Japan, Afghanistan, China, Malaysia, South Korea, Sri Lanka, India, Philippines, Thailand, Taiwan); Africa (South Africa, Egypt, Niger, Angola, Kenya, Swaziland); Western Europe and Scandinavia (England, Scotland, Ireland, Germany, the Netherlands, Italy, Finland, Austria, Norway, Sweden, Denmark, France); Eastern Europe (Russia, Latvia, Ukraine, Yugoslavia, Northern Ossetra, Hungary, Albania); and Australia/New Zealand. Many involve guns but also knives, swords, daggers, machetes, hammers, sickles, and even bombs.

It is a truism that shooters, whether students Eric Harris and Dylan Klebold at Columbine High School or South Korean college student Seung-Hui Cho at Virginia Tech University, seem alienated and estranged, both from their fellow students and from their school and larger cultural environments. As to the motives held by the attackers, we can say from media reports and speculation by human behavior experts (often after the fact, because the attackers are quickly dead following the attacks in most cases) that the apparent reasons provided range from acts of revenge, a result of alienation or estrangement from other classmates, to an act of rebellion to the power and authority of schoolteachers and administrators.

It is tempting to label most shooters as sociopaths, since they treat other flesh-and-blood students, teachers, and other victims as if these were mere targets in a carnival shooting gallery without human concerns or pain. Rather than "play" armchair psychiatrist, however, it is probably sufficient to say that anger and resentment, consistent with a sense of alienation due to perceived wrongs against them, fuel most of the perpetrators. Sometimes the anger is sparked by an encounter—with a student, teacher, or principal—and previous resentments that have festered (incubated with a sense of relative frustration) result in carrying out the attack plan (almost all massacres are premeditated to cause harm). According to a student enrolled in Columbine High School: "Harris and Klebold would walk with their heads down, because if they looked up they would get thrown into lockers and get called a fag" (Bender, Shubert, and McLaughlin, 2001, 106). Larkin (2009) contends that school shootings by students are political events aimed at challenging the legitimacy of school authority and a reaction to the rituals of humiliation, predatory behavior of elite students, and punishment of losers. "On March 2, 1987, N. Ferris, age 12, got tired of being teased: he brought a pistol to school and, when a classmate made fun of him, he killed the other boy. Then he turned the gun at himself" (De Venanzi, 2012, 13).

De Venanzi found in his analysis of the literature on school shootings "that it is at the intersection of factors such as (a) society's narcissistic culture, (b) schools' suburban locations and their punitive style of decision-making, (c) the idiosyncratic nature of status hierarchies in schools; and (d) popular culture's trivialization of the negative end of its code, where we can identify a social niche appropriate for the high incidence of school shooting events" (De Venanzi, 2012, 14). According to De Venanzi, popular culture's messages and symbols play a fundamental role in the construction of the status hierarchies that produce peer marginalization in schools. He further notes that these "grandiose and vulnerable narcissistic types often engage in antagonistic social interactions, thus producing a considerable level of physical and psychological abuse against weaker peers," which most often result in the withdrawal and diminished self-esteem for the victim, but which at times can lead to a violent attack of retaliation.

Clinically diagnosed mental illness can also be an undercurrent for some attackers, perhaps a few. For instance, seventeen-year-old Kip Kinkel, who caused the 1998 shooting mayhem at Thurston High School in Springfield, Oregon, had documented schizophrenia. Psychotropic medications (antidepressants) like Prozac, Ritalin, Paxil, and Luvox, used by teenagers, also have been found to encourage suicidal behavior and are not rare in the backgrounds of some young attackers (High Beam, 2011).

But in the end, the entire possible range of personal problems that translate into attacks in schools runs an enormous gamut: from pure rage to (as in many Chinese attacks) job/interpersonal/romantic frustration to vendettas against particular students or faculty members. There is no single psychological category or profile of attackers, no single universal motive inspiring the school attacker. Nor are the attackers always students. Sometimes they are older ex-students of the school or even nonstudents. In almost every case they are male. Their victims seem indiscriminately divided between the sexes, and victims' ages depend on the potential victim pool attacked, that is, nursery or kindergarten schools, middle schools, high schools, or colleges and universities.

However, what is crucial in our understanding of institutional violence is to understand how the violence occurs as a result of the position and roles that actors play within the organization. The violence would not have occurred if it was not for the position and role behavior of the actors within this organizational context. Most, but not all, attackers are within the established institution of public or private education and are filling the conventional role of students. The examples mentioned above in Brazil and the People's Republic of China also point to ex-students and ex-employees of schools who choose vulnerable students as targets but seem to be enraged at the schools as entire entities. In China, in particular, the spring 2010 wave of attacks were committed by mostly middle-aged males: Zheng Minsheng, who stabbed eight elementary schoolchildren to death and injured five more, was forty-one years old; Yang Jiaqin, who killed a second-grade student and an elderly woman with a meat cleaver, was forty years old; Xu Xuyuan, who rampaged through an elementary school, injuring twenty-nine young students, a security guard, and two teachers, with an eight-inch knife was forty-seven years old; farmer Wang Yanglai, who went to a nursery school and injured five young pupils using a hammer before burning (self-immolating) himself to death, was also middle-aged (Campbell, 2010). In unraveling the interpersonal dynamics of specific school attacks from the institutional level, in nearly every case the attacker picked the school grounds for convenience of locating targets but also had some grievances related to personal school experiences (or those of a family member in school) either with fellow students or teachers/administrators.

CORPORAL PUNISHMENT

Corporal punishment, defined here as the official physical punishment of students for various misdemeanors, employs deliberate striking of students on the hands, back, buttocks, or face, with either an implement (by caning—whether rattan or bamboo—or by a wooden paddle or board plank or leather strap) or with an open human hand (slapping the face or spanking the buttocks and anterior thighs). It is an old form of educational discipline delivered by either teachers or administrators, perhaps as old as the formal educational institution itself. In the United States the practice took as its inspiration the mode of physical punishment employed in Anglo-British schools going back to the eighteenth and nineteenth centuries (Quigly, 1984; Chandos, 1984; Gould, 2007).

Corporal punishment of the types we have outlined above is currently legal in twenty American states (particularly in southern states such as Alabama, Arkansas, Mississippi, Tennessee, Texas, Oklahoma, Louisiana, and Georgia). It has been abolished in the other thirty. The inconsistency exists because the U.S. Supreme Court determined in 1977 that such punishment is lawful except where it has been outlawed by local authorities. A variety of northern states (such as Delaware, Ohio, and Pennsylvania) only outlawed CP (as corporal punishment is legally known) during the early years of the twenty-first century, while others (such as Wyoming, Missouri, and North Carolina) have resisted efforts to abolish it (CORPUN, 2011). Just because a state or local educational district permits CP, however, does not mean that the practice is frequent. In 2006, for example, Utah permitted CP but reported zero incidents (CORPUN, 2011). Where permitted in public schools by states, there are usually restrictions and regulations regarding the conditions of punishment: type of implement to be used, number of strokes to be administered, who on the school staff may administer the punishment, whether or not parents must be informed or consulted before/after, and so forth—a bureaucratization of the punishment ritual that may or may not be observed in specific instances.

A Human Rights Watch and American Civil Liberties Union report found that during the 2006–2007 academic year, the Office for Civil Rights at the U.S. Department of Education reported that 223,190 students nationwide received corporal punishment at least once during the school year. The largest number of students who were assaulted by school officials conducting a punishment ritual was in Texas with 49,197 students (Human Rights Watch, 2008). In Mississippi, 7 1/2 percent of public school students were struck

Figure 5.1.   Cartoon drawing of two students receiving the cane from Mr J. S. Kerr. One boy has just been caned and sucks his fingers. The other boy stretches out his hand for punishment. A blackboard lies on the ground with a chalk drawing depicting "Old Kerr." Caption reads: Kerr on the Cane; or Cane and Cure. "Strict discipline must be insisted upon, even to the extent of corporal punishment. No punishment is so economical of time. and so stimulating as the cane."— J. S. Kerr's Essay (delivered to the East Moreton Teachers' Association) on "The Teacher and his Position." Date 28 July 1888. Copied and digitized from an image appearing in *Queensland Figaro*, 28 July 1888, p. 140.

with paddles. An example cited in the report is the case of Tim L. "On August 18, 2003, 10-year-old Tim L. started the fifth grade at his public elementary school in rural east Texas. On the fourth day of school, Tim refused to run in gym class because he did not have his asthma medication. When the gym coach confronted him, Tim said, 'Coach sucks.'" The coach then took a wooden paddle and beat Tim severely on the buttocks. Faye L., Tim's mother, reported, 'There was blood in his underpants. . . . I had to pull the underwear off his behind from the dried blood'" (Human Rights Watch, 2008, 1). The report found that students can be physically punished for a wide range of misbehavior, including infractions such as chewing gum, being late, sleeping in class, talking back to a teacher, violating the dress code, or going to the bathroom without permission.

There is also indication of discrimination in the use of physical punishment. According to the research, "in the 2006–2007 school year, African-American students made up 17.1 percent of the nationwide student population, but 35.6 percent of those paddled. In the same year, in the 13 states with the highest rates of paddling, 1.4 times as many African-American students were paddled as might be expected given their percentage of the student population (Youseff, et al., 1998, 980)." This discriminatory application of physical punishment was found for both male and female students. There were also indications of discriminatory application for Native American children and children with mental and physical disabilities. The researchers found that use of physical discipline was also more likely to be found in schools where poverty and lack of resources created conditions of overcrowded classrooms and lack of counselors to assist teachers with particularly disruptive students.

Currently 106 countries have outlawed the practice of corporal punishment in schools. International instruments, including the United Nations Convention on the Rights of the Child, the UN Convention against Torture, and the International Covenant on Civil and Political Rights, prohibit the use of cruel, inhuman, or degrading treatment, regardless of circumstance. The U.S. Supreme Court has refused to impose constitutional restrictions on the practice of "reasonable" corporal punishment.

Liberals (to paint a broad stereotype) tend to see corporal punishment as something akin to unenlightened barbaric abuse while conservatives (another stereotype) attribute everything from teenage drug use, sexual promiscuity, disobedience in the classroom, poor grades, teenage pregnancies, and school shootings to a decline in CP. Many of these myths fall in the face of facts. For example, there is no question that more U.S. school shootings have taken place in states that allow corporal punishment than in states that do not permit it, and as paddling has decreased over time, violence against U.S. public schoolteachers has accordingly declined as well (CED, 2008a). In fact, states that allow corporal punishment (and where it is more prevalent, such as Missouri, Georgia, Alabama, Mississippi, and Louisiana) also have higher prison incarceration rates of adults.

Of course, it is simplistic to make one-to-one associations between school CP/no school CP and many adult social phenomena (though this is often done by partisans for and against the practice). But regardless of one's position on the morality or effectiveness of CP, its prevalence is declining in the

United States. Compared to the 1980s, by the 2005–2006 school year this prevalence of use of physical discipline had dropped 18 percent (CED, 2008b).

It is a truism in social psychology that aggression (or discipline) only stifles the aggression of the target if the latter happens to be weaker. That is, violence represses but does not eliminate the original aggression or disobedience. It only drives it under the surface and may actually feed it for the future. U.S. educators (and increasingly, legislators) have come to recognize this pattern. And not just in the United States. Corporal punishment of students as an educational tool has largely been outlawed in most European countries, Canada, Japan, New Zealand and most of Australia, and South Africa. It is still fairly common in most African countries, in Southeast Asia in places like Myanmar and South Korea, and in Middle Eastern societies such as Egypt (Youssef, Attia, and Kamel, 1998). At the risk of presenting a somewhat broad generalization, most industrial nations have recognized corporal punishment as a sometimes effective tactic to produce overt compliance (through fear, intimidation, and deterrence) in the short run but not one conducive to generating positive motivation to learn and master curricula.

SYMBOLIC VIOLENCE

Symbolic violence in the school context is the systematic and deliberate destruction of students' ethnic/racial/familial/religious identities by school administrators and other leaders. (Their intentions may be sectarian, political-civil, ethnocentric, or racist as well as—in those administrators' minds— benevolent.) It is, in its extreme form, cultural genocide. Bourdieu and Passeron (1977) defined symbolic violence as the imposition of a different or more likely dominant culture upon those who are in positions of domination as defined in terms of class, ethnicity, or gender. The violence stems from the denial of legitimacy of the other's knowledge based on their culture. Symbolic violence may manifest itself in physical violence like the physical beatings that took place in the Indian Schools throughout the United States and Canada when aboriginal children spoke their language and practiced their rituals. It may also take the form of psychological abuse resulting from the ridicule directed at those who resist or are slow to assimilate to the new dominant culture. But most of all, the violence was a result of the exclusion of the knowledge of the dominated and their resultant marginalization within their own communities and the larger society. For Bourdieu and Passeron (1977) symbolic violence was the internalized humiliations and legitimations of inequality based on ethnicity, gender, or class. Symbolic violence occurs as a result of the conquest of peoples throughout the world. It is a form of genocide (cultural) of those who practice competing ways of life. There have been a number of historical examples, but here we mention just several in North America and elsewhere.

The most spectacular cases have occurred in the United States and Canada involving the AmerIndian (or Native American or Aboriginal [a Canadian term]) population. These original inhabitants of the United States and Canada

Figure 5.2. A sewing class in Bismarck Indian School, North Dakota, taken be-tween 1909 and 1932. The Library of Congress Prints & Photographs Online Catalog.

have been the victims of horrific symbolic violence. As Tinker notes, the shift in policy from "annihilating to assimilating the residue of surviving Indians commenced in earnest following the end of a very uncivilized civil war in the U.S. when newly installed President Ulysses S. Grant, responding to the concerted lobbying of church reformers and liberal politicians, enunci-ated what was referred to as his 'Peace Policy' in 1869" (Tinker, 2004, xvi). A series of annual meetings of the "Friends of the Indian" were held at Lake Mohonk, New York, beginning in 1883, which formed the foundation of the policy of assimilation of the native population through the use of boarding schools. Tinker (2004, xvii) notes that three themes emerged in these confer-ences and provided the rational for the development of the policy of Indian education: "1) the 'need' for inculcation of individualism among native peo-ple, 2) that to achieve this end Indians should be universally 'educated' to hold Eurowestern beliefs, and that, 3) all Indians, duly educated and individ-ualized, should be absorbed as citizens into the U.S. body politic." As George Manypenny, an early U.S. Indian Commissioner, explained the need in 1856, for assimilation to occur, it was necessary that Indians learn to say "I" instead of "we," "me" instead of "us," "mine" instead of "ours" (Tinker, 2004, xvii).

The systematic removal of AmerIndian youths, males and females, from their tribal homes and their placement in "Indian residential schools" began in earnest in the 1890s after conquest of indigenous people was completed in both the United States and Canada. Churchill (2004) claims that by that time the indigenous population in North America had been reduced to 5 percent or less from the pre-invasion population. The ostensible purpose was to "assim-ilate" the AmerIndians into U.S. and Canadian societies. In Canada, the Canadian federal authorities entered into a partnership with four Christian denominations: the Roman Catholic Church, the Anglican Church of Canada, the Presbyterian Church of Canada, and the United Church of Canada (itself a merger of Methodist and Congregationist denominations). In the United States many of the schools were started by missionaries; however, the federal government took over their operation, retaining many of the missionaries that were employed in the schools. Churchill (2004, 28) notes that despite the secular control, "for most secular as well as missionary educators, 'civilization' was inconceivable unless grounded in Christian values."

During the nineteenth and twentieth centuries, over one hundred thousand First Nations children were removed from their homes by state authorities and placed into what sociologists call "total institutions," variously known by such official designations as "homes," "dormitories," "campuses," or "schools," all managed by religionist whites without AmerIndian input or oversight. Churchill (2004) contends that 80 percent of several succeeding generations of children were processed through the schools. He contends that at their peak of operation, the schools had the capacity of housing half of all Native American children at any given point in time.

The pastors and other ecclesiastical leaders of the white religious denominations held transparently low (racist) opinions of the First Nations' various religio-cultural traditions. Their goal, judged by their strategies and actions, was to eradicate those First Nations' traditions in the minds of the students as completely as possible. This meant denigrating and forbidding usage of native language and cultural traditions, all in the name of nationalizing and Christianizing the students. As Captain Richard Henry Platt, army officer selected by the United States to create and supervise its system in 1879 (once warden of a military prison), stated in 1895, the objective was to "kill the Indian, save the man" in every pupil (Platt, 1895). The severe conditions in the residential schools at times more resembled concentration camps or prisons than actual educational facilities. Tinker summarizes the experience of native children in North America in the following passage:

> Taken, often by force, from their homes at ages as young as four, transported to facilities remote from their families and communities, confined there for a decade or more, relentlessly stripped of their cultural identities while being just as methodically indoctrinated to see their traditions—and thus themselves—through the eyes of their colonizers, chronically malnourished and overworked, drilled to regimental order and subjected to the harshest forms of corporal punishment, this was the lot of one in every two native youngsters in North America for five successive generations. Of those ushered into the steadily expanding system of residential schools during its first forty years or more, about half did not survive the experience. In other words, roughly one-quarter of the American Indian population during the early twentieth century was physically destroyed by the process of schooling. (Tinker, 2004, xviii)

In one typical Canadian Catholic school for the native population, students' daily schedule consisted of rising at 6:30 a.m.; attending required chapel for Latin Mass; performance of chores; one hour for religious training; two hours dedicated to reading, writing, and arithmetic; lunch; the rest of the afternoon spent at "assimilation training" (farming and manual labor for the males; gardening, sewing, and cleaning for females); supper; one hour of study time in the evening; cleanup, supervised recreation; prayer; and sleep (Ward, 2001; Religious News Service, 2002). The total supervision of students' every movement, the total control of supervisors, and the latter's general contempt for their wards provided a ripe opportunity structure for physical abuse and sexual exploitation by teacher-clergy. Within this situation of literal indentured servitude, there were regular physical beatings for disobedience, malnourishment used as punishment, and rapes. For example, in the Roman Catholic schools, in which 70 percent of the AmerIndian children were placed, life for students often resembled that of a slave system. Children were beaten and locked away in dark closets as punishment for even expressing resentment and were whipped and had their heads shaved in front of the other students for attempting to run away. Siblings were deliberately separated and forbidden to speak to one another. Rebellious students were frequently disciplined in front of the others as "examples." Says one First Nations document, replete with testimonies of former residential students:

> Variations on punishment included isolation for days, sometimes without food or water. . . . For many, it eventually led to feelings of mistrust and irrepressible rage. Occasionally, this rage was released, but the children usually kept their feelings suppressed. Public beatings of the children also created feelings of powerlessness. . . . The most profound form of physical woundings occurred through sexual victims. . . . Reported sexual violations vary, with incidences of fondling, intercourse, ritualistic washing of genitals, and rape, and some instances of pregnancy and forced abortions [by clergy and teachers]." (Assembly of First Nations, 1994, 49–51; Brown, 2000)

The schools in the United States had more of a military school orientation, although that was often present in the Canadian schools as well. Children were often dressed in military-style uniforms and marched and drilled carrying dummy rifles. Churchill notes that as the children progressed in language acquisition, there was increasing weight placed on learning the "lessons of citizenship" or "civilization." For this purpose he notes that text like Horace E. Scudder's *A History of the United States of America* was used. There, the youngsters learned that the country was "peopled by men and women who crossed the seas in faith [and that] its foundations [were] laid deep in a divine order." The "nation was entrusted with liberty," and that "carries with it grave duties: the enlargement of liberty and justice is the victory of the people over the forces of evil" (Scudder, 1884, iv). Churchill (2004, 27) describes Scudder's depiction of the "Indian race" in the following passage: "While the tribes differed from one another, all the Indians were in some points alike. They were brave, but they were treacherous. They could bear hunger and torture in silence, but they were cruel in their treatment of captives. . . . [They were] ignorant barbarians . . . like wild animals [who perpetrated gratuitous] massacres, and so on." In the American Indian Residential Schools there was also approximately two hours of Christian proselytizing in the course of a typical school day.

The forced assimilation of Native American children in total institutions followed three stages in the destruction of the cultural heritage of the students. After their capture, in most cases from their home, they were brought to the school and first stripped of their clothing and artifacts that reflected their culture. They were also stripped of their names and given Christian names that were deemed appropriate for their new status. "This stripping of their culturally based identity was often accompanied with 'a thorough scrubbing' and 'disinfection'—alcohol and kerosene were among the astringents used for the latter purpose—often accompanied by staff commentary about 'dirty Indians'" (Churchill, 2004, 19). Churchill notes that for boys the next step was to undergo the humiliating experience of having their hair cut off and being given military-style haircuts. Churchill notes that at the heart of the policy was the belief that long hair was symbolic of savagery and that removing the hair was central to "destroying their sense of themselves as Indians."

The next step was homogenizing the group into one for the purpose of assimilation. Once they were stripped of their clothing and artifacts that were part of their cultural identity, they were given uniforms and forbidden to speak their language or perform any rituals or acts that were part of their culture. Churchill notes that a consistent theme through autobiographical material written by Indians who went through the process was how they felt they had lost themselves and were thus now strangers to their former world with no possibilities for the future. According to Churchill such despair made the children readily malleable to the new culture that was to be imposed upon them.

Once stripped of their former selves that were rooted in their native culture and homogenized as part of a group of students, they were then subject to a form of assimilation that taught them the new culture and punished severely any attempts of preserving or practicing the culture of their past. Children were punished, often beaten severely for the speaking of their language or the carrying out of their rituals. The Bureau of Indian Affairs promulgated a regulation in 1890 requiring "pupils be compelled to converse with each other in English, and should be properly rebuked or punished for persistent violation of this rule" (Adams, 1995, 140). Canada followed the same policy in 1896. Miller (1996) notes that the attack on Native languages was part of a broader assault on Aboriginal identity and the individual Native person's sense of worth as an Indian or Inuit.

Sexual abuse and predation was widespread in the Canadian boarding schools. In 1995 a Supreme Court judge for British Columbia went on record describing his county's residential school system as having been nothing but a form of institutional pedophilia and sexual terrorism (Grant, 1996, 229). Churchill (2004) cites a report of the Cariboo Tribal Council that conducted interviews with former students at the Oblates of St. Joseph's (Mission) residential school in Williams Lake that indicated that out of the 187 interviewed 89 people answered that they had suffered sexual abuse as a child, 38 reported that they hadn't, and 60 refused to answer. A 1993 report of the Ministry of National Health and Welfare reported that in some schools all of the children were sexually abused during the period from 1950 to 1980 (Churchill, 2004). Smith (2005, 40) reported that the Truth Commission on Genocide in Canada issued a report in 2001 that maintained that "the mainline churches and the federal government were involved in the murder of over 50,000 Native children through the system. The list of offenses committed by church officials includes murder by beating, poisoning, hanging, starvation, strangulation, and medical experimentation. Torture was used to punish children for speaking Aboriginal languages. Children were involuntarily sterilized." Smith also notes that the report "found that clergy, police, and business and government officials were involved in maintaining pedophile rings using children from residential schools" (Smith, 2005, 40).

Both Churchill (2004) and Smith (2005) contend that the experience in the United States was as bad or worse. Smith argues that the reason for lack of acknowledgment on the part of the U.S. government and churches is that the abuses are not as well documented in the United States as they are in Canada. She does identify particular cases of abuse like the case of John Boone who was a teacher in the Hopi day school in Arizona. He had sexually abused 142 boys. The principal at the school never investigated any of the allegations of abuse. Smith notes that this was not unusual for in all cases that she reported the Bureau of Indian Affairs (BIA) supervisors ignored complaints from the parents before the arrests were made. She reports that one BIA official stated that "child molestation at BIA schools is a dirty little secret and has been for years. I can't speak for other reservations, but I have talked to a lot of other BIA administrators who make the same kind of charges" (Smith, 2005, 38).

Churchill (2004) describes a psychological dysfunction that in Canada has been referred to as RSS or Residential School Syndrome. He notes that the symptomology of the illness is similar to the symptoms experienced by victims of rape, domestic violence, and child abuse. He also notes that there are some similarities in behaviors between those with RSS and those soldiers who have undergone heavy combat and experience Post-Traumatic Stress Disorder (PTSD) and Concentration Camp Syndrome (CCS).

Resistance from native population of the forced transfer and assimilation began early on, requiring both the Canadian and U.S. governments to use force when necessary for parent and tribal refusal to cooperate with the agents that came to gather their children. The following is one scene reported by the Indian Agent of the Mescalero Apache Reservation in 1886 as recorded in the Annual Report of the Commissioner of Indian Affairs to the 49th Congress, 1st Session, 1886: "Everything in the way of persuasion and argument having failed, it became necessary to visit the [Indians'] camps with a detachment of police, and seize the children as were proper, and take them away to schools, willing or unwilling. Some hurried their children off to the mountains or hid them away in camp, and the police had to chase and capture them like so many wild rabbits. This proceeding created quite an outcry. The men were sullen and muttering, the women loud in their lamentations, and the children almost out of their wits with fright" (Churchill, 2004, 17). In regard to Indian resistance, Adams concluded "a major motivation for resistance [was] that a significant body of tribal opinion saw white education for what it was: an invitation to cultural suicide" (Adams, 1995, 217).

By the late twentieth century, there were over eight thousand complaints of sexual, physical, and cultural abuse. The last of the residential schools was not closed in Canada until 1996. In the United States most of the residential schools were closed soon after 1935 when then Commissioner John Collier issued an Indian Reorganization. Today there are only eight off-reservation boarding schools that remain in operation in the United States. The Canadian government, which had assumed responsibility for the schools in 1969, was still issuing extensive apologies to First Nations AmerIndians as late as 2000, and the Canadian Conference of Catholic Bishops published its own apologies in *From Pain to Hope: Report from the Ad Hoc Committee on Child Abuse* (Brown, 2000; Careless, 2002; Baglo, 2002). In the United States, buried in a 2010 defense authorization bill, there is a statement that the U.S. government "apologizes on behalf of the people of the United States to all Native Peoples for the many instances of violence, maltreatment, and neglect inflicted on Native Peoples by citizens of the United States" (McKinnon, 2009). Following this statement is a qualification that the statement is not intended to support any lawsuit claims against the U.S. government. Meanwhile, the First Nations had been filing lawsuits in Canada, and both the Canadian federal government and separate denominations began paying substantial financial settlements to living victims. Some experts believed a decade ago that the more than eight thousand lawsuits could require as much as $1.26 billion to settle, but like any victim-settlement estimate, that amount was far too low (Baglo, 2002; Careless, 2002). The settlements are still rising in amounts and being negotiated.

Something similar on a smaller scale, without so much deliberate cultural destruction, occurred in Mamou, Guinea, West Africa, during the years 1950–1971. There the victims were the school-aged children of mostly Presbyterian missionaries left in the care of a boarding school operated by the Christian and Missionary Alliance. (CMA is based in Colorado Springs, Colorado.) While the parents were absent in the jungles and villages, their children were turned literally into prisoners, unable to leave and subjected to a variety of abuses that included belt whippings, malnourishment, and sexual assault by "caretakers" (see the Missionary Kids Safety Net, a victims' website, at www.mksafetynet.net; also Kennedy, 1995).

VIOLENCE OF EDUCATIONAL INEQUALITY

One last area of educational violence is the violence that is derived from the differences in how educational resources are allocated and how this impacts the differences in levels of educational achievement and differences in health within the population. The manner in which educational resources are distributed in countries around the world is that those who enter schools with more of the cultural and material resources derived from their class and ethnic position (family income and wealth) will receive more school resources throughout their education. Those who enter school with the least amount of resources from their class and ethnic position receive fewer school resources throughout their education. There are exceptions to this overall pattern; however, they are exceptions to the general pattern as to how educational resources are distributed within a country throughout the world.

This process of unequal distribution of resources for education begins with the positions that one is born into as defined by gender, ethnicity, and class. The pattern of disparity varies in terms of the level of development of the society and the social policies related to inequality. Poorer, less developed countries generally have the greatest disparities in terms of position and access to schools. UNICEF reports that only 60 percent of children of the appropriate age attend secondary school worldwide. In sub-Saharan Africa, the world's poorest region, that number drops to only a quarter. Figures for primary schools are better where in this same region 65 percent of boys and 63 percent of girls who are of primary school age are attending primary schools (UNICEF, 2011). UNICEF estimates that in general the number of out-of-school children in the world today is 93,000,000. The majority are girls and almost 80 percent live in sub-Saharan Africa and South Asia (UNICEF, 2011). UNICEF claims that education enhances life and that it ends the generational cycles of poverty and disease. They contend that a basic education provides boys and girls the knowledge and the skills that are necessary to adopt healthy lifestyles and to protect them from contraction of sexually transmitted disease including HIV/AIDS and allow them to grow in terms of their human potentials as they transition to adulthood and to be more active in decision making to enhance their social, economic, and political lives (UNICEF, 2011).

The differences in education opportunity and quality translate into differences in life chances for people in the world today. These differences in life chances can be measured in terms of the differences in life expectancy, life free of debilitating disease and illness, and differences in the opportunities that are available to people in various social positions to achieve their human potentials. In general, the least educated in the world are also those who are least likely to develop their human potentials and are most likely to live in poverty, to live on the margins of society, and to die at an earlier age than those with the most education.

According to research conducted by Cutler and Lleras-Muney on the effect of education on people's lives in the United States, better educated people have lower morbidity rates from the most common acute and chronic diseases and these differences are independent of basic demographic and labor market factors (Gerald R. Ford School of Public Policy, 2007). Furthermore, life expectancy differences in the United States have grown between those who are college educated and those who are not college educated. In lesser developed countries like Ethiopia, where only 45 percent of children who are of age are in primary school, the differences between those who do and those who don't are likely to be even more dramatic.

In more developed countries, like the United States, some of the reasons for this relationship may be found in the results of the 2009 National Youth Risk Behavior Survey (Centers for Disease Control and Prevention, 2010). The results of the survey show that students who perform better in school are less likely to engage in health-risk behaviors when compared to their classmates who don't perform as well in school. These health-risk behaviors include differences in tobacco and alcohol use, being sexually active, being physically active and television watching, and carrying a weapon on at least one day, during the thirty days prior to taking the survey.

However, it is not just differential access to education; it is also the quality of the education that affects the quality of one's life. Again in the developing world the differences in quality are the greatest. As countries become more developed, the disparities decline. However, even in the most developed countries in the world, the disparities in the quality of education persist. The United States is a good example of how the disparities persist especially between minority and majority ethnic groups and in terms of class position. For example, let's look at two public schools in the state of Indiana in the American Midwest. These two public schools are a three-hour drive on an interstate highway, but represent two different worlds of educational opportunities in the state (Stockman, 2011). One school is located in Hammond, Indiana, an industrial city that is clearly in the U.S. rust belt. In the neighborhood that is serviced by Lafayette Elementary School, the median household income is $10,581.00. Seventy-five percent of families are headed by a single mother and 98 percent are eligible for free or reduced price meals. The majority of students are members of minority groups, African American and Hispanic. In Hammond 20 percent of the population received public assistance; 93 percent rented their home. At least one-third of the children live in public housing projects. Students who begin kindergarten at the school are often two years developmentally behind. At Lafayette Elementary only 45 percent of the students passed the state-mandated Indiana Statewide Testing for Educational Progress-Plus. Drive three hours south on I-65, which cuts through the center of the state, and you arrive in Carmel, a wealthy suburb of Indianapolis. Like all the public schools in Carmel, College Wood Elementary is a magnet school that draws students from all over the area. The median household income is $138,713.00, the highest in the state. The majority of the residents in the census tract for Carmel are white non-Hispanic; 0.2 percent of the households were receiving public assistance income and 7 percent of households rent their home. Not only are there significant differences in the backgrounds of the children, but despite additional state funding to the Hammond area (Hammond gets 19 percent more per student in state aid than Carmel), teachers in Carmel are paid an average of 12 percent more and administrators receive 8 percent more in salary. In Carmel, almost 90 percent of the students pass the state-mandated achievement tests.

This difference in resources and results is replicated throughout the United States and in most countries throughout the world. In many of the largest metropolitan areas in the United States, the schools that are in poorer areas systematically receive less funding per student than schools in the wealthier areas. A large portion of this is a result of the property tax as the principal basis of funding for public education. However, in the wealthier districts additional school taxes are usually accepted by the population to maintain the high quality of education. Those communities with wealthier residents and higher valued property have more resources available to their schools than communities with poorer residents and lower property values. For example reviewing 2002–2003 school year data for the New York city metropolitan area, in the Manhasset School District on Long Island where 5 percent of the students are from low-income families and 9 percent are black or Hispanic, the per pupil expenditure is $22,311. On the other hand, in the New York City school district, where 83 percent of the students come from low-income households and 72 percent are black or Hispanic, the per pupil allocation is $11,627 (Kozol, 2005). Throughout the nation, the schools that receive the lowest levels of per pupil expenditures are the schools that have the highest percentage of minority students who come from the poorest families. Those that receive the highest levels of per pupil expenditures are the schools with the lowest percentage of minority students and those who have the lowest percentage of students from poorer families.

Reviewing 2008 census data, the ten states with the lowest percentage of poor students gave their students on the average approximately 25 percent more in per pupil funding than states with the highest percentage of poor students, a difference of approximately $3,000 in funding per pupil (New America Foundation, 2011). Education in the United States is class and ethnically segregated. Focusing on ethnic segregation alone, almost 75 percent of black and Hispanic students in the United States attend schools that are primarily minority populated (Kozol, 2005). Class and ethnic segregation in schools are even more pronounced when private schools are added to the mix.

The differences between the schools based on who attends can be seen in terms of the quality of the buildings that the students are educated in, the experience and salaries of schoolteachers, the availability of schoolbooks and materials, the nature of the school curriculum and style of teaching, and the level of achievement of the student population (Kozol, 2005). "In general, students in states with lower student poverty rates in 2008 performed better on the National Assessment of Educational Progress (NAEP) in 2009 than those in states with higher student poverty rates" (New America Foundation, 2011). The consequences of unequal access to quality education go beyond measures of educational achievement. Given the centrality of education in modern societies, those who do not have access to it experience a life of less quality and more hardship that often results in earlier onset of disease and death. The actions and institutionalized practices that serve to deny this resource to those who need it the most can be described as an act of violence.

CONCLUSIONS

The acts of violence that occur in the context of the educational institution are at times a matter of school policy (corporal punishment and symbolic violence of forced assimilation, unequal allocation of school resources) or abuse of positions of authority (rape, assault, and murder), and in some cases they were a response to students' school experiences (assault and murder). What they all have in common is that the actors were occupying positions within organizations that are functioning to educate people. The institutional and organizational context is central to the occurrence of the violence. If the actors were not in positions within the schools, the violence would not have occurred. The offender either was operating from the position or in reaction to these positions in all cases of violence. What is also important in this case of violence is the hierarchical nature of the positions and the violence that occurs. Students are abused because they have less power relative to their abusers. This is not always the case, as shown in the cases of violence by students directed at other students and those in authority. In this case, those who are the offenders were often those who were powerless and were striking out at a structure of power either defined formally in the structure of the organization or informally in the case of the social structure of students within the school. The violence also takes all forms from physical to psychological to social harm.

The acts of violence in schools (rapes, bullying, corporal punishment, assault, and murder) that so vividly and dramatically catch our attention and symbolize the misgivings many persons hold for various reasons about mass education in democratic societies can be seen, in fact, *not* to be separate from the institutional roles that persons play in education and also from the macro issues affecting the larger society outside the schools. In order to understand the nature of violence within this institutional setting as well as others, it is crucial that we understand the nature of the context as defined in terms of positions and roles and its place in the personal dramas of violence that occur within these places. Focusing entirely on the offender personality or biography will miss this important context and its role in the occurrence of the violence.

DISCUSSION QUESTIONS

1. Have you been a victim of school bullying? Who could have intervened to stop it? Did your experience fit the patterns laid out in the first part of this chapter?
2. Some advocates of stopping school bullying say it is a general problem affecting both males and females, whatever their sexual orientation. Some other critics say the entire concern is part of a left-wing political agenda to protect a homosexual lifestyle in schools. Based on your personal observations and experience, which rings truer?
3. If there was one aspect of possible educational violence that affected or concerned you most as a teen in high school, what would you say it was?
4. Was forced assimilation through the "Indian Schools" of the native populations in the United States and Canada the only way to integrate these populations into the society? In what other way could it have been done without the violence that occurred?
5. With all the ways that bullying and harassment can occur electronically through social media, what ways could be employed to stop it from occurring? Should the schools be involved in bullying the occurs outside of school on the web?

Chapter Six

Religious Violence

The question of how many people at Jonestown willingly took the poison always will be open to debate. Certainly young children could not have evaluated very well what their actions would mean. The presence of armed guards shows at least implicit coercion, though the guards themselves reported their intentions to visitors in glorious terms and then took the poison. No one rushed up to tip over the vat of Flavor Aid. Wittingly, unknowingly, or reluctantly, they took the poison (Hall, 1989, xii).

Joshua continued his wars of conquest until a total of thirty-one kings and thirty-one cities were overthrown and all of the inhabitants put to death. Assuming the cities averaged 10,000 people, Joshua slaughtered about 310,000 people inhabiting that part of Palestine that was reduced to his command (Scott, 1979, 66).

In 1171 at Blois, France, thirty-eight Jewish leaders were sentenced to death because the mayor's servant thought he saw a Jew throw a child's body into the river—even though no body was found and no child was missing. The thirty-eight were given a chance to save their lives by converting to Christianity, but they refused. They were locked in a wooden shed, which was burned (Haught, 1990, 44).

Religious beliefs and values, as regarded by symbolic interaction theorists, are important components of the *social reality* in which virtually everyone lives. Even for those persons who are avowed atheists or agnostics, or even if they only nominally identify with some form of spirituality or religious tradition, religious standards of morality—of right and wrong—both explicitly and subtly permeate most cultural understandings of social behavior. Because many followers of *historical* religions (i.e., those with real, known founders, such as Judaism, Christianity, Islam, and Buddhism) believe their

Figure 6.1. *Entry of the Crusaders into Constantinople* by Gustave Doré (1832–1883).

faith's origins involve (to some extent) divine elements, such persons are predisposed to stress religion's contributions to society and humanity in general as positive, uplifting, and beneficial.

Indeed, religion is usually regarded as a force for goodwill and nonviolence among human beings, a positive set of beliefs and values undergirding social order, law, and harmony. This conventional wisdom holds that the greater the consensus among people about the fundamentals of religious truths, the greater the reduction in misunderstandings, discrimination, violence, and other social problems that have a moral dimension. In reality, the truth-claims of various religions often inspire invidiousness, hostility, and intolerance. Religion can inflame passions of outrage and fear that motivate not just individual believers but also, on occasion, entire societies to repress or eliminate "nonbelievers." Religious violence thereby becomes an ironic servant to the ultimate goal of ushering in, or enforcing, utopian schemes thought to be divinely ordained.

Thus, starting in 1979, a virtual reign of terror existed in Iran. It was in large part initiated by fundamentalist Muslim mullah (holy leader) the Ayatollah Ruhollah Khomeini in an attempt to turn his nation away from "satanic" Western influence toward a "pure" revolutionary Islam. Meanwhile, a group of virtually harmless non-Islamics called Baha'is literally became an endangered species in that country. The religion of Baha'ism originated in mid-nineteenth-century Persia. It is a faith that recognizes Moses, Jesus of Nazareth, and Mohammed as successive prophets of God, to be joined by a Persian mystic named Baha'ullah who felt called to spread a Quaker-like message of peace, love, and universal spiritual unity. The Ayatollah decided that the 300,000 Baha'is living in Iran presented a subversive presence to the Islamic revolution and began a systematic campaign of persecution. Tens of thousands of Baha'is fled the country. Thousands of those remaining were rounded up for summary kangaroo court trials, torture, and imprisonment and given a choice of either conversion to Islam or execution. By the late 1980s more than four hundred had been hanged or shot, and in some instances the government even coerced the families of victims to pay for the firing squads' bullets before letting them claim their loved ones' bodies (Wright, 1989, 106, 181). Since traditional Islamic law prohibits capital punishment for female virgins, some Baha'i women and girls were reportedly first raped in the prison cells by Iranian soldiers before being executed (Haught, 1990, 202).

A more recent example would be the Taliban regime, extremist Muslims in pre-American occupation Afghanistan, which enacted a series of social taboos (that movies and music be banned, that women follow severe restrictions on their dress and public appearances, that all men grow beards, and so forth) and destroyed artistic expressions of all non-Islamic religions. They appeared to have been sponsored by and harbored terrorists, particularly the Al Qaeda network and Saudi Arabian Osama bin Laden, who was one of the instigators of the horrific September 11, 2001, attacks on New York's World Trade Center towers and the Pentagon. Another series of examples would be the Palestinian suicide bombers and shooters who have indiscriminately killed Israeli citizens in public places such as markets, cafés, and shopping malls. They have been revered by their conationalists as heroes and martyrs. It is unknown as to whether the deaths of these Palestinians will ever hasten their goal of statehood, but such violence has indisputably achieved destructive reprisals by the Israeli army and many more resulting deaths among Palestinians than Israelis.

The French philosopher Blaise Pascal pessimistically observed about violence and religion: "Men never do evil so completely and cheerfully as when they do it from religious conviction" (cited in Evans, 1968, 210). Likewise, Thomas Jefferson (1954, 160), commenting on Christianity's tendency over the past two thousand years to enforce religion at the point of a sword, concluded: "Millions of innocent men, women, and children, since the introduction of Christianity, have been burned, tortured, fined, and imprisoned, yet we have not advanced one inch toward conformity. What has been the effect of coercion? To make one half of the world fools and the other half hypocrites. To support roguery and error all over the earth."

A conflict perspective on the spiritual aspect of the violence phenomenon points to the fact that a human symbolic creation, religion, over the past five known millennia has produced a myriad of cases wherein religionists have dehumanized, slain, and tortured countless millions of their fellow human beings. Such massacres are in no way abnormal. Religion is, in the end, about power: power not just to ensure one's salvation and immortality, or to be healed, or to find succor in times of grief, but also power to control, enslave, thwart, and destroy. Religion buttresses the social realities of believers and justifies that all-too-human tendency to create walls between in-groups and out-groups, between the "saved" and the "damned," between true believers and infidels. Religion also legitimizes regimes and systems of inequality and is often seized upon by elites, from the brutal empires of antiquity to such modern nation-states as pre–World War II Imperial Japan, Nazi Germany, and Khomeini-era Iran.

In this chapter we consider several general categories of religious violence. These cases are illustrative but in no sense comprehensive, since it would require many volumes to handle the topic in full detail.

RELIGIOUS WARS AND CRUSADES

Wars between the defenders of separate religions and crusades (which really amount to the same thing) are the violent outcomes of collisions among competing sacred symbol systems. To take one recent example: modern Lebanon, a once-beautiful, thriving urban center, lay largely in ruins during the 1980s, scarred with acres of crumbling bombed-out buildings and left with a shattered economy. There various Muslim and Christian sectarians (Sunnis, Shiites, Druzes, Marionites, Alawites, and Jews) who previously lived in peaceful tolerance now arm themselves in shifting, violent alliances for and against each other as well as with Syrians, Palestinians, Israelis, and numerous paramilitary organizations. Over 130,000 Lebanese citizens died in the civil war, not to mention 241 U.S. Marines killed in 1983 while sleeping in their barracks near the Beirut Airport when a terrorist on a suicide mission drove a truckload of explosives into the building (Martin and Walcott, 1988, 125–45).

Religious wars also serve to legitimate imperialistic conquest of other nations under the guise of the need to save those who are to be dominated by means of religious enlightenment. In reality they are conquests for territory, resources, and markets. Probably the most spectacular series of such religious conflicts were the nine separate Christian Crusades that took place between the eleventh and thirteen centuries. The First Crusade began in 1095 when Pope Urban II preached spiritual revival and a call to arms following the capture of Jerusalem by Turkish forces (and an appeal to the West for military assistance by Alexius, Emperor of Constantinople). Under the Truce of God the church had for a half century previously attempted to limit feudal warfare within European societies. Now, at the Council of Trent, Urban II was attempting to recruit knights for his Crusade. Urban offered that all "knights who with pious intent took the Cross would earn a remission from temporal penalties for all his sins; if he died in battle he would earn remission of his sins" (Cohn, 1971, 61). Urban also recognized that there would be material gains and that knights who were in constant battle over the shortage of land would reap new lands as an outcome of the Crusade. At the time the Christian church, as well as Europe in general, was in an expansionist mood. Agricultural improvements, swelling populations, developing urban areas, and religious passions for reform and conversion were all pressuring Western Europeans to look eastward. Moreover, the church was concerned with channeling the growing power of the military estate into an extended enterprise that did not threaten the church's own authority at home (Rowling, 1979, 106ff) while steering knights away from innumerable petty wars and violent exploitation of the peasantry (Gies, 1984, 17ff; Payne, 1984).

The Crusaders (whether French, German, English, Flemish, or Spanish) lustily raped, looted, and massacred both Muslim and unlucky Christian populations on their paths through the Middle East and perceived the gore and destruction they caused as part of a divine strategy. Raymond of Aquilers, a contemporary chronicler and eyewitness to the slaughter of Muslims in Jerusalem, recorded the violence with a relish for religiously inspired violence that compares well to the Ayatollah Khomeini's:

> Wonderful things were to be seen. Numbers of the Saracens were beheaded. . . . Others were shot with arrows, or forced to jump from the towers; others were tortured for several days, then burned in flames. In the streets were seen piles of heads and hands and feet. One rode about everywhere amid the corpses of men and horses. . . . In the temple of Solomon the horses waded in blood up to their knees, nay, up to the bridles. It was a just and marvelous judgment of God, that this place should be filled with the blood of the unbelievers. (Haught, 1990, 25–26)

When Richard the Lion-Hearted of England captured the city of Acre in 1191, he ordered that three thousand prisoners (the majority of them women and children) be slain, then their bodies slit open to see if they had concealed jewels by swallowing them (Haught, 1990). There have actually been many more localized wars of religious liberation and struggles for hegemony that are less well-known or recognized outside scholarly circles. Many have involved what anthropologists refer to as "revitalization movements" (Wallace, 1966). Such phenomena arise typically when a less technologically advanced people confront a more sophisticated industrial civilization. In the process of the former being subdued and colonized, prophets arise who speak a common message: a day of apocalypse is coming when the old gods (or ancestors) will join with the living in overthrowing the foreign oppressors. The victors will then have their sovereignty restored and enjoy the fruits of the advanced civilization minus the foreigners. Sometimes, as in Melanesian "cargo cults," the ghostly ancestors are to arrive on the same ships that bring colonial overlords and carry off raw materials, with the rebellious natives set to take possession of the desirable manufactured goods (i.e., the cargo) in the ship's holds (see Adas, 1979; Lanternari, 1963). Such prophecies resonate well with popular frustrations and discontent among groups of displaced and alienated persons.

In the North American case, the Ghost Dance movement among Native Americans predicted that their ancestors would arrive on trains (rather than ships) prior to purging their lands of whites in warfare. The familiar Hollywood stereotype of painted Indians chanting and whooping as they shuffle around a fire or totem pole is actually a caricature of the Ghost Dance ritual that included a prolonged dance that induced trances and mobilized Native Americans for battle. The Ghost Dance cult spread across North America as it became increasingly apparent to Native Americans that they were losing out to the hoards of whites inexorably pushing westward. Many of the so-called Indian Wars, such as the Great Sioux Uprising during the 1870s, were, from Native Americans' perspective, religious wars as much as political struggles over territory. Sitting Bull, the Sioux chief whose warriors wiped out General George Armstrong Custer's Seventh U.S. Calvary at the Little Big Horn River, was as much a religious prophet as military leader to his people (Lanternari, 1963, 63–122).

The Ayatollah Khomeini, Iran's late leader, exhorted literally hundreds of thousands of young Iranian men, including adolescents used as human mine-sweepers, to be slaughtered in human-wave assaults against better-armed Iraqi troops during the 1980s. The carnage was reminiscent of the bloody (and equally futile) trench warfare in Europe during World War I. An entire generation of Iranian males was subsequently decimated in the name of a nationalistic Muslim holy war.

Khomeini elevated death in battle to religious martyrdom. It did not matter if the enemy was the Great Satan of the Christian West (the United States) or other Muslim believers who opposed his uncompromising Islamic Revolution. In 1984 Khomeini proclaimed in a speech:

> War is a blessing for the world and for all nations. It is God who incites men to fight and kill. The Koran says, "Fight until all corruptions and all rebellion have ceased." The wars the Prophet led against the infidels were a blessing for all humanity. . . . Thanks to God, our young people are now, to the limits of their means, putting God's commandments into action. They know that to kill the unbelievers is one of man's greatest missions. (quoted in Haught, 1990, 203)

To this end, Iranian leaders have sponsored and harbored a variety of paramilitary organizations that kidnap, bomb, assassinate, and sabotage their Western enemies. But Khomeini was not adverse to spreading Islamic jihad (holy war) to other Muslim societies, such as Saudi Arabia, where leaders did not share his single-minded vision. In 1979, at Khomeini's instigation, more than two hundred Iranian "pilgrims" to the annual hajj (return) to the Grand Mosque in Mecca smuggled in automatic weapons, fired on a crowd of forty thousand worshippers, briefly occupied the mosque, and only after nine days of intense house-to-house fighting with police were all killed or captured. (The Saudis ordered sixty-three of the Iranian terrorists beheaded.)

In South Asia religiously inspired violence between Hindus and Muslims has been repeated again and again in India/Pakistan and between Hindus and Sikhs in the southern part of the Indian subcontinent. In 1984 alone, mobs of each faith near the Bombay region, inspired by a Hindu speaker's anti-Islamic barbs and returned Islamic insults, killed 216 persons, injured 256, left 13,000 homeless, and resulted in 4,100 arrests. That same year, an armed contingent of Sikh extremists (Sikhism is a mixture of Islam and Hinduism) barricaded themselves in Amritsar's Golden Temple, a Sikh shrine, in a demonstration aimed at gathering support for a separate Sikh theocracy to be called Khalistan. India's then prime minister, Indira Gandhi, ordered one thousand troops to retake the temple; then Sikhs among Gandhi's own personal guard assassinated her. In an enraged response that lasted over three days, Hindu mobs killed 5,000 persons. According to eyewitnesses, mobs dragged Sikhs from homes, stores, buses, and trains, slashing and pounding them to death. Some were doused with kerosene and burned alive. Sikh boys were castrated (Haught, 1990, 172).

The violence repeated itself in India early in 2002. Hindu extremists in Gujarat state, for example, killed more than 600 people in a week-long riot, most of the victims Muslim but some Christian. In the city of Ahmadabad hundreds of Hindu militants broke into a mosque where Muslims had gathered for daily prayers. Wielding sledgehammers, metal rods, and shovels, they smashed walls and minarets. During the previous week Hindu mob behavior killed hundreds of Muslims and drove thousands more out of the city. Muslim gravestones were desecrated and whole neighborhoods were burned.

The ethnic/racial/religious hatred behind such violence is complex and long-standing. Part of the Indian violence is due to Hindu revitalization sentiment; part of it is also grounded in the brutal poverty undoubtedly surrounding the rioters' lives. Many have nothing left to lose by immersing themselves in what, to many outsiders, seems transparently a self-destructive campaign. Thus the nonviolent alternatives offer little, if anything, better (Chandrasekaran, 2002; Mahapatra, 2002).

RELIGIOUS TERRORISM

Political scientist Walter Laqueur (1997, 9) wrote in his classic *The Age of Terrorism* concerning the problem of identifying terrorism that "the difficulty with terrorism is that there is no terrorism *per se* . . . but different terrorisms." In other words, like the so-called disease "cancer," we are really confronting many things lumped under the same umbrella rubric, in this case including states exterminating whole communities of their own citizens, armies wholesale murdering civilians, small cells of violent subversives dis-

rupting society with seemingly random bombings, and so forth. But to delimit religious terrorism, we need to be precise. First, what is terrorism? Then,
what is the subspecies we call religious terrorism?

Terrorism is a loaded and somewhat ambiguous word if used in a purely
relative sense, that is, if groups we approve of using indiscriminate violence
are referred to as heroic "freedom fighters" but groups that are seen as the
enemy are regarded as ruthless, homicidal, and sociopathic. And it is a mistake to limit the domain of terrorism to relatively small groups causing political, social, and/or economic disruption in a society (or in his words, "from
below"), as Laqueur does. Laqueur's analysis fundamentally bypasses the
issue of terroristic tactics used by government agencies against their own
society's members or foreign populations, though he admits that "no one is
likely to deny that the number of victims and the amount of suffering caused
by tyrannical and aggressive governments throughout history has been infi-
nitely greater than that caused by small groups of rebels. A Hitler or a Stalin
have killed in one year more people than all terrorists throughout recorded
history." We focus on this particular type of terrorism in our state violence
chapter. To be sure, Laqueur (1997, 5–9, 96–97) acknowledges characteristics of terrorism also recognized by other experts, such as:

1. Terrorism as a strategy for disrupting society is not new.
2. Terrorism is mostly effective as a tactic if it is part of a more far-
   reaching strategy not depending solely on violence; otherwise it generates more ill will than results in the support of the general population.
3. Terrorism is always more acceptable against society's "outsiders" than
   against its indigenous "insiders."
4. Terrorism is a serious problem in modern industrial (not just Western)
   societies, to be sure, but it rarely is "the" most serious problem confronting them.
5. Specific forms of terrorism can be seriously contained or even eliminated if enough terrorists are killed or arrested, rendering it virtually
   ineffective.
6. Terrorists are often not poor and desperate but at the same time nor are
   many terribly sophisticated in their ideological beliefs.
7. Terrorism is no monopoly of the Middle East nor are most victims in
   North America.
8. Harsh reprisals against terrorism are usually not effective, outraging
   more persons than the original terrorism, and thus counterproductive.

Terrorism in fact can be regarded as "normal," to paraphrase French sociologist Émile Durkheim's famous dictum on crime, because it is and has been
present in every society or civilization. And likely it will never disappear.
Laqueur (1997, 9) asks if it is realistic to expect governments, which are
incapable of stamping out crime or drug peddling or illegal immigration, to
have full success in the battle against terrorism. Governments cannot protect
all of the citizens all of the time against muggers and thieves; likewise, they
cannot protect everyone against a terrorist attack.

Actually, considering both the terrorism against a government or racial/ethnic/religious groups in society by small cells of activists using indiscriminate violence *and* ruthless terror against populations employed by governments and their agents (including police and armies) is, in our opinion, the only realistic approach to the subject. Military historian Caleb Carr (2003, 6) defines terrorism, in a rather straightforward way that encompasses both types: "Terrorism . . . is simply the contemporary named given to . . . warfare deliberately waged against civilians with the purpose of destroying their will to support either leaders or policies that the agents of such violence find objectionable." According to Carr's definition, terrorism is not simply some brutal tactic that the enemy, or only "the other side," employs during wartime or at any other time, and it really is a form of warfare. Says Carr (2003, 30): "One man's terrorist, in short, is most emphatically *not* another man's freedom fighter; but *every* man's murderer of civilians during hostilities is *every* man's terrorist" (emphasis in the original).

This uncompromising definition, focusing on who is a victim as opposed to any innate justness of the cause of the terrorists, thus includes not only the massacres of entire tribes, cities, and populations in Canaan by the ancient Israelites, as related in the Bible; or the slaughterous reprisals in the Europe and Middle East of antiquity by Roman legions (which operated under the stated policy of *destructive war* or *punitive war*, i.e., civilians and their living property were as much fair game for the sword as were identified combatants); or the equally bloody wars of conquest by the ancient Hittites, Assyrians, Babylonians, and Egyptians; or the Allied Forces mass bombing of Dresden; or the Nazi *Blitzkrieg* (Lightning War) over London; or Hitler's obsessive extermination of millions of Jews and other minorities; or the use of terror bombing in warfare beginning with Guernica during the First World War (Kramer, 2010). This definition *also* would include the intense allied aerial bombardment of Saddam Hussein's Baghdad during Operation Desert Storm, the devastating firebombing of Tokyo by Americans during World War II, and of course the two atomic bombings of the Japanese cities Hiroshima and Nagasaki, in which civilians—the elderly, the females, and the children and babies, all relatively greater in number than any soldiers present—as similar acts of terrorism. Kramer (2010) notes that the form of state terrorism from the bombing of civilians has become normalized by the United States in its method of warfare since World War II, including the recent wars in the Middle East the United States spearheaded. Thus civilian casualties, and not ideologies, define the essence of terrorism.

Recall that our definition of religious terrorism emphasizes military historian Carr's emphasis on civilian casualties, which essentially means noncombatants or persons with necessarily no intense ideological passion who are merely going about their lives when they fall victim to the spread of terror in spontaneous, unpredictable deaths and injuries. This is what occurred during the 1970s, when Northern Ireland became a bloodbath for not only British soldiers and Irish Republican guerrilla fighters but also for numerous citizens totally uninterested in participating in the violence. Following the establishment of the Irish Free State in 1921, Protestants (who were descendants of the settlers sent over after the conquest of Ireland by the British in the first step in creating their overseas empire) came increasingly to identify with

Britain whereas Roman Catholics saw the Free State areas as sovereign Irish territories. The Irish Republican Army, an offshoot of the political party Sinn Féin and a major terrorist group, initiated a wave of violence against Protestants starting in the 1960s; the Protestants in turn grouped themselves vigilante-style to form the Ulster Volunteer Forces; and violence and subsequent reciprocal reprisals occurred in Irish neighborhoods of both sides. On January 30, 1973, occurred Bloody Sunday (also called by Irish nationals the Bogside Massacre), when Roman Catholic activists were engaged in a peaceful demonstration and British troops fired in their midst (killing thirteen persons). This event initiated a vicious eye-for-an-eye series of exchanges. Snipings, bombings, and other retaliations continued among the two groups of Christians. Juergensmeyer (2008, 177) writes of the aftermath of Bloody Sunday that "the British embassy in Dublin was burned, British soldiers were attacked, police stations were bombed, and individual Catholics and Protestants were captured by opposing sides and sometimes hideously tortured or murdered."

Something more episodic happened in 1995 in East Asia when a Japanese-based cult (the Aum Shinrikyo), inspired by a charismatic leader who preached an apocalyptic Armageddon message of a coming World War III, utilizing a hodge-podge of Hindu, Buddhist, Jewish, and Christian beliefs (that also included an obsessive fear of Freemasonry conspiracies), released nerve gas into a Tokyo subway near the government district, killing twelve commuters and injuring five thousand more (Kisala, 1998).

Sometimes a "terrorist tradition" continues over vast periods of history, as it has in China for several thousand years, where religiously based secret societies (such as the Triads, the White Lotus Society, and the Boxers) often engaged in criminal activities (gambling, smuggling, and so forth) but also proved critical in aiding and fomenting popular revolutionary movements with their terror activities, such as in the Opium Wars of the 1830s, the Taiping Rebellion of the mid-nineteenth century, and the Boxer Rebellion of 1900. In addition, such groups played important roles in the political revolutions, Republican and later Communist, of the twentieth century (Chesneaux, 1992).

Religiously inspired terrorism was also a medium of political assassination during the late twentieth century when five separate heads of state in Asia, Africa, and the Middle East were the targets of fatal terrorist violence: Anwar al-Sadat (Egypt), Yitzhak Rabin (Israel), S. W. R. D. Bandaranaike (Sri Lanka), Indira Gandhi (India), and Muhammad Boadiaf (Algeria).

For the past seventy-five years, regions as disparate as Africa, South and East Asia, all of Europe, the United States, South America, and Indonesia, and religious traditions as varied as Hinduism, Buddhism, Christianity, Sikhism, and even Japan's indigenous Shintoism, have contributed directly or indirectly to religious terrorism resulting in hundreds of thousands of deaths. Most of these terrorist acts were not part of declared wars but rather were examples of what Shupe (2008a, 481) has termed *global fundamentalism*, a reaction against *institutional differentiation* in societies influenced by secular Western and industrial cultures. This phenomenon is a gradual compartmentalization of religion from other spheres of society and the activities of individuals. Such militant fundamentalist religionists, of whatever specific faith tradition, essentially issue "a proclamation of reclaimed authority over a sacred tradition which is to be reinstated as an antidote for a society perceived to have strayed from its cultural moorings." They intend in their separate (but parallel) ways to return their religion to center stage and restore its influence in politics, economics, medicine, education, the home, and virtually all other institutions.

Two Middle Eastern examples—one contemporary, one ancient—involving years, decades, even centuries of terrorism and strife, illustrate the fundamentalist religious themes in their violence and also the terrible toll that terrorist violence (with its reprisals, counter-reprisals, and so on) costs nations' inhabitants. The first example consists of the constant terrorist attacks of Iraqi Muslim Shi'a and Sunni fighters against civilians (though most civilians and Muslim clerics stay out of and do not incite violence against others) in the name of redressing the attacks of the others. These partisans were further aided by *jihadist* (holy war) fighters immigrating into Iraq from Lebanon, Syria, and elsewhere, both Sunni and Shi'a. Bombings of Shi'a and Sunni neighborhoods became commonplace during the first decade of the twenty-first century. Just one case in point: in February 2006 Sunni militants bombed the Samarra Mosque (among others) and ten Sunni *imams* (clergy) were killed. Soon fifteen more *imams* were kidnapped. Shi'a retaliations against Sunnis for these actions were encouraged by the Shi'a cleric Muqtada al-Sadr, who conducted a small theocracy of his own in a crowded area of Baghdad called (appropriately) Sadr City. Almost all the residents were poor Shi'a immigrants and refugees from violence elsewhere. Al-Sadr appointed himself commander of a large paramilitary force, the Mahdi Army, which drew members particularly from disbanded units of the former Iraqi army (and was said to have received support from Shi'a Iran). Observes Juergensmeyer (2008, 76):

> After the destruction of the Samarra mosque, rogue elements related to the Muqtada camps undertook unusually savage acts of terrorism, aimed at the Sunni population in retaliation for car bomb assaults in Shi'a neighborhoods in Sadr City. The Shi'a reprisals were equally brutal. Groups of ordinary Sunni citizens were rounded up, tortured, and murdered, their bodies mutilated by electric drills and dumped in the Tigris River or in fields outside the city of Baghdad.

Underlying all this sectarian infighting was an intense hatred of the threat seen from (Western) Christian secularization and its purported commercialization of culture, thus an affront to images of traditional Islam. Sunni and Shi'a infighting may really be seen as a struggle to determine which group would then triumph as Islam's primary sect in taking on the West. Concludes Juergensmeyer (2008, 76):

> Many Muslim activists are united in opposing the prospect of Western-style secular nationalism in the Middle East while espousing an Islamic nationalism of their own. Like religious activists elsewhere, they have criticized secular rule from a religious perspective; they employ religious language, leadership, and organization in their attempts to change it, and they hold up as their ideal the promise of a new religious order.

The second example deals with ancient Palestine and to an extent the social milieu in which Christianity originated. When Alexander III of Macedonia (Alexander the Great) died in 323 B.C.E., his empire was divided among his generals into regional satrapies (Syria, Egypt, and so forth). From the second century B.C.E. throughout the next four centuries, many in the Jewish populations of those areas were constantly engaged in resisting foreign and domestic rule, enduring terrorism committed as state policy by the Greeks, Syrians, Romans, and even by home-grown Jewish leaders. In a comprehensive overview of this turmoil, Horsley and Hanson (1985), utilizing biblical and historical texts, chronicle these terrorist and counter-terrorist events, noting that in the age of Jesus of Nazareth "nearly all of the separate movements were popular groups directed against the Jewish ruling elites as well as against Roman rule" (iv). Indeed, many years prior, the Israelite peasantry even participated in two widespread revolts against King David, and later ten of the twelve tribes of Israel rebelled against King Solomon, splitting Israel into northern and southern kingdoms. Repression of each conflict invoked ruthless violence.

One of the most significant violent episodes concerned the successful Maccabean uprising by Jews against Hellenistic cultural trends imposed by the Seleucids, a post-Alexandrian dynasty that ruled the territories spanning Syria to Persia. An enormous tax had burdened the peasantry, levied by the Jewish authorities (working on commission) from Jerusalem on behalf of the foreign rulers. Jewish priestly and aristocratic elites, including King Antiochus IV Epiphanes, were not merely becoming Hellenized (i.e., Greek) in lifestyles and numerous other ways but also collaborated with the ruling non-Jewish powers, fueling a powerful resentment among many loyal Jews. At one point, Antiochus put down one revolt, allowing his army to massacre thousands of Jews in Jerusalem, selling many other Jews into slavery, and leaving Syrian mercenary troops in charge of the city. Filled with the expectation of divine intervention and a coming apocalypse to overthrow the tyranny, certain of the Judeans in the south believed they were anointed as the "instruments of God's own battle against the intolerable heathen attack" (Horsley and Hanson, 1985, 19). Judas "The Hammer" Maccabee, of the Hasmonean family, led a successful revolt around 158–160 B.C.E. as his soldiers plundered the estates and slaughtered the households of noble Hellenized Jews accused of being collaborators. After a good deal of bloodshed and terrorist attacks/reprisals from both sides, the Syrian forces forged a truce with the Jewish Hasmoneans, who founded their own dynasty of Jewish rulers/priests but eventually became as "corrupt" (or cooperative) with the Syrians as had the previous Jewish elites (and were eventually deposed).

By the time the Roman General Pompey conquered the region of Palestine in 63 B.C.E., the Jewish population was faced with the standard terror tactics of the Roman army (i.e., its *punitive war*): in their initial conquest, and particularly in subsequent re-conquests, the Romans treated the inhabitants brutally in order to induce the people to submit. Repeatedly, the Roman armies burned and completely destroyed towns and either slaughtered, crucified, or enslaved their entire populations (Horsley and Hanson, 1985, 31).

The Jews once again witnessed the familiar collaboration (and enrichment) of Jewish priests and aristocrats, such as King Herod the Great, with Roman officials. Upon Herod's death, in fact, there was a persistent series of violent anti-Roman rebellions from 4 B.C.E. to 66 C.E. In 66 C.E. the Jews engaged in their most destructive rebellion against Rome, culminating in 70 C.E. with the Romans sacking Jerusalem, destroying the Temple of Solomon, besieging a handful of hold-out Zealots (revolutionaries) on the high mountain fortress of Masada, and eventually dispersing many of the fleeing Jewish civilians to other countries in the Mediterranean world.

One particular Jewish terrorist group of anti-Roman/anti-Jewish-elite notoriety were the Sicarii, active in the mid-first century (and named for the short curved dagger, the *sicarus*, that was their main weapon of choice). They were strictly urban (not rural) terrorists who were particularly adept at mingling in crowds and attending festivals and other public events where they stabbed *Jewish* officials, slitting their throats or disemboweling them. The Sicarii operated in the most public places, but because of their clandestine, virtually invisible manner of assassination could continue to lead normal lives alongside their unknowing neighbors and did not flee like ordinary bandits to secret mountain strongholds or hideouts. They were not the same as the Zealots (a guerrilla party of revolutionaries who only emerged briefly during the Roman siege of Jerusalem). The Sicarii restricted their terrorist strikes to Jewish officials, not Romans or ordinary Jewish citizens. They limited their activities to "(a) selective symbolic assassinations, (b) more general assassinations, along with plundering of the property of the wealthy and powerful; and (c) kidnapping for ransom" (Horsley and Hanson, 1985, 204–5). The Sicarii largely disappeared after the Jewish revolt against the Romans as did much of the Jewish population of Palestine.

In addition, note Horsley and Hanson (1985, 35), "This period is of special interest to Christians because it forms the context of the life and career of Jesus." Indeed, as portrayed in the Gospel of Mark (considered by most scholars the earliest Gospel to have been written), Jesus is belligerently vocal against the political and social leaders of his era. He challenged the Jewish authorities (who after all were puppets of the Roman occupiers), he proclaimed a "higher" allegiance and ultimately a kingdom on earth to replace the corrupt one of his society, and he condemned the Jewish leaders and denounced them as parasites. That he may have meant his possible messiahship (to Jews of that time, a messiah was to be a military leader) literally or metaphorically did not matter to the authorities. In their view he was yet another upstart revolutionary in a long succession of Jewish peasant troublemakers (also one of a series of such revolutionaries named Joshua, or in Greek, Jesus). It was not for mere mockery that the Romans allegedly placed a sign on the cross above Jesus's head proclaiming him as King of the Jews. The Romans, and their Jewish priestly allies, *very likely did believe* that Jesus's followers believed in his messiahship status; thus he was a credible political threat and had to be dealt with accordingly (Ehrman, 1999, in particular, 125–39, 217–23).

VIOLENCE AS AN INTEGRAL PART OF RELIGIOUS TRADITION AND THEOLOGY

Some religions explicitly incorporate violence into their theologies, making aggression a virtue. Two classic cases are the Assassins and the Thugs. These terms today commonly refer to hired murderers and violent thieves, respectively, yet both are derived from the name of past religious groups.

The Assassins were an extremist branch of Islam made up of professional cutthroats enlisted and trained to murder politicians and rulers. They were formed during the Christian-Muslim conflict of the First Crusade. They derived their name from the Arabic *hashishiyan*, or "users of hashish." They apparently used the drug deliberately to accentuate their violent tendencies, that is, "to become wired" for their violence. The Assassins' founder, Sheikh Sinan, was known as the Old Man of the Mountain and was believed during his lifetime to have commanded a force of one thousand men to contract out as ninja-like killers (Payne, 1984, 184ff, 252). One writer (Annan, 1967) has compared the Assassins to the modern Mafia in the way that the former's agents systematically employed violence and harassment, creating an extensive twelfth- to thirteenth-century extortion racket that gathered protection payments through Middle Eastern towns, villages, and along caravan routes. At times they even "cut deals" with Christian Crusaders if the politics were right and profits were high enough (Daraul, 1969, 1–33; Heckethorn, 1965, 116–22, 243). Their agents' modus operandi was to deliver death by way of a ceremonial dagger.

Similarly, the cult of Thuggee was a sect of polytheistic Hindu religion in India. The focus of its followers' devotion was the "Black" goddess Kali, deity of death. In Hindu theology Kali required human sacrifices and at the same time empowered her followers with spiritual merit when they robbed and murdered victims, particularly travelers on the highways. Thugs were part of an intergenerational/multifamily cartel, professional bandits/murderers who used sacred strangling scarves and ritually anointed pickaxes to kill, rob, and bury their victims (Heckethorn, 1965, 245–51). During the late eighteenth century, British colonial administrators began to investigate and prosecute this homicidal religious network. In 1810 alone magistrates discovered the bodies of thirty travelers ritually disemboweled and dumped down public wells (Annan, 1976, 53). This secretive cult is believed to have murdered twenty thousand victims a year since it began in the thirteenth century, perhaps dispatching as many as several million victims altogether before it was finally broken up by British officials (Haught, 1990, 34).

Some authors (Sutherland, 1987; Scott, 1979) have argued that major world religions such as Judaism, Christianity, and Islam graphically glorify and legitimize violence in their scriptures: from homicide to rape to genocide. It is undeniably true that the scriptures of these religions are replete with incidents of warfare, slaughter, and interpersonal aggression. For example, in the Bible the writer of 2 Kings 19:35 states that in one night alone an angel of Jehovah slew 185,000 Assyrians for the purpose of defending Jerusalem. The Book of Numbers (25:4, 9) details the beheading of 24,000 Israelites who married or cohabited with Moabite women and worshipped the pagan god Baal. 2 Chronicles 28 says that 120,000 Judeans were massacred by Israel's King Pekah for religious apostasy, to name only a few biblical references to bloody mayhem.

Nevertheless, to enumerate such cases out of context and ignore the ethical/theological purposes for including them in religious writings apart from the original authors' standpoints is to commit an obvious distortion. For example, an outraged Jesus of Nazareth taking a whip to drive the money-changers out of the Jerusalem temple cannot logically be used to develop a Christian theory of aggression or retribution. Likewise, the Prophet Mohammed, who led his earliest followers repeatedly into battles, "hated the idea of fighting even in self defense and had to be inured to it" (Pickthall, 1961, xvii).

Those who wish to read into Islamic theology some inherent justification for terrorism, violence, and fanaticism will just as surely find it as have those who have "proof-texted" (or cherry-picked selected segments) from the Bible to legitimize crusades, pogroms, slavery, or the arms race. Despite the visceral pro-violence statements that some religionists, such as Iran's Ayatollah Khomeini, have made, they speak no more for Islam's ultimate position toward violence or peace than did Richard the Lion-Hearted for Christianity when he butchered thousands of helpless Muslim prisoners.

Pathological, or "deviant," religions have incorporated violence into their principal tenets. For example, there is now substantial reason to regard Adolf Hitler's Nazi movement as more than just a fascist political phenomenon. It was also an ongoing religious concern of the first magnitude. Hitler did more than dabble in magic and the paranormal: he was obsessed with astrology, the Arthurian Holy Grail legends, German/Nordic mythology, racial mysticism, and other aspects of the occult (Sklar, 1977; Angebert, 1974; Brennan, 1974). Hitler also allegedly regarded his role in the growth of the Third Reich as a messianic one.

As historian Robert G. L. Waite (1977, 32) has observed about Hitler, "He did not view the (Nazi) Party and the Reich merely as secular organizations." Such a messianic view may in part explain the otherwise sociopathic zeal with which Hitler dispatched millions of Jews, gypsies, Slavs, and other ethnic minorities to concentration camps and gas chambers. Worse, it probably reveals his complete detachment in approving so-called scientific experiments where many unfortunate persons were sterilized and operated upon to discover, for example, how fast injected gangrene would spread in a patient's body, what the product of a female human inseminated with ape sperm would be like, and other aberrant investigations (Muller-Hill, 1988).

On a micro level, various racist tax-protesting/right-wing/survivalist groups in the Mountain West, including Christian Constitutionalists, The Order, The Aryan Nations, American Israelites, and the Posse Comitatus, have incorporated religious justifications for violence in their ideologies of militant resistance (Aho, 1990; Corcoran, 1990), and in recent decades there have been several sensational cases of groups integrating violence with theology. One was the Reverend Jim Jones (an ordained Disciples of Christ minister) and his People's Temple. There is no question that Jones, who claimed to be a reincarnation of both Karl Marx and Jesus Christ, systematically introduced abuse and intimidation of adults and children into his cultic congregation (Hall, 1989; Moore and McGhee, 1989; Levi, 1982), even to the point of having followers engage in macabre mock communions that he told them might or might not include poison instead of wine.

Eventually, when Jones perceived that his movement (the headquarters of which he had moved from San Francisco to a remote jungle compound called Jonestown in Guyana, South America) was about to be seriously investigated by the U.S. federal government, he ordered his followers to undergo suicide by drinking grape Flavor Aid (similar to Kool-Aid) mixed with cyanide. Not all followers eagerly or willingly drank it. A third of the group were, after all, infants and small children panicked by the screams and moans of those already dying. (Cyanide does not provide an instantaneous or painless death.) Even a dog had a pipe inserted down his throat to get the deadly drink down it. Whether passively or at rifle-point, more than nine hundred persons died of the poison, except Jones, who died mysteriously from a gunshot to his head.

Such suicidal tendencies are by no means unique. There were repeated outbursts of religious zealots known as "Old Believers" in eighteenth- and nineteenth-century Russia. The Old Believers mutilated, castrated, and even immolated (burned alive) themselves out of religious fervor and political protest long before Jim Jones ever chose to make a fatal statement of defiance with his followers' suicides in the jungles of Guyana. The Old Believers protested reforms in the Russian Orthodox Church regarding liturgy and hymns, attracting many peasants who also were unhappy with political centralization efforts of the czars. The Russian Skopzi, both males and females, believed strict, irrevocable celibacy was the spiritual ideal and mutilated their genitals with red-hot irons, knives, razors, hatchets, and glass (Heckethorn, 1965, 292–300; Robbins, 1986). Thousands died during these cultic revolts.

One of the most recent examples of violence and religion combined occurred during the spring of 1993 just outside the town of Waco, Texas. On a remote ranch known as the Mount Carmel compound, an apocalyptic Christian sect called the Branch Davidians followed a charismatic prophet named David Koresh (originally known as Vernon Wayne Howell). Koresh, a rock musician from California who had not passed the ninth grade in school, regarded himself as the person who could finally decipher the seven seals or mysteries in the Bible's final Book of Revelations, thereby bringing about the End of Time or Final Conflagration of Earth, which he believed was prophesied in various places in the Bible.

The Branch Davidians began in conflict and violence. In 1918 Victor Houteff, a Bulgarian immigrant, joined the Seventh-Day Adventist sect, but by 1934 he had disagreed with leaders over interpretations of last days prophecies in the Book of Revelations. He formed his own group, consisting of several dozen former Adventist members, and moved them to a location outside the small town of Waco, Texas.

In 1942 the group officially adopted the name Branch Seventh-Day Adventists. When Houteff died in 1955, his wife, Florence, took charge and publicized her own prophecy that the Kingdom of King David would be re-created on April 28, 1959 (tantamount to predicting the return of Jesus Christ to earth). About 1,400 persons responded with hope and flocked to her. With their property and assets all handed over to Florence, she bought the Mount

Carmel compound about ten miles east of Waco. After her prophecy failed, there was a split, the largest group going with Florence's rival leader, Ben Roden. Roden gave his faction the name with which most Americans are familiar: the Branch Davidians.

When Ben Roden died in 1978, there was further conflict as his son, George, and Vernon Wayne Howell (not yet Koresh) vied for leadership. Eventually the hostilities culminated in a shoot-out that drove Roden off the Mount Carmel property, charges of attempted murder filed against Howell and seven followers, and a trial in which those followers were found innocent, the charges against Howell eventually dropped, and Roden committed to a mental asylum for murdering another Texas man by reason of insanity (Wright, 1995).

Koresh had a fascination with guns and armaments that became an integral part of his doomsday theology. That is why the U.S. Bureau of Alcohol, Tobacco, and Firearms (BATF) initially came into contact with him. That was also the primary pretext behind a disastrous raid on the Mount Carmel compound on February 28, 1993, by 130 BATF agents. According to the search warrant issued by a federal judge (and ironically never served), Koresh had acquired grenade and flare launchers; numerous handguns, rifles, and semiautomatic weapons (evidence of almost three were found in the later wreckage); explosives; and the necessary parts to convert the weapons so as to make them fully automatic (Bureau of Alcohol, Tobacco, and Firearms, 1993, 193ff).

It is still debated who fired first, the Davidians who knew the federal agents were coming or the BATF agents. It is still contested as to whether either the fifty-one-day siege of the compound by a small army of Federal Bureau of Investigation agents or the final assault on compound buildings with armored vehicles was justified (Lewis, 1994). And we will likely never know the true extent to which Koresh and his followers posed any serious danger to citizens outside their doomsday group.

Inside the group, allegations by disillusioned ex-members that Koresh physically and sexually abused children were never verified by state social workers who visited the compound, yet President Bill Clinton and newly appointed Attorney General Janet Reno steadfastly maintained that the final assault on the compound had to be undertaken for the children. (One wonders, then, why all utilities and water had been cut off to the families inside for weeks and why a form of tear gas, outlawed by the Geneva Convention for use in warfare, was pumped into the compound buildings hour after hour.)

After becoming frustrated with Koresh's seemingly unlimited stalling tactics, their own inability to deal with an erratic religious leader, and the embarrassing negative publicity growing nationally day by day, on April 19 the FBI decided to end the standoff. Some eighty-six Davidians died in the fiery holocaust that resulted. Seventeen of the dead were children.

What most American citizens know of the events at Waco is based on information, some of it deliberately disinformational and provided by government sources for their own purposes, filtered through a noncritical mass media that had little access to independent data (Shupe and Hadden, 1995). What can be said is that not all religions manifest a clear potential for violence but that violence, as manifested in stored armaments, in theology, and in the everyday expectations of committed followers, was a clear theme running throughout the affairs of the Branch Davidians.

Likewise, there have been several other spectacular examples of cult violence at the end of the twentieth century. The Order of the Solar Temple was a Euro-American group associated with drugs and suicide. The Heaven's Gate UFO cult, believing a spaceship was coming to transport them to another planet and that males should have themselves castrated to be "purer," tried to recruit believers on the Internet and ended up committing suicide (all in uniforms, wearing Nike athletic shoes and covered in purple sheets). It is as if people destroying themselves as well as others is an episodic but continuing phenomenon through religion in virtually every culture (see, e.g., Hoffman and Burke, 1997; Kaplan and Marshall, 1996; and Boyle, 1995, for popular but reliable accounts of these groups).

In a previous chapter we also examined martyrdom as a time-honored cultural role in various religious traditions. It is a role both the Ayatollah Khomeini and the Reverend Jim Jones chose to offer up to their followers with grisly consequences. Human sacrifice as well was mentioned earlier. Given its widespread practice throughout history and on virtually every continent, there is absolutely no way to be sure how many victims altogether have perished at the hands of priests, Crusaders, and ecclesiastical executioners. Undoubtedly the numbers would run into many millions. One generalization, however, can be made with certainty about any "officially" sanctioned religious violence: the symbol-manipulating potential of human beings presents a capability to rationalize and justify virtually any activity, no matter how heinous, in the name of faith in the supernatural, and to regard it as consistent with the loftiest ideals.

PERSECUTION OF HERETICS AND NONBELIEVERS

Journalist James A. Haught (1990, 14) observes: "A grim pattern is visible in history: when religion is the ruling force in a society, it produces horror. The stronger the supernatural beliefs, the worse the inhumanity. A culture dominated by intense faith invariably is cruel to people who don't share the faith—and sometimes to many that do." One need look no further than the Iranian theocracy of the 1980s for evidence to support Haught's assertion. Closer to home the religiously minded colonists of seventeenth- and eighteenth-century North America also exercised their share of intolerance (Morgan, 1968). Despite the image of America as a land of religious freedom, it is just as accurate to say that this country has always been a cauldron of religious tension. The Calvinist Puritans, who fled England seeking religious freedom, in turn felt quite comfortable in denying it to others. In seventeenth-century New England, pacifistic Quakers who refused to pay taxes, serve in the military, or take oaths were hanged, flogged, deported, tortured, and sold into bondage by Puritan councils (Hill, 1980, 58). Between 1659 and 1661 the city fathers of Boston hanged four Quakers on Boston Common as public menaces.

During the eighteenth century the Shakers (a Pentecostal-style sect promoting strict celibacy and monastic-like piety) were accused of disturbing the peace, disloyalty and treason, heresy, and witchcraft (Foster, 1981, 30–35; Andrews, 1963, 58). Their refusal to fight in the American Revolution brought charges that they were really British spies (Holloway, 1966, 58–59). As a result, mobs broke into their dormitory-style homes and roughed up Shaker men or attacked them in the streets. Shakers were imprisoned for refusing to take oaths of loyalty and fined repeatedly.

The experiences of many Irish Catholic immigrants from the 1820s to the 1860s were no more tranquil. Accused of being the advance guard for a Vatican plot to take over the United States, the Irish confronted blatant discrimination and hostility from the dominant Protestant culture. Throughout the 1830s and 1840s there were numerous instances of anti-Catholic mobs destroying homes, churches, and convents. In 1834 an Ursuline convent in Charleston, Massachusetts, was looted and burned to the ground by a Protestant mob. The latter riot was incited by rumors that a young woman was being held inside against her will. Undoubtedly one of the worst riots occurred in Kensington, a suburb of Philadelphia, in 1844. There, a series of rumors inspired a mob to swarm into a predominantly Catholic neighborhood. Two churches and a convent were torched, and thirteen people died in the violence. The riot was halted only after the militia was called out and finally forced to fire point-blank into the crowd to quell it. Religious tensions continued. As late as 1871 a riot broke out in New York City between Protestant and Irish Catholic immigrants (Gilje, 1987; Marty, 1984; Wittke, 1970; Shannon, 1966).

Likewise, members of the Church of Jesus Christ of Latter-Day Saints, as is well known, experienced constant persecution from non-Mormons ("Gentiles") in mid-nineteenth-century America (Hill, 1989; Arrington and Haupt, 1988; Arrington and Bitton, 1980). Things became so bad for them in Missouri and Illinois, including the mob murder of founder Joseph Smith and his brother Hyrum, that most of the Mormons finally packed up and trekked to Utah, at that time one of the most desolate and inhospitable regions of North America.

However, the Mormon pilgrims were not just victims of religiously inspired violence. The 1857 Mountain Meadows Massacre occurred when a group of Mormon men attacked a wagon train of pioneers traveling through Utah to California, killing 120 men, women, and children. Bagley (2002) contends that the church leadership knew of the impending attack and covered up the involvement of the Mormon community. Walker, Turley, and Leonard (2008) place the blame on John D. Lee, a militia leader who feared an attack of federal soldiers. What all agree to is the fact that the violence directed at the Mormons and the attack by the Mormon militia group were inspired by the violence of religious intolerance.

The most systematically ruthless persecution of "heretics" was unquestionably the Spanish Inquisition, with the name of its most famous inquisitor general, Tomas de Torquemada, now a synonym for cruelty and religious fanaticism. The Inquisition functioned at a time when Spanish kings were retaking their kingdoms league by league from the Moors, who had ruled the greater part of Spain for eight centuries. At the same time, Christian intolerance of Jews was increasing.

The Inquisition began in the twelfth century in response to various pre–Protestant Reformation sects that arose and after Pope Innocent III urged secular and ecclesiastical officials to persecute such heretics. In Spain the tribunals of the Inquisition achieved a prominence unlike anywhere else. Calling it a "hideous monster," one historian observes:

> Thousands were submitted to the cruelest torture these (Inquisitors) could devise; the flesh of the victims was torn with red hot pincers, and molten lead poured into the wounds; many suffered the agonies of the hoist and the water torture; some were racked to death; some were burned at the stake; every means of dealing pain and indignity to the human body was explored, and all this was done in the name of One who had commanded his followers to love one another. (Plaidy, 1969, 16)

Christians, particularly political dissidents, were also among the victims. The Inquisition coincided with political events in Spanish history from the fifteenth to nineteenth centuries (the last Inquisitor General died in 1834). However, inquisitions and torture/executions of alleged heretics were well under way elsewhere in Europe earlier. As Norman Cohn (1975) chronicles so well in *Europe's Inner Demons*, the obsession to ferret out heretics was premised on the assumption that society and the church were under attack by a subversive conspiracy of satanists. This "subversion fantasy" maintained "that there existed, somewhere in the midst of the great society, another society, small and clandestine, which not only threatened the existence of the great society but was also dedicated to practices which were felt to be wholly abominable, in the literal sense of anti-human" (Cohn, 1975, xi).

We can go back even earlier in the history of Christianity during the first century when its institutional structure was less secure and messiahs who were supported by the most marginal elements of feudal society posed a serious threat to the social order. Cohn mentions a number of cases of messiahs who were killed because of the threat they posed to the church and the established order.

Cohn (1971) traces the growth of folklore about black masses, satanic covens, and witchcraft as church leaders, in their attempt to consolidate power over diversifying medieval society, used it as a pretext for imprisonment, torture, and execution. In related fashion, Phillip the Fair, king of mid-fourteenth-century France, used the mythology of witchcraft to break up the Knights Templar. The Templars were members of a military religious order of the church that not only fielded its own warrior-monk armies but also created an extensive, lucrative, influential banking system throughout Europe. Envious of the Templars' wealth and claiming that they actually constituted an underground cult of Satan-worshippers and heretics, Phillip attacked the order, driving its leaders into exile or torturing and burning them at the stake (Partner, 1987; Burman, 1986).

This concern to weed out heretics gradually focused on persons accused of being witches, the supposed tools of Satan and the real scapegoats for strains and fears of the power establishment in a Europe shifting from feudal to capitalist economies. Anthropologists (e.g., Marwick, 1968) and sociologists (MacFarlane, 1970; Bednarski, 1968) regard "outbreaks" of witchcraft as well as its alleged ongoing existence as indications, or "gauges," of social strain in societies, occurring particularly in times of widespread economic change. Discontent with social structural changes becomes focused on suspicions of interpersonal wrongdoing, in particular on alleged usages of antisocial means to get ahead or deal revenge. Old norms and vested interests, meanwhile, are threatened, while new ones compete for ascendance.

Thus witch hunts occurred throughout Europe during the sixteenth and seventeenth centuries, most victims of which were women who were also the most powerless, "convenient" scapegoats (MacFarlane, 1970, 160–61). Likewise, Karlsen (1987, 20, 47–49) relates how, between 1620 and 1725, 344 North American colonists were formally accused of being witches, 78 percent of them women. Women accounted for many more of the executions (usually by hanging) than men.

Massachusetts, with its staunch Puritan heritage, saw disproportionately more witch-hunting hysteria than other colonies. Most famous was the witch hunt that occurred at Salem in 1692. It is a classic example of the "strain-gauge" hypothesis. By the late seventeenth century, New England was witnessing a breakdown in its theocratic political structure, caused in large part by British trade policies and an influx of non-Puritan immigrants. There was an unmistakable clash between the strict values of the Massachusetts Bay Colony's original settlers and emerging religious pluralism. The colony was diversifying and urbanizing. As a consequence, the homogeneous "small town" quality of life among Puritan believers and neighbors was rapidly, and stressfully, disappearing. Amid these profound changes came charges of witchcraft that transformed much of Massachusetts, in the words of one sociologist (Bednarski, 1968, 156), into "a society gone mad—a society blind to rationality and reason, driven by fear and distrust."

According to the horrifying testimonies of a handful of adolescent and teenage girls, a network of demonically inspired witches was systematically hexing and possessing people as well as attempting to wreck the social order. It is generally agreed among modern scholars that there was no real outbreak of witchcraft, only a case of public panic. (The girls also later recanted their testimonies and apologized.) The witch-finding prosecutors at Salem nevertheless sent nineteen persons to the gallows. Two more died in jail awaiting hanging, and one man was crushed to death by heavy rocks piled on him during interrogation. Meanwhile, in response to public clamor for the satanic conspirators to be apprehended, more than 150 suspected witches were held in custody and an additional 200 had been accused. Only gradually, as the girls' accusations became more indiscriminate and incredible, did the scare collapse (Bednarski, 1968; Hansen, 1969; Starkey, 1969).

Recent fears of a rising satanist network of pornographers, ritual child abusers, cattle mutilators, and murderers (Raschke, 1990; Johnston, 1989; Kahaner, 1988) have caused alarm in communities across the United States as well as abroad, expanding on the demonological motifs of medieval witchcraft folklore. Reliable social science, law enforcement, and journalistic research (Richardson et al., 1991; Victor, 1993; Hicks, 1991), however, find that claims of satanic violence, like those of the alleged abducted "milk carton" children (the vast majority of which are abducted by parents) or the rumors of poison and razor blades hidden in Halloween trick-or-treaters' candy, are largely "urban legends," plausible because they feed off our worst fears of impersonal/potentially dangerous society but nevertheless empirically disconfirmed (Best, 1990). The FBI, for example, has yet to find a single case of a person murdered by an organized satanistic conspiracy, even though promoters of a satanic scare loudly proclaim (with absolutely no substantiation) that fifty thousand persons are ritually sacrificed (i.e., murdered) every year in the United States.

CLERGY VIOLENCE

A member of the clergy is a fiduciary, just like a physician, therapist, accountant, or attorney. Fiduciaries are the professionals who have special expert knowledge to help (biblically, "to minister") other less expert persons and are responsible for looking out for their best interests. Clergy fiduciaries are especially trusted when they occupy their sacred role because they are intermediary agents between the layperson or parishioner and the supernatural. As such, when clergy elites betray the trust placed in them by persons in the pews—whether sexually (molestations, rapes, seductions, or harassment), economically (as in theft from the congregation), or through misuse of their authority to overly control lives—we have a particularly painful, damaging, and egregious form of deviance that is often accompanied by violence.

A serious form of clergy religious violence first came to light in the United States during the mid-1980s, involving clergymen (though a few women were likewise accused) who physically and sexually abused prepubescent boys and girls, teenagers, and women. The molestations included oral and anal sex, rape, and outright seduction, all in unequal power situations within an otherwise trusted institution: the church. Much of the media attention, whether in the press, on investigative television magazines like *20/20* and *Prime Time Live*, or on talk shows like *Montel Williams* or *Oprah Winfrey*, has focused on Roman Catholic priests and children (Burkett and Bruni, 1993; Berry, 1992; Rossetti, 1990), though there are plenty of comparable cases of Protestant sexual abuse of laypersons (Enroth, 1992; Poling, 1991; Cooper-White, 1991; Brock and Lukens, 1988). In fact, several scholars have examined this sort of violence occurring across a broad array of religious traditions (see Shupe, 1995; Cartwright and Kent, 1992; Jacobs, 1989).

In 2002 many Americans suddenly became aware that the Archdiocese of Boston, at that time the fourth largest Roman Catholic diocese in North America, was immersed in a priest sexual abuse scandal of tremendous scale. Thanks to relentless reporting by news outlets such as the *Boston Globe* (which won a Pulitzer Prize for its coverage) and numerous lawsuits brought against the archdiocese and its leader, Cardinal Bernard Law, it was learned that the cardinal and various bishops under him had, over a period of years, hushed up laypersons' accusations against priests with money or intimidation. Meanwhile, Law and others with his knowledge had systematically reassigned those abusive priests from parish to parish without the next parish knowing what the abusive cleric had done in his previous assignment (in Catholic circles known cynically as "the geographic cure"). While the scandal continued to mount, Cardinal Law was deposed under oath by plaintiffs' lawyers multiple times and then suddenly was recalled by the Vatican to Vatican City in Italy and appointed to a relatively symbolic position (thus escaping the very real and serious likelihood of criminal prosecution—see Shupe, 2007, 1–4).

By the time the scandal was in full swing in early 2002, there were already 84 lawsuits filed against *just one* of the several dozens of accused priests and 118 suits filed against Cardinal Law. Over 275 persons claimed they had been sexually abused over the years. Then one lawyer announced to the media that he was representing 250 *new* clients claiming victimization on top of many others. Estimates of the portended damages sought ran into the hundreds of millions of dollars. Soon scandals erupted in virtually every state in North America, in Canada, and eventually around the world.

Many in the mass media, with an acute sense of historical myopia, kept asking the questions, "Why has this wave of scandals so abruptly surfaced now?" or "Why is this type of abuse suddenly happening?" Both questions essentially ignored the history and existence of pastoral abuse in this country and elsewhere. For, example, to consider just the Roman Catholic Church (the largest Christian group in North America as well as the world), historians have found a lengthy record of sexual exploitation of nuns, sisters, and male novitiates (young aspirants to holy orders and the priesthood) by older priests and church superiors stretching back more than nine hundred years into medieval times in Europe (for example, see Laudurie, 1978; Boswell, 1981; Daichman, 1990; Doyle, Sipe, and Wall, 2006).

Moreover, based on numerous historical studies, including lengthy case analyses (such as those by Johnson and Wilentz, 1994; Jenkins, 2002), we know that half a millennium later in North America, both in the United States and Canada, there has been a steady parade of hustlers, con-artists, charlatans, and lecherous clergypersons, many of them Protestant, during the eighteenth, nineteenth, and twentieth centuries, all preying on gullible, trusting believers. We have abundant evidence of pastoral chicanery in modern Reform/Conservative/Orthodox Jewish congregations (Schwab, 2002) as well as similar sexual/financial/power abuses in modern American Zen Buddhism (for a summary, see Shupe and Bradley, 2010, 161–63), among television preachers (with their continuous appeals for money and occasional sexual peccadilloes exploiting women and children) and lack of accountability (Hadden and Shupe 1988; Shupe and Eliasson-Nannini, 2012), and within the Church of Jesus Christ of Latter-Day Saints, among many other groups' abuses (Shupe, 2008).

Thus, there is nothing new about clergy abuse or malfeasance, only our periodic rediscovery of it. Nor is the problem of exploitation of layperson believers by clergy of various faith traditions contained within the borders of the North American continent. There are a variety of sources to inform us of this fact, such as Associated News Services worldwide and local/regional newspaper reports, television newsmagazine reports (not to mention numerous cable news outlets), and the various Internet websites and publications of watchdog victims' advocacy groups, such as SCAR (Survivors of Clergy Abuse Reachout), SNAP (Survivors Network of Those Abused by Priests), Survivors Connection, and Voice of the Faithful. These organizations have become literal clearinghouses of information for victim self-help, referrals to mental health and legal specialists, news of upcoming local/regional/national/international meetings, and so forth.

Thus researchers know of revelations and exposures of clergy abuse incidents and prolonged scandals in countries such as Australia (including Adelaide, Brisbane, Melbourne, Perth, and Sidney), Austria, Belgium, Canada, England, France, Germany, Iceland, India, Ireland (both Northern and Republic), Israel, Italy, Mexico, Nepal, the Netherlands, the Philippines, Poland, Scandinavian countries, most nations in South America, Switzerland, Taiwan, Trinidad, the United Kingdom and Scotland, even Vatican City as well as Rome. All this demonstrates that the domain of clergy malfeasance in time and geographic space is immense, sparing no continent, few countries, and virtually no major religious tradition.

Much of what is being studied about sexual violence among clergypersons is social psychological, concerned with the motives of both perpetrators and their victims who often remain silent (Sipe, 1990, 1995, 2003; Nason-Clark, 1991). Not surprisingly, analogies have been drawn between sexual violence by clergy directed at victims in the pew or serving at the altar and violations of sexual trust by other professionals, such as teachers, counselors, psychiatrists, and physicians (Rutter, 1989). But to focus only at the social psychological or interpersonal level is to lose sight of the larger significance of clergy violence, since (by our definition) it is a premier case of institutional violence.

Any religious organization, as we intimated at the beginning of this chapter, is a hierarchy of power, a system of levels of trusted authority, wherein followers/believers/congregants/laypersons often drop their guards when dealing with leaders they assume will show benevolence, integrity, and ethical professionalism toward them. Several authors (see Fortune, 1989; Shupe, 1995) have compared a religious leader's authority in this case to one that legal experts refer to as fiduciary responsibility, that is, that the professional is not supposed to substitute what is in his or her own best interest for what is in the best interest of the client or parishioner (i.e., the fiduciary).

In fact, Shupe (1995; 2008) developed a structural conflict theory of clergy malfeasance that bases its propositions on the organizational polity, or political structure, of individual religious groups. Polities, he maintains, recruit personnel and manage the handling of deviance (in this case, sexual violence against vulnerable church members) in different ways. He distinguishes between hierarchical groups, in which local congregations are part of larger systems or denominations to which they are accountable (such as United Presbyterians, United Methodists, Roman Catholics, Church of Jesus Christ of Latter-Day Saints, or Episcopalians) and congregational groups (such as Independent Baptist and Fundamentalist Christian churches, the Bhagwan Shree Rajneesh movement, various televangelist para-ministries, and numerous sect-cult groups).

Using this hierarchical/congregational model, Shupe has developed empirically based propositions about how hierarchical religious groups, with their accountability to authority outside the local congregation, would react to clergy deviance differently from congregational groups in terms of perpetration of abuse, official organizational response, and victims' responses. He concludes that hierarchical church groups, with their relatively greater bureaucratization, shield abusers longer than do congregational groups, but the former ultimately do better in discouraging the normalization, or members' acceptance, of clergy malfeasance. Shupe contends that hierarchical groups provide religious leaders with greater opportunities to rationalize or dismiss victims' claims of abuse but at the same time are more likely than congregational groups to develop policies addressing clergy abuse. Lastly hierarchical groups, thanks to their layers of authority and ecclesiastical traditions, at first promote ambivalence among victims and/or fear of elite retaliation for whistle-blowing on clergy but ultimately empower them to protest more so than in congregational groups.

The recognition and analysis of clergy violence against followers is relatively new in social science. The subject has not been subjected to much study and analysis except in spectacular cases like the People's Temple or the Branch Davidians. Shupe's more church-structure approach is rather novel and new. What emerges, however unpalatable it is to many believers, is the fact that the religious institution is itself a major source of violence.

MISSIONARIES, MILITARY CONQUEST, AND IMPERIALISM

Religious missionaries during the past five hundred years have played an important role in furthering the spread of empires throughout history, notably in the conquest of the Americas, Africa, and Asia by European imperial powers. Missionaries have played the role of assimilators of those who have been conquered. They function as a mechanism of social control as they establish symbolic internal mechanisms to coerce conformity to the culture of the imperial power. Unfortunately, the methods of assimilation have often had a devastating effect, often exerting violence on those who are the subject of their missionary work. Indeed, in 2001 Pope John Paul II even publicly apologized to the world for his church's role in aiding oppressors and conquerors. Missionaries serve to make the area safe for the later penetration of economic actors to secure valued resources. They also have made areas safe for settlement of citizens from the conquering nations.

Hayford (1970) states that "it is the favorite practice with European nations to precede the Flag with the Gospel of Jesus Christ. . . . The missionary points to the cardinal lesson of truth, love and brotherhood as proclaimed by the Gospel, which are in accord with the higher impulses of the Native, and commands his ready respect and obedience. In the course of time, the Flag makes its appearance, and with it boldly emerges the merchant and trades-man, who before were merely sneaking round the corner" (232).

Tinker (1993) argues that Christian missionaries throughout North Amer-ica were partners with the state in genocide of the indigenous populations. He argues that the missionaries were guilty of complicity in the destruction of Indian cultures, tribal social structures, and the devastating impoverishment and death of the people to whom they preached. Focusing on several major missionary efforts in North America (John Eliot in colonial Massachusetts, Junipero Serra in California, Pierre-Jean De Smet in Missouri, and Henry Benjamin Whipple in Minnesota), Tinker documents the role that their ef-forts played in the cultural, social, political, and economic destruction of the tribal groupings that they were assimilating and converting to the European and Christian way of life. He concludes that the European colonial conquest of the Americas was fought on two separate symbiotically related fronts. One front involved the political and military strategy that drove Indian peoples from their land to make room for the more civilized conqueror and worked to deprive Indian peoples of any continuing self-governance or self-determina-tion (120).

The second front, just as decisive in the conquest of the Indian popula-tion, was the religious one pursued by missionaries of all denominations. Tinker notes that missionaries arrived first, to be followed in due course by the flag, armies, farmers, and merchants. But the missionaries for the most part have stayed on and continue to this day to exert a subtle social control over Indian communities. For Tinker, the missionaries played a crucial role in the European conquest of Indian people, a conquest that resulted in geno-cide.

The genocidal violence directed at the indigenous populations of North America was cultural and spiritual as well as physical. These forms of geno-cide are linked. Destruction of a people's cultural system often resulted in their physical destruction. Tinker defines cultural genocide as the effective destruction of a people by systematically (intentionally or unintentionally in order to achieve other goals) destroying, eroding, or undermining the integ-rity of the culture and system of values that defines a people and gives them life (Tinker, 1993, 5). The cultural genocide the missionaries practiced began with destroying those cultural structures of existence that gave a people a sense of holistic and communal integrity. By limiting a people's freedom to practice their culture and to live out their lives in culturally appropriate patterns, they effectively destroyed a people by eroding both their self-es-teem and the interrelationships that bind them together as a community (5).

Tinker argues that missionaries utilized four interrelated vehicles of cultu-ral genocide. The first vehicle is the political. This is the use of political power, backed by the threat of military or police intervention, to control and subdue a weaker, culturally discrete entity. Tinker cites the "Civilization" Act passed by the U.S. Congress in 1819 that gave missionaries land grants and funding for mission schools as one example of the linkage of the mis-sionaries with the state. This act was important in indicating the state spon-sorship of the penetration of missionaries into Indian territories. He also cites the Grant Peace Policy of 1870, which delegated to the denominations the responsibility for filling the positions of Indian agent and parceling out particular nations or reservations to various denominations. Here missionaries were operating directly in their capacity as officers of the state in controlling the indigenous populations. Through these legislative actions, the government of the United States was utilizing missionaries as part of the larger strategy of territorial expansion.

In discussing the missionary work of Father Junipero Serra and how it was related to the goals of the Spanish colonial and imperial governments, Tinker notes that Serra and other missionaries were on the payroll of the viceroy and effectively functioned as a branch of the civil service in their mission endeavors. Tinker observes that this relationship had been in existence since the sixteenth century, whereas the "state assumed responsibility for the conversion of the natives in return for papal support for the Crown's colonial expansion and concessions permitting royal intervention in ecclesiastical affairs of the colonies" (Tinker, 1993, 43). Tinker does not doubt that the Franciscans, Dominicans, and Jesuit missionaries came to their task with pious intentions, while the government in New Spain saw their evangelistic outreach as serving the purpose of conquest in terms of pacification of the countryside. The development of the California mission system from its beginning was an integral part of Spain's strategy of colonization and conquest. He concludes that "Serra was a mere religious-political agent for imperial Spain, helping Spain achieve its colonial goals in the late eighteenth century" (Tinker, 1993, 46).

Tinker also discusses the link between the state (British imperial state) and the missionary efforts of John Eliot in Massachusetts. Not only were missionaries acting as an extension of the states that sponsored them by destroying the political independence of the people they were converting, through the assimilation process they destroyed the native forms of self-governance. The reducción system, which was based on the creation of separate Indian communities controlled by the missionaries for the purpose of assimilation and conversion, presupposed both the inability of the native people to govern themselves as civilized people and the need for authoritarian governance by the missionary in each locale. Tinker (1993) notes that the indigenous political leadership was recognized only to the extent that it could be exploited by either the colonial government or the missions themselves.

The second vehicle of cultural genocide is economic. Here Tinker is referring to the forced transformation of the indigenous population, removing them from their cultural roots and establishing relationships of domination between missionaries and Indians. "The economic aspects of genocide involve using or allowing the economic system, always with political or even military support, to manipulate and exploit another culturally discrete entity that is both politically and economically weaker. The results can range from enslavement and the direct exploitation of labor to the pillaging of natural resources that leaves a people unable to sustain themselves" (Tinker, 1993, 7).

In general these forced economic changes resulted in the transformation of a people who were economically self-sufficient to those who were dominated and dependent as they produced for their colonial overlords, the missionaries and the colonial state. The economic plight and role of these isolated communities, "praying towns," which were located on the frontier of white settlements, served as a military buffer. Tinker also notes how the economies of these praying towns were subservient and dependent in their development on the white colonial settlements.

> Essentially limited in their ability to compete, the praying towns became sup-
> pliers for the more substantial and stable Puritan economy. Allowed to pro-
> duce goods and services for Puritan trade, the praying towns became a depen-
> dent, client economy. The resulting economic codependency is a phenomenon
> that continues to this day. Indian tribes in the United States today function
> largely around a carefully conceived and federally controlled comprador sys-
> tem that rewards an educated class of tribal members for maintaining the well-
> behaved client status of their tribes. (Tinker, 1993, 33)

Tinker also notes that the reducción system Serra established and the resultant economic transformation of the indigenous population resulted in problems of famine that were unheard of previously among those populations.
Work on the missions was geared to the production of surplus that was
controlled by the missionaries. The Indian producers received the bare minimum as daily sustenance. It is not only nation-states that utilized missionaries to fulfill their own economic interests. Tinker notes the self-interest of the
fur trading companies was evident as they made substantial contributions to
both Protestant and Catholic missionaries for their pacification efforts, which
according to Tinker aided and abetted the companies' exploitation of Indians,
Indian lands, and Indian resources.

In regard to the religious vehicle of cultural genocide, Tinker states that
this involves the overt attempt to destroy the spiritual solidarity of a people.
One of the ways this was done was to outlaw native ceremonial forms of
worship. For example, the performance of the Sun Dance of the Plains Indians or the Hopi Snake Dance was defined as a punishable crime, and the
performance of the Ghost Dance resulted in the massacre of 350 people at
Wounded Knee on December 29, 1890.

Another way religion was used as a vehicle of cultural genocide was
through the forced participation of native populations in the conqueror's
religious ceremonials by means of the threat of physical punishment. Tinker
notes that Serra in his missionary work in the Sierra Gorda region of central
Mexico used the power of the military to force attendance at religious services for Indian converts and nonconverts alike. In describing the efforts of
Eliot in Massachusetts, Tinker cites "the imposition of Puritan theology and
theological language across the cultural chasm that separated Indian and
English certainly generated a sense of low self-worth on the part of Indian
converts from which Indian people have not yet recovered" (Tinker, 1993,
40).

This pattern of forced conversion has been going on for centuries in the
history of Christendom. In 1531, Pizarro invited the Inca ruler, Atahualpa, to
visit him. Atahualpa arrived along with thousands of unarmed Inca soldiers.
The priest that accompanied Pizarro on his mission, Vicente de Valverde,
was sent out to meet the ruler and to inform the Incan ruler that he must
accept Christianity and Spanish rule. The Incan ruler rejected the offer,
throwing the Bible that was handed to him down onto the ground. This was a

signal the armed Spanish soldiers were waiting for as they swooped in on their horses, killing more than 7,000 unarmed Incan soldiers and their attendants (Gage, 1991). For the Spanish it was a precondition of conquest to require that those whom they were about to conquer be given the opportunity to voluntarily accept conversion and their rule. If they chose not to accept, they would be slaughtered.

After conquest, the Spanish clergy throughout the Americas forbade the native population from practicing their religion. In 1614 the Archbishop of Lima announced to the native people of Peru that they were no longer allowed to perform their traditional songs or dances. Native instruments were burned and severe punishments were levied upon those who violated the rule (Gage, 1991). The social aspects of cultural genocide involved a wide variety of social changes imposed on Indian people with destructive consequences. These changes included seemingly minor changes of impersonal behavior as well as fundamental changes relating to the social organization of the community.

One major area of these latter changes was the attack on the Indian family. Attacks on extended and often polygynous family systems were particularly powerful in destroying the solidarity of the community and the self-identity of the population. The resultant displacement of wives and their children after husbands forced to convert to nuclear family structures abandoned them had a significant impact on the physical and psychological well-being of these abandoned elements of the community.

Tinker does not regard the actions of missionaries as a product of sinister motives designed to subjugate and dominate the Indians. This subjugation and domination resulted from their ethnocentric commitments to their own European cultures and social structures and institutions. The missionaries naturally assumed the superiority of their way of life and felt it was in the interests of the native populations to accept these ways, even if they had to be forced on them. A similar subtly exploitative role by religionists has been documented for the Mormons (i.e., members of the Church of Jesus Christ of Latter-Day Saints) and their modern-day relations with Native Americans (Heinerman and Shupe, 1985, 223–27).

The cultural genocide by religious missionaries is not a thing of the past. Today, especially in South American countries such as Paraguay, Bolivia, and Brazil, Protestant missionaries have succeeded the Catholic missionaries of an earlier era in representing the dominant imperial interests of Western capitalist countries. Munzel, in discussing the missionary work in Paraguay, documents that in one particular mission run by U.S. fundamentalist missionaries the minister himself has engaged in Indian hunts where the young child captives are sold into slavery. Munzel notes that those who are not sold are herded into reservations where they are subjected to psychological degradation to break their spirit to prepare them for assimilation.

> Fundamentalist missionaries have followed the official line of the Paraguayan Indian Affairs Department with greater cruelty than their predecessors; they have attempted and continue to attempt to secure the rapid cultural integration of the Ache at almost any cost. Their technique is "civilizing with a sledge-hammer," in the words of the Director of the South American section of the

Hamburg Ethnographic Museum, who discusses their "racist feeling of superiority" and suggests that their disdain for Indian culture may be the reason why
they were selected by the government to run the reservation. Indians are forced
to give up their names, customs, traditions, and taught to think that anything
connected with their own culture is shameful. (Munzel cited in Chomsky and
Herman, 1979, 112)

Chomsky and Herman (1979) discuss the role of the Summer Institute of
Linguistics (SIL) and the Wycliffe Bible Translators in missionizing the
Indian population in Bolivia. Chomsky and Herman note that the SIL, possibly the richest and most powerful of the North American religious bodies
devoted to missionary work in South America, is supported by the Bolivian
government under the Ministry of Culture and Education.

The standard missionary technique when an uncontacted group is found is
to leave gifts along forest paths to draw the Indians to the mission compound,
where "often at the end of a long journey, far from the Indian's source of
food, his fish, his game, (the trail) comes abruptly to an end." The Indians are
then taught that they must work for money on local farms and they agree,
"when they realize that there's no going back," according to the head of SIL,
an official of the Ministry of Culture and Education (1979, 122).

As noted, this form of violence has occurred in virtually every continent
throughout history. Today it occurs in South and Central America, Africa,
and Asia. Wilson and Kvale (1994) describe how in the Central African
Republic the Baaka people and their way of life are under threat from both
the government and Catholic missionaries. Both groups are trying to force
the Baaka to move from their villages deep in the forest to organized village
settlements where they can be under the control of the government and the
church. Wilson and Kvale note that as part of this move they are encouraged
to build wells and latrines and to adopt domestic agricultural techniques as
opposed to their traditional hunting and gathering. The authors note that the
government officials and missionaries justify their actions by arguing that the
Baaka need to be brought into the modern age in order to participate in the
national culture and economy. Behind these supposed humanitarian concerns
are economic interests. According to Wilson and Kvale, the government
wants to tax the Baaka and wants a freer hand in granting timber-felling
concessions to foreign companies in the forest where the Baaka currently
live.

There is resistance on the part of the Baaka. "We are happy in the forest
because it provides everything we need," says Theresa, a spokesperson for
the community of Sanguila in the forest of Haute-Sanga in the country's
southern region. "We want to carry on living here. . . . I do not think that the
forest will disappear; how can you think it would? People may damage the
forest but this village will continue. . . . When I die my children will live
here. . . . The village is expensive and there is a lot of hunger," according to
Theresa. "The villagers exploit us a lot. The missionaries would like our
children to go to school there but they cannot go because village children
tease them. It would be better to have a school in the forest. The missionaries

want to change us, but they will not change us. As for the Government, they do not give us anything—they do not know us yet" (quoted in Wilson and Kvale, 1994, 17).

In his discussion between globalization and empire, Iadicola (2008) discusses the importance of cultural penetration of the U.S. empire in new areas of conquest. He points to the media, market penetration of Western goods, and missionaries as important elements of this cultural penetration and force for conversion of newly conquered areas of the empire. As it relates to missionaries specifically, he points to the fact that U.S.-based mission societies have the greatest number of missionaries in all inhabited continents of the world. In the most recent front in the American Empire, the Middle East, one half of the missionaries are from the United States.

This is not to say that all missionary work is the product of empires, nor is it to say that missionaries are not acting at times to prevent the abuse of indigenous populations from the exploitation of newly arrived settlers or foreign corporations. They also have a record of nonviolence in their actions to defend the rights of indigenous people. Nevertheless, it is important to recognize the role they have played historically as both an arm of empires and as what they perceive as a humanitarian goal of conversion and civilizing the natives to the new order that is being thrust upon them.

CULT VIOLENCE

Sensational instances of violence among fringe religious groups in the United States give the impression that so-called cults are inherently dangerous. Media treatments of such groups are usually unsympathetic, so when cult violence is reported, it is invariably given a "spin" that is unflattering to all unconventional religious groups. J. Gordon Melton, director of the Institute for the Study of American Religion in Santa Barbara, California, conducted a two-year study of reported incidences of violence concerning cult groups. He looked at three types of reported violence: violence directed against cults, violence initiated by cults, and cult-on-cult violence.

> Overwhelmingly, nonconventional religious groups have been free of reported incidences of violence. Most groups in the survey were quite similar to the more familiar and established mainline church bodies; they experienced one or two scattered incidents atypical of their day-to-day life. Those few nonconventional religious groups which have suffered a history of violent interaction with society are very much the exceptions of those groups which have been labeled "cult." (Melton, 1986, 241)

His conclusion is that more violence has been aimed at unconventional religions by mainstream society than vice versa. Some reported instances of cult-related violence or public menace are overblown or just plain false. For example, it is true that the Hare Krishnas "stockpiled" weapons at their New Vrindiban temple/farm complex in West Virginia during 1978, but their entire weapons cache consisted of several .22-caliber weapons, which were never used and were purchased only after local rowdies had threatened and shot at Krishna members as they worked. There were several other cases involving Krishnas and guns during the 1980s, but these all involved maverick members who were disciplined and/or excommunicated for violating the Hare Krishna prohibition on violence (Melton, 1986, 243–44). Likewise, rumors that members of The Way International (a controversial Christian sect) were engaging in paramilitary and guerrilla warfare training at The Way College in Emporia, Kansas, during the late 1970s proved groundless; the college, among other schools in the state, actually offered only a state-approved course in hunting safety (Melton, 1986, 244).

Nevertheless, it cannot be denied that there are real instances of cult violence. We have already mentioned the People's Temple (a congregation in the Disciples of Christ denomination that was labeled a "cult" only after the massacre at Jonestown, Guyana), the Order of the Solar Temple, the Branch Davidians, and the Heaven's Gate UFO groups (all now extinct). Within Mormonism there always have been breakaway groups and splinter sects quarreling over issues of leadership or polygamy (plural marriage).

The longest running cult-on-cult violence involved the renegade Mormon LeBaron brothers: Ervil, Joel, and Verland. Joel founded the polygamous Church of the First Born of the Fullness of Time; then Ervil quit to form his own Church of the Lamb of God and demanded all other Mormon sect groups acknowledge him as God's leading prophet. When they refused, Ervil dispatched execution squads, particularly targeting his brothers. Joel and several other polygamous sect leaders were subsequently murdered. Ervil was arrested, convicted of murder, and incarcerated in Utah State Prison, where he died of a massive heart attack in 1981. The bloody family saga finally ended two days after Ervil's death when his brother Verland was killed in an automobile accident (Bradlee and Van Atta, 1981; LaBaron, 1981).

In Kirtland, Ohio, self-proclaimed prophet Jeffrey Lundgren and his followers broke away from the Reorganized Church of Latter-Day Saints (itself a breakaway Mormon group) and formed their own cult. Then they lured five members of a Mormon family, including three little girls, one by one into a barn on Lundgren's property. There Lundgren shot them with a .45-caliber Colt Combat Elite pistol, then had the five bodies dumped in a large pit dug in the barn's dirt floor. Lundgren explained the murders as a "blood atonement," a nineteenth-century Mormon notion that Mormons were justified in violence against "Gentiles" as blood atonement, or revenge, for the murder of Joseph and Hyrum Smith. Lundgren was sentenced to death five times over and to a maximum of five consecutive ten- to twenty-five-year terms for kidnapping.

The Nation of Islam (popularly known as the Black Muslims) was entangled in open civil war among rival factions during the 1960s. One charismatic dissenter from the leadership, Malcolm X, was machine-gunned in 1965, and various other leaders, including founder Elijah Muhammed's son-in-law, were shot or killed (Melton, 1986, 248).

One highly publicized form of violence directed at members of a wide variety of both conventional and unconventional religious groups during the 1970s and 1980s was deprogramming, a pseudo-scientific process of physical abduction, restraint, and coercive browbeating aimed at deconverting adult converts to groups such as the Hare Krishnas, The Way International, the Unification Church, the Children of God, even the Old Catholic Church. Often well-meaning parents and relatives rationalized deprogramming on the grounds that no sane person would voluntarily join such groups; thus their loved ones must have been programmed, that is, subjected to some little-understood procedures of brainwashing or mind control. Since most of the persons to be deprogrammed were legal adults, important issues of civil liberties and religious freedom were raised. (In one case, Greek Orthodox parents hired deprogrammers because their post-college daughters refused to attend church or continue to live at home and refused to allow their parents to select their husbands for them in the traditional Greek manner.)

Behavioral scientists, including sociologists who have done fieldwork and participant observation, have found little evidence that such extreme conditioning, or programming, ever existed in cultic groups, and retaliatory legal pressures from the groups themselves as well as from angry members who outwitted and escaped their deprogrammers pretty much ended coercive deprogrammings by the late 1990s (Shupe and Bromley, 1980, 1994; Bromley, 1989; Bromley and Shupe, 1981; Shupe and Darnell, 2006).

No one was ever killed by deprogrammers, but the tendency to go beyond gentle persuasion in matters of spiritual conviction runs like a red letter throughout American religion. This is not to make an argument against religion per se or to suggest that every group is capable of cruelty and violence and simultaneously justifying these. But religious coercion and persecution are staples of every major society's culture and history. And because the social reality that every religion proclaims is difficult to substantiate empirically, human beings will (if they feel they have to) at times fight, repress, even murder others who accept different social realities.

CONCLUSION: THE UBIQUITY OF RELIGIOUS VIOLENCE

Religious violence is no aberration. It is normal, patterned, and to be expected along the same structural, historical, and symbolic lines that all inequality, oppression, and rationalization thereof occur. When we look at who the victims of religious violence are, those who are least powerful appear to suffer from the highest levels of victimization. This is the case whether we are talking about the violence of crusades, missionaries, religious persecution of heretics or nonbelievers, witch hunts, or the abuse of small children or women by religious functionaries in the case of "clergy malfeasance." Religious institutions have been so interwoven with political and economic institutions that the same could hardly be otherwise. Religion is a two-edged sword: it can be a force for revolution and change (the Weberian vision) or a social influence to repress moral outrage and infuse acquiescence among those downtrodden with legitimate grievances (the Marxist vision).

The relation of religion and violence, therefore, is twofold. First, religious leaders and the beliefs they preach have led to direct violence in the name of the religious creed, and second, religion has served to facilitate or maintain some violent modes of political conquest and economic exploitation. Our point is neither to apologize for nor condemn religion per se. Instead, we want to indicate its role as a crucial human institution that is deeply involved in the otherwise political/economic/ideological matrix of violence by social groups acting against one another or against individuals.

DISCUSSION QUESTIONS

1. Can any religion's values be said to be inherently prone to violence?
2. How can religion be employed to construct justifications for violence?
3. Locate the physical harm/violence of an exploitive "bad pastor" (i.e., a minister/priest/rabbi) respectively at the interpersonal, institutional, and structural levels.
4. Should churches and the religious leadership who were aware of the abuse be held responsible for the violence? If so, what should be done?
5. Would there be less sexual abuse if priests were not celibate or if women were allowed to be priests in the Catholic Church?

Chapter Seven

Economic Violence

Toms River, New Jersey, is the location of one of the largest known clusters of childhood cancers in America. Union Carbide and Ciba-Geigy for many years disposed of chemical wastes from their operations into a number of sites that fed into the Dover County water supply (Shabecoff & Shabecoff, 2008).

Seventy-six-year-old Amy Selle had gotten out of her '77 Thunderbird to help a friend get in. When she saw the car jump, she grabbed for the wheel, but the door knocked her down. Onlookers, most of them elderly, watched in horror as she was run over twice, her skull fractured by the wildly circling Ford (Branan 1980, 41).

On February 10, 1985, Stefan Golab staggered from the cyanide tank he was working over, stumbled to the adjacent locker room, and collapsed. Some of his fellow workers dragged him outside and called an ambulance. When the ambulance arrived back at the hospital, Golab was dead. An autopsy was performed to determine the cause of death. . . . The autopsy findings led to an eight-month investigation, resulting in the indictment of five Film Recovery executives on charges of murder and the indictment of Film Recovery Systems, Inc., and two related corporations on charges of manslaughter (Frank, 1986).

The morning of the explosion, the factory was frantic. Rows of machines buffed cases as masked employees pushed buttons. Large air ducts hovered over each station, but they could not keep up with the three lines of machines polishing nonstop. Aluminum dust was everywhere. The iPad had gone on sale just weeks earlier, and workers were told thousands of cases needed to be polished each day. Aluminum dust is a known safety hazard. In 2003, an aluminum dust explosion in Indiana destroyed a wheel factory and killed a worker. Two hours into the second shift, the building started to shake, as if an earthquake was under way. There was a series of blasts, plant workers said. Then the screams began. The toll would eventually count four dead, eighteen injured. Months before the explosion, an advocacy group in Hong Kong published a report warning of unsafe conditions at the Chengdu plant, including problems with aluminum dust. The group Students and Scholars Against Corporate Misbehavior, or Sacom, had videotaped workers covered with tiny aluminum particles and sent the report to Apple. Seven months after the explosion in the Chengdu plant of Foxconn, the largest manufacturer of consumer electronics, another iPad factory owned by Foxconn, this time in Shanghai, exploded because of aluminum dust, injuring fifty-nine workers (Duhigg and Barboza, 2012) .

On September 3, there was a fire at the Imperial Food Products chicken-processing plant in Hamlet, North Carolina. As the fire spread through the factory, workers rushed to the exits only to find that six of the nine exit doors were shut tight, most padlocked by the owners to prevent workers stealing chickens. Twenty-five workers who were locked in the building died from the fire (Kerr and Hall, 1992).

These are some of the stories of economic violence. Thousands upon thousands of people each year are injured or die as a result of actions taken by agents of businesses to further their interests, placing the accumulation of profits above the health and safety of consumers, workers, and members of communities around the world. What is economic violence? What are the major types of economic violence? Who are the victims and perpetrators? Why does it occur? These are the questions we address in this chapter.

We begin by defining economic violence. First, economic violence is a category of institutional violence. In general, institutional violence is violence that occurs by the action of societal institutions and their agents. In referring to economic violence in particular we are focusing on actors or agents of economic entities, in most cases businesses or economic entities formed to produce or market commodities. This would include actors in a large chemical corporation, a small farmer, a state-owned steel mill, an automobile manufacturer, or a retailer. Friedrichs (2004) notes that corporate violence differs from interpersonal violence in five specific ways. First of all the violence is more likely to be indirect, not directly from person to person. This is because corporate violence is more likely to result from policies and actions undertaken on behalf of the corporation that result in the victims being exposed to harmful conditions, products, or substances. The second distinguishing characteristic is that the effects of the violence are removed in time from the implementation of the policy or action that caused the harm. In many cases of economic violence the effect may be twenty to thirty years after the exposure. This is the case with exposure to asbestos fibers that people come in contact with because of their work, products they purchase, or the asbestos-polluted environment. Third, in corporate violence we are typically describing action in which a large number of individuals are acting collectively. This is violence that is a result of organizational action, more so than the action of single individuals. Fourth, corporate violence is motivated by a desire to maximize corporate profits. These forms of violence are instrumental forms of violence in that they are calculated to create a gain, usually monetary, for the organizational and individual actors. Lastly, corporate violence receives a much more limited legal and justice system response than interpersonal violence. The offenders of the violence usually have taken steps to neutralize or minimize the social control system that would prevent the violence.

Thus, there is often collaboration between the economic organization and the state in allowing or facilitating the violence. Michalowski and Kramer (2006, 20) refer to cases where this occurs as cases of state-corporate crime or, in regard to our focus, state-corporate violence. They define state-corporate crime as "illegal or social injurious actions that result from a mutually reinforcing interaction between (1) policies and/or practices in pursuit of goals or one or more institutions of political governance and (2) policies and/or practices in pursuit of the goals of one or more institutions of economic production and distribution." Michalowski and Kramer identify two forms of this criminal relationship: state-initiated corporate crime and state-facilitated corporate crime. In the former case, corporations employed by a government engage in organizational deviance at the direction of, or with the tacit approval of, that government. In the latter case, this occurs when government social control or regulatory agencies are guilty of a failure to create the necessary regulations or failed to enforce the regulations that would prevent the harm. They observe that this occurs because of direct collusion between business and government or because they adhere to shared goals whose attainment would be hampered by regulation.

The creation of control systems for economic violence is fairly recent in U.S. history. Many of the controls regulating the safety of food and drugs have their origins in the reforms developed in response to the progressive movement in the beginning of the twentieth century. Control systems preventing harm in the workplace, products other than food and drugs, and the environment are much more recent, many established in the early 1970s. These control systems have from their origins been areas of conflict between proponents of public safety and the profit-making corporations who would be impacted by the controls. As the power of corporations has increased as a result of their growth in size and political power, these regulatory systems have been reduced in their effectiveness to prevent violence.

In general, the response of agencies of social control has been principally reactive as opposed to preventive. This is especially the case in most areas of economic violence with the exception of drugs where testing on safety and effectiveness is required before approval for sale and distribution. In most other areas of economic violence, the creation of regulations and the enforcement of regulations principally occur after a significant number of deaths or injuries become known and linked to economic action. The presumption is that the substances that are produced, worked with, or released to the environment are harmless to humans, unless proven otherwise. Furthermore, in the United States, the testing of the safety of the product, production process, or what is released into the environment is often done by the same economic entities that profit from the practice. And as illustrated in the cases that will be discussed, even when they are aware of the potential dangers, they will often withhold the information from the public and the regulatory agencies that are designated to provide these safeguards.

When dangerous substances are uncovered by scientific research, Michaels (2008) describes how an entire industry of public relations, product defense lawyers, and scientists in the service of large corporations work to "manufacture doubt" about the claims of harm, often delaying the necessary regulations to protect the public. Michaels, former assistant secretary for environment, safety, and health in the Department of Energy, argues that "the regulatory agencies in Washington, D.C., are intimidated and outgunned and quiescent." He notes that polluters and manufacturers of dangerous products tout "sound science," but what they are promoting just sounds like science but is not. In his book, *Doubt is Their Product: How Industry's Assault on Science Threatens Your Health*, Michaels documents case after case of corporations that spend billions of dollars each year lobbying politicians to pressure regulatory agencies, hiring public relations and legal firms to create doubt in the scientific research, and hiring scientists to conduct research in the interest of making profits from the sale of dangerous products and polluting production methods.

Lastly, those who are in charge of the agencies to prevent the violence usually come from and often return to the same industries that are being regulated. This is oftentimes referred to as a "revolving door" between industry and the regulatory agencies created to prevent them from doing harm as they pursue profits (Meghani and Kuzma, 2011). Personnel from all levels within these regulatory agencies can most often find employment in the various companies they were regulating at much higher salaries. Lawyers and former corporate officials appear to be prime candidates to run the various agencies that they were regulated by when they were working in the private sector.

For example, since leaving government service, Gale Norton, secretary of interior under President Bush, became Shell's general counsel. J. Steven Griles, a deputy secretary of interior, lobbied for numerous oil and gas industries, including BP; and Randall Luthi, the most recent former director of Mineral Management Service (now named Bureau of Ocean Energy Management, Regulation and Enforcement), became president of the National Oceans Industries Association, whose mission is to secure a "favorable regulatory and economic environment for the companies that develop the nation's valuable offshore energy resources." Bill Buzenberg, executive director of the Center for Public Integrity (an independent think tank that investigates government operations), after what seemed like a quick succession of failures of the regulatory system that led to the collapse of Enron, one of the largest coal mine disasters occurring at the Big Branch Mine in West Virginia, and the BP oil spill in the Gulf of Mexico, concluded that "we're seeing the consequences of inadequate regulation stemming from the revolving door, lobbying and the impact of money on both Congress and the agencies" (Powell, Dunham, and Gaffney, 2012). Another study pointed out that approximately half of the EPA officials who left top-level jobs in toxics and pesticides during the past fifteen years went to work for chemical companies, their trade associations, or their lobbying firms (Fagin et al., 1999, x).

While there is little centralized collection of statistics on the various forms of economic violence, there is some data on specific forms of economic violence that are generated by the agencies that have been created to regulate economic actors who are likely to commit the acts of violence. However, the quality of the data is limited to the level of enforcement of the rules, which can vary significantly depending on which political party is in power and the economic interests who support them, and whether the regulations exist in the first place. Furthermore, there are no victimization studies done by government agencies on forms of economic violence as there are for forms of interpersonal crimes or with family violence. Most of the data on economic violence comes from case studies of economic violence. The quality of the information and the availability of information also vary significantly from country to country. More developed countries generally have a more developed regulatory system that attempts to control or at least collect some information on the incidence of several forms of economic violence. However, even in these more developed countries, enforcement levels will vary over time as there are changes in state leadership from parties that promote regulation and those that don't. Thus, it is very difficult to assess changes in the incidence or rates of economic violence within countries because of these changes in enforcement levels, and the difference between countries becomes almost impossible because of the differences in the nature of the regulatory climate and differences in the quality of the data collected between countries. Most recently international organizations such as the World Health Organization and International Labor Organization have improved their abilities to collect data across societies. However, there are still significant problems in attempting to compare rates across different societies

In discussing economic violence we can identify three major types of violence: product violence, production violence, and environmental violence. Product violence refers to producing commodities that because of the nature of the product, a defect in design, or a defect in manufacturing are known to lead to the death and injury of consumers and not informing consumers of these hazards, preventing them from avoiding victimization. Production violence is a result of establishing a work environment that leads to the death and injury of workers and not informing the workers of the hazards, preventing them from avoiding victimization. Environmental violence results from the manner of disposing of harmful waste from economic production and not informing those who are affected by the disposal of the potential harms, preventing them from avoiding victimization.

PRODUCT VIOLENCE

There is no way to know specifically how many people die from the use of faulty products. In the United States a number of agencies may receive reports of deaths or injuries to the public as a result of the use of consumer products. The one agency that is principally responsible for this type of violence is the Consumer Products Safety Commission (CPSC). The CPSC has noted that as many as 33.1 million Americans are injured and more than 27,000 die because of incidents connected with consumer products each year (Weintraub, 2007). There is no way of estimating the numbers of deaths or injuries worldwide. Given the paucity of regulations on product safety for the majority of the world's population, levels of product violence are likely to be significantly higher in many developing countries. Many of the injuries and deaths as a result of consumer product use are a result of unsafe use of the product. These are obviously not the fault of the products' manufacturers and therefore not defined as cases of violence. However, there are a number of cases where the dangers of the product as a result of the design or its intended use are known but this information is withheld from the consuming public, resulting in death and injury.

Product Violence and Product Dumping

One particular area where there is a callous disregard for consumer safety is when products that are either about to be banned or are banned from sale in one location because of the potential harm to consumers are sold in another location where the public and the governing authorities are unaware of the dangers. This has been referred to as a form of "product dumping." The European Union has taken steps to safeguard European consumers by providing an alert system to member countries when dangerous products enter the markets of its members. RAPEX is a rapid alert system for dangerous products that ensures that information about dangerous products withdrawn from the market and/or recalled from consumers anywhere in Europe is quickly circulated between member states and the European Commission, so that appropriate action can be taken everywhere in the EU. There are thirty countries that currently participate in this notification system. According to the annual report of RAPEX, a record 2,244 unsafe products were banned, withdrawn from the market, or recalled from consumers in 2010 (European Business Ltd., 2011). The major categories of unsafe items that were banned from sale in the EU in 2010 were clothing, textile, and fashion items (625 notifications, 32 percent); toys (488 notifications, 25 percent); motor vehicles (175 notifications, 9 percent); electrical appliances (158 notifications, 8 percent); and child-care articles and children's equipment (72 notifications, 4 percent). There is not a comparable system in any other region of the world.

The practice of selling unsafe products in foreign markets after they have been banned in the United States is not illegal in the United States. Product dumping was made illegal temporarily by an executive order issued by President Carter just before leaving office. This order was rescinded by President Reagan, and there have not been any orders or legislation since to prevent this practice by U.S.-based corporations. Let's illustrate the problem by describing some cases of product violence as a result of product dumping.

The range of dangerous products that are dumped is quite broad, from pharmaceuticals, chemicals used in agriculture, building materials, and children's toys, to clothing and various adulterated food products. There is reason to suspect that this is a greater problem in less developed countries because of the weakness of the regulatory systems in these countries to safeguard consumers. A recent report of the Food and Agricultural Organization Council of the UN expresses a continued concern over the distribution of hazardous farm chemicals (United Nations Food and Agricultural Organization Council, 2005). Pesticides and fungicides such as chlordane, DBCP, DDT, and heptachlor, which, although produced in the United States, have been banned from sale in the United States because of their carcinogenic effects on consumers and farm workers, have been shipped to foreign countries for use there. For example, Velsicol Chemical Company between 1987 and 1989 exported thousands of pounds of chlordane and heptachlor to Argentina, Australia, the Dominican Republic, India, the Netherlands, the Philippines, Singapore, Thailand, and many other countries (Bray, 1989).

Another example is that of DBCP, a pesticide banned in the United States after workers who produced the chemical became aware of research conducted by some of the developers that showed exposure to the chemical caused testicular cancer and sterility. As early as 1955, Dow and Shell both knew that low doses of DBCP caused profound organ changes in animals, and in 1958 Dow knew that exposure caused testicular atrophy in laboratory rats. In the United States, the DBCP hush-up ended abruptly in 1977 when workers in California brought Dow and Shell to court. Dow temporarily stopped sales of DBCP in the United States. In 1985, a nationwide ban went into effect. There have been reports of cases of sterility at a Shell Chemical plant in Mobile, Alabama, and reports of sterility among workers in an Occidental Chemical plant in California. One report issued by an Environmental Working Group (EWG) analysis of recent state data concluded that the tap water of more than one million Californians, mostly in the Central Valley, has been contaminated with the banned pesticide. The *Sacramento Bee* reported that EWG's computer-assisted analysis of water utility test results found that DBCP contaminates tap water in thirty-eight water systems in nine counties. Fresno, Riverside, Clovis, Lodi, and Madera were the largest communities with serious problems (Environmental Working Group, 1999).

However, DBCP continued to be produced after it was banned for use in the United States for shipment overseas. Latin American countries were a particular region where sales were high. In 1979, the Costa Rican government finally pressured Standard Fruit to stop using DBCP after hundreds of Costa Rican agricultural workers discovered that they were sterile. Mokhiber (1994) notes that fifteen thousand Costa Rican workers made similar claims in Texas state courts. Other countries, such as Peru and Honduras, where governments are not as concerned about the health and safety of farm workers, continue to be a target for the exportation of this deadly chemical (e.g., Brown and Thrupp, 1991).

DDT is another pesticide banned in the United States that continues to be produced and exported to developing countries. Burbach and Flynn (1980) reported that a UN study revealed that in the cotton-producing regions of Guatemala and Nicaragua, the average DDT content in human blood is 520 parts per billion (compared with 46 in Dade County, Florida). Mokhiber (1988) notes that DDT levels in cow's milk in Guatemala is ninety times as high as that allowed in the United States. Nursing mothers in many Guatemala and Nicaragua villages have levels of DDT in their breast milk that is two hundred times greater than levels in women's breast milk in the United States. In 1989 the World Bank approved a $99 million loan for Brazil's mosquito control program. The loan was to be matched by the Brazilian government and was to be used for the purchase and application of three thousand tons of DDT in the ecologically sensitive Amazon region (Gold, 1989).

Bissio (1990, 71) contends that dangerous pesticides have killed, injured, and poisoned more people in rural Brazil than were affected by the chemical disaster in Bhopal, India. He notes that foremen will often send out the youngest workers, fourteen and fifteen years old, to apply pesticides. They are chosen as the sprayers because they'll last longer. They haven't built up chronic poisoning yet, and when they're eighteen or twenty, they're moved to other jobs.

In 1995 the Commission on Human Rights adopted its first resolution specifically concerning the adverse effects of the illicit movement and dumping of toxic and dangerous products and wastes on the enjoyment of human rights (resolution 1995/81, confirmed by Economic and Social Council decision 1995/288 of July 25, 1995). A 2001 UN report noted that the sale of banned pesticides is a particularly large aspect of this problem of dumping unsafe products. The report noted that more than fifty kinds of dangerous pesticides and organophosphorus compounds such as parathion methyl, mevinphos methamidophos, and monocrotophos have been illegally exported. The report also noted that there was an increasing trend in the exporting of production of these banned chemicals to developing countries where worker and consumer safety regulations are weak (Ouhachi-Vesely, 2001, 6).

One major problem with the sale of banned products in developing countries that were banned in developed countries is what Dowie (1979) called *the boomerang effect*. For example, the pesticides banned in this country, as well as other more advanced countries in the world, come back to these countries in the foods treated with these pesticides that are imported. In an article on the problems of the use of banned pesticides, the *New Internationalist* (2000) gave the following example of the problems of pesticide residue. They noted that the average Westerner consumes more than eleven kilograms of apples a year. Apples are exported from at least forty different countries. They are among the most contaminated fruits; 98 percent of all apples have pesticides on them. Chocolate is another example; the *New Internationalist* reports that "in 1994 75 per cent of 72 samples of European chocolate tested contained low levels of lindane (or gamma-HCH), a pesticide that is banned in six countries and severely restricted in 18" *(New Internationalist, 2000, 23)*.

In the United States, three federal government agencies share responsibility for the regulation of pesticides. The EPA regulates residue on domestically produced food products, except animal products (which are regulated by the Department of Agriculture), and the FDA is responsible for imported foods and domestic food shipped in interstate commerce. In regard to the FDA monitoring for 2004 to 2006, they found that an average of 2 percent of domestic and 6 percent of imports sampled, such as sweet basil, ginseng, and peas, were in violation of standards. They report that these proportions have been consistent in the fifteen years they have been monitoring foodstuffs for residue (U.S. Food and Drug Administration, 2011).

Although many agricultural pesticides that are defined as carcinogenic are banned for sale to farmers in the United States, they are still sold in this country as home insecticides. According to one report, tens of millions of homes in the United States are contaminated with varying levels of chlordane/heptachlor, both pesticides still registered by EPA for termite treatment.

In one study conducted by a medical team from Mt. Sinai Hospital in New York, the researchers asked eighty major chemical industries whether they had done any epidemiological studies on carcinogens they were using. Most of the companies reported that they had conducted no such research (Bissio, 1990).

Medical researchers, however, have found that the hazards of these pesticides used in the home and on lawns and gardens indicated that children were four times more likely to develop lymphocytic leukemia if their parents used pesticides in the home and six times more likely if pesticides were used on lawns and gardens (Lowengart, Peters, and Cicioni, 1987). Another study found that pesticide use around the home can more than double the chance of a child developing neuroblastoma, one of the most common cancers (10 percent of cancerous tumors) found in infants and children, which develops in nerve tissue (Daniels, 2001). The research concluded that using pesticides in and around the home resulted in a 60 percent increased likelihood of children developing the disease. Another study on the link between pesticides and breast cancer found that cancerous human breast tissue contained the chemical heptachlor epoxide (found in the common home pesticide chlordane) at levels four times higher than noncancerous breast tissue. Chlordane, a pesticide banned for agricultural use, was used as the primary termite prevention pesticide in over thirty million U.S. homes between the mid-1950s and 1988. It is estimated that approximately fifty million U.S. residents are currently exposed to this chemical from previously treated pre-1989 homes (Cassidy, Sridhar, and Vaughan, 2005). One review article described thrity-one studies of pesticides and childhood cancers reported during the period 1970–1996. The review concluded that results from leukemia studies suggest that no-pest strips and frequent use of pesticides in the home may be strongly associated with childhood leukemia (Daniels et al., 1997).

One final (and classic) example of product dumping would be the contraceptive Dalkon Shield manufactured by the A. H. Robins Company during the late 1970s. After Robins had already learned that their product was responsible for twenty thousand North American cases of serious uterine infection, and several thousand women required subsequent hysterectomies, the company arranged (with assistance from the U.S. Agency for International Development) to distribute the product in a number of developing countries. Meanwhile, there was no movement to recall the Shield in the United States until 1984 (Dowie and Johnston, 1976; Mintz, 1985).

PRODUCT VIOLENCE IN THE PHARMACEUTICAL INDUSTRY

The pharmaceutical industry is one industry that has had particular problems with product violence. One classic case is that of Richardson Merrell Company and MER 29 (Ungar, 1972). MER 29 was a drug designed to lower cholesterol levels in the blood. Before it was to be marketed, the FDA routinely requested further testing to determine potential hazards and drug side effects. Merrell assured the FDA that animal tests had been completed and that the results were satisfactory. The required test results were submitted to the FDA for drug approval. In 1960 Merrell began a large-scale sales campaign praising the drug to physicians. Soon after it was introduced, physicians began to notice side effects from the drug that were not indicated in the drug literature. Some of these problems were inflammation of the skin, loss of hair, color change of hair, and loss of sex drive. Merrell instructed its sales personnel to shift the blame to other drugs the patients might be taking, a result not of the drug itself but rather due to an interaction effect.

Not until 1962 did the FDA discover that Merrell had falsified test results. In tests using monkeys and dogs, several had become ill using the drug. The researchers replaced sick animals with new animals and continued the study. In rat studies in which whole samples had died, the results were not reported. Permission was awarded to market the drug after the test results were reviewed. After physicians had reported many harmful consequences, however, permission to market the drug was withdrawn by the FDA. The Health Department of the State of California later discovered that five hundred people developed cataracts while using the drug. This was not the only case of corporate violence committed by Merrell and its subsidiaries. During the 1960s, Merrell was responsible for distributing thalidomide, a drug given to pregnant women to treat morning sickness during the first three months of pregnancy. Thalidomide was never tested to determine if it caused birth defects. Unfortunately, this was the case. Later, Merrell was involved in withholding information from the FDA on the link between Bendectin and birth defects (Dowie and Marshall, 1980; Mokhiber, 1988).

Consider several more recent cases:

When Roche Pharmaceuticals learned of a possible association between its drug Accutane and inflammatory bowel disease in 1984, it failed to alert patients and prescribing physicians. In February 2010 a New Jersey jury awarded $25.2 million in compensatory damages to a man who proved his colon was removed after suffering from a disease caused by Accutane (AboutLawsuits.com, 2010)

SmithKline Beecham produced and sold Avandia as a treatment for diabetes. Over a ten-year period the company was aware of risk for heart attacks and strokes before finally alerting the FDA. Otherwise, it is estimated, the drug company would have seen a loss of $600 million in sales from 2002 to 2004 alone (Harris, 2010).

The GlaxoSmithKline Corporation was found in 2004 to have repressed data that showed its antidepressant Paxil could lead children and teenagers to have more (rather than fewer) suicidal thoughts and behaviors (Michaels, 2008).

Likewise, the pharmaceutical giant Merck misrepresented its data so that the FDA allowed the deadly drug Vioxx onto the market. The FDA later estimated that Vioxx caused 88,000 to 139,000 heart attacks before it was recalled (Michaels, 2008).

Since the early 1970s, and until twenty years after, the trade association manufacturers of PPA (phenypropandolamine—both a decongestant and an appetite suppressor) insisted the drug was safe. The FDA received reports of strokes in young women who had been taking the drug. Paid scientists and lobbyists managed to keep the drug available on an over-the-counter basis. An independent study done at the Yale University School of Medicine in

1999 confirmed that PPA causes hemorrhagic strokes. But the drug's annual sales were at $500 million, so the manufacturer GlaxoSmithKline attacked the Yale study, hired a consulting company, and refused to withdraw the drug from markets. The FDA finally advised the manufacturer to stop marketing PPA in late 2000, but meanwhile it estimated PPA had caused between two hundred and five hundred strokes annually among a relatively young (eighteen to forty-nine years) population (Mundy and Sack, 2004).

There are other cases of pharmaceutical companies producing and marketing hazardous products that are not reported to the public or the medical profession that prescribes them. Eli Lilly and their products Oraflex and DES, SmithKline and Beckman and the product Selacryn, Upjohn and the product Halcion, and the Cordis Corporation and defective heart pacemakers are all examples of this. In all these cases, the manufacturers knew of the hazards they did not report, which resulted in the death and injury of consumers (Mokhiber, 1988, 1994; Simon, 1999).

Another area of violence related to the pharmaceutical industry is the violence directed at animals for research. If violence is not restricted to humans but to other animals as well, then we cannot avoid mentioning the violence directed at animals in the testing of drug safety for humans. Remember, that regardless of the supposed legitimacy of the use of animals in research, although there is a vigorous debate as to the necessity of using animals in many types of research done in product development, it nevertheless is still an act of violence. In regard to vertebrates, most testing is done on mice, which share approximately 99 percent of their genetic makeup with humans. Rats are second to mice in the number used in experiments. Each year approximately twenty million rats and mice are used in experimentation in the United States (Trull, 1999). This number composed about 90 percent of vertebrate animals used in research. All of these animals experience pain, distress, and the vast majority death in the process of research.

According to the USDA, another 1.2 million larger animals, mostly mammals, were used in experiments in 2005. Of these many would be considered animals that are often used as pets and are purchased from animal shelters and breeders. For example, cats are often used in neurological research. According to the American Anti-Vivisection Society, in 2000 more than twenty-five thousand cats were used in experiments that caused pain or distress. The U.S. Department of Agriculture Animal Welfare Report of 2005 reported that sixty-six thousand dogs were used in USDA-registered facilities. One particular breed, beagles, is most often used because they are gentle and easy to handle. According to the U.S. Humane Society, dogs are commonly used as models for diseases in cardiology, endocrinology, and bone and joint studies. For nonhuman primates, it is estimated that approximately seventy thousand are used each year in the United States and European Union (Commission of the European Communities, 2007; U.S. Department of Agriculture, 2006). Most of the nonhuman primates used are macaques, but marmosets, spider monkeys, monkeys, chimpanzees, and baboons are also used. In all cases, the animals experience distress, pain, and oftentimes death from the experimentation.

Product Violence—The Slaughterhouse

One area of violence that is least likely to be considered violence is the violence in acquiring the food that we eat. The statistics are staggering. One estimate based on data from U.S. government agencies, in particular the Department of Agriculture and Department of Commerce, is that in 2009 59 billion sea and land animals were killed for food in the United States (Mohr, 2012). Of the 59 billion, 8.27 billion were land animals (chickens being the largest single species at 7.8 billion; followed by turkeys, 274 million; pigs, 119 million; cattle and steers, approx. 40 million; ducks, 22 million; and rabbits, 2.4 million). Being socialized to define the animals we kill as food and the acts of violence that are used to take their lives are most often hidden from the consumers of the nicely packaged flesh of the animals.

Violence is not the term that we use when describing what is done in creating the diet of meat eaters. Mohr (2012) estimates that the average U.S. meat eater consumes sixteen thousand animals in their lifetime. These animals are referred to as livestock to be eaten. However, not all animals are defined as animals to be eaten. There are those who carry a special privilege as the designation of pet, a status that protects them from acts of violence including the act of killing them for food. Which animals are defined as pets and which are defined as those to be killed for entertainment or for clothing or food products can vary in different regions of the world. Animals that are considered pets in some countries in another may be considered food. A recent article in *China Daily* (Wei, 2011) reports how animal rights campaigners rescued 430 dogs from the dinner table after staging a fifteen-hour blockade at a toll station in Tongzhou district. The protestors ended up purchasing the dogs from the owner who was transporting them to slaughter to be served as "meat." China does not yet have animal protection laws for dogs and cats; they are still considered a food and not a victim of violence. When one thinks of this example, one cannot help but think of the relativity of the definition of violence as it pertains to animals. Dogs and cats are pets in the United States and in European countries, and thus can be victims of violence, but not cows, chickens, or pigs. In India the cow is seen as a sacred animal and thus often treated as a pet and not livestock to be rendered into meat. In the McDonald's restaurants in India meat from cows is not on the menu (Petrun, 2009). There is an interesting contradiction in the way that we define the chicken in the United States. If chickens were fighting in a ring for sport, that would be violence and outlawed, but if we slice their throat with a knife and let them bleed to death, that's considered food preparation, legal, and not violence.

Another interesting example of animals as pets and food is the case of horses. Generally there is no market for horsemeat in the United States other than to feed pets and other livestock. Horses are still considered pets or working animals in the United States. In 2006, animal rights activists successfully lobbied Congress to pass legislation that prevented the U.S. Department of Agriculture from using federal funds to inspect any meat processing plants that slaughter horses, and since plants that are not inspected by the USDA cannot ship meat across state lines, it effectively ended domestic horse slaughter (Shesgreen, 2011). However the GAO found that instead the horses were shipped to Canada where they are slaughtered and the meat was sold overseas to other countries where horsemeat was considered a delicacy. Congress lifted the ban in a spending bill President Barack Obama signed into law November 18 to keep the government afloat until mid-December (Juozapavicius, 2011). Current estimates are that a slaughterhouse could slaughter two hundred thousand horses per year generating a more than 67 million dollar industry in horsemeat. Many people in the United States would consider the horse to be something that should not be turned into meat.

Governments regulate the commercial methods of killing of animals. For mammals other than rabbits, U.S. federal law requires that the animals are stunned prior to slaughter. There is an exemption for ritual slaughter that follows religious rules. During religious slaughter, such as kosher and halal, animals are usually fully conscious as their throats are cut. In many cases, the animal is shocked with an electric current to induce a heart attack. This is the case with hogs. Hogs are then dunked in tanks of scalding hot water after they are stunned to soften the hides for skinning. When the electric current fails to create cardiac arrest, the hogs often drown in the scalding water.

In the case of cows, slaughterhouses use a compressed air gun that shoots a metal bolt into their heads, which knocks them unconscious. The natural life cycle of beef cattle is approximately twenty years. Beef cattle to be slaughtered as food live to about fourteen to sixteen months of age. Male dairy cattle are either killed soon after birth; placed in small confined pens at eighteen to twenty weeks and fed a liquid-, iron-, and fiber-deficient diet to create the tender and pale flesh that sells as "milk-fed," "white," or "fancy" veal; or sent on to live the sixteen months, the last three or four months of which are spent in highly concentrated feedlots that can contain as many as one hundred thousand head of cattle. These feedlots contain mounds of waste in which the animals often stand. Schlosser (2001) notes that during the months in these feedlots before they are slaughtered, they eat grain (corn) dumped into long concrete troughs that resemble highway dividers. The feed has also been supplemented with the blood of slaughtered cattle, pigs, poultry, and horses, as well as sawdust and old litter that contains chicken manure from poultry processing plants, to increase the protein content of the food.

Pollan (2006) notes that cattle that would normally eat grass rarely live more than 150 days on the feedlot diets. Many develop problems of a high level of acid in their stomach, leading to large amounts of gas that become trapped. Pollan notes that the rumen (first chamber of the cow's stomach) inflates until it presses on the animals lungs. If action is not taken, like forcing a hose down the animal's esophagus, the animal suffocates. He notes that over time the acid eats away at the rumen wall, allowing bacteria to enter the animal's blood and eventually leading to abscessed liver. Not only is this diet harmful to the cattle being rapidly fattened for slaughter, but it is also very dangerous to the humans who consume the beef. Pollan notes the new acid-resistant strains of E. coli have evolved that are dangerous to humans. According to Pollan, the problem with these bugs is that they can shake off the acid bath in our stomachs—and then go on to kill us. The corn fattens the cattle quickly, aided by anabolic steroids implanted in their ear. A typical steer can consume more than three thousand pounds of grain during its stay at a feedlot, just to gain four hundred pounds of weight. Dairy cows are usually sent to slaughter after about four or five years when their milk production begins to decline.

Schlosser (2001) describes the process at a ConAgra slaughterhouse that is one of the largest in the United States. The cattle are driven in long rows into chutes that then enter the building where they are to be killed and processed. Once inside the building the steer come to the knocker.

> He wears safety goggles and a hardhat. His face is splattered with gray matter and blood. He is the "knocker," the man who welcomes cattle into the building. Cattle walk down a narrow chute and pause in front of him, blocked by a gate and then he shoots them in the head with a captive bolt stunner—a compressed-air gun attached to the ceiling by a long hose—which fires a steel bolt that knocks the cattle unconscious. . . . For eight and half hours, he just shoots. . . . As soon as the steer falls, a worker grabs one of its hind legs, shackles it to a chain, and the chain lifts the huge animal into the air. (Schlosser, 2001, 171)

Next the animals are carried into the air to the "sticker." "For eight and a half hours a worker called a 'sticker' does nothing but stand in a river of blood, drenched in blood, slitting the neck of a steer every ten seconds, or so, severing its carotid artery. He uses a long knife and must hit exactly the right spot to kill the animal humanely" (Schlosser, 2001, 171). The cattle are then suspended overhead on hooks, some still moving from the life reflexively leaving their bodies. Men operating whizzards, which are small electric knives, begin peeling meat off decapitated heads. Schlosser then waded through blood that's ankle deep and that pours down drains into huge vats below that collect the blood that is draining from their bodies. "I see a man reach inside cattle and pull out their kidneys with their bare hands, then drop the kidneys down a metal chute, over and over again, as each animal passes by him; a stainless steel rack of tongues" (Schlosser, 2001, 171–72). The skin is cut off and he then describes another worker with a power saw who slices cattle into halves as they are carried into the cooler along a conveyer belt to other workers who continue the butchering process, creating the cuts of meat that are eventually sold in the supermarkets in the nicely wrapped plastic to be purchased by the meat-eating consumer.

The highest efficiency slaughterhouses slaughter four hundred cattle per hour, approximately six steer per minute. It takes approximately twenty-five minutes to transform a living steer to a porterhouse steak. *Washington Post* investigative reporters found that many times the cattle do not die quickly enough after they have had their carotid artery cut. "The cattle were supposed to be dead before they got to Moreno. But too often they weren't. 'They blink. They make noises,' he said softly. 'The head moves, the eyes are wide and looking around.' Still Moreno would cut. On bad days, he says, dozens of animals reached his station clearly alive and conscious. Some would survive as far as the tail cutter, the belly ripper, the hide puller. 'They die,' said Moreno, 'piece by piece'" (Warrick, 2001).

The U.S. Department of Agriculture oversees the treatment of animals in meat plants, but Warrick notes the enforcement of the law varies dramatically. In one example he cites, the government took no action against a Texas beef company that was cited twenty-two times in 1998 for violations that included chopping hooves off live cattle. In a case in Florida, agency supervisors fired an animal health technician who complained to the Humane Society for skinning cows while they were still alive. The basis of the firing was that the technician "irreparably damaged" the agency's relations with the packing plant. At another Texas plant, Supreme Beef Packers in Ladonia, which earned twenty-two violations in six months, during one inspection, federal officials found nine live cattle dangling from an overhead chain. "Privatization of meat inspection has meant a quiet death to the already meager enforcement of the Humane Slaughter Act," said Gail Eisnitz of the Humane Farming Association, a group that advocates better treatment of farm animals. "USDA isn't simply relinquishing its humane-slaughter oversight to the meat industry, but is—without the knowledge and consent of Congress—abandoning this function altogether" (Warrick, 2001).

More than 95 percent of U.S. land animals killed for food are birds, chickens, turkeys, and ducks. There is no federal law requiring they be handled humanely. In the case of chickens, those raised for meat are referred to as broilers. These birds have been genetically modified to increase the size of their breast and thigh tissue. These are the most popular parts of the animals for human eating. These birds are kept in confined pens and fed high-protein diets to rapidly increase their weight in the usually six to seven weeks before they are killed. The growth of abnormally heavy bodies causes crippling and painful skeletal deformities, and the overburdening of the birds' underdeveloped cardiopulmonary systems often causes congestive heart failure before they are six weeks old. Other common causes of death pre-slaughter are heat prostration, cancer—in an animal less than seven weeks old—and infectious diseases. The buildings that house broiler chickens tend to be highly overcrowded with tens of thousands of birds crammed into a single closed broiler house (Murray, 2007). Each chicken is given less than a square foot of space, so hardly any floor is actually visible. The birds, which are unable to roam, to scratch, or, indeed, to avoid each other at all, will peck and fight with each other. The solution to this problem is the process of debeaking chicks shortly after they hatch; without anesthesia the chicks are placed beak-first into an apparatus that quickly cuts the tips off the beaks with a hot blade. In about six or seven weeks the chickens have attained slaughter weight; they are loaded into crowded trucks that offer no protection from extreme temperatures, where many of them die before they reach the processing facilities. The most efficient processing plants can kill approximately 8,400 birds per hour. This process is highly automated as the machines operated by workers automatically stun the birds, cut their throats, and scald and pluck them. The process begins by the workers strapping the live chickens into leg shackles on a moving rail, from which the birds hang upside-down as they move on to baths of electrified water, which stuns them in order to render them insensible before their throats are cut. However, Murray notes that some observers believe it is done to make it easier to carry out the process of killing them. The stunned birds move on to a mechanical blade that cuts their throats. After the slicing of their throats, they are plunged into a scalding bath that removes feathers. Murray notes that with the high-speed assembly-line processing, there are missteps where the voltage in the electrified bath may be too low, resulting in the rapid recovery of the chickens, who are then well aware of the throat-cutting machine as they approach it. The blade then can miss many chickens who are still conscious and moving, and it leads them to a more painful fate of being boiled alive in the scalding bath.

Joy (2009) contends that humans have developed a belief system that she refers to as "carnism," which allows us to believe that we "love" and "care for" nonhuman animals, yet enslave, torture, slaughter, dismember, process, and consume billions of them each year as food. First of all the animals that we slaughter are invisible to us. Other than seeing these animals in a replica of a farm at a local zoo in most cases, these animals are invisible to us and so is their slaughter. Only a very small percentage of meat eaters have witnessed the killing of their meal. Then according to Joy there is the three "n's": it's normal, natural, and necessary to eat animals. The three n's are culturally defined and therefore relative to the culture of which we are part. Normality refers to the presence of a normative environment that promotes eating of the flesh of animals. In our own society, this normative environment has changed as has the marketing of different food products and as the cultural orientation of the population has changed with the immigration of people from other cultures. Natural and normal implies that it is by the nature of humans to eat the flesh of animals. However, the nature of humans is that they are omnivores, meaning that the can consume a whole range of foods to meet their dietary needs, thus the eating of meat is an option that can be easily replaced with other foods to meet nutritional requirements for health.

Joy discusses other elements of the ideology of meat eating including objectification, the reducing of nonhumans to objects or property; deindividualization, stripping the animal of their individual identities; dichotomization, creating categories of food/not food, cute/ugly, dirty/clean; rationalization; and dissociation. As noted previously, the vast killing of non-human animals by humans far exceeds the number of nonhuman animals killing of humans. Humans have created a hierarchy of animals that places themselves at the top, supreme, followed by pets, livestock, game, and pests. Which animals reside in the categories of pets, livestock, game, and pests can be quite arbitrary depending on the culturally defined utility of the animal. As we move down the lists the violence toward the animals becomes increasingly less regulated and more wanton. To deny this form of violence as violence, whether it is for entertainment, food, or to protect property or person, is an example of speciesism in which the more powerful species exercises its power by killing and consuming the less powerful one. Whether we define this violence as appropriate, legitimate, or necessary is irrelevant to whether it is violence.

Product Violence: Food Adulteration

Let's now turn to a more conventional form of economic violence in the food industry, the selling of unwholesome or spoiled food. Schlosser notes that "every day in the United States, roughly 200,000 people are sickened by a foodborne disease, 900 hospitalized, and fourteen die" (Schlosser, 2001, 185). Research by the Centers for Disease Control analyzed information from multiple surveillance systems and other sources and found that foodborne diseases cause approximately 76 million illnesses, 325,000 hospitalizations, and 5,000 deaths in the United States each year (Mead et al., 1999). The report notes that just three pathogens, Salmonella, Listeria, and Toxoplasma, are responsible for 1,500 deaths each year, more than 75 percent of those caused by known pathogens. Schlosser notes that a 1996 nationwide survey of hamburger produced in the United States published by the USDA found that 7.5 percent of the ground beef samples taken at processing plants were contaminated with Salmonella, and another 11.7 percent were contaminated with Listeria monocytogenes. Schlosser contends that the problem is because of the highly centralized and industrialized processing of meat where cost cutting and profits take precedence over food safety.

> The problem begins in today's vast feedlots. A government health official, who prefers not to be named, compared the sanitary conditions in a modern feedlot to those in a crowded European city during the Middle Ages, when people dumped their chamber pots out the window, raw sewage ran in the streets, and epidemics raged. The cattle now packed into feedlots get little exercise and live amid pools of manure. "You shouldn't eat dirty food and dirty water," the official told me. "But we still think we can give animals dirty food and dirty water." Feedlots have become an extremely efficient mechanism for recirculating the manure, which is unfortunate, since E. coli 0157:H7 can replicate in cattle troughs and survive in manure for up to ninety days. (Schlosser, 2001, 201–2)

The cattle in feedlots are more prone to all sorts of illnesses and what they are fed often contributes to the spread of disease. Schlosser notes that up until August of 1997, about 75 percent of the cattle in the United States were routinely fed livestock waste. Cattle were fed millions of pounds of dead cats and dead dogs that were purchased from animal shelters. The FDA banned the practice after evidence from Great Britain suggested it was responsible for "mad cow disease." Despite some restrictions, the current FDA regulations allow dead pigs and dead horses to be rendered into cattle feed, along with dead poultry (including the sawdust and old newspapers used as litter to hold the birds' waste); cattle can also be fed the blood from other cattle, and poultry are allowed to be fed dead cattle. Schlosser contends that because of the concentration of slaughterhouses and grinders (thirteen provide most of the meat for the nation; each one can produce eight hundred thousand pounds of hamburger a day), one animal that is infected with E. coli can contaminate thirty-two thousand pounds of ground meat. The goal of maximizing profit and reducing costs together with a regulatory environment that has been regularly underfunded and pressured by powerful interests to weaken or not vigorously enforce regulations that would protect the public from harm have resulted in this form of economic violence.

One case of product violence in the food industry involved the death of at least twenty-one consumers of Ball Park hot dogs and other processed meat products produced by Bil Mar Company, a subsidiary of Sara Lee. The deaths resulted from a listeriosis outbreak. It was suspected that the outbreaks were caused by the replacement of an air conditioning unit in the processing plant. This work dislodged some dangerous bacteria on the ceiling of the plant. When the plant reopened, steam from the passing hot dogs went up to the ceiling, condensed, and dripped back down with the dangerous bacteria onto the hot dogs. According to a series of reports in the *Detroit Free Press*, plant workers were regularly testing work surfaces for the presence of cold-loving bacteria, a class of bacteria that includes the deadly Listeria monocytogenes as well as some harmless bacteria.

After the replacement of the old refrigeration unit, workers recorded a sharp increase in the presence of cold-loving bacteria. "'Sara Lee was doing testing of the environment in the plant for cold-loving bacteria,' says Caroline Smith DeWaal of the Center for Science in the Public Interest. 'Then their tests started coming up positive, so they stopped testing. They knew they had a problem with bacteria in the plant. But instead of solving it, they chose to ignore it.' The company paid a $200,000 fine" (Mokhiber and Weissman, 2001a, 17).

In some cases the food processors have washed and cleaned spoiled meat and resold it. Simon reported the following cases:

> In 1984, Nebraska Beef Processors and its Colorado subsidiary, Cattle King Packing company—the largest supplier of ground meat to school lunch programs and a major supplier of meat to the Department of Defense, supermarkets, and fast-food chains, was found guilty of (1) regularly bringing dead animals into its slaughterhouses and mixing rotten meat into its hamburgers, (2) labeling old meat with phony dates, and (3) deceiving U.S. Department of Agriculture inspectors by matching diseased carcasses with the healthy heads from larger cows. . . . In 1979, a New Jersey firm was convicted of making pork sausage with an unauthorized chemical that masks discoloration of spoiled meat. And in 1982, a California company used walkie-talkies to avoid inspectors while doctoring rotten sausage. (Simon, 1999, 134)

Another case of selling adulterated food was reported by employees of Food Lion, a grocery store chain. Employee whistleblowers charged Food Lion with adding Clorox bleach to old fish to remove the spoiled smell, then putting the repackaged fish out for sale; pouring barbecue sauce on old chicken, repackaging it, and selling it; grinding dirty and spoiled beef to resell as hamburger; and sending employees into dumpsters to pick out thrown-away food to resell (Mokhiber, Gozan, and Knaus, 1992).

Product Violence—Tobacco

One of the most deadly cases of product violence is tobacco. As early as 1900, medical experts noted an increase in cancer of the lungs linked to tobacco consumption. In 1925 a British scientist established the link between tar in tobacco and skin cancer. In 1938, Dr. Raymond Pearl noted the reduced life expectancy among smokers. When *Reader's Digest* in 1941 kicked off a series of articles informing the public of the potential hazards of cigarette smoking, the tobacco industry countered with an advertising campaign extolling the health virtues of smoking. Claims such as smoking cigarettes was good for digestion, that more doctors smoke Camels than any other cigarette, and that nose, throat, and accessory organs are not adversely affected by smoking Chesterfields were made by the tobacco companies to counter this attack by the medical community (Mokhiber, 1988). Meanwhile, research continued to be produced illustrating the link between cancer and tobacco products. The Sloan-Kettering Institute study of 1953 found that cancer could be induced in test animals by spreading tars from cigarettes on their skin. In 1964 the U.S. Surgeon General's report concluded that cigarette smoking is a health hazard of sufficient importance that immediate action was warranted and that cigarette smoking is causally linked to lung cancer in men. Since the first report in 1900, Mokhiber (1988) notes that more than thirty thousand reports have documented the link between tobacco products and pulmonary emphysema, chronic bronchitis, coronary heart disease, and cancer of the lung, mouth, esophagus, bladder, kidney, pancreas, stomach, uterus, and cervix.

By 1989, the U.S. Surgeon General declared cigarette smoking as the chief preventable cause of death in our society. Estimates at this time put the number of deaths in the United States at one thousand a day due to cigarette smoking alone. As more evidence came in demonstrating the link, the tobacco industry increasingly got their message across, linking cigarette smoking to sex appeal, the good life, enjoyment, youth, and vitality through their advertisements. In 1988 the tobacco industry spent $2.5 billion on advertising. Mokhiber (1994) reports that since 90 percent of smokers start before the age of twenty-one and 60 percent before the age of fourteen, much of the tobacco industry's marketing and promotion is geared toward children and youth (14).

As part of the 1998 multi-state settlement with the tobacco industry, the tobacco companies were to eliminate advertising techniques that would appeal to teenagers. A catalyst for the tobacco companies for signing this pact was that the R.J. Reynolds Corporation was discovered to have specifically marketed their Camel brand cigarettes to young people with the use of a cartoon character named "Joe Camel." Company memos detailing the plan and strategies to market to the young were released by Rep. Henry Waxman, D-California, who said they provide the first detailed look at how R.J. Reynolds spurred youth sales. "These documents . . . show us that RJR's most senior executives developed and implemented a sophisticated plan to market their cigarettes to our children" (CNN, 1998). Mokhiber and Weissman (2001) recently reported that the tobacco industry continues to target young people in the United States with cigarette ads. They cite a *New England Journal of Medicine* study that found in the year 2000, magazine advertisements for youth brands of cigarettes (defined as cigarettes smoked by more than 5 percent of eighth, tenth, and twelfth graders) reached more than 80 percent of young people in the United States an average of seventeen times each.

Since the market of male, white, educated consumers had declined rapidly over the most recent years in the United States, the tobacco industry has also increasingly targeted minority populations and blue-collar males as important market areas in their advertising (Simon, 1999; Lewis, 1992; Mattera, 1992). Two new brands being developed by R.J. Reynolds that particularly target African American and working-class women are Uptown and Dakota (Mattera, 1992).

The U.S. tobacco industry also increasingly expanded overseas. Consider these patterns:

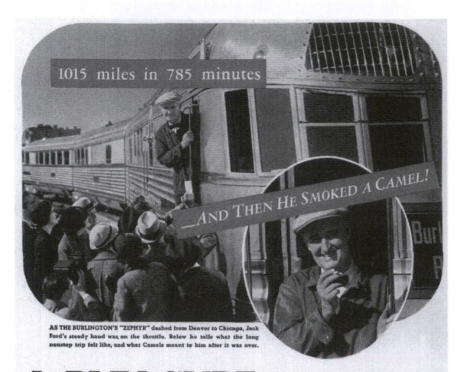

Figure 7.1. Caption under graphic, from a Camel Cigarettes ad in Popular Science, November 1934 promoting the smoking of Camel Cigaretts gives you an "energizing lift."

Philip Morris sells more than 175 brands in 160 countries.

The U.S. government has been an important ally of the tobacco companies in increasing this expansion overseas. Under authority of Section 301 of the 1974 Trade Act, the U.S. Trade Representative has threatened to impose severe trade sanctions against any country that denies U.S. tobacco companies market access.

U.S. companies increasingly protest any foreign nations' attempts to protect their public with anti-tobacco health measures (Weissman, 1992).

South Korea and Taiwan are two countries that were recently unsuccessful in overcoming U.S. pressure in their attempts to block the importation of tobacco products. The U.S. General Accounting Office reported that in Korea, one year after the lifting of import restrictions on cigarettes made by U.S.-based multinational corporations, the smoking rate among teenage girls rose by more than 300 percent (Mokhiber, 1994).

With the passage of treaties such as the North American Free Trade Agreement (NAFTA) and the General Agreement on Trade and Tariffs (GATT) that attempt to open markets and expand trade internationally by in part removing such technical barriers to trade as consumer safety, environmental safety, and workplace safety regulations, countries have been less able to protect their citizens from the tobacco products pushed by some of the largest companies in the world.

Countries in Africa and Latin America are also being targeted by American and British tobacco companies. One marketing technique of Philip Morris was to donate street signs to some South American cities that say Marlboro along with the name of the street. In Uganda, the British American Tobacco Company is marketing high-nicotine cigarettes with no warning label at far-reduced prices (12 cents per pack of twenty cigarettes). The goal is obvious: addict the population with high doses of the drug and then increase the price to increase profits.

Other areas of expansion are Eastern Europe and the People's Republic of China (Weissman, 1992b). Tobacco companies in capitalist nations are not the only purveyors of this form of product violence. In Eastern Europe prior to the early 1990 economic transformation to capitalism, most of the tobacco industry was state-owned. Estimates are that more than one-third of all deaths among middle-aged East European men in 1985 were due to tobacco. Rates were highest in Poland and the Soviet Union, where 40 percent of middle-aged males died because of tobacco use (Weissman, 1992b). However, there is an indication that rates of smoking may have increased with the increased advertising and sales by multinational corporations in Eastern Europe. Dr. Jiri Kozak, an adviser to the Czech Ministry of Health, noted that until the arrival of the transnational tobacco companies and the beginning of aggressive advertising, the prevalence of smoking was decreasing (Mokhiber, 1994, 14).

The largest population of smokers in the world is in the People's Republic of China. Approximately 250 to 300 million smokers live in the PRC. Richard Peto, an Oxford University epidemiologist, estimates that of all the children alive today in China under the age of twenty years, fifty million of them will eventually die from tobacco (Mackay, 1992, 9). Two recent studies have concluded that China has the largest number of smoking-related deaths in the world (British Broadcasting Company, 2003). Estimates are that two thousand people a day are currently dying of smoking in China. By 2050, the researchers expect this number could rise to eight thousand a day—some three million people a year.

The China National Tobacco Corporation, the government monopoly, controls at least 90 percent of the market. But U.S. and European tobacco companies are placing more and more attention on this largest market for tobacco products. With their increasing market penetration, it is likely the tobacco consumption will increase. Overall, the United Nations estimates that five hundred million people in developing countries will die within the next decade from smoking-related illness. This together with the millions of people who die each year in the more industrialized developed world makes tobacco the largest single instance of product violence in the world today. The *New York Times* reported that a study of schoolchildren thirteen to fifteen in sixty-eight countries, conducted by the WHO and the Centers for Disease Control and Prevention, found that about 11 percent of the children in Latin America and the Caribbean were offered free cigarettes by a tobacco company representative in 1999 and 2000. In Russia, nearly 17 percent said they had been given free cigarettes. In Jordan, it was 25 percent (Winter, 2001).

Product Violence in the Automobile Industry

This industry has such a history of product violence against the public that we only present in brief some classic and more recent examples. The Ford Pinto is a classic case of product violence by the auto industry. Dowie (1977) points out in his now classic story on the case that Ford engineers discovered in preproduction crash tests that rear-end collisions at a speed exceeding twenty-five miles per hour would result in rupture of the gas tank, which was positioned directly behind the rear bumper. Altogether, in more than forty crash tests, ruptured gas tanks occurred every time. Eleven of these tests occurred prior to production for sale.

Despite these test results, Ford, which had made a significant investment in retooling for production, decided to go ahead with the manufacture and sale of the automobile. Later, when Ford discovered that the defective design could be corrected by minor modifications in the design of the gas tank, costing between $5.67 and $11, they conducted a cost/benefit analysis to determine whether it was cost effective to make the changes in design. In this analysis Ford executives assigned approximately $200,000 to the value of a human life and then calculated that the estimated number of deaths in fiery crashes of the Pinto and small pickup trucks that had the same design defect would be 180. They also estimated that 180 persons would be injured at an estimated cost of $67,000 per injury, and 2,100 vehicles would be damaged at an estimated cost of $700 per vehicle. The total savings in lives, injuries, and damage to vehicles if the defect was corrected was estimated to be $49.5 million. The cost of the modification in design was calculated to be $11 for each of the 11 million Pintos produced and 1.5 million light trucks, for a total cost of $137 million. Therefore, according to the analysis it was not cost effective to correct the design. But Ford made a bad decision. By the time the

1977 Dowie article was published, estimates were that between 500 and 900 people had died, and the cost to Ford Motor Company resulting from the double and triple damage lawsuits was well beyond what Ford had anticipated.

A similar case of product violence, again involving the Ford Motor Company, was a defect in the design of automatic transmissions that resulted in cars that were placed in park with the engine idling shifting into reverse unexpectedly. Ford Motor Company executives knew the defect for at least ten years before the public was made aware of the hazard. Automobiles and trucks with automatic transmissions manufactured between 1962 and 1979 had this defect. As early as 1971, office memos issued by an engineer in the Chassis Safety Systems Department to his superiors indicated that the improper position (of the transmission shift lever) appears to the customer as proper and that this situation had resulted in an actual high accident incidence. In November, one month before the National Highway Traffic Agency's investigation, a Ford engineer's ankle was run over after he placed the shift lever of a test vehicle into park, put the emergency brake on, and left the car in idle. The car lurched backward, ran over Hare's ankle, barely missed four other test cars, and was headed at twenty-five miles per hour for the high-speed track when a technician corralled it with a van (Branan, 1980, 46). By the time the correction was made, 70 people had died, 1,100 were injured, and 3,700 accidents had occurred. Ford was never required to recall and correct the defect in 26 million vehicles produced between 1962 and 1979.

Another recent case of product violence in the auto industry, this time involving General Motors, was the X-car design. General Motors executives were repeatedly warned by test drivers and internal company documents of a serious braking problem and later withheld information from federal officials regarding these cars (the 1980 Chevrolet Citation, Pontiac Phoenix, Oldsmobile Omega, and Buick Skylark). Hebert, reporting in the *Denver Post*, noted that by August 1983 the government had received more than 1,700 complaints about brakes locking in the X-body cars, including accidents involving fifteen deaths when the cars went into spins (Hebert, 1983).

A more recent General Motors case involves pickup trucks and the side-mounted fuel tanks outside the frame rails on all "C" and "K" style pickups manufactured between 1972 and 1987. Mokhiber (1994) notes that the Center for Auto Safety charged that GM manufactured and marketed pickup trucks with hazardous gas tanks that have led to six hundred deaths. The center claims that GM covered up the exploding gas tank problem and the company's decision not to install safety liners that would have reduced crash fires in the vehicles. Secretary of the United States Department of Transportation Federico Peña noted that of critical importance in this matter is the evidence that GM was aware, possibly as early as the mid-1970s, but certainly by the 1980s that this design made these trucks more vulnerable and that fatalities from side-impact fires were occurring. However, GM chose not to alter the design for fifteen years (Mokhiber, 1994, 8).

Another auto-related example involves the production of tires. Firestone Tire and Rubber Company produced and sold the defective Firestone 500 radial tire. The company was aware of the defect as early as three years after manufacture in 1975, yet continued to manufacture and market the defective tire, which was subject to blowouts, until 1978. A House of Representatives committee reported that the tire had caused thousands of accidents, hundreds of injuries, and thirty-four deaths (Mokhiber, 1988).

More recently Ford Motor Company and Firestone Tire and Rubber Company have had to settle millions of dollars in lawsuits as a result of problems of rollover accidents and tire blowouts from the underinflating of tires on their Ford Explorer brand SUV. Mokhiber reports that Joan Claybrook, president of Public Citizen, presented evidence before Congress in September of 2000 that "Ford internal documents show the company engineers recommended changes to the vehicle design after it rolled over in company tests prior to introduction, but other than a few minor changes, the suspension and track width were not changed. Instead, Ford, which sets the specifications for the manufacture of its tires, decided to remove air from the tires, lowering the recommended psi to 26. The Firestone-recommended psi molded into the tire for maximum load is 35 psi." Claybrook notes that within a year of introduction of the product, lawsuits against Ford and Firestone were filed for tire failures that resulted in crashes and rollovers. Almost all were settled and settled with gag orders prohibiting the attorneys and the families from disclosing information about the cases or their documentation to the public or Department of Transportation. She testified that there is no question the companies knew they had a problem. But they kept it secret.

By 1996, state agencies in Arizona were reporting problems with Firestone tires on Explorers. By 1998, Ford and Firestone had entered into discussions over tire failures with authorities in Middle Eastern, Asian, and South American countries. "Ford eventually decided to conduct its own recall without Firestone and replace the tires in the various countries in 1999 and 2000. More than 90 deaths and hundreds of injuries occurred before either company took action to notify owners of the potential defect. Company action was eventually motivated by a National Highway Traffic and Safety Administration investigation that began in 2000" (Mokhiber and Weissman, 2001).

Recently, Bridgestone/Firestone Inc. reached a $7.5 million settlement in a $1 billion lawsuit filed by a Texas family involved in a Ford Explorer rollover accident that left a thirty-nine-year-old mother paralyzed. CBS News reported that internal Firestone documents showed that executives wanted to cut costs at a Decatur, Illinois, plant that made the recalled tires. The documents also showed Firestone declined to use 90-cent nylon strips that company research found would have reduced the risk of tread separation by three to five times. An attorney for one of the victims stated that "this tire has killed more people than Timothy McVeigh. That is the awesome nature of the tragedy" (CBS.Com, 2001). At the time of this report, Firestone had settled two hundred cases and there were another three hundred cases pending.

There are thousands more cases of products that were known to be unsafe and yet the information was never presented to regulators or the consuming public, which resulted in deaths and injuries. Markowitz and Rosner (2002) in their work, *Deceit and Denial*, detail the history of lead poisoning in workers and consumers who used leaded paint and gasoline for years after the dangers were known. The story is the same: corporations knew of the danger of their product, withheld the information, and obstructed regulatory agencies from attempting to control the violence by limiting use or banning the product.

Product Violence and the Research Industry

One major case of product violence involved fraudulent product safety testing by independent testing labs. These labs contract with the companies that are to profit from positive safety tests for their product. The incentive for these companies is to provide positive test results in order for their customers to receive approval for marketing the company's products. One massive example of this type of product violence occurred in the case of Bio-Test Labs. This company was one of the major test labs determining product safety for many of the largest manufacturers in the United States. An investigation by the U.S. government determined that 80 percent of some nine hundred tests they reviewed were invalid. Shredding of product test results, which was against the law, was extensive. The Federal Trade Commission investigation, completed in 1980, identified 157 cases of compromised and deceptive product standards and testing lab actions, many of which led to thousands of deaths or serious injuries caused by unsafe playground equipment, toxic art materials, hazardous electrical appliances, unsafe occupational protective gear, and inadequately designed vehicles, all of which had been labeled or certified safe (Dowie, Foster, Marshall, Weir, and King, 1982).

Recently, an increasing number of private laboratories have been caught falsifying pollution test results (Rosoff, Pontell, and Tillman, 2007). The Inspector General of the EPA has called the rise of laboratory fraud a disturbing trend. An environmental contractor in South Carolina by the name of James Edward Adams was sentenced to twenty-seven months in prison. His company employees were instructed by Adams to provide false test reports for companies that had underground petroleum storage tanks in a number of southern states. Tanknology-NDE International, which was the country's largest provider of underground storage tank testing, was sentenced to pay a $1 million criminal fine and $1.29 million in restitution for false testing services it performed.

In another case, the owner of Quality Water Analysis Laboratories in Pittsburgh, Kansas, was sentenced to eighteen months in prison after pleading guilty to making false statements in violation of the Clean Water Act. The company deliberately falsified tests on water samples performed for clients needing CWA permits. The fraudulent results allowed water to be discharged into the environment with illegally high levels of pollutants. Intertek Testing Services Environmental Laboratories of Richardson, Texas, was fined $9 million for falsifying tests of air and soil at federal Superfund sites, defense department facilities, and other locations.

A larger problem than the fraud in testing is the industry bias in the U.S. government control systems developed to prevent unsafe and hazardous products from entering the marketplace. In the United States, the companies that produce a product are responsible for providing evidence to the government of its safety. Fagin, Lavelle, and the Center for Public Integrity in their work *Toxic Deception* (1999) analyze the cases of four dangerous chemicals that are in use throughout the United States. Two of the products, atrazine and alachlor, are herbicides widely sold to farmers and homeowners to control weeds and are listed as probable carcinogens. These herbicides are found in drinking water throughout many Midwestern states. The two other cases are perchlorethylene, which is a degreaser used by dry cleaning establishments, and formaldehyde, which is used as a preservative and binding agent for everything from cosmetics, pesticides, cleaners, and adhesives. Both products are listed as probable carcinogens by the International Agency for Research on Cancer.

Fagin et al. focus on the use of formaldehyde in building products such as particleboard used in cabinets, flooring, and furniture. Formaldehyde was discovered to cause cancer in laboratory animals in the early 1970s. The problem is that the companies that benefit from the marketing and sale of the products are responsible for presenting evidence to the government regarding the hazards for their use. An indication that this is not working very well is when the EPA offered an amnesty from large fines if companies turned in health studies that they should have provided to the government earlier. "Manufacturers suddenly produced more than 10,000 studies showing that chemicals already on the market could pose a 'substantial risk of injury to health or to the environment'—the king of never-published data that the law says must be presented to the government immediately" (Fagin et al., 1999, 14). Fagin notes that several of the studies not reported to the government included research on the health risk of alachlor, atrazine, formaldehyde, and percholoroethylene. The EPA is still wading through the deluge of studies to determine the safety of these products and hundreds of others that may pose significant health risks to consumers. Furthermore, the authors note that these companies have an army of lobbyists and lawyers who work with legislators in crafting the regulations and the agencies that are charged with executing them. There is also a revolving door phenomenon where employees for these same agencies that police the private corporations end up working for them or worked for them previously.

The Enronization of Science refers to private companies in the service of corporate clients that will conduct research to produce favorable results for their clients (Michaels, 2008). In most cases, the role of these companies is to prove or to create enough doubts in research claims of harms of product, production processes, or the release of chemicals into the environment that they block the creation of regulations to safeguard the public. One company Michaels discusses is Exponent, Inc., which began its existence as an engineering firm, calling itself Failure Analysis Associates and specializing in assisting the auto industry in defending itself in lawsuits involving crashes. However, the company has branched in the service in the industry to create enough doubt in scientific claims to block government regulation. An article in the *Annals of Emergency Medicine* claimed that the new generation of amusement park rides exposed thrill seekers to g-forces (a measure of acceleration) that exceed those experienced by astronauts and recommended that emergency physicians consider these rides as "a possible cause of unexplained neurologic events in healthy patients." Michaels notes that twelve Six Flags Theme Parks, Inc., commissioned Exponent to produce an "Investigation of Amusement Park Roller Coaster Injury Likelihood and Severity." The press release on the report was headlined "Roller Coasters, Theme Parks Extraordinarily Safe."

Another case of Exponent research for hire was done under contract of the American Beverage Association, which became increasingly concerned when school districts around the nation became concerned about research linking the availability of high sugar soft drinks with childhood obesity and were removing the vending machines from schools. The research that Exponent conducted concluded that the number of beverages consumed from school vending machines "does not appear to be excessive."

When a study by consulting epidemiologists discovered a high rate of prostate cancer cases at a Syngenta plant that produced the pesticide atrazine, Exponent's scientists produced a study that found no relationship between the chemical and the disease. After numerous studies that linked pesticide exposure and Parkinson's disease appeared in prestigious scientific journals, Exponent's scientists produced a literature review for *CropLife America*, the trade association of pesticide producers, whose conclusion maintained that "the animal and epidemiologic data reviewed do not provide sufficient evidence to support a causal association between pesticide exposure and Parkinson's disease."

A crucial part of the scientific method is to replicate results to provide a level of certainty of the claims. However, when research is particularly contracted to refute scientific research, the results can be a distortion of the research process in the service of the industry. One way that this is done is through the manipulation of the peer-review process, which provides a mechanism of quality control for research.

> The credibility given peer-reviewed studies encourages product defense firms to manipulate and distort the process. They play the peer-review card beautifully. They understand that their studies and re-analyses need this imprimatur, but how do they get this seal of approval? Easy. They establish "vanity journals" that present themselves to the unwary as independent sources of information and science, but the peer reviewers are carefully chosen, like-minded corporate consultants sitting in friendly judgment on studies that are exquisitely structured to influence a regulatory proceeding or court case. (Michaels, 2008, 63)

Michaels refers to these journals as "captured" journals. He cites the example of the tobacco industry, which secretly financed the journal *Indoor and Built Environment* to promote for its legal defense of their product the idea that indoor air pollution was a problem caused not by secondhand smoke but by inadequate ventilation.

Another case is the journal *Regulatory Toxicology and Pharmacology*, which is listed as the official journal of the International Society for Regulatory Toxicology and Pharmacology (ISRTP). Michaels points out that the association's membership is dominated by scientists who work for industry trade groups and consulting firms. He notes that the sponsors of the ISRTP include many of the major tobacco, chemical, and drug manufacturing companies and the leadership of the organization consists of corporate and product defense scientists and attorneys. There are hundreds if not thousands of think tanks that sponsor "research" on the behalf of their corporate sponsors to attempt to create enough doubt to block regulations to safeguard the public, organizations like Foundation for Clean Air Progress, run by Burson-Marsteller, the major corporate public relations firm, using funds provided by the petroleum and trucking industries, or the Annapolis Center for Science-Based Policy, which was started by a vice president of the National Association of Manufacturers for fighting the EPA's Clean Air standards. The Center for Media and Democracy is one group that is trying to keep track of the large number of corporate-funded think tanks that are trying to reduce regulations in the interest of corporations. Their website provides information as to the sponsors of these "think tanks," important information for those who are trying to determine what is science and what is corporate-sponsored public relations.

In general there is a significant problem when the companies that are to profit from the research results are hiring scientists to conduct the research. Michaels concludes that beginning in the 1990s, the link between corporate sponsorship of research and the propensity for pro-industry conclusions was uncovered. "When a scientist (or the scientist's employer) is hired by a firm with a financial interest in the outcome, the likelihood that the result of that study will be favorable to that firm is dramatically increased. This close correlation between the results desired by a study's funders and those reported by the researchers we now call the 'funding effect'" (Michaels, 2008, 143). Michaels notes that there is little doubt of the existence of the "funding effect"; research on a whole range of pharmaceutical products concludes that there is a high correlation between corporate-funded research and corporate-favorable results. However, he notes that what may come as a surprise to the research community is the nature of the bias of the research.

A recently retired editor of the *British Medical Journal* (BMJ), Dr. Richard Smith, observed that it took him "almost a quarter of a century editing to wake up to what was happening." According to Smith, "companies seem to get the results they want not by fiddling the results, which would be far too crude and possibly detectable by peer review, but rather by asking the 'right' questions—and there are many ways to do this . . . many ways to hugely increase the chance of producing favourable results, and there are many hired guns who will think up new ways and stay one jump ahead of peer reviewers" (Smith, 2005). According to Michaels, the manufacturers have strong motivation to promote the certainty that the drug is effective, while downplaying any possible risk. When such a risk is indicated, however, the strategy flips, and the new objective is to create uncertainty about the danger. Product defense experts may be called in to save the day, as defined in terms of the profitability of their clients, but at the same time ruin the day, as defined in terms of increasing the level of product violence victimization.

PRODUCTION VIOLENCE

According to 2010 preliminary data from the U.S. Bureau of Labor Statistics and the Department of Labor, 4,547 people died from fatal work injuries. Highway work–related deaths composed that largest single percentage of deaths, 21 percent; followed by falls, 14 percent; homicides, 11 percent; struck by an object, 9 percent; exposure to harmful substances, 9 percent; and fires and explosions, 4 percent. Ninety-two percent of the victims were male. Older workers, those fifty-five years of age and older, have the highest rates of workplace fatalities. The rate of those sixty-five and older is more than three times higher than the average for all age groups.

The highest rates of workplace fatalities occur in the agriculture, forestry, fishing, and hunting category, 26.8 per 100,000; followed by mining, 19.8 per 100,000; transportation and warehousing, 13.1 per 100,000; and construction, 9.5 per 100,000. The International Labour Organization (ILO) estimates that for the year 2008 every day, 6,300 people died as a result of occupational accidents or work-related diseases, that is, more than 2.3 million deaths per year. They also claim that there over 337 million accidents that occur on the job each year (International Labour Organization, 2011). The overall current number of fatal accidents and the fatal accident incident rates are the lowest they have been for the past ten years. Levels of employment may be a factor because of the impact of the recent worldwide recession. However, changes may be related to other factors including more regulatory controls and policing.

There are some areas where rates of occurrence and fatalities have increased. This is true in the case of the incidence of nonfatal accidents and fatalities from exposure to hazardous chemicals at work. There has been an enormous growth in the use of industrial chemicals that have not been adequately tested. There are significant differences in numbers of and incidence of work-related fatalities across different regions of the world. The highest incidence rates for fatal industrial accidents are found in Africa where the rate is more than five times the rate in high-income countries. The rates in low- and middle-income counties in Latin American, Eastern European, and Southeast Asia and Western Pacific regions are at least twice the rate in higher-income countries.

Occupational disease is one of the most under-researched, underfunded, and ignored areas of public health today. The occurrence of death from occupational diseases is much higher than workplace fatalities noted above. One calculation from a reputable source using 1997 U.S. mortality data estimated the annual occupational disease mortality resulting from selected respiratory diseases, cancers, cardiovascular disease, chronic renal failure, and hepatitis was forty-nine thousand (Steenland, Burnett, Lalich, Ward, and Hurrell, 2003). The rates of occupational disease and mortality from work are believed to be significantly higher in developing countries. The World Health Organization estimates that deaths from coming into contact with carcinogens while at work are approximately five times higher in low- and middle-income countries compared to high-income countries. Deaths from airborne particulates are more than ten times greater in low- and middle-income countries compared to high-income countries (World Health Organization, 2009).

When we review mortality and injury statistics, it is important to recognize that one cause may be worker carelessness or negligence or a result of events that were unforeseeable or outside of the worker's or management's control, in short accidents that were unpreventable. In these cases, this would not be violence. However, when there are dangers that workers are required to be exposed to as part of their job and these dangers are hidden from them or safeguards are not put in place to prevent injury or death, we are describing acts of violence. Let's review some examples of production violence across a series of different industries.

Asbestos

One of the major causes of worker violence in the United States and throughout the world concerns asbestos. The *British Medical Journal* in 1924 reported a link between asbestos exposure and disease (Rosoff, Pontell, and Tillman, 2007). In 1928, the *Journal of the American Medical Association* reported on a young woman who died of asbestosis (Mokhiber, 1987). Castleman (1984) reports that according to internal company documents Johns Manville Corporation was aware of the hazards as early as 1930. The company along with Raybestos-Manhattan conspired to distort a 1935 study sponsored by the industry that indicated the hazards of the product (Kotelchuck, 1987). In 1949, Manville conducted its own research indicating that lung damage had occurred in the 534 out of 780 asbestos workers tested. A confidential report written by the medical director of the Johns Manville Corporation issued that same year recommended that workers stricken with asbestosis who had not developed symptoms should not be informed of their illness, noting, "As long as the man feels well, is happy at home and at work and his physical condition remains good, he should be permitted to live and work in peace" (Castleman, 1984, 27). People working with the materials, as well as those who purchased products made from asbestos, were not told of its hazards until the 1970s. An explanation for the delay in notifying workers of the hazards of working with the substance is illustrated in a statement made under oath by the medical director, Kenneth W. Smith, in 1976 when asked about whether he had advised the placement of warning labels on asbestos products. He stated that the company "had to take into consideration the effects of everything they did, and if the applications of a caution label identifying a product as hazardous would cut out sales, there would be serious financial implications" (Mokhiber, 1987).

Research done on asbestos workers who had worked with the material for twenty years indicated that mortality rates for the group was 50 percent higher than for average white males, and the rate of lung cancer was seven hundred times greater than expected. The rate for all types of cancer was four times greater (Epstein, 1978). Mokhiber notes that the industry cover-up of the harms of asbestos came to light in 1978 as a result of congressional hearings. What became known as the asbestos "Pentagon Papers" revealed a pattern of cover-up and deception by the industry as early as the 1930s. South

The roofing problem of this building has been solved

Figure 7.2. Advertisement for Asbestos roofing by Johns-Manville, Inc., depicting the Detroit Public Library. From page 35 of Architectural Forum Vol 35 Issue 1, 1921.

Carolina Judge James Price ordered a new trial for a deceased asbestos insulation worker whose claim had earlier been dismissed. Judge Price noted in the reopening of the case that the internal documents reflected "a conscious effort by the industry in the 1930s to downplay or arguably suppress the dissemination of information to employees and the public for fear of promotion of lawsuits" (Epstein, 1978, 75). As late as 1972, Johns Manville decided against the installation of a dust-control system to protect its workers that would have cost $5 million a year to operate. In the logic of the corporation, it was more cost effective to pay an estimated $1 million per year in workmen's compensation for workers disabled or killed by asbestos dust (Rosoff, Pontell, and Tillman, 2007).

Up until the 1970s, asbestos was used in everything from roofing materials and insulation materials to hair dryers and other small and major appliances. Furthermore, in many countries around the world these products are still available and the materials are still in use in homes and public buildings. An agency of the United Nations recently called for global trade restrictions on the sale of all forms of asbestos. On February 21, 2002, an announcement was made by the United Nations Environment Programme (UNEP). In a press release issued by the agency it stated that "all forms of asbestos should be added to an international list of chemicals subject to trade controls" (United Nations Environment Programme, 2002). This decision follows a review of asbestos that had been triggered by unilateral bans adopted by the European Union and Chile. The committee of government experts, which studied the issue, noted that the inhalation of asbestos fibers causes cancer and other illnesses and that asbestos is still used in seals, gaskets, joints, brakes, armaments, and other applications. The report noted that cost-effective substitutes are increasingly available for most applications.

Meanwhile, about 125 million people in the world are exposed to asbestos at the workplace. According to the most recent WHO estimates, more than 107,000 people die each year from asbestos-related lung cancer, mesothelioma, and asbestosis resulting from exposure at work. One in every three deaths from occupational cancer is estimated to be caused by asbestos. In addition, it is estimated that several thousand deaths annually can be attributed to exposure to asbestos in the home (World Health Organization, 2010). In the United States it is estimated that the number of deaths from asbestos will peak around 2015. Mesothelioma develops usually twenty to forty years after exposure.

According to the U.S. Centers for Disease Control, an estimated 1.3 million construction and general industry workers potentially are being exposed to asbestos. The CDC's National Institute for Occupational Safety and Health (NIOSH) analyzed annual multiple-cause-of-death records for 1999–2005, the most recent years for which complete data are available, and calculated that a total of 18,068 deaths of persons with malignant mesothelioma were reported. This was an increase from 2,482 deaths in 1999 to 2,704 in 2005 (Centers for Disease Control, 2009).

In addition to this relatively rare form of cancer, an additional 1,400 people will die from asbestosis, 4,800 from asbestos-related lung cancer, and approximately 1,200 people will die from gastrointestinal cancer (Environmental Working Group, 2004). Thus, for all forms of cancer related to asbestos, approximately 10,000 people die each year in the United States.

Vinyl Chloride

Vinyl chloride is another illustration of production violence. Vinyl chloride is a chemical intermediary that is used to produce PVC, which is the third most common plastic, used in the production of plastic bottles and plastic pipes, clothing and upholstery, electrical cable insulation, inflatable products, and many applications in which it replaces rubber. Up until 1974 it was also used as an aerosol spray propellant. As early as 1970, a study indicated that long-term intermittent exposure of rats to vinyl chloride in the air resulted in the production of several types of cancers. In 1972 research confirmed this earlier finding. Representatives of U.S. industries were given the full details of these studies in January 1973. These companies then entered into an agreement with the European consortium not to disclose the information without prior consent.

The Manufacturing Chemists Association, which was aware of the research, failed to disclose the dangers of vinyl chloride despite a request from a government agency for all available data on the toxic effects of vinyl chloride. The data were finally revealed to the government when three workers exposed to vinyl chloride at a B. F. Goodrich plant died of angiosarcoma of the liver. According to a special committee report of the American Association for the Advancement of Science, the Manufacturing Chemists Association had deliberately deceived the government and "because of the suppression of these data, tens of thousands of workers were exposed without warning, for perhaps some two years, to toxic concentrations of vinyl chloride" (Epstein, 1978).

In 1974, Congress passed the Safe Drinking Water Act. This law requires EPA to determine safe levels of chemicals in drinking water that do or may cause health problems. These nonenforceable levels, based solely on possible health risks and exposure, are called Maximum Contaminant Level Goals. The MCLG for vinyl chloride has been set at zero because EPA believes this level of protection would not cause any of the potential health problems described below.

Production of vinyl chloride pollution in 1993 was nearly fourteen billion pounds. Its major release to the environment is as air emissions and wastewater at polyvinyl chloride (PVC) plastics manufacturing facilities. Small quantities of vinyl chloride are also released to food since it is used to make many food wrappings and containers. From 1987 to 1993, according to EPA's Toxic Release Inventory, vinyl chloride releases to water and land totaled over thirty-eight thousand pounds. These releases were primarily from plastics materials and resins industries. The largest releases occurred in Louisiana and Delaware (U.S. Environmental Protection Agency, 2001).

According to the National Toxicology Program of the U.S. Department of Health and Human Services ninth report on carcinogens, the primary routes of potential human exposure to vinyl chloride are inhalation and dermal contact. Potential human exposure to vinyl chloride occurs principally in the workplace, through general air and water pollution, and to a limited extent from the use of fabricated products (U.S. Department of Health and Human Services, 2001).

In a recent case, the Taiwan-based Formosa Plastics Corporation facility in Louisiana has been fined several times since 1987 for excessive releases of vinyl chloride. Holley Knaus reported that in 1986, a Delaware judge ordered a six-week shutdown of a Formosa plant in that state in response to a vinyl chloride monomer release so extreme that the factory's sprinkler system went off and employees were forced to wear breathing equipment. In Point Comfort, Texas, Formosa has been hit with two of the largest environmental fines in Texas history. In spring 1990, the Texas Water Commission fined the company $247,000 for seventeen violations over a three-year period, including improper storage of oil and other waste, cracked wastewater retention ponds, and releases of extremely acidic wastewater into surface water. In October 1990, the five-state Region Six office of the EPA handed Formosa a proposed $8.3 million fine for illegal disposal of hazardous waste (Knaus, 1991). According to Chemical Industry Archives (2001), in 1998, Formosa Plastics Corporation in its plant in Delaware City, Delaware, produced 13 percent of the total vinyl chloride emissions in the United States.

Film Recovery Systems

Rarely are cases of production violence officially defined as criminal violence. One exception concerns Stefan Golab and Film Recovery Systems, Inc. Golab, a Polish immigrant, was employed by Film Recovery. He worked with other workers in reclaiming silver from used X-ray film. The process involves the use of cyanide. Workers frequently became ill breathing in the fumes coming off the large vats of cyanide. When they became ill, they were allowed to go outside the shop, often to catch a breath of fresh air and at other times to vomit. February 10, 1985, Stefan Golab staggered from the cyanide vat he was working over, stumbled to the adjacent locker room, and collapsed. Some of his fellow workers dragged him outside and called an ambulance. But it was too late. The cause of death: cyanide poisoning. A Cook County, Illinois, Hospital study of Golab's fellow workers, undertaken following his death, found that "at least two thirds of Film Recovery's workers suffered ten times a month or more from each of four major symptoms of cyanide intoxication; they were told to 'go outside so you can have some fresh air.' Investigators found that many workers were not aware that they were working with cyanide" (Frank, 1987).

A former bookkeeper for Film Recovery stated that illegal aliens were specifically chosen to work in the plant because they could not read English. Thus they could not read the warning labels on the drums of cyanide. Also, several employees observed skull and crossbones markings being painted or burned off the drums. Since company managers had never informed workers of the hazards of working with the chemical, workers who did see the skull and crossbones assumed that the chemical was dangerous only if it was swallowed. They did not know that it could be lethal if inhaled or absorbed through the skin. Three executives were convicted of murder and fourteen counts of reckless conduct; two corporations were convicted of involuntary manslaughter and fourteen counts of reckless conduct (Frank, 1987, 104). But the sentences were overturned on appeal, and two of the executives pleaded guilty to involuntary manslaughter (Felsenthal, 1993).

Coal Mining—Black Lung and Mining Disasters

Coal is one of the major sources of energy in the United States and the world. However, there are some serious hazards to the use of coal as a source for the generation of energy. The first problem results from how it is acquired through mining. According to the CDC, during the past decade more than ten thousand miners have died of coal workers' pneumoconiosis, or what is commonly called black lung disease (Centers for Disease Control, 2008). According to the CDC, the prevalence of black lung disease had decreased by about 90 percent from 1969 to 1995 as a result of the enactment of the Coal Mine Health and Safety Act. However, they note that the downward trend of this disease has leveled off and that many current underground miners are developing severe and advanced cases. It was not just long-time miners who had the disease, but some were as young as twenty-five, and five had less than ten years of experience working in coal mines.

The increases may be also a result of the change in mining techniques. Richer coal reserves have been depleted or mined out. What's left in these areas are thinner seams that one CDC researcher claims may pose a greater risk to health, particularly if dust regulations haven't been adjusted to accommodate increased exposure. Thinner-seam mining is much more difficult to do because miners are often cutting the rock that's adjacent to the coal seam. That adjacent rock contains silica in many cases, and silica is about twenty times more toxic than coal mine dust. There are questions of whether mining companies are monitoring silica and coal dust levels and keeping them at appropriate levels and whether those levels are low enough. United Mine Workers estimate that 1,500 former coal miners die each year from black lung disease (James, 2011).

For most of the twentieth century, the coal mining companies have worked to deny the existence of the disease; however, in recent times mine workers have been successful in having the government recognize the significant health hazard caused by breathing coal dust in mines. A congressional committee noted that "the dreadful high incidence of black lung is an immediate consequence of the coal dust created by the increased production rates of the industry. . . . The incidence of this disease can be completely prevented by implementing existing technology and undertaking the research necessary to reduce the levels of respirable dust. The problem lies not in the lack of technical competence but in the lack of will to invest in health and safety" (U.S. House of Representatives, 1979, 1230).

In 1969, Congress placed strict limits on airborne dust and ordered operators to take periodic air tests inside coal mines. The law has significantly reduced black lung among the nation's fifty-three thousand underground coal miners. But according to an investigative report that appeared in the *Courier-Journal* of Louisville, Kentucky, because of cheating and lack of federal regulatory diligence, the law has fallen far short of its goal of virtually eliminating the disease (Harris, 1998). The investigative report claims that because of widespread cheating by the mining companies in the Appalachian region of the United States, miners' lives are endangered. In a series of interviews it was revealed that two dozen mine owners or managers admitted submitting fraudulent tests. The report also notes that the government regularly ignores these obvious fraudulent reports. This is confirmed by the autopsies that were done on twenty-four miners who died in the mine explosion at the Upper Big Branch mine in West Virginia, which revealed that seventeen of them or 75 percent showed signs of black lung disease (James, 2011).

Mining accidents as a result of preventable unsafe working conditions are another area of violence. Regarding the Scotia mine disaster that occurred in 1976 and killed twenty-six people, Caudill (1987) notes that the mine had been inspected hundreds of times before March 9, 1976, and 652 violations of safety laws and regulations had been cited. Of these at least sixty infractions dealt with serious ventilation problems, including insufficient air circulating at the workers' face, line brattices out of position, inoperative methanometers, failure to follow the ventilation plan, and findings of imminent danger of explosions, due to methane concentrations of 1.2 percent. Penalties amounting to $164,352 had been imposed by assessment officers, but the company had actually paid only $78,877 (98).

More recently on Easter morning, April 5, 2010, a powerful explosion ripped through the Upper Big Branch in West Virginia, an underground mine owned by Massey Energy and operated by Performance Mine Company, killing twenty-nine miners. The company had a long list of violations of mine safety regulations. A statement from the report to the governor of West Virginia summarized its conclusion on the reasons for the disaster.

> Ultimately, the responsibility for the explosion at the Upper Big Branch mine lies with the management of Massey Energy. The company broke faith with its workers by frequently and knowingly violating the law and blatantly disregarding known safety practices while creating a public perception that its operations exceeded industry safety standards. The story of Upper Big Branch is a cautionary tale of hubris. A company that was a towering presence in the Appalachian coalfields operated its mines in a profoundly reckless manner, and 29 coal miners paid with their lives for the corporate risk-taking. (McAteer and Associates, 2011, 108)

Mokhiber (1988) notes that 100,000 miners have been killed in mining accidents in the twentieth century, and 1.5 million injuries have been reported since 1930. Between 2005 and 2006 there was an 84 percent increase in the rate of fatal injuries from coal mining (Bureau of Labor Statistics, 2007).

Textile Industry and Brown Lung

Brown lung or byssinosis is another disease that has affected a large number of working people in this country and around the world. Like black lung, the disease has been known for more than a hundred years. As early as 1713, an Italian physician reported the problem among flax and hemp workers. During the nineteenth century, French, English, and Belgian doctors reported the occurrence of the disease. Despite hundreds of reports regarding the disease, textile mill owners have regularly denied its existence and have used their political power to block regulation and the enforcement of regulations. According to the American Lung Association (2000) between 1979 and 1996, byssinosis caused 120 deaths and an estimated 35,000 current and former textile workers have been disabled.

Much of this problem in the United States is located in the South. Guarasci (1987) notes that there are about 400,000 textile workers in the Carolinas. Of those, 115,000 are exposed to cotton dust in their work and it is estimated that between 18,000 and 35,000 Carolinians suffer from byssinosis. Guarasci concludes in his analysis of two textile mill towns in North and South Carolina that the problem of brown lung is a result of industrial negligence, authoritarian rule in the workplace, and pernicious misadministration of government regulations.

Farming and Use of Pesticides

We mentioned earlier pesticides that are carcinogenic and banned in the United States but are sold overseas to be used by farm laborers in South and Central America. But there is a very serious problem of pesticide poisoning in this country from pesticides defined by the government as suitable for agricultural production. One of the most lethal pesticides used in agriculture in the United States is parathion, a nerve-gas insecticide. Moses (1993) claims that this particular poison is responsible for more occupational deaths throughout the world than any other single pesticide. The EPA notes that this pesticide causes poisoning among all categories of workers who come into direct contact with it. EPA further notes that these poisonings occur under conditions where workers are following label directions.

Moses (1993) cites epidemiological studies of workers exposed to pesticides that portend increased risks of developing a wide range of cancers. Furthermore several studies indicate an increased risk to children exposed to pesticides. The State of California Department of Health Services (1988) found a significantly higher rate of cancer among children in agricultural communities in the San Joaquin Valley than what would be expected given the national average. There is additional research that illustrates a correlation between pesticide exposure of workers and the risk for birth defects. Moses (1993) notes that research has established the linkage between various pesticides and facial clefts, spina bifida, anencephaly, and neural tube defects. Also, research suggests a link between exposure to agricultural chemicals and spontaneous abortions or stillbirths. In one large U.S. study of 6,386 stillbirths, pesticide exposure of either parent increased the risk (Savitz, Whelan, and Kleckner, 1989).

The World Health Organization (WHO) estimates that pesticides poison at least three million people annually and kill some twenty thousand. They note in a 2008 bulletin that studies in developed countries have demonstrated the annual incidence rates of pesticide poisoning in agricultural workers to be as much as 18.2 per 100,000 full-time workers and 7.4 per million among schoolchildren (Thundiyil, Stober, Besbelli, and Pronczuk, 2008). As mentioned earlier, in developing countries in South and Central America and Africa, rates of injury and death are expected to be many times higher, not only because of the laxness of regulations and safety procedures but also because of the dumping of toxic pesticides in these countries. One study estimated that 75 percent of the pesticides applied in Central American are either banned, restricted, or unregistered in the United States (Alston and Brown, 1993). Seventy to 80 percent of all poisonings occur in developing countries where regulatory, health, and education systems are weakest (Forastieri, 1999).

Child Labor

One area where the work itself is dangerous to the person is the area of child labor. Child labor is considered violence because the nature of the work stunts the development of children. Article 32 of the United Nations Convention on the Rights of the Child states: "State Parties recognize the right of the child to be protected from economic exploitation and from performing any work that is likely to be hazardous or to interfere with the child's education, or to be harmful to the child's health or physical, mental, spiritual, moral or social development" (UNICEF, 1989). The convention has been ratified by 191 countries. Only the United States and Somalia have not ratified the convention at the time of this writing.

Examples of child labor as economic violence are where children are employed to spray dangerous pesticides and fungicides on the crops of the labor contractors employed by large multinational corporations. Another example is the case of young children working in the sweatshops in countries south of the equator sewing the seams on clothing and athletic shoes. And another is millions of young children who are forced into the sex trade. Regarding the latter example, in a recent article in *Time* magazine, the reporters purchased the freedom of two young girl prostitutes from a brothel for less than $1,000. The brothel owner, Mama San, says that "their mothers or the middlemen bring them to me. There are always fresh ones" (Perry and Sai, 2002, 7). The article notes that according to the International Labour Organization, at least one million children are working as prostitutes in Asia. We will discuss this topic more when we discuss slavery and forced labor in the structural violence chapter.

A preliminary analysis by UNICEF shows that in more than thirty countries covering 35 percent of the developing world population, 19 percent of five- to fourteen-year-old boys and girls are working. UNICEF (2001) notes that there are substantial urban-rural differences, with 21 percent of children aged five to fifteen working in rural areas as compared to 13 percent in urban areas. Two-thirds of those working do so for a family farm or business and less than 5 percent do paid or unpaid work and/or domestic work for four or more hours a day. Sub-Saharan African countries show the highest proportions of children working.

The ILO estimated that 250 million children between five and fourteen worked for a living, and that more than fifty million children under age twelve worked in hazardous circumstances. It also estimates that domestic work is the largest employment category of girls under age sixteen in the world. According to International Labour Organization statistics, some 61 percent of this total, or nearly 153 million, are found in Asia; 32 percent, or 80 million, are in Africa; and 7 percent, or 17.5 million, live in Latin America (International Labour Organization, 2002).

The ILO has begun a program to improve the knowledge on the extent and nature of some of the worst forms of child labor through its Statistical Information and Monitoring Programme on Child Labour (SIMPOC). This program has carried out thirty-eight rapid assessments in nineteen countries and one border region. The investigations explore "urgent and often sensitive" issues such as children in bondage; child domestic workers; child soldiers; child trafficking; drug trafficking; hazardous work in commercial agriculture, fishing, garbage dumps, mining, and the urban environment; sexual exploitation; and working street children. For example, one of these reports assesses the problem of trafficking in Nepalese girls for prostitution. Based on their surveys of villages, they estimated that twelve thousand young girls have trafficked out of Nepal to become prostitutes (Kumar et al., 2001). Another study focuses on child labor in mining in Tanzania (Mwami et al., 2002), and another on the work of street children in Turkey (Aksit, Karanci, and Gunduz-Hosgor, 2001). A most recent ILO report (2011a) found that the number of children engaged in hazardous work has declined by 50 percent from 2000 to 2008.

In the United States, just in the fifteen-to-seventeen-year age group, 374 children died at work in a ten-year period, 1998–2007 (a fatality rate of 2.9 deaths per 100,000 full-time equivalents) and an estimated 598,000 children sustained work-related injuries and illnesses severe enough to be treated in hospital emergency departments (an injury/illness rate of 4.2 per 100 full-time equivalents) (International Labour Organization, 2011). This rate of injury for children aged fifteen to seventeen is nearly twice that of workers twenty-five years and older. The largest portion of children working is in agriculture, which also has the highest rates of injury and death. Human Rights Watch (2000) estimates that in the United States between three hundred thousand and eight hundred thousand children work in agriculture each year.

ENVIRONMENTAL VIOLENCE

This is one area of violence that is less likely to be defined as violence, although this is more a result of who has the ability to define what is violence and who does not. Ralph Nader notes that those who define violence are those who perpetuate most of it. While the government focuses its attention on the violence that occurs from street crimes, it tends to ignore the violence that occurs from the chemical assault on the environment. More is lost in money and health through pollution than crimes of street violence, yet only the latter is defined officially as violence (Simon and Eitzen, 1993, 154). According to a recent study, pollution levels around the world today are estimated to cause 40 percent of the deaths of humans worldwide (Pimentel, Cooperstein, Randell, Filiberto, and Sorrentino, 2007). Most of these deaths are caused by poor sanitation and the water pollution that results. However, the authors estimated that air pollution from smoke and various chemicals kills three million people a year. In the United States alone about three million tons of toxic chemicals are released into the environment contributing to cancer, birth defects, immune system defects, and many other serious health problems.

In considering environmental violence we will consider four categories. The first is knowingly disposing of wastes from production in an unsafe manner so that it kills or injures community residents. Another is knowingly emitting toxic gases into the air that result in the death or injury of residents. A third category refers to knowingly emitting toxic liquids or solids into water systems so that they result in the death or injury of residents. The last category of environmental violence we discuss is knowingly removing a resource in such a way and extent that it leads to further environmental damage and to the death or injury of residents.

No official statistics are collected regarding the number of deaths resulting from environmental violence. All that is available is a series of case studies from around the globe that highlight these different categories of environmental violence.

TOXIC WASTE

There is an increasing crisis throughout the world connected with the disposal of hazardous waste. The problem principally originates in the richest countries in the world and then spreads to poorer countries. The United States has the greatest problems in this area. In 2009, Americans generated about 250 million tons of trash and recycled and composted approximately a third of it (U.S. Environmental Protection Agency, 2010). Approximately 60 percent of this waste is generated by households and the remainder by non-households including commercial business, government and offices, schools, and hospitals. The largest percentage is placed in landfills throughout the United States. Approximately 10 percent is incinerated, but 40 percent of the waste remains as ash, which is then disposed of in landfills. When discussing economic violence as it relates to waste disposal, we are focusing on the waste generated by economic organization and disposed in a manner that leads to the death and injury of the members of a community who are affected by the manner of the disposal.

Love Canal is a classic example of this type of environmental violence. In 1942 Hooker Chemical and Plastics Corporation negotiated an agreement to use land owned by the county power company to dispose of chemical wastes from its plant in Buffalo (Mokhiber, 1988). In 1947 Hooker bought Love Canal, drained it, lined it with clay, dumped thousands of fifty-five-gallon metal drums of waste, and then covered it with dirt. Grass and weeds grew on the surface of the dump site. Mokhiber (1988) notes that in 1953, after Hooker had filled the canal with deadly chemicals (tricholorophenol and dioxin, two highly toxic chemicals), the company sold the land to the town of Love Canal for one dollar with the stipulation that they were not liable for any consequences resulting from use of the land. The company at the time of the sale knew that the town planned on developing an elementary school on the land. Housing developers planned on constructing homes around the school site. Mokhiber points out that the transfer deed warned that the land "had been filled, in whole or in part, to the present ground level . . . with waste products resulting from the manufacturing of chemicals [by Hooker]" and that "the [Board of Education] . . . assumes all risks and liability incident to the use thereof" (Mokhiber, 1988, 271). Hooker gave no information about the danger posed by the wastes. A school and houses were built on the perimeter of the site, and the playground for the school was located on the site.

As early as 1958, Hooker knew that some chemicals buried on the site were coming in contact with children who played on the playground. Hooker investigated the problem and found that carcinogenic chemicals were surfacing in the north and south perimeters of the site. Hooker also was aware at the time that the site was being used by children as a playground. Hooker informed the school board of the potential problem of the leakage. However, Mokhiber notes that the corporation did not warn residents of the danger. Mokhiber cites the testimony before Congress of Jerome Wilkenfeld, the Hooker Chemical executive who wrote the memo to the school board: "We did not feel that we could do this without incurring substantial liabilities for implying that the current owners of the property were [taking] . . . inadequate care [of] . . . the property" (Mokhiber, 1988, 271).

The chemicals continued to leak out of the containment system of the landfill at an increased level during the 1970s and migrate to the homes that belted around the site. There were problems in the baseball field next to the schoolyard where large holes appeared in the outfield. Eventually, the chemicals began to leach into the basements of several homes surrounding the site. A black sludge would come up through the drainage holes into the basements. Besides the effects on the homes, there were serious health effects that became apparent. Women who had lived near the site an average of 18.5 years had 3.5 times the expected number of miscarriages, as well as a disproportionate number of birth defects and spontaneous abortions.

> Mrs. Timothy Schoeder, a canal resident, suffered from burning eyes and skin ailments. Her daughter, Sheri, was born with a cleft palate, a double row of bottom teeth, a deformed ear, eardrums that disintegrated, bone blockage in her left nasal passage, a hole in her heart, and slight retardation. In 1978, Sheri began to lose her hair in large clumps. . . . One women living in the area had three successive miscarriages before giving birth to a child. The baby was born with three ears. Her second child also was born with deformed ears. (Mokhiber, 1988, 273)

Mokhiber notes that Hooker denied responsibility for the damages caused by the site. They first attempted to place the blame on contractors who built houses around the site, claiming that they may have damaged the containment system in their excavation work for house construction. Hooker disowned any liability for the damages, citing the deed the Board of Education accepted when they purchased the land for a dollar in 1953. Mokhiber cites a discussion Hooker vice president John Riordan had on *The Today Show*, a popular morning news program, claiming that Hooker was not aware of the hazards of the waste when they dumped them. This claim was countered by Dr. Robert Mobbs, who had conducted research into the hazards of lindane, one of the chemicals dumped at the site. Mobbs was furious over Riordan's comments and charged that Hooker "'damn well knew that the compounds it deposited in the canal were extremely dangerous to human beings. . . . I presented evidence that it was a possible cancer-causing agent in 1948.' Mobbs' findings were published in the December 1948 issue of the *Journal of the American Medical Association* and had been publicized further by Washington columnist Drew Pearson. Hooker chemical eventually settled with the 1,300 residents of Love Canal paying close to $20 million" (Mokhiber, 1988, 274). Nevertheless, as Mokhiber concludes, this hardly pays for the physical damage and death to residents in the area.

Unfortunately, the case of Love Canal is not an isolated incidence. There have been other "Love Canals." According to the EPA there are approximately 77,000 toxic waste dumps in the United States and an additional 9,267 more discovered each year (Heilprin, 2004). Less than 1 percent of the projected average number of sites that would need to be decontaminated by 2033 are part of EPA's Superfund program for the worst toxic waste messes. In addition to these land-based dumps there are approximately 180,000 toxic pits, ponds, and lagoons throughout the states (Zastrow, 1992).

In Anniston, Alabama, the Monsanto Company had been dumping toxic waste unsafely for almost forty years without telling residents. *The Washington Post* reported that company memos dating almost forty years ago, many with warnings such as "CONFIDENTIAL: Read and Destroy," indicated that the company knew of the danger of their dumping of polychlorinated biphenyls (PCBs) into creeks and open pit landfills in West Anniston, the poor minority section of the community. In 1966, Monsanto managers discovered that fish submerged in that creek turned belly-up within ten seconds, spurting blood and shedding skin as if dunked into boiling water. They told no one. In 1969, they found fish in another creek with 7,500 times the legal PCB levels. They decided "there is little object in going to expensive extremes in limiting discharges." In 1975, a company study found that PCBs caused tumors in rats. They ordered its conclusion changed from "slightly tumorigenic" to "does not appear to be carcinogenic" (Grunwald, 2002, A01). Grunwald notes that Monsanto enjoyed a lucrative four-decade monopoly on PCB production in the United States and battled to protect that monopoly long after PCBs were confirmed as a global pollutant. "We can't afford to lose one dollar of business," one internal memo concluded (Grunwald, 2002, A01).

A case of toxic dumping that directly affected workers of the company that conducted the dumping was that of General Electric Company. *Multinational Monitor* reported in a June 1988 investigation that an employee parking lot had been built on a toxic dump site that had a radioactive contamination level many times higher than the New York State safety level. Though GE was aware of the contamination at the site, the company allowed employees to park there without any warning for more than twenty years. *Multinational Monitor* reports that in March 1988, GE sold the parking lot to the U.S. government, effectively removing the jurisdiction of the state of New York over the property and placing the clean-up bill in the hands of U.S. taxpayers. *Multinational Monitor* reports that the GE weapons plant, Knolls Atomic Power Lab, is alone responsible for thirty-nine sites contaminated with radioactive waste (Mokhiber et al., 1992).

General Electric has been required to pay approximately $500 million to pay for the dredging of the Hudson River. GE discharged 1.3 million pounds of PCBs in the river over a forty-year period from plants in Fort Edward, New York, and Hudson Falls, New York (Shapely, 2002). Cray notes that "between the 1940s and 1976, when the U.S. Congress outlawed PCB manufacture, sale and distribution (except in 'totally enclosed' systems), GE discharged about 1.3 million pounds of PCBs into the Hudson River. The contamination ruined a once-thriving commercial fishing industry and devastated recreational fishing, which was only opened on a 'catch and release' basis in the 40-mile long upper Hudson in 1996, after being closed for two decades" (Cray, 2001, 11). Cray notes that the potential impact doesn't stop at the tip of Manhattan. He notes that because of PCBs' chemical stability and their ability to travel long distances, PCBs can migrate around the planet and are part of a global class of chemicals known to migrate from warmer regions to colder regions. "Inuit people living in the Arctic thousands of miles from any industrial source carry some of the highest body burdens of PCBs on the planet" (Cray, 2001, 11). GE has other sites of dumping of PCBs in other waterways in Massachusetts and Georgia (Cray, 2001).

In another case, the A.C. Lawrence Leather Company was convicted of violating the Clean Water Act, defrauding the U.S. government, falsifying reports to the government, and illegally disposing of hazardous waste. The company had received $1.5 million from the U.S. government to construct a demonstration affluent-waste-treatment system at its plant in Winchester, New Hampshire. Company executives decided that it would be lot cheaper to use the money to build a pipeline to dump the waste directly into the Ashuelot River. The company also had buried six hundred fifty-five-gallon drums of hazardous waste on the company property (Adler, 1985). Adler notes that the illegal disposal of toxic waste has been so pervasive that an EPA survey estimates that one out of every seven companies that generate toxic wastes may have disposed of them illegally during the past few years.

The Velsicol Chemical Company of Memphis contaminated the wells of a number of farms in Toon, Tennessee, by illegally dumping waste. Families were suffering from unexplained cases of chronic depression that was eventually linked to chloroform in their drinking water that was equivalent to a daily dose of a sedative. The truck driver who hauled Velsicol's leaking barrels of chemical waste from Memphis to Toon went blind after continued exposure to the corrosive fumes (Setterberg and Shavelson, 1993). In Pocono, Oklahoma, Conoco oil company had contaminated the drinking water of the residents, requiring them to move to another location (Rosoff, Pontell, and Tillman, 2007). In Woburn, Massachusetts, the Cryovac Division of W.R. Grace Corporation negligently had dumped chemicals that led to the deaths of children who were stricken with leukemia and adults with kidney cancer. Company officials admitted in U.S. District Court that they had provided false information to the EPA in 1982 in response to questions about its toxic waste disposal. A criminal indictment was handed down in 1988. The company negotiated a plea agreement that resulted in a maximum fine of $10,000 (Rosoff, Pontell, and Tillman, 2007).

In 1981, DuPont's scientists in Parkersville, West Virginia, had discovered that perflouroctanoic acid (PFOA) produced at that plant had contaminated the local drinking water supplies and that the children of workers from the plant had PFOA in their blood. It was also discovered that childbearing female workers also had high levels and that some of the children were born with birth defects of the eyes and nostrils. Company officials suppressed the information for more than twenty years until lawyers of a class action suit discovered the information in 1983. The company paid more than $300 million to as many as sixty thousand residents of West Virginia and Ohio and paid $17 million to settle the Environmental Protection Agency's allegations, the largest civil administrative penalty the EPA had ever obtained under a federal environmental statute.

The illegal dumping of toxic waste has become big business and, according to Representative John Dingell, chairperson of the House Subcommittee on Oversight and Investigations, has connections to organized crime. On the day before Earth Day in 1980 in Elizabeth, New Jersey, the Chemical Control Corporations plant exploded, sending fireballs of fifty-five-gallon drums of toxic waste hundreds of feet into the sky, spewing toxic pesticides, acids, and plasticizers over the community. The fire at the plant took firefighters ten hours to put out. Area schools were closed and residents were urged to stay indoors. For years before the fire, residents tolerated the smell of noxious chemicals that had been illegally stored at the plant. According to Miller and Miller (1985), New Jersey's Department of Environmental Protection removed ten thousand barrels of the explosive, poisonous materials prior to the explosion; twenty-four thousand barrels remained, however, and they turned into a time bomb. A confidential federal government report found that crooked stashing of chemical wastes and pesticides at Chemical Control could have sent poisonous fumes, drifting like an angel of death, over New York City (60). A federal grand jury investigating the company found that it had links to organized crime.

Rosoff, Pontell, and Tillman (2007) note that some of the most reckless tales of toxic dumping involve the waste-hauling practices of illicit trucking operations. They noted that one week prior to a federal waste monitoring system was to take effect in late 1980, thousands of tons of toxic waste were hurriedly disposed of in a last-minute rush to circumvent the new law. One way this was done was by simply opening the spigots of the tanks that the truckers were carrying, allowing the waste to be released as they drove along the interstate highways. These truckers became known as "sludge runners" and one popular venue for these truckers was the Mianus River Bridge in Connecticut. Rosoff, Pontell, and Tillman (2007, 153) note that "gallons of corrosive liquid would drain off the span, not only polluting the river below but eventually weakening the metal support joints of the structure. When the rotting joints finally broke apart in 1987, the bridge collapsed."

In 1980, Congress passed the Comprehensive Environmental Response, Compensation, and Liability Act (CERCLA), which is better known as "Superfund." The legislation was intended to address the problem of abandoned toxic waste sites across the country in response to the public outcry over the Love Canal scandal. Under the legislation, the companies responsible are supposed to clean up the site or reimburse the government for the cleanup. Rosoff, Pontell, and Tillman contend that the legislation is one of the most ineffective pieces of legislation passed by Congress. The cost of cleanup is paid for by the taxpayers, and they estimate the costs will exceed the cost of the savings and loan crisis caused by government deregulation in the early 1980s. The estimate of the cost to tax payers for bailing out more than 1,600 savings and loan companies in the 1980s and early 1990s was $160 billion. As of November 29, 2010, there were 1,280 Superfund sites on the National Priorities List. Three hundred and forty-seven sites have been cleaned up and removed from the list. But as noted earlier there is believed to be thousands more that need to be added to the list. Given current rate of cleanup and the number of sites that need to be added, it will be hundreds of years before it is completed and people in the United States will be safe from this form of environmental violence

In another publicized case, dishonest haulers of medical waste from hospitals bypassed the cost of using the special dump sites they were required to by law. Instead they dumped in the ocean. During the summer months of 1988, large amounts of this illegally dumped medical waste, including hypodermic needles, IV tubing, catheter bags, and vials of blood (some testing positive for AIDS), washed ashore at public beaches in New York and New Jersey (Rosoff, Pontell, and Tillman, 2007).

Dumping on the Poor and Toxic Terrorism

Increasingly, advanced industrial countries have resorted to dumping toxic wastes in poor countries or, within the United States, in areas in the country where the poor reside. For example, the U.S. government and waste brokers have increasingly sought to dump industrial and household waste on Native American land. Since 1990 toxic waste disposal companies have approached more than fifty U.S. indigenous groups, offering millions of dollars in exchange for the right to dump U.S. trash on Native American grounds. These waste companies seek to avoid state, county, municipal, and many federal waste-facility operating standards that do not apply to Native American reservations because of their sovereign status.

They sell these disposal plans to these impoverished indigenous communities as opportunities for "economic development" and increased employment for residents of the reservations. They do not mention the serious health threats posed by the incineration and storage of hazardous and other waste (Weissman, 1992a). Weissman cites a 1989 case in which a subsidiary of Amoco named Waste Tech Incorporated approached the governing council at Dilkon, a remote Navajo community. This community had an unemployment rate of 72 percent. The company proposed taking over one hundred acres of community land to build an incinerator for the burning of hazardous waste and a landfill to bury the toxic ash. For the use of the land, the company promised the creation of 175 new jobs, a new hospital, and a $100,000 signing bonus to be distributed to the residents of the community.

In another case, O&G Corporation approached the leadership of the Rosebud Lakotas in South Dakota with a proposal to build the largest landfill in the United States on the reservation. The dump would hold solid waste, incinerator ash, and sewage sludge. Weissman notes that the most significant effort of dumping waste on Native American land does not come from private corporations but from the U.S. government's Department of Energy (DOE). The DOE is responsible for securing radioactive materials and disposing of the radioactive waste from the production of nuclear weapons as well as nuclear power plants. Weissman notes that they have contacted every Native American nation with a proposal to become either an interim or permanent recipient of nuclear waste.

One particular plan is for the carving out of a portion of Yucca Mountain, eighty-five miles from Las Vegas, Nevada, on the Shoshone reservation, and disposing of seventy thousand metric tons of high-level waste in the mountain (Weissman, 1992a). Weissman also notes that the government has been involved in issuing grants to minority businesses for the establishment of dump sites on reservations. He cites the case of the U.S. Department of Commerce awarding a $248,000 minority business grant to a promoter who arranged for a company to bring hazardous waste to an Oklahoma Kaw reservation. The United States is not alone in trying to dump toxic waste on its indigenous population. Cohen (1995) notes that Taiwan solved its problem of disposing of nuclear waste by shipping the waste to Orchid Island, off Taiwan's southeast tip. This island is the home to three thousand Yami aborigines.

The problem of dumping waste in the United States is not isolated to reservations. Gozan (1993) notes that it is estimated that 60 percent of all hazardous waste or toxic-emitting facilities are located in or adjacent to communities of color, and that 65 percent of U.S. commercial hazardous waste is dumped in the South. In 1990, 437 of 3,109 counties and independent cities failed to meet at least one of the EPA ambient air quality standards: 57 percent of whites, 65 percent of African Americans, and 80 percent of Hispanics live in 437 counties with substandard air quality. Out of the whole population, a total of 33 percent of whites, 50 percent of African Americans, and 60 percent of Hispanics live in 136 counties in which two or more air pollutants exceed standards (Wernette and Nieves, 1992, 16–17).

Bullard (1993) described places like Chicago's South Side, Louisiana's Cancer Alley (those communities along the eighty-five-mile stretch of the Mississippi River from Baton Rouge to New Orleans), and East Los Angeles as human sacrifice zones. They are characterized as having severe environmental problems because of the placement of dump sites and highly polluting industries and are attracting new polluters as a result of their relatively politically powerless position. These are examples of environmental racism and classism, where those who are the poorest and the most powerless in the society experience the greatest levels of violence from environmental pollution.

Besides the dumping of waste in the United States, companies in the United States, as well as other advanced countries, are dumping waste in developing countries. Feagin and Feagin (1990) note that in 1988 some three million tons of hazardous waste from the United States and Western Europe were transported to impoverished countries in Africa and Eastern Europe that desperately need hard currency. The Feagins refer to this as "trash imperialism," whereby the richer countries push off their problems onto poorer countries. They observe that many Third World countries lack the technical ability to deal with toxic wastes.

U.S. law requires that companies shipping toxic materials abroad notify government officials who are responsible for ensuring that the receiving countries dispose of the waste properly. But EPA officials report that U.S. shippers frequently ignore this requirement. Some shippers have even tried to sell toxic ash to Third World countries as landfill, claiming the ash was nontoxic and nonhazardous. Others have referred to the practice as a form of "toxic terrorism." Dumping of toxic waste, the dumping of unsafe products (product dumping), and the relocation of highly polluting industries to developing countries that don't have the regulatory system in place to protect their citizens are other forms of toxic terrorism (Rosoff, Pontell, and Tillman, 2007).

One case of a company selling toxic waste as fertilizer occurred in Bangladesh (Leonard, 1993). Leonard reports that in 1991, three U.S. corporations located in South Carolina gathered what is called baghouse dust, waste captured in the smokestack filters of the metal smelting furnaces of Gaston Cooper Recycling Corporation. This dust contained toxic levels of lead and cadmium. The waste was then handled by Hy-tex Marketing Company, a hazardous waste broker. Hy-tex Marketing sold the waste to Stoller Chemical Corporation, which mixed other materials with the waste to make fertilizer. Stoller Chemical then transported the toxic waste/fertilizer mixture to Bangladesh. The toxic waste/fertilizer mixture was then purchased with funds from the Asian Development Bank by the Bangladesh Agricultural Development Corporation, a government institution.

The U.S. embassy did notify the Bangladesh government that the waste contained lead and cadmium. Samples were collected from the toxic waste/fertilizer mixture by the U.S. embassy and the Bangladesh government. The Bangladesh Agricultural Research Institute concluded that the amount of waste contained in the fertilizer did not pose a health threat. However, the U.S. test results conducted by the South Carolina Department of Health and Environmental Control indicated that the waste was a threat to human health and the environment. The results of these tests were not released to the public and the government of Bangladesh until three months after the waste had been distributed to farmers. Farms visited by Greenpeace found that children were often given the task of applying fertilizer without any protective clothing or gloves.

Leonard reported that a public outcry in Bangladesh developed over the scandal. Newspapers reported in September 1992 that the toxic fertilizer was no longer being distributed. But in November, representatives from Greenpeace were still able to purchase the fertilizer in a local market in Dinajpur and the waste was still seeping into the ground and the foodstuffs grown on the contaminated land (Leonard, 1993). In June of 1992, a U.S. federal grand jury indicted all three corporations and three individual employees who were responsible for the creation of the toxic mixture.

In another case, a hazardous waste shipping company was indicted for dumping toxic waste on a beach in Haiti. *Multinational Monitor* reports on the case of the owners of the *Khian Sea*, a ship that sailed the world's seas to find a place to dump incinerator ash from Philadelphia. The operators of the ship were indicted on July 14, 1992, in a Wilmington, Delaware, U.S. District Court for making false statements to a federal grand jury. In 1986 Palino and Sons, a waste management company hired by the city of Philadelphia, contracted with John Dowd, of Amalgamated Shipping Corporation, and William Reilly, of the Coastal Carriers Corporation, to dispose of ash from the city's municipal garbage incinerator. The ash was carried aboard the ship *Khian Sea* for twenty-seven months. In January 1988, the ship unloaded four thousand tons of waste, labeled as fertilizer, on the beach of Gonaives, Haiti, in violation of Haitian law prohibiting waste imports. In May 1988, the ship sailed to the former Yugoslavia, where it docked with approximately eleven thousand tons of the remaining ash in its cargo holds. In Yugoslavia, the ship's name was changed to *Felicia*. It left Yugoslavia shortly thereafter and arrived in Singapore in November 1988 with its cargo holds empty (Gozan, 1992, 4). *Multinational Monitor* reported that testimony by a member of the ship's crew led to the indictment of Dowd and Reilly on dumping the waste in the Indian Ocean. An EPA analysis revealed hazardous levels of lead, cadmium, and dioxin in the Philadelphia incinerator ash. The waste remains exposed in Gonaives, Haiti, without fencing or warning signs. It is believed that the rest of the waste was dumped in the Indian Ocean.

Mpondah (1990) notes that many companies, under pressure from environmental groups in Europe and North America, are increasingly turning to poor countries with less stringent regulations to get rid of toxic and dangerous wastes. The World Health Organization (WHO) has sharply criticized this practice. In 1989 an international treaty was introduced into the United Nations to stop this practice, but it was defeated by parliamentary maneuvers introduced by the United States and the United Kingdom that served to strip the treaty of any power to control these dumping practices (Heong, 1990). Mpondah (1990) observes that the opportunity for dumping this hazardous waste is occurring because a number of impoverished Western African countries are lured by the prospect of millions of dollars. The Nairobi-based UN Environmental Program (UNEP) reported that about twelve African countries either have "quietly" signed contracts to accept industrial wastes or are in the process of negotiations to that effect, which has placed the leaders of the Organization of African Unity in a difficult situation. Mpondah documents that African countries have increasingly been recruited because sites in the South Pacific and the Caribbean that have been used as dumps for years began to fill up in the mid-1980s. An example of this practice is Equatorial

Guinea, which signed a ten-year contract with a British company based in Buckingham to bury a minimum of five million tons of nuclear waste a year. A down payment of £1.6 million was made.

In another case, Congolese officials agreed to accept a million tons of "heavily polluted chemical waste," as it was described, for storage or incineration over a period of eight years in return for $92.6 million. The waste was to be shipped from the Netherlands, Belgium, Luxembourg, and West Germany. Mpondah (1990) points to the profitability of this arrangement for many of these poor countries by citing the case of Guinea-Bissau, one of the poorest countries in the world. Guinea-Bissau canceled plans to import fifteen million tons of toxic waste from industrialized countries. The contract would have earned the country $600 million, twice its foreign debt. Unfortunately, the wastes in many of these countries are again dumped in areas in which the poorest populations within these very poor countries are most likely to experience the deadly consequences. Feagin and Feagin (1990) refer to this practice of economic violence as toxic terrorism. Nigeria, one of Africa's most populous states, is one of the most outstanding opponents of dumping. Incensed by reports of the illegal waste dumping, Nigeria threatened to impose the death penalty on those found responsible (Mpondah, 1990).

Foster (1994) writes that since 1989, there have been more than five hundred attempts to export more than two hundred million tons of waste from the twenty-four wealthy nations that make up the Organization for Economic Cooperation and Development (OECD) to 122 non-OECD countries (7). He notes that between 1986 and 1991 waste shipments were principally targeting Africa, the Pacific, the Caribbean, and Latin America. More recently, there has been a shift to include Eastern Europe and Asia. Each day, enough toxic waste is shipped to Asia to fill 185 forty-foot seagoing containers (Foster, 1994).

In a report issued by Greenpeace and the Basil Action Network (2000), they list a number of recent cases of toxic dumping. At the Cambodian port of Sihanoukville, three thousand tons of highly toxic mercury-tainted waste from Formosa Plastics of Taiwan was unloaded. The toxic wastes, initially dumped on open ground fifteen kilometers outside Sihanoukville, were later packed into containers following the deaths of two workers who had direct contact with the waste. The report also notes that in December 1999, Philippine authorities seized 122 forty-foot containers carrying infectious medical wastes from Japan. The consignment was disguised as used plastic scrap for recycling purposes. The waste shipment exported by Japanese company Nisso Ltd. consisted of needles for intravenous injections, medical rubber hose and tubes, used adult and baby diapers, used sanitary napkins, discarded intravenous syringes used in bloodletting, and used bandages. In both these cases, the shipment was shipped back to its home country after public protest.

Eastern Europe also is being recruited for toxic dumping sites. Poland signed an agreement in the 1970s to store radioactive waste from former West Germany (Slocock, 1992). These shipments took place until 1983 when they were finally stopped because of increasing citizen concern about pollution. Germany and other Western countries have continued to seek access to

Poland's land to dump its waste. Since the capitalist transformation of Poland, more offers have been made to use land for disposal purposes, and there are increasing problems of Polish entrepreneurs bypassing the government's restrictions on dumping by importing waste as industrial materials and then dumping them once they are in the country.

Poland is one of the most polluted countries in Europe. Most of the pollution is a result of the operation of state-run industries. Environmental violence is economic in nature and is authorized by the state, which directly profits from the costs. Poland's level of sulfur dioxide pollution is almost twice that of the United Kingdom. This level of pollution is only exceeded by the former Czechoslovakia (Slocock, 1992). Water pollution in Poland is in a critical condition. Slocock reports that over 68 percent of surface water is unfit for human consumption. The Vistula River, which runs through Warsaw, is so polluted by saline discharges from coal mining operations, chemical wastes, and heavy metals that it corrodes the metal barges that travel the river.

One of the most polluted regions in Poland is Katowice Province, where 55 percent of industrial wastewater is discharged into the rivers. Water for human consumption has to be trucked in from outside the area. The infant mortality in Katowice is 40 percent above the national average. The Katowice environmental director states that there is an annual death rate of 878 persons per 1 million population from environmentally related illnesses in the area. Another area is Upper Silesia, where an estimated 50 percent of the population live in conditions hazardous to their health. In total, more than a quarter of the population of Poland live in areas deemed to be an immediate health hazard, according to the World Health Organization.

The United Nations Environmental Program proposed an international convention to control the dumping of wastes in developing countries. The Basel Convention on the Control of Transboundary Movements of Hazardous Wastes and their Disposal was adopted in Basel, Switzerland, on March 22, 1989. One of the guiding principles of the Basel Convention is that, in order to minimize the threat, hazardous wastes should be dealt with as close to where they are produced as possible. Under the Convention, transboundary movements of hazardous wastes or other wastes can take place only upon prior written notification by the state of export to the competent authorities of the states of import and transit (if appropriate). In addition, there are outright bans on the export of these wastes to certain countries. At the Second Meeting of the Conference of the Parties (COP—2) in March 1994, parties to the agreement agreed to an immediate ban on the export from OECD to non-OECD countries of hazardous wastes intended for final disposal. They also agreed to ban the export of wastes intended for recovery and recycling (Decision II/12). As of March 2, 2002, 149 countries had ratified the convention; the United States, Afghanistan, and Haiti have not.

Besides the dumping of waste produced in advanced countries, increasingly there is the dumping of factories that are heavy polluters to poor countries that do not have the government regulations in place to protect its citizenry from the violent consequences of the pollution. Today, 850 U.S. corporations operate one or more *maquiladora* plants, foreign-owned plants operating in Mexico along the U.S. border. More than 80 percent of the *maquiladoras* are U.S. owned. There is an increasing problem of occupational disease and injury to workers at these plants. One study conducted by the Work Environment Program of the University of Massachusetts at Lowell concluded that the working conditions identified in this study are reminiscent of the nineteenth-century sweatshops of the U.S. industrial towns (LaBotz, 1993, 22). This study revealed that workers were suffering from muscular-skeletal disorders and chemical poisoning resulting from their work.

But there may be even greater problems of death or injury resulting from the environmental violence due to the migration of factories to poor countries with few environmental protection regulations in place. More than eighty chemical plants, metalworking plants that use lead and zinc, and electronic assembly plants (40 percent of the *maquiladoras*) that use benzene and other toxic chemicals in the production process operate along the border (LaBotz, 1993, 22). These plants release their toxic waste in streams, open pits, the air, and dump sites close to the residential areas of workers at the plants. As a result, there are increasing problems of death or injury to people who have less ability to protect themselves from this violence.

One example is the city of Matamoros, which lies directly across the Rio Grande from Brownsville, Texas (Knaus, 1993). This community is one of many along the Mexican border of the United States that has experienced a dramatic influx of *maquiladoras*. Recently the region has suffered a dramatic rise in the birth of encephalic babies (infants born without brains). In the Brownsville/Matamoros area, confirmed cases of encephalic babies now stand at fifty since January 1989. Knaus (1993) notes that this is the largest cluster of encephalic babies ever documented and four times the U.S. national average. She reports that physicians and health activists believe that the cause of the high incidence is the industrial chemical xylene used at the Matamoros facility of the Chicago-based Stepan Chemical. This chemical is known to cause liver and kidney damage and is linked to birth defects. Samples taken from a drainage ditch at Stepan's Matamoros facility contained xylene at fifty-three thousand times the allowable U.S. level. Community residents have long borne witness to the company's practice of dumping chemicals into open, unlined canals that run through the colonia. Since most of the dwellings around the plant do not contain indoor plumbing, residents will draw water from the canals for everyday purposes: bathing, cleaning, and drinking. Some residents will boil the water; however, the result is a higher concentration of the toxic chemical in the water. The residents claim that contaminated soil samples can be found just a few feet below ground level.

Another example is the impact of Texaco's drilling operations in the Amazon region of Ecuador (Jochnick, 1995). The Organization of American States began an investigation into human rights abuses by the Texaco and Maxus Oil companies. It was estimated that the oil drilling operations, 90 percent controlled by Texaco, had discharged 4.3 million gallons of toxic waste into the Orientes environment every day of operation. In this region of operation, documented toxic contamination of water has reached levels that are one thousand times the safety standards recommended by the U.S. Environmental Protection Agency. Local workers report increased health problems including birth defects, cancer, and gastrointestinal problems related to this contamination. Texaco's twenty years of operation in the region has resulted in contaminated rivers, soil, and environment and destroyed forests, fish, and other wildlife. Indigenous populations in the area have been severely reduced in size as a result of the displacement and disease resulting from the pollution in their environment and the encroachment from settlers participating in Texaco and related operations. Contact with outsiders and the vital loss of land have broken down traditional bonds, brought malnutrition and new diseases, and pushed indigenous communities to the bottom rung of a hostile market economy. Alcohol and prostitution, endemic to the Orientes oil towns, are among the most visible signs of the social and cultural deterioration. The World Bank has described the region's socioeconomic state as calamitous (Jochnick, 1995, 13). Jochnick notes that the government of Ecuador has discovered that several indigenous groups have been pushed to the edge of extinction. One such group, the Tetetes, has completely disappeared. There is no evidence that any people from this tribe exist today. Another group is the Cofan, whose population of fifteen thousand in 1950 has been reduced to three hundred people. Similar examples of genocidal destruction as a result of the impact of oil exploration and drilling by Unocal and Total can be found in Thailand (Strider, 1995).

Barry Commoner summarized this pattern of environmental violence:

> The result of this division is a painful global irony: the poor countries of the south, while deprived of an equitable share of the world's wealth, suffer the environmental hazards generated by the creation of that wealth in the north. The developing countries of the south will not only experience the impact of global warming and ozone depletion, which are now chiefly due to the industrialized countries, but are also victimized by the north's toxic exports. For example, as bans have been imposed on particularly dangerous pesticides in industrialized countries, manufacturers have marketed them in developing countries instead. There, poorly regulated, they have created in the bodies of local populations the world's highest concentrations of pesticides. Similarly, as environmental concerns have limited disposal sites for trash and the toxic ash from trash burning incinerators in the United States, efforts have been made to get rid of these pollutants—not always successfully—in developing countries. (Commoner, 1990, 142)

AIR POLLUTION

A second area of environmental violence results from air pollution. A survey of air quality conducted by the EPA revealed that in 1987, large U.S. companies (those producing 75,000 pounds or more of toxic substances annually) emitted a total of 2.4 billion pounds of chemicals into the air (Feagin and Feagin, 1990). Air pollution is a major source of cancerous diseases. According to the World Health Organization, lung cancer causes the largest disease burden of all cancers globally, or about 15 percent of the burden of all cancers. By far the largest risk factor for lung cancer is smoking, at 66 percent (WHO, 2002). About 9 percent of the disease burden of lung cancer has been attributed to occupation (WHO, 2002; Concha-Barrientos et al., 2004), about 5 percent to outdoor air pollution (WHO, 2002; Cohen et al.,

Figure 7.3.   Sulfur dioxide and particulate matter from plant burning fossil fuels in New Mexico. Source: National Park Service.

2004), and 1 percent to exposure to indoor smoke from solid fuels (Smith, Corvalán, and Maeusezahl-Feuz, 2004). In particular, polluted urban air has been linked to not only cancer, but an increased probability of other respiratory diseases, eye irritation, and asthma. Those who are already ill, children, the aged, and the poor are the most likely to be the immediate sufferers from air pollution (Feagin and Feagin 1990). Erickson (1992) claims that in the United States today 60 percent of the population live in areas where the air does not meet the standards set by the 1970 Clean Air Act. A recent report by the CDC indicates that the number of people diagnosed with asthma grew by 4.3 million from 2001 to 2009 (Center for Disease Control, 2011). The CDC estimates that approximately one in twelve persons or 8 percent of the U.S. population suffers from asthma. For children the rate is higher than it is for adults: one in ten children, one in twelve adults. From 2001 through 2009 asthma increased the most among black children, almost a 50 percent increase. Asthma was linked to 3,447 deaths (about nine per day) in 2007. The estimate costs for asthma treatment in the United States grew from about $53 billion in 2002 to about $56 billion in 2007, about a 6 percent increase.

Kepone and Allied Chemical Company

Allied Chemical, producers of Kepone, a pesticide used to kill ants, cockroaches, and pests that attack bananas, is a good example of air pollution as environmental violence. Allied Chemical initially produced the chemical in the 1960s and was aware of research that indicated that the chemical was highly toxic and that it was linked in animal studies conducted in the 1940s and 1950s to sterility, damage to nerves, and liver cancer. Here we first have a case of product violence. Allied shipped Kepone to Life Sciences Company (a company formed by former executives for Allied) in 1973. Mokhiber states that "by contracting with Life Sciences, Allied could have its Kepone and the profits too, without the headaches involved in complying with the environmental laws" (Mokhiber, 1988, 252).

The Life Sciences plant emitted sulfur trioxide, a Kepone ingredient, into the air. Mokhiber (1988) found that emissions were so bad that those who worked or resided in the area around the plant had trouble seeing the plant because of the thick white clouds emanating from it. Blood analysis done of residents in the neighborhoods near the plant indicated the presence of Kepone. Not only was there a problem of air pollution, but Kepone wastes were dumped into the sewage system, which made the sewage system inoperable by the spring of 1974. "As a result, the city began pumping the Kepone-laden effluent into a nearby open field known as Kepone Lagoon. Kepone Lagoon grew enormously, eventually holding 800,000 to 1,000,000 gallons of the contaminated sludge. Traces of Kepone found their way into the city's industrial water pipeline, a pipeline that services a nearby federal reformatory and the U.S. Army's Fort Lee, as well as industrial users" (251).

Before this period, Allied directly dumped Kepone into the James River, contaminating it. Before the river was closed to fishing in late 1975, about nine hundred thousand catfish, hundreds of thousands of pounds of shad, and five hundred thousand bushels of oyster were removed from the river each year for sale throughout the nation. All of the catch is believed to contain trace elements of Kepone. Hundreds of workers from both the Allied and Life Sciences suffer from neurological damage from exposure to Kepone (Mokhiber, 1988).

Union Carbide and Bhopal, India

A second case study, one of larger proportions, is that of Union Carbide and Bhopal, India. At 12:30 a.m. on December 3, 1984, there was an explosion in one of the storage tanks holding methyl isocyanate (MIC), a highly toxic chemical used to produce pesticides at the plant. Water had entered the tank when a maintenance worker attempted to clean out a pipe leading from the tank. The pipe leading from the storage tank had been improperly sealed, which led to the gases from the tank mixing with the water. This led to a chain reaction that created heat and pressure and an explosion that led to the release of forty tons of deadly gases into the atmosphere over Bhopal.

There were problems with the plant in Bhopal, many of which were originally anticipated by the executives in charge of the subsidiary of Union Carbide headquartered in Connecticut. In February 1985, Edward Munoz, a retired Union Carbide official and former managing director of Union Carbide of India Limited (UCIL), claimed in a sworn affidavit that in the early 1970s, Union Carbide insisted, over UCIL's objections, that large amounts of MIC be stored at the plant in Bhopal. UCIL's position was to store only token amounts in small, individual containers. But Union Carbide's corporate engineering group imposed the view that Bhopal would be the site for the construction of large bulk storage tanks patterned on similar Union Carbide facilities at Institute, West Virginia (Mokhiber, 1988, 90). Union Carbide, U.S.A. owned 51 percent of Union Carbide LTD, Bhopal, India.

Mokhiber (1988) cites several serious problems at the plant, problems that were well known to company officials. One problem was the refrigeration unit that was designed to keep the gas in the storage tank at a low enough temperature to prevent runaway chemical reactions. The refrigeration unit was not working at the time of the disaster and had been inoperable five months before the accident. The gas was at a temperature that was higher than what was defined as safe by the plant's operating manual. Mokhiber notes that with the refrigeration unit out of commission, the instruments to measure the temperature and pressure of the gas in the tank were crucial. Workers perceived the gauges to be unreliable. The emergency scrubber system that was to function to neutralize the gas in the event of a leak was not working at the time of the disaster and had been inoperable for six weeks before the accident. The flare tower that was to be the last line of defense to burn off the escaping gas had been closed down for ten days prior to the accident because the gas line to the flare tower had corroded as a result of neglected maintenance. To make matters worse, the workers at the plant were inadequately trained because of a high turnover of personnel.

Company officials in the United States were aware of the problems at the plant as early as 1982. At that time a team of American experts, at the request of Union Carbide, pointed out major safety concerns at the plant including deficiencies in instrumentation and safety valves, lax maintenance, and high turnover of operating and maintenance staff (Mokhiber, 1988). The team of experts made several recommendations to correct the deficiencies. Soon after the report was released, Mokhiber notes that union organizers in India appealed to the U.S. management team to improve the safety conditions at the plant; however, according to spokespersons, none of the recommendations was implemented.

If the report of experts and pleas of union organizers were not enough, there was also the recent history of accidents at the plant. Between 1978 and 1984, there were six serious accidents at the plant. Each accident should have told the executives in Connecticut of the dangers at the plant. In November 1978 there was a fire at the plant that took ten hours to bring under control and resulted in $5 million in property damage. A plant operator was killed in December 1981 because of a phosgene gas leak. Another phosgene gas leak occurred in January 1982 and caused twenty-eight injuries. There were three MIC leakages reported between October 1982 and 1984. Several residents in the area surrounding the plant reported problems in breathing and burning of eyes. Four workers were seriously injured in the mishaps. Union Carbide never informed residents of the community of Bhopal of the extreme toxicity of the gas being stored at the plant. Furthermore, only a few in the medical community had been informed. When the disaster occurred at midnight on December 3, the warning siren failed to go off until two hours after the explosion. Most of the residents around the plant were asleep at the time of the leak. They woke up choking and vomiting from the fumes; many did not wake at all. Praful Bidwai, a chemical engineer and journalist, described the situation in a hospital three days after the leak: "The scene is compelling in its display of death. There is something indescribable about the horror, the squalor, the sheer magnitude and force of death here. No one is counting numbers any longer. People are dying like flies. They are brought in, their chests heaving violently, their limbs trembling, their eyes blinking from photophobia. It will kill them in a few hours, more usually minutes" (cited in Mokhiber, 1988, 87).

Weissman (1994) quotes estimates of the death toll range from a low of three thousand to a high of sixteen thousand. Hundreds of thousands more suffer from blindness, permanent lung damage, gas-related cancers, post-traumatic stress disorder, and other ailments. One recent study found that 40 percent of the 865 pregnancies at the time of the disaster did not end in a live birth. This is almost four times greater than the rate in previous years.

WATER POLLUTION

It is estimated that one in ten Americans has been exposed to drinking water that contains dangerous chemicals or fails to meet a federal health benchmark in other ways (Duhigg, 2009). According to an investigative report by the *New York Times*, an estimated 19.5 million Americans fall ill each year from drinking water contaminated with parasites, bacteria, or viruses. More than 23 million people receive drinking water from municipal systems that violate a health-based standard. The number may be much higher since wells that are not regulated under the Clean Water Act are usually more likely contaminated and the contamination rates are not systematically collected.

The *New York Times* report found that the Clean Water Act has been violated more than 506,000 times since 2004, by more than 23,000 companies and other facilities, according to reports submitted by polluters themselves. The number could be much higher since companies test what they are dumping only once a quarter, so the actual number of days when they broke the law is suspect to be far higher. They also note that the number of facilities violating the Clean Water Act grew more than 16 percent from 2004 to 2007, the most recent year with complete data. Sixty percent of the polluters were deemed in "significant noncompliance"—meaning their violations were the most serious kind, like dumping cancer-causing chemicals or failing to measure or report when they pollute. The *New York Times* investigative research also uncovered that fewer than 3 percent of Clean Water Act violations resulted in fines or other significant punishments by state officials. Furthermore, they found that the EPA often declined to prosecute polluters or pressure states to strengthen their enforcement levels. They contend that the enforcement lapses were particularly frequent under the administration of President George W. Bush. "For the last eight years, my hands have been tied," said one EPA official who requested anonymity for fear of retribution. "We were told to take our clean water and clean air cases, put them in a box, and lock it shut. Everyone knew polluters were getting away with murder. But these polluters are some of the biggest campaign contributors in town, so no one really cared if they were dumping poisons into streams" (quoted in Duhigg, 2009).

Feagin and Feagin (1990) illustrate the problem of water pollution result-ing from the dumping of industrial and agricultural runoff in the Mississippi River:

> Beginning in Minnesota, where more than ten million pounds of toxic chemi-cals are dumped into its waters each year, the Mississippi River continues to be assaulted by the effluent of industries, cities, and agricultural lands along its bank as well as by the pollutants carried by its many tributaries. Thousands of toxic waste dump sites are to be found in the river's basis; hidden dump sites are discovered each year. There are an estimated 112 toxic waste dump sites in the Memphis area alone. The Mississippi River basin, once called the "Body of the Nation," is referred to today by its residents as "Cancer Corridor" or "Chemical Alley." The basin's fertile soil and fresh water once made it one of the world's ideal habitats. Today, it is one of the most dangerous. Toxic wastes have poisoned groundwater as well as river water. Industrial toxins are re-leased into the air from chemical manufacturers, power plants, pulp and paper mills, and hazardous waste incinerators. Areas that rely on the Mississippi River for drinking water have disease rates for certain types of cancers that are among the nation's highest. The waste the Mississippi River pours into the Gulf of Mexico has created a seasonal "dead zone" covering nearly 2.4 million acres of prime fishing ground from the river's mouth in Louisiana to the Texas border. (Feagin and Feagin 1990, 368)

Feagin and Feagin (1990) go on to say that there has been a significant increase in cancers and other illnesses among the residents of Natchez, Mis-sissippi. When citizens began to investigate the causes of the problem, they found that carcinogens were found in private well water. The wells had been poisoned by toxic wastes from oozing barrels in abandoned dump sites, many of which belonged to Armstrong Tire Company (368).

Unfortunately, Natchez, Mississippi, is not an isolated incident. Accord-ing to Feagin and Feagin, petrochemicals are polluting a growing number of underground wells in the United States, wells that supply half of all our drinking water. Underground water pools, called aquifers, are seriously con-taminated with chemical wastes in several New Jersey townships, twenty-two towns in Massachusetts, and a number of areas in Minnesota and Michi-gan.

In regard to some specific cases of dumping by corporations, General Electric routinely dumped water contaminated with cesium-137, strontium-90, uranium, and plutonium into the Mohawk River in the early 1950s. GE claims to have stopped this dumping in 1964, but trace amounts of plutonium were detectable in the river in 1989, according to tests conducted by the state of New York (Mokhiber, Gozan, and Knaus, 1992).

Feagin and Feagin (1990) report that in 1988 residents living near East-man Kodak's eighty-year-old Kodak Park plant in Rochester, New York, learned that highly toxic chemicals from the plant had been seeping into their groundwater for years. Although many chemical spills had occurred over the years, Kodak only noticed the problem in the fall of 1987. Still, the authors note that residents were not notified until March 1988. By this time, chemi-cals had leached into yards adjacent to the land and had eaten through carpets in the basements of some homes. Strong chemical odors were also reported by residents, and children who lived in the area were developing eye lesions and experiencing dizziness.

In another case, Chevron was fined by the California Regional Water Quality Control Board for dumping forty-eight million gallons of extremely toxic wastewater daily into San Francisco Bay. And many people remember how medical wastes including stained bandages, containers of surgical sutures, vials of AIDS-infected blood, needles, and syringes, as well as miscellaneous household waste washed ashore along the beaches of Long Island during the summer of 1988 (Feagin and Feagin, 1990).

Minamata

In the 1950s in a fishing village in Japan, Minamata, the first signs of a problem were birds that fell out of the sky dead and cats that appeared to commit suicide as they staggered and then jumped into the ocean off the docks (Mokhiber, 1988). The first human case of poisoning was a five-year-old girl who developed severe symptoms of brain damage believed to be from eating the fish that were found to carry traces of mercury ethyl from the Chisso chemical plant. Mokhiber reports that the chemical plant had been dumping more than sixty poisonous chemicals directly into the bay. By the summer of 1956 the symptoms exhibited by this young girl had reached epidemic proportions. In August 1956 a research group from the local university discovered that the cause of the disease was heavy metal poisoning caused by eating fish and shellfish taken from Minamata Bay.

Mokhiber notes that the response of the company was to deny the claims of the research team and to continue dumping the chemicals into the bay and then in 1958 to begin pouring its waste into Minamata River, ignoring the warning signs of their own company doctors. The disease then spread to river residents who fished out of the river. One study, conducted by one of the company doctors, Dr. Hajim Hosokawa, clearly established the linkage between the disease and the effluent from the plant. The company's response was to remove the doctor from the research and seal the evidence.

> After receiving Hosokawa's findings, the company did not immediately halt the dumping of mercury-tainted waste into Minamata Bay, nor did it warn people not to eat the tainted fish. Chisso's first reaction was to offer the victims payments in consolation for their misfortune (in Japanese, mimai)—an offer many victims were in no position to refuse. Although Chisso knew about Hosokawa's findings, the affected residents did not. They only suspected that the disease was somehow contagious and that they were catching it from their neighbors. Taking advantage of the legal and scientific ignorance of their victims, Chisso negotiated one-sided contracts that limited the company's liability to the initial, minimal payment. Chisso initially accepted no legal responsibilities for the damage done and disclaimed any future monetary liability. (Mokhiber, 1988, 303)

Eventually, Chisso admitted wrongdoing, two company executives were convicted of involuntary manslaughter, and the corporation threatened to go bankrupt because it could not pay all the damage claims.

Reserve Mining Company

Mokhiber (1988) notes that for more than thirty years, the Reserve Mining Company dumped thousands of tons of taconite wastes into Lake Superior on a daily basis. By the middle of the 1950s, the company was dumping sixty-seven thousand tons of waste rock into the lake every day, almost twenty-five million tons a year. In 1947, when the company applied for and obtained a permit to dispose of its wastes into Lake Superior, the company assured the public that the dumping would not affect the lake.

By the late 1960s, Reserve Mining's dumping of wastes into the lake came to the notice of the Department of Interior. An unofficial report written by a staff member of the department that was drafted in response to Reserve Mining Company's application for a renewal of their permit to continue the dumping suggested that a permit be granted only for another three years to give the company time to develop a land-dumping strategy. The staff member reported that Reserve Mining was polluting the lake by increasing the concentration of particulate matter. Reserve joined with Armco and Republic (the two companies that had jointly purchased Reserve Mining) to pressure the government to not release the report.

The Environmental Protection Agency picked up the fight against Reserve Mining. The company took the battle to federal court to gain permission to continue its dumping into the lake. But the evidence that came out of the court hearing showed that Reserve Mining was dumping fibers into the lake that resembled cancer-causing asbestos fibers and that the fibers were floating in the drinking water used by residents of Duluth and smaller cities in the area. In July 1973 the drinking water of several of these cities was defined as unfit for human consumption. Judge Lord of the federal court ruled in April 1974 that the Reserve Mining Company had to cease all discharges into Lake Superior and into the air.

Within days, Reserve had successfully appealed the order. The case was returned to Judge Lord, who was subsequently removed from the case because of the pressure by Reserve Mining and its parent corporations. The company continued to dump waste into the lake despite evidence of the health risk to residents in various cities in the area. Finally, in 1980, the federal government ordered the Reserve Mining Company to stop dumping into the lake—eleven years after the initial analysis by the Department of the Interior indicating that the dumping was polluting the lake and causing a health hazard to residents of the surrounding communities.

RESOURCE DEPLETION

As companies put short-term interests, profits, and the generation of surplus ahead of long-term interests, and the health and well-being of residents, there are increasing problems resulting from the nonsustainable extraction of resources. Furthermore, corporations will exercise the power in influencing the nature of government regulations that are developed to reduce the harm caused by unsustainable resource extraction activities.

Mountain Top Removal Mining

One such example of this is mountain top removal (MTR) mining. Yes, it is just as it is titled. The tops of mountains, up to four hundred vertical feet, are blasted off in order to get to the underline coal seams. Legislation requires that the mining companies return the topsoil after the coal is extracted and reshape the mountain to its former contours. Unfortunately, there are exemptions to this requirement and most mining operations receive the exemption. Instead the tops of mountains that are blown away with explosives go into the air, leading to higher levels of particulate matter pollution as well as other airborne toxins. The excess rock and soil laden with toxic mining byproducts are often dumped into nearby valleys. At times streams and watersheds are covered with the mining byproducts leading to an increase of minerals in the water—zinc, sodium, selenium, and sulfate levels may increase and negatively impact fish and macroinvertebrates leading to less diverse and more pollutant-tolerant species (U.S. Environmental Protection Agency, 2011). This practice of mining is done in the Appalachian mountain region of West Virginia and Kentucky, areas that have high rates of poverty. Estimates by the Environmental Protection Agency were that 2,200 square miles ($5,700 \text{ km}^2$) of Appalachian forests would be cleared for MTR sites by the year 2012.

A scientific review of the impact of mountain top removal mining concluded that there are serious environmental impacts that mitigation practices have not been able to address. In particular the scientists reported that there is extensive destruction of forests that support several endangered species in one of the areas of North America that has some of the highest levels of biodiversity (Palmer et al., 2010). Research also indicates that there is an increase in hospitalization of adults for pulmonary disorders and hypertension and increased rates of morality related to lung cancer and chronic heart, lung, and kidney diseases in counties with increased levels of this type of mining activity. These rate increases are for both males and females, which indicates that it is more likely to be caused by environmental effects and not occupational exposure (Palmer et al., 2010).

The battle between mining interests and environmentalists has been ongoing over the past fifteen years. In 1998, a court blocked the corps from allowing mining debris to be placed in streams. This was overturned in appeal court. In 2001, a court found that the mining debris violated the definition of "fill" allowed in waterways. The Bush administration changed the wording of the fill regulation to cover mining debris. In 2004, a court blocked the corps from issuing streamlined general permits and ordered individual permits, which require more scrutiny. The appeals court returned the case to the trial court. In 2007, Judge Chambers found "alarming cumulative stream loss" and ordered more thorough environmental reviews before permits are approved (Parker, 2007). More recently, the EPA in 2011 revoked permits for mining granted by the Bush administration. The EPA claimed that the coal mining would do permanent damage to rivers, wildlife, and communities. The mining project was owned by Arch Coal of St. Louis and would have buried 6.6 miles of streams under tons of mining waste. In March 2012, a United States District Court judge wrote that the EPA's unilateral decision in January 2011 to retroactively revoke the waste disposal permit for the Spruce No. 1 mine in Logan County, West Virginia, overstepped the agency's authority (Broder, 2012). The EPA is appealing the court's ruling. And so the legal battle continues over a practice of mining that is unsustainable in its destruction to the environment and has deleterious health effects on poor communities in the coal mining regions of Appalachia.

This is just one example of resource extraction that is not done in a sustainable way and that can have significant impact on the bio-system. In the United States in the past two hundred years we have lost 50 percent of our wetlands, 90 percent of northwestern old-growth forests, 99 percent of tall-grass prairies, and up to 490 species of native plants and animals (*Information Please Environmental Almanac*, 1993). Each year we lose one million acres of cropland to erosion (Pimentel, 1993). In general, the people of dominant countries in the world use most of the resources. The U.S. population comprises 5 percent of the total world population. Yet this 5 percent consumes 30 percent of the world's resources (Hayes, 1993). To compound this damage of resource depletion is the pollution in the poorest communities around the world as a result of the overconsumption patterns in the most advanced countries. What has been the impact on the people who depended on these resources or were affected by other environmental calamities resulting from this resource depletion?

Violence in the Amazon

Currently a great deal of violence is associated with the exploitation of resources in the Amazon region. This is an old story that has been repeated on every continent of the world. Our national history of violence connected to driving indigenous populations off their land to get access to minerals, game, land for farming, timber, and so on is well known. Today, those indigenous populations that have not been eliminated are the poorest in terms of access to resources, and where these populations reside as we have indicated is sought after as a site for the dumping of toxic waste. The story has been repeated in Africa and, most recently, South America, Brazil in particular. In the Amazon, the violence is between the indigenous populations, which are increasingly shrinking in numbers because of disease and violence; *garimperios* (small miners, many of them sons of farmers); large ranchers and plantation owners; small farmers; rubber tappers; foreign corporations; and the military. Since 1980, more than one thousand people have been murdered in land disputes in rural Brazil, but no more than ten people have been convicted and sent to jail (Revkin, 1990). Indigenous populations are increasingly being displaced and the government in recent years has established a reservation system to protect these populations. Missionaries are plentiful in converting and re-socializing the native populations to the new order and their appropriate position in it.

Besides the murders connected with land disputes, there is environmental violence in the Amazon as a result of the method of extracting raw materials that has been more violent to many tribal societies within the region. One example of this is gold mining. Mercury poisoning is an increasing problem among the indigenous population because of the gold mining activity. This results from the technique of gold and silver mining by which the ore is passed over mercury-coated copper plates. The gold and silver adhere to the plates and the mercury-contaminated water runoff flows into streams and rivers. Fishing grounds are polluted as well as drinking water. A study by the Brazilian Department of Mines and Energy in 1988 found that Kaypo Indian children have mercury levels in their blood almost as high as the miners. In another study, conducted by Rogerio da Silva, that analyzed the blood, urine, and hair of people directly or indirectly exposed to mercury, found that 25 percent of Kaypo Indians tested had excessive amounts of mercury (Hecht and Cockburn, 1989). This pollution together with being driven from their land by more powerful groups interested in quick access to the resources that lie beneath the land is having devastating consequences for many indigenous people in the Amazon.

Buffalo Creek

One classic case of economic violence resulting from environmental damage is the case of Buffalo Creek. Buffalo Mining Company, a subsidiary of Pittston Corporation, is one of the largest coal mining companies in the United States. In February 26, 1972, it was involved in an environmental disaster that claimed the lives of 125 persons and left between 4,000 and 5,000 residents homeless.

As noted previously in our discussion of mountain top removal mining, there are problems of disposal of waste from coal mining. Mokhiber (1988) notes that with every four tons of coal a company digs out of the ground, there is one ton of slag or gob, a mixture of mine dust, shale, clay, and other impurities. Coal companies usually dispose of this waste by dumping it in a river or at the base of a mountain. Buffalo Mining Company dumped its waste in the middle of the waters of Middle Creek, one of the three streams that feed Buffalo Creek.

The dumping of waste began as early as 1957. By 1972, the company was dumping one thousand tons of slag per day into Middle Fork, at the top of the mountain, within eyesight of five thousand residents who resided in the valley below. The tons of waste clogged up the creek and formed a huge bank of waste, 200 feet deep, 600 feet wide, and 1,500 feet long. Mokhiber notes that the company also had a liquid waste problem. Buffalo Mining used more than half a million gallons of water per day to clean the thousands of tons of coal it mined. Before the creation of EPA, mining companies would dump the waste into nearby rivers and streams. With the new environmental awareness of the 1960s, coal companies were expected to hold on to this water until some impurities settled. Buffalo Mining dumped its wastewater behind the dam created by the slag.

It rained hard for a few days before February 26, 1972. On that day in Appalachia at 8:00 in the morning, Buffalo Mining's slag dam, situated nine miles above Amherstdale, collapsed, sending a black torrent of 132 million gallons of water and a million tons of solid waste roaring through the breach. The gigantic wave caused a series of explosions as it thundered down the valley like a mass of rolling lava—a mud wave, as one engineer put it—on a roller-coaster ride of destruction aimed to disturb the stillness at Amherstdale and demolish everything in its path (Mokhiber, 1988, 121). The mud wave totally demolished the town of Saunders. It took everything with it, sweeping the town clean. Saunders was only the first town in line for destruction. By the time the black wave reached the mouth of Buffalo Creek, seventeen miles down the hollow, 125 people were dead and 4,000 Buffalo Creek residents were left homeless.

The tragedy in this disaster, and what makes it a case of economic violence as opposed to an unavoidable accident, is that the corporation was well aware of the potential hazards. Mokhiber (1988) states that as early as 1926, *Coal Age*, the industry weekly, reported the dangers of dumping refuse from mining in a hollow that is the drain for a watershed in hilly or mountainous areas. The article in the magazine warned that trouble can be expected if there is no provision made to take care of potential overflows. Following the publication of this article, a West Virginia inspector checked the dam at Buffalo Creek and wrote to the company to tell them of the need for an emergency spill well. In 1966 a disaster occurred in Wales when a 300-foot coal slag mound collapsed, killing 145 persons. Following this disaster, a federal investigator visited Buffalo Creek and determined that the dam was subject to a large washout on the north side from overflow of the lake (Mokhiber, 1988, 125). Pittston was finally warned in 1971, when a 150- to 200-foot section of Dam 3 gave way, spilling debris into the second dam in the chain. Despite this problem, Pittston did not build an emergency spillway to avoid a future disaster. That disaster occurred the following year.

CONCLUSION: ECONOMIC VIOLENCE AND INEQUALITY

Are there patterns of economic violence and what factors explain these patterns? It is virtually impossible to compose a representative sample of all the types of economic violence we have discussed in this chapter in order to analyze patterns. Most governments in the world do not collect statistics on the incidence of this type of violence. But from what we know and what we suspect, the incidences of this violence are not random. Indications are that they follow a pattern that is duplicated repeatedly in the story of violence. That pattern is one where those who are least powerful are more likely to experience higher levels of violence than those who are more powerful. And like the story of all other forms of institutional violence, those who are dominant within the institutional spheres enact most of the violence directed at the most powerless segments of the population. Thus it would stand to reason that as societies and the world in general are stratified, higher levels of economic violence are to be found among the poor populations in a given nation-state and in the world.

For production violence it is clearly the poor segments of any given society that experience the most hazardous forms of production, agricultural or industrial, and bear the greatest cost in occupational diseases and accidents. For product violence, the poor segments of the population in a given country as well as the poor populations in the world are likely to be exposed to hazardous products. This is especially the case when we think of the impact of product dumping by which products banned from wealthier countries are sold in poor countries to unsuspecting consumers.

Lastly, for environmental violence, it is the poor segments of the population of a given society and the poor populations in the world that are likely to be exposed to hazardous air, water, and soil. Exceptions to this pattern might be a product of the population's geographic isolation. However, even in isolated areas there are serious problems of pollutions because of ocean pollution resulting from the dumping of toxic waste by developed countries. Furthermore, as valuable resources are stripped away from the poorest populations of the world, not only does their impoverishment have violent consequences via interpersonal violence and other types of institutional violence, but it has a violent consequence as a result of the pollution caused by the very stripping process employed to remove the resources in the largest amounts with the least cost to owners.

In sum, it is a statistical truth that more people die or are injured by economic violence than any other single category of violence that we have discussed thus far. Certainly more than the numbers of people injured or killed in interpersonal violence. In the next chapter we discuss the last form of institutional violence that we consider in this work: state violence.

DISCUSSION QUESTIONS

1. As consumers we are always looking for the cheapest price for the products that we buy. However, buying the cheaper product can actually contribute to the problem of economic violence in the world. These products could be made under violent conditions, using slave labor or unsafe working conditions or causing pollution. Can consumers be motivated to stop economic violence through their buying behavior if they are aware of the violence connected to the products that they are buying? Let's say you had an app that allowed you to scan the bar code on the packaging and discover whether the product was made with or without violence. Would you use such a phone app or not? Would it affect your consuming behavior?

2. If we accepted the fact that animals can be victims of violence, can we truly live a nonviolent life? How would you change your style of life?

3. Given the power of corporations and those who own them in our society, is there any way to stop economic violence? What would have to be done to stop it?

4. I had a discussion with a student from the People's Republic of China who after watching a film on the unsafe working conditions in a factory and the unsafe dumping of waste in his country said that this was necessary for his country to develop. He stated that the United States went through this same experience in order to develop. He stated that it was the cost of development. Is this the only path of economic development for developing countries, or is there a way to avoid this economic violence in the development of countries like China?

5. What role should the U.S. government play in reducing the levels of economic violence in the world today?

Chapter Eight

State Violence

In Crescent City, California, at the Pelican Bay State Prison on the morning of April 22, 1992, guards of the facility entered Vaughn Dortch's cell and ordered him to strip naked. The guards returned thirty minutes later, shackled his legs and arms, gagged him, and carried him to the prison infirmary where one guard told him that he would receive a Klan bath. Dortch testified that he was forced by six guards to remain in a steel tub of scalding hot water and scrubbed with a wooden brush until his skin peeled away from his body. He also testified that he was held down in the water for several minutes. Dortch collapsed after he was removed from the tub and was treated at the prison infirmary for burns before he was transferred to the burn unit of the University of California, Davis, hospital (Berma, 1994).

"Thirty heavily armed men wearing army combat vests, but masked with hoods lettered death squad came to my village and seized and killed a number of campesinos. They went then to the neighboring village of Santa Helen, seized Romilia Hernandez, aged 21, raped and then decapitated her. Her relatives buried her head: the rest of her body was burned by her murderers. The head had been left in front of her relative's house. The members of the death squad were evacuated that day by a Salvadoran army helicopter."—Testimony by a Salvadoran refugee to an Amnesty International mission visiting refugee camps in Honduras, August 1981 (Amnesty International, 1983, 11).

"We have been living under extreme terror, there is only one way in and out of the barrio and it is controlled by the paramilitaries. . . . In the last two weeks, six women have been killed, some because of their alleged relationship with the guerrillas, others because they refuse to give sex. One girl was raped before she was killed; they took out her eyes, pulled out her nails and cut off her breasts. One boy had his penis cut off and put in his mouth. . . . When the police arrive everything is calm and the paramilitaries mingle with the police as they walk around the barrio."—Testimony given to the United Nations Special Rapporteur on Violence against Women during her mission to Colombia in 2001 (United Nations Commission on Human Rights, 2002).

On September 3, 1992, Sdiq al-Karim Malallah, a twenty-three-year-old Shia Muslim and an advocate for improved civil rights in Saudi Arabia, was beheaded after he was found guilty of apostasy (renunciation of religious faith) and blasphemy (Amnesty International, 1993, 2).

During the mid-1960s more than half a million people were killed in Indonesia after the military took over the country and began a campaign to eliminate all political opposition to their rule (Amnesty International, 1977).

In Guatemala on May 29, 1978, Roman Catholic Church workers reported that 114 peasants were killed by the army in an Indian village when Indians attempted to present a petition protesting the takeover of their land by wealthy landowners (Chomsky and Herman, 1979, 282).

"Stalking from home to home, a United States Army sergeant methodically killed at least 16 civilians, 9 of them children, in a rural stretch of southern Afghanistan early on Sunday, igniting fears of a new wave of anti-American hostility" Shah and Bowley, 2012).

These are incidents of state violence. The scale of violence committed by governments is greater than interpersonal violence, yet when we think of violence what usually comes to mind is images of muggers, rapists, and teenage gangs on city streets. The state protects us from these criminals. Yet interpersonal violence makes relatively modest contributions to the overall violence phenomenon. This is consistent with the principles noted earlier regarding levels of violence. As we move from the interpersonal to institutional to structural forms of violence, the scale and scope of violence increase. Ironically, at the same time, these higher levels of violence are less likely to be defined as violence and thus are seen as nonproblematic. But before we discuss the details of state violence, we must define it.

DEFINITION

Any definition of state violence presupposes agreement on what we mean by the term *state*. A working definition will equate state with government. For classic German sociologist Max Weber the modern state was characterized by three particular dimensions: territoriality, legitimacy, and violence. Weber noted that only the state has a monopoly on the legitimate use of violence (1958). But one question that is immediately raised is how we distinguish the state's legitimate use of violence from the state's illegitimate use of violence, although this is not a question particularly relevant to a definition of violence. It is violence no matter if it is defined as legitimate or illegitimate by the state. In all cases the legitimacy issue is separate from the question of the existence of violence. As Michalowski writes, "The fact that state violence is legal within any given political context . . . should not tempt us to overlook the fact that it is nonetheless violence" (Michalowski, 1985, 279). Thus we pragmatically define state violence as referring to all forms of violence committed by government. This includes actions by police and military forces, or, as Michalowski observes, all forms of politically authorized violence.

Most researchers have focused on only illegitimate or illegal categories of violence. The obvious problem with this limitation is that the state is in a monopoly position of power to define the legal status of the violence. Consequently, most of the acts within the broader domain of violence that eventually become defined as violence are those acts that threaten the state. This can be seen in the use of the term *terrorism*. Terrorists are usually defined in terms of individuals or groups who threaten the social order. For example, Brian Jenkins (1984), a Rand think tank specialist on terrorism, defines terrorism as the use or threatened use of force designed to cause a political change.

But what about violence used to maintain the status quo? Laqueur (1987) describes terrorism as the illegitimate use of force to achieve a political objective when innocent people are targeted. The qualifier "illegitimate" again begs the issue. Who defines legitimacy? In both of these authors' works, most of what we would call state terrorism is precluded from their definitions. If the state is unlikely to define its own acts of violence as illegitimate, then who is left to do so?

We can turn to international organizations like the United Nations or private watchdog groups such as Amnesty International, the African Human Rights Research Association, Americas Watch, Asia Watch, Cultural Survival, Helsinki Watch, and Human Rights Advocates International, which have focused to a large extent on state violence or terrorism. Unfortunately, the power they have to bear on states that engage in illegitimate violence is determined by the distribution of power within the world system. Those states with the greatest amount of power in the world system have the greatest amount of power to define illegitimate state violence and terrorism. Their influence lies in their ability to inform citizens around the world of these crimes and to apply the normative pressure of world public opinion on the leaders of states that sanction such acts.

One international force that could be important in the future in controlling state violence is the International Criminal Court. This court has been formed specifically to try and convict those responsible for state violence, including genocide, crimes against humanity including rape, murder, enslavement, various war crimes including torture, and attacking civilians. On April 11, 2002, sixty-one countries ratified the International Criminal Court treaty. It went into effect July 2002. The U.S. government, the most powerful state in the world, has for many years attempted to block the ratification of the treaty. President Clinton signed the treaty but then never presented it to the U.S. Senate for ratification. Most recently Congress passed a law entitled the American Service Members Protection Act that exempts all U.S. government personnel from being prosecuted by the court and also denies all military aid to non-NATO signatories of the treaty. President George W. Bush announced that the treaty will not be ratified and that the United States will not be subject to the treaty's jurisdiction.

Amnesty International has indisputably been the premier organization that monitors state violence. It defines political killings as unlawful and deliberate killings of persons by reasons of their real or imputed political beliefs or activities, religion, other conscientiously held beliefs, ethnic origin, sex, color, or language, carried out by order of a government with its complicity (Amnesty International, 1983).

Violence by the state can be understood as accomplishing two general purposes. For one purpose, violence is used to maintain order, that is, the order that is in part defined in terms of particular systems of stratification that determine the distribution of resources and power and defined in terms of the particular functioning of institutions that maintain and reproduce the society from generation to generation. A second purpose is that violence is used by the state to extend the order to other territorial domains and to those who are outside of its legal jurisdiction.

The state's practice of executing offenders of particular crimes is one example of state violence that we take for granted. In the exercise of capital punishment, the state is defending the order by killing an individual who has threatened it and at the same time warning others that if they commit similar acts they will be dealt with in the same manner. In the United States since the 1930s there have been more than four thousand legal executions. Between 1972 and 1976 capital punishment was outlawed by the U.S. Supreme Court and thus executions were not conducted. However, after this period executions resumed and in several states resumed with a vengeance. Between 1977 and March 1, 2002, 761 convicted murderers have been executed in the United States. Of those executed, eight were female. Although the majority of those who were executed were white with 422 (55 percent), African Americans were overrepresented with 266 (35 percent). The majority of those executed were executed by lethal injection, 599 (79 percent), including all 110 of those executed since July 6, 2000. One hundred forty-six were executed by electric chair, eleven by gas chamber, three by hanging, and two by firing squad. Executions were held in thirty-two different states. However, the state of Texas had more than any other state with 261 or 34 percent of all executions during this post-1976 period.

Of these 761 executions, eighteen were of those who were under the age of eighteen at the time of their crime. The execution of juvenile offenders is rare in the world today. Amnesty International USA reports that since 1990, only seven countries in the world are known to have executed juveniles: Democratic Republic of Congo, Iran, Nigeria, Pakistan, Saudi Arabia, Yemen, and the United States (Amnesty International, 2002a). Yemen has since outlawed the practice, as did China in 1997.

The United Nations Convention on the Rights of the Child Article 37(a) states: "Neither Capital punishment nor life imprisonment without possibility of release shall be imposed for offenses committed by persons below 18 years of age." Only the United States and Somalia have not ratified this Convention. As of July 2001, eighty-five men on death row were sentenced as juveniles (Amnesty International USA, 2002a). Ten out of eighteen or 56 percent of the executions of juvenile offenders that have occurred between 1973 and 2001 were in the state of Texas. In 2005 the U.S. Supreme Court ruled in a five-to-four ruling that the execution of those less than eighteen years of age is cruel and unusual punishment and therefore abolished the execution of juveniles in the United States.

In looking at the population of those executed by the U.S. government, the majority have been members of ethnic minorities and generally from the poorer strata of society (Bowers, 1974; U.S. Department of Justice, 2000). Of the 211 federal death penalty prosecutions authorized by the attorney general since 1988, 75 percent have been against minorities. The U.S. General Accounting Office issued a report in 1990 which found that in 82 percent of the studies reviewed, race of the victim was found to influence the likelihood of being charged with capital murder or being sentenced to execution. Those who murdered whites were more likely to be charged and executed than those who murdered blacks (General Accounting Office, 1990). Amnesty International's report (1998) on human rights violations in the United States noted that blacks make up just 12 percent of the country's population, but 42 percent of the nation's condemned prisoners. In early 1998, of the twenty-six people under federal sentences of death (military and civilian), only five prisoners were white. The report also notes that between 1908 and 1962, all those executed for rape were black, although only 55 percent of those imprisoned for rape were black. Furthermore, blacks and whites in the United States are the victims of murder in almost equal numbers, yet 82 percent of prisoners executed since 1977 were convicted of the murder of a white person (Amnesty International, 1998, 109).

An argument increasingly used by abolitionists is the problem of false convictions. In recent years with the advent of DNA testing, there has been the discovery of a large number of inmates awaiting execution who were found to be innocent. The Innocence Project was founded in 1992 by Barry C. Scheck and Peter J. Neufeld at the Benjamin N. Cardozo School of Law at Yeshiva University to assist prisoners who could be proven innocent through DNA testing. As of 2012, 289 people in the United States have been exonerated by DNA testing, including 17 who served time on death row. The average prison term that these innocent men served before exoneration and release was 13.5 years. Approximately 70 percent of those exonerated were minorities (Innoncence Project, 2012).

Worldwide, Amnesty International reports that ninety-two countries and territories have abolished the death penalty for all crimes. Another ten countries have abolished the death penalty for "ordinary" crimes and an additional thirty-six countries can be considered abolitionist in practice in that they retain the death penalty in law but have not carried out any executions for the past ten years (Amnesty International, 2009). This would make the total number of countries that have abolished the use of death penalty in practice to a total of 138. During 2008, at least 2,390 prisoners were executed in twenty-five countries and 8,864 people were sentenced to death in fifty-two countries. These figures include only cases known to Amnesty International; it is expected that the true figures are higher.

According to Amnesty International data, the number of executions has increased worldwide, while the number of countries abolishing the use of the death penalty increased. This is because a relatively small number of states carry out most of the executions in the world. Six states conducted more than

95 percent of all executions. The following countries carried out executions in 2008: China (at least 1,718), Iran (at least 346), Saudi Arabia (at least 102), United States (37), Pakistan (at least 36), Iraq (at least 34) (Amnesty International, 2009). Amnesty International also notes that like in previous years, a large number of death sentences were handed down in trials that failed to meet internationally recognized standards of fairness. A concerning number of executions were carried out after proceedings that relied upon confessions solicited through torture in violation of international law.

One particularly gruesome case of state violence as it relates to executions is where there is a policy by the government to remove organs for their organ transplant program before prisoners are executed or that they are executed in such a way as to keep valuable tissue undamaged for transplant. The organization Human Rights Watch/Asia reports that three thousand executions conducted annually by the People's Republic of China have been an important source of organ transplants within the country as well as organs exported overseas. The group estimates that in 1992 alone between 1,400 and 1,700 kidneys were harvested from executed prisoners. Sometimes the executions are botched so that transplants can be conducted after the execution. In 1978 a young woman teacher, Zhong Haiyuan, accused of hiding clandestine literature, was executed in Ganzhou, Jiangxi Province. She was shot twice in the head but did not die. Instead of waiting for her death, medical personnel were allowed to take her body to a specially erected operating facility on the prison premises and to remove both kidneys while she was still living (Schmetzer, 1994, 5). According to the government-sponsored *China Daily* newspaper, executed prisoners currently provide two-thirds of all transplant organs in China (BBC News, 2009).

Another form of state violence is police use of deadly force. The police "justifiably" killed 343 persons in 2005 (U.S. Bureau of Justice Statistics, 2012). Justifiable homicides are defined as the killing of a felon by a law enforcement officer in the line of duty. According to the government data collected from police agencies, this figure is down from the high point during the past thirty years of 462 in 1994 when overall homicide rates were also high when there was a great deal of interpersonal violence connected to the war on drugs. However, the estimate provided in the report is believed to be conservative since not all police jurisdictions report to the federal government cases of killings by police and there are problems of misclassification. More accurately the numbers could be up to 29 percent higher (Loftin, Wiersema, and McDowall, 2003). In the Bureau of Justice report it notes that 39 percent of those killed justifiably were black, which is more than three times their representation in the population. The vast majority were young; the modal (most frequent) age was twenty-two years of age. In an earlier report, it was noted that young black males, who made up 1 percent of the total U.S. population, were 14 percent of felons "justifiably" killed by police in 1998. In 1998, the city of Detroit had the highest rate of killings by police (Brown and Langan, 2001).

However, there are a number of cases each year in which the justifiability is not present or is questionable. For example, on March 27, 2009, Nick Christie was strapped naked to a chair at Lee County jail in Florida and died of heart failure after being pepper sprayed. The medical examiner ruled his death was a homicide because he had been restrained and sprayed with pepper spray by law enforcement officers. There have been no charges filed against the officers (Smith, 2011). In another case, former Iraq veteran Jose Guerena was shot to death by Pima County Sheriff SWAT officers. They suspected Guerena of being part of a drug-dealing operation, which he was not. The officers prevented the ambulance from getting Guerena medical attention until they searched the house. The SWAT team was cleared of any wrongdoing by the Pima County Attorney's Office (Echavarri, 2011).

Jason Alan Kemp, thirty-one, was shot at point-blank range and killed when he refused to allow officers into his home without a search warrant. The state troopers were investigating a minor traffic accident when they kicked in the door and blinded Jason with pepper spray when he refused to let them in, and he was then fatally shot by one of the state troopers. The civil trial of the state troopers was scheduled for April of 2012 (Harrison, 2011). In 2011, five current and former New Orleans police officers were found guilty on all counts by a federal jury for shooting six citizens, killing two, and then conducting cover-up that followed the shootings that occurred in the aftermath of destruction caused by hurricane Katrina in 2005 (Robertson, 2011).

Historically, urban riots are very often connected to police violence. There have been riots in several major cities in the United States as a result of police violence and homicides. In 1980 the Liberty City Riots in Florida were sparked by the police killing of an unarmed black male who ran a red light. In the decade of the 1990s in Los Angeles, there were the riots in South Central Los Angeles after the acquittal of all the officers who were video-taped beating Rodney King with batons and stun weapons. In 2001, there was rioting in Cincinnati after police had shot and killed an unarmed black man. Mr. Bacre Waly Ndiaye, special rapporteur of the Commission on Human Rights, recently included the United States as one of several coun-tries to investigate for extrajudicial executions. In his report, Ndiaye issued urgent appeals to ninety-one countries, including the United States, to end extrajudicial, summary, or arbitrary executions (Ndiaye, 1996). A report is-sued by the Council of Europe on the problem of the recent urban rioting that occurred in Europe in 2006 and 2007 concluded that growing discrimination and worsening of relations between the police forces and residents was an important factor (R. Blum, 2008).

A final form of violence we often think of in terms of the state defending itself is the use of the military to defend the national interest. In most cases we think of governments using their military forces to defend their geograph-ic borders. But for states whose national interest extends beyond the territori-al boundaries of the country, violence is used as a means of extending eco-nomic and political control over people of other nation-states where these interests reside. Imperialist nations or nations whose development depends upon the increasing control of resources outside of the national boundaries blur the lines between violence used to defend its internal order and violence used to extend it. Although conceptually these two general forms of violence may be distinct, analytically the distinction in the practice of state violence becomes blurred. Violence to extend the order, in other words, becomes defined as violence to defend the order. The often heard phrase in the United

States by U.S. presidents and State Department officials to legitimate the use of military force to defend U.S. dominion overseas is to defend our national interest. These national interests are often in places far removed from the physical and legal boundaries of the United States. It would be more accurate to say that in defending U.S. imperial interests its leaders are utilizing military force to maintain economic domination of these regions. The rhetorical phrase "to defend our national interest" is employed to legitimize the violence, but there is also truth in this claim given the nature of imperialist societies. To maintain the socioeconomic/political and industrial system (which in part is based on military production) of the United States, it is necessary for the state to utilize violence or the threat of violence to continue its political and economic dominance over other people around the globe. The economic doomsday prognostications and regional complaints that occurred in the early 1990s as President Clinton began to make serious movements to cash in on the post–Cold War peace dividend are ample demonstration of the shock to a system otherwise oriented to a permanent state of war. With the election of President George W. Bush, and the beginning of the ever expansive war on terrorism, military spending skyrocketed and it has opened a new era of overt U.S. military interventionism worldwide.

EXTENT OF STATE VIOLENCE

Overall, there is no way of comprehensively knowing the extent of state violence in the world today. In most cases, what are counted by agencies concerned about state violence are the extralegal forms of state violence. These extralegal forms refer to the use of violence without justification or legitimization by the laws of the state that is conducting the violence. The extent of legal state violence, which includes executions by the state, police use of deadly force, and military actions, is in some respects more difficult to assess because it relies on data, if collected, that are created by the very state that is conducting the violence. One example that we have previously discussed is the statistics on police use of deadly force. The existence and quality of such statistics in countries around the world are even more problematic. At times there are reports that are developed by groups outside of the state concerned about the extent of police violence. For example in one recent report done by medical legal experts in Kenya, they note that six out of every ten Kenyans who are shot dead are victims of police. According to this same report, the 2001 rate increased to nine out of every ten victims (Leyan, 2002).

From what is known about extralegal state violence, it occurs in many countries throughout the world. There is no annual census of the numbers of people who are killed by governments. According to Balint, conflicts within and between states involving violence by the state "occurring between 1945 and 1996 have resulted in an estimated 98 million casualties; 87 million of which were in the course of conflicts of a non-international, internal, and tyrannical regime victimization character, and 11 million of which were in the course of conflicts of an international character" (Balint, 1996, 235). One estimate of the number of deaths by state violence, or as defined by Hobsbawm, "by human decision," in the period from 1914 to 1991 is 187 million (Hobsbawm, 1994). This figure was derived from another work by former Secretary of State and National Security Advisor Zbigniew Brzezinski (Brzezinski, 1993). Although according to Leitenberg the estimate is very rough given the various sources the estimate is based upon (Leitenberg, 2006). One example of state violence was in 1994 when up to a million men, women, and children were slaughtered in Rwanda in just one hundred days (Amnesty International, 2001b).

Since 1998 there have been a number of conflicts between states that may indicate that the occurrence of state violence is unabated. The second Congo War that began in 1998 has claimed an estimated 5.4 million lives (McGreal, 2008). The war in the Darfur region of the Sudan has claimed approximately four hundred thousand victims. The wars between the United States and coalition partners in Afghanistan, Iraq, and Pakistan are believed to have claimed somewhere between one hundred thousand to almost one million lives. State violence occurs throughout the world and the numbers for the twenty-first century, if trends continue, may be closer to the two hundred million number mark if we use the definition of state violence in this chapter.

According to the most recent annual report of Amnesty International (Amnesty International, 2011), extrajudicial executions or killings through excessive use of force were carried out in fifty-nine countries and people were reportedly tortured or ill-treated by security forces, police, or other state authorities in ninety-two countries in 2010. In this most recent report of Amnesty International, state violence is identified on all continents with the exception of Antarctica. In Africa, "confirmed or possible" extrajudicial executions were carried out in twenty-four countries. For example, "in May, the bodies of William Marques Luís 'Líro Boy' and Hamilton Pedro Luís 'Kadú' were found by their family in the Central Morgue of Luanda, [Angola]. They had been arrested without a warrant at their home in Luanda's Benfica neighbourhood by several police officers and were subsequently extrajudicially executed" (Amnesty International, 2011, 63). The report also cites cases in thirty-two countries where people were reportedly tortured or ill-treated by security forces, police, or other state authorities. In Mozambique, "in September, police fired live ammunition at crowds in Maputo and Manica provinces who were demonstrating against the rising price of bread and basic commodities, including by burning tyres and blocking roads. At least 14 people were killed and more than 400 injured" (Amnesty International, 2011, 234).

In the Americas, eight countries' governments were identified as committing extrajudicial killings. "On 19 March, Javier Francisco Arredondo and Jorge Antonio Mercado Alonso, two students at a private university in Monterrey, were killed when the military opened fire on suspected members of a criminal gang. A CNDH investigation into the case showed that the military planted guns on the students and destroyed crime scene evidence to falsely accuse the victims of belonging to a criminal gang" (Amnesty International, 2011, 225). People were reportedly tortured or ill treated by security forces, police, or other state authorities in eleven countries in the Americas. "On 4 September, peasant farmers Luis Alberto Cortes Mesa, Jose Wilmer Mesa

Mesa and Ilfo Boanerge Klinger Rivera were stopped by members of the Black Eagles paramilitary group as they walked home along the river Telembi in Barbacoas Municipality [in Columbia], Narino Department. On 5 September, the bodies of the three men were found hacked to death and bearing signs of torture" (Amnesty International, 2011, 110).

Amnesty International reported in the most recent report that

> in his memoirs, published in November, and in a pre-publication interview, former President Bush admitted that he had personally authorized "enhanced interrogation techniques" for use by the CIA against detainees held in secret custody. One of the techniques he said he authorized was "waterboarding," a form of torture in which the process of drowning a detainee is begun. On 9 November, the US Department of Justice announced, without further explanation, that no one would face criminal charges in relation to the destruction in 2005 by the CIA of videotapes made of the interrogations of two detainees— Abu Zubaydah and 'Abd al-Nashiri—held in secret custody in 2002. (Amnesty International, 2011, 343)

An earlier example of a case of torture within the United States listed by Amnesty International is the case of Corcoran State Prison in California where "in June, eight prison guards were accused of staging 'gladiator style' fights among prisoners between 1989 and 1995. The guards were acquitted of criminal charges after a jury trial." However, Amnesty International notes that "although the guards were acquitted, the state had earlier been forced to change its policies after an independent panel found that 80 percent of the shootings had been unjustified. State legislative hearings in 1998 had found a pattern of brutality at the prison." Last, confirmed or possible prisoners of conscience were held in four countries in the Americas (Amnesty International, 2001b).

In Asia and the Pacific Islands, "confirmed or possible" extrajudicial executions were carried out in twelve countries in the region in 2010. In Myanmar, in April 2010 "soldiers arrested two men in Pa Laai village, Nam-Zarng township, Shan state, accusing them of supporting armed Shan rebels. The soldiers beat one of the men to death, while the fate and whereabouts of the other are unknown" (Amnesty International, 2011, 236). People were reportedly tortured or ill-treated by security forces, police, or other state authorities in twenty-one countries in the region. The countries of China, India, Bangladesh, and Myanmar have been particularly monitored by Amnesty International. In Bangladesh, on "27 June, 2010 Rapid Action Battalion personnel used excessive force during a raid on the house of Mirza Abbas, a leading BNP politician and former mayor of Dhaka. They attacked those gathered peacefully inside the house during the general strike called by the opposition. They beat and injured at least 20 people, mostly women" (Amnesty International, 2011, 74). Confirmed or possible prisoners of conscience were held in thirteen countries (Amnesty International, 2001b).

In Europe, "confirmed or possible" extrajudicial executions were carried out in four countries in the region in 2001. For example, in Poland on "23 May, 2010 at a market in Warsaw's Praga district, a police officer shot a 36-year-old Nigerian trader who died on the spot. The incident happened during a police action which reportedly involved a license check of the market traders" (Amnesty International, 2011, 265). People were reportedly tortured or ill-treated by security forces, police, or other state authorities in fifteen countries in the region. For example, in Ukraine "on 30 June a group of 15 prisoners were due to be taken to court. The police officers escorting them ordered one of them to strip naked. When he refused to remove his under-pants, he was beaten, handcuffed and tied to the wall" (Amnesty International, 2011, 335).

Last, in the Middle East Amnesty International reports "confirmed or possible" extrajudicial executions were carried out in seven countries in the region. For example, in Israel and the Occupied territories in September 2010 Israeli military killed three Palestinian shepherds—Ibrahim Abu Said, aged ninety-one, his sixteen-year-old grandson Hosam Abu Sa'id, and seventeen-year-old Isma'il Abu 'Oda were killed by Israeli tank shells while grazing their sheep inside the Gaza "exclusion zone" near Beit (Amnesty International, 2011, 183). They were mistakenly suspected to be terrorists. In Iraq, Riyadh Mohammad Saleh al-'Uqaibi, a former army officer, died on Febru-ary 12 or 13 at the Muthanna airport prison. Arrested in late September 2009, he was alleged to have been beaten so severely under interrogation that he sustained broken ribs, liver damage, and internal bleeding. His body was returned to his family weeks later with a death certificate giving heart failure as the cause of death (Amnesty International, 2011, 177–78).

The use of torture was widespread in many Middle Eastern countries. Amnesty International reports cases of torture in ten countries in the Middle East. For example, in Egypt, torture in police stations continued to be wide-spread. Taha Abdel Tawwab Mohamed, a medical doctor, said he was stripped and beaten by SSI officers in Fayoum on March 7 because of his public support for Mohamed ElBaradei, the former head of the International Atomic Energy Agency, who the authorities consider a government critic (Amnesty International, 2011, 132).

TARGETS OF STATE VIOLENCE

Conquered Indigenous and Ethnic Minority Populations

Who are the targets of state violence? In general, several groups are perennial prime targets of state violence. One of the largest categories of groups is made up of conquered indigenous and ethnic minority populations. Through-out the history of white conquest and colonization of lands occupied by nonwhite people, there has been a pattern of violence used to control, domi-nate, and exterminate these populations. Whether we are speaking about the Americas, Africa, Asia, Oceania, or Australia, the pattern is the same and it continues. In a report on racism and the administration of justice, Amnesty International (2001c) noted that there are three hundred million indigenous people worldwide and that despite the wide range of diversity of this popula-tion, there are striking similarities of the abuse they have suffered and contin-ue to experience. Amnesty International notes that government leaders will often incite racial or ethnic hatred against minority groups in order to stay in power. This often results in violence by state authorities against these ethnic minority populations. Violence has always been systematically used as a means to strip the indigenous populations of access to valued resources. Dee Brown (1970) begins the history of the systematic destruction of indigenous people of the Americas with a discussion of what happened to the Tainos and Arawak people after Columbus discovered America more than five hundred years ago:

> The Tainos and other Arawak people did not resist conversion to the Europeans' religion, but they did resist strongly when hordes of these bearded strangers began scouring their islands in search of gold and precious stones. The Spaniards looted and burned villages; they kidnapped hundreds of men, women, and children and shipped them to Europe to be sold as slaves. Arawak resistance brought on the use of guns and sabers, and whole tribes were destroyed, hundreds of thousands of people in less than a decade after Columbus set foot on the beach of San Salvador, October 12, 1492. (Brown, 1970, 2)

The violence directed at the native population in the United States has continued, as seen in the activities of the FBI, the military, and the Bureau of Indian Affairs against dissident groups of Native Americans (Churchill and Vander Wall, 1990; Matthiessen, 1991). The pattern is basically the same as it was in earlier times in North American history, although it is grounded more in covert forms of violence, as opposed to the overt military actions of the past. In each case the violence is used to acquire access to valued resources held by the indigenous population. This generalization holds whether we are talking about the genocide of the Arawak and Tainos by the Spanish military beginning with Columbus's invasion or the extinction of the Powhatan in the Virginias, to the Wampanoag and Narragansett in Massachusetts, to the six nations of the Iroquois, to the deaths resulting from the forced marching of the Cherokee (referred to as the Trail of Tears), or to the violence directed at various other tribes of North America, such as Pequot, Montauk, Nanticoke, Machapuga, Catawba, Cheraws, Miami, Huron, Erie, Mohicans, Shawnee, Cherokees, Chickasaw, Choctaws, Creeks, Seminole, Apache, and Lakota, to name only a few. Similar stories of state violence directed at indigenous populations are repeated in Australia, Central and South America, Africa, Taiwan, and Oceania/Polynesia. Bodley has attempted to assess the level of depopulation of indigenous populations since first contacts with white Europeans. He observes:

> According to these figures, tribal populations in lowland South America (east of Andes and exclusive of the Caribbean) and North America (north of Mexico) were reduced by almost 95 percent or by nearly 18 million by 1930. . . . In Polynesia, Micronesia, and Australia, where fairly complete, although conservative, estimates have been made, the population was reduced by approximately 80 percent, or more than 1.25 million since 1980. If moderate allowances are made for further depopulation in areas not included, such as Siberia, Southern Asia, islands of southeast Asia, southern Africa, and Melanesia, and if Morel's modes of estimate for the Congo is accepted, it might be conservatively estimated that during the 150 years between 1780 and 1930 world tribal populations were reduced by at least 30 million as a direct result of the spread of industrial civilization. (Bodley, 1982, 39–40)

Today state violence persists in the United States where the mineral resources of the Lakota in the Black Hills constitute the prize to be acquired (Churchill and Vander Wall, 1990). We can also see a struggle in Wisconsin where the Lake Superior Chippewas have been subjected to federal and state pressure and harassment to give up their treaty rights to hunt and fish on northern Wisconsin lakes. While federal spokespersons are now suggesting that Congress may modernize the treaties first negotiated from 1834 to 1854, white protesters chant slogans like "Save a walleye. Spear a pregnant squaw." Two men were charged in 1990 with criminal conspiracy to interfere with the Chippewas' civil rights after they built and exploded a pipe bomb near Chippewa spear fishers at the same time that Wisconsin officials grumbled publicly about the high cost of law enforcement to protect Native American rights (Kerr and Hall, 1992). These are just some of the many examples of conflicts between indigenous people and federal and state governments.

Mineral wealth in the Amazon and other regions of South and Central America have led to increasing amounts of violence and the displacement of indigenous populations who inhabit such lands. Chomsky and Herman cite the writings of Munzel, a German anthropologist, who notes that at the time of his research in Paraguay, there was a campaign under way against the Ache Indians that included manhunts, slavery, and virtual cultural destruction:

> In manhunts with the cooperation of the military, the Indians are pursued like animals, the parents killed and the children sold. Machetes are commonly used to murder Indians to save the expense of bullets. Men not slaughtered are sold for field-workers, women as prostitutes, children as domestic servants. . . . The process of deculturation aims at the intentional destruction of Indian culture among those herded into the reservation. (Chomsky and Herman, 1979, 111)

Most recently in Paraguay signs of the uncontacted Ayoreo Indians have been found on land owned by Brazilian company River Plate. Illegal deforestation and attacks on Indians living in the forest have led to their increasing displacement and loss of life (Survival for Tribal Peoples, 2012). Shelton H. Davis's research cited in Chomsky and Herman's (1979) work details a history of extermination of Brazilian Indians similar to the North American pattern, that is, genocide conducted in order to permit Western colonization.

> From 1900 to 1957, Davis estimates, the indigenous population of Brazil dropped from 1 million to less than 200,000, and by the latter day many were enduring the most precarious conditions of life in the greatest misery. Hideous atrocities came to light in 1968 when a government commission released a 5,000-page report documenting widespread corruption and sadism and the use of biological as well as conventional weapons to wipe out Indian tribes (deliberate spread of smallpox, tuberculosis, measles, etc.). (Chomsky and Herman, 1979, 127)

The Guarani were one of the first peoples contacted after Europeans arrived in South America around five hundred years ago. According to the NGO Survival for Tribal Peoples, Brazil's Guarani suffer at the hands of violent ranchers. For the Guarani, land is the origin of all life. Violent invasions by ranchers have devastated their territory and nearly all of their land has been stolen. Guarani children starve and their leaders have been assassinated. Hundreds of Guarani men, women, and children have committed suicide. In Brazil, there are today around forty-six thousand Guarani living in seven states, making them the country's most numerous tribe. Many others live in neighboring Paraguay, Bolivia, and Argentina. Today they are squeezed onto tiny patches of land surrounded by cattle ranches and vast fields of soya and sugar cane. Some have no land at all and live camped by roadsides (Survival for Tribal Peoples, 2012).

Only recently has the Brazilian government taken steps to protect the indigenous populations in the Amazon and often policies to promote economic development work at cross purposes to this goal, oftentimes assisting them in the displacement of the peoples who have inhabited the land for hundreds, if not thousands of years (Sponsel and Headland, 1996; MacMillan, 1995; Carvalho, 2000). The story of the Amazon is similar to the story of displacement and destruction of indigenous populations throughout the Americas, Africa, Australia, and everywhere else the more than three hundred and seventy million indigenous peoples reside in more than seventy countries.

In Northern Territory of Australia under an intervention by the state to protect the children of aboriginal people, 73 indigenous communities were taken over by the Australian army, police, and government officials. Collective control over Aboriginal lands—only handed back to indigenous peoples in 1976—was revoked, community assets frozen, and indigenous-run social programs closed down. Despite assertions that an "emergency" response was needed to tackle child abuse, rehabilitation programs for abused children were not put in place. Three major police investigations failed to back up allegations that Aboriginal children are systematically abused in their communities. "The Northern Territory has major deposits of other minerals, including aluminum and coal, many of them on Aboriginal lands. Since the Intervention, the Territory's government has allocated AU$14.4 million to expanding its mining industry" (Irving, 2011).

In India mining policies have overlooked the existence of the Adivasi (aboriginal) communities and the constitutional provision for the protection of their land and resources, the report notes. One estimate is that between 1950 and 1991 at least 2,600,000 people were displaced by mining projects of which only 25 percent received any resettlement. Among those displaced 52 percent belonged to the Scheduled Tribes. Indian Law automatically assumes all minerals found underground are state property (Sebastian, 2011).

In Ethiopia, a hydroelectric dam threatens the tribes of the Lower Omo River. The Lower Omo River in southwest Ethiopia is home to eight different tribes whose population is about two hundred thousand. The tribes have lived in this area for centuries and when the dam is completed it will destroy a fragile environment and the livelihoods of the tribes, which are closely linked to the river and its annual flood (Survival for Tribal Peoples, 2012).

Organizations like Survival for Tribal Peoples and Cultural Survival have been in the forefront of preventing the modern-day genocides as a result of state actions to promote economic development and the displacement of indigenous populations around the world.

The use of state violence is not restricted to indigenous minority populations. It extends to other ethnic minorities. In the experience of the United States, following the conquest and subjugation of Native American tribes, violence was directed at African populations who were brought here as slaves and at Hispanic populations who were inhabitants of conquered lands in the Southwest. Churchill and Vander Wall (1990) describe the efforts of the federal and state government in attempting to neutralize the efforts of what was perceived to be radical wings of the civil rights movement, in particular the Black Panthers. In some cases these efforts resulted in the use of violence in the form of assassination or instigating violence by other organized groups.

A recent report by United Nations Committee on the Elimination of Racial Discrimination documents the widespread abuse by police of people of color and minorities. They note that this abuse has increased with the increased powers assigned to police in the United States in the wake of the September 11, 2001, attack (Ritchie and Mogul, 2007). They also note that law enforcement officials in the United States enjoy impunity with respect to the use of excessive force against people of color since criminal investigations are rarely convened, charges are seldom brought, and convictions are rarely sought or obtained against officers responsible for such violations.

The pattern of targeting ethnic minorities for state violence is not unique to the United States but can be found in other countries throughout the world. For example, in Sri Lanka the military has targeted the Tamil Sinhalese populations. Amnesty International reports that government troops have caused the disappearances or deaths of, "at a minimum, thousands of civilians, including babies and elderly villagers" (Amnesty International, 1993, 2). Another case is Chad, which is made up of two hundred distinct ethnic groups and is split in terms of religion: approximately 44 percent are Muslim, 33 percent Christian, and 23 percent members of indigenous tribal religions. In Chad a commission established by President Derby concluded that approximately forty thousand people had been killed by previous regimes. But Amnesty International (1994a) reports that since taking office, the government under Derby carried out hundreds of extrajudicial executions and that security forces have been responsible for a number of massacres of unarmed men, women, and children.

One term that has developed in recent years to describe the use of state violence directed at minority populations is "ethnic cleansing." The term has been used to describe the state violence directed by agents of the Serbian government in the civil war that broke out with the breaking away of several regions of the former Yugoslavia from central government (Serbian) control. However, in the wars that broke up the former country, there were charges of "ethnic cleansing" in several of the former regions as ethnic minorities were pushed out or in some cases killed by government and militia forces to promote ethnic and in some cases religious homogeneity in the regions that eventually became independent in the wake of the civil war. This was the case for both sides in Croatia and Kosovo, though Western media focused on the practice of the Serbian government as they were promoting the breakup and engaged in combat with the former central government in Belgrade, Serbia.

Similar violent acts labeled ethnic cleansing occurred in the breakup of the former Soviet Union. In particular, in North and South Ossettia regions, which are part of the border with the new republic of Georgia and Russia, and Abkhazia, which is seeking independence from Georgia. The ethnic cleansing in Chechnya when the region attempted to break away from Russia led to forced expulsion of Russians from the region seeking autonomy. The war in Chechnya has continued on for more than twenty years.

Another example in which the violence persists after programs of ethnic cleansing is the case of Israel. Pappe (2006), an Israeli scholar, details the history of ethnic cleansing by Zionist forces who were creating a state that would be controlled by Jews (mostly new settlers in the aftermath of the Holocaust) in an area dominated by Palestinian Arabs who were under the control of various empires, the Ottoman and British. For more than fifty years the conflict has continued as a result of this ethnic cleansing. A major issue of the conflict is the "right of return" for Palestinians who were violently forced off their land beginning in 1947 and continuing today. Pappe describes many villages that were destroyed and erased from maps and the population driven out. In one case he describes the village of Sirin, which was occupied by the Israeli army in May 1948. The village of seven hundred residents composed of two Muslim clans and a small Christian community was an isolated agricultural settlement that dated back to the Ottoman period. The village owned the agricultural land collectively and shared in the harvest of its fruit trees.

> The villagers did not put up a fight. The Jewish troops gathered the Muslims—of both clans—and Christians together and ordered them to start crossing the River Jordan to other side. They then demolished the mosque, the church and the monastery, together with all the houses. Soon, all the trees in the bustans had withered away and died. Today, a cactus hedge surrounds the rubble that was Sirin. Jews never succeeded in repeating the success of the Palestinians in holding on to the tough soil in the valley, but the springs in the vicinity are still there—an eerie sight as they serve no one. (Pappe, 2006, 106)

More recently, in the Darfur region of Sudan there has been ethnic conflict between the Arab-dominated government of the north and the southwestern portion of Sudan or the Darfur region, which is dominated by a black African population. The conflict had been going on for hundreds of years but reached a peak in the 2003 when resistance groups in the Darfur region united. Militia groups, the Janjaweed, that had links to the government in the north carried out raids on civilians to terrorize and force them out of the territory. "The Janjaweed entered my school and caught some girls and raped them in the classrooms. I was raped by four men inside the school. When they left they told us they would take care of all us black people and clean Darfur for good" (Mullins and Rothe, 2008, 177). The death toll in South Sudan is estimated to be close to half a million with more than two million displaced. The president of Sudan, Omar Bashir, has been charged by the International Criminal Court with war crimes and crimes against humanity for the violence in the Darfur region.

The history of state violence in South Africa to control the black population (who compose more than 80 percent of the population) up until the end of white minority rule and the killings of almost one million people in Rwanda and Burundi between the Hutu and Tutsi are part of a pervasive pattern of state violence throughout the world, whereby violence is an instrument of the state employed to control ethnic minorities as they may pose a threat to the maintenance of the established order. In many of these cases the ethnic conflict is rooted in the legacy of colonial administration where the imperial power would empower one ethnic group to control another. After political independence the former dominant ethnic group will rule but oftentimes will use violence against the ethnic minority to maintain control.

This is the story of the ethnic conflict in Rwanda between the Hutu and Tutsi. Mullins and Rothe note that "the conflict between the Hutu and Tutsi was largely the product of the colonial system; largely the result of the administrative reforms initiated in 1926 by the Belgians which were crucial in shaping the existing ethnic relations. The Belgians explicitly used lineage conflicts to reinforce their control of the territory" (Mullins and Rothe, 2008, 103). The authors note that in many regions of Africa, the imperial power creates the ethnic stratification system by privileging specific groups, which they used in the lower levels of administration of the colonial regime. "By elevating certain ethnic groups over others, lines that were previously nonexistent or blurred were brought into sharp relief and given solidity. Political and economic competition and resentment began to simmer; even previously peaceful relations could easily deteriorate into open or latent hostility due to the new resource distribution" (Mullins and Rothe, 2008, 73). The ethnic stratification systems are often the product of imperial conquest and the establishment of colonial regime. Soon after political independence (although not necessarily economic independence since most of the valued assets are still controlled from outside the country by corporations from the former imperial power), conflicts along ethnic lines ignite and ethnic cleansing can be the result. Even in the imperial centers of empires, the ethnic conflicts and the ethnic stratification system are a product of the legacy of conquest where those who are at the bottom of the hierarchy are the populations that were conquered and in some cases enslaved and the ethnic group of the conquering group is at the top. In some cases, where the settler population is imported after conquest, the ethnic group of the settler population may be dominant. Look at the patterns of ethnic stratification in North, Central, and South America, Africa, and Asia and you will find this pattern of hierarchy. Unfortunately violence is often used to maintain this system that has its roots in a period of conquest.

Dissident Political Groups, Organized Labor, and Peasants

Other categories of targets of state violence are dissident political groups and organized labor and peasants who threaten the system of property ownership in a given country. Note that these categories are not distinct. For example, dissident political groups, organized labor, and peasant populations may also be composed of ethnic minorities. The state violence in South Africa, Guatemala, Indonesia, and Burundi fits this pattern. For example, Jenny Pearce (1982) reported that with regard to the assassinations conducted by or for the state in El Salvador, 69 percent were campesinos (farmers and farm laborers), 14 percent were workers, and 14 percent were students. She points out that the vast majority of workers murdered by death squads or the military were trade union leaders or union members. Campesinos in many cases had engaged in organized protests for better wages (Pearce, 1982).

In the United States, Churchill and Vander Wall (1990) find that a major focus of the Bureau of Investigation of the Treasury Department, the predecessor to the Federal Bureau of Investigation, was radical political movements. For example, these authors discuss the significance of the Slacker and Palmer raids as examples of this early activity by the bureau. Attorney General Thomas W. Gregory had seized upon the national war fever to act in concert with major financial supporters of the Democratic Party to make America safe for industry, crushing the radical opposition once and for all. The Slacker raids and similar broadly focused gambits were designed more than anything to intimidate the general public to a point where there was greatly diminished possibility of a popular radical resurgence after the war (20).

The United States does not illustrate the most severe cases of violence directed at dissident political groups. In Indonesia, the massive violence in the middle 1960s was targeted at members of the Indonesian Communist Party and its affiliated organizations: the trade unions, the women's organization (Gerwani), and the peasants' association (Barisan Tani Indonesia). Amnesty International (1983) observed that there was no set pattern to the killings that began during those years and claimed the lives of an estimated five hundred thousand Indonesians over a nine-month period. Nevertheless, certain features recurred. Everywhere local officials of the PKI (the Communist Party, the largest political party in Indonesia at the time) and its affiliated organizations were rounded up and shot. Amnesty International reported that often whole families were killed to eliminate the communist menace for all time.

The army initiated the first killings in nearly every province. In some areas the army was assisted by gangs of youths belonging to Ansor, an affiliate of the Nahdatul Ulama, a fundamentalist Muslim party. Amnesty International notes that in Java, Bali, and Sumatra, night after night for months on end local army commanders loaded lorries with captured PKI members—their names checked off against lists—and drove them to isolated spots for execution, usually by bullet or knife. The international agency reports that in the town of Kediri in Central Java, a PKI stronghold, some seven thousand PKI supporters are estimated to have been killed. In Banjuwangi in East Java, four thousand people were killed within a few days:

> As the purge accelerated in November 1965 headless bodies covered with red flags were floated down rivers aboard rafts and heads were placed upon bridges. Every day for several months riverside residents in Burabaya in East Java had to disentangle bodies that were caught on jetties. At one point so

many bodies from Kediri filled the Brantas river that the downstream town of Jombang lodged a formal protest complaining that plague might break out. In the small mill town of Batu so many were executed within the narrow confines of a small police courtyard that it was decided that it would be simpler to cover the piles of bodies with layers of cement rather than bury the victims. . . . In Bali, armed with machine guns, commandos scoured villages in groups of 25, in some cases executing the entire male population. . . . In one incident alone in the city of Medan, North Sumatra, some 10,500 prisoners were reportedly killed in the space of a few days. (Amnesty International, 1983)

Violence has continued throughout many of the seventeen thousand islands that make up Indonesia, the former Dutch colony, as they themselves seek independence.

Similar patterns of mass slaughter are found in other countries. In Kampuchea, under Khmer Rouge rule from 1975 to 1979, at least three hundred thousand persons were killed in a series of purges directed at counterrevolutionaries and other undesirable elements. In Guatemala the dramatic rise in political killings began with the presidency of Mendez Montenegro from 1966 to 1970. Estimates of the number of people who have been eliminated by the Guatemalan government are in the tens of thousands. In February 1981 Amnesty International issued a report stating that since President Lucas Garcia took office in July 1978 the organization had learned of the seizure without warrant and subsequent killing of some five thousand Guatemalans. The report disputed claims by successive governments that the death squads were not under official control. It concluded that there was no evidence of pro-government clandestine groups operating independently of government support. Citing testimony from recent defectors and from survivors of disappearances, Amnesty International (1983) stated that the links between the death squads and the authorities had been particularly blatant during the presidency of Lucas Garcia.

After Garcia came to power in the late 1970s a new death squad was formed by the government, Ejercito Secreto Anti-Communista (Secret Anti-Communist Army). Soon after it was formed, this group issued to the press a list of people it had sentenced to death. According to Amnesty International, the list included trade unionists, student leaders, lawyers, journalists, and academics. For example, Oliverio Castaneda, president of the Students' Association of the University of San Carlos, was murdered on a busy street corner in Guatemala City by heavily armed assailants as armed security officers watched. By the end of the year, Pedro Quevedo y Quevedo, secretary general of the trade union organizing at the Coca-Cola bottling plant, was murdered. Then Manuael Lopez Balan replaced the slain leader and in turn was knifed to death in Guatemala City the following spring. In May 1980 union activist Marlon Mendizabal was killed as he waited for a bus outside the plant. In June almost the entire leadership of the Central Nacional de Trabajadores, the trade union congress (which included several labor leaders at the Coca-Cola bottling plant), were kidnapped as they met to discuss funeral plans for still another union leader. Eyewitnesses recognized some of those carrying out the abduction as members of the official security forces; vehicles used in the abduction were official issue models, and the street was closed off to traffic by uniformed National Police officers, while approximately sixty plainclothes officers raided CNT headquarters. Various officials denied that the arrests had taken place, but the late minister of labour, Carlos Alarcon Monsanto, informed Amnesty International (1983) that those detained had subsequently been released. The fact is that none of the trade unionists has ever been seen again.

John Booth (1991) estimates that approximately 150,000 people were killed in Guatemala between 1982 and 1985. In a recent report on state violence in Guatemala, 34,363 killings and disappearances in Guatemala were identified as committed by the state and part of a deliberate government policy of extrajudicial killing from 1960 to 1996. As noted earlier, the vast majority of these killings occurred during the Garcia regime (Ball, Kobrak, and Spirer, 1999). In December 1996 the Guatemalan government and rebels of the National Revolutionary Unity of Guatemala (URNG) signed peace accords ending the civil war.

One case brought by survivors of this war centers around ten massacres in the Ixcán and Ixil regions of the Quiché and in Rabinal in Baja Verapaz. The survivors believe that Lucas Garcia and two other top military officers conspired to commit genocide against the indigenous peoples of Guatemala. The Guatemalan Truth Commission Report substantiates their claims. The report, which was an outcome of the 1996 Peace Accords, concluded that two hundred thousand unarmed civilians were murdered or disappeared and more than six hundred Mayan villages were completely destroyed during the thirty-six-year civil war. According to the report, government agents committed 97 percent of the atrocities.

The report also highlighted the role of the United States in supporting the Guatemalan military. According to the report "the United States government and U.S. private companies exercised pressure to maintain the country's unjust socioeconomic structure. In addition, the United States government, through its constituent structures, including the Central Intelligence Agency, lent direct and indirect support to some illegal state operations. On May 3, 2000, Guatemalans from around the country brought before the national court system an unprecedented case. They charged former dictator Romeo Lucas García and top officials of his 1978–1982 regime with genocide and crimes against humanity" (Guatemalan Historical Clarification Commission, 1999).

Amnesty International found that six years after the peace accords were signed in Guatemala, there had been an upsurge in death squad lynchings. According to the UN Human Rights Verification Mission (MINUGUA), 390 lynchings occurred between 1996 and 2001; in 97 percent of the cases, no one has been brought to justice (Amnesty International, 2002e).

The documented role of the United States in promoting assassinations in Guatemala goes back to the 1954 coup engineered by the United States. In 1997, the CIA released 1,400 pages of an estimated 100,000 pages of secret archives on the 1954 overthrow, "Operation PBSUCCESS" (Doyle and Kornbluh, 1997a). In the documents released are lists of persons identified by the CIA for assassinations including members of the communist party and "collaborators." The released documents note that as early as January 1952, CIA headquarters began compiling lists of individuals in Arbenz's government "to eliminate immediately in event of [a] successful anti-Communist coup." The list contained names of Arbenz government leaders, members of the Communist Party, and individuals "of tactical importance whose removal for psychological, organizational or others reasons is mandatory for the success of military action" (Haines, 1997). The CIA planning for assassination included budgeting, training programs, creation of hit teams, drafting of target lists of persons, and transfer of armaments. There was also a how-to guidebook on the art of political killing. The nineteen-page manual offers detailed descriptions of the procedures, instruments, and implementation of assassination. "The simplest local tools are often much the most efficient means of assassination," counsels the manual. "A hammer, axe, wrench, screw driver, fire poker, kitchen knife, lamp stand, or anything hard, heavy and handy will suffice." For an assassin using "edge weapons," the manual notes in cold clinical terms, "puncture wounds of the body cavity may not be reliable unless the heart is reached. . . . Absolute reliability is obtained by severing the spinal cord in the cervical region." The manual also notes that to provide plausible deniability, "no assassination instructions should ever be written or recorded." Murder, the drafters state, "is not morally justifiable," and "persons who are morally squeamish should not attempt it" (Doyle and Kornbluh, 1997a). Unfortunately, "Operation Success" had a deadly after-math. "After a small insurgency developed in the wake of the coup, Guatemala's military leaders developed and refined, with U.S. assistance, a massive counterinsurgency campaign that left tens of thousands massacred, maimed or missing" (Doyle and Kornbluh, 1997a).

Similar acts of state violence have occurred in other countries in Central and South America, many times with U.S. government support. El Salvador has had a particularly brutal history of state violence. In one event in El Salvador in 1932, National Guard members, the army, and paramilitary groups, with the collaboration of local landowners, carried out a massacre known as "La Matanza," in which they murdered at least ten thousand peasants in the western part of El Salvador in order to put down a rural insurrection (Betancur, 1993). The UN Truth Commission Report on El Salvador reported that in the most recent civil war, which killed more than seventy thousand people and lasted from 1981 to 1991, death squad activity killed more than eight hundred people. According to the report, the death squads, often operated by the military and supported by powerful businessmen, landowners, and some leading politicians, have long acted in El Salvador, and it was particularly concerned that the U.S. government tolerated the activities of Salvadoran exiles living in Miami who directly financed and indirectly helped run certain death squads (Betancur, 1993).

In 2005, *Newsweek* reported that Secretary of Defense Rumsfeld and the Pentagon were considering a strategy referred to as the "Salvador Option," which referred to the U.S.-sponsored death squads in El Salvador to combat leftists in the early 1980s (Barry and Hirsh, 2005). In September 2004 Counselor to the U.S. Ambassador for Iraqi Security Forces James Steele was assigned to work with a new elite Iraqi counterinsurgency unit known as the Special Police Commandos, formed under the operational control of Iraq's Interior Ministry. Previously from 1984 to 1986 then Col. Steele had led the U.S. Military Advisory Group in El Salvador, where he was responsible for developing special operating forces at brigade level during the height of the

conflict. Fuller reports that soon after the Steele appointment multiple victims of extrajudicial killings began turning up in 2005 around Baghdad and
Mosul (Fuller, 2005). Ralph McGehee, former CIA officer, created a list of
CIA-supported death squad activities in more than thirty-nine countries
around the world (McGehee, 1999).

For most of the deaths by the state, the principal targets were peasant
organizations, unions, and political dissidents. According to Amnesty International, Colombia is the world's most dangerous country for trade unionists.
Ninety-five percent of the roughly three thousand cases of assassination of
union members committed over the past thirty years remain unprosecuted
(Amnesty International, 2012). Colombia for many years has been a principal
recipient of U.S. military aid and assistance. Over the past ten years, the
United States has given more than six billion dollars in military aid and has
opened seven new military bases in the country to work with the Colombia
military in its battle with drug traffickers and a long-standing leftist insurgency movement, FARC (Suárez, 2009).

Women

Rape of women has long been a tactic of war. It was practiced by the Greeks
and Romans during their imperial period. The Vikings during the Middle
Ages raped as a spoil of war. At times, the military has organized brothels of
captured young women to service the soldiers, as occurred in Poland during
World War II. The Germans organized in Warsaw a wholesale official abduction of young girls from the Solec district and the streets of the suburb of
Czerniakov. An estimated 80 percent of the young women were arrested in
and outside their houses and sent to the hospital of Saint Lazare, where they
were examined by military doctors. After the examination for venereal diseases, healthy girls were placed in brothels to service the German soldiers
(Creel, 1944, 31). Similar accounts are reported for the Japanese in their
abduction of between fifty thousand to two hundred thousand young Korean,
Chinese, Taiwanese, and Filipina women, who were then forced to perform
the role of "comfort women" for Japanese troops (Soh, 2001). In December
2001, the Women's International War Crimes Tribunal at The Hague made
its final judgment and found that Japan is responsible under international law
for the internationally wrongful acts—the rapes and sexual slavery—committed by the Japanese army against Korean women and seeks restitution and
reparation for the women victimized by these crimes.

Rothe (2009) finds that rape was widespread in the conflicts in the Ivory
Coast, Central African Republic, Uganda, Democratic Republic of Congo,
and the Darfur region of Sudan. She notes that the use of sexual assault is an
orchestrated tactic of warfare. "Countless reports of the 'typical' elements of
genocidal rape have emerged: families being force to watch the rapes, gun
barrels being used as tools of sexual assault and the pattern of moving into a
neighborhood and raping every female found" (Rothe, 2009, 53). The following is testimony from a witness to the mass rapes that occurred in Darfur:

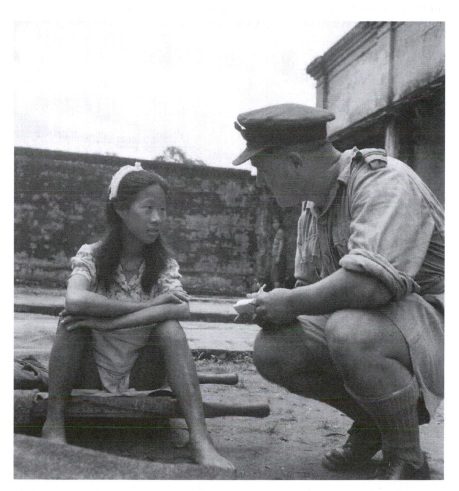

Figure 8.1.   A Chinese girl from one of the Japanese Army's "comfort batta-lions" sits on a stretcher, awaiting interrogation at a camp in Rangoon. Source: IWM Collections.

> If you look, you could see the evidence, even in the whitened skeletons. The legs bent and apart. A broken bottle, a rough branch, even a knife between them. Where the bodies were fresh, we saw what must have been semen pooled on and near the dead women and girls. There was always a lot of blood. Some male corpses had their genitals cut off, but many women and young girls had their breasts chopped off, and their genitals cut apart. They died in a position of total vulnerability, flat on their backs, with their legs bent and knees wide apart. It was the expressions on their dead faces that assaulted me the most, a frieze of shock, pain, and humiliation. (Rothe, 2009, 53)

In response to the sexual violence directed at women in the conflicts in Bosnia, Liberia, and the Congo, the United Nations Security Council adopted a resolution (1820) on June 19, 2008 that "*Demands* the immediate and complete cessation by all parties to armed conflict of all acts of sexual violence against civilians with immediate effect" (UN Security Council, 2008, 2). The Security Council noted that "women and girls are particularly targeted by the use of sexual violence, including as a tactic of war to humiliate, dominate, instill fear in, disperse and/or forcibly relocate civilian members of a community or ethnic group" (UN Security Council, 2008, 1).

One recent report documented conflict-related sexual violence in fifty-one countries in Africa, the Americas, Asia, Europe, and the Middle East that have experienced armed conflict over the past twenty years (Bastick, Grimm, and Kunz, 2007). In many conflicts, indigenous people or people from specific population groups are targeted for sexual violence based upon their ethnicity. The perpetrators of sexual violence in armed conflict include members of official armed and security forces, paramilitary groups, nonstate armed groups, humanitarian and peacekeeping personnel, and civilians. The authors note that sexual violence is used to punish or humiliate an enemy group and in situations where a person or persons are targeted in the knowledge that such abuse will have a broad impact on terrorizing the population.

Not all victims are females, although most of the cases documented appear to be women and young girls. Women are particularly targeted because the sexual violence is intended to humiliate the victim's families and communities, especially the men who are shamed for failing to protect "their" women. The sexual violence is used as a means of destroying family and community structures, most overtly when armed groups commit public rapes in front of the community, force family members to witness each other's rape, or even force people to commit acts of sexual violence against their own family members. The sexual violence can also serve to affirm aggression and brutality of the armed forces and groups and is also used as a "morale booster" or a "reward for bravery" (Bastick, Grimm, and Kunz, 2007).

The report lists twenty countries in Africa where sexual violence was widespread as a result of civil and interstate warfare. This has contributed to the HIV pandemic on the continent.

> The Democratic Republic of the Congo since its independence in 1960 has endured a number of conflicts over access to natural resources. After the overthrown of the Mobutu regime in 1997 more than 3.8 million people have died in the conflict. Sexual violence has been committed by all parties to the conflict. The motives of the perpetrators include revenge for previous sexual violence, organized rape by troops as a "morale booster," and ethnic cleansing. Ritualised rape is also committed by the belief among combatants that the rape of a virgin conveys magical powers and invincibility. The number of victims are the thousands. The rapes in the DRC were particularly brutal often times includes "public rape in front of the family and the community, forced rape between victims, the introduction of objects into the victims' cavities, pouring melted rubber into women's vaginas, shooting women in the vagina and inducing abortion using sharp objects." (Bastick, Grimm, and Kunz, 2007, 42).

Rape by both the Ethiopian and Eritrea governments was committed by both sides in the thirty-two-year-old war (Bastick, Grimm, and Kunz, 2007). In the fourteen-year war in Liberia beginning in 1989 an estimated 40 percent of the population was affected by sexual violence (Bastick, Grimm, and Kunz, 2007). In Rwanda the estimate of the number of rapes that occurred during the four-month period in 1994 of the genocide is between 15,700 to 500,000 victims (United Nations Commission on Human Rights, 1996).

The report lists six countries in the Americas where there are documented cases of sexual violence. In Colombia in its more than forty-year civil war, Amnesty International has documented how government and paramilitary forces have used counterinsurgency tactics involving sexual violence, including sexual slavery, forced prostitution, sexual mutilation, and rape, to punish communities in rebel-controlled territory for allegedly supporting rebels (Bastick, Grimm, and Kunz, 2007). In Guatemala, the Commission for Historical Clarification's investigations found that acts of sexual violence including extremely cruel forms of sexual violence involving raping and killing orgies organized by soldiers were an integral part of the military's counterinsurgency strategy (Bastick, Grimm, and Kunz, 2007). In Haiti during the period of military rule from 1991 to 1994 "political rape" was a common practice. Those who were believed to be Aristide supporters were attacked at night in their houses by masked men (sometimes in uniform) and women were raped because of the alleged political activity of their husbands (Bastick, Grimm, and Kunz, 2007). Eight countries are listed in Asia that have documented cases of sexual violence as a result of warfare. In Afghanistan in the post-Taliban after the U.S. invasion period, rape as a tactic of warfare continues. Often women who participate in public life are targeted. Women who report rape risk being accused of adultery and even fined, imprisoned, or murdered in honor killings by family members. In Myanmar (formerly called Burma) soon after becoming independent from Britain in 1948, a civil war broke out. The conflict between the military government and ethnic insurgency groups in the provinces of Shan, Karen, Karenni, Rakhine, Mon, and Chin, among others, has been ongoing and continues today.

> The next day on June 11, 2002 Nan Bway Poung was released. After she arrived back home she told her husband and her father-in-law that about 20 Burmese soldiers at Pah Klaw Hta SPDC troops' camp raped her. She said, "I was raped by the column commander Captain Ye Htut first, then he ordered his soldiers to rape me." Captain Ye Htut also said to his soldiers, "You all must rape that woman; those who refuse to rape will be shot and killed." Nan Bway Poung was very ashamed and said, "I am not willing to live in this world anymore." Then before anybody noticed, she drank poison and committed suicide the same evening she arrived back. (The Karen Women's Organization, 2004)

In six European countries during the twenty-year period of study, sexual violence was documented as a result of the warfare within these countries (Bastick, Grimm, and Kunz, 2007). In the civil war in the former Yugoslavia, rape was used systematically as an instrument of war and as a strategy of ethnic cleansing or genocide. Thousands of women were raped, in some cases in camps that were established to rape and impregnate women to give birth to children claimed by the ethnic groups of the rapist. Sexual violence was committed against women of all ethnicities; however, Bosnian Muslim women were particularly targeted. In Georgia, since independence in 1991, there has been violence and civil war related to the secessionist aspirations of the regions of Abkhazia and South Ossetia. Rape was systematic and widespread in the Abkhazian conflict as a means of ethnic cleansing (Bastick, Grimm, and Kunz, 2007).

Rape in the Military

Not only do civilians experience rape during warfare, but also women who serve in the armed forces experience sexual violence at an alarming rate.

> It was the 1991 convention of the Tailhook Association, a group of retired and active naval aviators. Coughlin, a helicopter pilot and admiral's aide, hurtled down a gantlet of groping, poking and pawing officers, who grabbed her breasts and tried to remove her panties. "Help me," she implored a pilot, who then molested her too. "It was the most frightened I've ever been in my life," Coughlin, the daughter of a retired navy aviator, told *The Washington Post* last week. "I thought, 'I have no control over these guys. I'm going to be gang-raped.'" (*Newsweek*, 1992)

Eighty-three women were sexually assaulted at this convention that was attended by more than four thousand Navy and Marine Corp aviation servicemen in Las Vegas. The term "military sexual trauma" (MST) was developed when the Veterans Health Care Act of 1992 was passed by Congress in the wake of the scandal.

One study of 125,729 Afghanistan and Iraq veterans found that 15.1 percent of women and 0.7 percent of men reported MST when screened at a VA facility (Kimerling, Street, and Pavao, 2010). Another study of 33,259 women and 540,381 men, found 19.5 percent and 1.2 percent, respectively, reported MST (Kimerling, Street, Gima, and Smith, 2008). Van Pelt reports that the "studies conducted by the Government Accountability Office in 2007 indicated that 25% to 50% of all military women experienced some type of sexual harassment, and 20% experienced overt sexual assault during military service" (Van Pelt, 2011).

The U.S. Department of Defense estimates that more than nineteen thousand service members were raped or sexually assaulted in 2010. This estimate is believed to be very conservative due to a culture within the military that often leads to retaliation and minimal prosecution. It is estimated that only 13.5 percent of the victims report the rape (Speier, 2011). According to U.S. Congresswomen Jackie Speier, "the Pentagon has largely ignored the recommendations of 18 reports on sexual assault and rape in the military over the past 16 years. As a result, the problem is now worse than ever" (Speier, 2011, F-3). Even in the military academies where the military leadership is trained, there has been a significant increase. In a 2011 report on sexual assault in the military academies, the number of reported cases of sexual assault more than doubled from twenty-eight cases in 2008 to sixty-two cases in 2010 (U.S. Department of Defense, 2011). In March 2012 lawyers for eight current and former members of the U.S. military filed a federal lawsuit charging that during their military service they were raped, assaulted, or harassed and when they reported it to their military superiors suffered retaliation (Associated Press/*NY Daily News*, 2012).

Children

Tragically, another group that has been systematically targeted for state violence in the modern world is children. In a recent report of the Special Representative of the Secretary-General for Children and Armed Conflict, it found that in the last decade, two million children have been killed in situations of armed conflict, while six million children have been permanently disabled or injured (U.N. Special Representative of the Secretary-General for Children and Armed Conflict, 2005). The report also notes that more than 250,000 children continue to be exploited as child soldiers and tens of thousands of girls are being subjected to rape and other forms of sexual violence. They found that child abductions are becoming more systematic and widespread. Since 2003, over fourteen million children have been forcibly displaced within and outside their home countries and between eight thousand and ten thousand children are killed or maimed every year as a result of landmines.

The forced conscription of children as soldiers is one particular area of state violence. According to Amnesty International, Worldwide, hundreds of thousands of children are recruited into government armed forces, paramilitaries, civil militia, and a variety of other armed groups (Amnesty International, 2012). Sometimes they are abducted at school, on the streets, or at home. Some may enlist "voluntarily" because they see few alternatives.

For example, according to UN figures in 2007, between seven thousand and ten thousand children may have been used as fighters or associated with Chadian and Sudanese armed opposition groups and the Chadian army (United Nations, 2007). Liberian leader Charles Taylor gave young boys their own fighting unit called Small Boy Unit (Frankel et al., 1995). A UNICEF worker in Liberia, Esther Guluma, states that children make more brutal fighters because they haven't developed a sense of judgment (Frankel et al., 1995, 45). The authors note that in Mozambique children fought on both sides of the civil war. Save the Children estimated that the average age for rebel leader Renamo's recruits in one region was eleven. Children are often terrorized to commit acts of violence. Renamo's commanders first terrorized the boys—often by hanging them upside-down from trees. They forced many to shoot or slit the throats of their parents (Frankel et al., 1995, 45).

Drugs are also used to pump up the youth for battle. Before battle in Liberia children were given Valium tablets to prepare them for battle. Amphetamines and marijuana are also mentioned as drugs used to prepare children for combat. The children who are recruited are poor. They are enticed by ownership of a weapon, new clothes (uniform), three meals a day, and medical care. In Sierra Leone, both the government and the rebel forces forced children as young as seven years old into military service. A similar pattern is found in Burundi (Amnesty International, 2002d).

The most recent report of the Secretary-General's Special Representative for Children and Armed Conflict indicated that were sixteen different armies and insurgent groups in conflicts from the Philippines and Myanmar to Darfur, the Democratic Republic of the Congo (DRC), and Colombia that have recruited or used child soldiers for at least the past five years (UN General Assembly Security Council, 2010). Just recently, the International Criminal

Court convicted a Congolese warlord, Thomas Lubanga, on March 14, 2012, of using child soldiers. This verdict was hailed as a legal landmark in the fight against impunity for the world's most serious crimes. It is the first judgment in the court's ten-year history that may serve as a deterrent to the use of children in armies.

In addition to child victimization during warfare, poor and homeless children can also be victims of violence committed by police. For example, in Brazil, a Parliamentary Commission of Inquiry reported that some seven thousand homeless children had been killed during the previous four years (Amnesty International, 1993). A Brazilian Parliamentary Commission report indicated that many children had been killed by death squads composed of off-duty police officers. In the first six months of 1992, 667 children and adolescents were killed in the states of São Paulo and Rio de Janeiro. Between 1988 and 1990, federal police reported that 4,611 children (82 percent of them black) had been killed.

The problem is that homeless children were engaging in begging and petty thievery in several large cities in Brazil. The begging and stealing interfered with the businesses of the shopkeepers in certain areas. The solution was to remove the children through wholesale abductions and executions. The children come from peasant families and/or indigenous populations who have been economically displaced as land ownership becomes more concentrated and there is an increasing shift to cash crops for the world export market. Street children have also been killed by police officers in Guatemala City and in other countries in Central and South America.

However, Colombia may lead the world in child murders. In Bogota, there are between five thousand and ten thousand street children. UNICEF claims there are more street children in this city than any other in South America. A report by Human Rights Watch/Americas noted that 2,190 children under the age of eighteen were murdered in Colombia in 1993, six children murdered per day. The report concluded that Colombia has the highest child murder rate in the world (Luft, 1995).

Another particular area of state violence that particularly affects children is the use of economic sanctions as a means to punish or topple government. The strategy has been used for thousands of years. The laying of a siege of a town, village, or nation was a way to force a people to capitulate through cutting off necessary supplies to sustain human life. In the twentieth and twenty-first centuries, economic sanctions were often the first stage in warfare that often led to the use of more conventionally understood means of warfare.

Since the 1990s with the fall of the Soviet Union, the United States through its alliances have used economic sanctions in Iraq, the Yugoslav federation of Serbia and Montenegro, Libya, and Haiti, all having a significant loss of life, especially to children and the elderly. Prior to this period the United States had an economic embargo against Nicaragua in the 1980s and Chile after the election of Allende to the point of the U.S.-assisted military overthrow. The longest running economic embargo by the United States is the case of Cuba, which has been in effect since 1961 and continues as of 2012. The effect of this economic embargo has been much less deadly because of a highly organized food distribution system and universally access-ible and highly skilled public medical care system (Garfield, Devin, and Fausey, 1995).

The impact of the embargo of Serbia and Montenegro was that the overall death rates reportedly increased by 10 percent and hospital mortality is re-ported to have increased by 30 percent (Garfield, Devin, and Fausey, 1995). In the early 1990s, the embargo against Haiti led to a rise from 5 percent to 23 percent in malnourished children in rural areas and deaths among children aged one to four years rose from ten to eighteen per one thousand (Garfield, Devin, and Fausey, 1995).

However, of recent cases, the most deadly case of economic sanctions was in the case of Iraq. The UN National Security Council authorized the embargo proposed by the United States and its allies that began four days after Iraq invaded Kuwait. The economic sanctions were a near total finan-cial and trade embargo. The ban, which did not include medicines and "in humanitarian circumstances" foodstuffs, nevertheless affected the supply of these vital items as a result of the difficulty of exporters getting licenses to export products to Iraq. Companies that requested permission to export had to make application to individual UN member states who then sent the appli-cation to the UN Sanction Committee. Decisions of the committee were secret and only one committee member voting against the request was suffi-cient to block the license. Anything that could be interpreted to be used for military purposes would be denied export; this included clothing, pencils, paper, tractors, among other widely interpreted items that could be used for military purposes. If the Committee granted approval for the export license, it was then sent back to the governing authorities of the country of export who then would grant permission. However, the items shipped were subject to inspection and impoundment if officials of that country determined that there were violations of the license. Lastly, because there were restrictions on exports from Iraq, it was difficult for Iraq to fund necessary imports.

According to the executive director of UNICEF, if the trend or reductions in child mortality that were occurring the 1980s had continued into the 1990s, there would have been an estimated half million fewer deaths of children under five. The rate at which children were dying in 1999 was two times the rate that occurred ten years before at the end of the 1980s (UNICEF, 1999). An article printed in *Lancet*, one of the oldest and best known medical journals, reported that infant mortality rose from 47 per 1,000 live births during 1984–1989 to 108 per 1,000 in 1994–1999, and under-five mortality rose from 56 to 131 per 1,000 live births (Ali and Shah, 2000). Citing information on maternal and child mortality rates collected by UNICEF, Professor Richard Garfield (1999) conservatively estimates that between 1991 and 1998, the number of excess deaths in Iraq among children under age five is approximately 106,000.

Lesley Stahl interviewed Secretary of State Madeleine Albright on May 12, 1996, during the network newsmagazine *60 Minutes* about the impact of U.S. sanctions against Iraq. Stahl stated to Albright, "We have heard that a half million children have died. I mean, that's more children than died in

Hiroshima. And, you know, is the price worth it?" Secretary of State Madeleine Albright replied, "I think this is a very hard choice, but the price—we think the price is worth it" (Mahajan, 2001).

Children are also victims of state violence because of their political activity. The killing of children by state security forces in South Africa during the turbulent times of political unrest directed at the system of apartheid is an example of this. During the latter half of the 1970s, organized school boycotts in the black townships were often responded to with violence by the state security forces. The victims of this violence were primarily school-age children who were participants in the boycotts. In Guatemala, the national police in April 1992 entered two secondary schools whose students were involved in political demonstrations and arrested 170 students; they later tortured many of those arrested (Amnesty International, 1993).

AGENTS OF STATE VIOLENCE

Police and Military

Who commits these acts of violence on behalf of the state? In most cases it is military or government police forces. In South Africa both the police and the military were regularly involved in state violence to control the black minority population. A three-year study of torture under detention by the Institute of Criminology of the University of Cape Town in the middle 1970s concluded that the vast majority of people held were physically abused and that the average South African security detainee was subjected to ten different forms of coercion, both physical and psychological (Herman and O'Sullivan, 1989). D. Jonathan Gluckman, at the time South Africa's most prominent independent pathologist and a strong supporter of the de Klerk regime, contends that the police were totally out of control and were killing at least one black suspect a week. Gluckman examined the bodies of two hundred victims of police torture during a two-year period. He is convinced that the police killed 90 percent of these people. According to a 1993 Amnesty International report:

> Dr. Gluckman pointed specifically to the case of 19 year-old Simon Mthimkulu who died after police arrested him in Sebokeng Township on July 14, 1992. A friend arrested with Mthimkulu, himself beaten and then released, later stated that he saw officers viciously kick and beat Simon and drop a huge rock on his rib cage. Police had told Simon's mother that they had released the youth. However, two days later, she found her son's body at a mortuary. His face was caked in blood. Dr. Gluckman performed a post-mortem examination on the dead youth and said his own findings were entirely consistent with the witness's account. South Africa's Ministry of Law and Order denied any police responsibility for any deaths in detention, suggesting that suicide was responsible for the high number of deaths in police custody. (Amnesty International, 1993, 1)

In 1988 the Independent Board of Inquiry into Informal Repression (IBIIR) corroborated the testimony of Butana Nofomela, a disaffected former police-man who claimed to have been for years part of an assassination squad. A former police captain, Dirk Coetzz, commanded Nofomela and others in death squads known as Askaris. These officially sanctioned groups targeted in particular African National Congress members and citizens suspected of being dissidents or sympathizers, both black and white. In the early 1990s, the African National Congress claimed that police had been involved in the killings of more than eleven thousand people since 1990 (Associated Press, 1994).

Uganda, mentioned earlier, is another extreme case of the state's use of the military and police to kill civilians. Amnesty International has reported that systematic and deliberate killings by government forces began in the first month of President Idi Amin's military government in 1971. The prac-tice became thereafter institutionalized as a means of eliminating those be-lieved to be opponents of the regime.

> Those arrested were often bundled into the back or trunk of a security forces vehicle and taken to a military barracks, the Bureau of State Research, the Public Safety Unit, or to a secret safe house under State Research Control. . . . . Prisoners were arrested and detained without legal formalities or judicial pro-cesses, held incommunicado and often without official records. . . . Nearly all prisoners were severely tortured; most either died under torture or were killed in other ways. . . . Prisoners were sometimes ordered at gunpoint to kill other prisoners. In this method of execution prisoners were lined up; one was given a hammer and ordered to beat another prisoner to death with it; he in turn was then killed by another prisoner, and so on, with the last survivor of the group being shot by a prison guard. . . . Prisoners' bodies were frequently dumped in rivers or forests. Occasionally, the bodies (usually mutilated) were returned to relatives by security officers on payment of large bribes. (Amnesty Interna-tional, 1978, 6–7)

During the entire period of President Amin's government, no security official was ever charged, fairly tried, convicted, or punished for any act of arbitrary arrest, illegal detention, torture, or murder.

The case of Argentina after the 1976 military coup is similar. Regional commanders were placed in charge of anti-subversive operations throughout the country. Amnesty International reports that typically the victims were dragged from their homes in the evening by those identifying themselves as members of the police or armed forces. Between the coup in 1976 and 1979, at least six thousand persons disappeared, often in gruesome ways. As Am-nesty International found, prisoners were forced to remain in their cells in silence. Around 5:00 in the evening each Wednesday, prisoners were se-lected for transfer. They were each led alone to the infirmary just as they were, dressed or not, whether in hot or cold weather. At the infirmary they were given an injection, they were told, because hygiene conditions in the camps to which they were going were so poor. In reality they were given sedatives. Then they were taken by lorry to the Aeroparque (a military air-field) in Buenos Aires and put on a Fokker airplane belonging to the navy's multipurpose air squadron. From there they were flown southward out to sea to a point where the Gulf Stream would ensure the disappearance of the bodies. Then the prisoners were thrown alive out of the plane (Amnesty International, 1983, 57). These claims by Amnesty International were later confirmed by Captain Adolfo Scilingo of the Argentine military, who stated before a federal court in Argentina that he and fellow officers threw as many as two thousand drugged, nude prisoners into the Atlantic Ocean from naval planes (Associated Press, 1995).

Amnesty International recently expressed grave concern regarding the use of U.S. funds to fight the drug war in Colombia by funding state violence. Much of this money has gone to the military and police, who have conducted an anti-subversive campaign in the cities and countryside. Amnesty International contends that more than 70 percent of the twenty thousand political murders since 1986 in Colombia were committed by army personnel or backed by the military. In many cases, the killings are directed at political parties deemed to be threatening to the interests of the military. According to Amnesty International more than 1,500 members and supporters of the Patriotic Union (UP) have been killed since the political party's inception in 1985. Most of the dead are peasants, who are killed in the military's attempt to neutralize guerrilla forces in the countryside. Amnesty International cites one example of the state violence conducted by the military against peasants in the countryside: "In October, 1993 . . . there was a massacre in El Bosque, Riofrio, Valle del Cauca department. Some 25 Colombian troops appeared early in the morning and by mid-day had taken 13 people from their homes, tortured and killed them. They raped and killed four women; two babies and several children were orphaned" (Amnesty International, 1994b, 3).

Stewart (1994) estimates that in 1993 the murder rate in Colombia was twenty-eight thousand a year, more than in the United States, whose population is eight times the size. She cites the findings of the Andean Commission of Jurists that 56 percent of the political killings (excluding combat) where the killer could be identified in the first nine months of 1993 were carried out by government forces. Stewart contends that Colombia's political death toll is approximately eleven a day. She claims that each year more people die in Colombia than in the entire seventeen-year reign of General Pinochet in Chile. As noted previously, the United States has been the major funder of the military in its war against the drug trade and the leftist rebels. Unfortunately, this often means a war against the Colombian people, who pose a threat to the established rule of the elite in Colombia. In a report by the UN Special Rapporteur on extrajudicial, summary, or arbitrary executions, Philip Alston describes the practice of unlawful killings of civilians staged by the security forces to look like lawful killings in combat by leftist guerrillas or criminals as "Falsos positivos" or false positives: "In some cases, civilian victims are lured under false pretenses—usually with the promise of a job— by a paid 'recruiter' (a civilian, demobilized armed group member or former soldier) to a remote location. Once there, victims are killed by members of the military, often within a matter of hours or days of when they were last seen by family members" (Alston, 2010).

Military forces are also agents of state violence in the process of invading a foreign country and engaging in killing civilians and military of the enemy. The major wars of the twentieth century are examples of the tremendous levels of state violence. Since World War II, however, there is no country that has been more involved in military invasions outside its borders than the United States. The United States has been either directly or (especially more recently) indirectly involved in more than sixty wars since World War II (Blum, 2000). Frappier (1983) contends that just in the period from 1946 to 1975, during a time of the United States being the dominant world power immediately after World War II, there were 215 instances in which U.S. armed forces were used as a political instrument. The most recent U.S. war (the War on Terror), which is the longest in U.S. history, a more-than-ten-year war, has killed more than 225,000 people, mostly civilians, in Afghanistan, Iraq, and Pakistan (Watson Institute for International Studies, 2011).

Prior to World War II U.S. military activity was confined principally to the Western Hemisphere, its principal sphere of political and economic influence at the time. Frappier (1983) notes that prior to World War II, for the purpose of protecting American lives and property and maintaining order, the United States used armed forces in: Argentina (1833), Peru (1835–1836), Argentina (1852–1853), Nicaragua (1853–1853, 1857), Uruguay (1858), Paraguay (1859), Mexico (1859), Colombia (1860), Panama (1865), Mexico (1866), Nicaragua (1867), Uruguay (1868), Colombia (1868, 1873), Mexico (1873), Panama (1885), Haiti (1888), Argentina (1890), Haiti (1891), Chile (1891), Brazil (1894), Nicaragua (1894), Colombia (1895), Nicaragua (1896, 1898–1899), Colombia (1901–1902), Honduras (1903), Dominican Republic (1903–1904), Panama (1903–1914), Cuba (1906–1909), Honduras (1907), Nicaragua (1910), Honduras (1911–1912), Panama (1912), Cuba (1912), Nicaragua (1912–1925), Mexico (1913–1919), Haiti (1914–1934), Dominican Republic (1914, 1916–1924), Cuba (1917–1922), Panama (1918–1921), Honduras (1919), Guatemala (1920), Honduras (1924–1925), Panama (1925), Nicaragua (1926–1933), and Cuba (1933) (4).

After World War II the U.S. sphere of economic and political dominance expanded throughout the world; today we have more than eight hundred military bases that encircle the globe and a fleet of war ships in every major body of water throughout the world. In one analysis, bases were listed in sixty-one countries and territories around the world (*Monthly Review*, 2002). Most recently the pattern is that after each U.S. military engagement, new bases are established in the region of the military engagement. This is certainly the case in the Middle East where many new bases were developed during the Gulf War and the wars in Afghanistan, Iraq, and Pakistan. The irony is that it is alleged that the attack on the World Trade Center that precipitated the U.S. attack on Afghanistan was in response to the increasing military occupation by the United States in the Middle East and by the development of airbases in Saudi Arabia that developed after the U.S. and Britain's war with Iraq that continues to this day. Johnson (2004) referred to the United States as an empire of military bases.

At any given time, there are numerous ongoing wars occurring around the globe that annually cost thousands of civilian lives. The average annual number of major armed conflicts around the world for the twenty-first century is sixteen; the range is fourteen to nineteen conflicts per year. In the most recent yearbook of the Stockholm International Peace Institute, the institute lists fourteen conflicts: Rwanda, Somalia, Uganda, Colombia, Peru, United

States, Afghanistan, India, Myanmar, Pakistan, Philippines, Iraq, Israel (Palestinian territories), and Turkey (Kurdistan) (Stockholm International Peace Research Institute, 2011). The number of armed conflicts is down from twenty-seven reported by the institute in 1999.

A second calculation of the number of armed conflicts, which builds upon the Stockholm institute calculation but includes conflicts of lesser scale, identifies twenty-four active armed conflicts occurring in 2010 (Ploughshares, 2011). They list additional conflicts in Yemen, Algeria, Chad, Democratic Republic of the Congo, Kenya, Nigeria, Somalia, Sudan, South Sudan-Darfur, Thailand, and Russia. Ploughshares defines an armed combat as one that involves the armed forces of at least one state (or one or more armed factions seeking to gain control of all or part of the state), and in which at least one thousand people have been killed by the fighting during the course of the conflict. They noted that the total number of armed conflicts was lower than the previous year by four; the conflicts in Uganda, Nepal, Burundi, and Sri Lanka were deemed to be over. Three quarters of the conflicts are currently in Africa and Asia (Ploughshares, 2011). From 1987 until 2010, the number of armed conflicts has declined from thirty-nine to twenty-four. For 2010, almost half of the conflicts were in countries that are classified as low on the Human Development Index and most of the conflicts were internal wars over resources that are valued on the world market. Many of these conflicts are supported by the major powers in the United States through the sale and funding of weapons under military aid programs.

The United States is the largest spender in terms of military spending in the world, accounting for approximately 46 percent of total world military spending (Ploughshares, 2011). This is more than the combined military spending of the next twenty-four countries. From 2002 to 2009, $310 billion worth of arms were delivered to countries around the globe; 61 percent went to underdeveloped countries. The five permanent members of the UN Security Council, some of the wealthiest countries, accounted for 71 percent of the deliveries of arms (Ploughshares, 2011). The United States delivers more weapons to the rest of the world, and especially poorer countries, than any other country. The United States also has the most powerful military in the world and its reach is global and is involved directly or indirectly in the vast majority of the wars occurring in the post–World War II era.

The U.S. military has since 1946 trained many members of foreign military and police in state violence. The U.S. Army School of the Americas (SOA) was established in 1946 in Panama. Since the Panama Canal Treaty, the school has moved to Fort Benning, Georgia. At the time of the move, the Panamanian newspaper *La Prensa* referred to SOA as the School of Assassins. President Jorge Illueca of Panama called it the biggest base for destabilization in Latin America (Imerman, 1994). In response to increasing public protests, the school's name was changed to the Western Hemisphere Institute for Security Cooperation.

According to Chomsky and Herman (1979), by the mid-1970s, more than two hundred thousand Latin American military personnel had been trained in the United States, and since 1949, more than thirty-five thousand Latin American officers have trained in the School for the Americas alone. Herman (1987, 14) notes that altogether between 1950 and 1987, the United States trained more than 500,000 military and more than 7,500 police personnel from eighty-five countries. He also notes that between 1950 and 1979, U.S. military aid programs transferred $107.3 billion in arms and ammunition to various U.S. client states, in addition to some $121 billion in arms sales. The vast majority of these weapons and training programs are used in internal conflicts and social control within these countries.

During 1993 alone, approximately two thousand soldiers from Latin American and Caribbean countries were trained in low intensity conflict (LIC). According to Imerman (1994, 13), LIC aims to maintain U.S. military influence south of our borders without using (or losing) large numbers of U.S. troops. Instead, soldiers from Latin America and the Caribbean are trained in dirty little war techniques by U.S. personnel. Imerman points out that consistently those countries having the worst human rights records and those where the vast impoverished minorities have no political representation have the most graduates of this school.

An example of this is El Salvador. On March 15, 1993, the UN commission that studied human rights violations in El Salvador released its findings. In comparing the list of individuals involved in assassinations and massacres of citizens, the SOA Watch group and Witness for Peace discovered that forty-six U.S. School of Americas graduates were implicated (Imerman, 1994). SOA Watch found that often those military personnel who had received the most training at SOA had committed the worst atrocities. For example, of the three officers cited in the assassination of Archbishop Oscar Romero of San Salvador on March 24, 1980, two were SOA graduates. Of the five officers cited in the murder and rape of three U.S. nuns and a Catholic layworker, three were SOA graduates. Of the twelve officers cited in the El Mozote Massacre, December 1991, where several hundred unarmed civilians were killed and their corpses mutilated and burned, ten were SOA graduates. SOA Watch (2002) claims that this is a pattern that is repeated throughout Latin America. SOA Watch notes that currently, Colombia, with more than ten thousand troops trained at the SOA, is the school's largest customer. Not surprisingly, Colombia currently has the worst human rights record in all of Latin America.

National and International Secret Police

Besides the military and the domestic police force, foreign secret police are involved in violence. Roebuck and Weeber (1978, 82) note that evidence from Senate investigating committees has shown, for example, that over a twenty-year period, one government agency—the CIA—was involved in more than nine hundred foreign interventions, including paramilitary operations, surreptitious manipulation of foreign governments, and assassinations.

A major program of assassinations orchestrated by the CIA was Operation Phoenix. William Colby, who was later to become head of that agency, directed this program. The program was formed to incarcerate and assassinate members of the Viet Cong and the National Liberation Front. Members of the program engaged in massive arrests, murder, and torture of thousands of Vietnamese citizens. Chomsky and Herman (1979) report that more than forty thousand civilians were murdered between 1968 and 1971 as part of this program. Other secret police or spy networks by other governments (Libyan, Iranian, French, British, or Russian) have also been involved in assassinations overseas. However, since World War II, the scale of activity of these foreign police forces is dwarfed by the documented activities of the U.S. government through the CIA (Blum, 1988).

Savak, the secret police that operated during the rule of Reza Pahlevi, the former shah of Iran, along with the Iranian military, were involved in widespread murder and torture of dissidents. After the United States and Great Britain engineered a coup overthrowing the Mossadegh regime in 1953, the U.S. CIA and military trained Savak at the Marine base at Quantico and CIA headquarters in Langley, Virginia, and exported over \$18 billion worth of weapons to Iran over the next twenty years. Simon and Eitzen (1993) report that while the shah was in power, close to 1,500 Iranians were arrested monthly. On one day, June 5, 1963, Savak and the shah's army allegedly killed as many as 6,000 citizens. Chomsky and Herman (1979) report that political prisoners (i.e., those arrested and incarcerated because they disagreed with government policy) numbered as high as 100,000 each year in Iran. Amnesty International stated that twenty years after the CIA coup, Iran had the highest rate of death penalties in the world and a brutal record of torture of political prisoners. While the shah was in power, Amnesty International reported that no country in the world had a worse record in human rights than Iran. Since the overthrow of the shah, the Khomeini regime has continued a pattern of violence directed at religious minority populations and groups, which were perceived to pose a political threat to the government.

Another case in which the CIA has been implicated in assisting in state violence is Operation Condor. According to Herman (1982) in the latter half of the 1970s, six South American countries—Argentina, Bolivia, Brazil, Chile, Paraguay, and Uruguay—began a joint monitoring and assassination program of dissident refugees in each other's countries. A recently released document, a cable sent by U.S. Ambassador to Paraguay White to the Secretary of State Cyrus Vance, discussed the coordinated activity of intelligence agencies of the Southern Cone and its use of U.S. communication systems that operated from Panama to coordinate communication (White, 1978).

McSherry states that "Operation Condor was inspired by a security doctrine that targeted ideological enemies. The military states in the Condor system engaged in terrorist practices to destroy the 'subversive threat' from the left and defend 'Western, Christian civilization'" (McSherry, 2005, 1). In her research based on CIA and State Department documents, she concluded that the Condor apparatus was a secret component of a larger, U.S.-led counterinsurgency strategy to preempt or reverse social movements demanding political or socioeconomic change. She described the Condor system as having three levels of operation. The first was mutual cooperation among military intelligence services, to coordinate political surveillance of targeted dissidents and exchange intelligence information. The second level was covert action, a form of offensive unconventional warfare in which the role of the perpetrator remains concealed. She contends that multinational Condor squadrons carried out covert cross-border operations to detain-disappear exiles and transfer them to their countries of origin, where most disappeared permanently. The third and most secret level was Condor's assassination

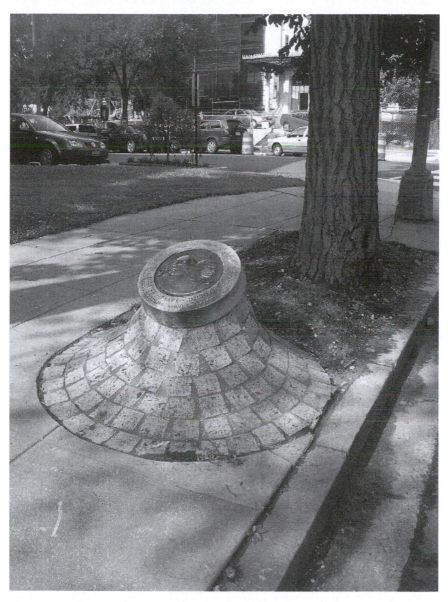

Figure 8.2.   Letelier's Memorial. Sheridan Circle, Washington D.C. In this place Orlando Letelier and Ronni Moffitt were murdered on September 21st, 1976 as part of Operation Condor. Source: Pepe Robles.

capability, known as "Phase III." Under Phase III, special teams of assassins from member countries were formed to travel worldwide to eliminate "subversive enemies." Phase III was aimed at political leaders especially feared for their potential to mobilize world opinion or organize broad opposition to the military states (McSherry, 2005, 4).

On September 21, 1976, Orlando Letelier, a Chilean economist, Socialist politician, and diplomat during the presidency of Socialist President Salvador Allende, was killed by a car bomb explosion in Sheridan Circle in Washington, D.C. Letelier was a long-time critic of the Pinochet regime that had come to power with the military overthrow of the Allende regime in Chile. Along with Letelier was his U.S. assistant, Ronni Moffit, who was also killed. Several people were convicted of the crime including Michael Townley, a member of DINA, the Chilean Secret Police, and a U.S. expatriate who had once worked for the CIA. General Manuel Contreras, former head of the DINA, and Brigadier Pedro Espinoza, also formerly of DINA, were also convicted. The assassination has been alleged to be part of Operation Condor. Five days before the assassinations, U.S. Secretary of State Henry Kissinger rescinded an order to U.S. ambassadors stationed in countries that were involved in Operation Condor including Chile to notify the military governments that the assassinations conducted in foreign countries would damage the international reputations and status of the countries involved. According to Kornbluh, "The bombing remains the most infamous attack of 'Condor'—a collaboration between the secret police services in Chile, Argentina, Uruguay, Paraguay, Brazil and several other Latin American military dictatorships, to track down and kill opponents of their regimes. Until 9/11, the Letelier-Moffitt assassination was known as the most significant act of international terrorism ever committed in the capital city of the United States" (Kornbluh, 2010).

Private Groups Organized and Sponsored by the State

Another major category of actors in state violence consists of private groups organized, sponsored, or sanctioned by the state to carry out violence. As mentioned earlier, death squad activity is frequently tied to the military or police in a given country and may be sponsored by foreign powers. Herman and O'Sullivan note that the occurrence of death squad activities throughout Latin America parallels the funding and training programs made available to these governments' military and police forces by the United States for the specific purpose of civilian control:

> The death squad made its appearance in ten different Latin American countries in the 1960s and 1970s, all of them recipients of U.S. military and police aid and training, which stressed counterinsurgency and unconventional warfare against subversion from the Kennedy era onward. In a number of countries, including Brazil, Guatemala and the Dominican Republic, death squads appeared immediately following a major U.S. intervention. Disappearances followed the same pattern of spread in the U.S. sphere of influence, with the death squad frequently the instrument of the disappearances. At a 1981 gather-

ing of relatives of the disappeared in Latin America, it was estimated that the number of disappeared in Latin America over the prior two decades had reached 90,000. (Herman and O'Sullivan, 1989, 37)

L. Fletcher Prouty is a retired U.S. Air Force colonel, a former professor of air science and tactics at Yale University, and a former chief of special operations for the Joint Chiefs of Staff during the Kennedy administration. In the latter role he was directly in charge of the global system designed to provide military support for the clandestine activities of the CIA. He concurs that most of the subcontracted state violence occurring in Third World countries following World War II has been a product of U.S. training and funding:

> Foreign nations from all over the world were trained in the methods of secret operations—that is, the use of high explosives, sabotage, communications, etc.—at a military base in the United States under CIA sponsorship. The CIA developed many of its own facilities around the world, but in most cases the agency concealed its presence on military facilities in one guise or another. Many of the skilled saboteurs and terrorists of today are CIA students of yesterday. Many skilled terrorists in Iran have gone to CIA schools and other training facilities and have become experts with the weapons and tactics of the trade. (Prouty, 1992, 36–37)

Likewise, Nairn (1984) contends that over the past twenty years, officials of the U.S. State Department, Central Intelligence Agency, and the U.S. armed forces conceived and organized ORDEN, the rural paramilitary and intelligence network described by Amnesty International as a movement designed to use clandestine terror against government opponents. Out of this organization grew the notorious Mano Blanco, the White Hand, which former U.S. ambassador to El Salvador, Raul H. Castro, has called nothing less than the birth of the death squads.

Agents of the U.S. government also conceived and organized ANSESAL, a special presidential intelligence service in El Salvador that gathered files on dissidents. The U.S. government supplied ANSESAL with electronic, photographic, and personal surveillance of individuals who were later assassinated by death squads (Nairn, 1984).

One example of how the death squad ORDEN worked with the El Salvadoran and a foreign military is the massacre at Rio Sumpul on May 14, 1980. Approximately eight hundred peasants (mostly women, children, and elderly) were relocated to Las Aradas, next to the Sumpul River, under the government's assumption that as rural citizens many of them were potential revolutionaries. Army patrols prevented them from leaving the areas. Accordingly, the peasants began to cultivate the land and carry on life as best as possible. On May 12 Honduran soldiers set up protective stone barricades along the other side of the river. At seven in the morning of Wednesday, May 14, 1980, the massacre at the Salvadoran villages of San Jacinto and Las Aradas began. Two armed helicopters, hundreds of Salvadoran National Guardsmen, army soldiers, and members of ORDEN assassinated some six hundred defenseless campesinos. The peasants who tried to cross the river seeking refuge in Honduras were returned by the Honduran soldiers to the zone of the massacre where they were killed (Herman and O'Sullivan, 1989,

240). Herman and O'Sullivan note that ORDEN has also received U.S. support in terms of training funds and weapons indirectly through programs that funded civilian security forces of friendly governments.

More recently as a result of the release of more than twelve thousand U.S. government documents on policy in Central America that were declassified and made available to the public in 1993, it was discovered that U.S. military officers in El Salvador trained a group of wealthy Salvadorans who called themselves Los Patrioticos (the Patriotic Ones). According to a *New York Times* article, "American officers were giving weekly training to fifty to sixty wealthy Salvadorans. The American officers referred to the group as the BMW Brigade." Citing U.S. intelligence reports, the article notes that the unit "was being used as a cover for death-squad activities" (Weiner, 1993).

The United States has also been involved in organizing and funding death squads in Southeast Asia and Cuba. We have already mentioned Operation Phoenix, in which the CIA together with death squads and the secret police of South Vietnam systematically assassinated thousands of civilians believed to be involved in subversive actions. During this same period, the CIA was also organizing terrorist groups such as Alpha 66 and OMEGA 7, the Cuban terrorist groups whose goal was to destabilize the Castro regime in Cuba as well as other left-wing groups in Latin America. OMEGA 7 has been described by the FBI as the most dangerous terrorist group operating within the United States in the 1970s, and the CIA itself reported that the group was responsible for eighty-nine separate terrorist incidents within the United States and the Caribbean (Churchill and Vander Wall, 1990). Hinckle and Turner (1981) argue that Cuban exile terrorism began with assassinations and bombings in the United States, picked up tempo during the 1970s, and by the end of the decade had spun a murderous web linking Cuban exiles with elements of the American CIA, the Chilean gestapo (known as DINA), the Venezuelan secret police, the Korean CIA, and European paramilitary fascist groups.

The CIA has also been involved with organized crime in the planning and attempted assassinations of Fidel Castro. Sam Giacana, a reputed crime boss, was given a contract to kill Castro during the Kennedy administration (Church Committee, 1975; Hinckle and Turner, 1981). Before awarding this contract, the CIA had been involved in recruiting syndicate crime figures to create a criminal terror squad to force recalcitrant Marseilles dockworkers to load ships with arms for use in Vietnam. For their assistance, these syndicate figures were permitted to continue to refine heroin in Marseilles for export to the United States. Beirne and Messerschmidt (1991) report a similar deal cut between the CIA and Meo tribespeople. "In return for fighting the Pathet Lao opposition forces, the Meo tribespeople of the area were compensated by the CIA's own airline—Air America—which helped to transport opium to heroin laboratories, and ultimately into the arms of GIs in Vietnam and users in the U.S." (261).

The United States has also been frequently involved in organizing and training mercenary forces for terrorist activities. One recent example is the Contras composed of former President Somoza's National Guard and peasants forced into conscription and trained and armed by the U.S. government. The Contras were used to conduct terrorist acts in Nicaragua to destabilize the Sandinista government (Emerson, 1988). During the 1980s the United States provided nearly $300 million in overt aid and $4 to $6 billion in covert aid (Sharkey, 1990). The Nicaraguan government ruled by the Sandinista party took the United States to the International Court of Justice for its terrorist actions. The Court ruled in favor of Nicaragua, ordering reparations estimated at $17 billion (International Court of Justice, 1986). The United States has refused to recognize the Court's decision, and when a new government supported by the United States (Violeta Chamorro) came to power, it quickly rescinded the request.

Similar examples can be found in Afghanistan in the training of the Moujahedeen, including the Taliban and other Islamic extremist groups who were organized and funded by the U.S. military to overthrow the government in an Afghanistan that was allied with the Soviet Union. The now infamous Osama bin Laden was running a front organization known as Maktab al-Khidamar (the MAK) that funneled money, arms, and fighters from the outside world into the Afghan war. The MAK was nurtured by Pakistan's state security services, the Inter-Services Intelligence agency, which was the CIA's primary conduit for conducting the covert war against the Afghan government headed by Najibullah who was supported by the government of the Soviet Union (Moran, 1998).

Blum notes that throughout the 1980s, the Karmal, and then the Najibullah regimes, despite the exigencies of the war, pursued a program of modernization and broadening popular support. This included bringing electricity to villages, along with health clinics, a measure of land reform, and literacy, as well as releasing numerous prisoners unlawfully incarcerated and bringing mullahs and other nonparty people into the government. Through the U.S. funding of warlords and fundamentalist groups (referred to as the Afghan Freedom Fighters by President Reagan), they drove the Soviet-backed government out of power. The fundamentalist Taliban came to power in the wake of a power struggle following the collapse of the government. Osama bin Laden and the Taliban, who were previously recipients of U.S. aid in their fight against the government of Afghanistan, were later charged by the U.S. government with attacking and destroying the World Trade Center on September 11, 2001.

This is an example of the problem of blowback, and according to Johnson it is the cost and consequences of an American empire (Johnson, 2000). According to Johnson "the term 'blowback,' which officials of the Central Intelligence Agency first invented for their own internal use, is starting to circulate among students of international relations. It refers to the unintended consequences of policies that were kept secret from the American people. What the daily press reports as the malign acts of 'terrorists' or 'drug lords' or 'rogue states' or 'illegal arms merchants' often turn out to be blowback from earlier American operations" (Johnson, 2000, 8). Johnson cites a 1997 report to the undersecretary of defense for acquisition and technology by members of the Defense Science Board warning of the problem of terrorist attacks. "Historical data show a strong correlation between U.S. involvement in international situations and an increase in terrorist attacks against the United States. In addition, the military asymmetry that denies nation states the ability to engage in overt attacks against the United States drives the use of transnational actors [that is, terrorists from one country attacking in another]" (9). Johnson notes that "terrorism strikes at the innocent in order to draw attention to the sins of the invulnerable. The innocent of the twenty-first century are going to harvest unexpected blowback disasters from the imperialist escapades of recent decades. Although most Americans may be largely ignorant of what was, and still is, being done in their name, all are likely to pay a steep price—individually and collectively—for their nation's continued efforts to dominate the global scene" (32).

There are many other examples of the U.S. government sponsoring terrorist or mercenary forces to overthrow governments that were not under the control of the United States. Blum (1995, 2000) outlines more than fifty interventions (overt and covert) by the United States in the overthrow of governments around the world since World War II. And the legacy of interventions and military attacks by the United States against relatively powerless foes continues into the twenty-first century.

In the United States, the CIA is not the only agency involved in utilizing private groups for violence. As we observed earlier, the Bureau of Investigation, predecessor to the FBI, had been involved in working with a vigilante group (the American Protective League) in conducting violence directed at the labor union IWW (Churchill and Vander Wall, 1990). More recently, there has been evidence submitted to the Senate Select Committee on Intelligence that the FBI succeeded in resurrecting a previously disbanded right-wing paramilitary organization known as the Minutemen and placing an FBI informant, Howard Godfrey, in a leadership position (Coleman, 1989). Not only did the FBI pay Godfrey a regular salary, but it also provided the Secret Army Organization (the group's new name) with firearms, explosives, and other equipment, and supplied at least 75 percent of the SAOs operating expenses.

An SAO cell directed by Godfrey engaged in repeated acts of violence and terrorism against the left, including the destruction of newspaper offices and bookstores, the firebombing of cars, and assaults on political activists. In one incident, Godfrey and another SAO member fired two shots into the house of a well-known leftist, seriously wounding a young woman. The following day Godfrey turned over the gun and jacket he wore during the assault to his FBI supervisor, who in turn helped conceal the evidence from San Diego police. Even after this information came to light, the FBI succeeded in protecting its operatives from prosecution (Coleman, 1989). Churchill and Vander Wall (1990) discuss other examples of the Bureau of Investigation organizing and utilizing established vigilante groups to carry out violence.

Another interesting example of another government using private groups to conduct violence is in the case of South Africa. The South African police was secretly funding the Inkatha movement, a more conservative black South African organization, to further fragment the black population and take away support from the left-oriented African National Congress (ANC). In the following excerpt from one report, the police are implicated in organizing and assisting in a violent attack on supporters of the ANC by members of the Inkatha movement:

Reports of the massacre of at least forty South African blacks in Boipatong and an adjacent squatter's camp on June 17 followed a familiar pattern. The attackers were Zulu-speaking supporters of the Inkatha movement from a nearby hostel. They were ferried to the scene by the South African Police, who prevented the victims from escaping and shot down some of them as they fled. If the police organized this attack, as press accounts indicate, it served a dual purpose. By further inflaming tensions between Inkatha and the African National Congress (or, in ethnic terms, between the Zulus and the Xhosas and other tribes that predominantly support the A.N.C.), it almost inevitably will lead to further violence, lending support to those who claim that a transition from apartheid to a nonracial state would produce a bloodbath. (Neier, 1992, 129)

TYPES OF STATE VIOLENCE

War

War is usually the single largest form of state violence. Between 1946 and 1986, there were more than thirty-one wars worldwide and 237 wars with estimated deaths of one thousand for each year. Sivard also points out that since the eighteenth century there has been an increase in the level of violence in terms of war deaths. Twelve times as many people died in the twentieth century compared to the nineteenth century, and twenty-two times more than the eighteenth century. In the nineteenth century there were only two wars with deaths exceeding one million, while in the twentieth century there have been thirteen such wars. Sivard notes that in 1986, there were twenty major ongoing wars that had at least an annual death rate of one thousand. According to Sivard, the numbers of deaths since the beginning of the twentieth century because of war is 83,642,000 (Sivard, 1986).

Project Ploughshares defines war or armed political conflict as "a political conflict in which armed combat involves the armed forces of at least one state (or one or more armed factions seeking to gain control of all or part of

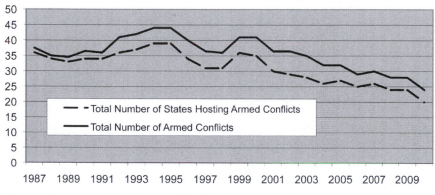

Figure 8.3.   Armed Conflicts, 1987–2010 (Borum, 2011)

the state), and in which at least 1,000 people have been killed by the fighting during the course of the conflict" (Ploughshares, 2011). The chart from their most recent report illustrates the annual frequency of wars since the Sivard estimate. On the average for the remainder of the twentieth century, there was an average of thirty-eight wars going on per year. Since the end of the twentieth century, the number of wars has declined to the twenty-four recorded.

As to the number of deaths from war during the twentieth century, the estimation of the number of dead as a result of war is a complex task. As Leitenberg notes there is first the problem of the reliability of the various estimates (Leitenberg, 2006). Depending on which side of the conflict, the number of dead, especially civilian deaths, can vary tremendously. In his comprehensive analysis of the numbers reported, he concludes that the best sources are from international organizations like the UN or international human rights oriented NGOs like those that have been used previously throughout this text. However, he notes that it would incorrect to think that these organizations operate in a political vacuum as it relates to wars. The most powerful countries who are the principal funders of many of these organizations, including the United Nations, are not without influence. Nevertheless, they are the best given the availability of sources worldwide, especially in areas where data of war deaths are not systematically recorded.

Leitenberg also points to the fact that there is no uniform operationalized definition of deaths from war used by various estimates. Some record only the battlefield deaths; others have excluded deaths that occur by bombing in noncombat areas; others may exclude deaths that occur from disease and starvation that are a result of the effect of the war on the economy and supplies of necessities for the population. He claims that such use of restrictive criteria seriously underestimates the consequences of war. He arrives at a definition of deaths caused by war as "the total number of deaths caused to the nation or the warring party, military or civilian, and irrespective of what the means of killing was, whether by high explosive or by other means, and whether in active combat or not" (Leitenberg, 2006, 5). His estimate of the number of deaths using this definition comes to between 136.5 and 148.5 million.

Sivard also noted that there is an increasing internationalization of violence in the Third World:

> Taking World War II as the turning point, there were more and bloodier regional and national wars after it than before it. Of the 120 wars recorded since World War II, only one, Hungary, was in a developed country, while in the period pre–World War II, 28 percent of all wars took place in developed countries and, if World War I is included, 88 percent of all war deaths were in the developed world. (Sivard, 1986, 27)

Sivard concludes that the rise in conflict in the Third World is associated with a complex of causal factors including rebellion rising out of intolerable deprivation, injustice, and frustration. She also observes that the superpowers play an important role in stimulating the conflicts and utilizing them for what she refers to as their own ideological crusades, or more precisely put, utilizing them to maintain their position in the hierarchy of countries in the international political and economic system or world system. With the collapse of the USSR in 1990, there has been a decline in the number of proxy wars.

One important role that the superpowers played in these regional conflicts was serving as arms suppliers and providing for technical support in using the weaponry. Throughout the history of the post–World War II period, the United States has consistently led the world in arms sales and technical assistance in conducting wars in the Third World. Now being the only superpower in the world, it has extended its role as arms merchant. Klare and Arnson (1981) note that under both the Military Assistance Program and the Foreign Military Sales Program, the United States became the largest single supplier of armaments in the world. According to Klare and Aronson (1981), most of the armaments sold under the Military Assistance Program were for internal repression of populations who were rebelling against the extreme conditions of poverty and inequality. Officially, U.S. arms programs are designed to strengthen the capacity of countries to defend themselves against external attack. But an examination of U.S. weapons trade data suggests that much of the equipment involved is intended for internal use, to control strikes and disorders and to suppress dissent. Thus, recent arms deliveries to these countries have included armored cars, shotguns, tear gas, riot clubs, and other weapons unsuitable for anything other than internal political warfare (5).

For example, Klare and Aronson note that U.S. arms were used by the Thai Border Patrol Police to massacre several hundred students killed during the military coup of October 6, 1976. The Iranian military used weapons purchased under military aid programs to kill thousands of unarmed demonstrators during the 1978 uprising against the shah. The Indonesian military used U.S. weapons supplied under aid programs to slaughter more than one hundred thousand civilians in East Timor. More recently, the Turkish military has killed more than thirteen thousand people, one thousand villages have been depopulated, and approximately two million civilians displaced (Wheat, 1995). Most of these killings and displacements have occurred since 1993. Wheat notes that "between 1987 and 1991, 77 percent of arms delivered to Turkey came from the United States. . . . For fiscal years 1986–1995, Congress has appropriated $5.1 billion in military aid for Turkey" (Wheat, 1995, 18). And the list goes on. Klare and Aronson state that the United States stands at the supply end of a pipeline of repressive technology that extends to many of the world's most authoritarian regimes (7).

But supplying armaments and U.S. involvement in various Third World wars continues. Today, in the purported New World Order, the United States is either fighting alone or in conjunction with alliances it can construct to maintain the world political economic order and its dominant position in it. As noted previously, the United States alone has about 48 percent of the armaments market. An estimated one-third of U.S. arms exports are paid for not by foreign governments buying arms but by U.S. taxpayers. Hidden subsidies take the form of loans for sales, forgiveness for past military debts—$7 billion to Egypt for its role as an ally in the Gulf War—and arms-related training. Wheat (1995) reports that prior to 1989, the United States delivered 11 percent of the Third World's arms; in 1994 it delivered 51 percent. Wheat claims that the U.S. taxpayers are subsidizing $4 billion a year in foreign arms purchases.

The *New Internationalist* (1994) reports that at least 20 percent of Third World debt is incurred by buying weapons. The ratio of military spending to social spending was found to be highest in those countries with the lowest per capita incomes (Stålenheim, Perdomo, and Sköns, 2008). Thus poor countries are expending a greater portion of their limited funds on weapons and war than on reducing the impact of poverty on their citizen's lives. Nigeria could have immunized two million children with the money its government spent on eighty British battle tanks in 1992. India could have provided basic education for all the fifteen million girls not in school with the money it spent on twenty Russian MiG-29 fighter aircraft, in the same year. And Iran could have provided essential machines to the whole country several times over for the cost of two submarines (*New Internationalist*, 1994, 9).

The report goes on to reveal that countries are encouraged to purchase additional arms with development aid, such as the British Overseas Development Agency, which was ordered to fund the unpopular and uneconomic Pergau Dam project in Malaysia in exchange for arms contracts. In general the *New Internationalist* (1994) concludes that globally, poor countries with big arms budgets get twice as much aid per person as those that spend less on military goods. They cite El Salvador, which gets five times as much aid as Bangladesh, even though the latter has twenty-four times more people and is five times poorer. Furthermore, today's world nuclear stockpile provides the equivalent of the explosive power of 1.8 tons of TNT for every child, woman, and man on earth—enough to erase the human race several times over. In the world today a conservative estimate, since countries are reluctant to report exact numbers, is that there are nine countries that possess 19,500 nuclear weapons. The United States and Russia possess approximately 95 percent of these weapons that are the most violent in terms of the killing of life.

Genocide

The United Nations Genocide Convention that went into force January 12, 1951, defines genocide as any of the following acts committed with intent to destroy, in whole or in part, a national, ethnic, racial, or religious group: (a) killing members of the group; (b) causing serious bodily or mental harm to members of the group; (c) deliberately inflicting on the group conditions of life calculated to bring about its physical destruction in whole or in part; (d) imposing measures intended to prevent births within the group; and (e) forcibly transferring children of the group to another group. There have been eight persons convicted of genocide under the United Nations Convention. The first case was that of Jean Paul Akayesu, the Hutu mayor of the Rwandan town of Taba at the time of the killings. Between April 7 and June 1994, at least two thousand Tutsis were killed in Taba. In his capacity as burgomaster, Jean-Paul Akayesu was in charge of the maintenance of law and order in his commune. During this period of the massacre, he did not act to prevent the massacre nor did he ask for the assistance of regional or national authorities to intervene. In a landmark ruling, a special international tribunal convicted him of genocide and crimes against humanity on September 2, 1998. Seven other Rwandans have since been convicted of genocide.

The story of the genocide in Rwanda is one of the most recent cases of genocide. Human Rights Watch (1999) has provided the most detailed account of the genocidal violence. During a thirteen-week period following the mysterious assassination of the president of Rwanda on April 6, 1994, at least half a million people perished, estimated to be as many as three-quarters of the Tutsi population. Human Rights Watch notes that thousands of Hutu were also slain because they opposed the killing campaign and the forces directing it. The report discusses the cause of the genocide.

> This genocide resulted from the deliberate choice of a modern elite to foster hatred and fear to keep itself in power. This small, privileged group first set the majority against the minority to counter a growing political opposition within Rwanda. Then, faced with RPF success on the battlefield and at the negotiating table, these few power holders transformed the strategy of ethnic division into genocide. They believed that the extermination campaign would restore the solidarity of the Hutu under their leadership and help them win the war, or at least improve their chances of negotiating a favorable peace. They seized control of the state and used its machinery and its authority to carry out the slaughter. (Human Rights Watch, 1999)

Human Rights Watch describes how this slaughter occurred through control of the hierarchical structures in the government and the organization of civilian militias who carried out the civilian defense program that was directed at the Tutsi minority. Rwanda, a country that has been racked by bitter poverty as a result of a history of colonialism, was in many ways ripe for the escalation of conflict along class and ethnic groups.

Genocide has been a frequent part of the story of imperialism since Christopher Columbus's conquest of the people on the Isle of Hispaniola. In the earlier stages, genocide is a product of conquest. On pre-Columbian Hispaniola in 1492, it was estimated that there was a robust population of almost three million; by 1542, fifty years later, approximately two hundred remained. Chomsky (1993, 5) states that the conquest of the New World set off two vast demographic catastrophes, unparalleled in history: the virtual destruction of the indigenous population of the Western Hemisphere and the devastation of Africa as the slave trade rapidly expanded to serve the needs of the conquerors and the continent itself was subjugated. This was the beginning of the history of modern genocide.

This tragic story of mass extermination continued into the eighteenth and nineteenth centuries by the genocidal policies of the American colonists and U.S. military in eliminating the majority of the tribes of indigenous people in North America (Glauner, 2001; Churchill, 1997). Haviland (1987) describes the case of the Pequot Indians, who were exterminated in 1637 by the colonists when they burned their village in Mystic, Connecticut, and then shot all of the people, including women and children who tried to escape. Dee Brown's (1970) history of the indigenous population is a history of this genocide across the land that would become the forty-eight states of the United States. Similar patterns of genocide were repeated on virtually every continent in the world, and continue to this day.

Genocide is directed at an outgroup or minority group or in the case of empires it may be the people who are conquered. Levinson (1995) notes that the term *genocide* was first used in this century to describe the Nazis' attempted extermination of Jews in Europe. The Holocaust of the Jewish population throughout Europe is the case that most people think about when they hear the word *genocide*. In 1933, the Jewish population of Europe stood at over nine million. By 1945, close to two out of every three European Jews had been killed as part of the "Final Solution" of the German government. Harff (1986) defines genocide as the mass murder, premeditated by some power-wielding group linked with state power, directed against any target group within the state however defined. She points out that genocide is likely to occur when (1) a national upheaval has occurred, (2) there exists sharp internal cleavages between majority and minority populations prior to the upheaval, and (3) there is strong group identification between competing groups. Harff cites Burundi as illustrative of her preconditions. During the spring and summer of 1972, approximately 250,000 people were systematically murdered by a tribal minority government that attempted to kill every possible Hutu male of distinction over the age of fourteen.

Another example of genocidal violence in this century is the murdering of more than one million Armenians in Turkey in the first quarter of the century. Another million Armenians were killed in Iraq about the same time. In what was known as German South-West Africa, today Namibia, German soldiers slaughtered one hundred thousand Hereros for the land and livestock the tribe held. German soldiers also killed more than one hundred thousand Africans in what is now Tanzania when they resisted German government orders to grow cotton for export instead of food for domestic consumption.

Sybil Milton, senior historian at the United States Holocaust Memorial Museum in Washington, D.C., notes that the modern scale of violence required for genocide requires both government power and technological ability to deliver it (Levinson, 1995). According to Levinson (1995), approximately 170 million people were killed in genocidal violence in the twentieth century.

What is important to note about the history of genocide is that it is a long history that dates back to the earliest agrarian-based imperial systems. Most of the recent research focuses on the most recent cases of genocide (World War II and the remaining twentieth century) and does little to draw connections between these most recent cases of genocide and its long history. Kiernan's (2007) world history of genocide begins to establish the linkages by noting the importance of technological advancement and the role of agrarian-based empires from the fifteenth century to the first half of the twentieth century. Moses also notes the importance of putting genocide in historical and imperial context (Moses, 2008). He notes that there are conceptual blinders by Western scholars who ignore the long history of genocide as it is a product of imperial expansion and see that the solution to the recent genocide in the periphery is for these states to adopt Western institutions, which themselves are a product of the history of Western imperial development.

Levene (2008) describes three trajectories or tendencies in imperial genocides: genocides resulting from the direct settlement and displacement of the indigenous from 1600 to 1890; colonial genocides in Africa, Asia, and the Pacific 1880 to 1910; and genocides of retreating empires (China, Russia, Ottoman, and Austria-Hungary) 1869 to 1915. For Levene modern genocide is understood as a state enterprise but one that is a product of a world system that develops from the history of empires of the nineteenth and twentieth centuries, with its own arrangement of states of the imperial center (the United States being at the very center of the system), and creates an intense competition in the semi and peripheral sectors for development. As Levene describes it, the dynamic that leads to the genocides of the modern day is "the pressure that a competitive, indeed Darwinistic, system of state economies places on national leaderships to establish and maintain sovereign viability. In some cases, usually among the second tier late-comer states (postcolonial) to the club established by Westerners, desperate shortcuts had been taken to accelerate and institutional modernization: by exterminating a native people who live in an area desired for economic exploitation, or by exterminating a minority associated with an external enemy that is held responsible for endangering the nation in a security crisis, or holding back the country's independent development by effectively representing the interests of a competitor" (Levene, 2005, 223–24). Thus according to these authors, to understand the genocides of the past fifty years is to not only consider the ethnic conflicts within societies where the genocides take place but to look to how these societies are part of a world system of inequality that was formed by imperial powers of the past and today, which creates competition and conflict between states for position and power. This is not to say that the dominant world powers are not directly involved in these genocides. For as we discussed previously, the technological military means to enact the genocide is often supplied by these same powers and the most powerful economic organizations (multinational corporations) often have a vested interest in the conflicts that develop (Jones, 2004). Or, as Levene concludes in his essay critiquing the dominant Western research on genocide:

> For decades, Westerners have been—to use an English colloquialism—"having their cake and eating it," reaping the rewards of the plundered peripheries while at the same time preaching to those whom they have plundered and/or aggrieved of the unacceptability of their human rights behaviour. Genocide, it is true, is currently not part of the Western domestic scene. But then the phenomenon is not a cause but an effect. An interconnected world without genocide can only develop in one in which economic domination as well as political hubris have been outlawed, in others words, in which principles of equity, social justice, environmental sustainability—and one might add genuine human kindness—have become the "norm." (Levene, 2004, 440)

Assassination

Assassination, the targeting of a specific individual for murder, is another form of state violence. As mentioned before, between 1960 and 1965 the CIA initiated at least eight plots to assassinate Fidel Castro. The unsuccessful and sometimes bizarre attempts included applying instantly lethal botulinium toxin to a box of Castro's cigars, hiring the Mafia to poison him, and presenting him a gift of a wetsuit treated with a fungus. The Senate Select Committee on Intelligence in 1975 found strong evidence that President Eisenhower had ordered the death of Congolese (Zaire) leader Patrice Lumumba and that CIA officials had planned the assassination. Furthermore, the United States was implicated in the assassination of Dominican dictator Rafael Trujillo, South Vietnam's President Ngo Dinh Diem, and General Rene Schneider of Chile. Simon and Eitzen (1993, 271) note that as recently as 1985, CIA Director William Casey arranged for the assassination of Sheikh Mohammed Hussein Fadlallah, a Lebanese Shiite Muslim leader, in coordination with Saudi Arabian intelligence. During the assassination attempt in Beirut eighty innocent people were killed when a car bomb exploded. Blum (2000) identifies thirty-five persons who were assassinated or who were targets of assassination plans by agents of the U.S. government since 1949.

Another case of planning the assassination of a world leader by the United States involved Libya's Muammar Qaddafi. In February 2011 a riot in response to the arrest of human rights activist Fethi Tarbel led to a full-scale rebellion that ended in less than eight months with the assassination of Qaddafi. On March 19, the United States launched "Operation Odyssey Dawn" and attacked Muammar Qaddafi's air defenses with strikes along the Libyan coast that were launched by Navy vessels in the Mediterranean (Associated Press/Huff Post World, 2011). The attack was in response to the government's attempt to repel rebel forces in Benghazi and to attack air defense around the capital city, Tripoli. The U.S. and NATO air and special forces units would then lead an attack on Libya and would help arm, train, and guide the rebel forces in completing the overthrow.

The Libyan coup is part of what has become referred to in the West as the Arab Spring in which riots and coups occur throughout the Middle East, a wave of revolts that President Bush had hoped to stimulate with his invasion and conquest of Iraq and Afghanistan. Libya, along with Syria and Iran, was defined as one of the countries in the "axis of evil" that needed regime change. The United States had been planning Qaddafi's assassination for more than thirty years, beginning in the early 1980s, when the CIA Director was William Casey under President Reagan (*Newsweek*, 1981). The plan to remove Qaddafi from power was presented to the House Select Committee on Intelligence by former deputy director of covert operations Max Hugel. The plan was approved by Casey and the White House crisis management team. According to members of the committee, the CIA's goal was Qaddafi's "ultimate" removal from power, which to members of the House intelligence committee who reviewed the plan seemed to imply Qaddafi's assassination.

Assassinations were declared to be illegal by presidential executive issued by President Ford in response to government hearings in the wake of the Watergate investigation that revealed assassination plans to kill Castro. *Newsweek* reports that the committee who reviewed the plans to remove Qaddafi sent a "strongly worded letter of protest directly to Ronald Reagan" (*Newsweek*, 1981). The plan was referred to as a classic CIA destabilization campaign. "One element was a 'disinformation' program designed to embarrass Kaddafi and his government. Another was the creation of a 'counter government' to challenge his claim to national leadership. A third—potentially the most risky—was an escalating paramilitary campaign, probably by disaffected Libyan nationals, to blow up bridges, conduct small-scale guerrilla operations and demonstrate that Kaddafi was opposed by an indigenous political force" (*Newsweek*, 1981, 19).

Chambliss (1989) describes another plot to assassinate Qaddafi by the Reagan administration. The plan was to lure Qaddafi into some foreign adventure of terrorist exploit that would give a growing number of Qaddafi opponents in the Libyan military a chance to seize power, or such a foreign adventure might give one of Qaddafi's neighbors, such as Algeria or Egypt, a justification for responding to Qaddafi militarily. Earlier in 1986, the United States accused Libya of bombing a discotheque in Berlin and the United States under President Ronald Reagan attempted to assassinate Qaddafi by bombing his residence at Bab al-Azizia in Tripoli. Qaddafi's daughter and over one hundred Libyans were killed (Perreira, 2011). Perreira reports that in 1996 the British Intelligence Service MI5 had offered $100,000 to members of an Al Qaeda cell operating in Libya to kill Qaddafi (Perreira, 2011).

On October 18, the day before the assassination of Qaddafi in 2011, Secretary of State Hillary Clinton met with rebel leaders in Libya to encourage the rebel leaders to unify and reportedly stated, "'We hope he can be captured or killed soon" (Sadeghi, 2011). No doubt Hillary Clinton's entourage had met with Colonel Khalifa Haftar, who was a former commander of the Libyan army in Chad and was captured and changed sides in 1988, setting up the anti-Gaddafi Libyan National Army with CIA and Saudi backing. Before the uprising Haftar had been living for the past twenty years in Virginia before returning to Benghazi to lead the fight against Gaddafi (Cockburn, 2011). The next day, a convoy leaving Sirte was spotted by a U.S.-flown drone operated out of Creech air force base in Nevada and began the attack on the convoy, which was later joined by British Air Special Forces (SAS) (Farmer, 2011). Rebel forces intercepted the fleeing convoy where Gaddafi was captured and then assassinated by the rebel forces. On October 23, the National Transitional Council declared that the country had been liberated. On October 31, a little-known engineering professor from the University of Alabama, Abdul Raheem al-Keeb, was chosen by the council to serve as the first interim prime minister of the new Libyan nation.

The United States has attempted to increase its influence and control of the oil reserves in the Middle East by means of U.S.-based multinational oil corporations and increasing military presence throughout the Middle East since World War II. As noted earlier, the U.S. policy regarding assassinations for most of the period since President Ford was a response to the Church Committee hearings that detailed CIA murder plots against Cuba's Fidel Castro, the Congo's Patrice Lumumba, and Dominican president Rafael Trujillo, among others. The Ford policy stated that "no employee of the United States shall engage in, or conspire to engage in, political assassinations" (Blum, 2000). Presidents Carter and Reagan issued similar orders.

However, Reagan canceled his executive order less than a year later. The prohibition was reinstated after a foiled plot to kill Sheikh Mohammed Hussein Fadlallah using a car bomb that killed eighty innocent persons in Beirut. However, the prohibition on the so-called license to kill was reinstated again. However, President George H. Bush (former head of the CIA under President

Ford) issued a "memorandum of law" that would, according to Blum (2000), allow for "accidental killings." This provided the loophole for the U.S. bombing of Qaddafi's home that resulted in the killing of his daughter and other members of his family and the bombing of command posts in Baghdad in the attempts to kill the Iraqi head of state, Saddam Hussein.

More recently it appears that the executive order was rescinded entirely during the George W. Bush administration in the war against terrorism (Cable News Network, 2002). As President George W. Bush is quoted in a recent *Newsweek* magazine article regarding Saddam Hussein, "We're taking him out" (Eisenberg, 2002). Saddam Hussein was captured by U.S. forces after the invasion of Iraq and was executed in a trial conducted by the interim Iraqi government, which was under control of U.S. provisional governing authorities.

The Obama administration has increased the level of assassinations using remote control missile firing drones attacking suspected terrorists in Afghanistan, Pakistan, Iraq, Yemen, and Somalia. Since 2010 there have been stepped-up attacks in North and South Waziristan region of Pakistan, a poor area of Pakistan where suspected terrorists operate from and live. In 2010 alone there were 117 drone strikes that killed 801 suspected terrorists and 14 civilians (Roggio and Mayer, 2012). Investigative journalists at the London-based Bureau of Investigative Journalism claim that there have been "260 strikes by Predator and Reaper drones since President Obama took office, and it said that 282 to 535 civilians had been 'credibly reported' killed in those attacks, including more than 60 children" (Shane, 2012). The report contends that the CIA drones have attacked rescuers after the attack as well as funeral processions for those who were killed in the attacks.

One controversial assassination was the assassination of two U.S. citizens, Anwar al-Awlaki and Samir Khan, who were propagandists for Yemeni terrorists. The principal target of the drone attack was Anwar al-Awlaki defined in the media as a "radical American-born Muslim cleric." The United States had at least two previous unsuccessful attempts of assassinations (Mazzetti, Schnutt, and Worth, 2011). The *Times* reported that "after several days of surveillance of Mr. Awlaki, armed drones operated by the Central Intelligence Agency took off from a new, secret American base in the Arabian Peninsula, crossed into northern Yemen and unleashed a barrage of Hellfire missiles at a car carrying him and other top operatives from Al Qaeda's branch in Yemen, including another American militant who had run the group's English-language Internet magazine" (Mazzetti, Schnutt, and Worth, 2011).

The assassinations of U.S. citizens appear to be the first since the 2001 War on Terrorism began. A secret fifty-page memo from the Justice Department's Office of Legal Counsel provided the legal justification for the assassination of a U.S. citizen (Savage, 2011). Overall, given the difficulty of trying suspected terrorists and the questionable legality of holding suspected terrorists indefinitely, assassinations or targeted killings may be the chosen method used by government officials.

Assassinations by the U.S. government do not occur only in foreign countries. Churchill and Vander Wall (1990) present information indicating the FBI's involvement in the assassination of two Black Panther leaders, Fred

Figure 8.4.   An MQ-1B Predator unmanned aircraft from the 361st Expeditionary Reconnaissance Squadron takes off July 9 from Ali Base, Iraq, in support of Operation Iraqi Freedom. Source: U.S. Air Force.

Hampton and Mark Clark. They detail how William O'Neal, Hampton's personal bodyguard and an FBI infiltrator, gave the agency a detailed floor plan of the Chicago apartment in which the Panther leaders were staying and the information that it contained two illegal shotguns. In response to this unsubstantiated report of illegal firearms, Chicago police conducted a pre-dawn raid on December 4, 1969, and shot Hampton and Clark to death while they were still in their beds:

> Groth assembled and briefed his force at approximately 4 a.m. on the morning of December 4, using O'Neal's floorplan and other information provided by Mitchel. . . . Once there, they divided into two subteams with eight of their number deployed to the front of the apartment and six to the rear. At about 4:30, they launched an outright assault upon the Panthers, as Gloves Davis kicked open the front door and promptly shot Mark Clark point-blank in the chest with a .30 caliber M-1 carbine. Clark, who had apparently nodded off in a front room with a shotgun across his lap, barely had time to stand up before being killed more or less instantly. His reflexive response to being shot discharged the shotgun. It was the only round fired by the Panthers during the raid. David immediately proceed to pump a bullet into eighteen-year-old Brenda Harris, who was lying (unarmed) in a front room bed; Groth hit her with a second round. Groman, joined by Davis and his carbine, then began spraying automatic fire from his .45 caliber Thompson submachine gun through a wall into the bedrooms. All forty-two shots fired by the pair converged on the head of Hampton's bed, pinpointed by O'Neal's floorplan. One of the slugs fired by Davis struck Hampton in the left shoulder, seriously wounding him as he slept.

While this was going on, the second subteam, firing as they came, crashed through the back door. This was followed by a brief lull in the shooting, during which Carmody and another (unidentified) raider entered Hampton's bedroom. They were heard to have the following exchange: That's Fred Hampton. . . . Is he dead? Bring him out. He's barely alive; he'll make it. Two shots were then heard, both of which were fired point-blank into Hampton's head as he lay prone, followed by Carmody's voice stating, He's good and dead now. The chairman's body was then dragged by the wrist from the bed to the bedroom doorway, and left lying in a spreading pool of blood. At that point, the raiders mopped up, with Gorman directing fire from his submachine gun at the remaining Panthers who were attempting to cover themselves in the apartment's other bedroom. Doc Satchell was hit four times in this barrage, and Blair Anderson twice. Seventeen-year-old Verlina Brewer was also hit twice. The victims were then beaten and dragged bodily to the street, where they were arrested on charges of attempting to murder the raiders and aggravated assault. (Churchill and Vander Wall, 1990, 71 and 73)

Churchill and Vander Wall note that it was not until 1983 that the victims' families won a judgment against the U.S. government. Judge John F. Grady ruled that there had been an active governmental conspiracy to deny Hampton, Clark, and the Black Panther Party plaintiffs their civil rights. The defendants were found to have been culpable, sanctions were imposed on the FBI for its cover-up activities, and an award of $1.85 million went to the survivors and families of the deceased.

Of course, the United States is not alone in conducting assassinations. The assassination of Sergei Kirov on December 1, 1934, by Leonid Nikolaev, an agent of Stalin's government, is claimed to have set off a chain of events that culminated in the pogroms of the 1930s in the Soviet Union, which resulted in the deaths of millions of people in the Ukraine who resisted Stalin's centralization of power (Snyder, 2010). Another example of assassinations by the Soviet government are the assassination of the Communist leader Leon Trotsky in Mexico City in 1940. More recently, it is alleged that the KGB tried twice to assassinate the Shah of Iran, who was a key U.S. ally, and in 1979, Soviet forces killed Afghan President Hafizullah Amin during the Soviet invasion of Afghanistan (U.S. Council on Foreign Relations, 2002).

Hougan (1978) indicates that during the 1960s the French Intelligence Agency hired an international mercenary to assassinate the Moroccan leader Ben Barka. The French Intelligence Agency in 1985 bombed Greenpeace's flagship in New Zealand, killing one member of its crew. The ship was preparing to set sail to disrupt French nuclear tests in the South Pacific. Herman and O'Sullivan (1989) list a number of assassinations conducted by the South African security forces, among these: the murder of a wounded ANC member in his hospital bed in Maseru, capital of Lesotho; a car bomb in Maputo, capital of Mozambique, maimed South African writer and lawyer Albie Sach; the assassination of an ANC representative in Paris in 1987; and a bomb in a TV set that exploded in the Harare house of a senior ANC exile, killing his Zimbabwean wife; the murder of a member of the ANC's national executive committee in Swaziland; and the murder of a teenager, Sicelo Dlomo, in South Africa a few weeks after he told CBS television of his experiences as a torture victim. Most recently, Israel has carried out a program of assassinations of Palestinians whom they have accused of being terrorists and responsible for killings in Israel. The Israeli government refers to these assassinations as "targeted attacks" (Lewis, 2001).

In Amnesty International's report entitled *Political Killings by Government*, numerous other cases of assassinations by government officials are cited, including Jean-Bedel Bokassa, self-proclaimed emperor of the Central African Empire, who killed fifty to one hundred schoolchildren in Ngaragba prison between April 18 and 20, 1979. Amnesty International (1983) also reports that in Guinea President Sékou Touré's government failed to account for approximately 2,900 prisoners who disappeared after being arrested for political reasons between 1969 and 1976. In Ethiopia sixty prominent political prisoners (fifty-nine were shot without trial) were executed by firing squad. Every year Amnesty International reports hundreds of cases known to them of assassinations by governments throughout the world.

Torture

Torture is another form of state violence. Amnesty International (1977) reports that in Chile under General Pinochet the most common forms of physical torture were prolonged beating using truncheons, fists, or bags of moist material; electricity to all parts of the body (especially the genitalia); and burning with cigarettes or acid. Such physical tortures were accompanied by the deprivation of food, drink, and sleep. In one Chilean case, for example, Amnesty International reported that a prisoner was found dead with his testicles burned off. He had been subjected to intensive beatings and electric shocks. One day later, another prisoner in the custody of the Chilean security police died from torture. He also showed the marks of severe burns on his genitals.

Amnesty International (1984) contends that today much of state torture is carried out by the military forces, usually elite or special units, which displace the civil police in matters of political security. The organization maintains that torture is often an institutionalized part of the state-controlled machinery to suppress dissent. It has become most often used as an integral part of a government's security strategy. When threatened by guerrillas, a government may condone torture as a way of extracting information from captured insurgents. Should the government broaden its definition of security, the number of people who appear to threaten it will naturally become larger. Under these new circumstances, many persons, such as students, trade unionists, publishers, and lawyers, may suddenly become suspect, and the rationale for torture expands. Amnesty International also claims that torture has been used to intimidate rural populations in many Latin American countries for the purpose of bringing increasing amounts of land under government control. An example is Guatemala, where government agents during the 1980s during its civil war displayed tortured, dying villagers to relatives and neighbors as a means of intimidation.

Torture also exists in many countries as a way of extracting confessions. In Northern Ireland, frequent use of torture by government security forces has been reported as a way to obtain confessions. Israel is the only state that has legally authorized the use of torture as a technique of interrogation.

According to Amnesty International (2001b) people were reportedly tortured or ill-treated by security forces, police, or other state authorities in 125 countries.

But torture is not only used as a technique of interrogation. In many countries torture has become institutionalized as a part of the legal system of punishment for crimes. Flogging, caning, and amputations or dismemberment are used in many countries as methods of punishment. Several Middle Eastern countries, such as Iran, Saudi Arabia, and Sudan, frequently apply torture as a punishment for those convicted of common crimes. In Iran in 1991 there were several known cases of common criminals being subjected to one hundred lashes before being executed. In Sudan, several people in 1991 were sentenced to be hanged and then publicly crucified for armed robbery. That same year in Iran, one woman was stoned to death for being convicted of adultery, while in Saudi Arabia four Kuwaiti nationals were sentenced to prison terms ranging from fifteen to twenty years and to receive between 1,000 and 1,500 whip lashes (Amnesty International, 1993).

In the United States there have been several reports of torture in prisons and police departments that have been settled out of court. In one case Gregory Banks confessed to a murder as a result of torture conducted by three officers of the Chicago police force. Banks described the nature of the interrogation:

> The sergeant kicked me out of the chair and put a nickel-plated .45 in my mouth. They was threatening to blow my head off and kicking me and hitting me across my chest with a flashlight . . . but I still persisted in denial. [Detective Peter] Dignan came back in the room . . . and said, We have something special for niggers, and he took out a plastic (garbage) bag and placed it over my head. He left it on there for about a minute. I almost suffocated. After the second time they put the plastic bag over my head, I gave them the confession. (Berma, 1994, 22)

This is not an isolated case in the Chicago Police Department. Another officer, Commander Jon Burge, was suspended for electroshocking and beating Andrew Wilson, a suspected cop killer. Berma (1994) notes that Commander Burge had also participated in or had knowledge of fifty cases of electroshock, bagging (placing a plastic bag over a suspect's head to the point of near suffocation), or excessive beating during interrogations.

These cases are not isolated. Berma (1994) notes that at the Montana State Penitentiary, dozens of prisoners were allegedly stripped naked and forced to run through a gauntlet of approximately sixty guards who punched and kicked at them. In a jail in Syracuse, New York, guards have shackled inmates' feet to their bunk and cuffed their arms to the bars above their heads in such a way that they are stretched tight, hanging above the mattress. They are left suspended for hours at a time. Berma notes that after a twenty-five-year delay, the United States ratified a UN covenant that prohibits torture in 1992. This signing occurred only after the U.S. Congress had weakened the measure by forbidding injured parties to use the treaty's definition of torture to sue the U.S. government.

Not only has the United States been involved in acts of torture nationally, but also through its training programs of military and police, where the use of torture may be a part of the curriculum. There is a strong linkage between U.S. aid and training programs and the use of torture in many countries around the world (Herman, 1987). Of thirty-five countries using systematic torture throughout the 1970s, 75 percent of them were clients of the United States. Herman furthermore contends that there is a great deal of evidence of U.S. training in methods of torture and the provision of torture technology.

On September 20, 1996, the Pentagon released seven training manuals prepared by the U.S. military and used between 1987 and 1991 for intelligence training courses in Latin America and at the U.S. Army School of the Americas (SOA), where the U.S. trains Latin American militaries. Haugaard (1997) notes that "the manuals show how U.S. agents taught repressive techniques and promoted the violation of human rights throughout Latin America and around the globe." The manuals provide the paper trail that proves how the United States trained Latin American and other militaries to infiltrate and spy upon civilians and groups, including unions, political parties, and student and charitable organizations; to treat legal political opposition like armed insurgencies; and to circumvent laws on due process, arrest, and detention. In these "how-to guides," the United States advocates tactics such as executing guerrillas, blackmail, false imprisonment, physical abuse, using truth serum to obtain information, and paying bounties for enemy dead. Counterintelligence agents are advised that one of their functions is "recommending targets for neutralization," a euphemism for execution or destruction (Haugaard, 1997, 30).

McCoy (2006) describes the evolution of the use of torture historically and discusses the use of torture and the U.S. training of police and military in other countries in the use of torture from the period of the Cold War through the current War of Terror. He traces the use of torture techniques by U.S. personnel to the origins of the CIA program of mind control from 1950 to 1962. He notes that after experiments with hallucinogenic drugs, electric shocks, and sensory deprivation, there developed what he referred to as a revelation in "the cruel science of pain." McCoy notes that the CIA's new torture paradigm fused sensory deprivation with "self-inflicted" pain, the combination of which causes the victim to feel responsible for their own suffering and thus capitulate more readily to the torturers demands. Klein (2007) discusses how in the 1950s the CIA contracted with researchers at McGill University to develop many of the techniques that were used by U.S. CIA and military or under their supervision.

The recent cases of the use of torture by the United States occurred at Abu Ghraib, Guantanamo, and twenty-four additional sites including sites that were part of the Central Intelligence Rendering Program where suspects are kidnapped and then sent to countries that are known to use torture for interrogation (American Civil Liberties Union National Security Project, 2012). Torture also occurred at secret CIA bases, several of which are believed to be in Eastern Europe and Central Asia (Priest, 2005). Amnesty International (2002f) also notes that the U.S. government admits that as many as one thousand suspected torturers may have fled to the United States to escape justice, but has failed to prosecute a single case in the eight years since U.S. law made prosecution for acts of torture possible.

In the wake of the terrorist attack on the United States, U.S. direct involvement in torture appears to have expanded. U.S. Secretary of Defense Rumsfeld authorized the creation of a "special-access program," or SAP, with "blanket advance approval to kill or capture and, if possible, interrogate 'high value' targets in the Bush administration's war on terror" (Hersch, 2004). The operation, known as "Copper Green," was approved by Condoleezza Rice and known to President Bush (Hersch, 2004).

The list of acts of torture is extensive, from official government reports such as the Taguba report (2003) and Jones and Faye Report (Jones, 2004). U.S. Army Major General Taguba found that the intentional abuse of detainees by military police personnel included the following acts:

1. Punching, slapping, and kicking detainees; jumping on their naked feet;
2. Videotaping and photographing naked male and female detainees;
3. Forcibly arranging detainees in various sexually explicit positions for photographing;
4. Forcing detainees to remove their clothing and keeping them naked for several days at a time;
5. Forcing naked male detainees to wear women's underwear;
6. Forcing groups of male detainees to masturbate themselves while being photographed and videotaped;
7. Arranging naked male detainees in a pile and then jumping on them;
8. Positioning a naked detainee on a MRE Box, with a sandbag on his head, and attaching wires to his fingers, toes, and penis to simulate electric torture;
9. Writing "I am a Rapist" on the leg of a detainee alleged to have forcibly raped a fifteen-year old fellow detainee, and then photographing him naked;
10. Placing a dog chain or strap around a naked detainee's neck and having a female Soldier pose for a picture;
11. A male MP guard having sex with a female detainee;
12. Using military working dogs (without muzzles) to intimidate and frighten detainees, and in at least one case biting and severely injuring a detainee;
13. Taking photographs of dead Iraqi detainees.

Part of the torture strategy of the U.S. government was the rendition program that began in 1990 but increased dramatically after the September 11 attacks. In the rendition program suspected terrorists would be kidnapped and then flown to a site for torture. In many cases it was to other countries whose police and military regularly used torture. In 2003, an Italian court convicted twenty-three Americans of kidnapping an Egyptian cleric on the streets of Milan and flying him to Egypt to be to tortured. Robert Seldon Lady, the CIA Station Chief in Milan, was one of the convicted. This was the first case in which the United States has been successfully prosecuted for the kidnapping and torture (Wong, 2009). Previous cases in the United States by foreign nationals have failed because of the U.S. government's disallowing information because of state secrets.

One of these failed cases was the case of Maher Arar, a Canadian citizen who was traveling with his family back from a vacation in Tunisia. He was detained by U.S. officials and interrogated about alleged links to Al Qaeda. As part of the CIA's rendition program twelve days later, he was chained, shackled, and flown to Jordan aboard a private plane and from there transferred to a Syrian prison. In a time line of his abuse reported in Canadian Broadcasting Company News (2005), Arar states that "the beating started . . . and was very intense for a week, and then less intense for another week. The second and the third days were the worst. I could hear other prisoners being tortured, and screaming and screaming." In a *Washington Post* article, Arar states, "They kept beating me so I had to falsely confess and told them I did go to Afghanistan. I was ready to confess to anything if it would stop the torture. They wanted me to say I went to a training camp. I was so scared I urinated on myself twice. The beating was less severe each of the following days. At the end of each day, they would always say, 'Tomorrow will be harder for you.' So each night, I could not sleep—I did not sleep for the first four days, and slept no more than two hours a day for about two months" (Brown, 2003). Arar was held and tortured for ten months in a prison in Syria before finally being released. The Canadian Commission of Inquiry validated Mr. Arar's claims (Toope, 2005). The U.S. government under President Obama is continuing the rendition program (Johnston, 2009). In his memoir of his years as president, George W. Bush admitted that he authorized the use of torture to extract information from those who have been detained (Bush, 2011). This may be the first case of an official who has admitted authorizing torture, a violation of U.S. and international law. There is little chance that he will be prosecuted.

Experimentation on Populations

The most heinous case of experimentation on people was conducted by Nazi Germany. The concentration camp of Buchenwald was used for experiments by medical doctors interested in the effects of amputations, lethal germs, and poisons on the human body. More than fifty thousand persons died in this camp. Nazi Germany was not the only country to do experimentations on prisoners during wartime. Dr. Shiro Ishii and his medical research assistants carried out violent human experimentation on tens of thousands during the Second Sino-Japanese War and World War II (Iserson, 2002).

In more recent times, there are cases of experimentation by other governments, including the U.S. government. One classic case is the Tuskegee Syphilis Experiment (Jones, 1987). The U.S. Public Health Service conducted a forty-year experiment in which it studied the effects of untreated syphilis on 399 black male residents of Macon County, Alabama. Those who participated in the study were paid $50 in 1932 (this sum was periodically increased over the length of the study to compensate for inflationary effects), given free medical examinations and transportation to and from the clinics, hot meals on examination days, free treatment for minor ailments, and a burial stipend to be paid to their survivors. A physician with firsthand knowledge of the early years of the experiment noted that the participants were never informed that they had syphilis. Those selected were in the third stage of the disease. Treatment was available at the time, although it was painful and not always successful. Those in the test group did not receive treatment so that the course of the disease could be studied. Dr. J. W. Williams, who was serving his internship at Andrews Hospital at the Tuskegee Institute in 1932 and assisted in the experiments in early years, stated that neither the interns nor the subjects knew what the study involved. "The people who came in were not told what was being done," Dr. Williams said. "We told them we wanted to test them. They were not told, so far as I know, what they were being treated for or what they were not being treated for." As far as he could tell, "the subjects thought they were being treated for rheumatism or bad stomachs" (Jones, 1987, 4). By 1969, Jones estimates that as many as one hundred men died as a direct result of complications caused by syphilis. Others had developed serious syphilis-related heart conditions that may have contributed to their deaths.

It has also been revealed that the government throughout the post–World War II period has been conducting radiation experiments on the population. As late as 1981, Rosenberg (1981) reported that doctors at an Atomic Energy Commission clinic exposed at least eighty-nine cancer patients to large doses of radiation in order to get information for NASA on levels of radiation

Figure 8.5. Six of the 600 men who were test subjects in the Tuskegee Syphilis Experiments which ran from 1932 to 1972 in Tuskegee, Alabama by the U.S. Public Health Service. Source: National Archives and Records Administration.

tolerance before nausea. The House of Representatives Subcommittee on Energy Conservation and Power and the Committee on Energy and Commerce, headed by Representative Edward Markey, issued a report in 1986 detailing thirty-one experiments that took place from the 1940s to the 1970s, sponsored by the Department of Energy or its predecessors. In these experiments 695 people were exposed to radiation (Harris, 1994).

Other information released by the government indicates that what was previously reported was just the tip of the iceberg. Secretary of Energy O'Leary provided information to the public about experiments at major universities including MIT, University of Chicago, California, and Vanderbilt. Experimenters in this research exposed about two thousand Americans to varying degrees of radiation (Ensign and Alcalay, 1994).

The General Accounting Office (1993) reported that government scientists deliberately released radioactive materials into populated areas so that they could study fallout patterns and the rate at which radioactivity decayed. The report describes thirteen different releases of radiation from 1948 to 1952. These releases of radioactive fallout were part of the U.S. nuclear weapons development program.

Ensign and Alcalay (1994) note that in 1949 the Green River tests at Hanford (Washington) Nuclear Reservation were conducted. The nuclear weapons plant deliberately released thousands of curies of radioactive iodine-131. This is several times the amount released from the 1979 Three Mile Island disaster. This release of radiation was done to test its recently installed radiological monitoring equipment. The authors report that a team of epidemiologists is now looking into an epidemic of late-occurring thyroid tumors and other radiogenic disorders among the downwind residents of eastern Washington State.

Between 1946 and 1958, the United States exploded sixty-seven atomic and hydrogen bombs at Bikini and Enewetok, two Marshall group atolls. The largest and dirtiest of the Marshall Islands blasts was code-named Bravo. At fifteen megatons—more than one thousand times the size of the Hiroshima bomb—Bravo rained lethal radioactive fallout over thousands of unsuspecting islanders under circumstances that remain mysterious. The people of Rongelap atoll were especially hard-hit. They were evacuated from their home islands two days after Bravo, following the absorption of massive doses of high-level fallout (Ensign and Alcalay, 1994, 32–33). Ensign and Alcalay note that three years after the bombing, Dr. C. L. Dunham, head of the Atomic Energy Commission's Division of Biology and Medicine, expressed the commission's interest in studying the Rongelap victims to determine the long-term effects of exposure. To this day, the AEC continues to compile data on the victims of these bombings.

Additional reports of experimentation indicated a callous disregard for patients who were already suffering from terminal illnesses. In 1945 Albert Stevens, a fifty-eight-year-old California house painter suffering from a huge stomach ulcer, was injected with doses of plutonium 238 and 239 equivalent to 446 times the average lifetime exposure. Doctors recommended an operation and told his family that Mr. Stevens had only about six months to live. For the next year, scientists collected plutonium-laden urine and fecal samples from Stevens and used that data in a classified scientific report entitled *A*

Comparison of the Metabolism of Plutonium in Man and the Rat. Welsome (1993) has determined that there is little doubt scientists knew of the danger. The report concluded that chronic plutonium poisoning is a matter of serious concern for those who come in contact with this material.

In another case, which occurred in 1947, doctors injected plutonium into the left leg of Elmer Allen, a thirty-six-year-old African American railroad porter. After three days, the leg was amputated for an alleged preexisting bone cancer. Researchers then analyzed tissue samples to determine the physiology of plutonium dispersion. As late as 1973, scientists summoned Allen to the Argonne National Laboratory near Chicago, where he was subjected to a follow-up whole-body radiation scan and his urine was analyzed to ascertain lingering levels of plutonium from the 1947 injection (Ensign and Alcalay, 1994, 31).

In two additional cases, the subjects of the experiments were not allegedly terminally ill. Instead, they were institutionalized and therefore unable to give free consent. In one case, young boys classified as mentally retarded were subjects in an experiment conducted by the Quaker Oats Company, the National Institutes of Health, and the Atomic Energy Commission. Beginning in 1949, the children at the Fernald School for the mentally retarded in Waltham, Massachusetts, were fed minute doses of radioactive materials in their breakfast cereal to determine if the materials prevented the body from absorbing iron and calcium. The children were told that they were joining a science club. The consent form sent to the boys' parents stated nothing about the radiation experiment (*New York Times*, 1994).

In 1963, 131 prison inmates in Oregon and Washington were given $200 each to be exposed to 600 roentgens of radiation (one hundred times the allowable annual dose for nuclear workers). The prisoners signed consent forms agreeing to submit to X-ray radiation of their scrotum and testes; they were not warned about the dangers of contracting testicular cancer. Doctors later performed vasectomies on the inmates to avoid the possibility of contaminating the general population with irradiation-induced mutants (*Newsweek*, 1993, 15).

Ensign and Alcalay (1994) contend that the experiments that caused the greatest number of fatalities occurred from 1960 to 1971. In this research, Dr. Eugene Saenger, a radiologist at the University of Cincinnati, exposed eighty-eight cancer patients to whole-body radiation. Many of the guinea pigs were poor African Americans at Cincinnati General Hospital with inoperable tumors. All but one of the eighty-eight patients has since died. According to Schneider (1994), there is evidence that scientists forged signatures on the consent form for the Cincinnati experiments. Gloria Nelson testified before the House that her grandmother, Amelia Jackson, had been strong and still working before she was treated by Dr. Saenger. Following exposure to 100 rads of whole-body radiation (about 7,500 chest X-rays), Amelia Jackson bled and vomited for days and became permanently disabled. Jackson testified that the signature on her grandmother's consent form was forged.

State Environmental Violence

The U.S. government itself has been a major violator of its regulations as they relate to the disposal of radioactive waste from weapons and power plant production. Kohn (1992) contends that the problem of how governmental agencies have disposed of radioactive waste is widespread and may be greater than the toxic dumping law violation activities of private companies. He notes that billions of pounds of governments accumulated waste—containing plutonium, arsenic, cyanide, nerve gases, TNT, rocket fuels, pesticides, bacteria, and other harmful substances—pose the most immediate threat to public health (Kohn, 1992, 40). According to Kohn at the time of his writing, the government had more than fourteen thousand dump sites that threatened the health of the public. All nuclear weapons plants (Hanford, in Washington; Savannah River plant, South Carolina; Rocky Flats, Colorado; and the Fernald Plant in Ohio) have serious problems in the disposal of waste.

Kohn notes that in the Hanford plant alone, it is estimated that the toxic waste would be equivalent to a forty-foot-deep lake that could cover Manhattan Island. Radioactive materials have also been found in the Columbia River, which supplies water to eastern Washington and western Oregon. At the Savannah River plant, there are increasing problems of radioactive material seeping into the region's biggest water source for the surrounding community. At the Fernald Plant, located outside Cincinnati, Ohio, it was discovered that eighty-one tons of liquid uranium had entered the Great Miami River, the major freshwater body in the metropolitan area. Lastly, the water supply for some of the suburbs of Denver has been contaminated by chemical and radioactive waste from Rocky Flats. Kohn notes one strategy of the U.S. Pentagon for dumping waste involves the complicity of private interests. When Pentagon officials auction used equipment by lot, they will often dump acids, solvents, and other dangerous chemicals in with the valuable hardware. The toxins get pawned off on military surplus dealers, who discard them wherever they can. The Los Angeles police last year discovered fifty thousand gallons of military chemicals, highly corrosive and explosive, that had been left in a vacant lot under a freeway, just a few feet from a river (Kohn, 1992, 45).

The Brookhaven National Laboratory, located on Long Island near New York City, is a serious toxic hazard in one of the most populated regions of the country (Flanders, 1994). In 1989 the Environmental Protection Agency designated Brookhaven a "superfund site." Scattered within a five-mile stretch of land adjacent to the plant are landfills that contained radioactive contaminated lab garbage, animal carcasses, and sewage sludge. The plant is located above Long Island's sole-source aquifer, and well monitoring has indicated that local groundwater was contaminated with radioactive strontium-90 and tritium. The lab's own published reports stated that the lab had been a source of radioactive emissions and toxic waste for more than forty years. Flanders (1994) reports that in 1990 the Department of Energy estimated that the contamination from the buried waste could affect 15,400 people. The DOE also estimated that it would take more than twenty years and $338 million for the cleanup. Flanders notes that a 1994 New York State

Department of Health study found that women with postmenopausal breast cancer were 60 percent more likely than cancer-free women to have lived within one kilometer of a chemical plant. The state's own breast cancer statistics show elevated rates in several areas close to the lab, where there are few industrial plants.

According to *Safetyforum Research* (2002), this problem of toxic waste disposal by the U.S. government is not confined to our national borders, but is even a greater problem overseas. According to *Safetyforum*, the U.S. Department of Defense (DOD) is the world's biggest polluter. "DOD generates 750,000 tons of hazardous waste a year, more than the five largest U.S. chemical companies combined. The private agency in its analysis of public records claims that there are 14,401 probable 'hot spots' at 1,579 military facilities. It is also notes that the U.S. military is responsible for contamination at 53 private sites—contractor-owned weapons plants and property Department of Defense once owned or used as dumps" (Safetyforum.com, 2002). *Safetyforum* notes that in 1999, the DOD Inspector General reported "potentially significant liabilities" and pollution at U.S. bases in Canada, Germany, Great Britain, Greenland, Iceland, Italy, Japan, Panama, the Philippines, South Korea, Spain, Turkey, and other nations.

Safetyforum highlights the case of the Philippines in its report and notes that when the U.S. military operated the naval base at Subic Bay, 3.75 million gallons of raw sewage were pumped daily into the bay. They also note that toxic waste from storage and destruction of excess bombs and ammunition was either poured into a local stream or dumped in a landfill. According to workers at the site, drums of cyanide were emptied into a landfill. The federal government's estimated cost of cleaning up both Clark and Subic Bay bases: $1 billion. The U.S. government contends that its treaties with the Philippines exempt it from cleanup costs.

Of the four thousand people living near Subic Bay when the base was in operation, eight hundred have been diagnosed with asbestosis. After a political movement in the Philippines pressured the United States to abandon the site in 1992, it was used for evacuees from the 1991 Mt. Pinatubo volcano eruption. A Filipino official who monitored the evacuated population said that they experienced unusually high rates of illnesses traced to poisoned well water. The list of ailments included skin diseases; mouth, nose, and throat diseases; kidney diseases; miscarriages, reproductive disorders, stillbirths, and physical and mental birth defects; cancers; heart ailments; and leukemia. Surprisingly, federal agencies of the U.S. government are exempt from Clean Water Act enforcement and the U.S. Environmental Protection Agency has no authority to police overseas facilities. In 1999, Congress wrote into the Department of Defense's budget language that prohibits payment of environmental fines or penalties.

The Philippines is not an isolated case. Safetyforum reports that raw sewage from two military bases is dumped daily into local waters in South Korea. In Germany, the estimated cost of the cleanup of toxic waste improperly disposed by the U.S. military is at least US$1 billion. In 1990 the U.S. Department of Defense Inspector General estimated that cleaning up U.S. bases would cost $100–$200 billion (Safetyforum, 2002).

Black Jacketing, Bogus Mail, and Black Propaganda Campaigns

The last examples of state violence are less direct and tend not to involve the use of state agents in conducting acts of violence but rather promoting the use of violence by those targeted for control or destruction. One general strategy that follows this pattern is the use of false information by agents of the state to promote violence directed at someone by either members of his or her own group or by members of another group. The FBI uses several names to describe this method: black jacketing or snitch jacketing, bogus mail, and black propaganda campaigns.

The Senate Select Committee investigating the strategies used by the FBI in their COINTELPRO (counterintelligence program) operations found that the FBI used the systematic fabrication and transmittal of letters and other documents expressly intended to push ideological disagreements between party leaders Huey P. Newton and Eldridge Cleaver into the realm of open hostility. Churchill and Vander Wall (1990) report that after Los Angeles Black Panther Party leaders Jon Huggins and Alpertice Bunch Carter were killed on UCLA's campus in 1969 by gunmen from the rival United Slaves Organization (US), the FBI assigned itself a good measure of credit for having stirred up antagonism among the two groups. At least one FBI memo recommended a new round of cartoons, purportedly to be sent by US to the Panthers, designed to indicate to the Black Panther Party that the US organization felt they were ineffectual, inadequate, and riddled with graft and corruption. Churchill and Vander Wall (1990) cited a congressional report entitled *The FBI's Covert Action Program to Destroy the Black Panther Party*, which described the specific strategy to incite violence between the two organizations.

Black jacketing or snitch jacketing is intended to create dissent and conflict within organizations. The goal is the creation of suspicion through the spreading of rumors or the manufacture of false evidence. With militant black organizations during the 1960s, the goal was to target bona fide members, usually in key positions, and to convince others within the organization that they were actually FBI/police informers or, alternately, that they were guilty of such offenses as skimming organizational funds. Churchill and Vander Wall (1990) indicate that the purpose of such tactics was to develop suspicion of jacketed individuals and sow dissension in the ranks. They maintain that this was a very common strategy used by the FBI to disrupt dissident organizations.

Agents Provocateurs

Another indirect form of violence is the use of agents provocateurs. An agent provocateur is an agent of a law enforcement organization who is placed in a group targeted for disruption or destruction. The agent tries to persuade the leadership to engage in illegal (often violent) activity. Once this has occurred, the agent then tells the law enforcement agency the time and place of the illegal activity so that it can be there to apprehend the group's members. Andrew Karmen outlines the following steps in the agent provocateur strategy:

1. First, the FBI or local police agency selects a group, situation, or territory for infiltration.
2. Next, the agency finds an agent whose background is compatible with that of the intended victims. He or she is then sent in to join the appropriate group and begins doing minor tasks to help win acceptance.
3. After this goal is achieved, the agent seeks out militant individuals and begins urging them to commit violence. Oftentimes the agents provide guns, bombs, and other materials and even personally participate in the crimes themselves.
4. Finally, the police close in at the most compromising moment. The agent then withdraws, only to return for the trial with a carefully conceived story admitting complicity with the criminal events but denying entrapment (Karmen, 1974).

Karmen reports that thousands of infiltrators were used against the political left during the 1960s. For example, the FBI deployed 316 informers between 1960 and 1976 within the Socialist Workers Party (SWP) and its youth wing, Young Socialist Alliance (YSA). Forty-two of these FBI plants had held office within the SWP or YSA and had thus participated in shaping the very organizational policies that the bureau claimed were necessary to investigate. According to Karmen, agents provocateurs were also involved in provoking violence at the Democratic National Convention in 1968 and in instigating a violent confrontation between the Black Panthers and the Los Angeles police in 1969. Karmen also contends there is evidence that Terrence Norman, an agent of the FBI and the campus police, precipitated the volley of shots by the Ohio National Guard that killed four students at Kent State University in the spring of 1970.

Churchill and Vander Wall (1990) mention that one of the more notorious agents provocateurs paid by the FBI was Tommy the Traveler Tongyai. Tongyai roamed from campus to campus across the Northeast in the late 1960s, agitating for the bombing of military research facilities, the burning of ROTC buildings, and similar violent actions. Marx (1974), analyzing the pattern of infiltration by informants and agents provocateurs, found that eleven involved white peace and/or economic groups, ten were directed against black and Chicano groups, and only two involved right-wing groups.

PATTERNS OF STATE VIOLENCE

Are there patterns of state violence in terms of particular features of countries that make them more or less vulnerable to its occurrence? Political scientist Ted R. Gurr (1986) has developed a series of propositions that attempts to summarize the patterns of state violence worldwide. Gurr contends that there are some necessary conditions for state violence to occur. First, the existence of a group, class, or party regarded by ruling elites as an active threat to their continued rule is necessary. In our discussion of targets of state violence, we have identified indigenous populations, ethnic minorities, unions, political opposition groups, and children (in Brazil and Colombia) identified as potentially threatening or creating threatening conditions and where elites have seen violence as a means to eliminate the threat.

Gurr goes on to specify conditions that increase the likelihood of state violence. He finds that the greater the political threat posed by challengers, the greater the likelihood that a regime will respond with violence (Gurr, 1986, 53–54). The most important factor in determining the level of threat is whether the challenger's objective is to displace those in power. Another condition concerns the degree of latent popular support of those who challenge the regime. Gurr specifies that the greater the latent support within the larger population for such challengers, the greater the likelihood of state violence. On the other hand, if such groups have support among some of the elite, then the state is less likely to use violence against them. Furthermore, if the challengers of the state also rely on violence, this again increases the likelihood that the state in turn will utilize violence to counter those who threaten their rule.

Gurr maintains that the existence of a conflict situation and the presence of challengers are necessary conditions for state terrorism, but characteristics of the state and prevailing political traditions probably are more important and immediate considerations in the calculus of terror than traits of the challengers. Thus, weak regimes are more likely to use violence in response to challenges than strong regimes (Gurr, 1986, 53–54). He explains this by pointing out that weak regimes have limited material resources and low levels of political institutionalization and that these conditions constrain the policy options of elites who are threatened. Furthermore, Gurr contends that ruling elites who themselves have secured and maintained their positions by violent means are likely to choose violent responses to future challengers.

Following from this latter point, it is likely that the military coups promoted and engineered by international superpowers contribute to further state violence in these client states as they go on to be more likely to use violence against those who challenge their rule. Gurr says that "the successful situational uses of state terror in polarized societies are likely to lead to institutionalized terror and to the preemptive use of terror to maintain political control. . . . Once rulers find terror to be effective in suppressing challenges, they are likely to regard it as an acceptable tactic in future challenges . . . [and] they are likely to regard it as an acceptable tactic in future conflicts" (Gurr, 1986, 55). Gurr finds that this social learning of the effectiveness of state violence does not necessarily have to be from the elites' own actions but can be learned from the modeling of others in their successful use of state violence, similar to how many forms of violence are learned at the interpersonal level. He believes that the majority of episodes of state violence in this century have been patterned either on the historical use of state terrorism in the society in question or on the concurrent use of terrorism by other rulers, especially those of ideologically similar regimes.

Other features of societies that relate to the levels of state violence, according to Gurr, are the democratic nature of the state and the levels of social heterogeneity and inequality in the society. Regarding the first feature, Gurr contends that the patterns of state violence in the world today support the generalization that democratic principles and institutions inhibit political elites from using state violence. Thus he states that "state violence is general-ly less in democratic than authoritarian regimes, and state terror has seldom been used by elites within countries with a democratic political tradition. . . . Democratic political norms emphasize compromise in conflict and participa-tion and responsiveness in relations between rules and ruled, traits that are inconsistent with reliance on violence as an instrument of rule or opposition" (Gurr, 1986, 57–58). This finding is consistent with Sivard's (1986) analysis of state violence in the modern world. Sivard finds that the association be-tween institutionalized political violence and military-controlled govern-ments is particularly strong. She writes that of those governments most prone to use torture, there are almost three times as many among the military-controlled as in other Third World countries (5).

In regard to the relationship between inequality and state violence, Gurr (1986) finds that the greater the heterogeneity and stratification in a society, the greater the likelihood that a regime will use violence as a principal means of social control. He explains this pattern by first demonstrating that in ethnically and religiously diverse societies, social cohesion tends to be low. Therefore, challenges to the regimes are more common, and elites are more likely to respond violently. As far as stratification is concerned, ruling classes in highly stratified societies are ruthless in their use of violence to suppress threats to their domination.

As we discussed earlier with regard to the relationship between stratifica-tion and violence, when it comes to being socialized in societies that are greatly stratified, we learn to accept some people as being worth less than others. This idea contributes to a general acceptance of violence directed at those categorized as being of less worth. Thus, Legum (1966), in describing the factors that led to the 1966 massacres of six thousand to eight thousand Ibos in northern Nigeria, finds that the danger signal is when government officials talk about a minority in nonhuman terms. Wolf (1976) has found that the Guaran-speaking Paraguayans who hunt the Ache use terminology like "rabid rats" to describe the native population. In a public speech made in Denver not long before the Sand Creek Massacre that occurred on November 28, 1864, U.S. Army Colonel Chivinton advocated the killing and scalping of Indians, even infants. "Nits make lice!" he declared. At the Sand Creek Massacre there was indiscriminate killing of 105 Indian women and children and twenty-eight men who were unarmed and standing around a white flag of surrender when the slaughter began (Brown, 1970).

Gurr (1986) concludes that minority elites (i.e., elites drawn from an ethnic population that is a numerical minority) in a highly stratified society are likely to use terror routinely as an instrument of rule. South Africa, Rwanda, and Burundi are excellent examples of this pattern. As Gurr argues, when the potential for internal challenges is intrinsically high and the social distance between advantaged rulers and ethnically or religiously distinct sub-jects is particularly great, violence is likely to be used for social control.

Gurr also focuses on characteristics of the international environment that contribute to state violence. He concludes that "regimes facing external threats are likely to use violence against domestic opponents. . . . In heteroge-neous and politically divided societies, elites facing external enemies have strong incentives to suppress internal opposition" (Gurr, 1986, 60). Furthermore, regimes involved in proxy superpower conflicts (i.e., where satellite regimes aligned with superpower nations commit violence in the latter's political interests) are likely to use the most extreme forms of violence against challengers. When internal conflicts become polarized, as along lines of East-West (Communist and capitalist regimes) and increasingly North-South (developed and developing countries) conflict, for example, external sponsors are likely to encourage the use of warfare and to provide their proxies with the advisers, technology, and even troops to do so, as in Afghanistan and Vietnam, and the internal conflicts within Guatemala, El Salvador, Nicaragua, Brazil, and Haiti. Sivard's (1986) analysis of 114 developing countries confirms this pattern. She notes that with respect to institutionalized political violence, the worst offenders are clients of one or the other superpower.

Gurr (1986) also points out that the highest levels of state violence occur in the periphery of the world system: Uganda and Equatorial Guinea, Ethiopia, the Central African Republic, Burundi and Rwanda, and Kampuchea, to name a few. He reasons that executioners of state violence in such places have not been significantly dependent, politically or economically, on the world system. Thus they have not been deterred by the prospect of economic sanctions or embargoes because they have been largely self-sufficient or because their trade and aid partners have simply not cared enough to apply economic pressures.

Nevertheless, the cases Gurr raises as examples of the rule may actually be exceptions. For when we look at the levels of state violence in Latin America in particular, we see that the United States has played an important role in supporting and assisting state violence to suppress dissent and maintain stability, one of the central goals of U.S. foreign policy in its sphere of influence, which is now the entire world. Furthermore, in all the cases cited (and in many others), the colonial history of domination created the peripheral status of the nation and may have contributed to the economic and political climate that increased the likelihood of the use of state violence. Thus historical ties may be more significant than the current context in which the state violence occurs.

Furthermore, Gurr assumes that the international community has had an impact on deterring state violence. Unfortunately, when we look at the incidences of state violence today, the superpowers have ignored, supported, or sponsored the instances of state violence conducted by their allies, and international bodies such as the United Nations and the World Court have had minimal impact on stopping or deterring elites from conducting campaigns of state violence in their countries.

State violence ultimately is used to maintain the order defined in terms of ranking people within nations and ranking nation-states within the international order. This order is defined ultimately in terms of a pattern of a distribution of power, a distribution, moreover, in which the framework is defined in terms of systems of stratification within the nation-state and between nation-states in the world system. We have seen that in nations where there are high levels of inequality, state violence is more pronounced. Furthermore, in regard to the nature of the world system, as the position of states in terms of a power hierarchy becomes more unequal and as the relationships between states within the system are defined by relationships of domination or imperialism, there is an increasing likelihood of the occurrence of state violence sponsored both nationally and internationally. Thus, nations that are themselves highly stratified internally and positioned in dominated or exploited locations in the world system are more likely to suffer from higher levels of state violence than nations that have lower levels of inequality and are positioned at the higher end of the world system. The state violence throughout Africa and Central and South America confirms this pattern. The exceptions to this pattern, of course, are those dominant powers that, although they may not have high levels of state violence within their own societies, nevertheless sponsor it internationally in order to maintain stability in terms of the distribution of power within those systems and internationally. State violence, in other words, has a two-tiered (i.e., center versus peripheral) existence in which the center nations internally show lower levels of state violence but sponsor it rampantly externally in the periphery in order to maintain their positions of dominance in the world.

Chomsky and Herman (1979) recognize that U.S. economic interests in the Third World have dictated a policy of containing revolution, preserving an open door for U.S. economic interests and assuring favorable conditions of investment. Thus the aim of the violence is pacification, discouraging popular movements or radical and even social democratic governments that could threaten patterns of property ownership and wage and tax structures affecting investments. This is the goal of U.S. foreign policy as well as the policies of other advanced capitalist governments.

Since the nineteenth century the United States, in its own hemisphere and throughout the rest of the world, has played a dominant role (if not the dominant role) in maintaining order through its use of state violence: in wars and in its involvement in covert forms of state violence through the activities of the CIA or through the training, arming, and directing of surrogate forces in the international periphery to carry out state violence. The United States' past involvement in all these arenas of state violence is well documented in various countries throughout the world. Its role today is truly worldwide, operating more than eight military bases around the world, serving as the major arms supplier to developing countries, and providing funds to train and equip military and police forces (Klare, 1981; McClintock, 1985; Pierce, 1970; *New Internationalist*, 1994; Wheat, 1995). Through this web of sponsored repression, the United States alone does more to maintain and extend systems of stratification around the world, which again leads to an increase in levels of violence at all levels, from interpersonal to institutional, and to the last level that we discuss: structural violence.

State violence for resources, markets, and profit (riches) is as old story of empires. Violence is a principal instrument for conquest outside of their imperial domain and control of territories within (Iadicola, 2009). Today, in what is referred to as a unipolar world, there are few imperial rivals that can challenge the United States in extending its domain. The recent wars in the Middle East follow a familiar pattern of imperial expansion as a result of a vacuum created by the collapse of a competing imperial system, in this case the USSR. Imperial control also spawns the violence of terrorism of those who are resisting the system that they are being incorporated within and the state to terrorize a population to accept its control. The story of the violence of terrorism is as old as the story of the violence of empires. And the story of state violence is as old as the state and its most powerful form, the imperial state.

CONCLUSION—STATE VIOLENCE AND INEQUALITY

State violence is about the exercise of power over those who threaten its distribution. As we have discussed, it takes many forms. But one pattern seems to be persistent. Those who are the most powerless in the society and world are easy victims when they act in ways that threaten the state or possess resources that the state or those who have the most power to influence the state wish to possess or control. They may be children, women, members of minority groups, workers, or members of dissident political parties. In country after country, where state violence is present, the pattern of victimization is repeated. When the elite are victims of state violence, there is much publicity and public concern despite the fact that their victimization is an exception to the dominant pattern. This is not the case when the victims are from the lowest levels of society; there is often little public outcry or awareness of their victimization, despite the fact that they make up the greatest numbers.

There is no databank on state violence. We would expect that societies in the world that have the lowest levels of inequality would have the lowest levels of state violence, while those that have the highest levels would have the highest levels of state violence. Furthermore, following from this, we would expect that as societies in the world and the world itself become increasingly unequal in the distribution of wealth and power, state violence is increasingly likely to be used to maintain and extend those patterns of inequality as defined nationally and internationally. In the post–Cold War era, the concentration of power internationally is greater than it has ever been during the past two hundred years. The power of the United States as a military, economic, political, and cultural power, or an imperial power, dwarfs the power of all previous imperial systems. Given the reluctance of international justice agencies like the International Criminal Court or the United Nations to prosecute the government of the United States for its illegal actions of war, assassinations, and torture, there is little check on its future acts of state violence (Iadicola, 2008, 2009, 2010).

It makes little difference if we are looking at the state's legitimate use of violence (e.g., when it carries out executions of those who commit capital crimes) or illegitimate use of violence (e.g., sponsored death squad activities); the victims are in the vast majority of cases those who have the least. The violence of the state is one more piece of the puzzle in describing the nature of violence. And now to the last piece, which is the centerpiece of the puzzle of violence.

DISCUSSION QUESTIONS

1. The most powerful nations in the world are some of the worst viola-
   tors of international law and are the most violent. How do we control
   state violence in the world today? What needs to be done in order to
   protect people around the world from this form of violence?
2. Part of the problem of state violence is the violence of imperial systems. The United States is the most powerful empire in the history of
   the world. Does the American Way of Life depend upon the use of
   state violence around the world today?
3. What poses a greater threat to world peace: the violence of state terrorists or the violence of nonstate terrorists?
4. The United States currently is engaged in the use of assassinations or
   targeted killings in the War against Terror. These assassinations often
   occur in areas that would not be considered to be the battlefield and
   are often done with unmanned drone aircraft, in some cases in other
   countries that we are currently not at war with. Is the United States
   justified in conducting assassinations in its War on Terror?
5. During the invasion and occupation of Iraq and Afghanistan, the United States used torture to extract information from those who were
   alleged to be terrorists. Is a country ever justified in using torture
   against prisoners of war? What about citizens?

Chapter Nine

Structural Violence

Each day, more than twenty thousand children under the age of five die in the world from malnutrition and preventable infectious diseases. The vast majority are from the least developed countries in Asia and Africa (World Health Organization, 2011).

Eight hundred and fifty million people (approximately 13 percent of the world's population, 99 percent of which reside in developing countries) are undernourished (Food and Agriculture Organization of the United Nations, 2001).

Over the past five decades in the United States the maternal mortality rate of black women is four times greater than it is for white women (Tucker, Berg, Callaghan, and Hsia, 2007). According to 2007 data, the infant mortality rate for non-Hispanic black women was 2.4 times the rate for non-Hispanic white women. Other minorities such as American Indian or Alaska Native (AIAN) and Puerto Rican women also had relatively high infant mortality rates compared to non-Hispanic white infants (MacDorman and Mathews, 2011).

"When Siri wakes it is about noon. In the instant of waking she knows exactly who and what she has become. As she explained to me, the soreness in her genitals remind her of the fifteen men she had sex with the night before. Siri is fifteen years old. Sold by her parents a year ago . . ." (Bales, 2004, 34).

These are stories of structural violence. Maxine Waters, congresswoman from South Central Los Angeles, giving testimony before the U.S. Senate Banking Committee in the aftermath of the Los Angeles riots of 1992, quoted Robert Kennedy in a speech he made in 1968 after one of the most turbulent periods of urban rioting: "There is another kind of violence in America, slower but just as deadly, destructive as the shot or bomb in the night. . . . This is the violence of institutions; indifference and inaction and slow decay.

This is the violence that afflicts the poor, that poisons relations between men and women because their skin is different colors. This is the slow destruction of a child by hunger, and schools without books and homes without heat in the winter" (Medoff and Sklar, 1994, 245).

As we discussed in the introductory chapter, structural violence is violence that occurs in the context of establishing, maintaining, extending, or reducing hierarchical relations between categories of people within a society. For example, violence can be an outcome of how we have organized a society in terms of access to basic necessities of survival. Or it can be an outcome of how we have organized a society in terms of access to a pollution-free environment. Or it can be an outcome of how we have organized a society in terms of access to medical care and medicines to cure diseases. In short, it can be an outcome of how we have organized a society in terms of the distribution of life chances. Life chances refer to the opportunities in life to realize one's potential—intellectually, physically, and spiritually. Differences in infant mortality rates among groups that occupy different positions in systems of stratification are a violent outcome of this arrangement of people. We know that in the United States, if you are born black you are more likely not to survive your first year of life than if you are born white. If you are born black you will have less access to health care and safe and nonpolluted communities. In short, if you are born black, you will on the average live six to seven years less than if you were born white.

These differences also manifest themselves in life expectancy differences between countries. If you are born in Malawi, a former colony of the British Empire in southeastern Africa, you will live on average thirty-two fewer years than if you are born in the United States (World Health Organization, 2011). These life expectancy differences are a result of the differences in the quality and opportunity for life available to people who occupy different positions in systems of stratification within one society and differences in the position of their society in the world system of stratification. Each year as a result of transnational adoptions children are born into a status or position in one country that also has a position in the world political economic system and transported to another society to occupy another position in a society that also has a different position. This change in positions that results from transnational adoption can dramatically change the number and quality of life of years the adoptee lives. Think about a child who was born in a poor African, Asian, or South or Central American country to parents of the poorest strata in that society. Let's say that this child is born in Nepal to a poor farming woman who has lost her husband and she decides that she cannot adequately care for this child given that she has five other children that she is trying to keep alive and to give this infant up for adoption to an international adoption agency. The child is adopted by a professional couple, a doctor and lawyer, who lives in Stockholm, London, or Los Angeles. How would his or her life be different? How would his or her life expectancy change? How different would his or her opportunities for education, for fulfilling career, to travel, and so on, be? This story happens every day around the world, where children's lives are dramatically changed as a result of a change in the position that they occupy in the world. The differences in the life chances between people who occupy different positions in the world are part of the story of structural violence.

Structural violence can also be interpersonal or institutional violence. For example, the actions of individuals acting outside institutional roles to establish, maintain, extend, or reduce the hierarchical ordering of a category of people within a society would be both interpersonal and structural violence. In this chapter we discuss groups, such as the Ku Klux Klan and skinheads in this country and several other countries in Europe today, assaulting and killing members of minorities in order to maintain or extend ethnic/racial hierarchical relations in a community. On the other hand, the Palestinian suicide bomber terrorist who is killing Israeli civilians to end the oppression and domination of Palestinians by the Israeli government is also committing violence that is interpersonal and structural. We also discuss the violence between religious groups within a society to maintain, extend, or reduce hierarchical relations between them. For example, the violence in India today between Muslim, Hindu, and Christian groups is an example of this type of violence. The violence also may be a product of governmental or other institutional actions that serve to establish, maintain, extend, or reduce the hierarchical ordering of categories of people within a society. Some examples of violence we have previously discussed in the family, religious, economic, and state violence chapters are also examples of structural violence.

Galtung (1969), one of the first to use the term *structural violence* in his writings in peace studies, defined it as the violence that is built into the structure of the society and manifests itself in differences in life chances. Galtung stated that "in a society where life expectancy is twice as high in the upper as in the lower classes, violence is exercised even if there are no concrete actors one can point to directly attacking others, as when one person kills another" (Galtung, 1969, 171). It is "the everyday violence of infant mortality, slow starvation, disease, despair, and humiliation that destroys socially marginalized humans with even greater frequency and usually invisible or misrecognized" (Scheper-Hughes and Bourgois, 2004, 2).

HIERARCHICAL STRUCTURES WITHIN SOCIETIES

Before we begin discussing the violent outcomes or actions that stem from hierarchical relations in a society, it is important that we describe the nature of the hierarchies and how they are a fundamental structural feature of capitalist society and the world political economic system. Societies of the world today are organized in at least four fundamental hierarchical relations: class, gender, ethnic/racial identity, and age. All societies of the world today are either some type of capitalist society, in transition from a statist or state socialist system to a capitalist system, or a state socialist society integrated into a world political economic system that is capitalist dominated. Most societies are hybrid systems that contain a mixture of ownership and control by private, cooperative, and public or state ownership. The sector that dominates economically and politically determines on which side of the ideological spectrum from right to left (capitalist to socialist) is the development trajectory of the country. At the beginning of the twenty-first century, in the vast majorities of societies the capitalist mode of production and distribution dominates.

As you recall from our discussion of the mode of production in chapter 1, capitalism connotes a particular pattern of class stratification where there is an owning or capitalist class and a working class. Other class positions are also present. These positions may be remnants of a subordinate mode of production in societies that are less advanced in terms of capitalist development or they may represent an emerging class position that develops because of changes in the nature of production in the society. For example, in many Latin American countries there exists a remnant of a class system that is rooted in a previous mode of production. The *latifundia* system of agriculture, which was based on a class of large landowners and a class of peasants or *campesinos* who worked the land for the landlords in order to have access to their own plots, represents a different class relationship than the dominant class relations in capitalist society between owner and wage workers. Also, in many regions of the world there are institutional systems of bonded labor, which creates a distinct class of bonded laborers and/or slaves.

Other class positions that may or may not add stability to the system develop as the capitalist modes of production increase in size and dominance. For example, as capitalist systems develop, a managerial class arises to control production for owners. As mentioned previously, these managers, like workers, do not own production, but unlike workers they do control it for those who own. This class becomes increasingly important as production becomes larger and the holdings of the capitalist class become more extensive, fluid, and distant. There is also a class of independent producers; originally they are the highly skilled artisans who are not transformed into workers because of the nature of the work. Eventually many of these positions become absorbed into the working class. However, opportunities for "self-employment" continue to develop in areas where the level of surplus generated by the owner-worker relations is insufficient for the capitalist investment. This may be in new areas of production as a result of new inventions, which are high risk in terms of investment return, or in areas of highly technical and specialized labor, which is too costly and cannot be as easily controlled to maximize the surplus produced for owners.

An alternative to capitalist relations of production has also existed within many capitalist countries where workers generally own and control the production. The development of cooperatives where workers have joined together to own production is one case. The cooperatives in the Mondrigan region of Spain, the city of Sheffield in England, as well in the Pacific Northwest of the United States with its plywood cooperatives are examples of these alternative class relations (Zwerdling, 1980; Morrison, 1991). However, these alternatives are not promoted within capitalist society and generally are an exception to the dominant relations of the production in advanced societies.

In capitalist political/economic systems, the fundamental relationship between those who own and control production and those who sell their labor is characterized by a particular pattern of income and wealth inequality that in general is reflective of the nature of the class system. As a general pattern, capitalists have more power, income, and wealth than workers. The income and wealth positions of independent producers (self-employed) and managers are in part based on the size and the cost of the production system that they own or control. Capitalist systems in general are based on an unequal distribution of wealth and income that parallels the patterns of ownership and control of production within the society. There are exceptions to this general pattern where you will find workers who because of the high level of skill or talent may earn more than owners. One thinks of movie stars and high-paid athletes as the exception. But they are exceptions to the general pattern of income and wealth distribution in capitalist society.

The nature of the relationship between capitalists and workers is also characterized by exploitation. Exploitation simply refers to a pattern whereby workers produce more than is required for them to reproduce their position as defined in terms of customary standard of living of workers at that particular skill level, and the surplus resulting from their labor goes to those who own production as a right of ownership. In return for this surplus production, workers receive a wage, which allows them to acquire the necessities that are customary for members of this class within the society. Capitalists receive the surplus produced in production, that is, that which is not necessary to reproduce the production (workers and managers, machinery, and raw materials). This surplus is the basis of profit, but must be realized in the marketplace if the capitalist is to receive a profit from the production of the goods or services.

Capitalists attempt to acquire larger and larger amounts of surplus in order to have more profits and attract more investment capital to grow in the marketplace. For capitalists, the law of survival in the marketplace is that you grow or you die. Growth depends on increasing the efficiency of production either by having workers produce more during the time that they work through speeding up the production process (this can be accomplished by means of the introduction of technology) and/or by cutting labor costs through deskilling and wage cutting. Workers, on the other hand, are trying to acquire a larger and larger portion of the surplus that they produce by means of wage or employment benefit increases and to be able to have more control over their labor. These are the central points of conflict between owners and workers.

Workers are also in a coercive relationship with owners because they must sell their labor in order to acquire the necessities for survival. This coercion is most obvious in the transition to capitalist society. For example, British imperialists in many African countries placed a head tax on native populations that required the native population to sell their labor in the marketplace to acquire the currency to pay the taxes that were imposed on them. Similarly, missionaries played a role in coercing indigenous populations to produce a surplus for their new spiritual and political overlords. It also occurs today in many South and Central American countries, as small peasant landowners are forced off their plots of land and are forced to sell their labor to capitalists to survive as agricultural production undergoes a transition to cash crop production for export and increased mechanization. In Peru and Guatemala 85 percent of rural workers are landless. In fact, a billion people living in villages in the developing world have no land of their own to farm (*New*

Internationalist, 1995). This displacement around the world as a result of the transformation of agricultural systems has led to a growing problem of unemployment that goes beyond the problems caused by business cycles (Somavia, 2006). This is particularly the case in the poor regions of the world in Africa and Asia.

As a rule, in the development of capitalism, as production becomes privately owned and there is less and less access to production either through the elimination of common ownership or free land, workers are coerced to sell their labor to those who own and control production in order to have access to the means of survival. As ownership of production becomes more concentrated with the further development of capitalism, this process accelerates and the size of the working class increases dramatically as small owners and independent producers become increasing displaced. The changes in farm ownership in the United States during the past century are an example of this concentration and displacement. Work under these circumstances is not a choice; it is forced on those displaced, who become the working class.

In more advanced capitalist societies, the coercion is less transparent. The coercive force or violence is replaced by the coercion of the market, where workers are tied more and more to meet their needs in the marketplace in purchasing goods with money they acquire from increasing amounts of work. The goods-mediated market grows to the extent that all needs are fulfilled through purchasing them in the ever-expanding marketplace that penetrates all spheres of social life (Klein, 2009; Bakan, 2004). The power of the market increases in not only providing workers with the access to their basic needs, but also extends to creating new needs that become the elusive dreams that tie workers to increasing amounts of work (Schor, 1993). The coercion exists through dominance of the power of the market to meet one's needs and the manipulation of wants and desires that can only be fulfilled through the marketplace. In advanced capitalist societies, the condition of poverty is defined in terms of the relative deprivation that is experienced because of the gap between the increasingly created needs and the population's ability to have those needs met through their participation in the market. This is obviously a gross simplification of the complexities of the relationship between class positions. Nevertheless, it is an accurate description of the basis of the relationship between class positions and how this relationship is related to differences in income, wealth and power, and patterns of structural violence victimization.

Not only are all societies ordered in terms of social class but they are also ordered in terms of gender. All societies today are patriarchal as it relates to the distribution of power along gender lines. Men rule all the institutions that make up today's societies. In every institutional arena, men systematically have more power than women do. Women are directed and controlled by men in the performance of roles within all societal institutions. This is the case no matter what institution we discuss: family, political system, educational institution, religious institution, or economy. Furthermore, the ultimate power of men is expressed in their ability to define women as significant principally in terms of their relationship to men. This is the case whether we are discussing the form of address used to distinguish between married and single women, Mrs. and Miss, or how women are portrayed in literature or mass media (as weaker than men and thus in need of protection from other men, as objects of love or lust by men, and as servers to men as wives and mothers).

Previously, we discussed gender hierarchy as it relates to the mode of reproduction. Patriarchy ultimately provides men with control over their progeny. In most stable societies patriarchy is integrated with capitalism so that each system of stratification reinforces the other. Women are traditionally a cheaper source of labor for capitalists and engaged in most of the unpaid labor that directly or indirectly subsidizes the payers of the paid labor. How much would wages have to be for the average worker if we all paid for the cost of child care and housework? Discrimination directed at women in the workplace has also served to divide the workforce, which serves to keep wages in check. Lastly, patriarchy provides even poor, displaced men with a sense of power and control over others that is celebrated and promoted in hierarchical societies. It also provides a bridge across the division of social class for men. Thus men who are of very different economic positions can jointly celebrate their domination of women as they revel in their sexual exploits or conquests.

It is also important to note that the systems can become disarticulated where changes in one system of stratification may conflict with that of the other. We see this in the United States; as women's economic position has improved relative to men, there has been an erosion of the power of men in the home. Traditional divisions of labor that have justified women being entirely burdened with domestic and childrearing responsibilities together with work outside the home have increasingly been a point of contention in homes, leading to some change in the domestic division of labor. Nevertheless, the average married woman in the United States did about three times as much cooking, cleaning, laundry, and other routine housework in the 1990s as the average married man. Household work continues to be divided according to gender, with women performing the vast majority of the repetitive indoor housework tasks and men performing occasional outdoor tasks (Coltrane, 2000). Differences are greater in lesser developed countries (Fuwa, 2004).

The third crucial division within societies and the world in general is along ethnic/racial lines. Ethnic and racial conflict and hierarchies play an increasingly important role in the distribution of life chances within and between societies. The conflict over and competition for scarcities often fall along racial and ethnic lines because these distinctions are important in defining position in the labor market and world economy as determined in terms of the political and economic positioning of nations. This positioning is the result of the heritage of empires and imperialism that dominates the history of the relations between peoples and nation-states around the globe. Ethnic disadvantage or advantage becomes institutionalized by racist and ethnocentric attitudes and institutional practices that justify, maintain, and extend the hierarchical ethnic relations.

Where these patterns of stratification are most evident is when populations are segregated within a society and this leads to the overt institutionalized denial of opportunities for human development. The United States has had a history of segregation of ethnic minorities. The most overt case has been with the indigenous populations. Native Americans were conquered and driven out of their homelands and placed in remote areas of the country that were not of economic interest to the dominant white population. The history of treaty violations is a history whereby the lands that they were driven to were later deemed to be of value and thus taken away from them. This systematic denial of resources has led to the institutionalization of their impoverishment. The native populations on reservations in the United States have the highest rates of poverty, alcoholism, and mental illness compared to any other geographic locations. This same pattern is reproduced in other areas of white European conquest throughout Central and South America, Australia, Oceania, and Africa.

African American populations and Hispanic populations in the United States also experienced segregation and thus the denial of opportunities. Laws were established throughout many areas of the country that segregated populations. Legal changes began to occur in the early 1950s and have continued through executive orders and the passage of various civil rights acts beginning with the 1964 act. Only in the last half of the twentieth century has the white leadership within the United States begun (although today more reluctantly) to address the harms of this system of segregation. The patterns of distribution of income, wealth, education levels, and mortality and morbidity differences still reflect these institutionalized patterns of segregation and racism. Today's ghettos in the largest cities in the United States still reflect this history of segregation. The populations who reside there are those ethnic populations who experienced legal segregation previously. The system of legal segregation and racism has resulted in a persistent pattern of de facto segregation and racism in many cities in the United States today.

Another dramatic example of this geographic pattern of ethnic stratification is the case of South Africa prior to black majority rule. Mukonoweshuro (1991) described the establishment of the bantustans, native lands for black South Africans, as the one of the bases of structural violence in South Africa. These ten white-constructed areas of ethnic minority segregation or reserves were the poorest areas of South Africa. The population within these areas was totally dependent for energy, water, jobs, and consumer goods on white South Africa. The political leadership was generally puppet rulers installed by or with the consent of the white South African leadership. The bantustans were eliminated by the black majority government in 1994.

This is an excellent example of internal colonialism. The dominant white South African leadership established colonies within their own country with the hope that they would be recognized internationally as independent nations so that they would no longer be responsible for the black South African citizenship that resided there. It also provided the illusion that white South Africa was addressing its history of theft of the lands of the black African population by giving these tribal populations their own land and country. In reality, this institutionalized impoverished population would be a reserve of cheap labor that could be exploited to support the dominance of white South Africa. The land that was given was often barren of resources, and the black population had little capital for the technology to develop the land that was ceded to them. Thus the people of the bantustans were even more dependent on white South Africa, though they had lost the rights of citizenship in the process. Unfortunately for white South Africa, the international community could not embrace such a blatant racist strategy to solve their native population problem. Today there persists extensive problems of poverty and destitution, child malnutrition, shortage of medical personnel, and crime in the former bantustans, a legacy of this racist system.

The major division between countries of the north and countries of the south in the world economy is also characterized by ethnic/racial divisions. The countries of the north are populated by people of white European ancestry, while those of the south with a few exceptions are characterized by people of color who are of Asian, African, or Aboriginal or Indo-American heritage. The average annual income of people of the north is $12,510, while the average income of people of the south is $710 (Bello, 1994).

These systems of stratification (class, gender, and race) intersect to create positions along a hierarchy of life chances and patterns of victimization for violence. We can think of the dominant positions in our own society and in the world in general as occupied by whites of European ancestry, males, capitalists who reside in countries referred to as the center of the world political economy (United States, Western Europe, Japan, Canada, and Australia). Those who occupy this position have the greatest power within societal institutions and have the greatest ability to fulfill their potentials as measured in terms of life expectancy, illness rates, educational level, control over resources, and so on. Those who occupy the most dominated positions in society and the world in general are female, ethnic minority group members (i.e., African, Hispanic, Asian, or Native American), and members of the working class or another subservient position within a subordinate mode of production (peasantry). People who occupy this position have the least ability to fulfill their potential as measured in terms of life expectancy, illness rates, educational level, control over resources, and so on.

In a particular society, one dimension of stratification may have greater significance in defining one's position than another. For example, in South Africa until recently, race had greater significance in determining position than either class or gender. That is not to say that the other dimensions are insignificant, for life chances were certainly affected by class and gender position within racial categories. Thus, black or white South African males had more power than their female counterparts; however, black males generally had less power than white females in terms of life chances. The same applies to social-class positions across the two racial or ethnic categories. These patterns are less clear in societies that have less rigid systems of stratification and where the distances between positions within a given dimension of stratification are less extreme.

Also, although we have described these dimensions of stratification as more or less distinguishable and independent of each other, they become intertwined as they define a particular position of an individual (African American female worker, Hispanic male worker, white male owner, black female manager, etc.). Mobility may occur between class positions, and this may fluctuate during times of economic expansion and contraction, but during times of economic stability, most class mobility occurs within relatively short ranges (within classes) and is principally intergenerational. The other two dimensions of stratification (ethnic and gender) are generally more fixed;

the positions you are born into are permanent. In this latter case, mobility occurs by moving out of the social system based on that stratification or changes occurring in the system of stratification as a whole in a society whereby positions change in relationship to each other. A women's movement can have an impact in changing the position of women as a whole relative to men. Or, as in Iran as a result of the Islamic fundamentalist revolution, women's position, as a whole, has declined significantly relative to men. Ethnic positions can change as a result of a civil rights or a minority rights movement as in the case of the changes that have occurred post 1960s in the United States and post 1990s in South Africa.

It is important to emphasize this last point. Societies are in a constant state of change. Systems of stratification within societies are also constantly changing. The changes can be dramatic, as the revolutionary change that occurred in the United States in 1776, Russia in 1917 and during the end of the twentieth century, Cuba in 1952, China in 1949, or today's South Africa or Afghanistan. Or these changes can be more gradual and less fundamentally disruptive or shocking to the society, as are changes in systems of stratification in our own and many Western European societies that have had fairly stable, relatively speaking, systems of stratification. That is not to say that the levels of violence associated with the changes are any more or less in societies that experience quick, dramatic changes. For, as we see, the level of violence that occurs within a stable society as it relates to systems of stratification (class, gender, and ethnicity) may be far greater than what is found in societies that achieve more quickly more dramatic changes in systems of stratification, although we may be more likely to recognize the violence in the latter.

HIERARCHICAL STRUCTURES BETWEEN SOCIETIES

Not only is it crucial for understanding the nature of structural violence to look at the nature of systems of inequality within societies, but equally if not more important as it relates to violence is to look at the structure of inequality between societies. Societies in the world are part of a larger hierarchical system that has an impact on the life chances of their populations as a whole and the life chances of people who occupy different positions within systems of stratification within these societies.

Godrej (1995) notes that in Britain the richest ten people have as much wealth as twenty-three poor countries with over 174 million. Citizens of the United States spent $30 billion dollars on jewelry and watches in 1991. This sum is equivalent to the entire GNP of twenty low-income countries at that time. The wealthiest fifth of the world's population controls 85 percent of global income while the poorest fifth lives off 1.4 percent of the income. The wealthiest countries of the world control most of the world's grain production, most of which they use to feed livestock. At the same time almost a billion people in the world do not have enough access to grain to fulfill minimum nutritional requirements for a healthy life. Godrej notes that with money-economies firmly in place, the wealthy can pull markets in whichever direction they like. Something as basic as food is completely skewed by the demands of the wealthy. Industrial countries contain 24 percent of the world's population, but they manage to use 48 percent of the world's grain and 61 percent of its meat. In fact they stuff quite a lot of this grain into what will become the meat that they consume or in the pets of their owners (Godrej, 1995, 9). While people in the poorest countries die from diseases of malnutrition, people in the wealthiest countries die, although on the average much later, from diseases of overconsumption and gluttony (e.g., heart disease and diabetes). How did this pattern of distribution, this hierarchy of people of different nations, come about?

Imperialism refers to the institutionalized pattern of domination of some countries over others. Although imperialism precedes capitalism, it develops further into a worldwide system as a product of capitalist development. In this context, capitalism not only describes the nature of production in a given society but it is fundamentally an organizational framework for the world. Galtung's early work on the causes of structural violence in the world focused on the role of imperialism. In that work he defined imperialism to be beyond the economic and political dimensions. He focuses on the disharmony of interests and inequality within the periphery that is caused by its relationship with the center. As Galtung states its importance, "Our point of departure is once more that the world is divided into have's and have-not's, in have and have-not nations. To decrease the gap, one aspect of the fight against structural violence, redistribution by taking from the have's and giving to the have-not's is not enough: the structure has to be changed. The imperialist structure has inter-national as well as intra-national aspects and will consequently have to be changed at both levels" (Galtung, 1971, 107).

The study of capitalism as a world system is the study of imperialism, the control and dominance of more developed over less developed societies. Modern-day imperialism is rooted in the process whereby capitalists seek to preserve and increase their capital through the extension of markets and production to locations outside their home societies. The driving force behind this extension of capitalist relations is the competition between capitalists in the marketplace. Competition between capitalists compels them to keep expanding capital in order to preserve it; thus progressive accumulation of surplus is a necessity for the survival of individual capitalists. For the modern-day corporation, the rule still holds: you grow or you die in the marketplace. Owners must seek ways of generating and realizing increasing levels of surplus and must find additional outlets for the productive use of this increasing surplus to keep extending the process. In the first case, owners search the globe for cheaper costs of materials and labor, and for ways of making the process of production more efficient by reducing the amount of time required to reproduce the labor power of the workers. In the second case, they search the globe for new investment opportunities where their capital can produce more surplus and more markets to realize this surplus or profits. Dowd (1993, 61) notes that expansion and exploitation are central to capitalist development.

From its beginnings, capitalist economic expansion has depended upon intermittent and deepening waves of geographic expansion. Increasing access to exploitable cheap labor, natural resources, and broader markets has lifted the volumes of trade, investment, and production for the core (center or imperialist) national economies. This has allowed the maintenance or increase of profits and, in raising the level of socially defined subsistence, has helped to reduce social conflict in the core countries, but at the expense of external populations.

There are three broad stages of imperialism: plunder, trade, and finally direct investment (Edwards, Reich, and Weisskopf, 1978). In each stage, the societies that are dominated play a crucial role in the development of the dominating or imperialist societies. The plunder of the European explorers of the fifteenth, sixteenth, and seventeenth centuries served as an important source of primitive accumulation and the development of these European empires and the underdevelopment of the countries that they explored and conquered.

Societies in African, Asia, and Central and South America were divided up by the dominant European powers and later the United States to be sources for cheap resources and labor for the extraction of raw materials for the rapid expansion of the industries in the dominant countries. Populations were slaughtered and enslaved in order to enhance the riches of those who were dominant in these countries of the center of the world system. Agricultural systems and industries that existed and prospered in these dominated societies were destroyed in order to fit them into this new international system of exploitation. The economic and political systems of native peoples of India, South Africa, Mexico, and North and South America (such as the Cherokee, Aztec, Maya) were destroyed and reconstructed into a pattern of economic and political dependency on the colonizing power. Lord Lugard, one of the architects of British colonial rule in Africa, noted that "the partition of Africa was, as we all recognize, due primarily to the economic necessity of increasing the supplies of raw materials and food to meet the needs of industrialized nations of Europe" (Institute of Race Relations, 1982, 2). Racist belief systems were promoted to justify and extend the domination of people of color in these societies. Their history and their accomplishments were denied as they became defined as primitive, uncivilized, heathen, and savage. These beliefs of inherent inequality provided the justification for the violence and control of these populations. This is the same pattern of justification that we essentially see in most patterns of violence as noted in the third and fourth principles of violence outlined in chapter 1.

The second stage followed the industrialization of the capitalist nations of Western Europe. As industrialization ensued, the European owning class saw the lesser developed societies as not only a source of raw materials, disposing of surplus value (investment capital) and new markets to realize the surplus, but also a place to dispose of their surplus population (originally criminals, heretics, and the poor became the first settlers of the colonies). Cecil Rhodes, British financier and colonial statesman, made this point most succinctly:

> I was in the East End of London yesterday and attended a meeting of the unemployed. I listened to the wild speeches, which were just a cry for bread, bread, bread, and on my way home I pondered over the scene and I became more than ever convinced of importance of imperialism. . . . My cherished idea is a solution, i.e., in order to save the 40,000,000 inhabitants of the United

Kingdom from a bloody civil war, we colonial statesman must acquire new lands to settle the surplus population, to provide new markets for the goods produced by them in the factories and mines. The empire, as I have always said, is a bread and butter question. If you want to avoid civil war, you must become imperialists. (Institute of Race Relations, 1982, 21)

With the rapid growth of world trade, capitalists in the dominant societies increasingly exported capital to the dominated societies to develop both the extraction of raw materials and eventually the markets for the disposal of finished goods. Sherman notes that "from 1890 to the Second World War was the peak period of colonialism, when all the world was divided among the West European and North American powers. In the late 1940s and 1950s a new era began with formal independence achieved by hundreds of millions of people throughout Asia and Africa as a result of struggles unleashed by the impact of two world wars, the Russian and Chinese revolutions, and the long pent-up pressures for liberation" (Sherman 1987, 236). This period of imperialism during the nineteenth and early twentieth centuries is often referred to as the period of "Pax Britannica"; in short, the peace, or more accurately put the violence, of British Imperialism. The history of the British Empire is a history of conquest and often genocidal violence against those who resist the imperial penetration into the frontiers. This is the case whether we are discussing the conquest of Ireland, AmerIndians of North America, Aboriginals of Australia, conquest of the Indian subcontinent, Arab tribes of the Middle East, or Africans on the African continent. During the height of the British Empire, the British navy ruled the seas and the sun never set on the British Empire of the nineteenth and early twentieth centuries. It is important to note that there existed other competitive European and Asian imperial systems during this time as well. This competition and conflict over territorial and economic expansion eventually led to wars on a scale never seen before, which were referred to as World Wars. The outcomes of these wars between imperial systems led to a consolidation of imperial systems and the creation of a new world system dominated by two, and then eventually one superpower.

The last stage of imperialism emerged in the second half of the twentieth century. The indigenous populations of the first stage of conquest and domination have either been destroyed or make up the most impoverished dominated sectors of the population of the societies that they occupy. Settlers exported from the dominant countries during the second stage have long assumed dominant positions within these societies. However, control or political domination from the center is still maintained by the economic and political ties that have long been established and institutionalized. The colonial structures of the preceding period have been replaced by neo-colonial structures and capitalist penetration by multinational corporations. Overt, direct political domination by the imperialist powers is replaced by covert political domination. Sherman (1987) states, regarding the current hierarchy between nations of the world:

On the one side are all the under-developed and newly "independent" countries, still under foreign economic domination, still facing all the old obstacles to development. On the other side are the advanced capitalist countries, still extracting vast profits from the dependent Third World. The imperialist group includes all those who extract profits by trade and investment. Thus, it includes most of West Europe, Japan, and the United States. Most imperialist control now comes through economic and monetary penetration, not direct occupation. The control ranges from blatant forms such as subsidies and military supplies to highly complex monetary agreements. (236)

After World War II there is the period of Pax Americana where the United States has assumed dominance in the world system of imperialism. Within fifty years following the end of World War II, the U.S. imperial rival, the Union of Soviet Socialist Republics and its Eastern European and Middle East sphere, collapses and we are now going through a period of integration of these regions into the U.S. sphere or what used to be referred to as the "free world" during the height of the Cold War. The United States is the dominant military, economic, and political power in the world. Its responsibility and interests are in maintaining the world capitalist system with its hierarchy between the societies of the center and the periphery for the benefit of its dominant class: the U.S. capitalist class as well as the other capitalist classes in other countries that they compete with but with whom they share an interest in maintaining a system based on private ownership of production and open markets especially in the periphery. This dominant class has become more transnational than any other time in the history of empires. The U.S. capitalist class position is still the dominant position in the world and their interests are supported and protected by the U.S. government whose governing elites depend upon their support and outright sponsorship. This sponsorship in the United States is increasingly transparent as more unrestricted money enters the electoral system with Supreme Court decisions that elevated money to be equivalent to protected free speech. As originally stated by Secretary of Defense Wilson, who served during the Eisenhower presidency, "what was good for the country was good for General Motors and vice versa" (U.S. Department of Defense, 2012).

The effect of imperialism on the development of the dominated societies has varied with these different stages. Beginning with the second stage and advancing with the third stage, there is the implantation of capitalist development in countries in the periphery, although this form of capitalist development is of a dependent nature. This dependent economic development has three characteristics. The first is that of unequal trade. In the earliest stages it takes the form of an exchange of raw materials by the dominated country for finished products produced in the dominant countries. In the next stages it takes the form of the importation of light manufactured component products in exchange for the end product to be fully assembled in the dominant countries. Sherman notes that most foreign capital invested in less developed countries still goes into raw materials extraction, in spite of the recent spread of some foreign investment to manufacturing in certain countries. This pattern is more fully developed than earlier patterns of unequal trade like the case of West Africa during the first stage of imperialism, when slaves were shipped from West Africa to the West Indies and the United States. Coffee, cotton, sugar, and rum were then shipped from those areas to Europe. Lastly, manufactured products including guns were shipped from England to the West African slave traders to pay for the slaves (Gage, 1991).

The second characteristic of dependent development is that because the export trade in dominated countries is principally in agricultural products and minerals, there is minimal industrial development in these countries. The economy in the dominated country is geared principally to the needs of the world market. Agricultural production that was for the local market of the consumer is transformed into cash crops for world export. In exchange for these cash crops, there is the importation from the dominant countries of expensive durable goods for the small class of well-off consumers, capital goods or machinery to increase the production for export, and processed foods of lesser nutritional value to replace the fresh foods produced for export or displaced by cash crop production. Sherman (1987), citing a UN Development report, notes that through the first half of the 1980s, Third World countries had 79 percent of their exports in food, mineral fuels, and crude materials. The developed capitalist countries had 75 percent of their exports in machinery and equipment, chemicals, and other manufactured goods.

The third characteristic of dependent development is that capital flows are on balance out of the dominated country to the dominant countries. This net surplus outflow restricts the development to that which is subservient to the interests of capitalists in the dominant countries.

> At any rate, in the present stage of mature imperialism, the situation is that the export of capital is exceeded by foreign earnings of the imperialist countries. The profits (and interest payments) from the underdeveloped countries to the imperialist countries are greater than the flow of investments (and loans) going the other way. . . . Thus, for the entire period 1950–1975, the U.S. direct investment outflow was a total of $68.4 billion. In the very same period, investment income receipts flowing into the United States from direct investments were $110.6 billion. Hence, the U.S. economy gained $42.2 billion from abroad in that period in receipts minus costs. (U.S. Council on International Economic Policy, 1977, cited in Sherman 1987, 240)

From 1950 to 1965, Sherman observes that in Latin America U.S. corporations invested $3.8 billion but extracted $11.3 billion, for a net flow of $7.5 billion from that area to the United States. Similarly, in Africa and Asia from 1950 through 1965 American corporations invested $5.2 billion, while transferring to the United States $14.3 billion in profits, for a net flow of $9.1 billion to the United States. Sherman also notes that in general the rates of return are much greater overseas; in 1974 the rate of return on investment (income/average capital invested) was 21 percent in the underdeveloped countries and only 10.5 percent in the developed countries; in 1980 the rate of return was 13.3 from the developed, but 52.2 from the underdeveloped; and in 1984, the rate of return was 9 percent from the developed, but 13 percent from the underdeveloped (Sherman, 1987, 240-41).

Production in the dominated countries is increasingly controlled by foreign capital. Initially this production was land. As dependent capitalist development continues, it increasingly becomes factories, banks, and sales and distribution networks. In today's world economy the largest companies in the countries outside of the center are owned by foreigners or, if there are restrictions on majority ownership by the government, foreigners will generally have a controlling interest. For example, in the 1970s and early 1980s in Brazil more than half of total manufacturing sales were accounted for by foreign-owned companies (Bello, 1994). Today, almost 48 percent of the largest companies in the world are U.S. corporations, another 30 percent are from Europe, and another 10 percent are Japanese (Petras, 2002). Eighty-eight percent of the largest corporations in the world that dominate world's markets are headquartered in the dominant capitalist countries of the world. Petras notes that the world's markets are divided among 238 leading U.S. and 153 European companies and banks. This concentration and control according to Petras "defines the imperial nature of the world economy, together with the markets they control, the raw materials they pillage (80 percent of the leading oil and gas companies are U.S. and EU owned), and the labor they exploit" (Petras, 2002, 5). As Petras notes this corporate penetration cuts across broad areas of the economies of the world and the United States and its corporations controlled by its capitalist class are in a dominant position. "Within the imperial system, U.S. economic power is still dominant. Five of the top ten banks are U.S., six of the top ten pharmaceutical-biotech companies, four of the top ten telecommunications companies, seven of the top information technology companies, four of the top gas and oil companies, nine out of the top ten software companies, four of the top ten insurance companies, and nine of the top ten general retail companies" (Petras, 2002, 5).

The principal vehicle for economic penetration and imperialist relations is the multinational corporation, beginning with the British East India Company and the British and Dutch Banking houses of the sixteenth and seventeenth centuries to Chase Manhattan, General Motors, Nestlé, and Coca-Cola today. Jalee (1965, 22) states that "through the multinational corporations, American capital directly owns a large chunk of West European industry, and the capitalists of all the imperialist countries together own the major industrial enterprises of the underdeveloped countries. There are no reliable figures for the Third World as a whole which measure the extent of foreign economic intervention, but it is certain that many, perhaps even most of the industrial undertakings of the underdeveloped countries are foreign-owned or controlled." Godrej (1995) reports that in 1989 transnational corporations controlled 70 percent of international trade and 80 percent of all land growing export crops. At the same time, transnational corporations only employed 3 percent of the world's paid labor. The UN Development Program (UNDP) notes in its Human Development Report (1999) that many global corporations now wield more economic power than nation-states. Fifty of the largest one hundred economies in the world are run by multinationals, not by countries. For example, the revenues of General Electric are larger than the GDP of New Zealand, Nike bigger than Paraguay, Apple is bigger than Ecuador, and Walmart would be the twenty-fifth biggest economy in the world, surpassing the GDP of 157 countries (Trivett, 2011). The UNDP report notes that the combined annual revenues of the biggest two hundred corporations are greater than those of 182 nation-states that contain 80 percent of the world's population.

Ellwood notes that these corporate actors act in their short-term economic interests and not in the interests of the countries in which they have invested capital. "Giant private companies have become the driving force behind economic globalization, wielding more power than many nation-states. Business values of efficiency and competition at all costs now dominate the debate on social policy, the public interest and the role of government. The tendency to monopoly combined with decreasing rates of profit drives and structures corporate decision-making—without regard for the social, environmental and economic consequences of those decisions" (Ellwood, 2001, 53).

One result of dependent capitalist development is that the economic cycles in the dominated countries are rooted in the supply and demand of the few raw materials exported. In countries like Algeria, Bangladesh, Burundi, Gabon, Ghana, Guinea-Bissau, Iran, Libya, Mauritius, Nigeria, Uganda, and Zambia more than 75 percent of their income is derived from one product (Institute for Race Relations, 1982). Sherman (1987) concludes that the colonial era left the economies of the underdeveloped countries very dependent on foreign demand and consequently very sensitive to the capitalist world economy's business cycle of expansion and depression.

In addition to this dependence on a narrow export market, the dominated countries are very dependent on foreign investment. Both factors make the economies of dependent capitalist nations subject to enormous fluctuations as a result of forces beyond their control. Sherman mentions the case of Ceylon, where 80 percent of the population are employed directly or indirectly in the production and handling of raw material exports (tea, rubber, and coconuts). As the market for these products changes with demand in the world market, the economy of Ceylon is subject to change as well. Countries whose economies have been developed to fulfill the needs for a few raw materials used in production in dominant countries have also become increasingly vulnerable as a result of import substitution and increasing competition from other depressed dominated producers.

Not only do capitalists from the dominating countries in the world extract more capital than they invest in the dominated countries, but capitalists within these dominated countries also export their investment capital to banks and investment houses in the center for safety and high returns in the currency of the dominating nations. George (1988) observes that these dominated countries fall deeper into debt to subsidize the imperialist relationships by the funding of economic development strategies that are export oriented (production of raw materials for export to the center). The debt is also a product of the corruption of political elites and to pay for an increasing supply of weaponry to control a population that is increasingly displaced. Finance capitalists in the dominant counties of the world (especially those within the United States) extract increasing amounts of capital from the dominated countries to pay interest payments. For Latin America alone, new capital inflows (both aid and investment) came to under $38 billion between 1982 and 1985, while it paid back $144 billion in debt service—net transfer from poor to rich: $106 billion (George 1988, 63). This occurred during a time when per capita GNP had declined, and poverty and unemployment had increased. Thus the dominated countries become increasingly impoverished relative to those countries that are dominant, and those who do not own and control production continue to lose position relative to capitalists in their own society and capitalists in the dominating countries. Thus levels of inequality within dominated countries and between dominated and dominating countries increase as a product of imperialism.

A recent report by the Canadian Conference Board analyzing data provided by the World Bank found that of total world income, 42 percent goes to those who make up the richest 10 percent of the world's population, while just 1 percent goes to those who make up the poorest 10 percent (The Conference Board of Canada, 2011). In general, the income gap between nations is greater than the income gap of nations that have the greatest inequality within (Milanovic, 2006). The Conference Board research also found that the gap of incomes between rich and poor countries grew in the 1980s, the 1990s, and the first part of the 2000s, but inequality leveled off and declined slightly between 2007 and 2010. This leveling off was no doubt in part related to the world recession that began in 2007 and still persists or has not ended in a robust upturn today in 2012 in many of the most developed countries.

The overall trend over the past thirty years is that the level of income and wealth inequality internationally is growing within nations and between nations (Klugman, 2011). "From 1990 to 2005 within-country income inequality, measured by the Atkinson inequality index, increased 23.3 percent in very high HDI countries. The gap between the rich and the poor widened over the last two decades in more than three-quarters of the Organisation for Economic Co-operation and Development countries and in many emerging market economies" (Klugman, 2011, 29).

Of the seventeen most industrialized or developed countries, the United States has the highest levels of inequality. A 2011 report by the Congressional Budget Office found that "for the 1 percent of the population with the highest income, average real after-tax household income grew by 275 percent between 1979 and 2007" (U.S. Congressional Budget Office, 2011, VIII). For others in the 20 percent of the population with the highest income (those in the eighty-first through ninety-ninth percentiles), average real after-tax household income grew by 65 percent over that period, much faster than it did for the remaining 80 percent of the population, but not nearly as fast as for the top 1 percent. For the 60 percent of the population that can be considered the middle income (the twenty-first through eightieth percentiles), the growth in average real after-tax household income during this same period was just under 40 percent. For the bottom 20 percent of the population, the average real after-tax household income was only 18 percent higher in 2007 than it had been in 1979, twenty-eight years previous. In general, the CBO found that the levels of income inequality in the United States after taxes have increased dramatically between the top 1 percent of the population and the rest, especially the bottom 80 percent of the population as ranked in terms of income.

Wealth inequality also increased in the United States during the period from 1983 to 2007. Wolfe reports that the richest 1 percent received over one-third of the total gain in marketable wealth over this period (Wolff,

2010). He found that the next 4 percent also received about a third of the total gain and the next 15 percent about a fifth, so that the top 20 percent collectively accounted for 89 percent of the total growth in wealth, while the bottom 80 percent accounted for 11 percent. In the United States in 2009, the wealthiest 1 percent of the population held 35.6 percent of the wealth, slightly less than what is held by 95 percent of the population, which holds 36.5 percent (Economic Policy Institute, 2011). The top 5 percent of the U.S. population has 63.5 percent, more than twelve times their representation in the population if wealth was distributed equally and almost twice more than what the remaining 95 percent of the population possesses.

George analyzes the impact of dependent capitalist development throughout Africa and finds that the results are more extremes in income and wealth inequality and increasing levels of poverty and malnutrition as the economy is less and less responsive to the needs of the majority of the population. The result is also increasing economic displacement of the peasant population, which in these countries is the majority, as cultivable land becomes used for cash crop production for export and ownership becomes more concentrated; proletarianization of the population at very low wages and with unsafe and hazardous working conditions; and increasing despoliation of the environment. In regard to dependent development in Latin America, George (1988, 120) notes that

> the [South American] continent is the world's record-breaker for unequal income distribution. Brazilian, Mexican or Venezuelan elites need no lessons from the upper classes of New York, London or Milan in the fine art of money-flaunting. Latin American upper classes are, if anything, more opulent, more flamboyant in their conspicuous consumption. They can also draw on a larger pool of miserable and unprotected, unemployed people for servants than can their counterparts in the North. It is there elites that have made capital flight a national sport and a bonanza for the banking industry.

Gage (1991) notes that Brazil is the fourth largest food-exporter in the world, yet is the sixth hungriest country in the world. In Brazil, the richest 1 percent of the population has the equivalent income of the bottom 50 percent (Beghin, 2008).

Economic dependency leads to political dependency. In the dominated countries there is often a weak internal ruling class, but the military grows in importance to deal with civil unrest resulting from investment strategies that displaces and impoverishes peasants and increases the levels of inequality in the country. The United States as the dominant country in the imperialist system since World War II has increasingly played an important role in (1) policing (overtly by the U.S. military and covertly by the Central Intelligence Agency) the world to maintain the security of market relations and foreign investment, (2) subsidizing military control and policing in the dominated country through training programs and the sale of weaponry, (3) subsidizing increasing investment by the dominant capitalist class through aid programs and the operation of the World Bank, International Monetary Fund, and World Trade Organization, which it controls, and (4) subsidizing and influencing elections in developing countries to legitimate and maintain regimes that serve the interest of those who are dominant in the world system.

The role of violence should not be underestimated in maintaining the relations of domination in the imperialist system. In regard to Central America, the United States throughout the twentieth century has regularly used force to maintain its relationship of dominance. In 1927, Undersecretary of State Robert Olds stated: "We do control the destinies of Central America and we do so for the simple reason that the national interest absolutely dictates such a course. . . . Until now Central America has always understood that governments which we recognize and support stay in power, while those we do not recognize and support fail" (Barry, Wood, and Preusch 1982, 5). President Taft was quite clear as to the imperialist goals of the U.S. capitalist class when in 1912 he stated: "The day is not far distant when three Stars and Stripes at three equidistant points will mark our territory: one at the North Pole, another at the Panama Canal, and the third at the South Pole" (Pearce, 1982, 17).

The Monroe Doctrine clearly defined the U.S. Empire, and the Evart Doctrine developed under President Hayes further justified intervention in the internal affairs of Latin American countries to protect the foreign holdings of U.S. nationals, later to become multinational corporations. Since the 1898 invasion of Cuba, the United States has dispatched troops to protect American interests, or the interests of the capitalist class, in Central America and the Caribbean twenty times, the invasions of Panama and Grenada during the 1980s being the most recent. But covert operations are more frequent and less costly, as the recent U.S. involvement in Nicaragua illustrates. The U.S. government, beginning in 1981, organized, funded (weapons and supplies), and directed the Contra invasion and campaign of terrorism against the Nicaraguan population in order to force a second election in which the U.S.-funded, pro-free-market candidate could win the election (Mathews, 1986). Sharkey (1990) notes that by 1989, thirty thousand Nicaraguans had been killed and the United States had spent between $4 billion and $6 billion in training and arming the Contras and had spent an additional $12.5 million or $7.00 per voter for the promotion of democracy. Most of this money was directly or indirectly funneled into the election campaign of the U.S.-supported candidate Chamorro who won this second election.

General Smedley D. Butler, who headed many of the American interventions in the region during the early part of the twentieth century, provided a frank accounting of his achievements:

> I spent thirty-three years and four months in active service as a member of our country's agile military force—the Marine corps. I served in all commissioned ranks from a second lieutenant to major-general. And during that period I spent most of my time being a high-class muscle man for Big Business, for Wall Street, and for the bankers. In short, I was a racketeer for capitalism. . . . Thus, I helped make Mexico and especially Tampico safe for American oil interests in 1914. I helped make Haiti and Cuba a decent place for the National City Bank to collect revenues in. . . . I helped purify Nicaragua for the international banking house of Brown Brothers in 1909–1912. I brought light to the Dominican Republic for American sugar interests in 1916. I helped make Honduras right for American fruit companies in 1903. (Pearce, 1982, 20)

Although our military and political leaders would not be as blatant today in describing our role in maintaining and benefiting from a system of imperialism, the pattern continues. We are involved overtly and covertly around the world, maintaining stability and protecting and furthering our national interests as they are rooted in maintaining open markets and the rights of private property, both of which are in the interests of the dominant capitalist class in the world, those principally in the United States, Western Europe, and Japan. Table 9.1 summarizes imperialist forms of economic and political domination in the world today.

Petras describes the New Imperial Order as built on five pillars: "long term interest payments on external debt; buyouts and takeovers of lucrative public enterprises and financially troubled national enterprises, as well as direct investments in sweatshops, energy resources, and low-wage manufacturing and service industries; collection of rents from royalty payments on wide range of products, patents, and cultural commodities; and favourable current account balances based on the dominance of U.S. corporations and banks in the region through traditional market 'familiarity' and historical ties" (Petras and Veltmeyer, 2001, 78).

Imperialist Relations and World Debt

Debt has historically been a very important instrument of empire. It is through debt that imperial governments are able to raise the military forces for conquest and occupation. It is through debt that imperial governments are able to manage by means of police and welfare systems the class conflict both domestically and internationally that causes increased threats to the imperial system within the center and periphery. Lastly, it's through debt that imperial governments are able to sponsor the penetration of their multinational corporations into foreign countries. It is the debt they incur but increasingly it is the debt incurred by those that they are penetrating that is central to the imperial mission. Going back to the earliest period of the American Empire, debt was crucial in funding the military expeditions against the native populations, but it was also the debt incurred by the native populations at the trading posts that led to the confiscation of their territory. It is also crucial that the currency of indebtedness be controlled by the imperial power, as it is in the case of the United States and the rest of the post–World War II world.

One recent area where the actions of policy makers and the world's financial elite have clearly resulted in increasing the levels of death, especially among the most helpless, is in the resolution of the world debt crisis during the 1980s and 1990s. How this works is that the governing elites (usually, the military and the landed oligarchy) are persuaded by bankers and investors from the dominating countries that a development strategy based on the classic model of dependent capitalist development (cash crop production for the world market, capital-intensive, single-crop agricultural production, heavy investment in infrastructural development to encourage investment by multinational corporations, privatization of public resources and open markets) will provide a greater investment return on their investments and the most efficient path for the economic development of the country.

Table 9.1.   Imperialist Forms of Economic and Political Domination.

1. *Control of production*—Direct or indirect ownership in dominated countries is by outsiders (multinational corporations, finance capital, foreign entrepreneurs).

1. *Control over selection of leaders*—Foundation for Democracy/CIA—U.S. funding and assisting in the election of pro-U.S. candidates.

2. *Debt to finance capital* (World Bank and IMF)—Structural Adjustment Programs—Debt established to move development in the direction of dependency on dominant actors in world economy or market.

2. *Political stabilization and destabilization efforts*—State terrorism to counter groups that threaten the stability of a client state and to destabilize a regime that threats dominant capitalist interests.

3. *Direction of capital flows*—Capital flows principally from dominated countries to dominant countries. This is in terms of profit repatriation, debt payments, and investment capital from capitalists in dominated countries.

3. *Foreign military bases*—U.S. has more than 300 bases around the world in 60 different countries and a naval force in every major international body of water.

4. *Maldevelopment*—Stress on extraction industries—Development is for the export market—principally for dominating countries of the world economy. Production geared to world market controlled by wealthiest consumers. Importation in dominated countries principally caters to top 20 percent of the population.

4. *Arming and training of domestic military and police forces*—Military and police dependent on dominating countries (particularly the U.S.) for hardware and training.

5. *Economic displacement of peasant populations* as a result of transformation of agricultural production for cash crops to outside markets. Increasing problems of poverty and inequality.

5. *Propaganda activities*—U.S. Central Intelligence Agency has established direct (ownership) and indirect (establishing friendly sources for disinformation) control of foreign media. Electronic and print mass media is controlled by multinational corporations.

6. *Increasing economic concentration and inequality*—as a result of the penetration of multinational corporations and the increasing capital intensive nature of production.

6. *Military interventions*—U.S. police actions to stabilize countries that have unrest because of the impact of developmental strategy on majority of countries' population. Military interventions against "renegade" countries whose actions threaten imperialist market relations.

7. *Economic development decision making dominated by foreign interests.* World Trade Organization is principal coordinating agency of the world economy.

7. *Establishment of military alliances for stabilization*—OAS, SEATO, NATO, etc.—legitimate intervention by the dominant capitalist country and are a means of establishing informal controls through the linkage between client states.

8. *Economic stabilization and destabilization efforts* as a means of foreign control—CIA, World Bank, IMF, WTO, AID programs function to maintain and extend dependent capitalist relations.

8. *Educational/cultural exchanges* to promote modernization as defined in terms of dependent development.

9. *AID programs also function to maintain and increase dependency*—Most aid tied to purchase of U.S. goods and services; also aid is geared to development model that is export-oriented economy. Aid is also used as a form of international welfare that creates dependency.

9. *Political advisers* from dominant capitalist countries to promote "capitalist" forms of democratic government structures.

10. *Imbalance of trade*—Protectionism in the center (dominating countries) and open access in the periphery (dominated countries).

10. *Importance of imperialism* for domestic political stability in the dominant countries. Importation of cheap products reduces wage pressure from workers in dominant countries. Nationalism sentiments are generated by wars against dominated countries.

Ellwood (2001) notes that the debt of the non-oil-producing Third World increased fivefold between 1973 and 1982, reaching a staggering $612 billion. He notes that the foreign debts of developing countries are more than US$2 trillion (million million) and still growing. This translates to a debt of over $400 for every man, women, and child in the developing world where the average income in the very poorest countries is less than a dollar a day. In 1999 debt had reached $3,000 billion and an ever increasing portion of this new debt was to service interest payments on the old debt, to keep money circulating and to keep the system up and running (Ellwood, 2001).

Another feature of the debt crisis is the high level of corruption that occurs as leaders are persuaded through financial payoffs to follow this path of development. There are also many wasted projects (roadways to nowhere, airports in remote locations, production facilities that are extravagant and costly) for the benefit of generating graft and paybacks for the economic and political elite of the country. Corruption has historically been an important means to provide access by corporations from the dominant capitalist nations to the resources of poorer countries. "The largest single debt of the Philippines is the Bataan nuclear power station. Completed in the mid-1980s at a cost of $2.3 billion, it was built on an earthquake fault at the foot of a volcano, and has never been used. The nuclear power station was built by the US multinational Westinghouse, in spite of a much lower bid from General Electric. The then president of Philippines, Ferdinand Marcos, over-ruled the choice of General Electric. Westinghouse admitted it paid a commission to a Marcos associate, and the *New York Times* estimates Marcos was given $80 million by Westinghouse" (Hanlon and Pettifor, 2000). Hanlon and Pettifor note that the World Bank's own evaluation of project performance in the 1990s showed that in the poorest countries, and in South Asia and Africa, between 60 percent and 70 percent of projects failed. Another example noted by Hanlon and Pettifor is the case of Nigeria, where according to a government commission at least sixty-one development projects financed by more than $5 billion in foreign loans have either failed or were never completed. Hanlon and Pettifor note that Nigeria estimates that former military governments have stolen billions of dollars and deposited these in British, U.S., and Swiss banks. Nigeria's foreign debt is now $34 billion.

Hanlon and Pettifor also cite the case of Bolivia, where a lead and platinum refinery was built using untested technology and requiring more ore than could be produced by local mines. They note that the project doubled in cost to $250 million and was built with $100 million in Belgian and German export credits plus German bank loans. The project has never functioned but the loan is still being repaid. Peru also is still paying a $70 million loan for boats worth $18 million that never worked properly and for aircraft engines that were never delivered. In regard to the billions of dollars loaned to Russia by the IMF, the U.S. Central Intelligence Agency reported as long ago as 1995 that money from International Monetary Fund loans was going to Swiss banks, but nothing was done except to approve the second largest loan in IMF history to Russia. It is estimated that at least $20 billion has gone astray (Hanlon and Pettifor, 2000). And the list goes on about the corruption and ill-conceived projects that were more designed to facilitate access to markets and resources by multinational corporations of the dominant countries in the world and to provide for the graft for a corrupted elite who are ruling many of these countries.

Perkins describes his work for international development firms that encouraged developing countries to take on these types of projects. He describes his job as an "economic hitman." "If an EHM (Economic hit man) is completely successful, the loans are so large that the debtor is forced to default on its payment after a few years. When this happens, then like the Mafia we demand our pound of flesh. This often includes one or more of the following: control over United Nations votes, the installation of military bases, or access to precious resources . . . and another count is added to our global empire" (Perkins, 2006). Perkins details his work, which was to have developing countries take on increasing amounts of debt from foreign banks (usually from the United States) to take on development projects that are done by U.S. corporations and that would be boondoggles or assist in the further penetration or investment from outside. He also notes the corruption of the elites was an important ingredient to convince to essentially bankrupt their country by creating huge debts that there would be no way for them to get out from under.

Dependent capitalist development strategy is accelerated by the loans given by the IMF and World Bank to transform or modernize their agricultural sector shifting the production to cash crops for the world market and increasing the displacement of the peasant populations as their land is usurped by large landowners. Export-oriented production is more concentrated and in most areas of production controlled by a relatively few transnational corporations. Kneen (1995) points out that about twenty large transnational corporations control most of the world's agriculture. Seven of the twelve largest agribusinesses are based in the United States.

Local food prices in these dependent capitalist countries climb dramatically as the level of production for the local market shrinks and there is increasing importation of foodstuffs from the dominating capitalist countries. As mentioned earlier, the food that is imported from the dominant countries is most often processed. The processing results in lowering the nutritional value of the product, yet increasing the cost (corn flakes instead of corn or, worse yet, powdered baby formula for mother's milk). The size of the working class increases dramatically, lowering the price of wages as displaced peasants flood into the cities looking for work or sell their labor to large landowners. This displacement and concentration of land also may lead to serious problems of famine that we will discuss later in this chapter.

As the debt accumulates, and the economy of the dominated country is more vulnerable to swings in the world economy, especially as it relates to the cyclical swings of the few cash crops they are exporting, this makes it more and more difficult for the country to reduce the debt. More money is spent to encourage more investment to produce for the world market, attracting the investment of multinational corporations through tax-incentive and infrastructure development projects, and more money is spent on the ever increasing military and police forces to maintain control of the growing poor and displaced population within the country. What results is an increasing cycle of debt, dependent development, and violence.

As the debt problem reaches a crisis, there is a serious possibility of default. After Mexico defaulted on its loans in the early 1980s, there was greater pressure placed on debtor countries to speed up the access to their markets and resources. As the debt crisis increases, bankers from the World Bank and the International Monetary Fund, financial agencies of the dominant capitalist countries (principally the United States, the country with the largest debt, more than several times greater than the debt of all dominated countries combined), step in to impose a solution referred to as "structural adjustment," which places the burden of repayment increasingly on the poorest segment of the populations in these countries The United States, principally in control of the IMF and World Bank, applied this pressure beginning in the mid-1980s with the Baker plan during the Reagan administration on indebted countries to continue to (in the language of the bank) "structurally adjust" their economies. More money was made available by the World Bank and IMF to avoid the debt crisis and in exchange the countries had to open themselves up for a greater level of access for multinational corporations. This financial leverage pushed the developing countries of the Third World further down the road to development that was dependent upon the dominant capitalist nations for their markets and for their investment capital to compete in the world market. The multinational corporations, the largest based in the United States, received more access to cheaper labor as currencies were devalued and unemployment increased as a result of the reduction in government employment and subsidies to the poor.

As part of the structural adjustment, these indebted countries were required to reduce the size of their state budgets, principally in the areas of welfare, employment, and health care. State security sections of the budget, military and police forces, are usually increased to deal with the increasing unrest, as well as infrastructure development costs to increase further foreign investment for world market production. Increasing levels of social control (military and police) are required in these countries to control the majority of the populations of these countries as they became increasingly impoverished. The United States is the nation that provides the majority of aid to finance increases in military and police to maintain stability in these countries. More money is also loaned in order to provide for these increases in social control. The civil wars that are occurring around the globe—in the Philippines, throughout the sub-Saharan region of Africa, throughout Latin America—are increasingly rooted in this development strategy and the debt crisis and structural adjustments.

The world's largest banks and leading finance capitalists also received tremendous returns on Third World debt as they were loaning money for the transformations of these societies along a dependent capitalist development path. "More conditions were extended to countries to acquire new loan money to help pay off the debts that were due. They included 'privatizing' state-owned enterprises, reducing the size and cost of government through massive public sector layoffs; cutting basic social services and subsidies on basic foodstuffs; and reducing barriers to trade" (Ellwood, 2001, 48). According to Ellwood, this restructuring was highly successful from the point of view of the private banks that siphoned off more than $178 billion from the south between 1984 and 1990.

Currencies are also usually devalued as part of the structural adjustment strategy in order to cheapen the cost of the resources acquired by foreign investors and reduce the cost of the exports to the world market. This also directly affects the costs of the increasing amounts of imported foods in the marketplace that are difficult for the working population to purchase as a result of the reduction of wages and increases in the number of unemployed. This is all part of the structural adjustment strategy to encourage investment by foreign corporations. Countries are also strongly encouraged to remove restrictions on foreign investment in industry and financial services, to institute a system of incentives for producing for export markets, and to remove market restrictions on imports in order to make their local industry more efficient in response to the increased competition from multinational corporations. Lastly as mentioned, governments in these countries are required to privatize state enterprises as rapidly as possible and engage in deregulation of the marketplace in order to encourage foreign investment. The pattern is reproduced in Africa, Central America, South America, and Asia, in short throughout the Southern Hemisphere (Bolles, 1983; Korten, 1993; Ahmad, 1992; Dewitt and Petras, 1981; McAfee, 1991; Bello, 1994).

Bello (1994, 31) states that "with over 70 Third World countries submitting to IMF and World Bank programs in the 1980s, stabilization, structural adjustment, and shock therapy managed from distant Washington became the common condition of the South in that decade." Using panel analysis and a data set containing inequality measures for sixty-five nations at two points in time, Beer and Boswell (2001) find that high within-nation inequality is due in large part to greater dependence on foreign investment. Beer and Boswell contend that a shift in capital/labor relations brought about by globalization is responsible for increases in income inequality within countries of the developing world. This inequality has violent consequences of disease, impoverishment, and death.

According to Bello, Chile is the country with the longest-running structural adjustment program, beginning with the CIA-planned overthrown of President Allende in 1973. During this period, more than six hundred state enterprises were sold off. Trade barriers and tariffs were significantly reduced or eliminated. Foreign investment increased dramatically, and the Chilean economy was more integrated into the international economy than ever in its history. Foreign trade accounted for 57.4 percent of GDP in 1990, whereas in 1970 it accounted for only 35 percent. Financial markets were also deregulated and total debt throughout the 1970 and 1980s increased dramatically as the IMF and World Bank continued to loan money to the government to stabilize the economy and to continue its development along a path of dependent capitalist development. Deindustrialization and increasing dependence on the exportation of raw materials and processed goods were major forces in the transformation of the Chilean economy. In general, the economy experienced a slower economic growth rate per year during the period of structural adjustment than in the years prior to it. While the government continued to safeguard and subsidize the wealthy, it cut government services and welfare to the working class.

The impact of these policies by the government and imposed by the World Bank and International Monetary Fund was that the proportion of families living below the line of destitution rose from 12 to 15 percent between 1980 and 1990, and the percentage living below the poverty line (but above the line of destitution) rose from 24 to 26 percent. This meant that at the end of the Pinochet period some 40 percent, or 5.2 million, of a population of 13 million people were defined as poor in a country that had once boasted of having a large middle class. Poverty translated into hunger and malnutrition; for 40 percent of the population the daily calorie intake dropped from 2,019 in 1970 to 1,751 in 1980 and 1,629 in 1990 (Bello, 1994, 45). Bello further notes that during this same period the share of the national income going to the poorest 50 percent declined from 20.4 percent to 16.8 percent, while the share going to the richest 10 percent rose from 36.5 percent to 46.8 percent. At the same time that these measures were being imposed on the population, the level of state violence accelerated rapidly as the government terrorized the population in order to maintain control and preserve the system of inequality, and the level of economic violence increased as unions were outlawed and the industrial accident rate climbed dramatically.

Jamaica is another country that has experienced dramatic intervention by the U.S. government and multilateral lending agencies. In response to the structural adjustment program implemented in Jamaica to pay off its debt during the ten-year period from 1975 to 1985 (1) real expenditures on social services were cut by 41 percent; (2) government expenditures for debt service increased from 21 percent to 44 percent from 1981 to 1985; (3) real spending on education was cut by 40 percent between 1981 and 1985, which had an impact on the rate of passage of high school exit exams falling from 62 percent to 34 percent during the same period; (4) real spending on health was cut by 35 percent between 1982 and 1985; (5) capital spending on housing dropped in 1985, falling to 11 percent of the level of 1982; and (6) the cost of purchasing the least-cost basket of minimum food requirements for a five-person household increased by 429 percent from 1979 to 1985 (McAfee, 1991).

A similar pattern of cutbacks directed at the poorest elements of the society to pay for the cost of the dependent development strategy can be found in the Dominican Republic. According to the Working Group on Debt of the Association of Caribbean Economists, the result has been that the rate of infant malnutrition, grade III, in one of the principal hospitals in Santo Domingo increased from 14 percent to 30.8 percent for admitted infants between 1977 and 1986 and from 3.9 percent to 10 percent for infant outpatients. Maternal mortality in a major maternal hospital in Santo Domingo grew from 15 to 22 per 100,000 between 1981 and 1985 (McAfee, 1991, 17). McAfee notes that in regard to the impact of debt and structural adjustment programs on Caribbean countries, per capita food production for domestic use had declined in the vast majority of countries in the region and that 44 percent of the region's population consumed less than the minimum dietary requirement for protein and 56 percent had an insufficient caloric intake (McAfee, 1991).

Susan George notes in *A Fate Worse Than Debt* that nutritional studies of Peru between 1972 and 1983 show a steady increase in malnutrition for children under age six. "In the poorest neighborhoods of Lima and the shanty towns around it the percentage of undernourished children climbed from 24 percent in 1972 to 28 percent in 1978 to 36 percent in 1983" (George 1988, 135). She goes on to note that in Lima, as a result of the increasing impoverishment of the population, the restaurants have developed the practice of selling to the poor a plate of food at the back door that is called *siete sabores*, or "seven tastes," made up of the leavings and leftover scraps of all the dishes on the menu. The poor in Lima buy this when they have enough money. When they do not, they often eat nicovita, a fish-meal flour used for fattening chickens and manufactured under unsanitary conditions. George notes that the former governor of the Peruvian Central Bank, Manuel Moreyra, had to admit that the "'social costs of this (IMF adjustment) policy are tragic. It means the death of some 500,000 children. . . .' World Bank statistics cited by a Swiss author are said to have placed Peruvian IMRs (infant mortality rates) at 70 per 1,000 in the 1970s but over 80 per 1,000 in the 1980s. Still other sources placed the overall IMR in Peru at more than 100, and some said that in the worst shanty towns half the new-borns were dying before the age of one" (George, 1988, 135).

In Argentina and Brazil the pattern is repeated. Citing from official sources, George notes that 685,000 children in greater Buenos Aires alone do not eat enough to stay alive—a government minister said this plus another 385,000 children in the province of Buenos Aires. Thus, one-third of the children under fourteen in Buenos Aires province are starving. The tragedy is worse in poorer provinces in the northern part of the country where 40 to 50 percent of the children under fourteen are starving. In Brazil, the problem of malnutrition is believed to be the worst on the continent. The government in 1985 estimated that two-thirds of the population was suffering from malnutrition. The problem is worst in the northeastern sections of the country where the children's growth is so stunted as a result of nutritional deficiencies that nutritionists in Brazil have discovered an epidemic of dwarfism. The *nordeste* children are found to be 16 percent shorter and 20 percent lighter than children of similar ages in other sections of Brazil (George, 1988).

George quotes Cardinal Paulo Evaristo Arns, archbishop of São Paulo, a diocese of more than fifteen million people, regarding the impact of the debt crisis in Brazil:

> The huge effort of the past two years resulted in an export surplus of a billion dollars a month. Yet this money served only to pay the interest on the debt. It's impossible to go on this way; we have already taken everything the people had to eat, even though two-thirds of them are already going hungry. When we borrowed, interest rates were 4 percent; they're 8 percent now and at one point they went as high as 21 percent. Even worse, these loans were contracted by the military, mostly for military ends—$40 billion were swallowed by six nuclear plants, none of which is working today. The people are now expected to pay off these debts in low salaries and hunger. But we have already reimbursed the debt, once or twice over, considering the interest paid. We must stop giving the blood and the misery of our people to pay the First World. (George, 1988, 138)

The problem of debt and the result of the structural adjustment programs imposed on countries as a strategy to repay the debt have had a pervasive effect on infant mortality rates throughout the dominated countries. Research by Sell and Kunitz (1989) found that the greater a country's participation in world markets, as measured by the degree of indebtedness, the slower life expectancy increased. Based on this analysis, George estimated that for each additional $10 a year in interest payments per capita, there was an associated decline in life expectancy improvement of approximately four months from 1970 to 1980 (George, 1988).

Although we have focused our examples on Latin America, Bello (1994) reports that sub-Saharan Africa has been even more devastated. Total debt for the sub-Saharan region climbed dramatically to where it is now 100 percent of GNP, compared to 35 percent of GNP for other developing countries. One result of the structural adjustment program was that by the end of the 1980s some 200 million of the regions 690 million people were classified as poor; the World Bank estimated that by the year 2000 that number was sure to reach 300 million, 40 percent of the world's poverty population. Malnutrition among the population has grown. Bello cites one study of families in Zambia where the impact of the adjustment programs has been to reduce the number of meals per day from two to one in many families. Public health services have been collapsing as governments cut public expenditures per the guidelines of the structural adjustment program. This has resulted in the rapid spread of cholera. Furthermore, the spread of AIDS is having a devastating effect on the population. Bello cites statistics that indicate that 50 percent of the armed forces in Zimbabwe and 25 percent of women seen in maternity clinics in Kampala, Uganda, are infected with the virus.

Ellwood notes that

> in Africa, external debt has ballooned by 400 per cent since the Bank and the IMF began managing national economies, through structural adjustment. Today in Ethiopia, a hundred thousand children die annually from easily preventable diseases, while debt repayments are four times more than public spending on healthcare. In Tanzania, where 40 per cent of people die before the age of 35, debt payments are 6 times greater than spending on healthcare. From the whole of Africa where one in every two children of primary-school age is not in school, the government transfers four times more to Northern creditors in debt payments than they spend on the health and education of their citizens. (Ellwood, 2001, 51)

George places the debt of the dominated countries as part of the larger strategy of imperialism, whereby the Northern Hemisphere countries control the resources and development of the Southern Hemisphere dominated countries. She describes the strategy as consistent with the transition to the use of low-intensity military conflict to maintain control.

> Highly visible, debilitating and exhaustively reported interventions like Vietnam have given way to Low-intensity Conflict (LIC). LIC has become the officially sanctioned and widely practiced strategy against movements popular in the Third World and governments unpopular in Washington. LIC is also LCC, or Low-cost Conflict—for the perpetrator. It costs little in money and in manpower; above all, it costs little in political opposition and turmoil at home because it is so hard to focus on. . . . Now let me take the LIC concept a step further. I'll call it FLIC, or Financial Low-intensity Conflict. FLIC is, aptly enough, the French slang word for police, the equivalent of "cop" or "fuzz." Third World debt is now, perhaps, less a "crisis" than an ongoing, dialectical FLIC waged against the South, a permanent global struggle exactly like LIC but played out on another terrain. As with LIC, FLIC does not seek to win because total victory—complete payback—would also mean bankruptcy for the debtors and the consequent collapse of the international financial system. The war would be over, and everyone would have lost. FLIC does, however, help to prevent the Third World from posing a threat, from dictating its terms, from changing the political balance of forces in the world. When creditor nations and institutions wage FLIC, they are not engaged in "linear activity" comparable with traditional war in which debts are contracted, mature and are paid off. They are, rather, carrying out a process without any foreseeable end, one that allows the North to keep a check upon any pretensions to real independence on the part of the South and to ensure privileged access to the South's resources, and to its industrial capacity, on the cheapest possible terms. (George, 1988, 233–34)

George contends that the Third World War has already started, but it is a silent war, a war whose victims are children and the unemployed in the dominated countries principally in the Southern Hemisphere of the world.

The impact of debt and the structural adjustment programs of the World Bank and the International Monetary Fund are just the most recent strategies in a war that has been going on since the fifteenth century. According to

Chomsky the New World Order is a continuation of the pattern of domination that has been ongoing for the past five hundred years. "In the South, in contrast, the New World Order imposed by the powerful is perceived, not unrealistically, as a bitter international class war, with the advanced state capitalist economies and their transnational corporations monopolizing the means of violence and controlling investment, capital, technology, and planning and management decisions, at the expense of the huge mass of the population. Local elites in the southern dependencies can share in the spoils" (Chomsky, 1993, 45).

It is important also to recognize that structural violence, as it manifests itself in differences in infant mortality rates and problems of hunger, is not restricted to countries dominated by the most powerful countries economically and militarily, but also occur in countries that are in positions of dominance. Bello (1994) observes that the structural adjustment programs implemented in the Southern Hemispheric countries were one part of a Reagan administration strategy to roll back the position of working people in the United States. Cutbacks in welfare programs, deregulation, tax policies that favored the wealthy, tight fiscal policy by the Federal Reserve Board, and policies that facilitated the flight of investment capital overseas all had a significant impact in decreasing the standard of living of the bottom 60 percent of the working population, increasing the levels of wealth and income inequality and poverty in the nation. At the same time, the government conducted a war on drugs that was fought in the poorest communities in the country and increased the percentage of the population in prison to the highest it has been in history. Furthermore, military spending skyrocketed and national debt climbed to the highest level, far exceeding the deficits accrued by the spending policies of all previous U.S. presidential administrations combined. By the end of the 1980s, the United States was the world's leading debtor nation and the country with the largest percentage of its population in prisons and spent the most on weaponry for maintaining order nationally and internationally.

MEASUREMENT OF STRUCTURAL VIOLENCE

Galtung and Höivik proposed a method for measuring structural violence by using the differences in life expectancies. For these authors structural violence is the difference between the optimal life expectancy and the actual life expectancy (Galtung and Höivik, 1971). Köhler and Alcock (1976) build on this earlier formulation and attempted to measure the level of structural violence in two ways. First using Galtung and Höivik's conceptualization they contrasted the differences in life expectancy between the country with the highest life expectancy (for the data set available for the year 1965, Sweden was the highest) and other countries in the world. They contrasted this measure with what they referred to as the "egalitarian model which is based on what life expectancy would be if global wealth was distributed equally across the people of the world. The egalitarian model is based on establishing a relationship between Gross National Product per capita and Life Expectancy." The authors then standardized the value of GNP per capita into Life Expectancy units and then equalized GNP per capita and determined what life expectancy would be in this ideal world of equality. The estimate of life expectancy for the idealized condition of equalized distribution of income and resources would be 68.3 years in 1965 compared to Sweden, which provided 74.7 years. Thus, the estimated egalitarian model provided a systematically more conservative estimate of life expectancy. The authors concluded that the concept of structural violence can be measured using this technique and a calculation of life loss could be developed from this inequity (using the more conservative measure) and could then be compared to other forms of violence that occurred in the world in the same period. Based on this analysis structural violence was estimated to be at least twice the magnitude of what the authors referred to as behavioral violence from wars and crime and civil unrest.

Another way of measuring structural violence is to examine differences between countries in terms of the level of human development that they provide for their populations. Comparing the differences between the levels of human development that are afforded different countries could then provide an estimate of the level of structural violence. The Human Development Index (HDI) is a more comprehensive measure of structural violence since it not only considers differences in life expectancy but includes other measure of the loss of human potential occurring because of systems of structured inequality in the world and within societies.

The Human Development Index was developed by the United Nations Development Programme (UNDP) for its 1990 report. Since its original formulation, the HDI has grown in its sophistication although still retaining a definition that embodies Amartya Sen's "capabilities" approach to understanding human well-being. The index from its beginnings focused on three important goals of national development: providing a decent standard of living, access to health to prevent and treat disease and injury, and education for the development of human potentials (Sen, 1985). Although there are criticisms of some of the limitations of the measure, there is no single measure that is more generally agreed upon by the world community to be a measure of levels of human development within the world.

Why use human development as a measure of structural violence? If we can agree to the fact that violence is any action, inaction, or structural arrangement that results in physical or nonphysical harm to one or more humans, and that harm is fundamentally a condition that limits the development of human life potentials, then the differences in the development of humans within and across societies around the world and its measurement provide a comprehensive measure of structural violence. Ultimately, the differences in the levels of human development are a result of the differences in the positions that we act within and in response to conditions created by these positions. The positions are defined in terms of systems of stratification discussed earlier and the position of the geographic area in a world system of stratification created by empires throughout world history.

What are the violent outcomes of these structures of inequality that occur within a society and between societies in the world system? One outcome is the inability of the vast majority of the world's people to develop their human potential. In this context the hierarchical relations in a society and the world inhibit people from living in health as many years as possible and developing their intellectual and physical capabilities to their fullest potential. "Human development is a process of enlarging people's choices. In principle, these choices can be infinite and change over time. But at all levels of development, the three essential ones are for people to lead a long and healthy life, to acquire knowledge and to have access to resources needed for a decent standard of living. If these essential choices are not available, many other opportunities remain inaccessible" (UNDP, 1990, 10). In the most recent report the definition of human development incorporated other dimensions of human freedom, equity, and sustainable development. This most recent definition defines "human development as the expansion of people's freedoms to live long, healthy and creative lives; to advance other goals they have reason to value; and to engage actively in shaping development *equitably and sustainably on a shared planet*" (Klugman, 2011, 1).

As to the rationale to include equity in the concept of human development, Klugman states that "all inequitable processes are unjust: people's chances at better lives should not be constrained by factors outside their control. Inequalities are especially unjust when particular groups, whether because of gender, race or birthplace, are systematically disadvantaged" (Klugman, 2011, 1). She also explains the importance of sustainable development as a component of human development, quoting Anand and Sen (2000), "it would be a gross violation of the universalist principle if we were to be obsessed about *inter*generational equity without at the same time seizing the problem of *intra*generational equity" (Klugman, 2011, 1).

The most recent index is composed of the following indicators: health (longevity at birth), education (mean years of schooling compared to the expected years of schooling), and income (gross national income, which is based on law of diminishing returns of income relative to creating a sufficient standard of living). Each of the units is treated to be of equivalent value and is standardized so that the value of each dimension of the index varies from 0 to 1 as the index does itself. Klugman, Rodriguez, and Choi (2011) provide a more technical discussion of the method of calculation of the Human Development Index. A score of 1 on the index indicates that the country is highest on all measures of human development; a score lower than 1 indicates that the country is lower on one or more of the indicators of human development compared to the country that has achieved the highest. It is important to realize that since we are principally focusing on averages within a given country on the measures of life expectancy, income, and education, the measure is not sensitive to inequality within the country on these dimensions.

Three other indices have been developed to measure a country's development that measure the impact of inequality within the country on the HDI: Inequality-Adjusted Human Development Index, Gender Inequality Index, and the Multidimensional Poverty Index. For purposes of this discussion, we will focus on the first two of these scales since the Multidimensional Poverty Index is not used for the most advanced countries since they register very little poverty on the index score. The Inequality-Adjusted Human Development Index (IHDI) adjusts the Human Development Index (HDI) for inequality in the distribution of each dimension across the population. The value of the IHDI falls below the HDI as inequality rises. For example, if there are disparities within the population on each of the elements of the index (income, schooling, and health), the index is systematically lowered to take into account the levels of these disparities (see Human Development Report 2011 for more details on the method of calculation of the adjustment of the HDI). In some countries the disparity in income inequality is partially offset by increasing reduction in disparities in health care or education. As noted in the report this is a pattern that has occurred in many Latin American countries during the past decade.

The Gender Inequality Index measures the gender-based disadvantage in three dimensions—reproductive health, empowerment, and the labor market. The Gender Inequality Index illustrates the loss of potential human development due to inequality between female and male achievements in each of these dimensions. The score varies between 0 when women and men are equal and 1 where one gender fares as poorly as possible in all measured dimensions in comparison to the other gender (Klugman, 2011).

Tables 9.2 and 9.3 illustrate the distribution of scores of the countries that would be classified as high and low human development, respectively. The countries selected were the highest and lowest developed countries to reach a comparable size population of five hundred million people within each group of countries. The disparity in human development across the two classifications of high and low developed countries is dramatic. For example, the Human Development Index for Norway, which received the highest rating of development, is .943, while for Democratic Republic of the Congo, which received the lowest score, it is .286. The average HDI score for the eleven most developed countries comprising a total population of five hundred million people was .912, very close to maximum score on the index, 1, meaning that these countries provide the highest level of opportunities for the human development of their population. The average HDI score for the twenty-seven least developed countries comprising a total population of five hundred million people was .226, one-fourth of the level of the most developed countries.

Looking at the differences in the separate components of the Human Development Index reveal the human costs of this disparity in HDI scores. For example, the life expectancy in Norway is 81.1 years, while for Democratic Republic of the Congo it is approximately 32 years less at 48.4. Overall, the average life expectancy for the eleven most developed countries was 80.7 years, while for the twenty-seven least developed countries the average life expectancy was 53.9 years, almost 27 years less of life for those who reside in these countries.

Table 9.2. 2011 Human Development Indicators for Eleven Highest HDI Countries with Total Population of Approximately 500 Million.

Country	Pop.	Med Age**	HDI	IneqAdj HDI	Life Exp.	Age 15+ Literacy	Gender Inequality	Maternal Mortality*	Under 5 Mortality**	Percent Species Endangered***
Norway	4.9	38.7	.943	.890	81.1	100	.075	7	3	7
Australia	22.6	36.9	.929	.856	81.9	100	.136	8	5	22
Netherlands	16.7	40.7	.910	.846	80.7	100	.052	9	4	5
United States	313.1	36.9	.910	.771	78.5	100	.299	24	8	21
New Zealand	4.4	36.6	.908	—	80.7	100	.195	14	6	25
Canada	34.3	39.9	.908	.829	81.0	100	.140	12	6	7
Ireland	4.5	34.7	.908	.843	80.6	100	.230	3	4	7
Lichtenstein	0	14.4	.905	—	79.6	100	—	—	2	1
Germany	82.2	44.3	.905	.842	80.4	100	.085	7	4	9
Sweden	9.4	44.3	.904	.851	81.4	100	.049	5	3	5
Switzerland	7.7	41.4	.903	.840	82.3	100	.067	10	4	6
Total	499.8	39.6	.912	.841	80.7	100	.133	9.9	4.5	10.5

* Data collected for 2008 used.
** Data collected for 2009 used.
*** Data collected for 2010 used.

Table 9.3. 2011 Human Development Indicators for Twenty-Seven Lowest HDI Countries with Total Population of Approximately 500 Million.

Country	Pop.	Med Age**	HDI	IneqAdj HDI	Life Exp.	Age 15+ Literacy	Gender Inequality	Maternal Mortality*	Under 5 Mortality**	Percent Species Endangered***
Uganda	34.5	15.7	.446	.296	54.1	73.2	.577	430	128	7
Togo	6.2	19.7	.435	.289	57.1	56.9	.602	350	98	4
Comoros	0.8	18.9	.430	—	61.1	74.2	—	340	104	13
Zambia	13.5	16.7	.430	.303	49.0	70.9	.627	470	141	3
Djibouti	0.9	21.4	.430	.275	57.9	—	—	300	94	9
Rwanda	10.9	18.7	.429	.276	55.4	70.7	.453	540	111	6
Benin	9.1	17.9	.427	.274	56.1	41.7	.634	410	118	4
Gambia	1.8	17.8	.420	—	58.5	46.5	.610	400	103	4
Sudan	44.6	19.7	.408	—	61.5	70.2	.611	750	108	5
Cote d'Ivoire	20.2	19.2	.400	.246	55.4	55.3	.655	470	119	7
Malawi	15.4	16.9	.400	.272	54.2	73.7	.564	510	110	9
Afghanistan	32.4	16.6	.398	—	48.7	—	.707	1400	199	5
Zimbabwe	12.8	19.3	.376	.268	51.4	91.9	.583	790	90	3
Ethiopia	84.7	18.7	.363	.247	59.3	29.8	—	470	104	7
Mali	15.8	16.3	.359	—	51.4	26.2	.712	830	191	2
Guinea-Bissau	1.5	19.0	.353	.207	48.1	52.2	—	1000	193	5
Eritrea	5.4	19.0	.349	—	61.6	66.6	—	280	55	8
Guinea	10.2	18.3	.344	.211	54.1	39.5	—	680	142	8
Cent Africa Rep	4.5	19.4	.343	.204	48.4	55.2	.669	850	171	1

Sierra Leone	6.0	18.4	.336	.196	47.8	40.9	.662	970	192	7
Burkina Faso	17.0	17.1	.331	.215	55.4	28.7	.596	560	166	3
Liberia	4.1	18.2	.329	.213	56.8	59.1	.671	990	112	8
Chad	11.5	17.1	.328	.196	49.6	33.6	.735	1200	209	3
Mozambique	23.9	17.8	.322	.229	50.2	55.1	.602	550	142	7
Burundi	8.6	20.2	.316	—	50.4	66.6	.478	970	166	5
Niger	16.1	15.5	.295	.195	54.7	28.7	.724	820	160	3
Congo Dem Rep	67.8	16.7	.286	.172	48.4	66.8	.710	670	199	6
Total	501.3	16.8	.358	.228	53.9	55.0	.629	667	135	5.5

* Data collected for 2008 used.
** Data collected for 2009 used.
*** Data collected for 2010 used.

Major differences in life expectancy between the most developed and least developed can in part be accounted for by differences in access to clean water and access to medical care and as the result of disease patterns. In particular, when looking at the differences between countries in Africa and more developed countries in Europe and North America, the impact of the AIDS pandemic is a significant factor. In an earlier report the United Nations Population Division estimated that "in the 38 highly affected countries of Africa, the population by 2015 is projected to be 91 million less, or 10 per cent lower, than it would have been without AIDS" (United Nations Population Division, 2002). We will discuss the impact of AID as structural violence later in this chapter.

The differences in life expectancy are also accounted for in looking at differences in mortality rates for small children and women giving birth. The mortality rates for children under five years of age is on the average thirty times greater in the twenty-seven least developed countries (136 per 1,000 live births) compared to the eleven most developed countries (4.5 per 1,000 live births). Thus, a child born in the rich world would have a thirty times greater chance of surviving their first five years than a child born in the poor world. The differences in the rates for maternal mortality between the most and least developed countries are even more striking where on the average women in the least developed countries experience almost a seventy-five times greater chance of dying giving birth than if they resided in one of the most developed countries of the world, 667 per 100,000 vs. 8.9 per 100,000.

Although the differences are great between countries, greater differences may also be found within countries. For example, the rate of infant mortality in many poor neighborhoods in American cities such as Detroit, Washington, D.C., New York, or Chicago is equivalent to the average rates in many poorer developing countries. Similar disparities are found in countries throughout Africa and Latin America between urban and rural areas. Thus the structures of inequality within a society compound the disparities in mortality and morbidity that we find between countries.

There are three major reasons why people die in any society. They either degenerate as a result of cancer and circulatory ailments, they are killed by communicable diseases, or they are killed by the products of the social and economic environment. These three factors may be intertwined so that for many in the world today, their economic and social environment increases the likelihood that their bodies will degenerate at a more rapid rate or are more vulnerable to communicable diseases. When we look at patterns of disease and mortality, human beings' positions via systems of stratification form a crucial factor in accounting for who, when, and why people die. In all societies, those in dominated positions, especially as defined in terms of class and ethnicity, experience higher rates of morbidity and mortality than those who are in dominant positions (Wilkinson and Pickett, 2010). Furthermore, in terms of the stratification system that ranks countries in the world system, those countries that are in dominated positions as defined in terms of the world political economic order generally have higher rates of mortality and morbidity within their population as a whole than those who are in dominant positions. Much of these differences in patterns are accounted for by differences in availability of survival needs (diet, shelter, clean water, and air) and differences in access to medical services during times of need.

Each day, twenty thousand young children die from malnutrition and disease (World Health Organization, 2011). The vast majority of these children reside in the countries of the Southern Hemisphere, the periphery of the world political economic system. This tragedy of child death is a result of the structure of inequality that exists within and between nations of the world. In Yemen 58 percent of children under five are stunted in their development as a result of malnutrition. Similarly in Guatemala, on the other side of the world from Yemen, the percentage of children under five who are stunted is 54 percent. Many African and Asian countries that are listed as low human development countries also have more than 50 percent of their children under five stunted in their development as a result of malnutrition (Klugman, 2011). What these children all have in common are the relatively low position of their nation in terms of the world system and the high levels of inequality within their societies.

Another interesting measure of structural violence that stems from environmental racism and toxic imperialism discussed previously is the difference in the amount of deaths from pollution. The Human Development Report breaks down deaths from pollution in three broad categories: deaths from water pollution, deaths from indoor pollution, and deaths from outdoor pollution. Although there are important differences in terms of the sources of pollution and its relationship to differences in mortality rates between countries, combining the three sources into a composite measure of deaths per million attributable to pollution or pollution deaths provides a stark contrast between countries that are the most developed and are the beneficiaries of past and present imperial systems and the least developed countries. The average rate of deaths from pollution per million citizens of the eleven most developed countries is 74. The average rate of deaths from pollution per million citizens of the twenty-seven least developed countries is 2,478, a rate thirty-three times greater. Your position in respect to where you geographically reside between the most and least developed places means you have a thirty-three times difference in the chance of dying from a polluted environment.

Access to a nonpolluted environment (water, air, and soil), sanitation, and health care is a serious problem in many areas around the world. These conditions also relate to the presence of disease and high mortality levels in these countries. These three factors are also directly related to the socioeconomic conditions of people. For example, in Somalia 70 percent of the population does not have access to safe water (Klugman, 2011). In Niger 11 percent of the population is using adequate or "improved" sanitation facilities. In Ethiopia no more than 20 percent of the population has access to safe water and adequate sanitation (Klugman, 2011). In regard to access to health care as measured by access to essential drugs, throughout most of the sub-Saharan region of Africa more than half of the population is deprived of access. This lack of access to health care together with the problems of sanitation and access to safe water creates a serious assault on the quality and quantity of life as measured by mortality and morbidity rates.

To what degree can we talk of these problems as acts of structural violence? Of course in looking at what segments of the population are most likely to be denied access to these essential services and resources, it is uniformly the poorer segments of the society. Among the poor those who are most vulnerable are children and women, or in other words, those with the least amounts of power as defined in terms of systems of stratification. In the extremely poor countries noted, it is principally the wealthiest segments of the society that are shielded from these dangers.

Furthermore, decisions by the elite in many of these countries to purchase weaponry for the military and police to maintain the order and to maintain their positions of dominance, to provide for access to luxury goods, and to provide for investment credits to encourage investments that will benefit elite segments of the society, as well as the high cost of corruption among governing elites, constitute violence because they deny resources to the poorest segments to provide for access to safe water, sanitation, and health care to prevent disease and shortened life spans. But it is not just the decisions of the national elites that result in acts of structural violence. It may be the case that the actions of the international elite have a far greater impact as it relates to the occurrence of structural violence in the countries on the periphery of the world economy.

Differences are also large when we look at differences in the ability of humans to develop their human potentials. The one component of the HDI that represents this dimension is the differences between the mean level of education and the expected level of education as defined within each country. This measure was used instead of the measure of adult literacy used in previous indices in order to provide variation for more developed countries, all of which have very high adult literacy rates. However, it creates problems in underestimating the differences in educational resources and their impact on human development when comparing the most to the least developed countries. For example, a country like Norway has an expected level of education to be 17.3 years and the mean level of years of education in Norway is 12.6, 4.7 years difference. In the Democratic Republic of the Congo the expected years of education is 8.2 years and the mean level of education is 3.5 years, a difference of 4.7 years. However, we would not say that Norway and the Democratic Republic of the Congo are equivalent in providing educational resources to their population. On the other hand, it would be accurate to say that both countries have similar disparities in what their population has accomplished given the relative expectations of educational achievement within these countries.

A better measure of ability of adults to reach their potentials that comes from the educational resources of a society and provides a more universal measure of evaluation is adult literacy rate, the component of the HDI in previous editions. Whether one can read or not is a significant factor for humans to develop their intellectual capacity. This is not to state that the oral tradition is not an important means of learning. However, being able to translate the symbolic representation of language is essential to the growth of human knowledge and human intellectual potential. The rate of adult illiteracy in the most advanced countries of the world is negligible. On the other hand, the rate of adult illiteracy is very high in the least developed nations of the world. In the twenty-seven least developed countries, the average rate of literacy for those fifteen and over is 55 percent. The range, however, is quite large with Zimbabwe having the highest rate of literacy at almost 92 percent while countries like Ethiopia, Burkina Faso, and Niger report levels of approximately 29 percent of their populations fifteen and over being literate. Going back to our comparison of Norway and the Democratic Republic of the Congo, the differences in the levels of literacy in their respective populations are 99 percent for Norway compared to 66.8 percent for the DRC.

Lastly, it is also important to note that differences in position are not just between nation-states but also between positions within nation-states. There are two summary measures included in the report listed on tables 9.2 and 9.3. The first is the HDI value adjusted for inequalities in the three basic dimensions of human development (see Technical Note 1 of Human Development 2010 Report) (Klugman, 2011). All three components of the HDI (income, education, and life expectancy) are adjusted for the levels of inequality for each of these components within the country. Klugman notes that when the IHDI equals the HDI, there is no inequality across people in the society on the measures of human development. However, the IHDI falls further below the HDI as inequality rises. She claims that in these cases, "the IHDI is the actual level of human development (taking into account inequality), while the HDI can be viewed as an index of the 'potential' human development that could be achieved if there was no inequality" (Klugman, 2011, 169).

As can be seen from the comparisons of the two sets of averages for each of the two sets of countries (highest and lowest), the development index drops from .912 to .840, a 9 percent drop for the highest developed countries and from .358 to .228, a 36 percent in the average drop for the lowest developed countries, four times greater of a drop in the index. Thus in the poorest countries you have the greatest disparity in the various components of measures that compose the index, indicating a greater disparity in human development than what is found in the most advanced countries. This differential is not uniform across the three different components of the measure, the differences are principally in life expectancy and income to live a full life (however, this would be expected given the measure of education achievement used in the HDI). Because of the increased levels of inequality in the poorest countries, it affects the overall human development that is provided in that society. Thus, the least developed countries have levels of structural violence that are higher not only because of their national position in the world, but also because of the increased inequality within them.

The Human Development Report also presented trends in the IHDI since 1990 for sixty-six countries. The report notes worsening income inequality occurring in most countries and regions of the world. There were exceptions in some countries in Latin America. However, Klugman notes that this "had the effect of offsetting the large improvements in health and education inequality, the results is the aggregate loss in human development due to inequality sums to 24 percent" (Klugman, 2011, 28).

Another measure of inequality that the report develops is a gender inequality index. The index is a composite measure reflecting inequality in achievements between women and men in three dimensions: reproductive health, empowerment, and the labor market (Klugman, 2011). The score varies from 0, where there would be complete gender equality in the three areas, to 1, where there would be complete inequality. The average Gender Inequality Index score for the eleven most developed countries was .133. The average for the twenty-seven least developed countries was .629, an index value that is almost five times higher in gender inequality. What this means is that women are experiencing significantly higher levels of structural violence as a result of their position. This violence manifests itself across all areas of human development: a sufficient income to sustain a quality of life, higher levels of risk in terms of death and injury because of the resources available to them to experience a healthy childbirth, and access to political power to ensure their well-being in the society.

Lastly, there are two other characteristics that distinguish the two sets of countries and are related to patterns of violence, age, and ethnicity. When we look at the differences between these two groups of countries, we see that in general the most developed countries in the world have citizens who are predominantly of European ancestry or white and are also older with a median age of 39.6 years. While the poorer countries are for the most part of African ancestry and are younger, the median age for the twenty-seven countries was 16.8 years, a 23-year or generational difference. Age and ethnicity are also important factors in considering patterns of violence, whereby those who are younger and of minority status are more likely to experience higher levels of violence victimization in most of the types of violence we have discussed thus far, and structural violence is not an exception to this pattern. Those areas of the world where there are the highest levels of structural violence are the areas of the world where the young, poor, and minority populations reside. The distribution of resources for human development in the world is the cause of this form of violence.

Species Destruction as Structural Violence

When we are describing structural violence, it is important not to neglect other species as victims. Remember that in our definition of violence we don't exclude other species. And as we have discussed in our discussion of economic violence, their victimization is much higher than the rates of the human species. Structural violence, which is violence that is based on a system of inequality, certainly applies to the case of other species. Our knowledge system and belief systems are all based on human superiority and thus the destruction of other species for our entertainment, enjoyment, and nourishment is built in human culture almost as a universal. This is certainly the case when we are discussing civilized societies that are based on systems of stratification.

Furthermore, the nature of the (human) world system as it relates to the positioning of nation-states and humans, and the nature of the development strategy based on neo-liberal strategies of capitalist development with a goal of unlimited, endless growth in human production and consumption, results in differences in the levels of species destruction across the globe. In areas where there is more development as defined in terms of this path of development, there is a greater level of violence directed at other species. Ironically this is evidenced in the data presented in the Human Development Report.

The most recent Human Development Report includes a measure of the "percentage of animal species (including mammals, birds, reptiles, amphibians, fish and invertebrates) classified as either critically endangered, endangered or vulnerable by the International Union for the Conservation of Nature" (Klugman, 2011, 149). The cost of development as defined by the United Nations and the dominant governments of the world system weighs heavily on species other than human. For the twenty-seven least developed countries of the world the average percentage of species endangered is 5.5 percent. Five and a half percent of the species who geographically reside with these 500,000,000 people are endangered by human activity. The percentage of species that are endangered goes up to two times greater in the eleven most developed countries—10.5 percent of species who are sharing this geographic space with 500,000,000 people are endangered on the average in these countries.

However, it is important to recognize that the range of scores is particularly broad for these eleven countries, with New Zealand, the United States of America, and Australia with the highest rates of the group, between 21 and 25 percent of species that are endangered in these geographic areas, and Lichtenstein, Sweden, and the Netherlands with rates of 1 to 5 percent. It is also important to recognize that in the most developed countries of the world, the level of species destruction is systematically lower than what would be expected since in their development process, the levels of species destruction would have been much higher at earlier times in their history during the period of rapid industrialization when there were no systematic measures of species destruction being taken and recorded. Nevertheless, what this means for the present and future is that as the development strategies promoted and sponsored and sometimes forced upon the developing world by the international and national elite follows the path of neo-liberal capitalist development, there will be a greater level of species death and structural violence directed at nonhuman species throughout these areas of the world.

Many scientists claim that we are currently experiencing a period of mass extinction. Some estimates put the current extinction rate at one hundred to one thousand times the historical average (MacFarquhar, 2010). The United Nations member nations agreed in 2010 to cut the rate of extinction in half by 2020. The Nagoya Protocol calls on member states to set more protected land and ocean space aside from development to reduce the extinction. It also calls upon the wealthier nations to help the poorer nations reach these goals. One specific way that this was proposed is for wealthier countries to share in the benefits of the new pharmaceuticals, new crops, and new products derived from the genetic treasure trove discovered in the developing world in places like the Amazon. It will be important to see if this can be accomplished given the dictates of the economic systems and the systems of stratification that they are based upon.

AIDS, Tuberculosis, and Structural Violence

Let's look at the AIDS epidemic and ask to what degree we can consider the deaths from this disease an example of structural violence. The AIDS epidemic claimed 1.8 million lives in 2009 (Joint United Nations Programme on

HIV/AIDS [UNAIDS], 2010). This is a disease that since its discovery approximately thirty years ago has infected 60 million persons and killed approximately 30 million people (UNAIDS, 2010). Thirty-three million persons are currently infected. There were 2.2 million new infections in 2009. It appears that the rate of contraction may have peaked globally in 1999.

Is there a pattern to this rate of infection and death that is related to one's position in the world and society? Yes, those who reside in the poorest nations and are the poorest within those nations are those with the highest concentrations of the disease. Ninety-eight percent of the deaths occur in the Southern Hemisphere of the world. More than 80 percent of the deaths have occurred in the sub-Saharan region of Africa, that region of the world that is the poorest and, as we have discussed, where there are the lowest levels of opportunities for human development. Those who live in the poorest regions and who are the poorest (who live for the most part on less than one dollar a day) and with the least access to health care, sanitation, and safe water are most vulnerable. They are also least likely to afford the cost of the current drug treatment therapy: the antiretroviral combination cocktail that could sell for $10,000 to $15,000 a year in the United States in 2001.

For years the United States threatened countries that attempted to manufacture their own version of the drug therapy in violation of copyright laws. U.S. pharmaceutical companies that manufactured the products expressed concern about the reduction in profits that they would experience if they lowered the prices to give greater access to those in developing countries. Millions of people died each and every year. In May 2001, President Clinton stated that the United States would not challenge laws in African countries that seek to improve access to AIDS drugs. UNAIDS pressured the major manufacturers of effective drug treatment to set lower prices for developing countries. Finally, five major pharmaceuticals joined an "Accelerated Access" program to negotiate 60 percent to 80 percent reductions in AIDS-drug prices for poor nations. In accordance with this program, each country must negotiate the price of each AIDS-cocktail component with each company. McGeary (2001) notes that there has been barely any impact noted thus far in the sub-Saharan region. She notes that while Senegal might haggle down the cost by 75 percent or 80 percent, the therapy is still too costly at $1,200 a year for people who earn $510 a year, Senegal's per capita income. Thus, death occurs from the disease and as a result of the structural position of the victim in the world system of stratification.

There have been significant improvements during the past ten years. In 2004, only 700,000 in low and middle income countries had access to the antiretroviral treatment; in 2009 the number has climbed dramatically to 5.2 million. However, one must question why it took so long to provide access to life-saving drugs to people who were sick and dying. What were the barriers that caused the deaths of millions of people? Was it the positions that they occupied, in the world and in their own country, that led to the premature deaths of tens of millions of people? Their deaths were deaths of structural violence, deaths that were caused because of the positions that they occupied.

Farmer (1999) draws the parallel between the AIDS epidemic and the tuberculosis pandemics of the past. He notes that TB, like infectious diseases in general, disproportionately kills the poor. Throughout history this has been the case and it is the case today. He notes that by the 1960s TB had disappeared from the public's view. However, it had never disappeared from the life of the poor in poor countries around the world and in the shelters and among the poorest populations within the United States. Recently there has been a significant increase in tuberculosis among minority populations in the United States. This is despite the fact that there has been low-cost effective treatment available for more than fifty years.

However, the vast majority of victims will be within the poorest populations of the poorest countries throughout the world. "Fifty years after the introduction of almost 100 percent effective combination therapy, tuberculosis remains the world's leading infectious cause of preventable deaths. If the World Health Organization is correct, tuberculosis killed some three million people in 1996—more than died from complications of HIV infection, and more than have died of tuberculosis in any one year since 1900. If we've done such a poor job delivering effective and inexpensive cures to people in the prime of their lives, what are our chances with medications that are less effective and hundreds of times as costly?" (Farmer, 1999, 266).

Farmer claims that "it is difficult to document any impact of the new treatment regimens on worldwide tuberculosis incidence: in the current decade, an estimated 300 million people will become infected with tubercle bacilli; 90 million will develop active tuberculosis; and, if access to care does not become a global priority, 30 million will die" (Farmer 1999, 212). But it is not just this disease or another; it is how we distribute the life chances as defined in terms of health resources and a safe and healthy environment. Farmer contends that inequality itself constitutes our modern plague. The linkage between inequality and national mortality rates in countries in North America, Europe, and Asian was documented in an analysis of ten separate sets of data from eight different groups of researchers (Wilkinson, 1996). Wilkinson writes that "it is now clear that the scale of income differences in a society is one of the most powerful determinants of health standards in different countries, and that it influences health through its impact on social cohesion" (Wilkinson 1996, ix). What they are describing in looking at the differences in morbidity and mortality across the various positions within and between countries is structural violence. Just as we can look at the differences in life expectancy, so can we look at the differences in morbidity and mortality from deadly diseases.

Structural Violence and the New Slavery

Slavery is one of the more basic forms of structural violence. The extreme exploitation from slavery has long been outlawed throughout the world because of the recognition of the violence that slavery does to human beings. It is not just the violence to enforce the ownership and control, but it is the violence that is done to the human spirit and psyche and the violence that is done because of the sacrifice of the development of the person who is owned as a slave. It is structural violence because the violence exists because of the structure of the positions of slave and master or slaveholder. It is because one is defined as a slave that one experiences the violence of a loss of one's humanity.

Slavery is a booming business in the world today and its dramatic growth is linked to the growth of inequality between and within nations (Bales, 2004). Slavery is part of the globalization of the world economy. According to Bales's estimate, slave labor directly contributes to approximately $13 billion in profit in the world economy. However, he notes that the indirect benefits of slave labor are much greater. In his research on the "new slavery" he claims that slavery is found in virtually every country and that the products that slaves produce extend throughout the world economy. He states that the "impact of slave labor reverberates through the world economy in ways ever harder to escape. Workers making computer parts or televisions in India can be paid low wages in part because food produced by slave labor is so cheap" (Bales, 2004, 22). He also notes that steel that is imported from Brazil by many countries around the world is produced by the charcoal fires that heat the blast furnaces; the charcoal is produced by slaves. Governor Mitch Daniels of my home state of Indiana was so concerned about the number of female slaves trafficked as prostitutes coming to the city of Indianapolis during the 2012 Super Bowl that he asked the state legislature to toughen state laws on human trafficking (WLTL.com, 2012). From 2008 to 2010, some thirty-four task forces and working groups have been operating around the country, and nearly nine hundred children have been rescued from prostitution, and more than five hundred pimps have been convicted (Federal Bureau of Investigation, 2010).

Bales estimates that the total world population of slaves is approximately twenty-seven million. Based on his estimate, the slave population today is larger than all the slaves taken from Africa during the trans-Atlantic slave trade, and greater than the population of Canada. His definition of slavery is quite broad: "the total control of one person by another for the purpose of economic exploitation" (Bales, 2004, 5). His research methodology uses a case study method of several countries, using researchers to interview slaves about their estimates of number of people in their area who are slaves and the nature of their lives as slaves. It is unclear how Bales extrapolated the data that he acquired from interviews into what he contends is a conservative worldwide estimate. Nevertheless, it is an estimate that has been embraced by organizations in the twenty-first century that are part of the anti-slavery movement.

The International Labour Organization (ILO) defined slavery more narrowly as forced labor. Article 2, section 1 of the ILO Declaration on Fundamental Principles and Rights at Work defines forced labor as "all work or service which is exacted from any person under the menace of any penalty and for which the said person has not offered himself voluntarily" (International Labour Organization, 2005). The ILO defines slavery as one form of forced labor. Slavery is understood as the condition of forced labor where the situation is a permanent one, often based on descent, rather than one with a fixed duration. For Bales, the permanency of it or whether there is a fixed duration is not central to the definition. The ILO's estimate of the number of people who were engaged in forced labor is 12.3 million. The 12.3 million is broken down into the following categories: 9.8 million are exploited by private agents (this includes more than 2.4 million in forced labor as a result of human trafficking) and 2.5 million are forced to work by the state or by rebel military groups.

The ILO methodology relies on the statistical method of double sampling of reported cases of forced labor. According to the researchers, this sampling procedure, called "capture-recapture" in the statistical literature, was originally designed for estimating the abundance of wildlife. The data was based on reports of slavery from various sources including police, government officials, academic researchers, NGOs, and so forth for a geographic area for the time period 1995 to 2005. These reports were reviewed by researchers to determine if the methods of data collection provided could be validated. The validated number of cases were then used and multiplied times the average number of forced laborers in each reported case to form a census for a total world number for the period. As to which estimate is correct, because of the difference in definitions used, collection methods, and the general difficulty in recording amount of illegal behavior especially in areas where there is little law enforcement, it is almost impossible to know what the true number is. It may be safe to say that using Bales's broader definition, the number of "slaves" is somewhere between the two figures. Nevertheless, the case studies and the official reports provide us with information about the different types of forced labor or slavery and its relative proportions.

Bales finds that the largest proportion of slaves, 60 to 75 percent, are bonded labor in India, Pakistan, Bangladesh, and Nepal. This is consistent with the ILO estimates, which found that two-thirds of total forced labor occurred in Asia and the Pacific and is private-imposed for economic exploitation, mostly debt bondage in agriculture and other economic activities. The ILO find this same pattern of the dominance of forced labor for agriculture and other economic activities in other developing countries throughout Latin America, the Caribbean, North Africa, and the Middle East.

However, in more transitional (Eastern and Southeastern Europe) and advanced societies, the pattern of forced labor is different, where the dominant form is a result of illegal trafficking in most cases for sexual purposes. According to the ILO this form of forced labor composes approximately 11 percent of the total amount of forced labor in the world. The ILO also makes a distinction in its data between forced labor that is done by private individuals and that done by the state. State-imposed forced labor is least found in the more advanced countries and comprises approximately 20 percent of total forced labor. The occurrence of state-imposed forced labor is more likely to be found in Asia and the Pacific as well as Latin America and the Caribbean (International Labour Organization, 2005).

For Bales two factors explain the dramatic growth in slavery since World War II. The first factor is the dramatic growth in world population, more than tripling from two billion to more than seven billion today. Bales finds that the greatest growth in slavery has occurred in those areas of the world that have experienced the greatest population growth. Essentially in these areas, there is the largest "surplus population" where access to work or production is the most scarce. The second factor is the impact of the rapid social and economic changes occurring in those regions of the world that are increasingly being integrated into the world system. Those places on the periphery or the frontier of empires are where there is a concentration of conflict and competition for resources and where there are dramatic increases in levels of inequality as populations become displaced as a result of these economic transformations. The slaves today reside or have residences in these areas in Africa, Southeast Asia, the Indian subcontinent, South America, and Eastern Europe and states within the former Soviet Union that experienced the greatest transformations and economic and social displacement of the population.

> Throughout Africa and Asia the last fifty years have been scarred by civil war and the wholesale looting of resources by home-grown dictators, often supported by one of the super-powers. To hold onto power, the ruling kleptocrats have paid enormous sums for weaponry, money raised by mortgaging their countries. Meanwhile traditional ways of life and subsistence have been sacrificed to the cash crop and quick profit. Poor families have lost their old ways of meeting a crisis. . . . Modernization and the globalization of the world economy have shattered these traditional families and small-scale subsistence farming that supported them. The forced shift from subsistence to cash-crop agriculture, the loss of common land, and government policies that suppress farm income in favor of cheap food for the cities have all helped bankrupt millions of peasants and drive them from their land—sometimes into slavery. (Bales, 2004, 12–13)

Another area is in the Amazon; Bales describes how "transitional zones where the world's industrial economy meets the traditional culture of peasant farming are found throughout the developing world" (Bales, 2004, 30). In these locations there are often very bloody struggles over the control of natural resources. Bales notes that in the Amazon a terrible war continues over the region's mineral wealth and timber as the "line of exploitation," as he refers to it, advances. He notes that the Amazonian Indians have little to fight back with and are often pushed to extinction or sometimes before that enslavement.

The ILO claims there is little consensus as to the cause, although they point to the problem of persistent poverty and high levels of inequality as both a cause and effect of forced labor, especially in less developed regions of the world. The ILO report also points to long-standing patterns of discrimination against certain ethnic and caste minorities. In particular, the report notes "Scheduled Castes and Scheduled Tribes in India; among indigenous minorities in western Nepal; and among non-Muslims in Pakistan" (International Labour Organization, 2005, 30). They also point to the indigenous peoples of Latin America as more likely to be enslaved than the ethnic majority. Lastly, the ILO points to the fact that women in poverty are also more vulnerable than men, especially in the human trafficking sector of forced labor.

According to Bales, there are some very important distinctions between the old slavery of the nineteenth century and the new slavery of the twentieth and twenty-first centuries. The first major distinction is that there is no legal ownership asserted in the new slavery. In the past, slaveholders had title to ownership. Ownership of slaves was made illegal around the world in the nineteenth and early twentieth centuries. However, the new informal ownership without legal documents but through the use of violence or its threat is more potent. The new form of slavery circumvents the anti-slavery laws that essentially outlaw systems of legal ownership.

Also in the former system, the cost of a slave was quite high. Bales notes that in today's dollars a slave sold in the South in the 1850s could cost between $40,000 and $80,000, whereas the debt for bonded slavery in India can be as low as $12 to $15. Given the low cost of the slave, there are higher profits to be made from slavery today than in the past. In Thailand, according to Bales, "a girl between twelve and fifteen years old can be purchased for $800 to $2,000, and the costs of running a brothel and feeding the girls are relatively low. The profit is often as high as 800 percent a year" (Bales, 2004, 18).

Slaves today work under the most highly exploitive conditions, working most of their waking hours. Bales notes that they are easily disposable since the slaveholder has little responsibility and little investment in them, and they can be easily replaced. This leads to another distinction between the old and new slavery: the period of enslavement is generally much shorter in the new slavery compared with the slavery of old. For example, a young girl who is sold into slavery in Thailand may be a slave for three to five years. By that time, if she has not been infected by HIV, died from a back-alley abortion (abortion is illegal in Thailand), or become pregnant, she is no longer as profitable because of the effects of prostitution at a rate of between ten and fifteen men a day. In Thailand there is what is referred to in the prostitution business as a "virgin premium." Some Chinese and Sino-Thai customers are willing to pay large sums of money to deflower a virgin. An ancient Chinese belief is that sex with a virgin will make the man more virile and prolong his life.

> When a new girl is brought to the brothel she will not be placed out in the selection room with the other prostitutes but kept back in another room, the hong bud boree sut (the "room to unveil virgins"). Here she will be displayed possibly with other children, and her price will be negotiated with the pimp. To deflower a virgin these men pay between 5,000 and 50,000 baht ($200 to $2,000). Deflowering often takes place away from the brothel in a hotel room rented for the occasion. The pimp or his assistant will often attend as well, since it is usually necessary to beat the girl into submission. (Bales, 2004, 56)

Bales estimates that there are approximately 35,000 young girls who are working as sex worker slaves in Thailand.

A last important distinction that Bales makes between the old and new slavery is that in the earlier system ethnic and racial differences were important in distinguishing slaves from masters. There are types and places of slavery where this still exists today, for example the chattel slavery that occurs in some Northern and Western African and some Arab countries where the color of the skin is important in designating the position. But for the most part, the only distinction between the slave and slaveholder today is their economic position. Poverty is the one feature that distinguishes all slaves from slaveholders today. But it also may be related to gender and age as well; those who appear to be most vulnerable to being a slave are also young girls in the poorest regions of the world—those in the most dominated positions in the world system.

There are also cases where religion was an important factor in distinguishing the slave from the slaveholder. For example, Bales notes that many enslaved brickmakers are Christians while the slaveholders are Muslim in Pakistan. However, one case where the connection between religion, poverty, gender, and age in terms of slavery is illustrated is in the case of the "devadasi" in India. In India poor families may attempt to appease local gods by marrying their daughter to the god. The "devadasi" as she is called is declared a saint but must move into the local temple and under the control of men who run the temple. For hundreds of years these women have been turned into prostitutes and the temple turned into a brothel. The girls must do no other work and cannot leave the village or marry anyone else. Furthermore, any female children born to the "saints" are raised to be "devadasi" as well.

Another case is in the case of "fetish priests" in southeastern Ghana, Togo, Benin, and southwestern Nigeria. Bales claims that thousands of girls and young women are given by their families to these priests in order to atone for sins committed by members of their families, often rape. The girls themselves may be the products of rape. Their slavery is seen as a way of appeasing the gods for that or other crimes committed by their male relatives. According to the custom "a girl, who must be a virgin, is given to the local priest as a slave when she is about 10 years old. The girl then stays with the priest—cooking, cleaning, farming, and serving him sexually—until he frees her, usually after she has borne several children. At that point the slave's family must provide another young girl to replace her. Ghana's constitution forbids slavery, but the practice is justified on religious grounds by villagers and priests" (Bales, 2004, 21–22).

Bales identifies the three forms of slavery that are dominant in the world today. The first, which is closest to the old slavery, is chattel slavery. In this form of slavery a person may be forced into slavery by means of capture or born or sold into permanent servitude. The children of these slaves are also considered slaves of the slaveholder. Chattel slaves are found in Northern and Western Africa and some Arab countries. As mentioned above this form of slavery is similar to the old slavery because ethnic or racial differences are important in distinguishing the slave from the slaveholder. Bales estimates that this form of slavery represents a very small portion of slaves in the modern world.

The largest number of slaves is a result of debt bondages (Bales, 2004). In this form of slavery the person who is to be enslaved gives him- or herself as collateral for the loan of money. The length of their servitude or the nature of their service is not defined and the labor performed by the slave does not reduce the amount of the original debt. The debt can be passed down to subsequent generations as a result of lack of payment or default on the debt. Children are often enslaved as a result of this failure to pay. Like the new forms of slavery, ownership of the slave is not official; however, Bales notes there is complete physical control of the slave. This form of slavery is found in the subcontinent of India. For example in the city of Sivakasi in the state of Tamil Nadu, forty-five thousand children work in the fireworks and matches factories. The children are picked up between 3 and 5 in the morning from the homes of their indebted families to work until 7 in the evening. A UNICEF survey uncovered thirty-three buses packing 150 to 200 children in each and picking up and dropping off the children each day at these factories.

> The children roll and pack the fireworks in dark and dingy sheds. The gun powder mixture is corrosive, and over time it eats away the skin on a child's fingers. When this happens, blisters form and the child can't work. . . . To wait for the blisters to heal takes five or six days, but to stay off this long means they will be fired. Instead, a hot coal or a lit cigarette normally is applied to the blister, bursting it and cauterizing the wound. In time the children's finger tips become a mass of scar tissue. The powdered potassium chlorate, phosphorous, and zinc oxides also fill their lungs and lead to breathing problems and blood poisoning. (Bales, 2004, 200)

The third form of slavery in the world is "contract slavery" (Bales, 2004). Bales notes that contracts are offered to the potential slave as a guarantee of employment either in a workshop or factory or as a domestic servant. But when the workers are taken to the place where they are to perform their work, they find themselves enslaved, forced to work for no pay and no longer free to return to their homes. Bales claims that this is the most rapidly growing type of slavery in the world today and it is the second largest as to the number of people who are enslaved. This form of slavery is found in Southeast Asia, Brazil, some Arab states, and some parts of the Indian subcontinent. The contract is used as an enticement to trick an individual into slavery, as well as a way of making the slavery look legitimate. The contract worker is a slave, threatened by violence, lacking any freedom of movement, and paid nothing.

Bales notes that although these are distinct forms of slavery, they are not mutually exclusive. He notes in his research that chattel slaves may have been issued contracts in order to hide their enslavement. Girls who are enslaved as prostitutes by debt bondage may also have contracts. However, the threat of violence is key to distinguishing free and un-free labor. He also notes that there are some other forms of slavery that are unique to political situations in certain regions of the world. War slavery, which has occurred throughout sections of Africa where there have been civil or proxy wars between imperial powers, will occur when young children are captured and forced into slavery to fight the wars. We discussed this previously in discussing child soldiers in the chapter on state violence.

This is an interesting case of structural violence committed by institutional actors (institutional structural violence). Both the ILO report and Bales's research cite the example of slavery that is committed by the government of Burma or Myanmar. Under the military dictatorship in Burma, ethnic communities that were fighting the military for independence were enslaved by the government. The motive behind the enslavement is economic gain, but not to generate profits. The labor forced by the military government was used principally in construction projects. Bales mentions the gas pipeline project in Burma built by the government in partnership with Unocal, a U.S. oil company; Total, a French oil company; and a Thai pipeline and exploration company. "In the pipeline project thousands of enslaved workers, including old men, pregnant women, and children, were forced at gunpoint to clear land and build a railway next to the pipeline" (Bales, 2004, 21).

Bales notes that these forms of slavery are unique because of the government sponsorship of the slavery; he notes that in most cases the government officials are not the sponsors but either are paid to look the other way or help the slaveholders by serving as the slave patrol capturing runaway slaves and returning them to the slaveholders. Other cases of slavery by government are also noted in the ILO report, including the governments of Tajikistan and Uzbekistan using forced labor in the cotton industry, which affected mainly women, children, and young students (International Labour Organization, 2005). There are also cases of prison labor. Within the United States, prisoners are forced to work to earn a reduction in sentence and to make a small amount of money (usually wages are between 20 and 30 cents an hour). These workers sometimes are producing directly for the state government, but in many cases they are working for private industry. Flounders (2011) reports that some major corporations including Motorola, Compaq, Honeywell, Microsoft, Boeing, Revlon, Chevron, TWA, Victoria's Secret, and Eddie Bauer are profiting from the slave labor of prisoners. Prison labor is considered to be slavery by the definitions of slavery (as punishment) and forced labor.

Another form of slavery directed specifically at children is the case of the "restavecs." Here children are sold into domestic service. The word "restavecs" from the French means "stays with" and this form of child slavery is found in parts of the Caribbean and Western Africa. The children are taken from desperately poor rural parents in the hope that they will find a better life in the city. In exchange for domestic work, they are supposed to receive food, clothing, shelter, medical care, and an education. Unfortunately, this is not often the case, as the children are often given over to poor families living in cities. The desperate plight of the "restavecs" in Haiti came to light in the wake of the hurricane that struck the island in 2008. The children were abandoned and forced to try to survive on their own. UNICEF estimates that there are three hundred thousand "restavecs" in Haiti (Lacey, 2008).

According to Bales, slavery is the ultimate human rights violation short of murder. However, despite the abolition of slavery throughout the world more than one hundred years ago, the practice persists in a new form and is more widespread than ever before. He notes that extreme poverty and economic displacement on the imperial frontiers establish the fertile ground for slavery to grow. He contends that two conditions must change in the world for slavery to be ultimately eliminated. First is the political will among governments to uncover the practice throughout the world and second is for governments to protect the victims of slavery. In the world today, there has been some progress on the legal front in several countries (see the ILO 2005 report on efforts in Brazil, many European countries, the United States, and Japan); however, the practice continues making billions of dollars in profits for those who hold the slaves and cheaper goods for the consumers around the world that search out the great deals on the products that are produced by slavery.

Famine as Structural Violence

Famine is the most extreme case of malnutrition and hunger. To what degree can we talk about the occurrence of famine and widespread patterns of hunger as cases of structural violence? Spitz (1978, 868) states that the "crisis created by a famine reveals the workings of the economic and social system and affords an insight into the structural violence which has the effect of denying the poorest members of society the right to feed themselves in order to stay alive." The problem of famine is a human-made problem. It is not the product of environmental disasters independent of human action, nor is it a result of overpopulation. George (1988, 1990) and others point out that environmental disasters may serve as a catalyst to preexisting situations of extreme poverty that in turn result in widespread death due to starvation. Furthermore, population size relative to size of the arable land in a country is not important when we consider countries with greater populations relative to available arable land that have never experienced famine in their modern histories.

Fundamentally, famine is a result of the extreme inequality in ownership and control over food production in a given society and in the world as a whole. For George (1982), famines are caused by people having no power over land and income. When people in rural agrarian economies have too little or no land or there is little or no income from other economic sources, it leads to hunger and a threat to physical existence. When this condition hits large segments of the population, we label this a famine (George, 1982, 98). When hunger is more dispersed and exists over long periods of time, we accept this as a condition of humanity or an artifact of underdevelopment.

A number of factors have been specifically identified as central to the problem of famine and extreme cases of malnutrition. We have already discussed the problems of debt, dependent capitalist development, and the structural adjustment programs imposed on dominated countries. All these factors point to the fact that famine in the modern world is ultimately an outcome of imperialism in the world economy. Spitz (1978) indicates how the legacy of classical colonialism of the European powers from the eighteenth century to the first half of the twentieth century had a significant impact on land-tenure customs, land rights, and farming systems, all of which contributed to making the colonized people less capable of producing enough food for themselves and inhibited them from building up the excess production needed to be used during emergency situations. Two studies on the problem of famine in the Sahelian region of Africa trace this legacy of colonialism and its impact on the problem of famine today in this region (Franke and Chasin, 1980; Watts, 1983). Tinker (1993) points to the impact of missionaries on forcing economic changes on the indigenous populations in North America, which at times resulted in hunger and famine, problems they did not experience in the past. There is an old African saying: When they first came they had the bible. We had the land. We now have the bible. They have our land (Institute of Race Relations, 1982, 3).

George (1982, 1990) sees hunger as a direct product of the hierarchical political economic ordering in the world. For George, hunger means the Third World. George maintains that because of tariff barriers that the domi-

Figure 9.1.   The Famine in India: Natives Waiting for Relief at Bangalore (original caption). Scan of image from *The Illustrated London News* (no artist given), Saturday, October 20, 1877.

nant capitalist countries establish against the underdeveloped or dominated countries, their industrial development is held back and their dependent status is maintained. Bello (1994) argues that the Reagan administration targeted the newly industrial countries (NICs) for differential trade policies in order to reduce the U.S. trade deficit with the NICs. These countries were targeted to reduce their government's involvement with the economy, reduce the restrictions on foreign ownership, and reduce import tariffs. The Omnibus Trade and Competitive Act of 1988 and the General Agreement on Tariffs and

Trade (GATT) were established mechanisms for U.S. overt retaliatory action against those deemed to be unfair traders. South Korea, Taiwan, and Singapore became targets of U.S. action. Universalism and the GATT, in short, are two faces of the same process of re-subordination directed at those countries that threaten to make the breakthrough to developed status. In much the same way that structural adjustment programs seek to contain the poorer countries of the South, the GATT and aggressive unilateral trade policy aim to roll back the NICs and aspiring NICs (Bello 1994, 85).

Moreover, industries in dependent capitalist countries do not create enough jobs to fulfill the needs of the millions of new workers displaced from land as a result of the transformations in agricultural production (cash crop production, large-scale mechanized farming, etc.). Jobless people with no money are hungry people. The economies in these poor countries are dominated by the interests of multinational corporations, finance capital, and the governments of the dominant capitalist countries.

> Today, political colonialism is nearly dead. Either the mother countries granted independence or national liberation movements fought for it and won. But economic colonialism lives on. Its effects on peoples' diets are still disastrous. In many former colonies, the new leaders, usually educated in and by the mother countries, have made no efforts to change colonial crop patterns. Thus Senegal still devotes over half its arable land to peanuts and the Philippines grows coconut oil-palms and sugar on over half their cropland. What happens when a still-dominated country depends on just one or two cash crops for most of its income in hard currency? Sugar-cane, coffee, tea, cocoa, etc. are grown in poor countries, but the prices these crops fetch are set on rich country commodities markets. Individual producing countries have no control over world prices which are vulnerable to speculation. (George 1982, 54)

The domination is reinforced because the processing of food occurs principally in the industrialized countries, and the processed foods are shipped back to the dominated country, which then pays more for them than the raw materials exported. Furthermore, the cost of manufactured goods is higher than the cost of raw materials. The overall result is unequal exchange in trade, whereby the dominated country continually falls behind economically relative to the dominated country.

Another factor is the concentration of land ownership in the countries where famine occurs. The very structure of the society as defined in terms of ownership of production, in particular agricultural production, leads to a limitation on food production and thus problems of famine. Four percent of the world's big landowners control half the world's cropland (just .23 percent of owners control over half of all land worldwide). Fifty-eight percent of the world's landholders, small producers, must make do with 8 percent of the world's cropland. George notes that in eighty-three poor countries, 3 percent of the landholders own or control four-fifths of the land. In Java, Egypt, Bangladesh, Venezuela, Mexico, and parts of India, a third to a half of the rural population has no land at all (George, 1982, 76–77). In Guatemala 22 percent of the country is made up of 482 huge plantations. At the same time, 54 percent of all farms are less than 1.4 hectares (Gage, 1991). In Brazil, where there are widespread problems of malnutrition in the population, eighteen large landowners control an area six times the size of Belgium (Shankland, 1995). Unequal distribution is not reserved for the Third World. In the United States, 5 percent of the farmers control over half the cropland. This is so despite the fact that small farmers produce more food per acre than large ones (George, 1982).

This concentration of ownership is related to the history of colonialism and the current position of the country in the world economy. The dependent capitalist development model promoted and fostered by the dominant capitalist countries and the leading banking institutions in the world is based on large-scale cash crop production. Furthermore, many of the largest farms in dominated countries are owned by multinational corporations or their subsidiaries. Small farmers and peasants are forced off their land by means of increases in taxes or forcibly by police, military, or thugs hired by the large landowners. The rural peasant population becomes marginalized economically and politically, increasing their vulnerability to famine. The agricultural production for the local market becomes reduced as more and more production is for the export market. Increasingly, foodstuffs are imported from the dominant capitalist countries at higher prices than could be produced locally and more often than not with less nutritional content.

Another important factor that leads to the problem of famine is, ironically, foreign aid by the dominant capitalist countries. Most foreign aid by dominant capitalist countries serves to maintain the relations of domination in the world economy. This is accomplished in three ways. First, foreign aid is a vehicle for disposing of excess agricultural production of farmers in the dominant capitalist countries. In this way it is a means of maintaining an agrarian producer class in the dominant countries by a system of subsidies. Those who are most likely to benefit from this subsidy system are the largest producers, corporate owners. Many of these same corporations are involved in agrarian production in the same dominated countries of the world to which the surplus is being shipped. Thus these large corporate producers receive a subsidy in the dominant country to ship foodstuffs to the same dominated countries that were increasingly impoverished, in part, as a result of these corporate owners' control of land in these countries producing foodstuffs for exportation. As small producers are not able to keep up with the cost of subsidized food aid, they lose their production (the land often being absorbed by the largest landholders in the country—contributing to further land concentration) and join the swelling ranks of the displaced working class. These same corporations also often receive subsidies from both the dominant and dominated countries for this production for exportation from the dominated country.

The system of subsidies also allows for the continued technical development of agriculture in the dominant countries, giving them an increasing market advantage relative to small producers. Another function of most aid is to further the economic dependency of the dominated countries as the aid economically displaces the local producers of foodstuffs in the dominated country, thus destroying any chance of economic self-sufficiency. As mentioned earlier food aid from the center is many times given away or sold at such low prices that it destroys the local producing sector. As a result, the country becomes increasingly dependent on the importation of foodstuffs from the dominant countries, and there is further integration of their own agricultural production (cash crop production) into the world market. This pattern of agricultural development that is promoted by foreign aid furthers the pattern of inequality as it relates to power and land ownership.

> Aid from the rich countries has made it possible to promote, not the development of the poor countries, but a certain type of industrial and agricultural growth, the unequally distributed benefits of which have enabled the dominant social classes in the poor countries to strengthen their domination. This increase in the wealth concentrated in the hands of a few aggravates structural violence in the poor countries. The rich in the poor countries then need to strengthen their military and police forces in order to maintain their domination. The rich countries are thus afforded fresh opportunities to make further profits, as is shown by the substantial growth of arms sales throughout the world. (Spitz, 1978, 889)

Aid also serves as a form of welfare that maintains the political stability of client regimes in the dominated country by keeping the poorest populations dependent on the government for survival. This dependency also keeps the poorest populations from rioting as they continue to receive the bare minimum nutritional requirements for their existence.

Lastly, technical aid serves to further the penetration of the dominated country by multinational corporations and furthers the dependent relationship as the production is geared increasingly to the export market and is increasingly dependent on the importation of agricultural chemicals and equipment to maintain the production. One example of this technical aid is the Green Revolution, a program of agricultural development created by the Ford and Rockefeller foundations and pushed by American universities and USAID. This program of technical aid was based on the distribution of genetically engineered seed that produced high-yielding plants (usually wheat or rice) that required lots of fertilizer, chemical protection, herbicides, and controlled irrigation and drainage. The increased need for chemical fertilizers and herbicides and tractors created new markets for U.S. multinational corporations.

The Green Revolution was promoted by the United States as an alternative to land reform, which would change the structural relations in the societies. George (1982) reports that from 1966 onward, the U.S. government made its food aid to poor countries conditional on their adoption of Green Revolution techniques. By means of the Green Revolution, peasant farmers would be able to produce more on their small plots, thus not requiring more access to the large concentrations of land held by a small segment, oftentimes the ruling oligarchy, of the population. Instead, according to Spitz (1978), this program increased the disparities between rich and poor and between regions well-endowed with natural resources and less fortunate regions. Furthermore, it replaced the poor's direct dependence for food supplies with a more insidious form of dependence consisting of the need to acquire fertilizers, pesticides, agricultural machinery, and sources of energy, thus providing transnational corporations with ample opportunity to step in. Spitz contends that the Green Revolution, by magnifying inequalities and aggravating the effects of the process of dispossession on the lives of the poorest, helps to exacerbate structural violence (884). The aid that was part of the Green

Revolution served to increase the concentration of land ownership by large producers as they were able to produce more, which required larger amounts of capital for equipment and chemicals. Poor farmers who could not keep up with the cost of the technological inputs increasingly required to maintain the higher level of crop yields were forced off their land and became vulnerable to famine.

> Rich countries and international agencies with their "aid" programmes and "development solutions" contribute to making an already calamitous situation even worse. They push "population control" (and dump unsafe contraceptives in Third World countries) instead of trying to change the conditions that make people need children. They encourage cash-crop production and refuse most other Third World goods through trade barriers. They consistently give economic, political, and military support to regimes that have no intention of improving the lot of their own poor people. And they do everything to wreck the efforts of those who do strive for agrarian reform and fairer distribution. . . . Essentially, rich countries are trying to make Third World food systems resemble or serve their own. If they could manage it (which they can't, entirely, yet), the most powerful countries would set up a single world food-system which they controlled. (George, 1982, 103)

According to George, the Green Revolution increased both production and hunger. Countries such as India, Bangladesh, the Philippines, parts of Africa, and Indonesia—big recipients of the Green Revolution—are testaments to the impact of this development strategy. In these countries more than half the population is living below the poverty line. At the same time that the wealthy landowning class dramatically increased its holdings, there has been increasing agricultural production for the export market and increasing levels of imports of agricultural chemicals and equipment, along with food aid from the dominant capitalist countries, which promoted the revolution. George notes that these outcomes of the Green Revolution were foreseen. She cites testimony to Congress in 1969, where experts said there would be further markets for industrial products in these countries, the peasant land tenants would become a diminishing breed, and the rich may get richer from this "revolution" (George, 1982).

The end result of this pattern of domination internationally and nationally in countries around the world is a level of violence that surpasses all other forms of violence. For example, it resulted in an estimated ten million people who died in India in 1769–1770, or in more modern day-examples, more than 250,000 dead in the Sahelian region of Africa in 1972 and 100,000 dead in Bangladesh in 1974, all from famine created by the structural relations within and between countries. Today, hundreds of millions of people around the globe are struggling to get enough nutrition to fulfill one day of life, a result of a legacy of systems of inequality within and between nations. In 1996 the United Nations sponsored the first global gathering at the highest political level to focus solely on food security. At that time the United Nations estimated that 800 million persons (of which 300 million were children) around the world were not receiving the minimum nutrition to sustain life. The meeting established a goal of reducing the number of starving people by one half by 2015. In a recent review of progress, United Nations officials say the world is falling short of targets to reduce hunger and chronic malnutrition, but it is reported by food security experts that the situation is far worse and that the number of hungry people in many developing nations is rising (Knight, 2001).

The last point to note regarding patterns of hunger throughout the world is that although we can look at how the problem is distributed along a hierarchy of countries in the world system from richest to poorest, the problem of hunger is distributed from richest to poorest within countries. Those who are in most dominated positions via systems of stratification within countries around the globe are most vulnerable to the violence of hunger. Women and children of workers and peasants of ethnic minority populations are the most vulnerable. For example in Southeast Asia 64 percent of pregnant women are anemic, passing along a legacy of malnutrition to the infants they bear (del Nevo 1995, 21).

INTERPERSONAL AND INSTITUTIONAL STRUCTURAL VIOLENCE

Hate Crimes

As mentioned earlier, structural violence intersects with interpersonal and institutional violence. Violence that stems from hate crimes is an example of structural violence that is also interpersonal. An FBI report noted that racial bias prompted 47.3 percent of the 6,624 single bias hate crimes reported in 2010. Of the remaining cases, 20 percent were committed because of religion; 19.3 because of sexual orientation; 12.8 percent because of ethnicity/national origin bias; and 0.6 because of physical or mental disability (Federal Bureau of Investigation, 2011). The number of hate crimes reported for 2010 was about the same reported to policing agencies in 2009 (6,604 incidents reported in 2009). The FBI reported that 4,824 offenses were crimes against persons; intimidation accounted for 46.2 percent of these offenses, simple assault for 34.8 percent, and aggravated assault for 18.4 percent. The remaining crimes reported (2,861) were crimes against property; the majority (81.1 percent) were acts of destruction/damage/vandalism. Of the known offenders almost 59 percent were white and 18 percent were black. In 2011, a Washington state man was sentenced to thirty-two years in prison for attempting to bomb a Martin Luther King Jr. Day parade in Spokane (Federal Bureau of Investigation, 2012b). Deryl Paul Dedmon, nineteen, John Aaron Rice, nineteen, and Dylan Wade Butler, twenty, from Brandon, Mississippi, pleaded guilty in March of 2012 in U.S. District Court in Jackson to federal hate crime charges in connection with an assault culminating in the death of James Craig Anderson, an African American man, in the summer of 2011.

> After Dedmon and the other two co-conspirators arrived in Dedmon's Ford F250 truck, Dedmon and Rice physically assaulted Anderson. Rice first punched Anderson in the face with sufficient force to knock Anderson to the ground, and then Dedmon punched Anderson in the face multiple times while he was on the ground. After the assault, Rice, Butler, and two co-conspirators

left the motel parking lot in the Jeep. As they left, one of the occupants of the Jeep yelled, "White Power!" Prior to getting back into his truck, Dedmon responded by also yelling "White Power!" Once back in his truck, Dedmon deliberately used his truck to run over Anderson, causing injuries which resulted in Anderson's death. (Federal Bureau of Investigation, 2012a)

In a major case that occurred in the early 1990s in which the United Klans of Alabama was successfully sued in civil court, requiring them to sell off most of their assets, Michael Donald was killed by members of an Alabama chapter of the Ku Klux Klan.

For Bennie Hays, the 25 policemen gathering around Michael Donald's body represented the happy conclusion to an extremely unhappy development. That week, a jury had been struggling to reach a verdict in the case of a black man accused of murdering a white policeman. . . . To Hays—the second highest Klan official in Alabama—and his fellow members of Unit 900 of the United Klans, the presence of blacks on the jury meant that a guilty man would go free. According to Klansmen who attended the unit's weekly meeting, Hays had said that Wednesday, "If a black man can get away with killing a white man, we ought to be able to get away with killing a black man." On Friday night, after the jurors announced they couldn't reach a verdict, the Klansmen got together in a house Bennie Hays owned on Herndon Avenue. According to later testimony from James (Tiger) Knowles, then 17 years old, Tiger produced a borrowed pistol. Henry Frances Hays, Bennie's 26 year old son, took out a rope. Then the two got in Henry's car and went hunting for a black man. Michael Donald (19 years old) was alone, walking home, when Knowles and Hays spotted him. They pulled over, asked him for directions to a night club, then pointed the gun at him and ordered him to get in. . . . When they stopped, Michael begged them not to kill him, then tried to escape. Henry Hays and Knowles chased him, caught him, hit him with a tree limb more than a hundred times, and when he was no longer moving, wrapped the rope around his neck. Henry Hays shoved his boot in Michael's face and pulled on the rope. For good measure, they cut his throat. . . .They then looped the rope over a camphor tree, raised Michael's body just high enough so it would swing. (Bullard, 1991, 31)

The Southern Poverty Law Center and the Justice Department's own research indicate that there is significant problem of underreporting hate crimes (McDevitt, et al., 2000; Southern Poverty Law Center, 2001). The Southern Poverty Law Center estimates that the occurrence of hate crimes is five times greater than what is reported in the government's statistics. But the peak activity of hate crimes probably occurred much earlier in our history: lynchings of African Americans reached their peak in the South in the late nineteenth century and declined sharply after 1935. Beginning with the Reconstruction era in the United States and up to the mid-1930s, an estimated 3,402 lynchings of African Americans occurred (New Grolier Multimedia Encyclopedia, 1993). Between 1882 (when reliable statistics were first collected) and 1968 (when the classic forms of lynching had disappeared), 4,743 persons died of lynching. Dray (2002) points out that from 1882 to 1944, the number of people of color lynched averaged more than one a week. Silberman (1978) notes that between 1882 and 1903, no fewer than 1,985 blacks were killed by southern lynch mobs.

The United States is not alone with a problem of interpersonal violence directed at maintaining ethnic hierarchy. In Germany there are numerous cases of neo-Nazi extremists targeting immigrant populations (Lee, 1993). In a recent case, five members of a Turkish family, two young women and three girls, were burned to death when their home was set afire by a group of neo-Nazis (Whitney, 1993). On November 25, 1990, fifteen masked youths, identified as members of an organization of skinheads, in the town of Eberswalde attacked Amadeu Antonio Kiowa, a guest worker from Angola, outside a disco, beating him to death. In Dresden on April 18, 1991, Jorge Gomondai of Mozambique was killed as a result of being thrown from a moving streetcar by a group of skinheads. In another Dresden case in 1991 masked skinheads knocked down the door to the apartment of a pregnant Vietnamese woman and brutally beat her. One of the most widely publicized cases in Germany occurred in August 1992 in Rostock. A large number of skinheads gathered in front of a hostel housing Rumanian Gypsy asylum seekers and Vietnamese guest workers. While local police and federal border guards stood by, the skinheads set fire to one of the buildings, trapping 140 Vietnamese inside. Most escaped with minimal harm (Neier, 1992).

More recently, Anders Behring Breivik bombed government buildings in Oslo on July 22, 2011, which resulted in eight deaths, and then carried out a mass shooting at a camp of the Workers' Youth League (AUF) of the Labour Party on the island of Utøya, where he killed sixty-nine people, mostly teenagers. In a 1,500-page manifesto released just before the attacks, Breivik ranted about Europe being overrun by Muslim immigrants and blamed left-wing political forces for making the continent multicultural (Amland and MacDougall, 2011).

Rape is another example of interpersonal violence that is also structural. As noted earlier, since the vast majority of rape victims are female, the structural position of women relative to men is reinforced and extended because of this pattern of victimization. Women's freedom is limited by the occurrence of rape. Their ability to develop their human potential is reduced because certain opportunities are not available to them because of the occurrence of rape. Rape is a form of power, a power that men have over women. It is used as a means of control and domination. Thus the motivation for rape is to maintain and extend the patriarchal structure that is the root cause of the violence. All unequal power relationships must, in the end, rely on the threat or reality of violence to maintain them (Clark and Lewis, 1977, 176). Rape is one form of violence that serves to maintain the institutionalized dominance of men over women.

Institutional Structural Violence

In regard to structural violence that is also institutional, we have in previous chapters discussed examples of state violence directed at minority populations, peasants and union movements, and political dissident groups. In all cases, the goal of the violence is to maintain or extend the structures of dominance in that society. Similarly, military interventions by the dominant capitalist powers throughout history with very few exceptions have been designed to maintain the imperialist relations (oftentimes defined in terms of

Figure 9.2.   Lynching of Laura Nelson, Okemah, Oklahoma, accused of killing a deputy sheriff. While in custody a gang of forty armed white men tied up the guard and kidnapped her and her son at the jail where they were held. Both she and her son were hanged from a bridge over the North Canadian River. Photographs like this were sold as postcards. The killers were never identified.

preserving a free market and defending the right of private property) threatened by political movements within the dominated country. With economic violence, again, those who are more likely to be victims are workers or peasants. Whether we are talking about product, production, or environmental violence, it is those who are in dominated positions in the society who are the victims. Thus, we can look at most cases of economic violence as structural in that the outcome of the violence is the maintenance or extension of the dominance, as victims are placed at a disadvantage relative to those who are victimizing them. In family violence, again the pattern is repeated as it relates to age and gender. Women and the young are more likely to be victimized relative to adult men. Thus the pattern of victimization extends the hierarchical structure rooted in patriarchy. Lastly, as we discussed in religious violence, its role in conquest and the establishment of imperialist relations is central to the purpose of the activity. Those who are most likely to be victimized by missionaries are those who have least power.

THE WEB OF STRUCTURAL VIOLENCE: THE CASE OF GUATEMALA

Hierarchical Structures within Guatemala

Let us illustrate how the many forms of structural violence can be interwoven by focusing on Guatemala. Guatemalan society contains two modes of production: a dependent capitalist mode of production and a remnant of what approximates a tributary mode of production (Amin, 1980). The capitalist mode of production is clearly the dominant mode: The capitalist class structure is composed of a small, dependent bourgeoisie (Ladino agricultural export, traditional landowning class, and merchant bourgeoisie), medium size agricultural entrepreneurs, and what is referred to as a puppet bourgeoisie composed of those who occupy positions in public and private institutions that make them instruments of exploitation, that is, leaders in the military and high-level government bureaucrats (Jonas and Tobias, 1981; Black, 1983b). Since the economic changes of the 1960s determined by the shift in U.S. investments, the capitalist class has become increasingly segmented into agrarian, industrial, financial, and commercial. The nature of their development has become dictated by the needs of transnational capital.

More important than this fragmentation, however, has been the increasing power of the military and their inclusion into the capitalist class as a separate element. Beginning in the 1970s with the Arana regime, the military developed its own economic interests. Initially brought into the government as a coercive protector of the established order, senior officers have increasingly used state power as a basis for owning production: agro-exporting, industrial, financial, and real estate enterprises. In the process they have become Guatemala's strongest political and economic force, which has at times threatened the traditional national owning class (Black, 1983a). This development in the capitalist class has created some interesting fragmentation and political alignment. Black contends that what may be more worrisome than this wealth of the military is the machinery created for its acquisition and protection. According to Black (1983b) an array of institutions fused the armed forces with the state. This merging of economic and state interests, together with the monopoly of force and violence that the military holds, was a formula for extreme violence and repression of those who threaten this distribution of power. The estimated size of the capitalist class during this period is 3 percent of the population.

The petite bourgeoisie includes members of the bureaucracies, small merchants, owners of family-sized artisan establishments, and owners of family-sized farms (14.88 hectares on the average). The petite bourgeoisie is estimated to be 20 percent of the population. The working class and peasantry are the remaining 77 percent of the population. This includes 21 percent who are industrial/service workers and 56 percent agricultural (including 30 percent semi-proletariat and 6 to 10 percent seasonal workers). The semi-proletariat is growing rapidly as the Indian population becomes increasingly displaced in the countryside.

There is also a tributary mode of production in Guatemala. A tributary mode of production is one where the surplus produced is not appropriated by an exploiting class. Instead, according to Amin (1980), it is centralized by a ruling group for the collective use and redistributed according to the needs of the population. This mode of production, although distinct from the capitalist mode of production, has become intertwined with it. Because communal land ownership has been severely limited, and most of the fertile land in the country has been stripped from the indigenous peasants, they cannot survive without participating in the dominant capitalist mode of production. These Indian or Indios populations become a convenient pool of cheap seasonal workers for the large landowners and the multinational corporations who own the plantations. This tributary mode of production is increasingly eliminated as there is further encroachment on their lands by the government and the large landowners, a further redivision of land in the form of inheritance to their children that creates problems of efficient use of the land and a need to export an increasingly large portion of their young to urban areas because the system cannot provide for all its members, and an increase in the amount of time the Indians need to participate in the capitalist mode of production in order to make up for what the tributary mode of production cannot provide. At the same time, mechanization of production on the large plantations and the switch to raising beef and other livestock, both of which require less labor, drives the Indian or Indios population into the cities to find work.

The society is also stratified in terms of ethnicity and gender. The society is divided ethnically in terms of three general ethnic strata: *criollos* (native-born Spaniards, a very small percentage of the population), *ladinos* (the product of intermarriage between Spaniards and natives, approximately 40 to 45 percent of the population), and *Indios* (or what the native population refers to as *naturales*, a little more than half of the population) (Jonas and Tobias, 1981). This last group is divided into at least three major ethnic groupings with twenty-two dialects and cultural groups with distinguishable dress and customs. Almost all the wealthy are *criollos* or *ladinos*; petite bourgeoisie, principally Ladino, with a small segment of *Indios* in rural areas; 45 percent of the working class (industrial and agrarian, including semi-proletariat and seasonal workers) is *ladinos*, 55 percent *Indios*. In general, the poor are disproportionately *Indios* and the wealthy disproportionately *ladinos*.

Most women in Guatemala work for poor wages under hazardous conditions in the textile and food processing industries, as well as working as domestics in the cities. Middle- and upper-class women, on the other hand, are entering traditionally female professional jobs (Chinchilla, 1978). Guatemala's Gender Inequality Index for Human Development is the most unequal in Central America (Klugman, 2011).

Impact of Dependent Capitalist Development

The Guatemalan economy, like others in the periphery of the world capitalist system, is plagued by problems of instability because of its dependence on export trade. This dependence on the world market has been worsened by the problems of inflation and the debt crisis. As an open economy whose external trade equals half of its Gross Domestic Product, Guatemala is tied to swings in the world market. Thirty percent of its trade is with the United States. In 1979 and 1980 the U.S. recession hit Guatemala hard, pulling down GDP growth rates, which had been running around a vigorous 5 percent, and pushing inflation, which had been running a rate lower than that of the United States, above 15 percent (Nairn, 1983, 100).

Guatemala's economy is highly concentrated. Over 80 percent of the land is held by 2 percent of farm families; 83 percent of farm families live on land too small to maintain a family; 87 percent of landowners own 19 percent of arable land (Jonas and Tobias, 1981). Guatemala's levels of poverty and land ownership concentration are the highest in the region (Lastarria-Cornhiel, 2003). There has been and continues to be increasing problems of displacement of the peasantry resulting from the stealing of their land by the military and plantation owners who are increasing the size of their holdings. Over the 1970s, peasants lost 26 percent of their acreage, while the area devoted to export crops swelled 45 percent. The average size of a highland Indian's farm was cut in half in the twenty-year period between 1955 and 1975; this pattern has continued to the present. In the industrial sector, monopoly patterns are found principally in oil refining and distribution, bonded paper production, steel tubing, tires, chemicals, and a large portion of food processing.

The pattern of market concentration is a direct product of U.S. multinational corporate penetration. The major shift from agriculture to manufacturing investments by U.S. corporations after the U.S-sponsored coup in 1954 took three forms. First, U.S. corporations purchased local companies. Twenty out of forty-six of the Fortune 500 corporations that have investments in Guatemala acquired Guatemalan companies as a means to enter the marketplace. The second form of penetration involves joint ventures with Guatemalan businessmen, with controlling interest residing with U.S. capital. The third method is production arrangements with competing firms, including product licensing agreements. Aside from these direct methods of U.S. penetration, the influx of foreign capital has the effect of driving out of business local companies not tied to transnationals. The access of transnationals to credit and higher technology, as well as their ability to withstand temporary losses, contributes to increasing concentration and foreign domination of the Guatemalan economy. Companies that employ one hundred or more employees are foreign owned or controlled, the majority U.S. owned. There are two sectors to the economy, one of which is labor intensive and the other capital intensive. Labor-intensive industries are generally referred to as offshore industries or runaway shops. Guatemala has become a haven for this type of investment, where the products are produced by Guatemalans to be sold in the United States. Textile and electronic assembly industries have utilized this resource. Although there has been a growth of jobs in these areas, the mechanization in agriculture has led to an increasing surplus population, which holds down wages.

As with all other countries in the Western Hemisphere, this pattern of dependent capitalist development is directed principally by the United States. After the 1954 coup and the installation of the Armas government, and through the 1970s, the United States spent $45 million in creating one of the most effective military machines in Central America. President Kennedy's Alliance for Progress and the formation of the Agency for International Development (AID), formed after the Cuban revolution to prevent the need for future Communist revolutions, have been major pipelines for U.S. influence on Guatemalan society. Millions of dollars of AID money has been spent to strengthen the free enterprise system through providing seed money for the development of new businesses and loans for the purchase of U.S. capital goods and services (85 percent of bilateral aid is tied so that the money would be spent on U.S. capital goods and services) (Tobis, 1983). The first administrative provision of the Foreign Assistance Act of 1961 states: "It is declared to be the policy of the United States to encourage the efforts of other countries to increase the flow of international trade, to foster private initiative and competition . . . and to encourage the contribution of United States enterprise toward the economic strength of less developed friendly countries through private trade and investment abroad (and) private participation in programs carried under this Act" (Barry et al., 1982, 83). Another large part of AID has been its efforts in counterinsurgency, through a civilian pacification campaign. After the guerrilla-based movement was neutralized in the late 1960s, AID continued its involvement in counterinsurgency through its Office for Public Safety (OPS). OPS trained more than thirty thousand Guatemalan police personnel between 1961 and 1970 in methods of policing and the control of dissidents.

The OPS program pre-dates the Kennedy administration. The program was established under the Eisenhower administration to train Latin American police. This program expanded dramatically under Kennedy. A part of the program was the creation of the International Police Academy in Washington as well as training schools in several locations in the United States established to train Latin American police and military personnel. In the early 1960s public safety advisers were in forty-five foreign countries. U.S. money was available for local policing agencies for the purchase of equipment, training in the United States, and training at the local site by U.S. police trainers. The result in these countries was the strengthening of counterinsurgency warfare at the local police level and more repressive control of the population. As mentioned previously in the chapter on state violence, several authors tie the expansion of these programs in several Latin American countries with the creation of death squads coming out of local police forces (Herman and O'Sullivan, 1989; Nairn, 1984).

The OPS program ended in 1975. By this time $200 million worth of arms and equipment had been disbursed to local policing agencies, more than 7,500 senior police officers had been trained in the United States, and more than a million rank-and-file police had been trained by U.S. personnel at local academies in the home country (Klare, 1981). A new program performing the same function (training police personnel in counterinsurgency warfare and riot control) is the International Narcotics Control Program that operates out of the State Department and works directly with the CIA. Much of the same personnel as under the OPS were initially used. Under this program the amount of money expanded rapidly, especially during the Reagan and Bush administrations. State violence in Colombia is in part funded by the United States under the guise of fighting the drug war.

New economic aid packages have the same intent in promoting capitalist relations of production within the dependent capitalist framework through providing investment opportunities for U.S.-based corporations. Landes and Flynn (1984) state that the new economic programs promote export-led development and nontraditional industries, such as tourism, new agricultural exports, and light assembly industries, thus increasing the pattern of dependency. Since the late 1970s, the resources of every aid program have been marshaled in an effort to bolster the status quo as defined in terms of dependent capitalist development. This was and is still the case in Guatemala.

Structural Violence in Guatemala

What has been the outcome of this pattern of dependent capitalist development as it relates to structural violence? Since the Spanish conquest the plight of the indigenous population has become worse as measured in terms of nutritional levels. The life expectancy in Guatemala is 71.2 years, the lowest in Central America. According to a UN Development report, Guatemala has the highest percentage of children under five who are suffering from stunting and wasting, 54.3 percent and 17.7 percent respectively. In 2000, 56 percent of the population lived below the poverty line; approximately 30 percent of the population lives in extreme poverty (Hammill, 2007).

Furthermore, Guatemala has one of the worst human rights records in the Western Hemisphere. Beginning with the eight thousand peasants (many union organizers and Indian village leaders) murdered in two months after the U.S.-sponsored military coup in 1954, approximately two hundred thousand unarmed civilians have been killed or have disappeared. Chomsky (1993) cites a recent report of the archbishop's office of human rights for the first half of 1992. The report identifies at least 399 assassinations, many of them extrajudicial executions conducted by the state security forces. The CIA had called its 1954 covert action against Guatemala "Operation Success." The year following the coup land reform stopped and any land distributed to poor peasants was returned to large landowners, 533 unions were banned, strikes were outlawed (punishable by execution), and political parties were outlawed (Gage, 1991). Military dictators ruled the country for thirty years after the coup and the United States has been the major supplier of armaments and training to the military that has waged a war on the poorest sectors of the population for almost forty years (Jonas and Tobias, 1981; Moyers, 1988).

The activity of right-wing death squads connected to the military and state security officers is very significant in creating a level of violence and fear among the poorest populations in Guatemala (Amnesty International, 1983). Herman and O'Sullivan (1989, 18) write that death squads made their appearance in ten different Latin American countries in the 1960s and 1970s, all of them recipients of U.S. military and police aid and training, which stressed counterinsurgency and unconventional warfare against subversion from the Kennedy era onward. Guatemala was the largest recipient of this aid and training in Central America throughout the 1960s and 1970s. This was an insurance policy provided by the United States to protect U.S. investments and the oligarchy in Guatemala. For example, the "U.S. intervention in Guatemala in 1954, followed by military-police aid and training and political support for the regime, provided a safety net to the Guatemalan elite, giving it assured control of the state and ending any need for reform or nonviolent response to mass demands and needs. . . . The insurance policy thus encouraged and stimulated an institutionalization of state terrorism as an ongoing and permanent policy response to popular demands" (Herman and O'Sullivan 1989, 18–19).

As part of the 1996 peace accords ending the civil war in Guatemala, an investigation was to be conducted on the scope of the political violence that occurred in Guatemala. Bishop Gerardi of Guatemala was the driving force behind the project for the Recovery of Historical Memory (REMHI). The report concluded that 150,000 people died, 50,000 "disappeared," one million became refugees, 200,000 children were orphaned, and 40,000 women became widows. The Guatemalan army was involved in most of the atrocities committed and was blamed for at least 85 percent of all massacres, tortures, disappearances, and killings during the civil war. It carried out 626 massacres during a scorched-earth counterinsurgency campaign in the early 1980s. Four hundred and forty Mayan villages were eliminated by the government during the civil war.

Two days after the bishop delivered a speech marking the end of their investigation, he was assassinated. He was bludgeoned to death in his garage. He was struck seventeen times to the face and head with a chunk of concrete. According to autopsy findings it took fifteen to thirty minutes for the elderly bishop to die, drowning on his own blood. Nothing of value was stolen. The death squad, the Jaguar Avengers, a group that has been linked to the military, claimed responsibility. Three persons were convicted and sentenced to thirty years of imprisonment for participating in the crime: Colonel Byron Disrael Lima and his son, Captain Byron Lima, and José Obdulio Villanueva.

According to a recent Amnesty International report, six years after the signing of the United Nations–brokered Peace Accords that ended thirty-six years of civil war in Guatemala, the country was once again descending into lawlessness and terror (Amnesty International, 2002). The report cites a UN

Human Rights Verification Mission (MINUGUA) report that listed 390 lynchings that occurred between 1996 and 2001. In 97 percent of the cases, no one has been brought to justice.

Aside from military- and police-sponsored death squads, there is ethnographic evidence of *ladino* landowners organizing death squads to remove peasants from the land they have occupied for hundreds of years (Carmack, 1988). In many cases, the ancestral Indian land is merely taken away because the occupants do not have a legal title.

> The ancestral farming rights of the Kekchi of Alta Verapaz were abused more than most. As the Emibal Nickel mine began operations, Indians on the banks of the Rio Polochic were forcibly relocated to make way for strip mining. Plans for a new highway through the Franja made matters worse. Attracted by soaring land values, coffee-grower Ricardo Sapper Cordua ravaged long-settled Kekchi lands. In July 1976, Sapper claimed ownership of 3,375 acres of farmland embracing the Kekchi villages of Secuachil, Semocaoch and Yalicoc. Without formal deeds to the land, the Indians were simply expelled. Disputes escalated into the massacre of May 29, 1978 when peaceful Kekchi protesters marched into the town of Panzos to discuss land grievances at the government's invitation, they were met with a hail of bullets from the troops called in by a local landowner, 119 Kekchi dead. (Black 1983a, 14)

Even where there is legal title, this does not assure people of their rights. The Indian relocation program, part of the strategic hamlet strategy to fight the guerrillas (a U.S. military strategy directly adopted from the Vietnam War and in some respect the conquest of indigenous populations on the North American continent), has resulted in the trading of better-quality Indian land for poor-quality farmland. Under this program, whole villages of peasant landholders are forcefully removed and relocated to another part of the country that is a distance from guerrilla activity. This strategy is intended to eliminate all local support and resources to guerrillas and supposedly to protect the peasants from becoming war casualties. Large landowners eventually acquire the land for production for export after the Indians are relocated.

In general, estimates are that over one half of Central America's agricultural land is devoted to export crops. The result is that agricultural production increases at the same time that there is less food available for internal consumption, and the region's import food bill has increased dramatically. This is the pattern of dependent capitalist development. In Guatemala, peasants work land that once was theirs, now owned by large plantations and agribusiness corporations, producing inexpensive food and cotton fibers for the North American consumer. At the same time, their subsistence plots have become smaller and smaller and increasingly of poor quality, and the prices of imported foods are further from their reach.

Economic violence directed at workers is widespread in Guatemala. Agricultural workers suffer from severe problems of pesticide poisonings. According to Murawski (1993, 6), it is common practice for landowners to spray fields with dangerous pesticides as they are being worked. According to the Central American Research Institute for Industry, the average DDT content in human blood in Guatemala's cotton areas is 520.6 parts per billion, in contrast to 46.4 parts per billion of the residents in Dade Country, Florida. A study conducted by the Central American Nutritional Institute concluded that the amounts of DDT in mother's milk in Guatemala were the highest in the Western world, over 185 times higher than the established safety limit (Barry et al., 1982). The average wage for agricultural workers who cut cane and pick cotton is between $1 and $2 a day, far below the $56 a month necessary for the average family to stay out of poverty. Union organizers are regular victims of harassment and violence by death squads and the security forces. Coats (1991) notes that in the Guatemala maquiladoras, workers are paid between $1 and $2 a day for long workdays that may stretch to sixteen hours. Most factories require workers to work on Saturdays. Only 5 percent of the country's workforce is organized. Coats notes that the figure in the maquila sector is close to zero. Today a small minority of the workers in U.S.-owned maquiladoras that are scattered throughout Mexico, Central America, and the Caribbean have been unionized, a testament to this strategy of intimidation. Guatemala has one of the highest rates of child labor in the Americas. The International Labour Organization reported in 2008 that 16.1 percent of children aged five to fourteen are obliged to work, many in unsafe conditions. Some of these children are employed in the construction, mining, and sex industries.

Chomsky (1993, 174) describes this interconnection between state, economic, and structural violence:

> As terror improved the investment climate, export oriented economic programs led to rapid growth in production in agricultural commodities and beef for export, destruction of forests and traditional agriculture, sharp increases in hunger and general misery, the world championship for DDT in mothers' milk (185 times World Health Organization limits), and gratifying balance sheets for US agribusiness and local affiliates. The new maquiladoras are having a similar impact. Current economic plans, under the guidance of US advisers, are intensifying this range of effects.

Finally, rates of homicide are very high as levels of interpersonal violence are in general high in response to the impact of the displacement and impoverishment on the lives of the poorest segments of the population. Alcoholism and drug abuse are also high, especially among the young. Gangs of displaced youth live on the streets of the capital, Guatemala City. According to Human Rights Watch, "violence against women is a chronic problem in Guatemala, and most perpetrators are never brought to trial. Despite legislative efforts to address this violence, there has been wide impunity for crimes against women" (Human Rights Watch, 2012). Guatemala historically has received its foreign aid principally from the United States. U.S. aid programs provided more than $112,000,000 in 2010 for a population of approximately thirteen million people. From 2006 to 2010, the United States provided more than $49 million in aid to the military and police (Guatemala Human Rights Commission/USA, 2011).

CONCLUSION

This chapter focused on structural violence, which is a product of systems of inequality. This form of violence is the largest in terms of victimization, but it is also the least recognized and acknowledged as violence. It is the violence that occurs because of lack of access to a clean environment, medical care, and resources to manifest one's potentials as a human being because of one's position in a society and in the world system of society as both are ordered hierarchically. It is also the violence of the extremes in exploitation one experiences because of one's position, as in the case of the slave. We described this new slavery, which is a product of the extremes of poverty that occur in part because of the increases in economic displacement as a result of the transformation of societies that were on the frontier of empires and now are experiencing the disruption as a result of their integration into the world system.

We also discussed structures of inequality within societies and between societies and how these systems are maintained and develop. In particular, we discussed the nature of imperialism as a force that serves to maintain and expand hierarchical relations within and between countries. When we compare countries throughout the world in terms of differential disease rates, death rates, and life chances, we clearly see the impact of the hierarchical relations that exist between countries. The exploitative relationships that deny populations a chance to live to their fullest potential are reproduced on an international scale when we examine the relationship between countries that are part of the capitalist core and countries that are part of the periphery of the world system.

We also looked at ways to measure structural violence in terms of life expectancy differentials; disease patterns, like AIDS and tuberculosis; and differences in the levels of human development between the rich and poor world and within societies between position along class (income), gender, and ethnic systems of stratification. We also looked at how other species experience structural violence as a result of the dominant human development strategies that are promoted by the richest and most powerful countries in the world.

We discussed how the system of international debt is used as a means to further the goals of the dominant capitalist countries, the United States in particular, as it accelerates the pattern of dependent capitalist development in countries that forcibly enroll in structural adjustment programs supposedly to pay off debt. We have discussed the structural violence that follows from the imposition of the structural adjustment program, violence that manifests itself in higher infant mortality rates and malnutrition among the poor populations in Latin America and Africa. We also discussed how famine, a form of structural violence, is a direct outcome of stratification within and between countries. Lastly, we discussed how structural violence overlaps with institutional violence, as in the cases of much of state and economic violence in particular, and interpersonal violence, as in the case of hate crimes.

So far, we have discussed the many forms of violence in the world today. We began our discussion with acts of interpersonal violence: murder and rape. We then discussed the different forms of institutional violence such as family, education, religious, economic, and government. Finally, we discussed structural violence, violence that is an outcome of the very systems of stratification that organize societies and the world. Is there a single thread that runs through all the forms of violence we have discussed? Is there a root cause to most of the violence that exists in the world today? In the concluding chapter we discuss the threads that tie all these forms of violence together. And we ask, how, then, do we begin to reduce the levels of violence in the world today?

DISCUSSION QUESTIONS

1. Is it possible to end all forms of structural violence in the world today? What would be necessary to do this? What would the world be like if there was no structural violence?
2. What role does the United States have in the problem of structural violence today? What role should it have?
3. What are some examples of structural violence in your own community? What can you do about reducing this violence?
4. Most people in our society are not aware of structural violence yet it is all around them. It is invisible to them. What could you do to make people more aware of structural violence?
5. In thinking about your own life, have you been a victim of structural violence? If so, how? Have you ever victimized someone else through your participation in the systems of stratification in your own society or in the world? If so, how?

Chapter Ten

Conclusion: Violence, Inequality, and Human Freedom

VIOLENCE AND INEQUALITY

Throughout this work a major focus has been the relationship between violence and inequality. We have discussed how inequality itself may be a cause of violence as offenders learn to define others as of less worth than they, and as they themselves have been defined by others. The structures of inequality that we experience, that we learn to accept, and that we maintain and extend through our everyday interpersonal interactions and in role performances within institutions contribute to our ability to separate ourselves from others and define others as in need of control, punishment, or subjugation.

Inequality » Violence

We have discussed how violence is caused by inequality. Beginning with our discussion of culture, we noted how culture itself is a product of the structures of inequality. In particular, our cultural understanding of violence is constructed for us by those who have more power in defining our understandings of the reality we experience. This is via the media, by our political leaders, our educators, our religious leaders, our leaders in the economic arena, and others who are in leadership positions in social institutions. In particular, entire books have been written on the functions that the mass media (television and radio, newspapers and magazines, most recently the Internet) serve to shape and limit news and shape our perceptions. Many of these sources are critical of the media and how it creates false "social realities" but are generally unknown outside of social science. For instance, as political critic and media analyst Michael Parenti (1986, ix) wrote almost thirty years ago: for many people an issue does not exist until it appears in the news media. How we view issues, indeed, what we even define as an issue or event, what we see and hear, and what we do *not* see and hear are greatly determined by those who control the communications world. Be it labor unions, peace protesters, the Soviet Union, uprisings in Latin American elections, crime, poverty, or defense spending, few of us know of things except as they are depicted in the news. And even earlier, before the advent of cable or the Internet, Mander (1978, 261) wrote in the same vein as Parenti of the commercial corporate control of just the television medium: along with the venality of its controllers, the technology of television predetermines the boundaries of its content. Some information can be conveyed completely, some partially, some not at all. The most effective telecommunications are the gross, simplified linear messages and programs that conveniently fit the purposes of the medium's commercial controllers. Television's higher potential is advertising.

Regarding violence, the mass media tends to *decontextualize* such phenomena as episodic and report news of violent events (except in many *foreign* countries like Libya, Syria, or Myanmar) as unconnected and certainly unconnected to the social structure. Relatively rarely are some of the forms of violence we have discussed here, such as economic, state, or structural violence, reported on as violence or even recognized as such. The forms of violence that are least damaging in scope (e.g., stranger rape and murder) are defined for us as posing the greatest threats. Those forms of violence that are most damaging in scope (for example, forms of institutional and structural violence) are defined for us as posing the least threats or are defined as not violent in the deviant context or as necessary or justified. Thus inequality is related to the occurrence of violence by first establishing the relationships that give those who are in dominant positions the power to define forms of violence that are most destructive and that they benefit by as not violence to be addressed by agents of social control or even to be recognized by those who are victims. In this way, structures of inequality contribute to the further occurrence of the forms of violence that are greatest in scope.

For example, when we think of rape, what comes to mind is the stranger lurking in the shadows waiting to attack the innocent women walking home in the evening. We do not think of the husband or boyfriend who, by means of threats of violence, forces himself sexually on his wife or girlfriend, although these forms of rape are more frequent. They are precluded from our concern by the system of inequality, patriarchy, which questions whether these acts are to be considered rape, and the ideologies that legitimate this system of structured inequality and that form the basis of the law and its enforcement.

Another example would be production violence. Again, when we think of violence, we think of interpersonal violence where approximately fifteen thousand people are murdered each year in the United States. We do not think of the more than hundred thousand or more people who die of work-related illnesses or injuries. We do not think of Bhopal, India, as a case of violence or mass murder, nor do we think of the large number of people whose life is cut short from brown lung or black lung disease as victims of violence. The class relations we take for granted in our society preclude us from considering that these are acts of violence; after all, didn't these people volunteer to work under these conditions? The inequality and coercion that affect the bargaining position of workers relative to owners are not even recognized because we have internalized the dominant ideology that defines this system as normal, just, and appropriate.

On the other hand, when we discover pesticide poisoning in child farm workers in Peru who are sent into the fields to assist in the spraying of DDT and chlordane, pesticides that have been banned in this country because of their carcinogenic effects, we may see the coercion rooted in the inequality of social relations between the poor peasants and their children and the wealthy landowners. This is in part because it takes place outside our own societal context. Nevertheless, in both cases, violence has taken place. This is violence that is larger in scope than the interpersonal violence that we read about daily in our newspapers, that we are entertained by in our movies and television programs, and that we think is the principal threat to people throughout the world and to the very existence of order. In general, the cultural understandings we have learned from those who are dominant allow us only to recognize forms of violence that are least in scope and to recognize these forms of violence as more threatening than forms that they commit that are larger in scope and more threatening.

There is one more step. As our understanding of violence is mediated by the ideologies that are a product of systems of inequality and how they serve to legitimate these systems of inequality, they contribute to the maintenance and extension of these systems through acts of violence. Those who are victims of the more devastating forms of violence that are not defined as violent are disempowered to address the causes of them. In this way, our understandings regarding violence and our resultant acceptance of violence lead to furthering the systems of structural inequality that are ultimately their cause. Thus the woman who is raped by her husband may not even recognize the act as rape or violence, thus furthering the pattern of male privilege as rooted in patriarchy. The worker who is victimized by production violence, or the consumer who is victimized by product violence, may not recognize the act as violence, thus furthering the pattern of class privilege as rooted in the class system. The U.S. citizen who supports his troops (disproportionately composed of working-class and minority members) in battle during the recent wars with Iraq and Afghanistan may not see these acts as forms of illegitimate violence or violence itself, thus furthering the pattern of the stratification internationally and the system of imperialism in the world.

Another way that systems of inequality can cause violence is through the effect it has on the social conditions of the actors involved. Beginning with interpersonal violence, to what degree do the conditions of one's life, as they are a product of systems of stratification, lead to acts of homicide and rape? In looking at patterns of homicide and rape, we see that those who are most likely to be victims and offenders are concentrated among the poorer segments of society. Could we not say that if we removed young children who were born in East Los Angeles, Brownsville in Brooklyn, or the south side of Chicago and transplanted or adopted them at birth into families who reside in wealthy suburbs of these same cities, the probability that they will be involved either as a victim or offender or a witness to a violent attribute of the positions that they occupy would diminish? The following is based on an interview of a sixteen-year-old boy who lives in the inner-city section of Indianapolis. Violence is an integral part of this boy's environment.

> Big Daddy, 16, Indianapolis. In my neighborhood, people are getting shot, getting killed, running around. People selling dope every day. They say average life span for a young black male is twenty-one years. Violence is definitely on the rise cause ain't nothing getting better. . . . But maybe a world without violence would be stupid 'cause people need something to talk about. I ain't saying its right to have violence and talk about it, but you never know. Sometimes you need violence to get your point across. I mean, violence was probably here for a reason. . . . We ain't got no relations with the police or nothing like that. Just as long as they go home, they don't care who they hurt or what they do. I mean, look at our little kids growing up, my nieces and nephews, how can they call the officer Mr. Friendly when they got guns all over? If you just go around popping each other, I don't think it'll never change cause that's all kids see nowadays. Just that. (Goodwillie, 1993, 161–62)

Would this young man have the same understanding of the nature of violence if he grew up in a wealthy suburb, say in Carmel, Indiana, the richest in the state? Or what about if he was adopted by a wealthy Swedish couple who reside in the suburbs of Stockholm? Thus, is it not the condition of one's existence as defined in terms of systems of class, ethnicity, and stratification that frame our understanding of violence that in part causes violence? Another example of how systems of inequality can cause violence is the case of patriarchy. Most violence is the violence of men. If we socialize males to view themselves as superior to females, train them to view themselves as in control of women, and train them to believe that aggression and violence are signs of masculinity, are we not contributing to the occurrence of male violence? If our male gender role models on the playing fields, in the cinema, and in public life teach the expediency of violence to address problems and to assert power and control, again signs of masculinity, are we not contributing to the occurrence of male violence? If we teach our male population to exercise this aggression in recreation and in work, at times to reward it, especially when it is most violent as in the case of a war hero or president who takes military action, are we not contributing to the occurrence of male violence? If toy weapons are given to male children and toy babies are given to female children to play and simulate adult behavior, are we not contributing to this male-dominated pattern of violence? The socialization of males to be masculine in patriarchal, capitalist society is one of the causes of the violence between men and women, and between men in pursuit of ownership and control of women and other valued possessions.

On another level, because of the position of men in the society, they are more likely to have access to weapons and to be empowered to use them in acts of violence. In this way the positions that men occupy in patriarchal society provide them with greater opportunities to be violent. When we looked at motives for interpersonal violence, the overwhelming reasons were controlling women, acquiring access to material wealth, or asserting power to gain position. In all cases, the relevance of the action exists only in the context of systems of inequality, where conditions of scarcity are created.

Systems of inequality also cause institutional and structural violence. When we address each form of institutional violence, we see a repeated pattern whereby those who are most likely to be victims tend to be those who are in dominated positions. Alternately, those who are perpetrators of violence are those who are in dominant positions or are acting as agents of those who are dominant. Systems of inequality cause the occurrence of institutional violence in that the function of institutional violence is to maintain or extend those systems of domination that a society is based on. This is true whether we are discussing spousal assault and the system of male privilege rooted in patriarchy, production violence and private property rights rooted in the class system, or state-sponsored genocide rationalized as national security, or, more accurately put, the maintenance of power relations in a nation-state or internationally as defined in terms of a system of imperialism.

Lastly, in structural violence, systems of inequality play a direct role. Structural violence is the form of violence that is most invisible; for it is by means of the dominant ideologies that by definition legitimate the basic structures of the society that we are rendered blind, or at least myopic, to the recognition of this form of violence. Because of such blinders, we are most likely to recognize the existence of this form of violence in other societies but not our own. Thus, we are more likely to see the violence of a system of apartheid in South Africa, but not see the violence of racial stratification in our own society. As we discussed in the chapter on structural violence, this is the form of violence most directly linked to the hierarchical relations that exist within a society, and the hierarchical relations that exist between societies. Structural violence is the relatively high occurrence of infant mortality among lower-income and minority populations throughout the world. It is also the high rate of abortions of female fetuses in rural health clinics in rural areas in India. It is the life expectancy differences between positions within a society. It also is the difference in infant mortality and life expectancy between countries positioned as dominant and dominated in the world system.

These differences in the quality and extent of life are direct products of the systems of stratification that are part of a nation-state system and an international system of imperialist relations. How long and what quality of life an individual will experience are significantly caused by the ranking of positions nationally and internationally and one's place within that rank. Whether we view the rankings as legitimate or not is irrelevant to our discussion of violence.

Violence » Inequality

We have discussed how violence can be caused by the structures of inequality that exist in a society and the world system. But violence can cause inequality as well. By this we mean that the consequences of acts of violence may serve to maintain and extend levels of inequality. In interpersonal violence, the pattern of victimization of both rape and homicide leads to increasing levels of inequality in our society. As the poorer and less powerful segments of our society experience higher rates of victimization compared to those in positions that are dominant in the society, these forms of violence serve to further the distance between the positions. For instance, as women are victimized by rape, the occurrence and fear of the occurrence reduce the power of women relative to men. As poorer and minority working-class populations experience a higher rate of homicide relative to the owning class and majority populations, their power is reduced relative to these higher positions.

Not only does the occurrence of acts of interpersonal violence serve to maintain and extend systems of inequality, but how we respond to this victimization does so as well. Formal state agents of social control are increasingly part of our everyday life. There is an increasing presence of armed authority and social control in our lives, more than at any other period in human history. In the United States, the proportion of the population that is performing an official role of social control as police officer, security guard, military personnel, prison guard, and the like is far greater than any other country in the world and far greater than any other moment in our history. Along with this pattern, the proportion of the population placed under intensive surveillance either by means of incarceration or probation is far greater in this society than any other society in the world and far greater than any other moment in our history. The number of state and federal prisoners and those on parole and probation (those under correctional personnel supervision) in the United States has quadrupled since 1980 (U.S. Bureau of Justice, 2001). In 1980, 1,842,100 persons were under correctional personnel supervision; for the year 2008 that number had climbed to 7,274,600, approximately a 400 percent increase (Glaze, 2010). This translates into a prisonization rate of 751 people in prison or jail for every 100,000 in population. In South Africa during the system of apartheid, another leading country in prison rates, 311 out of every 100,000 South Africans was in prison during the tumultuous early 1990s (Sniffen, 1994). The United States composes approximately 5 percent of the world's population, yet the U.S. prison population is one-fourth of the total world's prison population (Liptak, 2008). The population is not under more control with the threat of prison and the number of laws, but there is a greater level of surveillance of the population and a larger portion of its population as social control agents than any other country in the world. This is all the product of what the dominant ideology, education, and media outlets define as a free society.

Yet the presence of these agents in monitoring and surveying our activities and our geographic space is not uniform throughout the population. Those subpopulations that are in dominated positions, especially as defined in terms of class, gender, and ethnicity, are more likely to experience their presence. The inequality of power that the layperson experiences in the presence of agents of social control becomes magnified when the layperson is in a dominated social position. The experience of lower-income, minority, and female populations is often one of intimidation, humiliation, and subservience, if not violence, in interaction with representatives of the state. Furthermore, the operation of policing agencies in general in addressing problems of interpersonal violence does not result in empowering the victims and other residents with the means to address the problem. Instead, it functions to remove the solution to the problem from the victim and community and to create greater dependence on the power of the state to address these problems in the future. This does not serve to reduce power inequalities in public life among these populations but does just the opposite.

As to how institutional and structural violence maintains and extends structures of inequality, we only have to look at the differences in patterns of victimization. Again, as with interpersonal violence, the pattern of victimization is not uniform throughout the population. As noted earlier, with few exceptions, those populations that are in dominated positions experience higher rates of institutional violence compared to those populations that are in dominant positions. This differential experience of victimization serves to maintain and extend the structures of inequality. Furthermore, the intent of institutional violence is the maintenance or extension of patterns of structured inequality. The husband who beats his wife, the activities of a death squad, the occurrence of production violence: all maintain and extend the patterns of structured inequality in the society.

The same pattern applies even more to structural violence. Populations in dominated positions experience higher levels of disease, shorter life spans, and in general less of an opportunity to develop their human capacities than those who are in dominant positions in the society. On another level, as poorer countries throughout the world are devastated by civil war, overt and covert military interventions, and famine, their positions are reduced relative to the positions of those countries dominant in the world system. In general, as these structures of inequality are maintained and extended within and between nations, the more violence there is throughout the world, and the result is the extension of these very structures of inequality that are the cause of the violence.

Of course, not all violence serves to maintain and extend inequality; violence may also reduce levels of inequality. The organized and unorganized violence of those who are dominated or in the interest of those who are dominated may cause a reduction in levels of inequality. Riots and rebellions throughout history have often resulted in a response by the elite to reduce the harshness of living conditions that are a product of systems of inequality. In our own society, whether we are talking about Shays's Rebellion during the eighteenth century, the rioting of the poor and unemployed throughout periods of economic crisis, slave rebellions sporadically in the South during the nineteenth century, the rioting that occurred around the country during the 1930s, the race and class riots of the 1960s, or the riots in the Miami and Los Angeles during the 1980s and 1990s, the result has often been the establishment or extension of economic or political rights that have reduced levels of inequality in the society (Cloward and Piven, 1977; Zinn, 1980).

VIOLENCE AND HUMAN FREEDOM

Violence » Freedom

Violence ultimately refers to a denial of human freedom. In societies and more specifically in geographic and social space where there are high levels of violence, there is less freedom than in societies and geographic and social space where violence is at lower levels. Violence as an act is often intended to lessen human freedom. The outcome of violence is always to lessen human freedom for those who have been successfully victimized. Whether we are discussing interpersonal violence, institutional violence, or structural violence, the outcome is less freedom for those who are victimized. But, as with all hierarchical interactions, those who are victims, in most cases those who are in dominated positions, have less freedom in the society to begin with and experience less freedom as a result of the violence. Those who are the perpetrators or beneficiaries of the actions of the perpetrators, in most cases those who are in dominant positions, experience greater freedom as a result of the violence.

The husband, friend, acquaintance, or stranger who rapes the wife, friend, acquaintance, or stranger experiences a sense of control and power over his victim. He feels a sense of freedom of action, while his victim experiences the denial of that freedom. The murderer experiences a sense of control and power over his victim, and the victim experiences the ultimate denial of freedom: death.

Similarly, in acts of institutional violence, those who are the agents of institutions who commit the acts and those who are in dominant positions who are more or less the beneficiaries of the institutional actions experience a greater freedom, and those who are the victims of the institutional violence experience less freedom. Thus, whether we are talking about the violence of missionaries in their attempt to control indigenous populations, the actions of employers to generate more surplus in production by forcing workers to engage in unsafe production methods or work or live in unsafe environments, the husband who uses violence as a means to control his wife, or the military or police who use violence to control dominated populations that threaten the power of the state and the interests of those who have most power in directing the actions of the state, the result is to deny freedom to those who are victimized.

Lastly, the occurrence of structural violence as it manifests itself in mortality and morbidity differentials lessens the freedom of victims and increases the freedom of those who are the beneficiaries of the resources that allow them to maximize their human potential. The differences in access to health care, safe drinking water, shelter, and an adequate diet all manifest themselves in differences in the quality of one's existence and greater or lesser freedom in living. For example, the freedom that we have because of the availability of food in every variety and form results in less freedom for the billion people who struggle to achieve the minimum caloric requirement for daily survival.

Freedom » Violence

Not only does violence cause a loss of freedom, but a lessening of freedom causes violence as well. As some people are less free relative to others, they are prone to victimization. This is not only true in institutional and structural violence, but also by means of interpersonal violence by those who are also in oppressive conditions and who are attempting to assert freedom through exerting power and control over others in similar or poorer circumstances. Those who are less free experience this higher level of victimization because they have less of an ability to respond to their victimization. The pattern is present in all forms of violence. This relationship between freedom and violence is also evident globally. As Gurr, Sivard, and others have pointed out, societies where there is less freedom are prone to higher levels of violence.

The exception to the pattern whereby violence reduces human freedom is the case where violence is used to extend human freedom. Organized or unorganized violence by the oppressed or in the interest of the oppressed can serve to extend freedom. Liberation movements and revolutions around the world have at times resulted in the granting of greater freedoms to people in dominated positions. Nevertheless, as these movements have been successful in reducing levels of exploitation, they have reduced the freedom of those who have been the exploiters. Thus, if we can think for a moment of the Civil War in the United States as a war that had a liberation thrust (although this was not the principal motive behind the war), the result was in granting more freedom to those who were former slaves. At the same time, it granted less freedom to those who lost the right to this form of exploitation.

CYCLE OF VIOLENCE, INEQUALITY, AND FREEDOM

What we have been describing thus far is a cycle of violence, inequality, and freedom. As violence increases, freedom is reduced in a society. There is a greater level of fear that inhibits one's action, and as violence occurs those who are victimized lose their freedom as an outcome. Conversely, as the level of violence is reduced in a society, the level of freedom experienced by the population increases. This is especially the case for those who are most victimized with violence, those who have less freedom, and those who are in the most dominated positions in the society.

The level of freedom in a society also serves as a causal agent in its relationship with violence. As the level of freedom in a society declines, the level of violence increases. The population becomes more vulnerable to levels of repression as they have less freedom to respond to it. The wife whose every action is controlled by her husband is more vulnerable to violence than the wife who is less controlled and dominated. The workers who are more desperate to find work, who are less free in this sense, are more vulnerable to violence than the workers who have many choices. The citizens of a repressive government where there is little political freedom are more vulnerable to violence than the citizens of a liberal government where there are extensive rights for citizens.

As to the link between violence and inequality, as violence increases so do the levels of inequality in a society. Those who are most vulnerable to violence in any society are those who are in the most dominated positions. As violence increases in a society, they are the ones who experience the highest victimization, and this serves to reduce their position relative to those who are most dominant, which results in an increase in the levels of inequality. Conversely, as inequality increases, the level of violence increases. This was noted in the above discussion regarding freedom and its relationship to violence. As inequality increases, those whose position declines have less freedom, which leads to an increased likelihood in their victimization. Furthermore, those who decline in position have less of an ability to respond to violence, thus again making them more vulnerable to victimization.

The last connection in the cycle is that between inequality and freedom. As inequality increases, freedom is reduced in a society for those in dominated positions. This is in part self-evident. The least free in any society and in the world are those who are in the most dominated positions. As levels of inequality increase, there is less freedom. Another way this relationship manifests itself is that increases in inequality in a society result in more coercion and control as dominated populations become economically and politically desperate and are perceived to be more threatening to those who are in dominant positions. Historically concern about crime is connected not to recent upsurges in its occurrence but rather in the restlessness or perceived threat of dominated populations (Michalowski, 1985). The calls for law and order in our society often mean a call for control of those populations who are in the most dominated positions. When we look at the composition of our jails and prison populations this is obvious. The vast majority of those imprisoned come from the lowest income and most dominated ethnic positions.

Another way that increases in inequality lead to a lessening of freedom is through its impact on time and space freedom. Those who decline in their position spend more of their time and energy meeting their basic needs as defined by the society that they reside in. There is less free time to enjoy life and develop talents and abilities.

Conversely, as freedom declines, the level of inequality increases. One loses freedom relative to those who are in control. Those who are in control are in a better position to realize their interest relative to those who are controlled. Thus, increases in inequality are a logical outcome of increases in repression and a lessening of human freedom in a society (see figure 10.1).

In conclusion, violence, freedom, and inequality are linked to each other in a cycle. As violence in a society increases, freedom is increasingly denied for those who are most dominated and systems of inequality are extended. As violence in a society decreases, freedom increases and systems of inequality are reduced. As in the case of all cycles, the starting or end point may be at any of three points. One may start with changes in the levels of freedom and its impact on inequality and violence, or start with the changes in patterns of inequality and its impact on violence and freedom, or start with changes in the level of violence and how it impacts levels of freedom and inequality.

What are the policy implications of the cycle of violence, inequality, and freedom? The first implication relates to how we attempt to solve problems of violence in our society. Attempts to combat the problem of violence by means of violence or repression are likely to lead in the long run to increasing the levels of violence in the society. This is evident from the nature of the cycle described above. Violence ultimately lessens the level of freedom in the society, especially for the dominated in the society, which is likely in turn to lead to higher levels of inequality and consequently more violence. Thus, as we use increasing amounts of repression to control criminal violence, these populations who are criminalized when eventually released will have greater problems of inequality and freedom as a result of the stigmatization of their ex-convict status. The result is that there is a greater chance that they will commit acts of violence in response to their social position. Strategies to reduce gang violence in today's inner cities by increasing levels of law enforcement, or repression, are likely to lead to increasing levels of violence via its impact on freedom and inequality of these groups.

A second implication relates to the impact of changing social policies on systems of inequality and their impact on levels of violence and freedom. For example, as economic policies that result in increasing the levels of inequality are implemented in a society, as was the case of the economic and tax policies of the Reagan and George W. Bush administration (Philips, 1990; Fieldhouse, 2011), there is likely to be an increase in the levels of violence and a reduction in freedom in the society. During Reagan's first term, the tax burden of the richest 1 percent of the population fell by 14 percent, while the bottom 10 percent of the population increased their tax share by 28 percent. Under the pretense of balancing the federal budget, deep cuts were leveled against programs that provided a safety net for the working class and safeguarded the environment, working conditions, and product quality. By 1985, nondefense procurement was down $16 billion from 1981, and funds for entitlement programs were cut by close to $30 billion. At the same time, defense spending increased by over $35 billion. Under the ruse of the Star

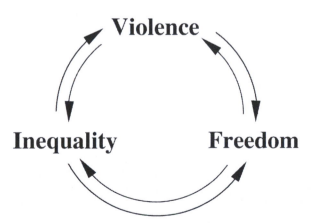

Figure 10.1.   The Cycle of Violence, Inequality, and Freedom.

Wars program, the military-industrial complex received a tremendous dose of corporate socialism to increase profits to stratospheric levels throughout the 1980s.

Another major area of growth in spending was in crime control. Expenditures on policing and prisons more than double in the wake of these economic reforms. These expenditures have continued to increase through the 1990s such that federal spending on the criminal justice system increased more than 400 percent during the past twenty years (U.S. Bureau of Justice, 2001). With the dramatic increase in defense spending after the terrorist attack on the United States in 2001 and the dramatic tax cuts for the wealthiest segments of the population and corporations, there appeared to be a repeat of the Reagan years under the administration of George W. Bush with increases in inequality and the use of violence internally and externally to maintain order.

These policies have led to an increasingly two-tiered society: the working class and middle-income sector lost position as the spread of income and wealth inequality grew in the society. A report of the Economic Policy Institute entitled the *State of Working America 1992–1993* noted that by the end of the conservative Republican era, the top 20 percent of the population had the highest share of income and the bottom 60 percent of the population had the lowest share of income ever recorded in U.S. history (Mishel and Bernstein, 1993). This trend also continued through the 1990s. After-tax income levels increased 14 percent for the bottom 80 percent of the population between 1977 and 1999, while they increased 43 percent for the top 20 percent and within that group the income of the top 1 percent of the population increased 115 percent during the same period (Shapiro and Greenstein, 2000). Levels of income and wealth inequality in the United States are at historic highs. The United States also has the highest rate of poverty among children compared to other advanced industrial countries in the world and two-thirds of the adult poor are women.

This growth of inequality and poverty was complemented by a growth in the proportion of the population in prison. Today, the United States has the highest proportion of its population incarcerated in its history and the highest or next to the highest (Russia may have the highest) in the world. Lastly, there is increasing fear of violence throughout the country. Communities throughout the nation have formed task forces to address the problem of violence, particularly youth violence that has increased in the aftermath of these policy changes. This ultimately impacts one's personal freedom in the society. As we become more fearful of the violence that is occurring in our society we are less free, and as we are victimized by the violence we experience less freedom. Furthermore, as our positions are reduced in the society in terms of systems of stratification it lessens our freedom. Today there is less freedom for working people as they spend increasing amounts of time working and holding onto their jobs in order to maintain their economic position, looking for one because they have recently become unemployed, or attempting to be employed for the first time (Schor, 1993). Another example is the impact of structural adjustment programs on levels of inequality, violence, and freedom. Throughout the world the imposition of conditions of lending that lead to further increases in the levels of inequality in the society and the world have led to increasing levels of violence and increasing loss of freedom.

A third implication relates to the cost of policies that result in reducing levels of freedom in the society and their impact on violence and inequality. As freedom is reduced in a society, it is likely to lead to increases in the levels of inequality and violence in the society. This may relate to the creation of laws that limit freedom of lifestyles that are not violent in themselves; for example, limiting gay lifestyles or drug use as a part of one's lifestyle may result in violence. In the first case, the denial of the freedom of gay lifestyles may result in increasing levels of violence via hate crimes and the state's response to those who violate the moral codes safeguarding heterosexuality and patriarchy. This violence impacts levels of inequality as that population is marginalized by the loss of freedom and violence. In the case of drug use, violence increases as a result of the government's violent tactics to control the behavior and the violence that stems from black market situations. Levels of inequality are affected by the marginalization and criminalization of the population of those who use drugs as part of their lifestyle. The recent strategies of employers to conduct drug testing and firing of employees that fail the test impact the economic position of those who use drugs as part of their lifestyle. Another case of how the lessening of freedom impacts violence and inequality is South Africa and its system of apartheid. The government regulations on travel and work of black South Africans led to the extension of levels of inequality and violence in that society.

Let's illustrate the cycle of violence, inequality, and freedom with the case of juvenile violence. There is a growing concern about youthful violence in our society. The response of governments at all levels has been increasing punitive measures to offenders and increasing restrictions on youths in general. As these responses lead to increasing the dependence of youth on adults and reducing their position relative to adults, it is likely to lead to increasing levels of violence as youth respond to the increase in forced dependency and status deprivation. Furthermore, dependency and status deprivation may make youths increasingly vulnerable to victimization by the adults in their lives. This may result from the fact that youths would have less ability to respond to their victimization in a way to deter future actions, or it may result from the increased strain placed on adults as a result of the increasing dependency and deprivation of youths.

As economic policies lead to reducing the opportunities for youth employment in the society, there is likely to be a decline in the freedom of youths in the society and a resultant increase in the level of violence. This occurs as youths become increasingly rebellious in response to their condition, and it occurs as they become vulnerable to acts of violence by other youths acting to exert power and control.

Lastly, as more and more laws and criminal justice and therapeutic strategies are implemented that reduce the freedom of youths, it is likely to lead to higher levels of violence and inequality for youths. Thus, as youth violence has increased in the society, the economic condition of youth has declined as measured by youth poverty and unemployment rates, and their freedom has lessened as a larger proportion of children are under treatment or incarceration for what is defined as abnormal or deviant behavior.

The impact of these policy interventions is higher levels of violence, inequality, and a loss of freedom for the youth population to the point that a crisis is reached where new strategies may be stumbled on that may reverse the cycle. These new strategies must reduce levels of inequality by integrating youths more into the adult world by giving them opportunities to develop their potential through participation in the society. This integration and reduction in status deprivation will increase levels of freedom as they achieve the rights of adulthood that have been denied to them. Lastly, as the levels of deprivation are reduced and levels of freedom are increased, there is a reduction in the levels of violence.

On another level is how parents' strategies for controlling their children's misbehavior have had an impact on their violence, inequality, and freedom. Think about how some parents respond to children with increasing restrictions or loss of freedom to control their behavior, how this leads to the levels of inequality between the child and the adult, creating a greater level of separation between them, all of which leads to increasing the probability of violence in their relationship. Rigoli and Hewitt (1994), in their theory of differential oppression, discuss how parental and adult oppression leads to youth adaptive responses such as the exercise of illegitimate coercive power and retaliation resulting in violence. Instead of parental strategies that restrict freedom, we should explore strategies that give our children more freedom. Instead of strategies that create further levels of inequality and separation, we should explore strategies that reduce levels of inequality and separation between parent and child. The impact of these strategies that create more freedom and less inequality will be less violence in the home.

What about the violence between men and women? Does the cycle of violence, inequality, and freedom provide any insight into explaining this violence? What about the violence directed at workers as in the case of production violence? Does the cycle of violence, inequality, and freedom provide any insight into explaining this violence? What about acts of state violence, as in Guatemala, Argentina, or Uganda? Does the cycle of violence, inequality, and freedom provide any insight into explaining this violence? What about the nature of structural violence, as illustrated by the tremendous disparities in life expectancies between Norway and Sierra Leone, or Germany and Ghana, or Sweden and Zambia? Does the cycle of violence, inequality, and freedom provide any insight into explaining this violence? In each case, as levels of inequality increase and levels of freedom decline, levels of violence increase. Conversely, as levels of inequality decrease, as levels of freedom increase, there are decreasing levels of violence. Where would you likely experience higher levels of violence within all spheres (interpersonal, institutional, and structural): in Zambia or Sweden, in Norway or Sierra Leone, or in Germany or Ghana? As indicated by the cycle of violence, inequality, and freedom, countries where there is more freedom and less inequality are places where there is less violence. Countries where there is less freedom and more inequality are places where there is more violence.

CHAIN OF VIOLENCE

Throughout this work we have described the different forms of violence in terms of three spheres: interpersonal, institutional, and structural. Although we can view these forms and spheres as distinct, they often overlap and may be linked to each other in a causal sequence. One of the principles of violence described in chapter 1 was the chain of violence. The basic idea is that spheres of violence are linked in a hierarchical manner, going from the more macro forms of structural violence to the micro level of violence at the interpersonal level.

Violence begins at the structural level. What allows us to victimize others is our ability to think less of those we victimize and our ability to separate ourselves from those we victimize. In an act of violence we think of our victim as less because we are conditioned to view others in our society differently, based on our perception of human value or quality. These differences of perception in the evaluation of others are rooted in the structural divisions that form the basis of the social order: class, gender, and ethnic systems of stratification. Inequalities of all kinds are fundamentally social constructions. Differences exist between people on a whole range of attributes. The transformation of these differences into inequalities is a social transformation based on systems of inequality within the society. The differences we perceive as hierarchies justify our violent behavior in terms of needing to control and punish those perceived to be less competent and forced to be our dependents. This is true whether we are victimizing children, women, ethnic minorities, or poor members of the displaced working class.

The violence that begins at the structural level (i.e., differences in illness rates, in infant mortality rates, in life expectancy rates, and in life chances to develop human potential) is the first link in the chain of violence. This violence is then linked to institutional violence. Those victimized at the structural level, at birth, are more likely to be victimized at the institutional level in schools, by religious organizations, in the family, in the economy, and in the political system. Lastly, the violence manifests itself at the interpersonal level, in some cases directed at those perceived as victimizers at the higher levels, in most cases at those who experience similar victimization.

The dominant pattern of interpersonal violence, whether we are talking about murder, assault, or rape, is that those who participate in violence at this level were more likely previously victimized at higher levels. Thus the causal chain of violence in any society begins with structural violence and ends with interpersonal violence. We noted earlier that it is at this point in the chain that the violence is officially recognized and defined as violence. The earlier links are made invisible. Thus, in searching for the causes of violence in a society, it is crucial to begin in assessing the society first in terms of patterns of structural violence and institutional violence and then to look at the patterns of interpersonal violence and how they are linked to the other two. Unfortunately, because we have been traditionally blinded from understanding violence as anything but interpersonal, we often look only at the causes of this violence at the interpersonal level, and our focus ends in blaming the victim in explaining the violence in our midst.

A corollary to this principle is that societies with high levels of structural violence will also have high levels of institutional and interpersonal violence. Conversely, societies that have low levels of structural violence will have low levels of institutional and interpersonal violence. Thus, to assess the level of violence in a society, it is crucial that we begin by measuring the violence at the highest levels.

How do we assess the United States in terms of levels of structural and institutional violence? As we noted previously, the levels of structural violence in our own society as measured by mortality and morbidity differentials are very significant. Those who are poor and of ethnic minority status (of African, Mexican, Hawaiian, or Native American ancestry) become ill and die six to ten years earlier than those in dominant positions via systems of stratification. Furthermore, the occurrence of interpersonal/structural violence and institutional/structural violence is also high relative to countries of a similar level of development. Hate crimes and economic and state violence have been and continue to be part of the American landscape. The result is that the ghettos for our poor minorities in cities across the nation are racked by high levels of violence at all levels.

This structural violence then affects the institutional violence in our society. The same populations who are victims of structural violence are primed for institutional violence victimization. As noted in our discussion of inequality and institutional violence, populations who are the most dominated in our society experience the highest rates of institutional violence. They experience the most hazardous employment, consume the unsafe products, and live in the most environmentally unsafe areas. They suffer from the greatest levels of violence from policing agencies, and their political movements have historically been the targets of state terrorism. Women and children from these positions disproportionately populate shelters for child and spouse abuse.

The last link in the chain is interpersonal violence. When we look at the pattern of homicide and rape, again, it is those populations that have experienced the greatest amounts of victimization at the higher two levels that with few exceptions have the highest rates of rape and murder victimization and perpetration. As we noted in the fourth principle, we generally learn that violence can be expressive in that it is learned to be an "appropriate" response to anger or frustration. Our ability to enact violence on those who have less power than ourselves allows us to experience the illusion that we have power and control over others and thus over our own lives when in most cases it is because of its absence that violence occurs. The learning provides the linkages between the levels of violence noted earlier. Violence that we are accustomed to at the structural level becomes a matter of policy at the institutional level and a mode of personal behavior at the interpersonal level. As we learn the cultural and ideological justifications for the structural violence, and learn the legitimacy of the violent policy actions at the institutional level, the violence we enact in our personal lives becomes "natural" or "normal."

INTERNATIONAL CHAIN OF VIOLENCE

The chain of violence is not only contained within a given nation-state, as the chain is international in nature. In order to comprehend the patterns of inter-personal violence in our own society, we must first recognize how it is a part of an international chain. This chain of violence begins at the highest levels of international systems of stratification within a world political economic system. The world system defined in terms of a hierarchy of nation-states is all part of a system of imperialist relations whereby those who have histori-cally dominated others militarily, politically, culturally, and economically begin the process of structural violence. Those who experience the highest levels of structural violence are those who experience the greatest levels of economic, political, cultural, and military domination from the center. Coun-tries in the Southern Hemisphere, which have been dominated historically by one imperialist power after another, have the highest levels of structural violence. We highlighted Guatemala in a previous chapter. Its history of domination by one empire after another continues to have a devastating impact on the levels of violence. Guatemala is not unique. We could have inserted a number of countries in Central and South America, Africa, and Asia to illustrate this pattern of the link between structural, institutional, and interpersonal violence.

The cause of the structural violence that begins the chain is a country's structural position in the world economy and the enforcement of the mainte-nance of this position by imperialist relations. Countries at the center experi-ence the violence that results from the displacement of working-class popula-tions because of the superexploitative relationships the multinational corpo-rations are able to create with workers in less-developed countries in the periphery. Workers in peripheral countries experience the deprivations that are a product of dependent capitalist development, deprivations in part caused by the increasing surplus populations as rural populations are dis-placed as the agrarian economy makes a transition to cash crop production. The impoverishment of peripheral nations and their people leads to interna-tional institutional violence. International institutional violence reproduces, maintains, and extends the hierarchy in social relations between nation-states and sectors of the world system. International structural violence is also linked to the structural violence within a given social system that is in part a product of world structural position and to the institutional violence that reproduces, maintains, and extends the hierarchy within nation-states.

Again in Guatemala, we see how the United States has played and contin-ues to play an important role in international institutional violence. This occurs through the economic violence by U.S.-based multinational corpora-tions, which have dumped unsafe products and utilized unsafe working con-ditions. It is also evident in the actions of the World Bank and International Monetary Fund, both largely controlled by the United States as the major contributor to both agencies, in instituting structural adjustment programs that have led to the further impoverishment and displacement of the poorest populations. The U.S. government policy of funding, arming, and training the military and police who have been linked to coups, death squads, and state terrorism against the poorest populations in Guatemala is another example. And lastly there is the role of U.S.-based missionaries in the cultural genocide of the indigenous population, converting them religiously and ideologically so that their thinking no longer poses a threat to the maintenance of dependent capitalist relations and the hierarchical relations within Guatemala. The international structural violence also leads to high levels of structural violence within Guatemala as evidenced by high levels of differences in mortality and morbidity between class positions and ethnic positions in systems of stratification within the society.

Finally, we arrive at the interpersonal violence between those who are acting in response to the social conditions and social relations that are a product of positions in social systems. Here we must recognize that the interpersonal violence concentrated in the most dominated positions within a society is linked to the higher levels. It may take the form of violence that is rebellious against the very organization of the society. Here the violence may be *interpersonal, institutional* or *interpersonal, structural* or *interpersonal, institutional, structural.* The gang violence on the streets of Guatemala City as a result of the rampant drug violence would be an example of the interpersonal violence that stems from the poverty in the country. Another example would be the violence of guerrilla bands that develop and begin a strategy of violence directed at the state and the classes that the state supports. Guatemala has had guerrilla activity that for the most part has been supported by the poorest segments of the society. Yet another example is the violence of death squads connected to the military and police that have reappeared attacking those that are suspected of supporting revolutionary groups.

The recent rebellion in Chiapas, Mexico, is another example of this violence. Chiapas, with a population of 3.5 million, is one of the poorest regions in Mexico. One-third of the homes are not electrified, 40 percent of the dwellings have no running water, a third of the population is illiterate. Chiapas has the highest tuberculosis rate in the nation, and Reavis (1994) reports that in 1994, fifteen thousand residents died of malnutrition and curable diseases. The revolt that started on January 1, 1994, was in response to the economic dislocation experienced by residents of the region. These economic dislocations were in part a product of changes in economic agreements (NAFTA) between nation-states linked via imperialist relations in the world system and the structural adjustment program imposed by world lending agencies. Whether the end result will be more repression or less inequality and more freedom is yet to be determined (Reavis, 1994).

The interpersonal violence may be adaptive and instrumental as a means to achieve power and control over others and one's own life. The responses may be an act of violence to achieve an end that the structural arrangement may block one from achieving. In this way, violence is an instrumental adaptive response to the structures. Violence connected to theft or black markets is an example of this form of violence.

Lastly, the violence may be expressive. In this case, the violence is an emotional expression of frustration in response to the social conditions stemming from the structures. Here the violence may appear to be the most vicious and the most dangerous because there does not seem to be any rationale for it. The explosion of anger and violence of young minority males against innocent victims happens often in the drama of the inner city today.

If we focus only on the lowest levels, we see the trees but we miss the forest of which they are a part. And we fail to understand the forces that are beyond the individual actors who are in their own personal drama of violence. This is true of interpersonal violence in the ghettos of the United States. If we do not understand how this violence is part of a larger web of violence that is national and international in scope beginning at the highest levels of violence, structural, then we lose the ability to address its causes.

WHAT LESSON CAN BE LEARNED?

What forms of violence do we begin with and at what level (national or international) and with what strategies do we address violence? All forms of violence are ultimately linked. The violence that we experience in our inner cities is linked to the international structural violence and institutional violence experienced in remote areas of the world. As people are victimized in countries on the periphery of the world system, they create an economic and political disadvantage for those dominated in the center countries. Populations in Brazil, Guatemala, Bolivia, and Ghana become more desperate to acquire access to the means of survival. State violence in the periphery directed at union organizing efforts, the structural adjustment programs imposed on poor indebted countries that are following the path of dependent capitalist development, the international and state repression of political parties that attempt to represent the interest of the dominated sectors of peripheral societies, all serve to make this rapidly growing working class of displaced persons increasingly desperate for access to production in the center and the periphery.

Investments in jobs that once appeared to be secure for the working class in the center nations now become insecure as owners discover new opportunities for the generation of surplus as another population is more desperate for access to production so that they will work for cheaper wages and with less concern for safety and security of employment. As capital is exported to the periphery to these desperate and more oppressed working-class populations, economic displacement occurs in the center, leading to increases in unemployment and increases in inequality between the classes in the center countries affected by the capital export.

As the displacement occurs there is an increase in the level of violence in response to the changes in the social environment. It manifests itself at the interpersonal level with an increase in the level of violent crime by populations that are most desperate, and there will be increasing opportunities for black market situations that circumvent the blocked opportunities that are a result of the capital export. Violence will manifest itself at the institutional level as more families experience strain resulting from the economic stress of unemployment and falling wages. Violence directed at children and spouses often occurs during these times. It will manifest itself in more economic violence as the economically displaced population within the center nation becomes increasingly desperate for access to jobs and are increasingly willing to trade safe working conditions and a healthy living environment for jobs. It will manifest itself in increased state violence as the state responds to actual or perceived threats to the systems of stratification as defined in terms of property, gender, and ethnic relations. Lastly, it will manifest itself in increases in structural violence within the center nations, as differences in life chances expand between those who are in dominated position and those in dominant positions.

Ultimately the levels of violence are interwoven because they are rooted in the same social conditions—conditions characterized by inequality (exploitation) and a lack of freedom. All violence is ultimately a means to control another, to force him or her to act in ways that he or she has chosen not to. This other can be a child or a spouse or a neighbor or someone who threatens your pursuit of the scarcity created by the system of inequality.

How we respond to violence ultimately leads to either increasing or decreasing levels of violence. If we respond, as we have increasingly done in recent years, by increasing the levels of repression against those who are most powerless and engaging in violence, we increase the level of violence in the society as these populations experience less freedom and more inequality. If we recognize that people choose their actions, even violent actions, then we stand to reduce violence, not by decreasing the choices available to people as occurs with increased government repression and control and increasing inequality. Rather we decrease violence by providing people with more choices of action, more freedom, and less inequality in opportunities to develop their potential.

The current policies of increasing police presence, levels of punishment, and levels of inequality through economic deregulation will in the long run increase the levels of violence and increase the perceived need for more repression. This has the potential of leading to a downward spiral of violence and repression that may eventually reach crisis proportions within the population. Thus, more resources should not be channeled into agencies of repression, but in creating opportunities for people to choose other paths of behavior.

More attention needs to be focused on patterns of structural and institutional violence in the society and internationally, which are more destructive in themselves and eventually lead to problems of interpersonal violence. We need to intervene at the beginning of the chain, not at the end. The violence experienced at birth by those who are in the most dominated positions in the society and world, and then occurs as a result of institutional action as the life cycle continues, in most cases manifests itself at the interpersonal level.

In conclusion, in order to comprehend the patterns of interpersonal violence in society, we must first recognize how it is a part of an interaction chain. This chain of violence begins at the highest levels of international systems of stratification within a world political economic system (international structural violence). It then leads to international institutional violence that reproduces, maintains, and extends the hierarchy in social relations between nation-states and sectors of the world system. This then leads to the pattern of structural violence within a given social system stemming from the patterns of stratification that are in part a product of world structural position and to the institutional violence that reproduces, maintains, and extends the hierarchy within nations-states. Finally, we arrive at the interpersonal violence between those who are acting in response to social conditions and social relations that are a product of positions within social systems. If we focus only on the lowest levels, we fail to understand the forces that are beyond the individual actors in their personal drama of violence. And if we respond to violence by decreasing the range of choices to those who are in most dominated positions, we will eventually increase the levels of violence in the system.

As in ecological theory, a web of life connects us to each other across all living things, across and within species. This web of life connects each person to another across groups, structures, and systems. The web of violence is the antithesis to the web of life. It is not a social Darwinian cleansing mechanism that strengthens the vitality of the whole. For, unlike other species, humans grow and develop because of interaction with their own, creating and re-creating themselves and their social world in a developmental spiral that extends their life. Thus, as members are lost, opportunities are lost for growth and development for all. The loss of a member of your primary group (a family) is a loss of opportunity through social interaction for growth. Similarly, the loss of members of your community, state, nation, or world community is a loss of opportunity for growth for the individual and the species. Thus, from the smallest scale or level of interpersonal relations to the highest, the web of violence systematically leads to destruction and injury, beginning with the least powerful, but eventually affecting us all as it serves to destroy the entire system of interconnectedness that makes life possible.

DISCUSSION QUESTIONS

1. Using the idea of the cycle of violence presented in this chapter, what would you do to prevent violence in the schools? What would be an example of a social invention that would use the cycle of violence idea to reduce the problem of school violence? What would be some of the obstacles to applying this idea to prevent violence in schools?

2. Using the idea of the cycle of violence presented in this chapter, what would you do to prevent gang violence? What would be an example of a social invention that would use the cycle of violence idea to reduce the problem of gang violence? What would be some of the obstacles to applying this idea to prevent gang violence?

3. Using the idea of the cycle of violence presented in this chapter, what would you do to prevent violence in the home? What would be an example of a social invention that would use the cycle of violence idea to reduce the problem of violence in the home? What would be some of the obstacles to applying this idea to prevent violence?

4. Illustrate the chain of violence with an example of violence that recently occurred in your community. Describe what you would think would be each of the links that led to the occurrence of this example of violence.

5. This chapter describes an international chain of violence. How is the violence that is occurring on the streets of Monterrey, Mexico, an example of an international chain of violence?

References

PREFACE

Pinker, S. 2011. *The Better Angels of Our Nature*. Viking: New York.

CHAPTER 1

Allen, James, editor. 2000. *Without Sanctuary: Lynching Photography in America*. Santa Fe, N.M.: Twin Palms.

Archer, Dane, and Rosemary Gartner. 1984. *Violence and Crime in Cross-National Perspective*. New Haven, Conn.: Yale University Press.

Ball-Rokeach, S. J. 1980. "Normative and Deviant Violence from a Conflict Perspective." *Social Problems* 28: 45–62.

Bell, Daniel. 1953. "Crime as an American Way of Life." *The Antioch Review* 13: 131–54.

Blum, William. 2000. *Rogue State*. Monroe, Maine: Common Courage Press.

Bourdieu, Pierre, and Jean-Claude Passeron. 1977. *Reproduction in Education, Society and Culture*. Beverly Hills, Calif.: Sage.

Budiansky, Stephen. 1992. *The Covenant of the Wild*. New Haven, CT: Yale University Press.

Bureau of Justice Statistics. 2010a. *Homicide Trends in the US: Trends by Race*. Accessed December 10, 2010, from U.S. Department of Justice: bjs.ojp.usdoj.gov/content/homicide/race.cfm.

———. 2010b. *Homicide Trends in the US: Trends by Gender*. Accessed December 10, 2010, from U.S. Department of Justice: bjs.ojp.usdoj.gov/content/homicide/gender.cfm.

———. 2010c. *Victim Characteristics*. Accessed December 10, 2010, from: bjs.ojp.usdoj.gov/index.cfm?ty=tp&tid=92.

Carbone, Larry. 2004. *What Animals Want*. New York: Oxford University Press.

Center for Disease Control and Prevention. 2010. "Youth Violence: Facts at a Glance." Accessed September 5, 2012, from: www.cdc.gov/ViolencePrevention/pdf/YV-DataSheet-a.pdf.

CNN. 2001, July 5. "Annan Condemns 'Targeted Assassinations' by Israel." Atlanta: Cable News Network: www.cnn.com/2001/WORLD/meast/07/05/un.mideast/.

Croce, Pietro. 1999. *Vivisection or Science? An Investigation into Testing Drugs and Safeguarding Health*. Baltimore, MD: Second Books.

Davis, Kingsley, and Wilbert Moore. 1945. "Some Principles of Social Stratification." *American Sociological Review* 10: 242–44.

Dentler, Robert, and Kai T. Erickson. 1959. "The Functions of Deviance in Groups." *Social Problems* 7: 98–107.

Durkheim, Émile. 1938. *The Rules of the Sociological Method*. New York: Free Press.

Fishbein, Diana H. 1990. "Biological Perspectives in Criminology." *Criminology* 28, no. 1: 27–57.

Gardner, Linzey. 1976. *Animal Rights: A Christian Perspective*. London: SCM Press.

———. 1995. *Animal Theology*. London: SCM Press.

Harris, Marvin. 1974. *Cows, Pigs, Wars and Witches*. New York: Vintage Books.

Heelas, Paul. 1982. "Anthropology, Violence and Catharsis." In *Aggression and Violence*, edited by Peter Marsh and Anne Campbell. New York: St. Martin's Press.

Herman, Edward S. 1987. "U.S. Sponsorship of International Terrorism: An Overview." *Crime and Social Justice* 27–28: 1–29.

Herman, Edward S., and David Peterson. 2010. *The Politics of Genocide*. New York: Monthly Review Press.

Hernstein, Richard. 1973. *I.Q. in the Meritocracy*. Boston: Little, Brown.

Hook, Sidney. 1934. "Violence." In *Encyclopedia of Social Sciences*, edited by R. A. Seligman and Alvin Johnson, Vol. 15, 264–67. New York: Macmillan.

Human Rights Watch. 2001. *The "Sixth Division" Military-Paramilitary Ties and U.S. Policy in Colombia*. New York: Human Rights Watch: www.hrw.org/reports/2001/colombia/.

Ianni, Francis A. J. 1973. *Ethnic Succession in Organized Crime*. National Institute of Law Enforcement and Criminal Justice. Washington, D.C.: Government Printing Office.

Jensen, Arthur R. 1969. "How Much Can We Boost IQ and Scholastic Achievement?" *Harvard Educational Review* 39: 1–123.

Koning, Hans. 1976. *Columbus: His Enterprise*. New York: Monthly Review.

Kozol, Jonathan. 1991. *Savage Inequalities: Children in America's Schools*. New York: Crown.

Lee, Richard B. 1979. *The !Kung San: Men, Women and Work in a Foraging Society*. New York: Cambridge University Press.

Lewis, Flora. 2001, January 12. "Israel Defiles Itself with These Assassinations of Palestinians." Accessed from the *International Herald Tribune*: www.iht.com/frontpage.html.

Masood, Naveen Naqvi. 2002, July 7. "A Brutal Rape Case Riles Pakistan." Accessed from MSNBC: www.msnbc.com/news/776838.asp.

Mauss, Armand, L. 1975. *Social Problems as Social Movements*. New York: J.B. Lippincott Co.

Michalowski, Raymond. 1985. *Order, Law, and Crime: An Introduction to Criminology*. New York: Random House.

Miliband, Ralph. 1983. *Class Power and State Power*. London: Verso.

Mills, C. Wright. 1959. *Sociological Imagination*. New York: Oxford University Press.

Parsons, Talcott. 1991. *The Social System*. London: Routledge.

Parsons, Talcott, Robert Bales et al. 1955. *Family Socialization and Interaction Process*. New York: Free Press.

Pepinsky, Harold. 1991. *The Geometry of Violence and Democracy*. Bloomington: Indiana University Press.

Report of the National Advisory Commission on Civil Disorders. 1968. New York: Times Books.

Schwendinger, Julia, and Herman Schwendinger. 1975. "Defenders of the Order or Guardians of Human Rights?" In *Critical Criminology*, edited by Ian Taylor, Paul Walton, and Jock Young, 113–46. London: Routledge and Kegan Paul.

Scully, Matthew. 2002. *Dominion: The Power of Man, the Suffering of Animals, and the Call of Mercy*. New York: St. Martin's Griffin.

Silberman, Charles E. 1978. *Criminal Violence, Criminal Justice*. New York: Random House.

Singer, Peter. 1975. Animal Liberation: A New Ethic for The Treatment of Animals. Sidney, AU: Pimlico.

Straus, Murray A. 1991. "Physical Violence in American Families: Incidence Rates, Causes, and Trends." In *Abused and Battered*, edited by JoAnn L. Miller and Dean D. Knudson. New York: Aldine de Gruyter.

Straus, Murray A., and Richard J. Gelles. 1991a. "Societal Change and Change in Family Violence from 1975 to 1985 as Revealed by Two National Surveys." In *American Families*, edited by Murray A. Straus and Richard J. Gelles, 113–31. New Brunswick, N.J.: Transaction Books.

Tallman, Irving. 1976. *Passion, Action, and Politics*. San Francisco: W.H. Freeman and Co.

Trippett, Frank, and Priscilla Painton. 1989, September 11. "Death on a Mean Street: A Murder in a White Section of Brooklyn Ignites Racial Discord." *Time Magazine*, 28.

Turner, Jonathan, 1997. *The Institutional Order*. New York: Longman.

UPI. 2010, September 29. "U.S. Marriage Rate Continues to Decline." Accessed December 8, 2010, from: www.upi.com/Health_News/2010/09/29/US-marriage-rate-continues-to-decline/UPI-77271285810979/.

U.S. State Department. 2001, April 30. *Overview of State-Sponsored Terrorism: Patterns of Global Terrorism—2000*. Released by the Office of the Coordinator for Counter-terrorism: www.state.gov/s/ct/rls/pgtrpt/2000/2441.htm.

Weiner, Neil Alan, Margaret A. Zahn, and Rita J. Sagi. 1990. *Violence: Patterns, Causes, and Public Policy*. New York: Harcourt Brace Jovanovich.
Zinn, Howard. 1980. *A People's History of the United States*. New York: Harper & Row.

CHAPTER 2

Associated Press. 2002, January 11. "Jury Deliberating Hockey Dad's Fate." Fort Wayne (Ind.) *Journal Gazette*.
Azizah, Al-Hibri. 1981. "Capitalism Is an Advanced Stage of Patriarchy: But Marxism Is Not Feminism." In *Women and Revolution: A Discussion of the Unhappy Marriage of Marxism and Feminism*, edited by L. Sargent. Boston: South End Press.
Baker, Robert A. 1992. *Hidden Memories*. Buffalo, N.Y.: Prometheus Books.
Bandura, Albert. 1965. "Influence of Model's Reinforcement Contingencies on the Acquisition of Imitative Responses." *Journal of Personality and Social Psychology* 1: 589–95.
———. 1973. *Aggression: A Social Learning Analysis*. Englewood Cliffs, N.J.: Prentice Hall.
———. 1977. *Social Learning Theory*. Englewood Cliffs, N.J.: Prentice Hall.
Bandura, Albert, D. Ross, and S. S. Ross. 1963. "Imitation of Film-Mediated Aggressive Models." *Journal of Abnormal and Social Psychology* 66: 3–11.
Bandura, Albert, and Richard H. Walters. 1963. *Social Learning and Personality Development*. New York: Henry Holt.
Barak, Gregg. 1994. *Media, Process, and the Social Construction of Crime*. New York: Garland Publishing.
Barnouw, Victor. 1963. *Culture and Personality*. Homewood, Ill.: Dorsey Press.
Bayley, David H. 1976. *Forces of Order: Police Behavior in Japan and the United States*. Berkeley: University of California Press.
Benedict, Ruth. 1946. *The Chrysanthemum and the Sword*. New York: Houghton Mifflin.
Bernadt, Catherine H. 1978. "In Aboriginal Australia." In *Learning Non-Aggression: The Experience of Non-literate Societies*, edited by Ashley Montagu, 144–60. New York: Oxford University Press.
Bersani, Leo, and Ulysse Dutoit. 1985. *The Forms of Violence*. New York: Schocken Books.
Billington, Ray. 1974. *The Origins of Nativism in the United States, 1800–1844*. New York: Arnor Press.
Bilton, Michael. 1992. *Four Hours in My Lai*. New York: Viking Press.
Brody, Hugh. 2000. *The Other Side of Eden*. New York: North Point Press.
Brown, Richard Maxell. 1969. "The American Vigilante Tradition." In *The History of Violence in America*, edited by Hugh D. Graham and Ted R. Gurr, 154–226. New York: Bantam Books.
Browning, Christopher R. 1992. *Ordinary Men: Reserve Police Battalion 101 and the Final Solution in Poland*. New York: Harper Collins.
Burrows, William E. 1976. *Vigilante!* New York: Harcourt Brace Jovanovich.
Cater, Douglass, and Stephen Strickland. 1975. *TV Violence and the Child*. New York: Russell Sage Foundation.
Chagnon, Napoleon. 1968. *Yanomamo: The Fierce People*. New York: Holt, Rinehart and Winston.
Chambliss, William. 1988. *Exploring Criminology*. New York: Macmillan.
Cloward, Richard, and Lloyd E. Ohlin. 1960. *Delinquency and Opportunity*. New York: Free Press.
Cohen, Albert. 1955. *Delinquent Boys*. New York: Free Press.
Collins, T. 2005. *Encyclopedia of Traditional British Sports*. London: Routledge.
Davies, Nigel. 1981. *Human Sacrifice in History and Today*. New York: Dorsett Press.
Davis, David Brion. 1970. "Violence in American Literature." In *Violence: Causes and Solutions*, edited by Renatus Hartogs and Eric Artzt, 54–66. New York: Dell Books.
Devos, George, and Hiroshi Wagatsuma. 1972. *Japan's Invisible Race*. Rev. ed. Berkeley: University of California Press.
Dimsdale, Thos. J., 1953[1865]. *The Vigilantes of Montana*. Norman: Oklahoma University Press.
Dominick, Joseph R. 1978. "Crime and Law Enforcement in the Mass Media." In *Deviance and Mass Media*, edited by C. Winick, 105–208. Beverly Hills, Calif.: Sage.
Douglas, Jack D., and Frances C. Waksler. 1982. *The Sociology of Deviance*. Boston: Little, Brown.
Dowie, Mark. 1977, September/October. "Pinto Madness." *Mother Jones*, 18–32.
Dworkin, Andrea. 1976. *Our Blood*. New York: Harper & Row.

Elliot, Mabel A. 1944. "Crime and the Frontier Mores." *American Sociological Review* 9: 185–92.

Erbe, Bonnie. 2002, January 21. "Make an Example of Violent Parent at Youth Sports." Fort Wayne (Ind.) *Journal Gazette*.

Erickson, R. V., P. M. Baranek, and J. B. L. Chan. 1991. *Representing Order: Crime, Law, and Justice in the News Media*. Toronto: University of Toronto Press.

Eron, L. D., L. R. Huesmann, M. M. Lefkowitz, and L. O. Walder. 1972. "Does Television Violence Cause Aggression?" *American Psychologist* 27: 253–63.

Fishman, Mark, and Gray Cavender. 1998. *Entertaining Crime: Television Reality Programs*. New York: Aldine de Gruyter.

Franklin, John Hope. 1956. *The Militant South*. Cambridge, Mass.: Harvard University Press.

Frantz, Joe B. 1969. "The Frontier Tradition: An Invitation to Violence." In *History of Violence in America*, edited by H. D. Graham and T. R. Gurr, 127–54. New York: Bantam Books.

Futreli, Alison. 2006. *A Sourcebook on the Roman Games*. Oxford, UK: Blackwell.

Gellner, Ernest. 1988. *Plough, Sword and Book: The Structure of Human History*. Chicago: University of Chicago Press.

Gergen, David. 1989, May 8. "Secrets behind the Gun Lobby's Staying Power." *U.S. News and World Report*, 26.

Goldstein, Jeffrey H. 1986. *Aggression and Crimes of Violence*. New York: Oxford University Press.

Greenberg, Edward S. 1985. *Capitalism and the American Political Ideal*. Armonk, N.Y.: M. E. Sharpe.

Gubar, Susan, and Joan Hoff. 1989. *For Adult Users Only*. Bloomington: Indiana University Press.

Hackney, Sheldon. 1969. "Southern Violence." In *Violence in America: Historical and Comparative Perspectives*, edited by H. D. Graham and T. R. Gurr, 505–27. New York: Bantam Books.

Handlin, Oscar. 1957. *Race and Nationality in American Life*. Boston: Little, Brown.

Harris, Marvin. 1974. *Cows, Pigs, Wars and Witches*. New York: Vintage Books.

Hartman, Heidi. 1981. "The Unhappy Marriage of Marxism and Feminism: Towards a More Progressive Union." In *Women and Revolution: A Discussion of the Unhappy Marriage of Marxism and Feminism*, edited by L. Sargent. Boston: South End Press.

Hirschi, Travis. 1969. *Causes of Delinquency*. Berkeley: University of California Press.

Hofstadter, Richard, and Michael Wallace. 1971. "Reflections on Violence in the United States." In *American Violence: A Documentary History*, edited by Richard Hofstadter and Michael Wallace. New York: Vintage Books.

Humane Society of the United States. 2010. "Unfair Chance: Ethic Objections from Both Ends of the Spectrum." East Lansing: Animal Law and History Web Center of the Michigan State University College of Law. Accessed September 19, 2012, from: www.animallaw.info/articles/arusfund22002.htm.

Hunt, E. K. 1981. *Property and Prophets: The Evolution of Economic Institutions and Ideologies*. 4th ed. New York: Harper & Row.

Huston, A. C., E. Donnerstein, H. Fairchild, N. D. Fashbach, P. A. Katz, J. P. Murray, E. A. Rubinstein, B. L. Wilcox, and D. Zuckerman. 1992. *Big World, Small Screen: The Role of Television in American Society*. Lincoln: University of Nebraska.

Iadicola, Peter. 2008. "Globalization and Empire." *International Journal of Social Inquiry* (June): 3–37.

Jenkins, Henry. 2006. "Reality Bytes: Eight Myths about Video Games Debunked." Accessed from: www.pbs.org/kcts/videogamerevolution/impact/myths.html

Jubera, Drew. 1991, August 17. "Tied to the Tube: is Television Hazardous to Our Children?" Fort Wayne (Ind.) *Journal-Gazette*.

Keynes, John Maynard. 1964. *The General Theory of Employment, Interest, and Money*. New York: Harcourt Brace Jovanovich.

Klinenberg, Eric. 2004. "Denaturalizing Disaster: A Social Autopsy of the 1995 Chicago Heat Wave." In *Violence in War and Peace*, edited by Nancy Scheper-Hughes and Philippe Bourgois. Malden, Mass.: Blackwell Publishing.

Kolson, Sally. 1993, December 17. "Put Boss' Kids Faces on Video Games." Fort Wayne (Ind.) *Journal-Gazette*, 1D.

Kramer, Ronald C. 2010. "From Guernica to Hiroshima to Baghdad: The Normalization of Terror Bombing of Civilians." In *State Crime in the Global Age*, edited by William J. Chambliss, Raymond Michalowski, and Ronald C. Kramer. Portland: Willan Publishing.

Kyle, Donald G. 1998. *Spectacles of Death in Ancient Rome*. London: Routledge.

Lacayo, Richard, Michael Duffy, and Steven Holmes. 1989, March 15. "A Partial Vindication." *Time*, 34.

Leo, John. 1990a, July 2. "Polluting Our Popular Culture." *U.S. News and World Report*, 15.

———. 1990b, December 3. "Marketing Cynicism and Vulgarity." *U.S. News and World Report*, 23.

Litwack, Leon F. 2004. "From Hellhounds." In *Violence in War and Peace*, edited by Nancy Scheper-Hughes and Philippe Bourgois. Malden, Mass.. Blackwell Publishing.

Lynn, Kenneth. 1969. "Violence in American Literature and Folklore." In *Violence in America: Historical and Comparative Perspectives*, edited by H. D. Graham and T. R. Gurr, 226–42. New York: Bantam Books.

Malamuth, N. M., and E. Donnerstein. 1984. *Pornography and Sexual Aggression*. New York: Academic Press.

McGrath, Roger D. 1984. *Gunfighters, Highwaymen and Vigilantes: Violence on the Frontier*. Berkeley: University of California Press.

McMurtry, John. 1978. *The Structure of Marx's World-View*. Princeton, N.J.: Princeton University Press.

Messerschmidt, James W. 1986. *Capitalism, Patriarchy, and Crime*. Totowa, N.J.: Rowman & Littlefield.

Michalowski, Raymond. 1985. *Order, Law, and Crime: An Introduction to Criminology*. New York: Random House.

Milgram, Stanley. 1974. *Obedience to Authority*. New York: Harper Colophon.

Montagu, Ashley. 1978. *Learning Non-Aggression: The Experience of Non-Literate Societies*. New York: Oxford University Press.

Mullins, Christopher W. 2006. *Holding Your Square: Masculinities, Streetlife, and Violence*. Portland: Willan.

Nakane, Chie. 1970. *Japanese Society*. Berkeley: University of California Press.

Newman, Graeme. 1979. *Understanding Violence*. Philadelphia: Lippincott.

Nisbet, Robert. 1962. *Community and Power*. London: Oxford University Press.

Ollman, Bertell. 1972. *Alienation: Marx's Conception of Man in Capitalist Society*. Cambridge: Cambridge University Press.

Olson, James Stuart. 1979. *The Ethnic Dimension in American History*. New York: St. Martin's Press.

Pagelow, Mildred Daley. 1981. *Woman Battering: Victims and Their Experiences*. Beverly Hills, Calif.: Sage.

Parenti, Michael. 1986. *Inventing Reality: The Politics of the Mass Media*. New York: St. Martin's Press.

Pierce, Chester M. 1970. "Violence and the National Character." In *Violence: Causes and Solutions*, edited by R. Hartogs and E. Artzt, 119–26. New York: Dell Books.

Potter, David Stone, and D. J. Mattingly, eds. 1999. *Life, Death and Entertainment in the Roman Empire*. Ann Arbor: University of Michigan Press.

Reckless, Walter C. 1962, March/April. "A Non-Causal Explanation: Containment Theory." *Excerpta Criminologica*.

Rousseau, Jean-Jacques. 1967. *The Social Contract and Discourse on the Origin and Foundation of Inequality among Mankind*. New York: Washington Square Press.

Rowland, Willard D., Jr. 1983. *The Politics of TV Violence*. Beverly Hills, Calif.: Sage.

Scheper-Hughes, Nancy, and Philippe Bourgois. 2004. *Violence in War and Peace*. Malden, Mass.: Blackwell Publishing.

Scully, Matthew. 2002. *Dominion: The Power of Man, the Suffering of Animals, and the Call to Mercy*. New York: St. Martin's Griffin.

Shapiro, Judith. 1971. "Sex Roles and Social Structure among the Yanomamo Indians in North Brazil." Ph.D. diss., Columbia University.

Sherizen, Sanford. 1978. "Social Creation of Crime News: All the News Fitted to Print." In *Deviance and Mass Media*, edited by C. Winick, 203–24. Beverly Hills, Calif.: Sage.

Sherman, David M. 2002. *Tendering Animals in the Global Village*. London: Blackwell.

Shupe, Anson. 1991. *The Darker Side of Virtue*. Buffalo, N.Y.: Prometheus Books.

Shupe, Anson, William A. Stacey, and Lonnie R. Hazlewood. 1987. *Violent Men, Violent Couples: The Dynamics of Domestic Violence*. Lexington, Mass.: Lexington Books.

Smith, Adam. 1937. *The Wealth of Nations*. New York: Modern Library.

Smith, Michael. 1983. *Violence and Sport*. Toronto: Butterworths.

Stacey, William A., and Anson Shupe. 1983. *The Family Secret: Domestic Violence in America*. Boston: Beacon Press.

Swift, Richard. 1990, August. "Fundamentalism: Reaching for Certainty." *New Internationalist*, no. 210.

Toffler, Alvin. 1990. *Powershift*. New York: Bantam Books.

Video Game Procon.org. Accessed April 12, 2010, from: videogames.procon.org/.

Vogel, Lisa. 1981. "Marxism and Feminism: Unhappy Marriage, Trial Separation or Something Else?" In *Women and Revolution: A Discussion of the Unhappy Marriage of Marxism and Feminism*, edited by L. Sargent. Boston: South End Press.

Williamson, John B., Linda Evans, and Anne Munley. 1985. *Social Problems: The Contemporary Debates*. Boston: Little, Brown.

Wood, Owen. 2001, May. "The Firestone Tire Recall." Accessed from CBC News Online: cbc.ca/news/indepth/background/tirerecall_timeline.html.

Young, Kevin. 2000. "Sport and Violence." In *Handbook of Sport Studies*, edited by Jay Coakley and Eric Dunning. London: Sage Publications

CHAPTER 3

Abel, Gene, Judith Becker, and Linda Skinner. 1980. "Aggressive Behavior and Sex." *Psychiatric Clinics of North America* 3: 133–51.

Adler, Jerry. 1994, August 15. "A Week in the Death of America." *Newsweek*, 41.

Ageton, S. S. 1983. *Sexual Assault among Adolescents*. Lexington, Mass.: D.C. Heath.

Amir, Menachem. 1971. *Patterns in Forcible Rape*. Chicago: University of Chicago Press.

Amnesty International. 2002. *Kenya: Rape the Invisible Crime*. Accessed from Amnesty International: www.amnestyusa.org/stoptorture/women/kenya_invisible.pdf.

———. 2007. *Maze of Injustice: The Failure to Protect Indigenous Women from Sexual Violence in the USA*. Accessed April 6, 2011, from Amnesty International: www.amnestyusa.org/women/maze/report.pdf.

Archer, Dane, and Rosemary Gartner. 1984. *Violence and Crime in Cross-National Perspective*. New Haven, Conn.: Yale University Press.

Avison, William R., and Pamela L. Loring. 1986. "Population Diversity and Cross-National Homicide: The Effects of Inequality and Heterogeneity." *Criminology* 24: 733–49.

Bailey, W. C., and R. D. Peterson. 1995. "Gender Inequality and Violence against Women: The Case of Murder." In *Crime and Inequality*, edited by J. Hagan and R. D. Peterson, 174–205. Stanford, CA: Stanford University Press.

Barkan, Steven E. 2012. *Criminology: A Sociological Understanding*. Boston: Prentice Hall.

Barlow, Hugh D. 1990. *Introduction to Criminology*. Glenview, Ill.: Scott, Foresman/Little, Brown Higher Education.

Baron, L. 1985. "Does Rape Contribute to Reproductive Success: Evaluations of Sociobiological Views of Rape." *International Journal of Women's Studies* 8: 266–77.

———. 1989. *Four Theories of Rape in American Society*. New Haven, Conn.: Yale University Press.

Baron, L., and Murray Straus. 1988. "Cultural and Economic Sources of Homicide in the United States." *Sociological Quarterly* 29, no. 3: 371–90.

———. 1989. *Four Theories on Rape in American Society: A State Level Analysis*. New Haven, CT: Yale University Press.

Basile, K. C. 2002. "Prevalence of Wife Rape and Other Intimate Partner Sexual Coercion in a Nationally Representative Sample of Women." *Violence and Victims* 17, no. 5: 511–24.

Bastian, Lisa D., and Bruce M. Taylor. 1994. *Young Black Males*. Bureau of Justice Statistics Crime Data Brief. Washington, D.C.: Government Printing Office.

Beirne, Piers, and James Messerschmidt. 2011. *Criminology*. New York: Oxford University Press.

Bensing, Robert, Jr., and Oliver Schroeder. 1960. *Homicide in an Urban Community*. Springfield, Ill.: Charles C. Thomas.

Bergen, R. K. 1999. "Marital Rape." Accessed from *Applied Research Forum: National Electronic Network on Violence Against Women*: www.vaw.umn.edu/Vawnet/mrape.pdf.

———. 2008. Marital Rape/Wife Rape, "Marital Exemptions in Rape Statutes." In *Encyclopedia of Interpersonal Violence*, edited by Claire Renzetti and Jeffrey Edleson, 431–32. Thousand Oaks: Sage.

Blau, Judith R., and Peter M. Blau. 1982, February. "The Cost of Inequality: Metropolitan Structure and Violent Crime." *American Sociological Review* 47: 114–29.

Block, R. 1981. "Victim-Offender Dynamics in Violent Crime." *Journal of Criminal Law* 72: 743–61.

Bohannan, Paul. 1960. *African Homicide and Suicide*. Princeton, N.J.: Princeton University Press.

Bourgue, Linda Brookover. 1989. *Defining Rape*. Durham, N.C.: Duke University Press.

Box, Steven. 1983. *Power, Crime, and Mystification*. New York: Tavistock.

Brenner, Harvey. 1978. "Impact of Economic Indicators on Crime Indices." *Proceedings of the Hearings before the Subcommittee on Crime of the Committee on the Judiciary*, Washington, D.C.

Browne, Angela. 1987. *When Battered Women Kill*. New York: Macmillan.

Brownmiller, Susan. 1975. *Against Our Will*. New York: Simon and Schuster.

Bureau of Alcohol, Tobacco, and Firearms. 1991, May 22. "How Many Guns?" Press release.

Bureau of Justice Statistics. 2010. *Homicide Trends in the U.S.* Accessed February 18, 2011, from: bjs.ojp.usdoj.gov/content/homicide/homtrnd.cfm

————. 2011. *Victim Characteristics. National Crime Victimization Survey 2009*. Page last revised on January 4, 2011. Accessed March 10, 2011, from: bjs.ojp.usdoj.gov/index.cfm?ty=tp&tid=92

Centers for Disease Control and Prevention. 2010. *Leading Causes of Death in Males United States, 2006*. Page last modified on June 4, 2010. Accessed March 10, 2011, from: www.cdc.gov/men/lcod/2006/BlackMales2006.pdf.

Chagnon, Napoleon. 1968. *Yanomamo: The Fierce People*. New York: Holt, Rinehart and Winston.

Church, George. 1989, February 6. "The Other Arms Race." *Time*, 20.

Clark, L., and D. Lewis. 1977. *Rape: The Price of Coercive Sexuality*. Toronto: Women's Press.

Coleman, Diane H., and Murray A. Straus. 1986. "Marital Power, Conflict, and Violence in a Nationally Representative Sample of American Couples." *Violence and Victims* 1: 141–57.

Cooper, Alexia, and Erica L. Smith. 2011. "Homicide Trends in the United States, 1980–2008." Accessed June 19, 2012, from the Bureau of Justice Statistics: bjs.ojp.usdoj.gov/content/pub/pdf/htus8008.pdf.

Daly, Martin, and Margo Wilson. 1988. *Homicide*. New York: Aldine de Gruyter.

Davis, A. Y. 1979. "Rape, Racism and the Capitalist Setting." In *The Women Say, the Men Say*, edited by E. Shapiro and B. M. Shapiro. New York: Dell.

Dawson, John M., and Patrick A. Langan. 1994. *Murder in Families*. Washington, D.C.: U.S. Department of Justice.

DeKeseredy, W., M. Rogness, and M. Schwartz. 2004. "Separation/Divorce Sexual Assault: The Current State of Social Scientific Knowledge." *Aggression and Violent Behavior* 9: 675–91.

Dentan, Robert K. 1978. "Notes on Childhood in a Nonviolent Context: The Semai Case." In *Learning Non-Aggression*, edited by A. Montagu. New York: Oxford University Press.

Divale, William, and Marvin Harris. 1976. "Population, Warfare, and the Male Supremacist Complex." *American Anthropologist* 78: 521–38.

Donaldson, Stephen. 2004. "Hooking Up: Protective Pairing for Punks." In *Violence in War and Peace*, edited by Nancy Scheper-Hughes and Philippe Bourgois, 348–53. Malden: Blackwell Publishing.

Ellis, Lee. 1989. *Theories of Rape: Inquiries into the Causes of Sexual Aggression*. New York: Hemisphere Publishing.

Farley, Reynolds. 1980. "Homicide Trends in the United States." *Demography* 17: 177–88.

Federal Bureau of Investigation. 1988. *Crime in the United States*. Uniform Crime Reports. Washington, D.C.: Government Printing Office.

Fiala, R., and G. LaFree. 1988. "Cross-National Determinants of Child Homicide." *American Sociological Review* 53: 432–45.

Finkelhor, David, and Kersti Yllo. 1985. *License to Rape: Sexual Abuse of Wives*. New York: Free Press.

Fisher, Bonnie S., Francis T. Cullen, and Michael G. Turner. 2000. *The Sexual Victimization of College Women*. Washington, D.C.: National Institute of Justice and Bureau of Justice Statistics, U.S. Department of Justice. Accessed March 29, 2011 from: www.ncjrs.gov/pdffiles1/nij/182369.pdf Viewed March 29, 2011.

Foster, C. D., M. A. Siegel, D. R. Plesser, and N. R. Jacobs. 1987. *Gun Control*. Plano, Tex.: Information Aids Inc.

Fox, James Allen, and Jack Levine. 2001. *The Will to Kill: Making Sense of Senseless Murder*. Needham Heights: Allyn and Bacon.

Fox, James Allen, and Marianne W. Zawitz. 2001. *Homicide Trends in the United States*. Washington, D.C.: Bureau of Justice Statistics, U.S. Department of Justice. Accessed from: www.ojp.usdoj.gov/bjs/homicide/homtrnd.htm#contents.

Frieze, I. 1983. "Investigating the Causes and Consequences of Marital Rape." *Signs: Journal of Women in Culture and Society* 8: 532–53.

Gibson, Thomas. 1990. "Raiding, Trading, and Tribal Autonomy in Insular Southeast Asia." In *The Anthropology of War*, edited by J. Haas. Cambridge: Cambridge University Press.

Goldstein, Paul J. 1985. "The Drugs/Violence Nexus: A Tripartite Conceptual Framework." *Journal of Drug Issues*: 493–506.

————. 1997. "Crack and Homicide in New York City: A Case Study in the Epidemiology of Violence." In *Crack in America: Demon Drugs and Social Justice*, by Craig Reinarman and Harry G. Levine. Berkeley: University of California Press.

Greenberg, D. F. 1981. "Methodological Issues in Survey Research on the Inhibition of Crime." *Journal of Criminal Law and Criminology* 72: 1094–1108.

————. 1985. "Age, Crime, and Social Explanation." *American Journal of Sociology* 91: 1–21.

Greenberg, James B. 1989. *Blood Ties*. Tucson: University of Arizona Press.

Groth, A. Nicholas, and Jean Birnbaum. 1979. *Men Who Rape*. New York: Plenum.

Gurr, Ted. 1979. "On the History of Violent Crime in Europe and America." In *Criminology Review Yearbook*, edited by Egon Bittnerr and Sheldon I. Messinger, 411–32. Beverly Hills, Calif.: Sage.

———. 1990. "Historical Trends in Violent Crime: A Critical Review of the Evidence." In *Violence: Patterns, Causes, and Public Policy*, edited by Neil Alan Weiner, Margaret A. Zahn, and Rita J. Sagi; under the general editorship of Robert K. Merton. San Diego: Harcourt Brace Jovanovich

Hall, E. R., and P. J. Flannery. 1984. "Prevalence and Correlates of Sexual Assault Experiences in Adolescents." *Victimology: An International Journal* 9: 398–406.

Hawkins, D. F. 1983. "Black and White Homicide Differentials." *Criminal Justice Bulletin* 10: 407–40.

Hewitt, John D. 1988. "The Victim-Offender Relationship in Convicted Homicide Cases: 1960–1984." *Journal of Criminal Justice* 16: 25–33.

Hite, Shere. 1976. *The Hite Report on Female Sexuality*. New York: Knopf.

Hoebel, E. Adamson. 1964. *The Law of Primitive Man: A Study in Comparative Legal Dynamics*. Cambridge, Mass.: Harvard University Press.

Hoskin, Anthony W. 2001. "Armed Americans: The Impact of Firearm Availability on National Homicide Rates." *Justice Quarterly* 18, no. 3: 569

Inciardi, James A. 1981. *The Drugs-Crime Connection*. Beverly Hills: Sage.

Johnson, Kevin. 2012, January 6. "FBI Changes Definition of Rape to Include Men as Victims." *USA Today*.

Jones, E. D., III. 1981. "The District of Columbia's Firearms Control Regulations Act of 1975: The Toughest Handgun Control Law in the United States—Or Is It?" *Annals of the American Academy of Political and Social Sciences* 455: 138–49.

Kantor, Glenda Kaufman, and Murray A. Straus. 1987. "The 'Drunken Bum' Theory of Wife Beating." *Social Problems* 34: 214–30.

Knauft, Bruce M. 1987. "Reconsidering Violence in Simple Human Societies." *Current Anthropology* 28: 457–500.

Kokopeli, Bruce, and George Lakey. 1994. "More Power Than We Want." In *Race, Class, and Gender: An Anthology*, edited by Margaret L. Andersen and Patricia Hill Collins. New York: Wadsworth.

Koss, Mary P. 1989. "Hidden Rape: Sexual Aggression and Victimization in a National Sample of Students in Higher Education." In *Violence in Dating Relationships*, edited by M. A. Pirog-Good and F. E. Stets. New York: Praeger.

Koss, Mary P., and Sarah L. Cook. 1998. "Facing the Facts: Date and Acquaintance Rape Are Significant Problems for Women." In *Issues in Intimate Violence*, edited by Racquel Kennedy Bergen, 147–56. Thousand Oaks, Calif.: Sage.

Koss, Mary P., C. A. Gidycz, and N. Wisniewski. 1987. "The Scope of Rape: Incidence and Prevalence of Sexual Aggression and Victimization in a National Sample of Higher Education Students." *Journal of Consulting and Clinical Psychology* 55: 162–70.

Krahn, Harvey, Timothy F. Hartnagel, and John W. Gartrell. 1986. "Income Inequality and Homicide Rates: Cross-National Data and Criminological Theories." *Criminology* 24: 269–95.

Krug, E. G., K. E. Powell, and L. L. Dahlberg. 1998. "Firearm-Related Deaths in the United States and 35 Other High- and Upper-Middle-Income Countries." *International Journal of Epidemiology* 27: 214–21.

Kuper, Hilda. 1963. *The Swazi*, edited by George and Louise Spindler. New York: Holt, Rinehart and Winston.

Kupers, Terry A. "Rape and the Prison Code." In *Prison Masculinities*, edited by Don Sabo, Terry A. Kupers and Willie London, 113. Philadelphia: Temple University Press, 2001.

Kutchinkski, B. 1988, June 16. "Pornography and Sexual Violence: The Criminological Evidence from Aggregated Data in Several Countries." Paper presented at the 14th International Congress on Law and Mental Health in Montreal, Canada.

LaFree, G. D., and E. L. Kick. 1986. "Cross-National Effects of Developmental, Distributional, and Demographic Variables on Crime: A Review and Analysis." *International Annals of Criminology* 24: 213–35.

Lee, Matthew R. 2000. "Concentrated Poverty, Race, and Homicide." *The Sociological Quarterly*: 189–206.

Lee, Richard B. 1979. *The !Kung San: Men, Women and Work in a Foraging Society*. New York: Cambridge University Press.

———. 1984. *The Dobe !Kung*. Chicago: Holt, Rinehart, and Winston.

Levine, Robert A. 1977. "Gusii Sex Offenses: A Study in Social Control." In *Forcible Rape: The Crime, the Victim, and the Offender*, edited by Duncan Chappell, Robley Geis, and Gilbert Geis, 189–226. New York: Columbia University Press.

Loftin, Colin, and Robert H. Hill. 1974. "Regional Subculture and Homicide." *American Sociological Review* 39: 714–24.

Loftin, Colin, D. McDowall, B. Wierseman, and T. J. Cottey. 1991, December 5. "Effects of Restrictive Licensing of Handguns on Homicide and Suicide in the District of Columbia." *New England Journal of Medicine* 325: 1615–20.

Loftin, Colin, and Robert Nash Parker. 1985. "The Effect of Poverty on Urban Homicide Rates: An Error in Variable Mode." *Criminology* 23: 269–87.

Luckenbill, D. F. 1977. "Criminal Homicide as a Situated Transaction." *Social Problems* 26: 176–86.

Maguire, Kathleen, Ann L. Pastore, and Timothy J. Flanagan. 1993. *Bureau of Justice Statistics Sourcebook of Criminal Justice Statistics—1992*. Washington, D.C.: U. S. Department of Justice.

Malamuth, N. M., and J. V. P. Check. 1985. "The Effects of Aggressive Pornography on Beliefs in Rape Myths: Individual Differences." *Journal of Research in Personality* 19: 299–320.

McCoid, Catherine Hodge. 1989. *Dowry Deaths in India: A Materialist Analysis*. Working papers, Women in International Development, Michigan State University.

McDermott, Joan M. 1979. *Rape Victimization in 26 American Cities*. Washington, D.C.: U.S. Department of Justice.

Messerschmidt, James W. 1986. *Capitalism, Patriarchy, and Crime*. Totowa, N.J.: Rowman & Littlefield.

Messner, Steven. 1989. "Economic Discrimination and Societal Homicide Rates: Further Evidence on the Cost of Inequality." *American Sociological Review* 54:597–611.

Messner, Steven F., Glenn Deane, and Mark Beaulieu. 2002. "A Log-Multiplicative Association Model for Allocating Homicides with Unknown Victim-Offender Relationships." *Criminology* 40: 457–79.

Messner, Steven, and Richard Rosenfeld. 1994. *Crime and the American Dream*. Belmont, Calif.: Wadsworth.

———. 1997. "Political Restraint of the Market and Levels of Criminal Homicide: A Cross-National Application of Institutional-Anomie Theory." *Social Forces* 75: 1393–1416.

Messner, Steven, and Kenneth Tardiff. 1986. "Economic Inequality and Levels of Homicide: An Analysis of Urban Neighborhoods." *Criminology* 88: 997–1007.

Mishel, Lawrence, Jared Bernstein, and John Schmitt. 2001. *The State of Working America*. Ithaca: Cornell University Press.

National Center for Injury Prevention and Control, Centers for Disease Control and Prevention (producer). 2010, June 14. Accessed March 8, 2011 from: www.cdc.gov/injury.

Neapolitan, J. L. 1994. "Cross-National Variation in Crime Rates: The Case of Latin America." *International Criminal Justice Review* 4: 4–22.

Neier, Aryeh. 1992, November 9. "Watching Rights." *The Nation*, 533.

Ousey, Graham C. 2000. "Explaining Regional and Urban Variation in Crime: A Review of Research." In *Criminal Justice 2000, Volume 1, The Nature of Crime: Continuity and Change*, by Gary LaFree. Washington, D.C.: National Institute of Justice, U.S. Department of Justice.

Ousey, Graham C., and Matthew R Lee. 2002. "Examining the Conditional Nature of the Illicit Drug Market-Homicide Relationship: A Partial Test of the Theory of Contingent Causation." *Criminology* 40, no. 1: 73–102.

Palmer, Craig. 1989. "Is Rape a Cultural Universal? A Re-examination of the Ethnographic Data." *Ethnology* 28: 1–16.

Parker, Robert Nash. 1989. "Poverty, Subculture of Violence, and Types of Homicide." *Social Forces* 67: 983–1005.

Perry, Steven W. 2004. *A BJS Statistical Profile, 1992–2002: American Indians and Crime*. Accessed April 6, 2011, from the U.S. Department of Justice: www.justice.gov/otj/pdf/american_indians_and_crime.pdf.

Peterson, Ruth D., and William C. Bailey. 1992. "Rape and Dimensions of Gender Socioeconomic Inequality in U.S. Metropolitan Areas." *Journal of Research in Crime and Delinquency* 29: 162–77.

Petras, James, and Christian Davenport. 1991. "Crime and the Transformation of Capitalism." *Crime, Law and Social Change* 16: 155–75.

Pokorny, A. D. 1965. "A Comparison of Homicides in Two Cities." *Journal of Criminal Law* 56: 479–87.

Polk, Kenneth, and David Ranson. 1991. "Homicide in Victoria." In *Australian Violence: Contemporary Perspectives*, edited by D. Chappell, P. Grabosky, and H. Strang. Canberra: Australian Institute of Criminology.

Porter, Roy. 1986. "Rape—Does It Have a Historical Meaning?" In *Rape*, edited by S. Tomaselli and R. Porter. New York: Basil Blackwell.

Rasmussen, Knud. 1932. *Intellectual Culture of the Copper Eskimo*. Gyldendalske, Boghandel: Nordisk Forlag.

Reiss, A. 1986. "Why Are Communities Important in Understanding Crime?" In *Communities and Crime*, edited by A. Reiss and M. Tonry. Chicago: University of Chicago Press.

Reiss, Albert J., and Jefferey A. Roth. 1993. *Understanding and Preventing Violence*. Washington, D.C.: National Academy Press.

Rennison, Callie Marie. 2001. *Criminal Victimization 2000 Changes 1999–2000 with Trends 1993–2000*. Washington, D.C.: U.S. Department of Justice Office of Justice Programs, Bureau of Justice Statistics.

Riedel, Marc. 1987. "Stranger Violence: Perspectives, Issues, and Problems." *Journal of Criminal Law and Criminology* 78: 223–58.

Riedel, Marc, and M. A. Zahn. 1985. *The Nature and Pattern of American Homicide*. Washington, D.C.: Government Printing Office.

Riger, S., and M. Gordon. 1981. "The Fear of Rape: A Study in Social Control." *Journal of Social Issues* 37: 4.

Robinson, Lillian S. 1993, November 1. "Touring Thailand's Sex Industry." *The Nation*, 492–97.

Russell, D. E. H. 1982, 1990. *Rape in Marriage*. New York: Macmillan.

———. 1984. *Sexual Exploitation: Rape, Child Sexual Abuse, and Workplace Harassment*. Beverly Hills, Calif.: Sage.

Rutherford, J., and R. Chapman. 1988. *Male Order: Unwrapping Masculinity*. London: Lawrence and Wishart.

Saad, Lydia. 2011. *Self-Reported Gun Ownership in U.S. Is Highest Since 1993*. Accessed June 18, 2011, from: www.gallup.com/poll/150353/self-reported-gun-ownership-highest-1993.

Sanday, P. 1981. "The Socio-Cultural Context of Rape: A Cross-Cultural Study." *Journal of Social Issues* 37: 5–27.

Scacco, Anthony M. 1982. *Male Rape: A Casebook of Sexual Aggressions*. New York: AMS Press.

Schwendinger, Julia R., and Herman Schwendinger. 1983. *Rape and Inequality*. Beverly Hills, Calif.: Sage.

Scully, Diana, and Joseph Marolla. 1985. "'Riding the Bull at Gilleys': Convicted Rapists Describe the Rewards of Rape." *Social Problems* 32: 251–63.

Sherman, L. W. 2000. "Gun Carrying and Homicide Prevention." *JAMA* 283:1193–1195.

Shields, W. M., and L. M. Shields. 1983. "Forcible Rape: An Evolutionary Perspective." *Ethnology and Sociobiology* 4: 115–36.

Silberman, Charles E. 1978. *Criminal Violence, Criminal Justice*. New York: Random House.

Sloan, John Henry, Arthur L. Kellerman, and Donald T. Reay. 1988. "Handgun Regulations, Crime, Assaults, and Homicides." *New England Journal of Medicine* 319: 1256–62.

Smith, M. Dwayne, and Nathan Bennett. 1985. "Poverty, Inequality, and Theories of Forcible Rape." *Crime and Delinquency* 31: 295–305.

Snyder, Howard N. 2011, September. *Patterns & Trends—Arrest in the United States, 1980–2009*. Accessed June 19, 2012, from: www.bjs.gov/content/pub/pdf/aus8009.pdf.

Sorenson, S. B., J. A. Stein, J. M. Siegel, J. M. Golding, and M. A. Burnam. 1987. "The Prevalence of Adult Sexual Assault: The Los Angeles Epidemiologic Catchment Area Project." *American Journal of Epidemiology* 126: 1154–64.

Straus, Murray A., Richard J. Gelles, and Suzanne K. Steinmetz. 1980. *Behind Closed Doors: Violence in the American Family*. New York: Doubleday/Anchor.

Sunday, S. R., and E. Tobach. 1985. *Violence against Women: A Critique of the Sociobiology of Rape*. New York: Gordian Press.

Sweet, Ellen. 1985, October. "Date Rape: The Story of an Epidemic and Those Who Deny It." *Ms. Magazine*.

Swigert, Victoria Lynn, and Ronald A. Farrell. 1976. *Murder, Inequality, and the Law*. Lexington, Mass.: Heath.

Taylor, William B. 1979. *Drinking, Homicide, and Rebellion in Colonial Mexican Villages*. Stanford, Calif.: Stanford University Press.

Thomas, Elizabeth Marshall. 1959. *The Harmless People*. New York: Knopf.

Thornhill, Randy, and Nancy Wilmsen Thornhill. 1987. "Human Rape: The Strengths of the Evolutionary Perspective." In *Sociobiology and Psychology: Ideas, Issues, and Applications*, edited by C. Crawford, M. Smith, and D. Krebs, 269–91. Hillsdale, N.J.: Lawrence Erlbaum Associates.

Tjaden, Patricia, and Nancy Thoennes. 2000. *Extent, Nature, and Consequences of Intimate Partner Violence*. Accessed March 22, 2002, from the U.S. Department of Justice: www.ncjrs.gov/pdffiles1/nij/181867.pdf.

Toufexis, Anastasia. 1989, June 12. "Our Violent Kids." *Time*, 52.

Truman, Jennifer L., and Michael R. Rand. 2010. *Criminal Victimization 2009*. Accessed April 6, 2011, from Bureau of Justice Statistics, U.S. Department of Justice: bjs.ojp.usdoj.gov/content/pub/pdf/cv09.pdf.

Turnbull, Colin M. 1961. *The Forest People*. Garden City, N.J.: Natural History Press.

UNICEF. 2000. "Domestic Violence against Women and Girls." *Innocenti Digests* 6. Florence: UNICEF Innocenti Research Centre. Accessed from: www.unicef.org/lac/ingles/urgente/deten5.htm.

U.S. Census Bureau. 2009 . *American Community Survey*. Accessed March 1, 2011, from: factfinder.census.gov/servlet/STTable?_bm=y&-geo_id=01000US&-qr_name=ACS_2009_1YR_G00_S0101&-ds_name=ACS_2009_1YR_G00_&-_lang=en&-redoLog=false&-state=st&-CONTEXT=st.

———. 2011a. *The 2011 Statistical Abstract*. Page last modified: January 20, 2011. Accessed March 7, 2011, from: www.census.gov/compendia/statab/2011/tables/11s0308.pdf.

———. 2011b. *Statistical Abstract of the United States*. Law Enforcement, Courts, and Prisons Table 308. Homicide Trends: 1980 to 2007. Accessed from www.census.gov/compendia/statab/2011/tables/11s0309.pdf.

U.S. Congressional Budget Office. 2011, October. *Trends in the Distribution of Household Income Between 1979 and 2007*. Washington, D.C.: Congressional Budget Office.

U.S. Department of Justice. 2001, June 13. "Rape Rates Declined Slightly between 1999 and 2000." Accessed from the Bureau of Justice Statistics: www.ojp.usdoj.gov/bjs/glance/rape.htm.

———. 2005. *Statutory Rape Known to Law Enforcement*. Accessed April 1, 2011, from: www.ncjrs.gov/pdffiles1/ojjdp/208803.pdf.

———. Federal Bureau of Investigation. 2010, September. Crime in the United States, 2009. Accessed February 17, 2011, from: www.fbi.gov/ucr/09cius.htm.

Vieraitis, L. M., and M. R. Williams. 2002. Assessing the Impact of Gender Inequality on Female Homicide Victimization across U.S. Cities: A Racially Disaggregated Analysis. *Violence against Women*, 8: 35–63.

Villaveces A., P. Cummings, V. E. Espitia, T. D. Koepsell, B. McKnight, and A. L. Kellermann. 2000. "Effect of a Ban on Carrying Firearms on Homicide Rates in 2 Colombian Cities." *Journal of the American Medical Association* 283: 1205-09

Vogelman, Lloyd. 1989. *The Sexual Face of Violence*. Johannesburg, South Africa: Ravan Press.

Winslow, Robert W., and Sheldon X. Zhang. 2008. *Criminology A Global Perspective*. Upper Saddle River, N.J.: Pearson Education Inc.

Wolff, E. N. 2010. *Recent Trends in Household Wealth in the United States: Rising Debt and the Middle-Class Squeeze—an Update to 2007*. Annandale-on-Hudson: Levy Economics Institute of Bard College.

Wolfgang, Marvin. 1958. *Patterns in Criminal Homicide*. Philadelphia: University of Pennsylvania Press.

Woodburn, James C. 1979. "Minimal Politics: The Political Organization of the Hadza of North Tanzania." In *Politics in Leadership: A Comparative Perspective*, edited by W. A. Shack and P. S. Cohen, 244–66. Oxford: Clarendon Press.

Woodbury, Richard. 1991, October 28. "Ten Minutes in Hell." *Time*, 31.

Wright, J. D., and P. H. Rossi. 1985. *The Armed Criminal in America: A Survey of Incarcerated Felons*. Washington, D.C.: National Institute of Justice.

Zahn, Margaret A., and Philip C. Sagi. 1987. "Stranger Homicides in Nine American Cites." *Journal of Criminal Law and Criminology* 78: 377–97.

Zawitz, Marianne, and Kevin J. Strom. 2000. *Firearm Injury and Death from Crime, 1993–1997*. NCJ 182993. Washington, D.C.: U.S. Department of Justice.

Zimring, F. E., and Gordon Hawkins. 1997. *Crime Is Not the Problem: Lethal Violence in America*. Oxford: Oxford University Press.

Zimring, F. E., S. K. Mukhergee, and B. Van Winkle. 1983. "Intimate Violence: A Study of Intersexual Homicide in Chicago." *University of Chicago Law Review* 50: 910–30.

CHAPTER 4

Abraham, Margaret. 1992. "Marital Violence among South Asians in the United States." Unpublished paper presented at the annual meeting of the American Sociological Association, Pittsburgh.

Adams, Carol J., and Josephine Donovan, 1996. *Beyond Animal Rights: A Feminist Caring Ethic for the Treatment of Animals*. New York: Continuum.

Ahmad, Mahnaz, and Mark S. Lachs, 2002. "Elder Abuse." *Cleveland Clinic Journal of Medicine* 69, no. 1: 801–8.

Archer, J. 2000. "Sex Differences in Aggression between Heterosexual Partners: A Meta-Analytic Review." *Psychological Bulletin* 126, no. 5: 651–80.

Ascione, Frank R. 1998. "Battered Women's Reports of Their Partners and Their Children's Cruelty to Animals." *Journal of Emotional Abuse* 1: 19–33.

Ascione, Frank. R., Claudia V. Weber, and David S. Ward. 1997. "The Abuse of Animals and Domestic Violence: A National Survey of Shelters for Women Who Are Battered." *Society and Animals* 5, no. 3: 205–18.

Attorney General. 1984. *Attorney General's Task Force on Family Violence.* Washington, D.C.: Government Printing Office

Bakan, David. 1971. *Slaughter of the Innocents: A Study of the Battered Child Phenomenon.* Boston: Beacon Press.

Baker, A. A. 1975. "Granny Battering." *Modern Geriatrics* 8: 20–24.

Beckman, Risa S., and Ronald D. Adelman. 1992. "Elder Abuse and Neglect." In *Assessment of Family Violence: A Clinical and Legal Sourcebook*, edited by Robert T. Ammerman and Michael Hersen, 236–52. New York: John Wiley.

Bennett, J. G. 1992. "Elder Abuse in Britain." *British Medical Journal* 305: 1998–99.

Berk, Richard A., Sarah Fenstermaker Berk, Donileen R. Loseke, and David Rauma. 1983. "Mutual Combat and Other Family Violence Myths." In *The Dark Side of Families*, edited by David Finkelhor, Richard J. Gelles, Gerald T. Hotaling, and Murray A. Straus, 197–212. Newbury Park, Calif.: Sage.

Besharov, Douglas J. 1988, August 4. "The Child Abuse Numbers Game." *Wall Street Journal.*

Best, Joel. 1990. *Threatened Children: Rhetoric and Concern about Child-Victims.* Chicago: University of Chicago Press.

Boswell, John. 1989. *The Kindness of Strangers.* New York: Random House.

Boyank, Payne, and Bruce L. Berg, 2003. "Perceptions about the Criminalization of Elder Abuse among Police Chiefs and Ombudsmen." *Criminal Delinquency* 49, no. 3: 439–59.

Bureau of Justice Statistics, Office of Domestic Programs. 2006. *Intimate Partner Violence in the U.S., 1993–2004.* Washington, D.C.: Department of Justice.

Burgess, Robert L., and James Garbarino. 1983. "Doing What Comes Naturally?" In *The Dark Side of Families*, edited by David Finkelhor, Richard J. Gelles, Gerald T. Hotaling, and Murray A. Straus, 88–100. Newbury Park, Calif.: Sage.

Butler, Kathy, 2006, February 28. "Beyond Rivalry, A Hidden World of Sibling Violence." *New York Times.*

Caffaro, John, and Allison Conn-Caffaro. 1998. *Sibling Abuse Trauma: Assessment and Intervention Strategies for Children, Families, and Adults.* New York: Routledge.

Cappell, Charles, and Robert Heiner. 1990. "The Intergenerational Transmission of Family Aggression." *Journal of Family Violence* 5, no. 2: 135–52.

Cardarelli, Albert P. 1997. "Violence and Intimacy: An Overview." In *Violence between Intimate Partners*, edited by Albert P. Cardarelli, 1–9. Needham Heights, Mass.: Allyn & Bacon.

Cazenave, Noel A., and Murray A. Straus. 1991. "Race, Class, Network Embeddedness and Family Violence: A Search for Potent Support Systems." In *Physical Violence in American Families*, edited by Murray A. Straus and Richard J. Gelles, 321–39. New Brunswick, N.J.: Transaction Books.

Chen, Andrew L., and Kenneth J. Koval. 2002, January–February. "Elder Abuse: The Role of the Orthopaedic Surgeon in Diagnosis and Management." *Journal of the American Academy of Orthopaedic Surgeons* 6, no. 1: 25–31.

Children's Bureau. 2011. *Child Maltreatment 2010.* U.S. Department of Health and Human Services, Administration for Children and Families, Administration on Children, Youth and Families. Washington, D.C.: United States Government.

Coleman, Diane H., and Murray A. Straus. 1991. "Marital Power, Conflict, and Violence in a Nationally Representative Sample of American Couples." *In Physical Violence in American Families*, edited by Murray A. Straus and Richard J. Gelles, 287–304. New Brunswick, N.J.: Transaction Books.

Collins, Randall. 1971. "A Conflict Theory of Sexual Stratification." *Social Problems* 19: 3–20.

Connell, R. W. 1987. *Gender and Power.* Stanford, Calif.: Stanford University Press.

Cooper, Caludia, Amber Selwood, and G. H. Livingstone. 2008. "The Prevalence of Elder Abuse and Neglect: A Systematic Review." *Age and Aging* 37, no. 2: 151–60.

Daly, Mary. 1978. *Gyn/Ecology: The Metaethics of Radical Feminism.* Boston: Beacon Press.

Diallo, Y., F. Hagemann, A. Etienne, Y. Gurbuzer, and F. Mehran. 2010. *Global Child Labour Developments: Measuring Trends from 2004 to 2008.* Geneva: International Labour Organization, International Programme on the Elimination of Child Labour (IPEC).

Dobash, Russell P., E. Emerson Dobash, M. Wilson, and M. Daly, 1992. "The Myth of Sexual Symmetry in Marital Violence." *Social Problems* 39: 71–91.

Dutton, A. 1988. *The Domestic Assault of Women: Psychological and Criminal Justice Perspectives.* New York: Allyn and Bacon.

Faver, L. A., and E. B. Strand. 2003. "Leave or Stay? Battered Women's Concern for Vulnerable Pets." *Journal of Interpersonal Violence* 18: 1367–77.

Felson, R., and M. Outlaw. 2007. "The Control Motive and Marital Violence." *Violence and Victims* 22, no. 4: 387–407.

Finkelhor, David. 1995, April. "The Victimization of Children: A Developmental Perspective." *American Journal of Orthopsychiatry* 65, no. 2: 177–93.

Finkelhor, David, Gerald T. Hotaling, and Murray A. Straus. 1991. "Physical Violence in American Families: Incidence Rates, Causes, and Trends." In *Abused and Battered*, edited by Dean D. Knudsen and J. Miller, 17–34. New York: Aldine de Gruyter.

Fox, James A. and Marianne W. Zawitz. 2007. *Homicide Trends in the U.S.* Washington, DC: U.S. Department of Justice, Bureau of Justice Statistics. Accessed September 12, 2012, from: http://bjs.ojp.usdoj.gov/content/homicide/homtrnd.cfm.

Gardner, Richard A. 1991. *Sex Abuse Hysteria: Salem Witch Trials Revisited.* Cresskill: Creative Therapeutics.

Gil, David. 1970. *Violence against Children.* Cambridge: Harvard University Press.

———. 1975. "Child Abuse: Levels of Manifestation, Causal Dimensions, and Primary Prevention." *Victimology: An International Journal* 2: 186–94.

Gillespie, Cynthia. 1981. *Justifiable Homicide: Battered Women, Self-Defense, and the Law.* Columbus: Ohio State University Press.

Gondolf, Edward W. 1988. "The State of the Debate: Review Essay on Woman Battering." *Response* 11: 3–8.

Goodwin, Megan P., and Bruce Roscoe, 1990. "Sibling Violence and Agonistic Interactions among Middle Adolescents." *Adolescence* 25, no. 98: 451–67.

Grant, James. 1994, February 3. *The State of the World's Children.* Oxford: Oxford University Press.

Herzberger, Sharon. 1983. "Social Cognition and the Transmission of Abuse." In *The Dark Side of Families*, edited by David Finkelhor, Richard J. Gelles, Gerald T. Hotaling, and Murray A. Straus, 317–29. Beverly Hills, Calif.: Sage.

Herzberger, Sharon D., and Noreen L. Channels. 1991. "Criminal Justice Processing of Violent and Nonviolent Offenders: The Effects of Familial Relationship to the Victim." In *Abused and Battered*, edited by Dean. D. Knudsen and J. L. Miller, 63–78. New York: Aldine de Gruyter.

Island, David, and Patrick Letellier. 1991. *Men Who Beat the Men Who Love Them: Battered Gay Men and Domestic Violence.* New York: Harrington Park Press.

Jaffe, Peter G., Marlies Sudermann, and Deborah Reitzel. 1992. "Child Witnesses of Marital Violence." In *Assessment of Family Violence*, edited by Robert T. Ammerman and Michael Hersen, 313–31. New York: John Wiley and Sons.

Kalmuss, Ebra S., and Murray A. Straus. 1991. "Wife's Marital Dependency and Wife Abuse." In *Physical Violence in American Families*, edited by Murray A. Straus and Richard J. Gelles, 369–82. New Brunswick, N.J.: Transaction Publishers.

Kaplan, Meg S., and Judith V. Becker. 1992. "Adolescent Perpetrators of Incest." In *A Clinical and Legal Sourcebook*, edited by Robert T. Ammerman and Michael Hersen, 332–47. New York: John Wiley.

Katy. 2009. "Sibling Sexual Abuse and Incest during Childhood." Accessed from: www.pandys.org/articles/siblingsexualabuse.html.

Knudsen, Dean D. 1992. *Child Maltreatment: Emerging Perspectives.* Dix Hills: General Hall.

Kohn, Melvin L. 1969. *Class and Conformity: A Study in Values.* Homewood, Ill.: Dorsey Press.

Kruger, Robert, and Marcella Pascuahy. 1997. "Elder Abuse and Neglect." *Southern Medical Journal* 90, no. 1: 107–18.

Kumari, Ranjana. 1989. *Brides Are Not for Burning: Dowry Victims in India.* New Delhi, India: Radiant Publishers.

Lachs, Mark S., Christina Williams, Shelley O'Brien, Leslie Hurst, and Ralph Horowitz. 1997. "Risk Factors for Reported Elder Abuse and Neglect: A Nine-Year Observational Cohort Study." *The Gerontologist* 37, no. 4: 469–74.

Lehman, Christine. 2002, October 20. "Elder Abuse." *Psychiatric News* 37: 5.

Little, Craig B. 1995. *Deviance and Control.* 3rd ed. Itasca, Ill.: F. E. Peacock Publishers.

Loring, M. T., and T. A. Bolden-Hines. 2004. "Pet Abuse as a Means of Coercing Battered Women into Committing Illegal Behavior." *Journal of Emotional Abuse* 4: 23–37.

McLeod, M. 1984. "Women against Men: An Examination of Domestic Violence Based on an Analysis of Official Data and National Victimization Data." *Justice Quarterly* 1: 171–93.

McNeely, R. L., and Gloria Robinson-Simpson. 1987, November–December. "The Truth about Domestic Violence: A Falsely Framed Issue." *Social Work*: 485–90.

McNulty, Faith, 1980. *The Burning Bed.* New York: Harcourt Brace Jovanovich.

Miller, Susan L., and Charles F. Wellford. 1997. "Patterns and Correlates of Interpersonal Violence." In *Violence between Intimate Partners*, edited by Albert P. Cardarelli, 16–28. Needham Heights, Mass.: Allen & Bacon.

Mooney, J. 2001. *Gender, Violence, and the Social Order.* New York: St. Martin's Press.

Moore, Angela M. 1997. "Intimate Violence: Does Socioeconomic Status Matter?" In *Violence between Intimate Partners*, edited by Albert P. Cardarelli, 90–100. Needham Heights, Mass.: Allen & Bacon.

Morrow, Betty Hearn. 1992. "Afro-Caribbean Women and Domestic Violence." Unpublished paper presented at the annual meeting of the American Sociological Association, Pittsburgh.

Neal, Andrea. 1992, June 20. "My Generation." *Indianapolis Star*.

Olson, Elizabeth. 2011, March 3. "When Abuse of Older Patients Is Financial." *New York Times*.

Phillips, Roderick. 1988. *Putting Asunder: A History of Divorce in Western Society*. New York: Cambridge University Press.

Pillemer, Karl A., and Rosalie S. Wolf, eds. 1986. *Elder Abuse: Conflict in the Family*. Westport, Conn.: Greenwood.

Pride, Mary. 1986. *The Child Abuse Industry*. Westchester, Ill.: Crossway Books.

Radbill, S. X. 1974. "A History of Child Abuse and Infanticide." In *The Battered Child*, edited by Ray E. Helfer and C. Henry Kempe, 3–24. Chicago: University of Chicago Press.

Rao, Neeraja. 1992. "Dowry Deaths in India." Unpublished paper presented at the annual meeting of the North Central Sociological Association, Fort Wayne, Ind.

Renzetti, Claire M. 1992. *Violent Betrayal: Partner Abuse in Lesbian Relationships*. Newbury Park, Calif.: Sage.

———. 1997. "Violence and Abuse among Same-Sex Couples." In *Violence between Intimate Partners*, edited by Albert P. Cardarelli, 70–89. Needham Heights, MA: Allyn & Bacon.

Richardson, James T., Joel Best, and David G. Bromley. 1991. *The Satanism Scare*. New York: Aldine de Gruyter.

Schechter, Susan. 1982. *Women and Male Violence*. Boston: South End Press.

Schlegel, Alice. 1977. "Toward A Theory of Social Stratification." In *Sexual Stratification: A Cross-Cultural View*, edited by A. Schlegel, 1–40. New York: Columbia University Press.

Schwartz, M., S. G. O'Leary, and K. J. Kendziora. 1997. "Dating Aggression among High School Students." *Violence and Victims* 12, no. 4: 295–305.

Shupe, Anson. 1991. *The Darker Side of Virtue*. Buffalo, N.Y.: Prometheus Books.

Shupe, Anson, William A. Stacey, and Lonnie R. Hazlewood. 1987. *Violent Men, Violent Couples: The Dynamics of Domestic Violence*. Lexington, Mass.: Lexington Books.

Silverman, Jay G., Anita Raj, Lorelei A. Mucci, and Jeanne E. Hathaway. 2001. "Dating Violence against Adolescent Girls and Associated Substance Abuse, Unhealthy Weight Control, Sexual Risk Behavior, Pregnancy, and Suicidality." *Journal of the American Medical Association* 286, no. 5: 572–79.

Sorenson, S., and L. Taylor. 2005. "Female Aggression toward Male Intimate Partners: An Examination of Social Norms in a Community-Based Sample." *Psychology of Women Quarterly* 29: 78–96.

Stacey, William A., Lonnie R. Hazlewood, and Anson Shupe. 1994. *The Violent Couple*. Westport, Conn.: Praeger Publishers.

Stacey, William A., and Anson Shupe. 1983. *The Family Secret: Domestic Violence in America*. Boston: Beacon Press.

Steinmetz, Suzanne K. 1977. "The Battered Husband Syndrome." *Victimology: An International Journal* 2: 499–509.

Stets, Jane E., and Murray A. Straus. 1991. "Gender Differences in Reporting Marital Violence and Its Medical and Psychological Consequences." In *Physical Violence in American Families*, edited by Murray A. Straus and Richard J. Gelles, 151–65. New Brunswick, N.J.: Transaction Books.

Straus, Murray A. 1983. "Ordinary Violence, Child Abuse, and Wife-Beating: What Do They Have in Common?" In *The Dark Side of Families*, edited by David Finkelhor, Richard J. Gelles, Gerald T. Hotaling, and Murray A. Straus. Beverly Hills, Calif.: Sage.

Straus, Murray A., and Richard J. Gelles. 1991a. "Societal Change and Change in Family Violence from 1975 to 1985 as Revealed by Two National Surveys." In *Physical Violence in American Families*, edited by Murray A. Straus and Richard J. Gelles, 113–31. New Brunswick, N.J.: Transaction Books.

———. 1991b. "How Violent Are American Families? Estimates from the National Family Violence Resurvey and Other Studies." In *Physical Violence in American Families*, edited by Murray A. Straus and Richard J. Gelles, 95–112. New Brunswick, N.J.: Transaction Books.

———, eds. 1991c. *Physical Violence in American Families*. New Brunswick, N.J.: Transaction Books.

Straus, Murray A., Richard J. Gelles, and Suzanne K. Steinmetz. 1980. *Behind Closed Doors: Violence in the American Family*. New York: Doubleday/Anchor.

Straus, Murray A., and Christine Smith. 1991a. "Family Patterns and Child Abuse." In *Physical Violence in American Families*, edited by Murray A. Straus and Richard J. Gelles, 245–61. New Brunswick, N.J.: Transaction Books.

———. 1991b. "Violence in Hispanic Families in the United States: Incidence Rates and Structural Interpretations." In *Physical Violence in American Families*, edited by Murray A. Straus and Richard J. Gelles, 341–67. New Brunswick, N.J.: Transaction Books.

Taves, Ann. 1989. *Religion and Domestic Violence: The Memoirs of Abigail Abbot Bailey*. Bloomington: Indiana University Press.

Tiger, Lionel. 1970. *Men in Groups*. New York: Vintage Books.

Tower, Cynthia Crossan. 1989. *Understanding Child Abuse and Neglect*. Boston: Allyn and Bacon.

U.S. Commission on Civil Rights. 1982. *Under the Rule of Thumb: Battered Women and the Administration of Justice*. Washington, D.C.: U.S. Commission on Civil Rights.

U.S. Department of Health and Human Services. 1988. *Study of National Incidence and Prevalence of Child Abuse and Neglect: 1988*. Washington, D.C.: Government Printing Office.

Walker, Lenore. 1979. *The Battered Woman*. New York: Harper and Row.

Whipple, E., and S. Finton. 1995. "Psychological Maltreatment by Siblings: An Unrecognized Form of Abuse." *Child and Adolescent Social Work Journal* 12, no. 2: 135–40.

Wiehe, Vernon R. 1997. *Sibling Abuse: Hidden Physical, Emotional, and Sexual Trauma*. Thousand Oaks, Calif.: Sage.

Wilson, Paul, and Gareth Norris. 2003. "Relationship between Criminal Behavior and Mental Illness in Young Adults: Conduct Disorder, Cruelty to Animals, and Young Adult Serious Violence." *Psychiatry, Psychology, and the Law* 10, no. 12: 239–43.

Yllo, Kersti A., and Murray A. Straus. 1991. "Patriarchy and Violence against Wives: The Impact of Structural and Normative Factors." In *Physical Violence in American Families*, edited by Murray A. Straus and Richard J. Gelles, 383–99. New Brunswick, N.J.: Transaction Books.

CHAPTER 5

Adams, D. W. 1995. *Education for Extinction: American Indians and the Boarding School Experience, 1875–1928*. Lawrence: University of Kansas Press.

Assembly of First Nations. 1994. *Breaking the Silence*. Ottawa, Ontario: First Nation Health Commission.

Associated Press. 1996, December 16. "Mom Takes Payoff from Principal Who Raped Son, 12."

———. 1998a, February 7. "Ex-teacher Back in Prison after Seeing Underage Love."

———. 1998b, March 15. "Teacher Jailed."

———. 2010, July 12. "9 Killed in Latest Attack at China School."

Baglo, Ferdy. 2002, July 9. "Canadian Churches Seek to Resolve Abuse Cases." *Christianity Today*, 21.

Barbassa, Juliana. 2011, April 18. "11 Children Shot, Die in Brazil." Associated Press.

Bauder, David. 2011, March 29. "Network Targets Bullying." Associated News.

Bender, A., T. Shubert, and P. McLaughlin. 2001. "Invisible Kids: Preventing School Violence by Identifying Kids in Trouble." *Intervention in School and Clinic* 37, no. 2: 105–11.

Bishop, John H., Matthew Bishop, Michael Bishop, Lena Gelbwasser, Shanna Green, Eric Peterson, Anna Rubinsztaj, and Andrew Zuckerman. 2004. "Why We Harass Nerds and Freaks: A Formal Theory of Student Culture and Norms." *Journal of School Health*, 235–51.

Bourdieu, P., and J.-C. Passeron. 1977. *Reproduction in Education, Society and Culture*. London: Sage Publications.

Brooks, Kara. 2010, September 14. "Teen's Suicide Prompts Call for Tougher Anti-Bullying Laws." Fox59.com.news.

Brown, DeNeen L. 2000, April 19. "In Canada, a Tougher Stand on Clergy Sex Abuse." *Washington Post*.

Bruce, Mary. 2009, July 8. "Congress Urged to Take Action against Bullying in Schools." ABC News.

———. 2011, October. "The Sins of the Fathers." *Washington Post*.

Campbell, Oliver. 2010. "China: School Attacks Point to Rising Social Tensions." World Socialist Web Site, May 11. Accessed September, 2012, from: www.wsws.org/articles/2010/may2010/chin-m11.shtml.

Careless, Sue. 2002, January 7. "Legal Bills Sink Canadian Diocese." *Christianity Today*, 20.

CDT. 2011. *China Digital Times*. Accessed from: chinadigitaltimes.net.china.

CED (Center for Effective Discipline). 2008a. "Facts vs. Opinion: School Corporal Punishment." Accessed from: www.ncpt.org.

———. 2008b. "Discipline in Schools." Accessed from: www.ncpt.org.

Centers for Disease Control and Prevention. 2010. "Youth Risk Behavior Surveillance—United States, 2009." *Mortality and Morbidity Weekly Report*. Surveillance Summaries, June 4, 2010. Vol. 59 / No. SS-5. Accessed September 12, 2012, from: www.cdc.gov/mmwr/pdf/ss/ss5905.pdf.

Chandos, John. 1984. *Boys Together: English Public Schools 1800–1864*. London: Hutchinson.

Campbell, Oliver. 2010. "China: School Attacks Point to Rising Social Tensions." *World Socialist Web Site* May 11. Accessed September 2012, from: www.wsws.org/articles/2010/may2010/chin-m11.shtml.

Churchill, W. 2004. *Kill the Indian, Save the Man: The Genocidal Impact of American Indian Residential Schools*. San Francisco: City Light Books.

Commentary Guest. 2008, August 11. "Adult Teacher Rapes Student: Comment."

CORPUN. 2008. "Corporal Punishment in US Schools." *World Corporal Punishment Research*. Accessed from the Center for Effective Discipline: www.stophitting.com.

———. 2011. "Corporal Punishment in US Schools." *World Corporal Punishment Research*. Accessed from the Center for Effective Discipline: www.stophitting.com.

Dakss, Brian. 2005, February 9. "Teacher-Student Rape: Another Case?" *CBS News, The Early Show*.

Davis, T. C., G. P. Peck, and J. M. Starment. 1993. "Acquaintance Rape and the High School Student." *Journal of Adolescent Health* 14: 22024.

De Venanzi, Augusto. 2012. "School Shootings in the USA: Popular Culture as Risk, Teen Marginality, and Violence against Peers." *Crime Media Culture*, 1–18.

Douglas K. A., et al. 1977. "Results from the 1995 National College Health Risk Behavior Survey. " *Journal of American College Health* 46: 55–66.

Dunn, Patricia C., Karen Vail-Smith, and Sharon M. Knight. 1999. "What Date/Acquaintance Victims Tell Others: A Study of College Student Recipients of Disclosure." *Journal of American College Health* 47: 213–19.

Fang, Lee. 2011, March 15. "The Pro-Bullying Lobby: Conservative Leader Explains Why He Is Mobilizing Anti-Bullying Measures." Accessed from *Think Progress*: thinkprogress.org/2011.

Fiegugh, Debra. 2002, May 25. "Denomination Thwarts Bankruptcy." *Christianity Today*.

Ford, Peter. 2010, May 12. "Another Gruesome School Attack Hits China." *Christian Science Monitor*.

Fort Wayne Journal Gazette. 1998, March 15. "Teacher Jailed for Affair with Young Male."

———. 2000, December 15. "Ex-Counselor Hears Sex Charges."

———. 2001, June 15. "Convicted Counselor Accused of More Sex with Teen."

———. 2002, June 5. "Coach Out after Giving Girl Gifts of Lingerie."

———. 2011, March 13. "Comment."

Fox, J., and J. Savage. 2009. "Mass Murder Goes to College: An Examination of Changes on College Campuses Following Virginia Tech." *American Behavioral Scientist* 52: 1465–85.

Freydis. 2011. "School Shootings II." Accessed February 22, 2011, from *Holology*: www.holology.com.

Gerald R. Ford School of Public Policy. 2007, March. *National Poverty Center Policy Brief #9, March 2007*. Accessed July 5, 2011, from Education and Health: www.npc.umich.edu/publications/policy_briefs/brief9/policy_brief9.pdf.

Goldman, R. 2007, October 18. "Kids 'Sitting Ducks' for Pedophile Teachers." Accessed May 18, 2011, from ABC News/International: abcnews.go.com/International/story?id=3743338&page=1.

Gottlieb, Robert, and Peter Wiley 1984. *America's Saints: The Rise of Mormon Power*. New York: Putnam.

Gould, Mark. 2007, January 9. "Sparing the Rod." *The Guardian*.

Grant, A. 1996. *No End of Grief: Indian Residential Schools in Canada*. Winnepeg: Pemmican Press.

Greenfield, L. A. 1997. *Sex Offenses and Offenders: An Analysis of Data on Rapes and Sexual Assaults*. Washington, D.C.: U.S. Department of Justice, Bureau of Justice Statistics.

Haynie, Devon. 2011, April 27. "EACS Teacher Has Been on Leave." *Fort Wayne Journal Gazette*.

High Beam. 2011. "Time Line of Worldwide School Shootings." Accessed March 22, 2011, from *High Beam Research*: www.infoplease.com.

Human Rights Watch. 2008, August 19. *A Violent Education: Corporal Punishment of Children in US Public Schools*. Accessed May 18, 2011, from Human Rights Watch: www.hrw.org/en/node/62078/section/1.

Javonen, Jaana. 2001. *Peer Harassment in Schools*. New York: Guilford Press.

Jimerson, Shane R. 2010. *Handbook of Bullying in Schools*. London: Taylor & Francis.

Kates, Brian. 2009, October 27. "Richmond High School Gang Rape: Cops Arrest 1 in Attack on California Teen Girl: Bystanders Did Nothing." *Richmond Daily News*.

Kaufman, P., Z Chen, S. P. Chang, S. A. Ruddy, A. K. Miller et al. 1999. *Indicators of School Crime and Safety*. Washington, D.C.: Departments of Education and Justice.

Kennedy, John W. 1995, September 13. "Probe of Mission Schools Demanded." *Christianity Today*, 14, 60.

Kennedy, Sheila. 2011, March 10. "Boys Will Be Homophobic Boys." Accessed from: Sheila-kennedy.net/2011.

Kozol, J. 2005. *The Shame of the Nation*. New York: Broadway Paperbacks.

Larkin, R. 2009. "The Columbine Legacy: Rampage Shootings as Political Acts." *American Behavioral Scientist* 52: 1309–26.

Malaby, M. 2007. "Elite Males and School Violence." *Curriculum and Teacher Dialog* 1–2: 157–70.

McKinnon, J. D. 2009, December 22. "U.S. Offers An Official Apology to Native Americans." Accessed June 30, 2011, from Washington Wirc: blogs.wsj.com/washwire/2009/12/22/us-offers-an-official-apology-to-native-americans.

Megan Meier Foundation. Accessed from: www.meganmeierfoundation.org.

Miller, J. 1996. *Shingwauk's Vision: A History of the Indian Residential Schools*. Toronto: University of Toronto Press.

Milner, Murray. 2004. *Freaks, Geeks, and Cool Kids: American Teenagers, Schools, and the Culture of Consumption*. New York: Rouledge.

Missionary Kids Safety Net. Accessed from: www.mksafetynet.net.

Moore, M. H., C. V. Petrie, A. A. Braga, and B. L. McLaughlin, eds. 2003. *Deadly Lessons: Understanding Lethal School Violence*. Washington, D.C.: National Academies Press.

National Center for Educational Statistics. 2004. *Indicators of School Crime and Safety: 2004 Executive Summary*. Washington, D.C.: National Center for Educational Statistics.

National Conference of State Legislatures. 2011. Washington, D.C. Accessed from: www.ncsl.org.

National School Safety and Security Services. 2010. *Sample of Reported School-Related Shootings Not Resulting in Deaths*. Accessed December 17, 2010, from: www.schoolsecurity.org/trends/school_violence09-10.html.

Netter, Sarah. 2010, October 27. "High School Rape Victim Spends Two Years in Court Fighting Ouster from Squad." *ABCNews/US*.

New America Foundation. 2011, April 6. *Federal Education Budget Project*. Accessed July 5, 2011, from Student Census Poverty Rate: febp.newamerica.net/k12/rankings/cenpov.

New York Times. 2009, March 11. "School Shootings."

Nhundu, T. J., and A. Shumba. 2001. "The Nature and Frequency of Reported Cases of Teacher Perpetrated Child Sexual Abuse in Rural Primary Schools in Zimbabwe." *Child Abuse and Neglect* 25, no. 11: 1517–34.

Pezanoski-Browne, Alison. 2010. "Top 5 Ways That Boys and Girls Bully." Accessed from *The Beehive*: www.TheBeehive.org.

Philadelphia Inquirer. 2002, March 7. "Teacher-Sex Ruling Sent for Review."

Platt, R. H. 1895. "The Advantages of Mingling Indians with Whites." *Proceedings and Addresses of the National Educational Association*, 761–62. Washington, D.C.: National Educational Association.

Quigly, Isabel. 1984. *The Heirs of Tom Brown: The English School Story*. London: Oxford University Press.

Religious News Service. 2002, March 11. "Churches Seek Help in Abuse Suits."

Rigby, Ken. 2001. *Bullying in Schools: And What To Do About It*. Austin, Tex.: Austin Council for Educational Research.

Saletan, William. 2006, January 16. "Teacher's Pet? Are Teachers Who Sleep with Boys Getting Off?" Accessed from *Slate Magazine*: www.slate.com.

Salmivalli, Christina, Kristi Legerspetz, Kaj Bjorkvist, Karin Osterman, and Ari Kaukiainen. 1996. "Bullying as a Group Process: Participant Roles and Their Relations to Social Status within the Group." *Aggressive Behavior* 22, no. 1: 1–15.

Scudder, H. E. 1884. *A History of the United States of America*. Philadelphia: J.W. Butler.

Smith, A. 2005. *Conquest: Sexual Violence and American Indian Genocide*. Cambridge: South End Press.

Smith, Peter K. 1999. *The Nature of School Bullying*. New York: Routledge.

Smith, Peter K., Debra J. Pepler, and Ken Rigby. 2004. *Bullying in Schools*. Boston: Cambridge University Press.

Solberg, Mona E., and Dan Olweus. 2003. "Prevalence Estimation of School Bullying with the Olweus Bully/Victim Questionnaire." *Aggressive Behavior* 29, no. 3: 239–68.

Southern Poverty Law Center. 2012. "SPLC Settlement to Protect Students from Bullying in Minn. School District." *SPLC Report* 42, no. 2: 1.

Staff, J., and Kreager, D. A. (2008). "Too Cool for School? Violence, Peer Status, and High School Dropout." *Social Forces*, 87: 445–471.

Stockman, D. 2011, May 29. "A World Apart." *The Journal Gazette*, 1A, 11A.

Swearer, Susan M. 2010, December 30. "Get Beyond 5 Bullying Myths." *Washington Post*.

Swearer, Susan M., Dorothy Lynn Espelage, and Scott A. Napolitan. 2009. *Bullying Prevention and Intervention: Realistic Strategies for Schools*. New York: Guilford Press.

Tinker, G. E. 2004. "Tracing a Contour of Colonialism: American Indians and the Trajectory of Educational Imperialism." In *Kill the Indian, Save the Man: The Genocidal Impact of American Indian Residential Schools*, edited by W. Churchill, xiii–xxxi. San Francisco: City Light Books.

Tjaden, P., and N. Thoennes. 1998. "Prevalence, Incidence, and Consequences of Violence against Women: Findings from the National Violence Against Women Survey." *Research in Brief*, 2–5. Washington, D.C.: National Institute of Justice, U.S. Department of Justice.

UNICEF. 2011, March 24. *Basic Education and Gender Equality*. Accessed July 6, 2011, from introduction: www.unicef.org/education/index.php.

———. 2011. *State of the World's Children: Adolescence: An Age of Opportunity*. New York: United Nations Children Fund (UNICEF).

U.S. Department of Justice. 1998. *Violence Against Intimates: Analysis of Data on Crimes by Current or Former Spouses, Boyfriends, and Girlfriends*. Washington, D.C.: U.S. Department of Justice, Bureau of Justice Statistics.

VH1. 2011. "Britney Spears Joins President Obama's Anti-bullying Campaign." Accessed from: vh1.com/newss20110310.

Ward, Kevin J. 2001, November 10. "The Path to Healing." British Columbia: Indiana and Northern Affairs Canada. Accessed from Provincial Residential Schools Project: www.prsp.bc.ca/history/history.htm.

Warsaw, R. 1994. *I Never Called It Rape*. New York: HarperCollins.

Youssef, R. M., M. S. Attia, and M. I. Kamel. 1998. "Children Experiencing Violence. II: Prevalence and Determinants of Corporal Punishment in Schools." *Child Abuse and Neglect* 22, no. 1: 975–85.

Zetter, Kim. 2007. "Cyberbullying Suicide Stokes the Internet Fury Machine." Accessed from: www.wired.con/politics/onlinerights/news/2007/11/vigilante_justice.

CHAPTER 6

Adas, Michael. 1979. *Prophets of Rebellion: Millenarian Protest Movements against the European Colonial Order*. Chapel Hill: University of North Carolina Press.

Aho, James A. 1990. *The Politics of Righteousness: Idaho Christian Patriotism*. Seattle: University of Washington Press.

Andrews, Edward Deming. 1963. *The People Called Shakers*. Enlarged ed. New York: Dover Books.

Angebert, Jean-Michel. 1974. *The Occult and the Third Reich*. Translated by Lewis A. M. Sumberg. New York: McGraw-Hill.

Annan, David. 1967. "The Assassins and the Knights Templar." In *Secret Societies*, edited by N. McKenzie, 88–108. New York: Penguins Books.

Arrington, Leonard J., and David Bitton. 1980. *The Mormon Experience*. New York: Vintage Books.

Arrington, Leonard J., and Jon Haupt. 1988. "Intolerable Zion: The Image of Mormonism in Nineteenth-Century American Literature." *Western Humanities Review* 22: 243–60.

Associated Press. 2002, March 4. "Sex Abuse Ravages Diocese Finances."

Bagley, Will. 2002. *Blood of the Prophets: Brigham Young and the Massacre at Mountain Meadows*. Norman: University of Oklahoma Press.

Bednarski, Joyce. 1968. "The Salem Witch-Scare Viewed Sociologically." In *Witchcraft and Sorcery*, edited by M. Marwick, 151–63. Baltimore: Penguin Books.

Berry, Jason. 1992. *Lead Us Not into Temptation: Catholic Priests and the Sexual Abuse of Children*. New York: Doubleday.

Best, Joel. 1990. *Threatened Children: Rhetoric and Concern about Child-Victims*. Chicago: University of Chicago Press.

Boswell, John. 1981. *Christianity, Social Tolerance, and Homosexuality*. Chicago: University of Chicago Press.

Boyle, James J. 1995. *Killer Cults*. New York: St. Martin's.

Bradlee, Ben, Jr., and Dale Van Atta. 1981. *Prophet of Blood*. New York: Putnam's.

Brennan, J. H. 1974. *The Occult Reich*. New York: Signet Books.

Brock, Raymond T., and Horace C. Lukens Jr. 1988. "Affair Prevention in the Ministry." *Psychology and Christianity* 8: 44–55.

Bromley, David G. 1989. "Hare Krishna and the Anti-cult Movement." In *Krishna Consciousness in the West*, edited by D. G. Bromley and L. D. Shinn, 255–92. Lewisburg, Penn.: Bucknell University Press.

Bromley, David G., and Anson D. Shupe Jr. 1981. *Strange Gods: The Great American Cult Scare*. Boston: Beacon Press.

Bureau of Alcohol, Tobacco, and Firearms. 1993, September. *Report of the Department of the Treasury on the Bureau of Alcohol, Tobacco, and Firearms Investigation of Vernon Wayne Howell also Known as David Koresh*. Washington, D.C.: U. S. Government, Treasury Department.

Burkett, Elinor, and Frank Bruni. 1993. *A Gospel of Shame: Children, Sexual Abuse, and the Catholic Church*. New York: Viking Press.

Burman, Edward. 1986. *The Templars: Knights of God*. Rochester: Thorsons Publishers.

Carr, Caleb. 2003. *The Lessons of Terror*. Revised ed. New York: Random House.

Cartwright, Robert H., and Stephen A. Kent. 1992. "Social Control in Alternative Religions: A Familial Perspective." *Sociological Analysis* 53: 345–61.

Chandrasekaran, Rajiv. 2002, March 5. "Militants Raze Mosque, Install Statue of Monkey God." *Washington Post*.

Chesneaux, Jean. 1972. "Secret Societies in China's Historical Evolution." In *Popular Movements and Secret Societies in China 1840–1959*, edited by Jean Chesneaux, 1–21. Stanford, Calif.: Stanford University Press.

Chomsky, Noam, and Edward S. Herman. 1979. *The Washington Connection and Third World Fascism*. Boston: South End Press.

Cohen, A. J., et al. 2004. "Urban Air Pollution." In *Comparative quantification of health risks*, edited by M. Ezzati, et al. Geneva: World Health Organization.

Cohn, Norman. 1971. *The Pursuit of the Millennium*. New York: Oxford University Press.

———. 1975. *Europe's Inner Demons*. New York: New American Library.

Concha-Barrientos M., et al. 2004. "Selected Occupational Risk Factors. In *Comparative Quantification of Health Risks*, edited by M. Ezzati, et al. Geneva: World Health Organization.

Cooper-White, Pamela. 1991, February 20. "Soul Stealing: Power Relations in Pastoral Sexual Abuse." *The Christian Century*: 196–99.

Cooperman, Alan. 2002, January 31. "Catholic Church Settles Suits Alleging Sex Abuse by Priest." *Washington Post*.

Corcoran, James. 1990. *Bitter Harvest*. Baltimore, Md.: Penguin Books.

Daichman, Graciela. 1990. "Misconduct in the Medieval Nunnery: Fact, Not Fiction." In *That Gentle Strength: Historical Perspectives on Women in Christianity*, edited by Lynda L. Coon, Katherin J. Haldine, and Elisabeth W. Sammer, 97–117. Charlottesville: University of Virginia Press.

Daraul, Arkon. 1969. *A History of Secret Societies*. New York: Pocket Books.

Doyle, Thomas P., A. W. Richard Sipe, and Patrick J. Wall, 2006. *Sex, Priests, and Secret Codes*. Los Angeles: Volt Press.

Erhman, Bart. 1999. *Jesus: Apocalyptic Prophet of the New Millennium*. New York: Oxford University Press.

Enroth, Ronald M. 1992. *Churches That Abuse*. Grand Rapids, Mich.: Zondervan.

Evans, Bergen. 1968. *Dictionary of Quotations*. New York: Delacorte Press.

Farragher, Thomas, 2002, March 8. "Law Adds Top Specialists to Abuse Prevention Panel." *Boston Globe*.

Fortune, Marie M. 1989. *Is Nothing Sacred?* San Francisco: Harper-Collins.

Foster, Lawrence. 1981. *Religion and Sexuality: Three American Communal Experiments of the Nineteenth Century*. New York: Oxford University Press.

French, Ron. 1993, December 12. "Shattered Trust." *Fort Wayne Journal-Gazette*, 5–6D.

Gage, Susan. 1991. *Colonialism in the Americas*. Victoria, British Columbia: Victoria International Development Education Association.

Gies, Frances. 1984. *The Knight in History*. New York: Harper & Row.

Gilje, Paul A. 1987. *The Road to Mobocracy*. Chapel Hill: University of North Carolina Press.

Hadden, Jeffrey K. and Anson Shupe. 1988. *Televangelism: Power and Politics on God's Frontier*. New York: Henry Holt.

Hall, John R. 1989. *Gone from the Promised Land: Jonestown in American Cultural History*. New Brunswick, N.J.: Transaction Publishers.

Hansen, Chadwick. 1969. *Witchcraft at Salem*. New York: New American Library.

Haught, James A. 1990. *Holy Horrors*. Buffalo, N.Y.: Prometheus Books.

Hayford, J. E. Casely. 1970. *Gold Coast Native Institutions, with Thought upon a Healthy Imperial Policy for the Gold Coast and Ashanti*. London: Cass.

Heckethorn, Charles William. 1965. *The Secret Societies of All Ages and Countries*. New Hyde Park: University Books.

Heinerman, John, and Anson Shupe. 1985. *The Mormon Corporate Empire*. Boston: Beacon Press.

Hicks, Robert D. 1991. *In Pursuit of Satan*. Buffalo, N.Y.: Prometheus Books.

Hill, Daniel. 1980. *Study of Mind Development Groups, Sects and Cults in Ontario: Report to the Ontario Government*. Ontario, Canada: Government of Ontario.

Hill, Marvin S. 1989. *Quest for Refuge: The Mormon Flight from American Pluralism*. Salt Lake City, Utah: Signature Books.

Hoffmann, Bill, and Cathy Burke. 1997. *Heaven's Gate: Cult Suicide in San Diego*. New York: HarperPaperbacks.

Holloway, Mark. 1966. *Heavens on Earth*. 2nd ed. New York: Dover.

Horsley, Richard A., and John S. Hanson. 1985. *Bandits, Prophets, and Messiahs: Popular Movements at the Time of Jesus*. San Francisco: Harper and Row.

Iadicola, Peter. 2008. "Globalization and Empire." *International Journal of Social Inquiry* 1, no. 2: 3–37.

Information Please Environmental Almanac. 1993. Compiled by World Resources Institute. Boston: Houghton Mifflin.

Jacobs, Janet Liebman. 1989. *Divine Disenchantment: Deconverting from New Religions*. Bloomington: Indiana University Press.

Jefferson, Thomas. 1954. *Notes on the State of Virginia*. New York: W. W. Norton.

Jenkins, Philip. 2002. *Mystics and Messiahs: Cults and New Religions in American History*. New York: Cambridge University Press.

Johnson, Paul E., and Sean Wilentz, 1994. *The Kingdom of Mattias: A Story of Salvation in the Nineteenth Century*. New York: Oxford University Press.

Johnston, Jerry. 1989. *The Edge of Evil: The Rise of Satanism in North America*. Dallas, Tex.: Word Publishing.

Juergensmeyer, Mark. 2008. *Global Rebellion*. Berkeley: University of California Press.

Kahaner, Larry. 1988. *Cults That Kill*. New York: Warner Books.

Kaplan, David E., and Andrew Marshall, 1996. *The Cult at the End of the World*. New York: Crown Publishers.

Karlsen, Carol F. 1987. *The Devil in the Shape of a Woman*. New York: Vintage Books.

Kisala, Robert. 1998. "The AUM Spiritual Truth Church in Japan." In *Wolves within the Fold*, edited by A. Shupe, 33–48. New Brunswick, N.J.: Transaction.

Kramer, Ronald C. 2010. "From Guernica to Hiroshima to Baghdad: The Normalization of the Terror Bombing of Civilians." In *State Crime in the Global Age*, edited by William J. Chambliss, Raymond Michalowski, and Ronald C. Kramer. London: Willan Publishing.

LaBaron, Verland M. 1981. *The LeBaron Story*. Lubbock, Tex.: Verland M. LaBaron.

Lanternari, Vittorio. 1963. *The Religions of the Oppressed*. Translated by Lisa Sergio. New York: Knopf.

Laqueur, Walter. 1997. *The Age of Terrorism*. Revised ed. Boston: Little, Brown and Company.

Laudurie, Emmanmuel Leroy. 1978. *Montaillou: The Promised Land of Error*. Translated by Barbara Bray. New York: Braziller.

Levi, Ken, ed. 1982. *Violence and Religious Commitment*. University Park: The Pennsylvania State University Press.

Lewis, James R. 1994. *From the Ashes: Making Sense of Waco*. Lanham, Md.: Rowman & Littlefield.

MacFarlane, Alan. 1970. *Witchcraft in Tudor and Stuart England*. New York: Harper & Row.

Mahapatra, Rajesh. 2002, March 6. "Christians Were Targeted in India." Associated Press.

Martin, David C., and John Walcott. 1988. *Best Laid Plans: The Inside Story of America's War against Terrorism*. New York: Harper & Row.

Marty, Martin E. 1984. *Pilgrims in Their Own Land: 500 Years of Religion in America*. New York: Penguin Books.

Marwick, Max. 1968. "Witchcraft as a Social Strain Gauge." In *Witchcraft and Sorcery*, edited by M. Marwick, 280–95. Baltimore, Md.: Penguin Books.

Melton, J. Gordon. 1986. *Encyclopedic Handbook of Cults in America*. New York: Garland.

Moore, Rebecca, and Fielding McGhee, III. 1989. *New Religious Movements, Mass Suicide, and Peoples Temple*. Lewiston: Edwin Mellen Press.

Morgan, Richard E. 1968. *The Politics of Religious Conflict*. New York: Pegasus.

Muller-Hill, Benno. 1988. *Murderous Science*. Translated by George R. Fraser. New York: Oxford University Press.

Nason-Clark, Nancy. 1991. "Broken Trust: The Case of Roman Catholic Priests in Newfoundland Charged with the Sexual Abuse of Children." Unpublished paper presented at the annual meeting of the Society for the Scientific Study of Religion, Pittsburgh, Penn.

New York Times. 2002, March 5. "Los Angeles Cardinal Removes Priests Involved in Pedophilia Cases."

Partner, Peter. 1987. *The Murdered Magicians*. Rochester: Thorsons Publishers.

Payne, Robert. 1984. *The Dream and the Tomb: A History of the Crusades*. New York: Dorset Press.

Pickthall, Mohammed Marmaduke. 1961. *The Meaning of the Glorious Koran*. New York: New American Library.

Plaidy, Jean. 1969. *The Spanish Inquisition*. New York: The Citadel Press.

Poling, James Newton. 1991. *The Abuse of Power: A Theological Problem*. Nashville, Tenn.: Abington.

Raschke, Carl. 1990. *Painted Black*. New York: Harper & Row.

Rice, Andrew. 1993, December 2. "Franciscans Admit 34 Boys Were Molested at St. Anthony's." *The Independent.*

Richardson, James T., Joel Best, and David G. Bromley. 1991. *The Satanism Scare.* New York: Aldine de Gruyter.

Robbins, Thomas. 1986. "Religious Mass Suicide before Jonestown: The Russian Old Believers." *Sociological Analysis* 41: 1–20.

Rossetti, Stephen J. 1990. *Slayer of the Soul: Child Sexual Abuse and the Catholic Church.* Mystic, Conn.: Twenty-Third Publications.

Rowling, Marjorie. 1979. *Life in Medieval Times.* New York: Paragon Books.

Rutter, Peter. 1989. *Sex in the Forbidden Zone.* Los Angeles: Jeremy P. Tarcher.

Sasse, Cynthia Stalter, and Peggy Murphy Widder. 1991. *The Kirtland Massacre.* New York: Donald I. Fine.

Schwab, Charlotte Rolnick. 2002. *Sex, Lies, and Rabbis: Breaking a Sacred Trust.* Bloomington, Ind.: 1st Books Library.

Scott, Ralph A. 1979. *A New Look at Biblical Crime.* Chicago: Nelson-Hall.

Shannon, William V. 1966. *The American Irish.* Rev. ed. New York: Macmillan.

Shupe, Anson. 1995. *In the Name of All That's Holy: A Theory of Clergy Malfeasance.* Westport, Conn.: Praeger.

———. 2007. *Spoils of the Kingdom: Clergy Misconduct and Religious Community.* Urbana: University of Illinois Press.

———. 2008a. "Religious Fundamentalism." In *The Oxford Handbook of the Sociology of Religion,* edited by P. Clarek, 478–90. New York: Oxford University Press.

———. 2008b. *Rogue Clerics: The Social Problem of Clergy Deviance.* New Brunswick, N.J.: Transaction.

Shupe, Anson, and Christopher S. Bradley. 2010. *Self, Attitudes, and Emotion Work: Western Social Psychology and Eastern Zen Buddhism Confront Each Other.* New Brunswick, N.J.: Transaction.

Shupe, Anson D., Jr., and David G. Bromley. 1980. *The New Vigilantes: Deprogrammers, Anti-Cultists, and the New Religions.* Beverly Hills, Calif.: Sage.

———. 1994. *Anti-Cult Movements in Cross-Cultural Perspective.* New York: Garland Publishers.

Shupe, Anson, and Susan E. Darnell. 2006. *Agents of Discord: Deprogramming, Pseudo-Science, and the American Anticult Movement.* New Brunswick, N.J.: Transaction.

Shupe, Anson, and Jannelle M. Eliasson-Nannini. 2012. *Pastoral Misconduct: The American Black Church Examined.* New Brunswick, N.J.: Transaction.

Shupe, Anson D., Jr., and Jeffrey K. Hadden. 1995. "Cops, News Copy, and Legitimacy: The Social Construction of Evil in Waco." In *Armageddon in Waco,* edited by Stuart A. Wright, 177–202. Chicago: University of Chicago Press.

Sipe, A. W. Richard. 1990. *A Secret World: Sexuality and the Search for Celibacy.* New York: Brunner/Mazel.

———. 1995. *Sex, Priests, and Power: Anatomy of a Crisis.* New York: Brunner/Mazel.

———. 2003. *Celibacy in Crisis: A Secret World Revisited.* New York: Brunner-Rutledge.

Sklar, Dusty. 1977. *Gods and Beasts: The Nazis and the Occult.* New York: Thomas Y. Crowell.

Starkey, Marion L. 1969. *The Devil in Massachusetts.* Garden City, N.Y.: Doubleday.

Sutherland, Charles W. 1987. *Disciples of Destruction.* Buffalo, N.Y.: Prometheus Books.

Tinker, George E. 1993. *Missionary Conquest.* Minneapolis, Minn.: Fortress Press.

Victor, Jeffrey S. 1993. *Satanic Panic.* Chicago: Open Court.

Waite, Robert G. L. 1977. *The Psychopathic God.* New York: Basic Books.

Walker, Ronald W., Richard E. Turley, and Glen M. Leonard. 2008. *Massacre at Mountain Meadows.* New York: Oxford University Press.

Wallace, Anthony F. C. 1966. "Revitalization Movements." *American Anthropologist* 58: 264–81.

WHO (2002). "World Health Report 2002—Reducing Risks, Promoting Healthy Life." Geneva: World Health Organization. Accessed March 2005, from: www.who.int/whr/2002/.

Wilson, Margaret, and Ingrid Kvale. 1994, June 17. "They Do Not Know Us Yet." *The New Internationalist.*

Wittke, Carl. 1970. *The Irish in America.* New York: Russell and Russell.

Wright, Robin. 1989. *In the Name of God.* New York: Simon and Schuster.

Wright, Stuart A. 1995. *Armageddon in Waco.* Chicago: University of Chicago Press.

CHAPTER 7

AboutLawsuits.com. 2010, February 17. "Accutane Lawsuit Over Inflammatory Bowel Disease Results in \$25M Verdict." Accessed August 2, 2011, from AboutLawsuits.com: www.aboutlawsuits.com/accutane-lawsuit-inflammatory-bowel-disease-verdict-8334/.

Adler, Bill. 1985, November/December. "Risky Business." *Sierra Magazine*, 21.

Aksit, Bahattin, Nuray Karanci, and Avse Gunduz-Hosgor. 2001. *Turkey: Working Street Children in Three Metropolitan Cities: A Rapid Assessment*. Geneva: International Labor Organization, International Programme on the Elimination of Child Labor (IPEC).

Alston, Dana, and Nicole Brown. 1993. "Global Threats to People of Color." In *Confronting Environmental Racism*, edited by R. D. Bullard, 179–94. Boston: South End Press.

American Lung Association. 2000. "Fact Sheet: Occupational Lung Disease." Accessed from the American Lung Association: www.lungusa.org/diseases/occupational_factsheet.html.

Bhagat, Dhiren. 1985. "A Night in Hell." In *Bhopal: Industrial Genocide?*, 23. Hong Kong: Arena Press.

Bissio, Roberto Remo. 1990. "A Creeping Bhopal." In *Third World Guide 91/92*, edited by R. R. Bissio, 70. Montevideo, Uruguay: Garamond Press.

Branan, Karen. 1980, June. "Running In Reverse." *Mother Jones* 5: 40–47.

Bray, Garth. 1989. "Poison Pushers." *Multinational Monitor* 10: 31.

British Broadcasting Company. 2003, January 26. "China's Cigarette Threat." Accessed January 26, 2012, from BBC News World Edition: news.bbc.co.uk/2/hi/health/216998.stm.

Broder, J. M. 2012, May 14. "E.P.A. Appeals Coal Mine Ruling."Accessed June 24, 2012, from *The New York Times*: green.blogs.nytimes.com/2012/05/14/e-p-a-appeals-coal-mine-ruling/.

Brown, Karen, and Lori Ann Thrupp. 1991, April. "The Human Guinea Pigs of Rio Frio." *The Progressive*: 28–30.

Bullard, Robert D. 1993. *Confronting Environmental Racism*. Boston: South End Press.

Burbach, Roger, and Patricia Flynn. 1980. *Agribusiness in the Americas*. New York: Monthly Review Press.

Bureau of Labor Statistics. 2007, August. "Coal Mining: Injuries, Illnesses, and Fatalities Fact Sheet and Charts." Accessed February 2, 2012, from Bureau of Labor Statistics: www.bls.gov/iif/oshwc/osh/os/osar0006.pdf.

Cassidy, R. A., G. Sridhar, and M. Vaughan. 2005. "Breast Cancer Linked to Home Pesticide Chlordane." *Breast Cancer Research and Treatment*: 55–64.

Castleman, B. T. 1984. *Asbestos: Medical and Legal Aspects*. New York: Harcourt Brace Jovanovich.

Caudill, Harry M. 1987. "Manslaughter in a Coal Mine." In *Corporate Violence: Injury and Death for Profit*, edited by S. L. Hills, 93–102. Totowa: Rowman & Littlefield.

CBS.Com. 2001. "Tire Giant Settles \$1B Lawsuit." Accessed August 24, 2001, from: www.cbsnews.com/stories/2001/08/10/national/main305944.shtml.

Centers for Disease Control. 2008, August 18. "Faces of Black Lung." Accessed January 31, 2012, from NIOSH Science Blog: blogs.cdc.gov/niosh-science-blog/2008/08/mining/.

———. 2009, April 24. *Malignant Mesothelioma Mortality—United States, 1999–2005*. Accessed January 31, 2012, from MMWR—Morbidity and Mortality Weekly Report: www.cdc.gov/mmwr/preview/mmwrhtml/mm5815a3.htm.

———. 2011, May. *Vital Signs—Asthma in the US, Growing Every Year*. Accessed February 16, 2012, from Centers for Disease Control and Prevention: www.cdc.gov/vitalsigns/Asthma/.

Chemical Industry Archives. 2001. "The Top 5 Facilities Accounted for over Half of All Vinyl Chloride Emissions in the Country." Accessed March 26, 2001, from: www.chemicalindustryarchives.org/dirtysecrets/vinyl/facilityrank.asp.

CNN Interactive. 1998. "Secret Memos Show Cigarette-Maker Targeted Teens." Accessed from: www.cnn.com/HEALTH/9801/15/tobacco.kid.settlement/#memos.

Cohen, Marc. 1995, January. "Choking on Growth." *New Internationalist*, 22–23.

Coleman, James W., and Donald R. Cressey. 1990. *Social Problems*. New York: Harper & Row.

Commission of the European Communities. 2007. *Fifth Report on the Statistics on the Number of Animals used for Experimental and other Scientific Purposes in the Member States of the European Union Commission of the European Communities*. Brussels: Commission to the Council and the European Parliament.

Commoner, Barry. 1990. *Making Peace with the Planet*. New York: Pantheon Books.

Cray, Charlie. 2001. "Toxics on the Hudson: The Saga of GE, PCBs and the Hudson River." *Multinational Monitor* 22, nos. 7–8: 9–17.

Daniels, Julie L, et al., 1997, October. "Pesticides and Childhood Cancers." *Environmental Health Perspectives* 105, no. 10: 1068–77.

————. 2001. "Neuroblastoma Linked to Homes Treated with Pesticides." *Epidemiology* 12, no. 1: 20–26.

Dowie, Mark. 1977, September/October. "Pinto Madness." *Mother Jones* 1: 18–32.

————. 1979, November. "The Corporate Crime of the Century." *Mother Jones* 4.

Dowie, Mark, Douglas Foster, Carolyn Marshall, David Weir, and Jonathan King. 1982, June. "The Illusion of Safety." *Mother Jones* 7: 35–49.

Dowie, Mark, and Tracy Johnston. 1976, November. "A Case of Corporate Malpractice." *Mother Jones* 2: 36–50.

Dowie, Mark, and Carolyn Marshall. 1980, November. "The Bendectin Cover-Up." *Mother Jones* 5: 43–56.

Duhigg, C. 2009, September 12. "Clean Water Laws Are Neglected, at a Cost in Suffering." *New York Times*. Accessed February 9, 2012, from: www.nytimes.com/2009/09/13/us/13water.html?pagewanted=all.

Duhigg, C., and D. Barboza. 2012, January 25. "In China, Human Costs Are Built into an iPad." *New York Times*.

Ehrlich, Paul R., Anne H. Ehrlich, and John P. Holdren. 1973. *Human Ecology: Problems and Solutions*. San Francisco: W.H. Freeman.

Environmental Working Group. 1999. "Tap Water in Central Valley Tainted With Banned Pesticide Bottle-Fed Infants May Exceed 'Safe' Dose Before Age 1." Press Release Memo. Accessed from: www.ewg.org/reports/dbcp/dbcpreport.html.

————. 2004. *Asbestos—Think Again*. Washington, D.C.: Environmental Working Group.

Epstein, Samuel S. 1978. *The Politics of Cancer*. San Francisco: Sierra Club Books.

Erickson, Jon. 1992. *World Out of Balance: Our Polluted Planet*. Blue Ridge Summit, Pa.: Tab Books.

European Business Ltd. 2011, May 12. *2010 RAPEX Report*. Accessed August 2, 2011, from EU Business: www.eubusiness.com/topics/consumer/rapex-2010.

Fagin, Dan, Marianne Lavelle, and the Center for Public Integrity. 1999. *Toxic Deception: How the Chemical Industry Manipulates Science, Bends the Law, and Endangers Your Life*. Monroe, Maine: Common Courage Press.

Feagin, Joe R., and Clairece Booher Feagin. 1990. *Social Problems: A Critical Power-Conflict Perspective*. Englewood Cliffs, N.J.: Prentice Hall.

Felsenthal, Edward. 1993, September 9. "Manslaughter Pleas: Legal Beat." *Wall Street Journal*, 12.

Forastieri, Valentina. 1999. *Safework: The ILO Programme on Occupational Safety and Health in Agriculture*. Accessed from: www.ilo.org/public/english/protection/safework/agriculture/agrivf01.htm.

Foster, John Bellamy. 1994, September/October. "Waste Away." *Dollars and Sense*, no. 195: 7.

Foundation for National Progress. 1984. "Dalkon Shield Executives Blasted by Federal Judge." *Insider* 15: 2.

Frank, Nancy. 1986. *Crimes against Worker Health and Safety*. San Francisco: Sierra Club Books.

————. 1987. "Murder in the Workplace." In *Corporate Violence: Injury and Death for Profit*, edited by S. L. Hills. Totowa: Rowman & Littlefield.

Friedrichs, D. O. 2004. *Trusted Criminals*. Belmont: Wadsworth.

Gold, Stuart. 1989, October. "The World Bank's Pesticide of Choice." *Multinational Monitor* 10: 7–9.

Gozan, Julie. 1992. "Toxic Traders Indicted." *Multinational Monitor* 13: 4.

————. 1993. "Demanding Justice." *Multinational Monitor* 14: 5.

Greenpeace and Basil Action Network. 2000. "Business As Usual: Case Studies of Hazardous Waste Dumping in Asia." Report prepared for the United Nations Conference on Trade and Development meeting held in Bangkok, Thailand, February 12–19, 2000. Accessed from: www.greenpeace.org/~toxics/toxfreeasia/unctad.html.

Grunwald, Michael. 2002, January 1. "Monsanto Hid Decades of Pollution: PCBs Drenched Ala. Town, But No One Was Ever Told." *Washington Post*, A01.

Guarasci, Richard. 1987. "Death by Cotton Dust." In *Corporate Violence: Injury and Death for Profit*, edited by S. L. Hills, 76–92. Totowa: Rowman & Littlefield.

Harris, Gardiner. 1998, April 19. "Dust, Deception, and Death." *The Courier-Journal* (Louisville, Ky.).

Harris, G. 2010, July 13. "Diabetes Drug Maker Hid Test Data, Files Indicate." *The New York Times*, A1.

Hayes, Denis. 1993, November 10. "Economic Power." *Seattle Weekly*, 15.

Hebert, H. Joseph. 1983, October 21. "Files Show GM Knew X-Car Brakes Locked." *Denver Post*, 1A, 12A.

Hecht, Susanna, and Alexander Cockburn. 1989. *The Fate of the Forest: Developers, Destroyers, and Defenders of the Amazon*. New York: Verso.

Heilprin, J. 2004, December 6. "EPA Projects Hazardous Waste Sites Growing in Number and Cleanup Costs." Accessed February 9, 2012, from Environmental News Network: www.enn.com/top_stories/article/520.

Heong, Yoke Chee. 1990. "Spotlight: Toxic Waste Treaty." In *Third World Guide 91/92*, edited by R. Bissio, 71. Montevideo, Uruguay: Garamond Press.

Human Rights Watch. 2000. *Fingers to the Bone: United States Failure to Protect Child Farmworkers*. Washington, D.C.: Human Rights Watch.

International Labour Organization 2002. *Statistics: Revealing a Hidden Tragedy*. Accessed from the International Programme on the Elimination of Child Labour: www.ilo.org/public/english/standards/ipec/simpoc/stats/4stt.htm.

———. 2011a. *Children in Hazardous Work*. Geneva: International Labour Organization.

———. 2011b. *ILO Introductory Report: Global Trends and Challenges on Occupational Safety and Health*. Turin: ILO.

James, S. 2011, May 21. *Black Lung Disease Seen Rising in U.S. Miners*. Accessed February 2, 2012, from Reuters: in.reuters.com/article/2011/05/20/us-black-lung-idINTRE74J6D J20110520.

Jeyaratnam, J. 1990. "Acute Pesticide Poisoning in Asia: A Major Global Health Problem." *World Health Statistics Quarterly* 43, no. 3.

Jochnick, Chris. 1995, January/February. "Amazon Oil Offensive." *Multinational Monitor* 16: 12–15.

Joy, M. 2009. *Why We Love Dogs, Eat Pigs, and Wear Cows: An Introduction to Carnism*. San Francisco: Conari Press.

Juozapavicius, J. 2011, November 30. "Horse Meat Inspection Ban Lifted In The U.S." Accessed June 23, 2012, from Huffington Post: www.huffingtonpost.com/2011/11/30/horse-meat-consumption-us_n_1120623.html.

Kerr, Mary Lee, and Bob Hall. 1992, January. "Chickens Come Home to Roost." *The Progressive* 56: 29.

Knaus, Holley. 1991, May. "The Front." *Multinational Monitor* 12, no. 5.

———. 1993. "Stepan Chemical: Poisoning Mexican Communities." *Multinational Monitor* 14: 28–29.

Kotelchuck, D. 1987. "Asbestos: 'The Funeral Dress of Kings'—and Others." In *Dying for Work: Workers' Safety and Health in Twentieth-Century America*, edited by D. Rosner and G. Markowitz, 192–207. Bloomington: Indiana University Press.

Kumar KC, Bal, Govind Subedi, Yogendra Bahadur Gurnung, and Keshab Prasad Adhikari. 2001. *Nepal: Trafficking in Girls with Special Reference to Prostitution: A Rapid Assessment*. Geneva: Central Department on Population Studies, International Labor Organization, International Programme on the Elimination of Child Labour.

LaBotz, Dan. 1993, May. "Manufacturing Poverty: The Maquiladization of Mexico." *Multinational Monitor* 14: 18–23.

Leonard, Ann. 1993, April. "Poison Fields: Dumping Toxic Fertilizer on Bangladeshi Farmers." *Multinational Monitor* 14: 14–18.

Lewis, Karen. 1992, January/February. "Addicting the Young: Tobacco Pushers and Kids." *Multinational Monitor* 13: 13–17.

Lowengart, R. A., J. M. Peters, and C. Cicioni. 1987, January. "Childhood Leukemia and Parents' Occupational and Home Exposures." *Journal of the National Cancer Institute* 79: 39–46.

Mackay, Judith. 1992, January/February. "China's Tobacco Wars." *Multinational Monitor* 13: 9–12.

Markowitz, G., and D. Rosner. 2002. *Deceit and Denial*. Berkeley: University of California Press.

Mattera, Philip. 1992, January/February. "RJR Nabisco: Transnational Tobacco Trafficker." *Multinational Monitor* 13: 38–41.

McAteer and Associates. 2011. *Upper Big Branch—The April 5, 2010 Explosion: A Failure of Basic Coal Mining Safety Practices*. Charleston: State of West Virginia.

Mead, P. S., L. Slutsker, V. Dietz, L. F. McCaig, J. S. Bresee, C. Shapiro et al. 1999. *Food-Related Illness and Death in the United States*. Accessed August 10, 2011, from Centers for Disease Control and Prevention: www.cdc.gov/ncidod/eid/vol5no5/mead.htm.

Meghani, Z., and J. Kuzma. 2011. "The 'Revolving Door' between Regulatory Agencies and Industry: A Problem That Requires Reconceptualizing Objectivity." *Journal of Agricultural and Environmental Ethics* 24, no. 6: 575–99.

Michaels, D. 2008. *DOUBT Is Their Product: How Industry's Assault on Science Threatens Your Health* (vol. 292). New York: Oxford University Press.

Michalowski, R. J., and R. C. Kramer. 2006. *State-Corporate Crime*. New Brunswick: Rutgers University Press.

Miller, Judith, and Mark Miller. 1985, March. "The Midnight Dumpers." *USA Today Magazine*, 60.

Mintz, Morton. 1985. *At Any Cost: Corporate Greed, Women, and the Dalkon Shield*. New York: Pantheon Books.

Mohr, N. 2012. "59 Billion Land and Sea Animals Killed for Food in the US in 2009." Accessed February 16, 2012, from Free From Harm: freefromharm.org/farm-animal-welfare/59-billion-land-and-sea-animals-killed-for-food-in-the-us-in-2009/.

Mokhiber, Russell. 1987. "Asbestos: An Industry's Lethal Cover-Up." *Multinational Monitor* 8, no. 4.

———. 1988. *Corporate Crime and Violence*. San Francisco: Sierra Club Books.

———. 1994. "The Ten Worst Corporations of 1994." *Multinational Monitor* 15: 7–16.

Mokhiber, Russell, Julie Gozan, and Holly Knaus. 1992. "The Corporate Rap Sheet: The 10 Worst Corporations of 1992." *Multinational Monitor* 13: 7–16.

———. 1994. "The Ten Worst Corporations of 1994." *Multinational Monitor* 15: 7–16.

Mokhiber, Russell, and Robert Weissman. 2001a. "Corporations Behaving Badly: The Ten Worst Corporations of 2001." *Multinational Monitor* 22: 8–19.

———. 2001b. "Enemies of the Future: The Ten Worst Corporations of 2000." *Multinational Monitor* 21: 12.

Moses, Marion. 1993. "Farmworkers and Pesticides." In *Confronting Environmental Racism*, edited by R. D. Bullard, 161–78. Boston: South End Press.

Mpondah, Dingaan. 1990. "Dumping on Africa and the Third World." In *Third World Guide 91/92*, edited by R. Bissio, 72. Montevideo, Uruguay: Garamond Press.

Mundy, A., and K. Sack. 2004, March 28. "A Dose of Denial: How Drug Makers Sought To Keep Popular Cold and Diet Remedies on Store Shelves after Their Own Study." *Los Angeles Times*.

Murray, L. 2007. "Factory Farmed Chickens: Their Difficult Lives and Death." Accessed February 19, 2012, from *Encyclopedia Britannica Advocacy for Animals*: advocacy.britannica.com/blog/advocacy/2007/05/the-difficult-lives-and-deaths-of-factory-farmed-chickens/.

Mwami, J. A., A. J. Sanga, and J. Nyoni. 2002. *Tanzania: Children Labour in Mining: A Rapid Assessment*. Geneva: International Labor Organization, International Programme on the Elimination of Child Labor (IPEC).

Nader, Ralph. 1972. *Unsafe at Any Speed: The Designed-In Dangers of the American Automobile*. New York: Bantam.

New Internationalist. 2000, May. "A is for Apple, P is for Pesticide." *New Internationalist* 323: 22–23.

Ouhachi-Vesely, Fatma-Zohra. 2001. *Economic, Social and Cultural Rights: Adverse Effects of the Illicit Movement and Dumping of Toxic and Dangerous Products and Wastes on the Enjoyment of Human Rights*. New York: United Nations Economic and Social Council. Accessed February 2, 2012, from United Nations Economic and Social Council: www.unhchr.ch/Huridocda/Huridoca.nsf/0/dd8f5b8876ef5101c1256a240058e30b/$FILE/G0110339.pdf.

Page, Joseph A. 1973. *Bitter Wages: Ralph Nader's Study Group Report on Disease and Injury on the Job*. New York: Grossman.

Palmer, M. A., E. S. Bernhardt, W. H. Schlesinger, K. N. Eshleman, E. Foufoula-Georgiou, M. S. Hendryx et al. 2010, January 8. "Mountaintop Mining Consequences." *Science* 327: 148.

Parker, L. 2007, April 18. *Mining Battle Marked by Peaks and Valleys*. Accessed June 24, 2012, from *USA Today*: www.usatoday.com/news/nation/2007-04-18-mines_N.htm.

Perry, Alex, and Mae Sai. 2002, March 11. "How I Bought Two Slaves, to Free Them." *Time* 159, no. 10: 7.

Petrun, E. 2009, February 11. "Where's The Beef?" Accessed June 23, 2012, from CBSNEWS World: www.cbsnews.com/2100-500522_162-2640540.html.

Pimentel, David. 1993. "United States Carrying Capacity Overview." Report presented at Carrying Capacity Network Conference, Washington, D.C.

Pimentel, David, S. Cooperstein, H. Randell, D. Filiberto, and S. Sorrentino. 2007. "Ecology of Increasing Diseases: Population Growth and Environmental Degradation." *Human Ecology* 35, no. 6: 653–68.

Pollan, M. 2006. *The Omnivore's Dilemma: A Natural History of Four Meals*. New York: Penguin Press.

Population Institute. 1990. *We Can Blame Billions of People for This*. Washington, D.C: Population Institute.

Powell, S., R. S. Dunham, and S. Gaffney. 2012, August 16. "Regulators' Ties to Agencies May Be Endangering Workers." *Houston Chronicle*.

Revkin, Andrew. 1990. *The Burning Season*. Boston: Houghton Mifflin.

Rosoff, S., H. Pontell, and R. Tillman. 2007. *Profit without Honor*. Upper Saddle River: Pearson Prentice Hall.

Savitz, D. A., E. A. Whelan, and R. C. Kleckner. 1989. "Self-Reported Exposure to Pesticides and Radiation Related to Pregnancy Outcome—Results from National Natality and Fetal Mortality Surveys." *Public Health Report* 104: 473–77.

Schlosser, E. 2001. *Fast Food Nation*. Boston: Houghton Mifflin Company.

Setterberg, F., and L. Shavelson. 1993. *Toxic Nation: The Fight to Save Our Communities from Chemical Contamination*. New York: Wiley.

Shabecoff, P., and A. Shabecoff. 2008. *Poisoned Profits: The Toxic Assault on Our Children*. New York: Random House.

Shapely, Dan. 2002, February 2. "Dredging Order Signed." *Poughkeepsie Journal*.

Shesgreen, D. 2011, December 1. "Horses Could Soon Be Slaughtered for Meat in U.S." Retrieved February 16, 2012, from *USA Today*: yourlife.usatoday.com/fitness-food/story/2011-11-30/Horses-could-soon-be-slaughtered-for-meat-in-US/51495306/1.

Simon, David R., and D. Stanley Eitzen. 1993. *Elite Deviance*. Boston: Allyn and Bacon.

———. 1999. *Elite Deviance*. Boston: Allyn and Bacon.

Slocock, Brian. 1992. *The East European Environment Crisis: Its Extent, Impact and Solutions*. London: Economist Intelligence Unit, 2109.

Smith, R. 2005. "Medical Journals Are an Extension of the Marketing Arm of Pharmaceutical Companies." *PLoS Med* 2, no. 5: 364–66.

State of California Department of Health Services. 1988. *Epidemiological Study of Adverse Health Effects in Children in McFarland, California*. Phase II Report. Sacramento: State Department of Health Services.

Steenland, K., C. Burnett, N. Lalich, E. Ward, and J. Hurrell. 2003. "Dying for Work: The Magnitude of US Mortality from Selected Causes of Death Associated with Occupation." *American Journal of Industrial Medicine* 43, no. 5: 461–82.

Strider, R. 1995, January/February. "Blood in the Pipeline." *Multinational Monitor* 16: 22–25.

Thundiyil, J. G., J. Stober, B. Besbelli, and J. Pronczuk. 2008. *Acute Pesticide Poisoning: A Proposed Classification Tool*. Accessed February 2, 2012, from Bulletin of the World Health Organization: www.who.int/bulletin/volumes/86/3/07-041814/en/index.html.

Trull, F. L. 1999. "More Regulation of Rodents." *Science* 284, no. 5419: 1463.

Ungar, Sanford J. 1972. "Get Away with What You Can." In *In the Name of Profit: Profiles in Corporate Irresponsibility*, edited by Robert L. Heilbroner et al. Garden City, N.J.: Doubleday.

United Nations Environment Programme 2002. "Three Deadly Pesticides and Asbestos Targeted for Action." Press Release of Third Session of the Interim Chemical Review Committee (ICRC), February 17–21, 2002, Geneva, Switzerland.

United Nations Food and Agricultural Organization Council. 2005. *International Code of Conduct on the Distribution and Use of Pesticides*. Rome: FAO.

UNICEF. 1989. United Nations Convention on the Rights of the Child. UNICEF: New York.

———. 2001. *Progress since the World Summit for Children—A Statistical Review*. UNICEF: New York.

U.S. Department of Agriculture. 2006. *Report on Enforcement of the Animal Welfare Act*. Washington, D.C.: U.S. Department of Agriculture.

U.S. Department of Health and Human Services, Public Health Service. 2001. *9th Report on Carcinogens*. Washington, D.C.: U.S. Government Printing Office.

U.S. Environmental Protection Agency. 2001. *National Primary Drinking Water Regulations: Consumer Factsheet on Vinyl Chloride*. Accessed from www.epa.gov/safewater/dwh/c-voc/vinylchl.html.

———. 2010. *Municipal Solid Waste Generation, Recycling, and Disposal in the United States: Facts and Figures for 2010*. Accessed January 12, 2012, from U.S Environmental Protection Agency: www.epa.gov/osw/nonhaz/municipal/pubs/msw_2010_factsheet.pdf.

———. 2011. *Mid-Atlantic Mountaintop Mining*. Accessed June 24, 2012, from U.S. Environmental Protection Agency: www.epa.gov/region03/mtntop/index.htm.

U.S. Food and Drug Administration. 2011. *Pesticide Residue Monitoring Program FY 2004–2006*. Accessed August 2, 2011, from U.S. Food and Drug Administration: www.fda.gov/Food/FoodSafety/FoodContaminantsAdulteration/Pesticides/ResidueMonitoringReports/ucm125183.htm.

U.S. House of Representatives Committee on Education and Labor. 1979. *Black Lung Benefits Reform Act and Black Lung Benefit Revenue Act of 1977*. Washington, D.C.: Government Printing Office.

Warrick, J. 2001, April 10. "Modern Meat: A Brutal Harvest—'They Die Piece by Piece.'" *Washington Post*, A01.

Wei, W. 2011, April 18. "Dogs Saved from Dinner Table." Accessed April 22, 2011, from *China Daily*: www.chinadaily.com.cn/cndy/2011-04/18/content_12341351.htm.

Weintraub, R. 2007, February 28. Hearing on Consumer Protections, Committee on Appropriations, U.S House of Representatives. Washington, District of Columbia, U.S.A. Accessed January 24, 2012, from: www.consumerfed.org/elements/www.consumerfed.org/file/health/CFA_Testimony_House_Fin_Serv_Approps_22807.pdf.

Weissman, Robert. 1992a, January/February. "America's Killing Ground." *Multinational Monitor* 13: 5.

———. 1992b, January/February. "The Marlboro Man Goes East." *Multinational Monitor* 13: 31–34.

———. 1994, December. "Remembering Bhopal." *Multinational Monitor* 15: 5.

Wernette, D. R., and L. A. Nieves. 1992, March/April. "Breathing Polluted Air." *EPA Journal* 18: 16–17.

Winter, Gregory. 2001, August 24. "Big Tobacco Is Accused of Crossing an Age Line." *The New York Times*.

World Health Organization. 2009. *Global Health Risks: Mortality and Burden of Disease Attributable to Selected Risk Factors.* Accessed January 31, 2012, from World Health Organization: Health Statistics and Health Information Systems: www.who.int/healthinfo/global_burden_disease/GlobalHealthRisks_report_part2.pdf.

———. 2010. *Asbestos: Elimination of Asbestos-Related Diseases.* Accessed January 31, 2012, from World Health Organization: Media Center: www.who.int/mediacentre/factsheets/fs343/en/index.html.

Zastrow, Charles. 1992. *Social Problems: Issues and Solutions.* Chicago: Nelson Hall.

CHAPTER 8

Ali, M. M., and I. H. Shah. 2000. "Sanctions and Childhood Mortality in Iraq." *The Lancet* 355, no. 9218: 1851–57.

Alston, P. 2010. *Report of the Special Rapporteur on Extrajudicial, Summary or Arbitrary Executions.* New York: United Nations.

American Civil Liberties Union National Security Project. 2012. *The Torture Report: What the Documents say about America's Post 9/11 Torture Program.* New York: ACLU.

Amnesty International. 1977. *Amnesty International's Report on Torture, 1975–1976.* New York: Amnesty International.

———. 1978. *Human Rights in Uganda Report.* London: Amnesty International.

———. 1983. *Political Killings by Government.* London: Amnesty International.

———. 1984. *Torture in the Eighties.* New York: Amnesty International.

———. 1992. *Amnesty International Report 1992.* New York: Amnesty International.

———. 1993. "Amnesty Action 1992: A Year of Trial and Triumph." *Amnesty Action.*

———. 1994a. *Amnesty International Report 1994.* New York: Amnesty International.

———. 1994b, Summer. "Colombia: Is U.S. Drug War Aid Financing Murder?" *Amnesty Action.*

———. 1998. *Rights for All—Amnesty International's Report on Human Rights in the United States of America.* New York: Amnesty International.

———. 1999, December 1. "Israel High Court Should End the Shame of Torture." *AI Index* MDE 15/005/1999.

———. 2001a. "China: Extensive Use of Torture—from Police to Tax Collectors to Birth Control Officials." *AI Index* ASA 17/003/2001. Accessed from: web.amnesty. org/ai.nsf/Index/ASA170032001? OpenDocument&of=COUNTRIES%5CCHINA.

———. 2001b. *Amnesty International Report 2001.* New York: Amnesty International. Accessed from: www.amnestyusa.org/scripts/exit.cgi?www.amnesty.org/ailib/inde.

———. 2001c. *Racism and the Administration of Justice.* New York: Amnesty International. Accessed from: web.amnesty.org/ai.nsf/Index/ACT400202001?OpenDocument&of=THEMES\RACISM.

———. 2002a. *Death Penalty Facts: Juveniles.* Accessed from: www.amnestyusa.org/abolish/juveniles.html.

———. 2002b. *Amnesty International Website against the Death Penalty.* Accessed from: www.amnestyusa.org/scripts/exit.cgi?www.amnesty.org/ailib/index.html.

———. 2002c, September 4. "Worldwide Executions Doubled in 2001." *AI Index* ACT 50/005/2002.

———. 2002d. "Red Hands to Stop the Use of Child Soldiers." *AI Index* ACT 76/001/2002. Accessed from: www.amnesty-usa.org/news/2002/world02122002.html.

———. 2002e. *Guatemala's Lethal Legacy: Past Impunity and Renewed Human Rights Violations.* Accessed from: www.amnestyusa.org/countries/guatemala/lethal_legacy.rtf.

———. 2002f. *USA: A Safe Haven for Torturers.* New York: Amnesty International.

———. 2009. *Death Sentences and Executions in 2008.* London: Amnesty International.

———. 2011. *Amnesty International Report 2011.* London: Amnesty International.

———. 2012a. *From Cradle to War.* Accessed March 14, 2012, from Child Soldiers: www.amnestyusa.org/our-work/issues/children-s-rights/child-soldiers.

———. 2012b. *Impunity.* Accessed March 16, 2012, from Amnesty International: www.amnestyusa.org/our-work/countries/americas/colombia/impunity.

Associated Press. 1994, March 20. "S. Africa Official Questions Validity of Violence Claims." *Fort Wayne Journal Gazette*, 2A.
————. 1995. "Argentine Officer Admits Military Killed Prisoners." *Fort Wayne Journal Gazette*, March 12.
Associated Press/Huff Post World. 2011, May 25. "Operation Odyssey Dawn: U.S. Launches Military Strikes In Libya." Accessed March 28, 2012, from Huff Post World: www.huffingtonpost.com/2011/03/19/operation-odyssey-dawn-us_n_838009.html.
Associated Press/*NY Daily News*. 2012, March 6. "U.S. Military Sued by Female Servicemembers Alleging Rape, Sexual Assault." Accessed from: NYDailyNews.com.
Balint, J. L. 1996. "Conflict, Conflict Victimization, and Legal Redress, 1945–1996." *Law and Contemporary Problems* 59, no. 4: 231–47.
Ball, Patrick, Paul Kobrak, and Herbert F. Spirer. 1999. *State Violence in Guatemala, 1960–1996: A Quantitative Reflection*. Annapolis Junction, Md.: American Association for the Advancement of Science.
Barry, J., and M. Hirsh. 2005, January 7. "The Salvador Option." *Newsweek*.
Bastick, M., K. Grimm, and R. Kunz. 2007. *Sexual Violence in Armed Conflict: Global Overview and Implications for the Security Sector*. Geneva, Switzerland: Geneva Centre for the Democratic Control of Armed Forces.
BBC News. 2009, August 26. "China Admits Death Row Organ Use." Accessed February 22, 2012, from BBC News: news.bbc.co.uk/2/hi/8222732.stm.
Beirne, Piers, and James Messerschmidt. 1991. *Criminology*. New York: Harcourt Brace Jovanovich.
Berma, Paige. 1994, July. "Torture behind Bars." *The Progressive* 58: 21–27.
Betancur, Belisario. 1993. *From Madness to Hope: The 12-Year War in El Salvador: Report of the Commission on the Truth for El Salvador*. UN Doc. S/25500/Annex. New York: United Nations.
Bissio, Roberto Remo. 1990. "A Creeping Bhopal." In *Third World Guide 91/92*, edited by R. R. Bissio. Montevideo, Uruguay: Garamond Press.
Blum, R. 2008. *Riots in European Cities: Lessons and Council of Europe Response*. Strasbourg: Council of Europe, Social, Health and Family Affairs Committee.
Blum, William. 1988. *The CIA, A Forgotten History: U.S. Global Interventions since World War 2*. London: Zed Books.
————. 1995. *Killing Hope: U.S. Military and CIA Interventions since World War II*. Monroe, Maine: Common Courage Press.
————. 2000. *Rogue State: A Guide to the World's Only Superpower*. Monroe, Maine: Common Courage Press.
Bodley, John H. 1982. *Victims of Progress*. Menlo Park, Calif.: Benjamin Cummings Publishing.
Booth, John A. 1991. "Socioeconomic and Political Roots of National Revolts in Central America." *Latin America Research Review* 26: 33.
Borum, Randy. 2011. "Science of Global Security and Armed Conflict." December 14. Accessed September 17, 2012, from: globalcrim.blogspot.com/2011/12/armed-conflicts-declined-worldwide-in.html.
Bowers, William. 1974. *Executions in America*. Lexington, Mass.: D. C. Heath.
Brown, Dee. 1970. *Bury My Heart at Wounded Knee*. New York: Henry Holt Company.
Brown, DeNeen L. 2003, November 12. "Ex-Detainee Details Fearful Path to Syria Torture Followed Handover By American 'Removal' Unit." *Washington Post Foreign Service*, A14.
Brown, Jodi M. and Patrick A. Langan. 2001. "Policing and Homicide, 1976–98: Justifiable Homicide of Felons by Police and Murder of Police by Felons." Washington, D.C.: Department of Justice Bureau of Justice Statistics. Accessed September 14, 2012, from: bjs.ojp.usdoj.gov/index.cfm?ty=pbdetail&iid=829.
Brzezinski, Z. 1993. *Out of Control: Global Turmoil on the Eve of the Twenty-First Century*. New York: Simon and Schuster.
Bush, G. W. 2011. *Decision Points*. New York: Broadway Books.
Cable News Network. 2002, November 4. *U.S. Policy on Assassinations*. Accessed November 1, 2011, from CNN.Com Law Center: archives.cnn.com/2002/LAW/11/04/us.assass ination.policy/.
Canadian Broadcasting Company News. 2005, October 27. "Indepth: Maher Arar: Timeline." Accessed June 26, 2012, from CBC Online: www.cbc.ca/news/background/arar/.
Carvalho, G. O. 2000. "The Politics of Indigenous Land Rights in Brazil." *Bulletin of Latin American Research*: 461–78.
Chambliss, William J. 1989. "State-Organized Crime—The American Society of Criminology, 1988 Presidential Address." *Criminology* 27: 183–208.
Chomsky, Noam. 1993. *Year 501: The Conquest Continues*. Boston: South End Press.
Chomsky, Noam, and Edward S. Herman. 1979. *The Washington Connection and Third World Fascism*. Boston: South End Press.

Church Committee. 1975. *Alleged Assassination Plots Involving Foreign Leaders.* Edited by U.S. Senate Select Committee to Study Governmental Operations with Respect to Intelligence Activities. Washington, D.C.: Government Printing Office.

Churchill, Ward. 1997. *A Little Matter of Genocide.* San Francisco: City Lights.

Churchill, Ward, and Jim Vander Wall. 1990. *Agents of Repression.* Boston: South End Press.

Cockburn, P. 2011, April 3. "The Shady Men Backed by the West to Displace Gaddafi." *The Independent.* Accessed from: www.independent.co.uk/opinion/commentators/patrick-cock-burn-the-shady-men-backed-bythe-west-to-displace-gaddafi-2260826.html.

Coleman, James S. 1989. *The Criminal Elite.* New York: St. Martin's Press.

Creel, G. 1944. *War Criminals and Punishment.* New York: R. M. McBride & Company.

Doyle, K., and P. Kornbluh. 1997a. *CIA and Assassinations: The Guatemala 1954 Documents.* Produced by National Security Archive and the Gelman Library, George Washington University. Accessed March 6, 2012, from National Security Archive Electronic Briefing Book No. 4: www.gwu.edu/~nsarchiv/NSAEBB/NSAEBB4/.

———. 1997b. *Document 2—"A Study of Assassination."* Accessed March 6, 2012, from National Security Archive: www.gwu.edu/~nsarchiv/NSAEBB/NSAEBB4/.

Echavarri, F. 2011, May 14. "SWAT Raid Fatal Drama Is Revealed in 911 Call." *Arizona Daily Star.* Accessed February 22, 2012, from: azstarnet.com/news/local/crime/article_b3177522-baa0-5c9e-9f0d-d3d7da6e9e4b.html.

Eisenberg, Daniel. 2002, May 13. "We're Taking Him Out." *Newsweek* 159, no. 19: 36–38.

Emerson, Steven. 1988. *Secret Warriors: Inside the Covert Military Operations of the Reagan Era.* New York: G. P. Putnam's Sons.

Ensign, Todd, and Glenn Alcalay. 1994, Summer. "Duck and Cover(up): U.S. Radiation Testing on Humans." *Covert Action Quarterly*: 28–35.

Farmer, B. 2011, October 22. "Gaddafi's Final Hours: Nato and the SAS Helped Rebels Drive Hunted Leader into Endgame in a Desert Drain." *The Telegraph.*

Flanders, Laura. 1994. "Brookhaven Lab: The Cancer Connection." *Covert Action Quarterly* no. 51 (winter).

Frankel, Mark, Joshua Hammer, Joseph Contreras, Ron Moreau, and Christopher Dickey. 1995, August 14. "Boy Soldiers." *Newsweek*: 44–46.

Frappier, Jon. 1983. "Above the Law: Violations of International Law by the U.S. Government from Truman to Reagan." *Crime and Social Justice* 21–22: 1–36.

Fuller, M. 2005, June 2. *For Iraq, "The Salvador Option" Becomes Reality.* Accessed March 6, 2012, from Centre for Research on Globalisation: www.globalresearch.ca/articles/FUL506A.html.

Garfield, R. 1999. "Morbidity and Mortality Among Iraqi Children from 1990 to 1998: Assessing the Impact of Economic Sanctions (1999)," Accessed September 17, 2012, from: www.casi.org.uk/info/garfield/dr-garfield.html

Garfield, R., J. Devin, and J. Fausey. 1995. "The Health Impact of Economic Sanctions." *Bulletin of New York Academy of Medicine*: 454–69.

General Accounting Office. 1990. *Death Penalty Sentencing: Research Indicates a Pattern of Racial Disparity.* GGD 90-57. Accessed from: 161.203.16.4/t2pbat11/140845.pdf

———. 1993, November. *Nuclear Health and Safety: Examples of Post World War II Radiation Releases at U.S. Nuclear Sites.* RCED 94-51FS.

Glauner, L. 2001. "The Need for Accountability and Reparation: 1830–1976: The United States Government's Role in the Promotion, Implementation, and Execution of the Crime of Genocide against Native Americans." *De Paul Law Review* 51: 911–62.

Guatemalan Historical Clarification Commission. 1999. *Guatemala: Memory of Silence.* Accessed from: hrdata.aaas.org/ceh/report/english/.

Gurr, Ted Robert. 1986. "The Political Origins of State Violence and Terror: A Theoretical Analysis." In *Government Violence and Repression: An Agenda for Research*, edited by M. Stohl and G. A. Lopez. New York: Greenwood Press.

Haines, G. K. 1997. *Document 3, "Selection of individuals for disposal by Junta Group," March 31, 1954.* Accessed March 6, 2012, from National Security Archive: www.gwu.edu/~nsarchiv/NSAEBB/NSAEBB4/cia-guatemala1_1.html.

Harff, Barbara. 1986. "Genocide as State Violence." In *Government Violence and Repression: An Agenda for Research*, edited by M. Stohl and G. A. Lopez, 45–71. New York: Greenwood Press.

Harris, Emily G. 1994, May/June. "Human Radiation Tests: An Old Story Finally Makes the Front Page." *Extra*, 8.

Harrison, W. 2011, May 24. "ACLU Sues State Troopers over Man's Shooting Death." *Denver News.* Accessed February 22, 2012, from: www.thedenverchannel.com/news/28011349/detail.html.

Haugaard, Lisa. 1997, September. "Textbook Repression: US Training Manuals Declassified." *Covert Action Quarterly*, no. 1: 29–39.

Haviland, William A. 1987. *Cultural Anthropology.* 5th ed. New York: Holt, Reinhart and Winston, 421–23.

Herman, Edward. 1982. *The Real Terror Network*. Boston: South End Press.

Herman, Edward, and Gerry O'Sullivan. 1987. "U.S. Sponsorship of International Terrorism: An Overview." *Crime and Social Justice* 27–28: 1–29.

———. 1989. *The Terrorism Industry*. New York: Pantheon.

Hersch, Seymour M. 2004, May 24. "Annals of National Security: The Grey Zone—How a Secret Pentagon Program Came to Abu Ghraib." *The New Yorker*. Accessed June 26, 2012, from: www.newyorker.com/archive/2004/05/24/040524fa_fact.

Hinckle, Warren, and William Turner. 1981. *The Fish Is Red*. New York: Harper and Row.

Hobsbawm, E. J. 1994. *The Age of Extremes: A History of the World, 1914–1991*. London: Michael Joseph.

Hougan, Jim. 1978. *Spooks: The Haunting of America—The Private Use of Secret Agents*. New York: Morrow.

Human Rights Watch. 1998. *Bosnia and Hercegovina, "A Closed, Dark Place": Past and Present Human Rights Abuses in Foca*. New York: Human Rights Watch.

———. 1999. *Leave None to Tell the Story: Genocide in Rwanda*. New York: Human Rights Watch.

Iadicola, P. 2008. "Globalization and Empire." *The International Journal of Social Inquiry*: 3–37.

———. 2009. "Violence of Empire." *International Journal of Contemporary Sociology* 46, no. 2.

———. 2010. "Do Empires Commit State Crime?" In *State Crime: Current Perspectives*, edited by D. L. Rothe and C. W. Mullins, 122–41. New Brunswick: Rutgers University Press.

Iadicola, Peter, and Gerry O'Sullivan. 1989. *The Terrorism Industry*. New York: Pantheon.

Imerman, Vicky A. 1994, Spring. "The US Army School of the Americas—School of Assassins." *Witness for Peace Newsletter* 11: 13–14.

Innocence Project. 2012. *Facts on Post-Conviction DNA Exonerations*. Accessed February 22, 2012, from Innocence Project: www.innocenceproject.org/Content/Facts_on_PostConviction_DNA_Exonerations.php#.

International Court of Justice. 1986, June 27. *Military and Paramilitary Activities in and against Nicaragua (Nicaragua v. United States of America)*. Accessed March 20, 2012, from International Court of Justice: www.icj-cij.org/docket/?sum=367&code=nus&p1=3&p2=3&case=70&k=66&p3=5.

Irving, S. 2011, April 1. "Aboriginal Peoples Lose Rights and Mineral Rich Land in Northern Territory Intervention." Accessed March 6, 2012, from The WIP: www.thewip.net/contributors/2011/04/aboriginal_peoples_lose_rights.html.

Iserson, K. V. 2002. *Demon Doctors: Physicians as Serial Killers*. Tucson: Galen Press.

Jones, Anthony R. 2004. *AR 15-6 Investigation of the Abu Ghraib Prison and 205th Military Intelligence Brigade: AR 15-6 Investigation of the Abu Ghraib Detention Facility and 205th Military Intelligence Brigade*. Buffalo: William S. Hein & Co

Jenkins, Brian. 1984, November. "The Who, What, When, Where, How, and Why of Terrorism." Paper presented at the Detroit Police Department Conference on Urban Terrorism: Planning or Chaos.

Johnson, Chalmers. 2000. *Blowback: The Cost and Consequences of American Empire*. New York: Henry Holt and Company.

———. 2004. *The Sorrows of Empire: Militarism, Secrecy, and the End of the Republic*. New York: Metropolitan Books.

Johnston, D. 2009, August 24. "U.S. Says Rendition to Continue, but With More Oversight." *The New York Times*.

Jones, A. 2004. *Genocide, War Crimes and the West: History and Complicity*. London: Zed Books.

Jones, James H. 1987. *Bad Blood: The Tuskegee Syphilis Experiment*. New York: Free Press.

Karen Women's Organization. 2004. *Shattering Silences*. Mae Hong Son Province, Thailand: The Karen Women's Organization.

Karmen, Andrew. 1974. "Agent Provocateur in the Contemporary U.S. Leftist Movement." In *The Criminologist: Crime and the Criminal*, edited by C. Reasons. Pacific Palisades, Calif.: Goodyear.

Kerr, Mary Lee, and Bob Hall. 1992, January. "Chickens Come Home to Roost." *The Progressive* 56: 1, 29.

Kiernan, B. 2007. *Blood and Soil: A World History of Genocide and Extermination from Sparta to Darfur*. New Haven: Yale University Press.

Kimerling, R., A. E. Street, K. Gima, and M. W. Smith. 2008. "Evaluation of Universal Screening for Military-Related Sexual Trauma. *Psychiatric Services*: 635–40.

Kimerling, R., A. E. Street, and J. Pavao. 2010. "Evaluation of Universal Screening for Military-Related Sexual Trauma. *American Journal of Public Health* 100, no. 8: 1409–12.

Klare, Michael T. and Cynthia Arnson. 1981. *Supplying Repression: U.S. Support for Authoritarian Regimes Abroad*. Washington, D.C.: Institute for Policy Studies.

Klein, N. 2007. *The Shock Doctrine*. New York: Picador.

Kohn, Howard. 1992. "America's Worst Polluter." In *The Rolling Stone Environmental Reader*, edited by R. Stone, 37–50. Washington, D.C.: Island Press.

Kornbluh, P. 2010, April 10. "Kissinger Blocked Demarche on International Assassinations to Condor States." Accessed June 26, 2012, from The National Security Archive: www.gwu.edu/~nsarchiv/NSAEBB/NSAEBB312/index.htm.

Laqueur, Walter. 1987. *The Age of Terrorism*. Boston: Little Brown.

Lewis, Flora. 2001, January 12. "Israel Defiles Itself with These Assassinations of Palestinians." *International Herald Tribune*.

Legum, Colin. 1966, October. "The Massacre of the Proud Ibos." *Observer*, 16.

Leitenberg, M. 2006. *Deaths in Wars and Conflicts in the 20th Century*. Ithaca: Cornell University, Peace Studies Program.

Levene, M. 2004. "A Dissenting Voice: Part II." *Journal of Genocide Research* 6, no. 3: 431–45.

———. 2005. *Genocide in the Age of the Nation-State*. 2 vols. London: I.B. Tauris.

———. 2008. "Empires, Native Peoples, and Genocide." In *Empire, Colony, Genocide: Conquest, Occupation, and Subaltern Resistance in World History*, edited by A. D. Moses, 183–204. New York: Berghahn.

Levinson, Arlene. 1995, September 24. "The Modern Face of Genocide." *Fort Wayne Journal Gazette* (Associated Press), C1.

Leyan, Brian. 2002, January 14. "Sharp Rise in Killings by Police, Says Report." *The Nation*.

Loftin, C., B. Wiersema, and D. McDowall. 2003. "Underreporting of Justifiable Homicides Committed by Police Officers in the United States, 1976–1998." *American Journal of Public Health*: 1117–23.

Luft, Kerry. 1995, January 15. "For Bogota's Street Children, Death is Just around the Corner." *Chicago Tribune*, 7.

MacMillan, G. 1995. *At the End of the Rainbow? Gold, Land, and People in the Brazilian Amazon*. New York: Columbia University Press.

Mahajan, R. 2001, November/December. "'We Think the Price Is Worth It.'" *Extra!*

Marx, Gary T. 1974. "Thoughts on a Neglected Category of Social Movement Participant: The Agent Provocateur and the Informant." *American Journal of Sociology* 80: 402–42.

Matthiessen, Peter. 1991. *In the Spirit of Crazy Horse*. New York: Viking Penguin.

Mazzetti, M., E. Schmutt, and R. F. Worth. 2011, September 30. "Two-Year Manhunt Led to Killing of Awlaki in Yemen." *The New York Times*.

McClintock, Michael. 1985. *The American Connection: State Terror and Popular Resistance in El Salvador*. London: Zed Books.

McCoy, A. W. 2006. *A Question of Torture*. New York: Metropolita Books/Henry Hold and Company.

McGehee, R. 1999, October 9. "CIA Support of Death Squads." Accessed March 6, 2012, from Serendipity: www.serendipity.li/cia/death_squads1.htm.

McGreal, C. 2008, January 22. "War in Congo Kills 45,000 People Each Month." *Guardian*.

McSherry, P. 2005. *Predatory States: Operation Condor and Covert War in Latin America*. Lanham: Rowman & Littlefield.

Michalowski, Raymond. 1985. *Order, Law, and Crime: An Introduction to Criminology*. New York: Random House.

Monthly Review. 2002, March. "U.S. Military Bases and Empire." *Monthly Review* 53, no. 10.

Moran, Michael. 1998, August 24. "Bin Laden Comes Home to Roost: His CIA Ties Are Only the Beginning of a Woeful Story." Accessed from MSNBC: www.msnbc.com/news/190144.asp.

Moses, A. D. 2008. *Empire, Colony, Genocide: Conquest, Occupation, and Subaltern Resistance in World History*. Herndon: Berghahn Books.

Mullins, C. W., and D. L. Rothe. 2008. *Blood, Power, and Bedlam*. New York: Peter Lang Publishing.

Nairn, Allan. 1984, May. "Behind the Death Squads." *The Progressive*: 19–29.

Ndiaye, Bacre Waly. 1996, 7 October. "Human Rights Questions: Human Rights Questions, Including Alternative Approaches for Improving the Effective Enjoyment of Human Rights and Fundamental Freedoms. Report of the Special Rapporteur of the Commission on Human Rights on Extrajudicial, Summary or Arbitrary Executions." Agenda item 110 (b), Fifty-first session of the United Nations General Assembly. Accessed from: www.unhchr.ch/Huridoc-da/Huridoca.nsf/TestFrame/10729ea00b7c34b0802567080052b7e4?Opendocument.

Neier, Aryeh. 1992, February 3. "Watching Rights." *The Nation*, 129.

New Internationalist. 1994, November. "That's the Way the Money Goes." *New Internationalist*, no. 261: 8–9.

New York Times. 1994, January 14. "Two Recall 1949 Radiation Tests on Them," A14. Cited in Todd Ensign and Glenn Alcalay, "Duck and Cover(up): U.S. Radiation Testing on Humans," *Covert Action Quarterly*, no. 49 (Summer 1994): 28–35.

Newsweek. 1981, August 3. "A Plan to Overthrow Kaddafi." *Newsweek*.

————. 1992, July 5. "Tailhook: Scandal Time." *Newsweek.*

————. 1993, December 27. "America's Nuclear Secrets." *Newsweek*, 15. Cited in Todd Ensign and Glenn Alcalay, "Duck and Cover(up): U.S. Radiation Testing on Humans," *Covert Action Quarterly*, no. 49 (Summer 1994): 31.

Pappe, I. 2006. *The Ethnic Cleansing of Palestine*. Oxford: One World Publication.

Parenti, Christian. 1994. "Urban Militarism." *Z Magazine* 7: 47–52.

Pearce, Jenny. 1982. *Under the Eagle*. Boston: South End Press.

Perreira, G. A. 2011a, March 25. "British Intelligence Worked with Al Qaeda to Kill Qaddafi." Accessed March 28, 2012, from GlobalResearch.ca: www.globalresearch.ca/index.php?context=va&aid=23957.

————. 2011b, March 25. "US and British Intelligence Have Repeatedly Tried to Kill Qaddafi CIA Involved in Libya's Civil War." Accessed March 28, 2012, from Project Censored: www.mediafreedominternational.org/2011/04/04/us-and-british-intelligence-have-repeatedly-tried-to-kill-qaddafi-cia-involved-in-libya%E2%80%99s-civil-war/.

Pierce, Chester M. 1970. "Violence and the National Character." In *Violence: Causes and Solutions*, edited by R. Hartogs and E. Artzt, 119–26. New York: Dell Books.

Ploughshares. 2011. "Armed Conflict Report 2011." Accessed September 17, 2012, from: www.ploughshares.ca/content/armed-conflicts-report-0.

Priest, D. 2005, November 22. "CIA Holds Terror Suspects in Secret Prisons: Debate Is Growing Within Agency About Legality and Morality of Overseas System Set Up After 9/11." *Washington Post*, A01.

Prouty, Fletcher L. 1992. *JFK: The CIA, Vietnam, and the Plot to Assassinate John F. Kennedy*. New York: Birch Lane Press.

Ritchie, A. J., and J. L. Mogul. 2007. *In the Shadows of the War on Terror*. New York: United Nations Committee on the Elimination of Racial Discrimination.

Robertson, C. 2011, August 5. "Officers Guilty of Shooting Six in New Orleans." *The New York Times.*

Roebuck, Julian, and Stanley C. Weeber. 1978. *Political Crime in the United States*. New York: Praeger.

Roggio, B., and A. Mayer. 2012, March 15. "Charting the Data for US Airstrikes in Pakistan, 2004–2012." Accessed March 28, 2012, from The Long War Journal: www.longwarjournal.org/pakistan-strikes.php.

Rosenberg, Howard. 1981, September/October. "Informed Consent." *Mother Jones*: 31–37, 44.

Ross, J. 2005. "A History of Torture." In *Torture*, edited by K. Roth M. Worden, 3–17. New York: The New Press.

Rothe, D. L. 2009. *State Criminality: The Crime of All Crimes*. Plymouth: Lexington Books.

Russian Archives. 1995. "Revelations from the Russian Archives—Kirov Murder and Purges." Library of Congress exhibit displayed through Spring 1992. Translated excerpts displayed on American Online. Vienna, Va.: America Online, Education and Reference Department (Electronic Communication Network).

Sadeghi, S. 2011, October 19. "Hillary Clinton Wants Gaddafi Killed." Accessed March, 28 2012, from Huff Post World: www.huffingtonpost.com/shirin-sadeghi/hillary-clinton-wants-gad_b_1020705.html.

Safetyforum Research. 2002. "Military Toxic Waste: Killing after the Wars are Over." Accessed July 21, 2002, from: www.safetyforum.com/mtw/.

Savage, C. 2011, October 8. "Secret U.S. Memo Made Legal Case to Kill a Citizen." *The New York Times.*

Schmetzer, Uli. 1994, August 29. "Transplant Coercion Charged." *Chicago Tribune*, 1–5.

Schneider, Keith. 1994, April 12. "Researchers are Accused of Forgeries" *New York Times*. Cited in Todd Ensign and Glenn Alcalay, "Duck and Cover(up): U.S. Radiation Testing on Humans," *Covert Action Quarterly*, no. 49 (Summer 1994): 28–35.

Sebastian, S. 2011, February 11. "India's Mineral Wealth Obtained by Violating Tribal Rights, Says ILO Study." *India Today.*

Shah, T., and G. Bowley. 2012, March 11. "U.S. Sergeant Is Said to Kill 16 Civilians in Afghanistan." *The New York Times*, A1.

Shane, S. 2012, February 5. "U.S. Said to Target Rescuers at Drone Strike Sites." *The New York Times.*

Sharkey, Jacqueline. 1990, May/June. "Nicaragua: Anatomy of an Election." *Common Cause Magazine*: 20–29.

Silverfarb, Daniel, and Majid Khadduri. 1997. *Britain's Informal Empire in the Middle East: A Case Study of Iraq 1929–1941*. New York: Oxford University Press.

Simon, David R., and D. Stanley Eitzen. 1993. *Elite Deviance*. Boston: Allyn and Bacon.

Sivard, Ruth Leger. 1982. *World Military and Social Expenditures*. Leesburg, Va.: World Priorities.

————. 1986. *World Military and Social Expenditures 1986*. Washington, D.C.: World Priorities.

Smith, D. 2011, December 15. "Photo Shows Pepper-Sprayed Prisoner." My Fox Tampa Bay. Accessed February 22, 2012, from: www.myfoxtampabay.com/dpp/news/investigates/photo-shows-pepper-sprayed-prisoner-12142011.

Snyder, Howard N., and Melissa Sickmund. 1995. *Juvenile Offenders and Victims: A Focus on Violence*. Washington, D.C.: Office of Juvenile Justice and Delinquency.

Snyder, T. 2010. *Bloodlands: Europe between Hitler and Stalin*. New York: Basic Books.

SOA Watch. 2002. "School of the Americas: School of Assassins, USA." Accessed from Third World Traveler: www.thirdworldtraveler.com/Terrorism/SOA.html.

Soh, C. S. 2001. *Japan's Responsibility toward Comfort Women Survivors*. San Francisco: Japan Policy Research Institute, University of San Francisco, Center for the Pacific Rim..

Sollenberg, Margareta, and Peter Wallensteen. 2001. "Patterns of Major Armed Conflicts 1990–2000." *SIPRI Yearbook 2001*. Stockholm, Sweden: Stockholm International Peace Research Institute.

Speier, J. 2011, April 17. "Rapes of Women in Military 'a National Disgrace.'" *San Francisco Chronicle*, F-3.

Sponsel, L. E., and T. N. Headland. 1996. *Tropical Deforestation: The Human Dimension*. New York: Columbia University Press.

Stålenheim, P., C. Perdomo, and E. Sköns. 2008. "Military Expenditure." Chapter 8 in *SIPRI 2007 Yearbook*, 267–97. Stockholm: Stockholm International Peace Research Institute.

Stewart, Sarah. 1994, June. "No Pablo, No Story." *New Internationalist*, no. 256: 20–22.

Stockholm International Peace Research Institute. 1994. *SIPRI Yearbook 1994*. Oxford: Oxford University Press.

———. 2011. *SIPRI Yearbook 2011: Armaments, Disarmament and International Security*. New York: Oxford University Press.

Suárez, D. M. 2009, November 25. "US Military Bases in Columbia and the Arms Race in South America." *Global Affairs—International Relations Magazine*.

Survival for Tribal Peoples. 2012, March 1. "Official Report Confirms Presence of 'Hiding Tribe' at Paraguay Ranch." Accessed March 6, 2012, from Survival for Tribal Peoples: www.survivalinternational.org/news/8140.

———. 2012, March 6. "The Guarani." Accessed March 6, 2012, from Survival for Tribal Peoples: www.survivalinternational.org/tribes/guarani.

———. 2012, March 6. "The Omo Valley Tribes." Accessed March 6, 2012, from Survival for Tribal Peoples: www.survivalinternational.org/tribes/omovalley/wayoflife#tribe-home-tabs.

Taguba, Maj. Gen. Antonio M. 2003. *US Army Report on Iraqi Prisoner Abuse*. Accessed June 26, 2012, from: www.antiwar.com/news/?articleid=2479.

Toope, S. J. 2005. *Commission of Inquiry into the Actions of Canadian Officials in Relation to Maher Arar*. Ottawa: Government of Canada.

UNICEF. 1999. "Iraq Surveys Shows 'Humanitarian Emergency.'" Accesseded March 14, 2012, from Information Newsline: www.unicef.org/newsline/99pr29.htm.

United Nations. 2007. *UN Security Council Working Group on Children and Armed Conflict: Conclusion on Children and Armed Conflict in Chad*. New York: United Nations Security Council.

United Nations Commission on Human Rights. 1996. *Report on the Situation of Human Rights in Rwanda submitted by Mr. René Degni-Segui, Special Rapporteur of the Commission on Human Rights under paragraph 20 of the resolution S-3/1 of 25 May 1994*. Geneva: Office of the United Nations High Commissioner for Human Rights.

———. 2002. *Integration of the Human Rights of Women and the Gender Perspective: Mission to Colombia*.

United Nations General Assembly Security Council. 2010. *Children and Armed Conflict*. New York: United Nations.

United Nations Security Council. 2008. "Resolution 1820." Accessed March 7, 2012, from United Nations Security Council: daccess-dds-ny.un.org/doc/UNDOC/GEN/N08/391/44/PDF/N0839144.pdf?OpenElement.

United Nations Special Representative of the Secretary-General for Children and Armed Conflict. 2005. *Report of the Special Representative of the Secretary-General for Children and Armed Conflict*. New York: United Nations.

United Nations World Food Programme. 2012. "Hunger Stats." Accessed March 22, 2012, from Hunger: www.wfp.org/hunger/stats.

U.S. Bureau of Justice Statistics. 2012. "Justifiable Homicides." Accessed February 22, 2012, from *Homicide Trends in the U.S.*: bjs.ojp.usdoj.gov/content/homicide/justify.cfm.

U.S. Council on Foreign Relations. 2002. *Assassination: Does It Work? Should America Try?* Accessed from: www.terrorismanswers.com/policy/assassination_print.html.

U.S. Department of Defense. 2011. *Annual Report on Sexual Harassment and Violence at the Military Service Academies*. Washington, D.C.: U.S. Department of Defense.

U.S. Department of Justice, Bureau of Justice Statistics. 2000. *Sourcebook of Criminal Justice Statistics Online*. Accessed from: www.albany.edu/sourcebook/.

Van Pelt, J. 2011, March/April. "Military Sexual Trauma." *Social Work Today* 11, no. 2: 8.

Watson Institute for International Studies. 2011. *The Costs of War since 2001: Iraq, Afghani-stan, and Pakistan.* Providence: Brown University.

Weber, Max. 1958. "Politics as a Vocation." In *Max Weber: Essays in Sociology,* edited by H. H. Gerth and C. W. Mills, 77–128. New York: Oxford University Press.

Weiner, Tim. 1993, December 14. "In 1990, U.S. Was Still Training Salvador Civilians Tied to Killings." *New York Times,* A1.

Welsome, Eileen. 1993, November 15. "The Plutonium Experiment: Elmer Allen Loses His Leg—And All Hope." *Albuquerque Tribune.* Cited in Todd Ensign and Glenn Alcalay, "Duck and Cover(up): U.S. Radiation Testing on Humans," *Covert Action Quarterly,* no. 49 (Summer 1994).

Wheat, Andrew. 1995, January/February. "Exporting Repression: Arms Profits vs. Human Rights." *Multinational Monitor* 16: 16–21.

White, R. 1978, October 20. *State Department Cable, U.S. Ambassador Robert White (Para-guay) to Secretary of State Cyrus Vance, Subject: Second Meeting with Chief of Staff re Letelier Case, October 20, 1978, Confidential, 1 p.* Accessed March 20, 2012, from the National Security Archive: www.gwu.edu/~nsarchiv/news/20010306/condor.pdf.

Wolf, Eric. 1976. "Killing the Aches." In *Genocide in Paraguay,* edited by R. Arens, 47–57. Philadelphia: Temple University Press.

Wong, K. 2009, November 9. "Italian Court Levies Judgment on U.S. Rendition Program." Accessed June 26, 2012, from ABC News: abcnews.go.com/blogs/politics/2009/11/italian-court-levies-judgment-on-us-rendition-program/.

CHAPTER 9

Ahmad, Nilufar. 1992. "Battling the World Bank." *Multinational Monitor* 13: 20–23.

Amin, Samir. 1980. *Class and Nation: Historically and in the Current Crisis.* New York: Monthly Review Press.

Amland, B. H., and I. MacDougall. 2011, July 29. "A Week Later, Norway Mourns 77 Victims of Massacre." Accessed 28 2012, June, from ABC News: abcnews.go.com/International/wireStory?id=14186416#.T-xGN_X8n7c.

Amnesty International. 1983. *Political Killings by Government.* London: Amnesty Internation-al.

———. 2002. *Guatemala's Lethal Legacy: Past Impunity and Renewed Human Rights Viola-tions.* London: Amnesty International. Accessed from: www.amnestyusa.org/countries/gua-temala/lethal_legacy.rtf.

Anand, S., and A. Sen. 2000. "Human Development and Economic Sustainability." *World Development* 28, no. 12: 2029–49.

Bakan, J. 2004. *The Corporation.* New York: Free Press.

Bales, K. 2004. *Disposable People: New Slavery in the Global Economy.* Berkeley: University of California Press.

Barry, Tom, Beth Wood, and Deb Preusch. 1982. *Dollars and Dictators.* Albuquerque: Re-source Center.

Beer, Linda, and Terry Boswell. 2001. "The Effects of Globalization on Inequality: A Cross National Analysis." Halle Institute Occasional Paper.

Beghin, N. 2008. "Notes on Inequality and Poverty in Brazil: Current Situation and Chal-lenges." Background paper for *From Poverty to Power: How Active Citizens and Effective States Can Change the World,* by Duncan Green. Brasilia: Oxfam International.

Bello, Walden. 1994. *Dark Victory: The United States, Structural Adjustment, and Global Poverty.* London: Pluto Press.

Bissio, Roberto Remo. 1990. *Third World Guide 91/92.* Montevideo, Uruguay: Garamond Press.

Black, George. 1983a. "Garrison Guatemala." *North American Congress on Latin America* 17: 1.

———. 1983b. "Guatemala: The War is Not Over." *North American Congress on Latin Ameri-ca* 17: 2.

Bolles, Lynn. 1983. "Kitchens Hit by Priorities: Employed Working-Class Women Confront the IMF." In *Women, Men, and the International Division of Labor,* edited by J. Nash and M. P. Fernandez-Kelly. Albany: State University of New York Press.

Bullard, Sara. 1991. *The Ku Klux Klan: A History of Racism and Violence.* 4th ed. Atlanta: Klanwatch, a project of the Southern Poverty Law Center.

Carmack, Robert M. 1988. *Harvest of Violence.* Norman: University of Oklahoma Press.

Chinchilla, Norma Stoltz. 1978. "Industrialization, Monopoly Capitalism, and Women's Work in Guatemala." *Signs: Journal of Women in Culture and Society* 3: 38–56.

Chomsky, Noam. 1993. *Year 501: The Conquest Continues*. Boston: South End Press.

Clark, L., and D. Lewis. 1977. *Rape: The Price of Coercive Sexuality*. Toronto: Women's Press.

Coats, Stephen. 1991. "Made in Guatemala: Union Busting in the Maquiladoras." *Multinational Monitor* 12, no. 11.

Coltrane, S. 2000. "Research on Household Labor: Modeling and Measuring the Social Embeddedness of Routine Family Work." *Journal of Marriage and the Family* 62: 1208–33.

Conference Board of Canada. 2011, September. *World Income Inequality*. Accessed April 20, 2012, from the Confernce Board of Canada: www.conferenceboard.ca/hcp/hot-topics/world-inequality.aspx.

del Nevo, Maria. 1995, May. "The Cost of Living." *New Internationalist* 267: 20–21.

Dewitt, Peter, and James Petras. 1981. "The Political Economy of Debt." In *Class, State, and Power in the Third World*, edited by J. Petras, 96–117. Montclair: Allanheld, Osmun.

Dowd, Douglas. 1993. *U.S. Capitalist Development Since 1776*. Armong, N.Y.: M.E. Sharpe.

Dray, Philip. 2002. *At the Hands of Persons Unknown: The Lynching of Black America*. New York: Random House.

Economic Policy Institute. 2011, January 24. *Wealth Holdings Remain Unequal in Good and Bad Times: Distribution of Wealth by Class, 1983–2009*. Accessed June 1, 2012, from Economic Policy Institute: The State of Working America: stateofworkingamerica.org/charts/distribution-of-wealth-by-class-1983-2009/.

Edwards, Richard, Michael Reich, and Thomas E. Weisskopf. 1978. The capitalist system: A radical analysis of American society. Englewood Cliffs: Prentice Hall.

Ellwood, Wayne. 2001. *The No-Nonsense Guide to Globalization*. Toronto: New Internationalist Publications.

Farmer, Paul. 1999. *Infections and Inequalities: The Modern Plagues*. Berkeley: University of California Press.

Federal Bureau of Investigation. 2010. "Sex Trafficking Convictions." Accessed June 6, 2012, from the Federal Bureau of Investigation: www.fbi.gov/news/stories/2010/may/trafficking_052010/sex-trafficking-convictions-seattle-gang-dismantled.

———. 2011, November 14. "Hate Crimes Remain Steady: 2010 FBI Report Released." Accessed June 6, 2012, from the Federal Bureau of Investigation: www.fbi.gov/news/stories/2011/november/hatecrimes_111411/hatecrimes_111411.

———. 2012a, March 22. "Three Mississippi Men Plead Guilty to Their Roles in the Racially Motivated Assault and Murder of an African-American Man." Accessed June 6, 2012, from Federal Bureau of Investigation—Jackson Division: www.fbi.gov/jackson/press-releases/2012/three-mississippi-men-plead-guilty-to-their-roles-in-the-racially-motivated-assault-and-murder-of-an-african-american-man.

———. 2012b, January 13. "MLK Parade Bomber." Accessed June 7, 2012, from the Federal Bureau of Investigation: www.fbi.gov/news/stories/2012/january/hatecrime_011312/hatecrime_011312.

Flounders, S. 2011, June 23. "The Pentagon and Slave Labor in U.S. Prisons." Accessed June 6, 2012, from the Center for Research on Globalization: www.globalresearch.ca/index.php?context=va&aid=25376.

Food and Agriculture Organization of the United Nations. 2001. *The State of Food Insecurity in the World*. Rome: Food and Agriculture Organization of the United Nations.

Franke, Richard W., and Barbara H. Chasin. 1980. *Seeds of Famine: Ecological Destruction and the Development Dilemma in the West African Sahel*. Montclair: Allanheld, Osmun.

Fuwa, M. 2004. "Macro-Level Gender Inequality and the Division of Household Labor in 22 Countries." *American Sociological Review* 69, no. 6: 751–67.

Gage, Susan. 1991. *Colonialism in the Americas*. Victoria, British Columbia: Victoria International Development Education Association.

Galtung, J. 1969. "Violence, Peace, and Peace Research." *Journal of Peace Research* 6, no. 9: 167–91.

———. 1971. "A Structural Theory of Imperialism." *Journal of Peace Research* 8, no. 2: 81–117.

Galtung, J. and T. Höivik. 1971. "Structural and Direct Violence: A Note on Operationalization." *Journal of Peace Research* 8, no. 1: 73–76.

George, Susan. 1982. *Food for Beginners*. New York: Writers and Readers Publishing.

———. 1988. *A Fate Worse than Debt*. New York: Grove Press.

———. 1990. *Ill Fares the Land*. London: Penguin Books.

Godrej, Dinyar. 1995, May. "Hunger in a World of Plenty." *New Internationalist* 267: 7–10.

Grant, James. 1994. *The State of the World's Children 1994*. Oxford, UK: Oxford University Press.

Guatemala Human Rights Commission/USA. 2011. "Fact Sheet: U.S. Foreign Assistance to Guatemala." Accessed June 28, 2012, from Guatemala Human Rights Commission/USA: ghrc-usa.org/Publications/factsheet_USassistance_Guatemala.pdf.

Hammill, M. 2007. *Growth, Poverty and Inequality in Central America.* Mexico City: United Nations Economic Commission for Latin America and the Caribbean.

Hanlon, Joseph, and Ann Pettifor. 2000. *Kicking the Habit: Finding a Lasting Solution to Addictive Lending and Borrowing—And Its Corrupting Side-Effects.* London: Jubilee Research. Accessed from: www.jubileeplus.org/analysis/reports/habitfull.htm.

Herman, Edward, and Gerry O'Sullivan. 1989. *The Terrorism Industry.* New York: Pantheon Books.

Human Rights Watch. 2012. *World Report 2011: Guatemala.* New York: Human Rights Watch.

Institute of Race Relations. 1982. *Patterns of Racism.* London: Institute for Race Relations.

International Labour Organization. 2005. *A Global Alliance against Forced Labour.* Geneva: International Labour Office.

Jalee, Pierre. 1965. *The Pillage of the Third World.* New York: Monthly Review Press.

Joint United Nations Programme on HIV/AIDS (UNAIDS). 2010. *Global Report: UNAIDS Report on the Global Aids Epidemic, 2010.* New York: Joint United Nations Programme on HIV/AIDS (UNAIDS).

Jonas, Suzanne, and David Tobias. 1981. *Guatemala.* Berkeley: North American Congress on Latin America.

Klare, Michael T. 1981. *Supplying Repression: U.S. Support for Authoritarian Regimes Abroad.* Washington, D.C.: Institute for Policy Studies.

Klein, N. 2009. *No Logo.* New York: Picador.

Klugman, J. 2011. *Human Development Report 2011—Sustainability and Equity: A Better Future for All.* New York: United Nations Development Programme.

Klugman, J., F. Rodriguez, and H. L. Choi. 2011. *The HDI 2010: New Controversies, Old Critiques. Development Research Paper 1.* New York: UNDP–HDRO.

Kneen, Brewster. 1995, May. "Captured by the Company." *The New Internationalist* 267: 23–25.

Knight, Danielle. 2001, May 29. "Food Security Worse, Outlook Dim—Experts." Accessed from Inter Press Service News Agency: www.ipsnews.net/interna.asp?idnews=10008.

Köhler, G., and A. Alcock. 1976. "An Empirical Table of Structural Violence." *Journal of Peace Research* 13, no. 4: 343–56.

Korten, Alicia. 1993. "Cultivating Disaster." *Multinational Monitor* 14: 20–22.

Lacey, M. 2008, September 14. "Children in Servitude, the Poorest of Haiti's Poor." *The New York Times,* A16.

Landes, David, and Patricia Flynn. 1984. "Dollars for Dictators: U.S. Aid in Central America and the Caribbean." In *The Politics of Intervention: The United States in Central America,* edited by R. Burbach, and P. Flynn. New York: Monthly Review Press.

Lastarria-Cornhiel, S. 2003. *Guatemala Country Brief: Property Rights and Land Markets.* Madison: Land Tenure Center, University of Wisconsin.

Lee, Martin A. 1993. "Hitler's Offspring." *The Progressive* 57: 28–31.

MacDorman, M. F., and T. J. Mathews. 2011, September. *Understanding Racial and Ethnic Disparities in U.S. Infant Mortality Rates.* Accessed April 4, 2012, from NCHS Data Brief No. 74: www.cdc.gov/nchs/data/databriefs/db74.pdf.

MacFarquhar, N. 2010, October 29. "U.N. Sets Goals to Reduce the Extinction Rate." *New York Times,* A6.

Mathews, Robert. 1986. "Sowing the Dragon's Teeth: The U.S. War against Nicaragua." *North American Congress on Latin America* 20: 13–40.

McAfee, Kathy. 1991. *Storm Signals: Structural Adjustment and Development Alternatives in the Caribbean.* Boston: South End Press.

McDevitt, Jack, Jennifer M. Balboni, Susan Bennett, and Justice Research and Statistics Association. 2000. *Improving the Quality and Accuracy of Bias Crime Statistics Nationally: An Assessment of the First Ten Years of Bias Crime Data Collection.* Washington, D.C.: Bureau of Justice Statistics. Accessed from www.dac.neu.edu/cj.

McGeary, Johanna. 2001, February 12. "Paying for AIDS Cocktails: Who Should Pick Up the Tab for the Third World?" *Time Magazine.*

Medoff, Peter, and Holly Sklar. 1994. *Streets of Hope: The Fall and Rise of an Urban Neighborhood.* Boston: South End Press.

Merrill Lynch/Gemini Consulting. 2001. *World Wealth Report 2000.* Accessed from: www.foxexchange.com/public/fox/news/industry_trends/world_wealth_report_2000.pdf.

Milanovic, B. 1999. "True World Income Distribution, 1988 and 1993." *Policy Research Working Paper* 2244. Washington, D.C.: World Bank.

———. 2006. *DESA Working Paper No. 26—Global Income Inequality: What It Is and Why It Matters.* Accessed June 1, 2012, from UN/DESA Working Papers: www.un.org/esa/desa/papers/2006/wp26_2006.pdf.

Morrison, Roy. 1991. *We Build the Road as We Travel.* Philadelphia: New Society Publishers.

Moyers, Bill. 1988. *The Secret Government.* Washington, D.C.: Seven Locks Press.

Mukonoweshuro, Eliphas G. 1991. "Between Verwoerd and the ANC: Profiles of Contemporary Repression, Deprivation, and Poverty in South Africa's Bantustans." *Social Justice* 18: 171–85.

Murawski, Anthony. 1993. "Challenging Guatemala's Labor Abuses." *Multinational Monitor* 14: 6–7.

Nairn, Allan. 1983. "Guatemala: Central America's Blue Chip Investment." In *Guatemala in Rebellion: Unfinished History*, edited by J. Fried et al. New York: Grove Press.

———. 1984, May. "Behind the Death Squads." *The Progressive*: 19–29.

Neier, Aryeh. 1992, February 3. "Watching Rights." *The Nation*: 533.

New Grolier Multimedia Encyclopedia. 1993. *Black Americans*. Novato, Calif: The Software Toolworks.

New Internationalist. 1995, May. "Hunger—The Facts." *The New Internationalist* 267: 18–19.

Pearce, Jenny. 1982. *Under the Eagle*. Boston: South End Press.

Perkins, J. 2006. *Confessions of an Economic Hit Man*. New York: Plume.

Petras, J., and H. Veltmeyer. 2001. *Globalization Unmasked*. London: Zed Books.

Petras, James. 2002, June. "Who Rules the World?" *Z Magazine* 15, no. 6 : 5–6.

Phillips, K. 2002. *Wealth and Democracy*. New York: Broadway Books.

Scheper-Hughes, N., and P. Bourgois. 2004. *Violence in War and Peace*. Malden: Blackwell Publishing.

Schor, J. 1993. *The Overworked American: The Unexpected Decline of Leisure*. New York: Basic Books.

Sell, Ralph R., and Stephen J. Kunitz. 1989, Winter. "The Debt Crisis and the End of an Era in Mortality Decline." *Studies in Comparative International Development*: 3–30.

Sen, A. 1985. *Commodities and Capabilities*. Amsterdam: North Holland.

Shankland, Alex. 1995. "Jacqueline's Garden." *The New Internationalist Magazine* 267 (May). Accessed September 17, 2012, from: www.newint.org/features/1995/05/05/garden/.

Sharkey, Jacqueline. 1990, May/June. "Nicaragua: Anatomy of an Election." *Common Cause Magazine*: 20–29.

Sherman, Howard J. 1987. *Foundations of Radical Political Economy*. Armonk, N.Y.: M.E. Sharpe.

Silberman, Charles E. 1978. *Criminal Violence, Criminal Justice*. New York: Random House

Somavia, J. 2006. *Changing Patterns in the World of Work*. Geneva: Office of Director General, International Labour Organization.

Southern Poverty Law Center. 2001, Winter. "Discounting Hate." *Intelligence Report* (a publication of the Southern Poverty Law Center).

Spitz, Pierre. 1978. "Silent Violence: Famine and Inequality." *International Social Science Journal* 30: 867–91.

Stolnitz, George J. 1983. "Three to Five Main Challenges to Demographic Research." *Demography* 20: 415–32.

Tinker, George E. 1993. *Missionary Conquest*. Minneapolis: Fortress Press.

Tobis, David. 1983. "The Alliance for Progress: Development Program for the United States." In *Guatemala in Rebellion: Unfinished History*, edited by J. Fried et al. New York: Grove Press.

Trivett, V. 2011, June 27. "25 US Mega Corporations: Where They Rank If They Were Countries." Accessed June 27, 2012, from Business Insider: www.businessinsider.com/25-corporations-bigger-tan-countries-2011-6?op=1.

Tucker, M. J., C. J. Berg, W. M. Callaghan, and J. Hsia. 2007, February. "The Black–White Disparity in Pregnancy-Related Mortality From 5 Conditions: Differences in Prevalence and Case-Fatality Rates." *American Journal of Public Health* 97, no. 2: 247–51.

UNAIDS. 2010. *The Global AIDS Epidemic*. Accessed June 27, 2012, from UNAIDS: www.unaids.org/documents/20101123_FS_Global_em_en.pdf.

United Nations Development Program. 1990. *Human Development Report*. New York: Oxford University Press.

United Nations Population Division. 2002. *World Population Prospects: The 2002 Revision*. New York: United Nations.

U.S. Congressional Budget Office. 2011, October. *Trends in the Distribution of Household Income between 1979 and 2007*. Washington, D.C.: U.S. Congressional Budget Office.

U.S. Department of Defense. 2012. "Charles E. Wilson, 5th Secretary of Defense." Accessed June 5, 2012, from U.S. Department of Defense Secretary Biographies: www.defense.gov/specials/secdef_histories/index.html.

Watts, Michael. 1983. *Silent Violence: Food, Famine and Peasantry in Northern Nigeria*. Berkeley: University of California Press.

Whitney, Craig R. 1993. "Bonn Suspects Neo-Nazi Arson as 5 Turks Die." *New York Times*, sec. 1, pt. 1.

Wilkinson, R. G. 1996. *Unhealthy Societies: The Afflictions of Inequality*. London: Routledge.

Wilkinson, R., and K. Pickett. 2010. *The Spirit Level: Why Greater Equality Makes Societies Stronger*. New York: Bloomsbury Press.

WLTL.com. 2012, January 11. "Super Bowl Raises Human Trafficking Concerns." Accessed June 3, 2012, from News 5 WLTL.com: www.wlwt.com/news/30192215/detail.html.

Volff, E. N. 2010. *Recent Trends in Household Wealth in the United States: Rising Debt and the Middle-Class Squeeze—an Update to 2007*. Annandale-on-Hudson: Levy Economics Institute of Bard College.

orld Health Organization. 2011. *World Health Statistics 2011*. Geneva: World Health Organization.

———. 2012, February. *Children: reducing mortality—Fact sheet No. 178*. Accessed April 4, 2012, from WHO Media Centre: www.who.int/mediacentre/factsheets/fs178/en/index.html.

Zwerdling, Daniel. 1980. *Workplace Democracy*. New York: Harper Colophon.

CHAPTER 10

Cloward, Richard A., and Frances Fox Piven. 1977. *Poor People's Movements*. New York: Pantheon Books.

Fieldhouse, A. 2011, June 4. *The Bush Tax Cuts Disproportionately Benefitted the Wealthy*. Accessed June 28, 2012, from Economic Policy Institute: www.epi.org/publication/the_bush_tax_cuts_disproportionately_benefitted_the_wealthy.

Glaze, L. E. 2010. *Correctional Populations in the United States, 2009*. Washington, D.C.: U.S. Justice Department.

Goodwillie, Susan. 1993. *Voices from the Future*. New York: Crown.

Liptak, A. 2008, April 23. "U.S. Prison Population Dwarfs That of Other Nations." *The New York Times*.

Mander, Jerry. 1978. *Four Arguments for the Elimination of Television*. New York: William Morrow and Company.

Michalowski, Raymond. 1985. *Order, Law, and Crime: An Introduction to Criminology*. New York: Random House.

Mishel, Lawrence, and Jared Bernstein. 1993. *The State of Working America*. Armonk, N.Y.: M.E. Sharpe

Parenti, Michael. 1986. *Inventing Reality: The Politics of the Mass Media*. New York: St. Martin's Press.

Philips, Kevin. 1990. *The Politics of Rich and Poor*. New York: Harper Collins.

Reavis, Dick J. 1994. "Chiapas Is Mexico." *The Progressive* 58 (May): 28–32.

Rigoli, Robert M., and John D. Hewitt. 1994. *Delinquency in Society: A Child-Centered Approach*. New York: McGraw-Hill.

Schor, Juliet. 1993. *The Overworked American*. New York: Basic Books.

Shapiro, Isaac, and Robert Greenstein. 2000. *The Widening Income Gulf*. Washington, D.C.: Center on Budget and Policy Priorities: www.cbpp.org/9-4-99tax-rep.htm#The%20CBO%20Data.

Sniffen, Michael J. 1994, June 2. "Prison Population Triples since 1980." *Journal Gazette*, 8A.

U.S. Bureau of Justice. 2001. "The Number of Adults in the Correctional Population Has Been Increasing." U.S. Bureau of Justice Statistics, Social Statistics Briefing Room: www.ojp.usdoj.gov/bjs/glance/tables/corr2tab.htm.

Zinn, Howard. 1980. *A People's History of the United States*. New York: Harper & Row.

Index

A.C. Lawrence Leather Company, 287
Afghan freedom fighters, 351
Afghanistan, 27, 37, 38, 43, 46, 87, 122,
    213, 312, 319, 343, 344, 351, 362, 364
Africa: AIDs and, 420, 426; capitalism
    and, 401, 408; child labor and, 170,
    282, 283; economic violence and, 273,
    282, 394, 397; educational violence
    and, 194, 199, 205, 206; environmental
    violence and, 291, 292, 293, 305, 421;
    extrajudicial executions, 319; famine
    and, 435, 440; genocide and, 47, 358,
    359; hierarchy and, 327; imperialism
    and, 327, 387, 389, 390, 396, 397;
    indigenous populations and, 321, 322,
    324, 387, 389, 390; infant mortality,
    420; malnutrition, 383, 421; organic
    conservative ideology and, 88, 89;
    religious violence and, 220, 235, 240;
    sexual violence and, 334; slavery and,
    357, 396, 397, 428, 429, 430, 431, 432,
    433, 434; state violence and, 379, 380;
    structural violence and, 48, 387, 388,
    390, 391, 394, 396, 397; tobacco and,
    265; war and, 344, 433; world debt,
    408, 411, 412
African Americans: arrest rates, 113, 140;
    capital punishment and, 314; child
    violence and, 172, 173; educational
    violence and, 198, 206, 207;
    environmental violence and, 290;
    experiments on, 372; hate crimes, 441,
    442; hierarchy and, 13, 14, 390;
    homicide and, 113, 114, 118; inequality
    and, 113, 390; infant mortality, 3, 25,
    26, 35; rape and, 140, 141, 149, 150;
    riots and, 36; state violence and, 325;
    statistics, 113, 114; structural violence
    and, 35; tobacco and, 263; victimization
    and, 113, 122, 149, 150; youth, 4
African National Congress (ANC), 341,
    352, 353, 364
agent provocateurs, 375–376
A.H. Robins Company, 253
AIDS, 136, 425; accelerated Access
    program, 426; pharmaceutical
    companies, 289, 302, 426; rape and,
    136; sub-Saharan Africa, 411, 420, 426;
    structural violence and, 425, 426;
    UNAIDS, 425, 426
Air America, 350
Allied Chemical, 297, 298
Alpha, 350
Al Qaeda, 37, 38, 39, 213, 361, 362, 369.
    See also Taliban
American Civil War, 65, 66, 83, 86, 87, 88,
    94, 119, 120, 121, 134, 155, 463
American Psycho (Ellis), 60
American Revolution, 134, 229
American Service Members Protection
    Act, 313
Amin, Idi, 341

About the Authors

Peter Iadicola is a professor of sociology at the joint campus of Indiana University and Purdue University, Fort Wayne. He received his doctorate from the University of California, Riverside. His research specialties include the study of violence, state crime, imperial systems, political economy, and applied sociology. He is the author of four books and more than forty articles and research reports. His current research is on the nature of crime and violence in neo-colonial imperial systems.

Anson Shupe is an emeritus professor of sociology at the joint campus of Indiana University and Purdue University, Fort Wayne. He received his doctorate from Indiana University, Bloomington. His research specialties include the study of violence, deviance, religion, and social psychology. He is the author/editor of thirty books and eighty articles. His most recent work has been in the area of deviance within religious organizations.